Exploring Child Welfare

THIRD EDITION

Exploring Child Welfare

A Practice Perspective

Cynthia Crosson-Tower
Harvest Counseling and Consultation

Boston • New York • San Francisco
Mexico City • Montreal • Toronto • London • Madrid • Munich • Paris
Hong Kong • Singapore • Tokyo • Cape Town • Sydney

Executive Editor: *Patricia Quinlin*
Editorial Assistant: *Annemarie Kennedy*
Marketing Manager: *Taryn Wahlquist*
Editorial Production Service: *TKM Productions*
Manufacturing Buyer: *JoAnne Sweeney*
Cover Administrator: *Linda Knowles*
Electronic Composition: *Omegatype Typography, Inc.*

For related titles and support materials, visit our online catalog at www.ablongman.com.

Between the time Website information is gathered and published, some sites may have closed. Also, the transcription of URLs can result in typographical errors. The publisher would appreciate being notified of any problems with URLs so that they may be corrected in subsequent editions.

Library of Congress Cataloging-in-Publication Data

Crosson-Tower, Cynthia.
    Exploring child welfare : a practice perspective / Cynthia Crosson-Tower.—3rd ed.
       p.   cm.
    Includes bibliographical references and indexes.
    ISBN 0-205-38127-8
      1. Child welfare—United States.   2. Social case work with children—United States.   3. Family social work—United States.   4. Social work education—United States.   I. Title.

HV741.T682 2003
362.7'0973—dc21

2002043725

Printed in the United States of America

10   9   8   7   6   5   4   3   08   07   06   05   04

To Muriel, my mother and friend, who saw me through the tough times,
and
to Jeri Niemela, whose dream was to make a
difference in the lives of children. And she did.

CONTENTS

3 Children and Poverty   63

by Judy A. Noel and Dee L. Whyte

PREFACE

We cannot forget that children are our most important resource. It is through our children that we can touch the future. But childhood is a time when children must depend on all of us to protect and nurture them to meet that future. Usually that task falls to the parents of children. But what if they are unable, or even unwilling, to carry the burden themselves? Hillary Clinton, in her book *It Takes a Village,* expanded the African saying, "It takes a village to raise a child," and spoke of how it is the responsibility of every citizen to ensure the well-being of children.

The tool that the "village," or society, uses to care for the well-being of its children is epitomized in the services provided under the child welfare system. These services vary greatly in purpose, intensity, cost, and procedures. For one who is unfamiliar with the services for children and their families, it may seem like a maze. This book is designed to help potential practitioners to understand that maze and become comfortable in using it and working within a variety of fields. The emphasis in the following pages is placed on the practice perspective both from the vantage point of the professional as well as understanding the experience of the child or family that is being helped. Since the intent is to empower the individual and family, the term *consumer* has become increasingly popular as a way of referring to those using services. By seeing the person as a consumer rather than a "patient" or a "client," as they were seen in the past, the practitioner becomes more of a guide or support as the family seeks to help itself. Thus, the analogy of the "village" becomes stronger by bringing to mind a community that helps its members rather than disempowers them. Certainly, there are times when the family is not able to care for its children and society must step in, but with increased community efforts to support family life, the hope is this is less likely to happen.

Plan for the Text

This book is designed to explore child welfare services from the least intrusive into family life to the more intrusive and finally those that substitute care for the family. The chapters are arranged so that, after a brief background of child welfare and the family, the reader will recognize the services that support family life, those that supplement the roles of the family, and those that substitute for what should be provided by the family.

Chapter 1 lays a framework for child welfare by considering the past—how children were perceived and treated, and the services available for them. Chapter 2 looks at the family, both traditional and nontraditional. The chapter explores the roles and rights of family members in diverse cultures. Further, internal and external stressors are outlined that may be responsible for bringing a family to seek help from the community.

Many children within our society live in poverty and this fact makes it difficult for them to develop normally. What are the implications of growing up in poverty? Chapter 3 answers this question. It also looks at the present methods of fighting poverty and speculates about some solutions in society's effort to reduce child poverty.

Poverty is not the only social problem that plagues today's children. Actually there are many issues with which they must deal. Three of the most prevalent are violence, addiction, and homelessness. Chapter 4 explores the problems facing children growing up in a violent society, children who are addicted to drugs or alcohol or whose parents are substance abusers, and children who have no place to call home.

Chapter 5 acquaints the reader with the services provided for children through education and socialization, outlining daycare and school-based services. Chapter 6 considers counseling for children and their families. Chapter 7 looks at situations in which families are having difficulty parenting properly and end up abusing or neglecting their children. Chapter 8 discusses family preservation services that strive to keep families together in their own homes and asks the question: What is *really* in the best interests of the child? Children may come to the attention of the court system for a variety of reasons. Court services for children are outlined in Chapter 9.

A problem of almost epidemic proportions today is teens, now, at a younger age than ever, having children and attempting the challenging role of parenting. Chapter 10 examines this phenomenon and its impact on both the teens and their children.

When families are unable to provide for their children, substitute arrangements must be made. The next three chapters explore these arrangements. Chapter 11 provides insight into the foster care system from entrance into the placement process to termination. The text describes the roles, feelings, and attitudes of both the birth parents and the foster parents. The role of the foster care social worker is also discussed. Chapter 12 outlines the adoption process from the ways children are released for adoption to the feelings of the adoptive parent or parents and the problems they face. But not every child is able to adjust to a home environment. Chapter 13 describes residential settings for children who may not have the family as a viable alternative.

The text concludes with Chapter 14, which explores the future for children and their families. What will this new century bring in the way of policy changes, resources, and new problems to be faced? These are topics of discussion for today and challenges to be faced by tomorrow's practitioners. The second edition of the text emphasized the importance of attachment in children's lives and how services must acknowledge this. Consideration was given to the problem of increased violence in schools and to new ways of addressing juvenile offenders. This third edition examines the pros and cons of family preservation services as well as reflects some of the changes that have taken place in the field. The chapters on school-based services and teen pregnancy have changed their focus, keeping with new programs and theories relating to these services.

Case examples from field experience have been woven throughout the text to help the reader see the "faces" behind the words. Each chapter is followed by Exploration Questions, developed to help the student review and pick out important material. The Suggested Readings suggest materials that enable the student to read books in the area covered by each chapter.

Exploring Child Welfare: A Practice Perspective is a suitable text for both undergraduate and graduate students in the fields of social work, human services, psychology, sociology, counseling, or education.

Acknowledgments

There have been many who have helped, either directly or indirectly, with the completion of this text. My thanks goes first to my family—my husband, Jim, my mother, and my sons—who have made allowances through the very busy period of this revision for Mom's need to work. My appreciation to my dear friends Kate Martin, Carolyn and Ed Thomas, and Mary Ann Hanley, who continue to cheer me on when need be. Very special thanks goes to Peggyann Prasinos, my invaluable research assistant, as well as to Judy Noel for being a great help and sounding board.

My contributors, both old and new, deserve note: Thanks to Denise O'Connell, Maureen Moorehouse, Judy Noel, Lynne Kellner, Lloyd Williams, Mary Ann Hanley, Dee Whyte, Elaine Francis, and Matthew Porter.

Also, I thank the reviewers—Carol Bisbee, Midwestern State University; Susan Mittendorf, Louisiana State University; and Maureen Braun Scalera, Rutgers University—for their many valuable comments.

This edition is dedicated in part to the memory of Jeri Niemela, one-time student, but ever a friend. As a strong advocate for children, Jeri gave of herself as long-time employee and director of a residential setting for adolescent girls. Her enthusiasm, her dreams, and her dedication are sorely missed by all who knew her. And to my other students, my thanks as they continue to give me new perspectives on how to best teach about the child welfare system and how to improve the provision of services to children. Thanks, too, to Janice Ouellette who is ever ready to embark upon one more library search for me— "due yesterday." And finally, my continued thanks to my editor, Patricia Quinlin, and her assistant, Annemarie Kennedy.

About the Author

Cynthia Crosson-Tower, M.S.W., Ed.D., is the author of numerous publications, including *Understanding Child Abuse and Neglect, When Children Are Abused: An*

Educator's Guide to Maltreatment, Secret Scars: A Guide for Survivors of Child Sexual Abuse, The Educator's Role in Child Abuse and Neglect and *Homeless Students*. She has also authored a monograph, *Designing and Implementing a School Reporting Protocol: A How-To Guide for Massachusetts Teachers*, for the Children's Trust Fund in Boston. Currently, she is at work on a text on child sexual abuse and a book to help clergy recognize and respond to child maltreatment.

Dr. Crosson-Tower brings to the writing of this text over 30 years of experience in child welfare practice. She has worked in protective services, foster care, adoption, and corrections, as well as with juvenile and adult courts and the homeless, and in a variety of counseling situations. She was also a regional trainer for the Massachusetts Department of Social Services. Dr. Crosson-Tower's recent book, *From the Eye of the Storm: The Experiences of a Child Welfare Worker*, chronicles some of her experiences in the field. She was also professor of Behavioral Sciences at Fitchburg State College in Massachusetts and still acts as the Director of the Child Protection Institute in the graduate program.

Recently, Dr. Crosson-Tower has taken an early retirement to devote herself to writing and counseling through Harvest Counseling and Consultation where she specializes in the treatment of survivors and perpetrators of sexual abuse. She offers workshops both nationally and internationally for educators, clergy, and other professionals. Dr. Crosson-Tower is also pursuing a Divinity degree and hopes to help clergy recognize the importance of their role in addressing child maltreatment.

Introducing the Contributors

As I began the writing of this text, with over 30 years in child welfare practice under my belt, it became evident to me that there are too many aspects of child welfare and too many varied services for me to know all of them in depth. It was for this reason that I enlisted the contributions of colleagues who are experts, and therefore current, in their fields and who were anxious to help me present a positive picture of these services to the future practitioner. The following introductions will give the reader insight into these authors and their contributions to the field.

Elaine Francis, Ed.D., is Professor and Chair of the Special Education Department at Fitchburg State College. She has been actively involved in schools for the past 25 years, providing consultation to school districts to assist them in meeting the needs of students with special needs. Dr. Francis has been an advocate of inclusionary practices, and has made presentations at state and national conferences on the subject.

Mary Ann Hanley, Ed.D., is Professor Emeritus from Fitchburg State College. She has 10 years of experience teaching and counseling in junior and senior high schools and has over 20 years of teaching counseling, psychology, and human services courses at the college level. She co-wrote the curriculum for School Guidance at Fitchburg State College and sits on the statewide committee of school counselors and counselor educators who are working on role statements and standards of practice.

Lynne Kellner, Ph.D., is Assistant Professor of Behavioral Sciences at Fitchburg State College in Massachusetts. She supervises graduate and undergraduate students in the field. She has 16 years of experience in community mental health, specializing in children and family services. Other research interests include resiliency in children, creating a model of treatment for male sexual abuse victims, and evaluating a Massachusetts-based Welfare to Work program. She is co-author of "She Even Walked the Dog: An Evaluation of a Welfare to Work Program" in *The Qualitative Report,* September 2001.

Maureen C. Moorehouse, Ed.M., is recently retired from a career that spanned 35 years in public school education. She worked in rural, suburban, and urban school districts and at preschool through grade 12. Her job titles included work as a school counselor, school psychologist, school social worker, and supervisor of pupil personnel services. Although her 21 years in direct service work are those most personally rewarding to her, she recognizes the importance of the 14 years she spent as an administrator facilitating the work of special educators, school counselors, school social workers, and school psychologists. Through this experience, Moorehouse expanded and implemented her philosophy for offering support to students and families and for affecting systemwide policy development.

Judy A. Noel, Ph.D., is Associate Professor of Social Work at the University of Arkansas at Fayetteville. She came to her 30-year teaching career in child welfare with a background in the juvenile court system. Dr. Noel was primary investigator for a child fatality grant from the State of Louisiana and the Children's Trust Fund, which served to provide data to develop a protocol to limit the number of deaths of children. She is also the author of "The Lower Income, Black Rape Victim: The Case for Hospital Based Services," in the *Journal of Alternative Human Services,* and is a consulting editor for the *Journal of Baccalaureate Social Work.*

Denise A. O'Connell, Ed.D., has recently joined the faculty at Fitchburg State College as an Assistant Professor and Program Chair of the Graduate Program in Moderate Disabilities. Dr. O'Connell has had 25 years of experience as both a teacher and administrator for a large urban school system in Massachusetts. This experience spans the prekindergarten to grade 12 levels, where she has worked as a learning disabilities specialist, resource room teacher, preschool special educator, school psychologist, and assistant to the pupil personnel supervisor. She has expertise in the area of IEP development, parent involvement, assessment, homeless education issues, and the history and legal aspects of special education. Dr. O'Connell has presented at several national conferences relative to her work with families who are homeless.

Matthew D. Porter, M.Ed., is the co-owner of Horizon Schools with a 20-year background in teaching and administration for both profit and nonprofit early childhood education programs, and is an adjunct professor at Springfield Technical Comunity College in Springfield, MA.

Dee L. Whyte, B.S., has written and spoken extensively about childhood poverty and child abuse for many years and is an advocate for family support as a critical strategy to address both of these issues. She brings with her experience as a general manager for Imagitas, a company that designs and implements innovative and unique public/private partnerships, and as Director of Programs and Evaluations for the Children's Trust Fund, the organization mandated to implement the child abuse prevention plan for the Commonwealth of Massachusetts.

Lloyd T. Williams, M.S.W., L.I.C.S.W., is a clinical social worker in full-time private practice with children, adolescents, and individual adults. He formerly served as staff clinician, intern and staff supervisor, and community consultant for Youth Opportunities Upheld, Inc., and as program director and clinician at the Worcester Youth Guidance Center, one of the oldest youth guidance centers in the United States. Among other areas, Williams has expertise in Jungian analysis, sandtray therapy, interpretation of drawings, hypnosis, and cognitive behavioral therapy.

My thanks and appreciation to all of the contributors.

Cynthia Crosson-Tower

Exploring Child Welfare

Children

Our Most Important Resource

*There is only one child in the world and the child's name
is All Children.... This child speaks our name.*

—Carl Sandburg

The fate of one child in the United States today can be the fate of all children. Likewise, we must seek, in the interest of serving all children, to help each individual child. It is this goal toward which the child welfare system strives.

There is no denying that America's children need our help. Each day one in five children is born poor. One in three children will be poor at some point in his or her childhood. For one in seven, a parent is employed, and yet the family is still below the poverty level. One in seven children has no health insurance and one in six is born to a mother who had no prenatal care during the first three months of her pregnancy. In addition to poverty, there are other factors that might impede the healthy development of children, and require that they be provided with services. One in eight children is born to a teen mother. One in twelve has a disability. One in sixty children will see their parents divorce. And one in twenty-four lives with neither of his or her parents (Children's Defense Fund, 2001).

As we consider the problems that plague our youth, we become aware that these figures often differ depending on racial or ethnic background. Table 1.1 provides an overview of many of these problems as they are distributed by ethnic group.

TABLE 1.1   Children's Problems According to Ethnic Group

	White	African Americans	Hispanic	Asian American	Native American
The number of children in the United States who					
Die in infancy	49	24	12	2	1
Are born in poverty	1,374	514	751	—	—
Have no health insurance	1,019	216	518	—	—
Are born to mothers who had no or late prenatal care	271	105	127	17	9
Are born at low birth weight (less than 5 lbs, 8 oz)	563	217	133	37	8
(less than 3 lbs, 4 oz)	99	52	24	5	1
Are born to teen mothers	939	343	349	24	22
Are suspended by public school	8,870	5,542	2,357	323	206
Are arrested	3,803	1,065	—	70	52
Are arrested for violent crimes	100	76	—	3	2
Are arrested for drug abuse	257	103	—	4	3
Drop out of high school	2,133	617	—	—	—
Die of HIV infection	1	1	—	—	—
Die from firearms	5	4	—	—	—
Commit suicide	4	1	—	—	—
Are homicide victims	4	4	—	—	—

Source: Adapted from Children's Defense Fund, 2002, at http://childrensdefense.org/everyday.htm.

All of these children are our future—our most important resource. It will be up to the adults in today's world to intervene so that all children will have a better future. This is the challenge facing the child welfare system.

To understand how we view children and our responsibility to protect and provide for them, we must look into the past and what the history of children's services has been. (A brief history follows, but individual chapters may expand on the etiology of specific services.)

A Brief History of Child Welfare

The concept of childhood as we know it is relatively new. At one time, children were seen as miniature adults with many of the responsibilities, albeit few of the rights, given to the adults of that time. Bremner (1995) points out that the plight of children was often reflected in the novels of various periods. For example, Disraeli's novel, *Sybil: The Two Nations* (1845), describes how children were subjected to horrendous conditions (sleeping on "moldering straw in a damp cellar…a dung heap at his head, and a cesspool at his feet"). A child was given drugs by his nurse and eventually left on the streets at age 2 to die. Charles Dickens writes of children apprenticed to cruel masters, and kept in poorhouses that treated them very badly. (See Dickens, *Oliver Twist*, 1838 [1987].) David Copperfield was neglected by his stepfather and eventually sent to a dirty, dark warehouse to work (Dickens, 1849 [1981]). Numerous other accounts throughout literature speak of how children were treated as chattel, abused and neglected because adults saw them as expendable.

Abortion, Infanticide, and Abandonment

The concept of abortion is not unique to our current society, nor is contraception. If contraception were ineffective, abortion was the traditional solution. Kadushin and Martin (1988) report that numerous studies of ancient societies reveal that abortion was widely accepted in all of them. Unwanted children who were not aborted were often dealt with in early times by abandoning or killing them. Infanticide was not an uncommon practice. During the Roman Empire and the flourishing of the Greeks, infanticide, although prohibited by law, appeared to be one of the responses to poverty and the burden of too many female children. In fact, Sumner (1959) comments that "for the masses, until the late days of the Empire, infanticide was a most venial crime" (319).

Stone (1977) reports that the history of infanticide in Western Europe dates back to antiquity, when it was widely practiced. He further comments:

> How far it remained a common deliberate policy for legitimate children in the Early Modern period is still open to question, although it is suggestive that as late as the early nineteenth century in Anjou, priests were instructed

to warn their congregations in their sermons every three months of the mortal
sin of killing an infant before baptism. (473–474)

We know too, from historical references and even popular ballads of early times, that infanticide was one solution for bearing children out of wedlock. The well-known old English ballad, "Mary Hamilton," tells how a lady-in-waiting to the Queen (believed to be Mary, Queen of Scots) became pregnant by the royal consort ("the highest Stewart of all") and was driven to solve her problem by drowning the baby at sea.

She tyed it in her apron
And she's thrown it in the sea;
Says, "Sink ye, swim ye, bonny wee babe
You'll ne'er get m'air o' me." (Friedman, 1956)

Infanticide was used to control the population and to ensure that the populace would remain a strong and healthy race. Langer (1974) reports that infanticide has "from time immemorial been the accepted procedure for disposing …of deformed or sickly infants" (354). In their early histories, such cultures as Hawaii and China used infanticide as a form of maintaining healthy populations. Hawaiians drowned sickly children and sometimes female children in the sea (Kempe and Helfer, 1968). Although it is outlawed by governments, some cultures still practice forms of infanticide today.

Sometimes infanticide took the form of abandonment. Parents who were unable to care for their children might leave them to die or be found by someone else. Kadushin and Martin (1988) cite Caulfield's (1931) assessment of England in the 1700s when "dropping [abandoning] infants was an extremely frequent occurrence…and was accepted by all classes without comment" (31). Even during the late 1800s, children were abandoned in the streets of New York City at an astonishing rate (Kadushin and Martin, 1988). Although we would like to think that abandonment is a practice of the past, the high incidence of drug addiction among parents of young children means that some continue to be abandoned and even killed.

Child Labor and Education

Children have always been expected to work along with their parents. Farm children in a largely agrarian society did chores to contribute to the family's livelihood. At one time children were also indentured to learn trades. *Indenture* was an arrangement whereby a child would be given over to an individual who could teach him (usually, though not always, the child was male) a trade. Some of these children were well treated but others were not. Dickens (1838) spoke of the plight of one such apprentice in *Oliver Twist*. Oliver was apprenticed to an undertaker who not only mistreated him, but exposed him to the fine points of death. Like Oliver's master, many of those using apprentices made them work long hours and in unreasonable circumstances.

But with the industrial revolution came a new way of using children in the workforce. Not only were children more plentiful than adults, but they were able to do jobs, due to their small hands and bodies, that adults were too large or too cumbersome to do. For example, children were frequently used in mining and chimney sweeping due to their ability to get into tight places. Little thought was given to the effect of the soot or mine dust on their growing bodies. In addition, they could be paid very little, and because children were thought to have no rights, little would be said by anyone about the long hours they were expected to work, the conditions under which they labored, or their treatment in general. Even the parents often depended so much on the child bringing in an extra income that they dared not protest their maltreatment, if they even knew about it. Other parents felt that their children owed them the wages they earned no matter the conditions.

It wasn't until the late nineteenth and early twentieth centuries that child labor was addressed in any significant way. It was through the efforts of such reformers as Jane Addams, Homer Folks, and Grace Abbott that the National Child Labor Committee (NCLC) was organized in 1904 to undertake reforms in the interest of working children (Stadum, 1995). Through its numerous publications that reported field investigations, the NCLC appealed to church, women's, and college groups to advocate for the reformation of child labor laws. The message was a straightforward one. Reformers believed that children could help with tasks around the farm or the home, but that they should also be allowed a childhood free from "unhealthy and hazardous conditions," "unsuitable wages," and "unreasonable hours" that could interfere with their "physical development and education" (Trattner, 1970, 9–10).

The first White House Conference on Children in 1910 stimulated the establishment of the U.S. Children's Bureau in 1912. It was the role of the Children's Bureau to advocate for children, and one of its first tasks became the furthering of reforms in the area of child labor. In reality the number of children in the workforce between ages 10 to 13 had dropped from 121 in 1,000 in 1900 to 24 in 1,000 by 1930 (Trattner, 1970), but large numbers of children were still being used as migrant labor and were often uncounted in the census. When the Fair Labor Standards Act of 1938 established rules governing both wages and hours for all workers, Grace Abbott of the Children's Bureau lobbied to extend the act to ensure that children under age 16 could not be used in certain industries (Stadum, 1995).

The economic needs of World War II put a strain on the enforcement of child labor laws, however, and the NCLC changed its focus to vocational training for children leaving high school. This change in focus would eventually culminate in the NCLC becoming the National Committee on the Employment of Youth in 1957 (Trattner, 1970).

Despite the fact that it would seem that early child labor laws would be applauded by all, some families found that the prohibitions dictated by the laws meant that there was one less wage earner in the family. Social workers, recognizing the families' need, questioned the stringency of the new legislation. At the same time, poor parents were often portrayed as lazy individuals who would prefer to send their children to work in factories than to become employed themselves. Rarely did the hard-working parents who labored along with their children to eke out a meager livelihood come to the attention of the media or the public (Stadum, 1995).

States began to allow children to be employed if a severe family need could be documented. The NCLC opposed such exceptions and in 1921 most states had eliminated this practice. In fact, argued the NCLC, allowing children to work for low wages actually contributed to family poverty by "driving down the pay for adults who should be the household supporters" (Stadum, 1995, 37).

Along with the argument against child labor came the push for mandatory school attendance. Thus school attendance laws piggy-backed on the child labor laws while some parents questioned the need for a formal education for the children who were needed more as wage earners. The first compulsory attendance laws in the 1920s addressed children under the age of 14; by 1927, most states had increased the age to 16. Still, if families could demonstrate an economic need, children were given a certificate that allowed an exception from school in favor of earning a wage. Even if a child did attend school, it was permissible for him or her to complete a full week's work after school hours (Stadum, 1995). It often fell to the Juvenile Courts to verify the family need to require their children to work. In some areas, this task fell to the Charity Organization Society (COS), which served as the first relief organization in the United States. It was the role of the COS (later to be called the Family Welfare Association) to coordinate services for families in need of assistance (Heffernan et al., 1997). When COS workers refused to grant the requests of parents to have their children work instead of attending school, tempers flared, and the debate became heated. To encourage children to stay in school, the COS began instituting "scholarships" for needy families, which equalled what the child would have earned in wages. Reformers discovered that these scholarships actually increased children's persistence in school. "Mother's Pensions" were also given to a select group of women who were raising their children on their own. It was these payments that actually became the forerunner of the later Aid to Families with Dependent Children (Stadum, 1995).

Today, most states decree that children must remain in school until the age of 16. More recent legislation protects children from unfair labor practices and insures that they have an opportunity for an education.

Responsibility for Children

Out-of-Home Care.   Because children were originally considered the property of their parents, the responsibility for them was expected to lie with these parents unless they were unable to assume it. Poor parents took their children with them to suffer the degradation of the almshouses. Other children remained at home with their parents receiving "outdoor relief," a form of "in kind" assistance. Children who had no parents or could not be kept by these parents were cared for by others, originally church-sponsored organizations. The first established orphanage in the United States was the Ursaline Convent, founded in 1727. But orphanages were initially slow in developing. By 1800, there were only 5 orphanages in the United States, and 77 by 1851. Once the idea took hold, however, orphanages multiplied quickly, with 400 in existence by the year 1900. By 1910, 110,000 children resided in 1,151 orphanages (Smith, 1995, 118). Orphan asylums, as they were sometimes known, might house few children or many, depending upon the facility. Although these institutions were established primarily to provide care for dependent children, Holt (2001) chronicles the development of orphanages for Native American children in an attempt to enculturate them into white society. The late 1800s also saw the moving of children from orphanages to "placing out." This practice, instituted largely by Charles Loring Brace, gave children an opportunity to live with families in the midwestern United States (Cook, 1995). (See Chapter 11 for more details.) But as farms in the West became fewer, the demand for dependent children as free labor also decreased at the turn of the twentieth century (Hegar and Scannapieco, 1999).

For the children who remained in orphanages, life varied, depending on the type of institution, the administration, and the personality of the individual environment. Corporal punishment was the norm and little thought was given to the developmental needs of children. Thurston (1930) describes orphanage life:

> *Life for a typical boy in an institution…meant essentially shelter, the actual necessities in the way of clothes, and food which primarily served the purpose of preventing starvation, rather than scientific or, may I say, common sense nourishment. The attitude of those responsible for the institution was that the boys and girls were unfortunate objects of charity. (70–71)*

Early child care institutions were also largely segregated. In fact, the only facilities for many African American children were jails or reform schools, even when they were not delinquents. In the early twentieth century, associations of African American women finally began to address the needs of African American children (Peebles-Wilkins, 1995). One such organization's first president, Mary Church Terrell (1899), described their mission:

> *As an Association, let us devote ourselves enthusiastically, conscientiously, to the children…. Through the children of today, we must build a foundation of the next generation upon such a rock of integrity, morality, and strength, both of body and mind, that floods of proscription, prejudice, and persecution may descend upon it in torrents, and yet it will not be moved. We hear a great deal about the race problem, and how to solve it…but the real solution of the race problem, both so far as we, who are oppressed, and those who oppress us are concerned, lies in the children. (346)*

Institutions specifically for African American children, such as the Colored Big Sister Home for Girls in Kansas City, Missouri, and the Carrie Steele Orphan Home in Atlanta, began to emerge (Peebles-Wilkins, 1995). Like the African American child, little was provided for the Native American child. Native American children were often sent to orphanages or boarding schools (whether or not they had parents to care for them) as a way of not only providing for their care, but also for enculturating them into the white society (Holt, 2001). It was not to be until the mid-twentieth century that child care institutions would be fully integrated.

During the 1920s, the institutions saw the need to modernize slightly. Increased recognition of the needs of children gave rise to attempts to provide more humane treatment and more "advantages" to the residents. Punishments continued to be severe in some cases, in spite of the reformers' criticisms of corporal punishment.

Another way to care for dependent children became the free boarding home. Here, children were placed with families who agreed to assume their care, initially for no compensation. Eventually, a fee was granted for room and board, and agencies began to study those wanting to provide homes. These "free homes" were a precursor of today's family foster homes (see Chapter 11).

It was expected that children in both orphanages and boarding homes would show how grateful they were for their care by being respectful, compliant, and generally well behaved. Children who "misbehaved" were threatened with expulsion. Children who complied with the rules of the institution could remain there until their majority (Holt, 2001; Hacsi, 1995; Smith, 1995).

With the recognition that children needed families, the use of orphanages declined in favor of family foster care. During the 1940s and 1950s, child welfare advocates spoke of the limitations of institutional care for children. Lillian Johnson, Executive Director of the Ryther Center in Seattle, likened an institution for a child to "a life jacket that holds the child above water but without putting solid ground beneath the child's feet" (Smith, 1995, 135). The numbers of children in child care institutions dropped from 43% in 1951 to 17.1% in 1989 (Wolins and Piliavin, 1964; Merkel-Holguin, as cited in Smith, 1995, 135).

Today, it is rare to find an institution dedicated to the provision of care solely for dependent children. Instead children are cared for through the provision of assistance payments to their parents or in family or group foster care. Current institutions are reserved for emotionally disturbed or delinquent children (see Chapter 13).

Daycare.   The daily care of children who had parents was also expected to be provided by them. During the years of the at-home mother, this was usually not a problem. But World War II and the advent of the mother who joined the work-force changed this picture considerably. Tuttle (1995) comments:

America's working mothers had to confront many obstacles during the Second World War, not the least of which was people's hostility to the idea of mothers working outside of the home, even in defense plants. Feeding this sentiment were not only longstanding gender roles, but also a slew of wartime magazines and speeches by Father Edward J. Flanagen of Boys Town, J. Edgar Hoover of the F.B.I., and other defenders of the father-led family in which the mother dutifully stayed at home. (93)

The advent of these working mothers, many of whose husbands were fighting at the front, necessitated that new programs be instituted for the care of their children. The Lanham Act of 1940, signed by Franklin Roosevelt, provided, among other funds for communities, money for daycare centers (Tuttle, 1995). Despite suppositions that the end of war would see mothers returning home to care for their children, "Rosie the Riveter" found that she enjoyed her new freedom and the family's increased income. Thus the era of working mothers had begun, and daycare outside the home increased. That trend has continued until today, as many families depend on the income of the mother to survive. (See Chapter 5 for additional information on the history of daycare.)

Advocacy in the Provision of Services for Children

Over the years, a number of agencies, individuals, and pieces of legislation have actively advocated the provision of services for children. One of the earliest agencies to advocate for children was the New York Children's Aid Society, founded in 1853. It was through this organization that Charles Loring Brace began to address the needs of dependent children through "placing out" (see Chapter 11). If the numbers attest to success, this agency's efforts were extremely successful. By 1873, Brace's program had placed 3,000 children and, in the year 1875, the peak year, 4,026 children found new homes in this manner (Hegar and Scannapieco, 1999; Heffernan et al., 1997; Popple and Leighninger, 2001; Zastrow, 2000).

The case of Mary Ellen Wilson in 1874 (see Chapter 7) brought with it the efforts of Henry Bergh, then director of the Society for the Prevention of Cruelty to Animals, and his colleague, Elbridge Gerry, who advocated not only for one child, but for all abused and neglected children by forming the Society for the Prevention of Cruelty to Children, the first agency with the specific mission of intervening in cases of child maltreatment.

Another group of advocates in the latter part of the nineteenth and early twentieth centuries were those individuals associated with the settlement house movement. Such figures as Jane Addams, Julia Lathrop, and others blazed the way for reform in child labor, the court system, and other matters affecting children.

In 1912, the United States Children's Bureau was established as a result of the first White House Conference on Children (1910). This marked the first recognition that the federal government had any responsibility in the provision of services for children. Julia Lathrop became the first director and led the efforts to institute programs to improve maternal infant care and decrease infant mortality. The Government Printing office still carries one of the Bureau's first publications, *Infant Care,* which has undergone over 20 revisions since its first printing (Heffernan et al., 1997; Downs et al., 1999; Johnson and Schwartz, 1996).

The years 1919 and 1920 saw the creation of the American Association for Organizing Family Social Work (which later became the Family Service Association of America) and the Child Welfare League of America (CWLA). Both of these organizations established standards for the provision of children's services and assistance in encouraging research, legislation, and publications related to child welfare issues (CWLA, 2001; Heffernan et al., 1997; Johnson and Schwartz, 1996).

Although it is not always thought of as specifically an advocate for children, the 1935 Social Security Act did establish mothers' pensions (later to become AFDC and Transitional Assistance) as well as mandating that states strengthen their child welfare services. Further, the act encouraged the views that poverty is a major contributor to family problems, that children be kept in their homes whenever possible, that states be allowed to intervene to protect family life, and that the federal government should have more of a role in overseeing child welfare services (Heffernan et al., 1997; Popple and Leighninger, 2001).

The 1960s and the War on Poverty saw the development of Project Head Start. This program was based on the research being done on the development of children and the effects of stimulation and poverty on children's ability to learn in school. Head Start strived to ensure that economically disadvantaged preschool children would receive the medical care, nutritional services, and educational preparation to help them succeed in school (Downs et al., 1999).

Another important advocacy agency for children was the Children's Defense Fund (CDF), founded by Marian Wright Edelman in 1973. Deeply involved in the civil rights movement of the 1960s, Edelman felt that there was a need to help children throughout the country regardless of their race or class. Thus the CDF encouraged parental involvement and change within the community. Early on, the CDF dedicated itself to several aspects of child welfare:

1. *Fighting the exclusion of children from school;*
2. *Promoting classification and treatment of children with special needs;*
3. *Ending the use of children in medical (especially drug) research and experimentation;*
4. *Guaranteeing the child's right to privacy with the growth of computerization and data banks;*
5. *Reforming the juvenile justice system;*
6. *Recognizing the importance of child development and child care; and*
7. *Monitoring the treatment of children in foster care. (Downs et al., 1999, 468)*

Since its beginnings, the CDF has also addressed child abuse and neglect issues, teen pregnancy, homelessness, and parenting issues.

In 1975, both the Title XX amendments to the Social Security Act and the Child Abuse Prevention and Treatment Act made major contributions to the provision of services for children. Public Law (PL) 94-142 (as part of the Title XX amendments) ensured the education of all handicapped children (see Chapter 5) and the Child Abuse Prevention and Treatment Act mandated reporting of child maltreatment, encouraged and provided funds for research, and mandated training for the recognition, prevention, and treatment of child abuse and neglect (Heffernan et al., 1997).

Perhaps a forerunner of the family preservation (see Chapter 8) and permanency planning emphasis of today, the 1978 Indian Child Welfare Act sought to protect tribal rights and stop the frequent removal of Native American children from reservations to Anglo homes, a practice that betrays their heritage and destroys their kinship networks. It may have been this act that impelled African American activists to insist that children from their cultural background also be kept within their own kinship and extended family systems (Downs et al., 1999).

The provision of services to Native American children was further extended by the 1991 Indian Child Protection and Family Violence Act (PL 101-630) that mandated reporting of child abuse on Native American reservations. Prior to this act, there was the potential for confusion as to whether abuse was handled by tribal councils or by the local child welfare agency. This discrepancy caused inconsistency in services (Pecora et al., 2000).

Permanency planning was further addressed by the Adoptions Assistance and Child Welfare Reform Act (PL 96-272) of 1980, which discouraged placement of large numbers of children in foster care and required case plans and reviews of services to be done every six months. Further, it provided federal funding to assist the adoption of special needs children. Following the institution of this law, the number of children in foster care dropped in the early 1980s, from an estimated 500,000 to an estimated 270,000. Unfortunately, some think that the numbers of abused and neglected children have also risen since the Act was instituted (Heffernan et al., 1997; Johnson and Schwartz, 1996).

During the 1980s and 1990s, several pieces of legislation affected the provision of services for children although they were not always directed specifically toward children. The Public Health Act of 1987 addressed teen pregnancy by establishing programs for pregnant and parenting teens. The Special Education for Infants and Toddlers Act (1989) enables developmentally delayed young children to receive services. The Developmentally Disabled Assistance and Bill of Rights Act (1990) requires that developmentally delayed individuals, including children, receive services in the least restrictive setting. Despite the passing of such acts, the funds to implement them are not always available. In addition, there have sometimes been ceilings placed on the amount of funds allocated to meet client needs (Heffernan et al., 1997).

The Family Preservation and Support Services in the Omnibus Budget Reconciliation Act of 1993 was the first major piece of legislation concerned specifically with child welfare since 1980. This act was directed toward vulnerable families and attempted to strengthen the services to parents in order to enhance parental functioning and protect children. The act was designed to be culturally sensitive and family focused with an emphasis on preserving the family unit (Downs et al., 1999). In addition to specific services, child welfare agencies were also encouraged to explore the resources of kinship and community care to meet the needs of children.

The Welfare Reform Act of 1996 also had an impact on children and the services provided to them (see Chapter 3). In 1997, the Adoption and Safe Families Act was signed into law. This legislation was designed to "improve the safety of children, to promote adoption and other permanent homes, and to support families" (Levy and Orlans, 1998, 214). (See Chapter 12 for more detail.) This law represents the most significant changes in the foster care and adoption system to date. In 1999, the Foster Care Independence Act sought to improve services for children as they "aged out" of the foster care system.

The Current Picture of Child Welfare Services

Currently there are discussions about various issues of public policy that greatly affect the provision of child welfare services. In addition, children are exposed to a variety of social problems that affect their well-being. The high incidence of drug use among both parents and their children influences healthy child development. Along with drugs goes the threat of HIV/AIDS and children's exposure to the virus. Further, the increase of violence in our society makes children especially vulnerable to harm, and the fact that the highest number of our nation's homeless are women and their children means that even the basic needs of some children are not being met (see Chapter 4).

In the provision of services to children, the minority child is still underserved. Although the majority of children in foster care are African American, the traditional foster family is white. Black advocacy groups argue that this robs black children of their cultural heritage (Hegar and Scannapieco, 1999). In addition, prejudice and discrimination are as present in the field of child welfare as in any other area of public service. Johnson and Schwartz (1996) cite the provision of services to African American children as an area of concern, and point out that

> only within the last fifty years have the needs of black children been considered. Prior to this time, the black community cared for its own children. Even though laws require that minority children receive the same standards of care as are given white children, such is not the case; widespread discrimination continues to exist within the system. (176)

The Native American community has been given the authority, under the Indian Child Welfare Act of 1978, to intervene in the care of children of its own culture, and therefore has more opportunity to protect its own children. It is the Asian community, however, that may be feeling some of the pressure of not having adequate services provided. Over the last few years, there has been an influx of Asian people to a variety of communities. The wide diversity of the cultures represented has created a challenge for the social service system. For example, one social worker in a large eastern city recounted the following story.

CASE EXAMPLE

Learning about Diverse Populations

We have had a large number of Cambodian families in our city for several years. Because of this, our social workers received training in some of the cultural issues so that we would know how to deal with these families. Then quite a few Hmongs moved here. The Hmongs are Laotian hill people who have customs that are quite different from the Laotians themselves. They have what we might consider somewhat archaic ideas of courtship and child-rearing and helping them to integrate into our culture has been a real challenge. Understanding these families, along with the Vietnamese parents, the several Chinese clients, and the families from India and Pakistan we serve, has kept us very busy. The cultural variations among these folks are great and to treat them all the same does them a great disservice.

Hispanic families are also increasing in many areas and, like the Asian population, cannot be assumed to share one specific set of cultural customs.

The emphasis today in child welfare services is first on family preservation (see Chapter 8) and on permanency planning. Child welfare advocates agree that, whenever possible, the best place for children is with their families. Thus the family must be given assistance in solving whatever problems make it difficult to deal with their parenting role. Kadushin and Martin (1988) cite eight factors that may affect the family's ability to care for and nurture its children adequately: parental role unoccupied; parental incapacity; parental role rejection; intrarole conflict; interrole conflict; role transitions; child incapacity and/or handicap; and deficiency of community resources (15).

Parental role unoccupied refers to the situation in which there is no parent in a particular role. This parent, either mother or father, might not be present due to death, physical or mental illness, imprisonment, migration, or because the child was born to an unwed mother. *Parental incapacity* describes the parent's inability to adequately provide for his or her children due to this adult's emotional immaturity, ignorance, illness, physical disability, mental retardation, or drug addiction. A parent is said to be involved in *role rejection* when she or he has neglected, abandoned, or physically abused her or his children. *Intrarole conflict* refers to parents who recognize their need to parent but are not clear about exactly how to do this. For example, parents may narrowly define their role, leaving some family needs unmet. One single father felt that, as long as he provided for his children financially, his obligation was met. He therefore expected his 10-year-old daughter to be the caregiver of her younger sister and to take care of the house and meals. Or the parent may overly restrict the child, assuming that she or he is doing what is best for the child. *Interrole conflict,* on the other hand, occurs when the role of parent conflicts with another role expected by society. For example, working mothers may find it difficult to attend to the needs of their children while giving full attention to their jobs. Assuming both roles simultaneously often requires some adjustments, especially for single mothers.

Some parents find themselves in the midst of *role transition issues.* When a parent is suddenly disabled or the spouse dies, accommodations are necessary to fill the parenting role. Each developmental stage, for both parents and children, has the potential for creating a crisis within the family. And divorce and remarriage may also be challenges for all parties.

Children who have a disability (*child incapacity or handicap*) can be difficult for their parents, requiring the parents to seek help to meet this challenge. And finally, even though parents may recognize a problem, the *deficiency of community services* can prevent their ability to address the need adequately (Kadushin and Martin, 1988).

All of these issues may require the child welfare system to intervene. If the family cannot be helped to deal with these problems and thereby remain intact, then substitute care, either temporary or permanent, may be necessary. When this is the case, the goal of the agency will be in favor of permanency planning or finding the best possible plan for the child as quickly as possible. The current emphasis on permanency planning originated with a study done by Henry Maas and Richard Engles, *Children in Need of Parents* (1959). These authors looked at nine communities and discovered that, of the 260,000 children in foster care at that time, only 25% of them would return to their parents. The remainder of these children appeared destined to remain in foster care throughout their childhood. Despite the fact that foster care was deemed a temporary arrangement, no permanent plans had been devised for them, and the authors recommended that the children be returned home, placed for adoption, or that another permanent plan be created for them. This study also prompted the writing of the landmark work, *Beyond the Best Interests of the Child* (originally published under Goldstein, Freud, and Solnit, 1973), which, in turn, alerted child welfare advocates to the need for permanent plans for children (Popple and Leighninger, 2001). The recognition of the need for permanency planning was the impetus for the Adoption Assistance and Child Welfare Act of 1980 (mentioned earlier).

In some instances, efforts to preserve the family are stymied by the controversy around getting families off welfare. Legislation that prevents unwed parents from receiving benefits under certain circumstances can serve to prohibit them from parenting. For example, in some states, an unwed mother cannot receive welfare unless she returns to or remains in her family of origin. For young mothers who have been abused at home, this plan is not safe for their baby or them. Other states propose that the birth of additional children should mean the cessation of benefits. In order for families to get off welfare and to parent effectively, they will require additional social supports that are, at this point, not available. Key components in President Bush's Welfare Reform program involve emphasis in child care funding and strengthening child support enforcement. It is part of the president's plan to direct funds to services that will "encourage healthy and stable marriages."

There is also an increased emphasis on serving children with special needs. Both in the educational setting (see Chapter 5) and for substitute care (see Chapters 11 and 13) practitioners recognize that the needs of children with a variety of disabilities require alternative methods of intervention.

Impact of Current Child Welfare Practices on Children

Experts have become increasingly aware of how the services offered to children and their families impact the consumers that they strive to benefit. We have long recognized the importance of early development on children's later ability to function. We know from the studies of Bowlby (1973, 1982, 1988) and others that maternal-infant bonding or attachment is important in the formation of the individual. Levy and Orlans (1998) comment:

> *Attachment is the deep and enduring connection established between a child and caregiver in the first several years of life. It profoundly influences every component of the human condition—mind, body, emotions, relationships and values. (1)*

Attachment is created through a consistent, reciprocal relationship between the parent and child. Not to provide the child with such a relationship is to compromise or disrupt this attachment and put the child at risk for a myriad of serious problems. Levy and Orlans (1998) suggest that *attachment disorder* can be created by such circumstances and events as parental substance abuse, child abuse or neglect, teen parenting, family violence, poor environmental stimulation, separation, and even poverty. These are the very circumstances that bring children to the attention of the child welfare system. So the neglected child of a drug-abusing mother who was battered by her husband is removed from the only home he knew through court intervention. This child demonstrates many of the characteristics that are associated with attachment disorder—difficulty with trust, inability to be affectionate or empathize with anyone, intense anger, lack of compliance with caregivers, self-destructive behavior, destruction of property, cruelty, and hyperactivity. What does such a child need to heal? Most needed are consistency, compassion, and patience (Levy and Orlans, 1998). Enter the child welfare system. The child is placed in a foster home, then another and then another. He is placed for adoption but the adoption placement fails and he returns to foster care. Finally, convinced that he is unable to make another transition to a family, he is placed in residential treatment where he is seen by a myriad of residential caregivers, numerous teachers, and several therapists. And we wonder why he does not improve.

We cannot totally condemn the child welfare system—as the previous paragraph would seem to imply. Practitioners have spent years trying to make the system work for children, yet experts feel that we are far from meeting that goal. Now it is up to the future generation of professionals to recognize the need for more consistency in the lives of troubled children. There are many ways that this can be accomplished, as will be demonstrated in the chapters following. We have the knowledge to improve the lives of children and their families. It is now up to us to reevaluate and make the system work.

Services in the Twenty-First Century

It is impossible to predict accurately the challenges for the provision of child welfare services during this century due to the unpredictable nature of environmental influences (i.e., political climate and economic fluctuations) in a constantly changing society. Many unresolved issues involving children and their families in the past century continue to plague us today. These include poverty, inadequate health and mental health care, domestic violence, child abuse and neglect, and alcohol and substance abuse. As a consequence, the need for preventive services and direct services for children and their families will continue. Throughout our history, this country has attempted to meet these needs through a residual approach by providing funds, at a level insufficient to meet the needs, for services if and only if problems become serious and affect larger numbers of people. The trend has been use one solution to fit the needs of those experiencing similar problems and to reinvent previous unsuccessful solutions with a slightly different twist and then blame the victims when these new programs are again proven unsuccessful. For example, the Temporary Assistance to Needy Families programs developed on the Personal Responsibility and Work Opportunity Act of 1996 is really a "workfare" program with another name. As is the case in many of these programs, some individuals have been successful in leaving welfare and others have not. Unfortunately, there is little or no research to evaluate the success of programs.

What direction should child welfare services and policy making relating to child welfare be taking in the twenty-first century? The ultimate goal would be to develop and implement a national family policy based on the models of other programs and services that exist in other family-friendly industrialized nations. In effect, residual services would be replaced by institutional services available to those in need as problems arise, with no stigma attached. Both prevention and treatment would be emphasized. A bureaucratic structure would continue to be necessary for deliver of services. However, agencies would have the flexibility to individualize services based on the specific needs of their clients. The foundation for services would be based on existing research concerning programs and services that have been successful in meeting the service goals for families. Additional research would continue to be the deciding factor in continuing, changing, or discontinuing services.

To accomplish this goal, effective lobbying of those with political power at the local, state, and national levels would have to occur. Lobbyists would need to be knowledgeable about research findings and realistic about costs. The tax structure would have to be changed to support comprehensive services that would involve higher tax rates for large, profitable corporations and equitable taxing of wealthy individuals. Funding for some services would be provided by employers or shared by employers and employees (e.g., health insurance, including coverage for mental health and child care centers on site or located in areas adjacent to several businesses). Comprehensive effective preventive services are less costly to society compared with intervention after the fact (e.g., building prisons and providing necessary services to those incarcerated is more costly than preventing the problems resulting in imprisonment). As a society, we need to accept that a small proportion of those in our society may need supportive services throughout their lifetime to function at the maximum of their capabilities.

Providing Services for Children Today

The child welfare worker assumes many different roles in the provision of services today. Each of these roles may require a different type of training. The first "child welfare workers" were volunteers, and it wasn't until the 1900s that child welfare became a field as such (Heffernan et al., 1997). What might a child welfare worker do? This is largely dependent on the type of service or agency in which he or she is employed. Table 1.2, based on the chapters to follow, gives an idea of what roles one might perform. It is far from inclusive of all the possible roles.

The roles mentioned in Table 1.2 require different levels of education. Some agencies will hire residential counselors or aides without a college education, but most prefer an associate or bachelor's degree. Although some agencies will hire people who have a degree in unrelated fields, most prefer that the degree be earned in such disciplines as human services, social work, or other subjects that prepare one for social service delivery. The more specialized the role, the more education required. For example, counseling often requires a master's in social work or counseling.

What a child welfare worker does from day to day depends largely on the type of agency. Most child welfare workers perform their roles in an agency or in some type of bureaucratic setting. This can add to the frustration of the job, as many bureaucracies, in order to maintain themselves and ensure quality, require that staff follow a great many procedures and document these through paperwork. "The paperwork can seem overwhelming at times," recounts a

TABLE 1.2 Examples of Child Welfare Roles

Type of Service	Agency	Possible Job Title	Roles Performed
Family Services	Family Planning Clinic	Counselor	Counsels on contraception, family planning, pregnancy, prenatal care, and so on
	Early Intervention	Home Visitor	Provides support for new parents, especially at-risk families
For Homeless	Homeless Shelter	Shelter Staff	Provides support, counseling in budgeting, housing, child care, homemaking, advocacy for families in shelter
	Housing Agency	Advocate	Provides support, advocacy, or counseling for families seeking housing; helps identify housing and places families
For Drug Addicted	Various Drug Agencies		Provides support and counseling for parents or teens who are drug addicted, and drug abuse prevention training in schools and the community
Daycare	Daycare Center (private or federal, e.g., Head Start)	Teacher or Aide or Family Worker	Provides services for children in day care setting; does outreach to parents
Education	Schools	School Counselor, Aide, Health Educator	Provides a variety of services to remove barriers to children's learning, such as counseling, groups, aid to special needs children; functions as a liaison to parents
Counseling	Family Service Agency	Counselor	Provides counseling to families and children
Child Protection	Child Protective Services	Child Protection Social Worker	Provides case management to families at risk for child maltreatment
Court Services	Juvenile Court	Social Worker Probation Officer	Provides counseling or case management for children and families seen by the juvenile court
Teen Parents	Agency for Teens Family Service Agency	Counselor Residential Staff	Provides support, counseling, or case management for teen parents, and serves as residential staff in homes for unwed mothers
Foster Care	Child Protection Agency Family Service Agency	Social Worker	Provides home studies of potential foster parents; places and supervises children in foster homes
Adoption	Adoption Agency Family Service Agency Child Protection Agency	Social Worker	Provides home studies on potential adoptive parents; places and supervises children in adoptive homes
Residential Care	Residential Treatment	Social Worker Residential Staff	Supervises children in residential settings, and provides counseling for children in care

veteran worker, "but it all seems worth it when a child and his or her family are receiving the service they need" (see Crosson-Tower, 2003).

Training is a vital part of child welfare. Unfortunately, some agencies in the past have used the "learning by doing" method to train staff to the detriment of the clients. Currently, the U.S. Department of Health and Human Services has available, under the Child Welfare Training Section 426 of the Social Security Act, funds for nonprofit agencies and educational institutions to train staff in public child welfare agencies (Johnson and Schwartz, 1996). Many professionals feel that it is also advisable to have college training in order to provide adequate services for families and children.

The field of child welfare can be a challenging one, but the role of the child welfare worker also has numerous rewards.

not just trad. services

Summary

The role of child welfare services is to provide a safety net for children. To better understand how today's services for children operate, it is helpful to consider the past. Children have always been at the mercy of their caregivers. Unwanted children were dealt with from earliest times by abortion, infanticide, and even abandonment. Children were also required to work alongside adults who may have disregarded the fact that the children were not as strong and not as able to work long hours. An early form of child labor was indenture, a system whereby children were apprenticed to tradesmen to learn by doing. It was not until the late nineteenth and early twentieth centuries that such reformers as Jane Addams, Homer Folks, Grace Abbott, and Julia Lathrop sought reform in child labor laws. Several agencies have advocated for children over the years. The U.S. Children's Bureau (founded in 1912), the Family Welfare Association (formerly the Charity Organization Society), and the Children's Defense Fund all had a role in protecting children and advocating for their well-being.

The responsibility for children originally rested entirely with their parents. Children were expected to follow their parents even to almshouses, in which the conditions could be unfit for adults let alone their offspring. Later, the care of orphaned children or children whose parents could not care for them shifted to orphanages. In the late nineteenth century, Charles Loring Brace, feeling that family life for children was preferable to an institutional setting, instituted "placing out" whereby children were sent by train to the midwestern United States to find homes with farm families.

Minority children were excluded from the programs aimed at white children. For African American children, this could mean being sent to a reform school rather than an orphanage or a private home. Native American children were often sent to boarding schools so that they could be better assimilated into the white culture.

With advances in research about child development came the recognition that children needed a family environment, and placement in foster and adoptive homes became the priority. In addition, the well-publicized case of the maltreated Mary Ellen Wilson in 1874 gave rise to the Society for the Prevention of Cruelty to Children and the first formalized efforts to protect children from abuse and neglect.

Since the early 1900s, there have been numerous advances in the provision of services for children. Today, the concepts of family preservation (that all reasonable attempts to maintain the family intact must be made) and permanency planning (finding a permanent arrangement for children whose parents cannot care for them as early as possible) are the key phases that characterize the provision of services. We are also beginning to recognize the issue of attachment in the lives of children and to seek new ways to provide the consistency needed to help children develop healthy relationships.

Funding, always an issue in the provision of child welfare services, is a major concern. Critics of the move to collapse funds into block grants contend that services to children would be cut substantially. Others argue that it is the "personal touch" that is lacking in today's agency efforts. The fact remains that children are our most important resource, and strengthening the safety net that protects them from harm and enables them to develop safely and healthfully is the obligation of all adults.

EXPLORATION QUESTIONS

1. What problems characterize the lives of children today?
2. Why did early people practice infanticide?
3. What is meant by the term *indenture*? Why might it not have served the best interests of the child?
4. What efforts were made toward reform in child labor? Who were some of the main advocates?
5. Trace the history of services for children whose parents could not care for them.
6. How did the services for minority children differ from those provided for white children?
7. Cite some key agencies that advocate for children. What do they do?
8. What is meant by *attachment disorder*? What role does this play in the provision of child welfare services?
9. What recent legislation has advocated for children?
10. What are the major trends in the provision of child welfare today?
11. What types of roles might a child welfare worker take in helping children?

REFERENCES

Bowlby, J. (1973). *Attachment and Loss. Vol 2: Separation*. New York: Basic Books.

Bowlby, J. (1982). *Attachment and Loss. Vol. 1: Separation*. New York: Basic Books.

Bowlby, J. (1988). *A Secure Base: Parent-Child Attachment and Healthy Human Development.* New York: Basic Books.

Bremner, R. H. (1995). "Child Welfare in Fact and Fiction," *Child Welfare,* 74(1), 19–31.

Caulfield, E. (1931). *The Infant Welfare Movement of the Eighteenth Century.* New York: Paul Locker. http://www.Childrensdefense.org (updated 2002)

Children's Defense Fund. (2001). *The State of America's Children Yearbook.* Washington, DC: Children's Defense Fund.

Child Welfare League of America. "Child Welfare History," at http://www.cwla.org (updated 2001).

Children's Defense Fund. At http://www.childrensdefense.org (updated 2002).

Crosson-Tower, C. (2003). *From the Eye of the Storm: The Experiences of a Child Welfare Worker.* Boston: Allyn and Bacon.

Cook, J. F. (1995). "A History of Placing-Out: The Orphan Trains," *Child Welfare,* 74(1), 181–197.

Dickens, C. (1981). *David Copperfield.* Oxford: Oxford University Press, 1849.

Dickens, C. (1987). *Oliver Twist.* Oxford: Oxford University Press, 1838.

Disraeli, B. (1845). *Sybil: The Two Nations.* London: Oxford University Press.

Downs, S. W., Moore, E., McFadden, E. J., & Costin, L. B. (1999). *Child Welfare and Family Services.* White Plains, NY: Longman.

Friedman, A. B. (1956). *The Viking Book of Folk Ballads of the English-Speaking World.* New York: Viking.

Goldstein, J., Freud, A., & Solnit, A. J. (1973). *Beyond the Best Interests of the Child.* New York: Free Press.

Hacsi, T. (1995). "From Indenture to Family Foster Care: A Brief History of Child Placing," *Child Welfare,* 74(1), 162–180.

Heffernan, J., Shuttlesworth, G., & Ambrosino, R. (1997). *Social Work and Social Welfare.* St. Paul: West.

Hegar, R. L., & Scannapieco, M. (1999). *Kinship Foster Care: Policy, Practice and Research.* New York: Oxford University Press.

Holt, M. I. (2001). *Indian Orphanages.* Lawrence: University of Kansas Press.

Johnson, D. (1999). *America's Children: Key National Indicators of Well-Being.* Washington, DC: U.S. Government Printing Office.

Johnson, L. C., & Schwartz, C. L. (1996). *Social Welfare: A Response to Human Need.* Boston: Allyn and Bacon.

Kadushin, A., & Martin, J. (1988). *Child Welfare Services.* New York: Macmillan.

Kempe, C. H., & Helfer, R. (1968). *The Battered Child.* Chicago: University of Chicago Press.

Langer, W. L. (1974). "Infanticide: A Historical Survey," *History of Childhood Quarterly,* 1, 353–365.

Levy, T. M., & Orlans, M. (1998). *Attachment, Trauma and Healing: Understanding and Treating Attachment Disorder in Children and Families.* Washington, DC: Child Welfare League of America.

Maas, H. S., & Engles, R. E. (1959). *Children in Need of Parents.* New York: Columbia University Press.

Mannes, M. (1995). "Factors and Events Leading to the Passage of the Indian Child Welfare Act," *Child Welfare,* 74(1), 264–282.

Merkel-Holguin, L. A., with Sobel, A. (1993). *The Child Welfare Stat Book 1993.* Washington, DC: Child Welfare League of America.

Pecora, P., Plocnick, R. D., Barth, R. P., Whittaker, J. K., & Maluccioo, A. N. (2000). *The Child Welfare Challenge.* New York: Aldine DeGruyter.

Peebles-Wilkins, W. (1995). "Janie Porter Barrett and the Virginia Industrial School for Colored Girls: Community Response to the Needs of African American Children," *Child Welfare,* 74(1), 143–161.

Popple, P. R., & Leighninger, L. (2001) *Social Work, Social Welfare and American Society.* Boston: Allyn and Bacon.

Schorr, L. (1989). *Within Our Reach: Breaking the Cycle of Disadvantage.* New York: Anchor.

Smith, E. P. (1995). "Bring Back the Orphanages? What Policymakers of Today Can Learn from the Past," *Child Welfare,* 74(1), 115–142.

Stadum, B. (1995). "The Dilemma in Saving Children from Child Labor: Reform and Casework at Odds with Families' Needs (1900–1938)," *Child Welfare,* 74(1), 33–55.

Stone, L. (1977). *The Family, Sex and Marriage in England, 1500–1800.* New York: Harper & Row.

Sumner, W. G. (1959). *Folkways.* New York: Dover.

Terrell, M. C. (1899). "The Duty of the National Association of Colored Women to the Race" *Church Review* (pp. 340–354). In Mary Church Terrell Papers. Washington, DC: Moorland-Springarn Research Center, Howard University.

Thurston, H. W. (1930). *The Dependent Child.* New York: Columbia University Press.

Trattner, W. I. (1970). *Crusade for Children: A History of the National Child Labor Committee and Child Labor Reform in America.* Chicago: Quadrangle Books.

Tuttle, W. M. (1995). "Rosie the Riveter and Her Latchkey Children: What Americans Can Learn about Child Day Care from the Second World War," *Child Welfare,* 74(1), 92–114.

U.S. Government. (1999). "America's Children: Key National Indicators of Well-Being 1999." Washington DC: U.S. Government.

Wolins, M., & Piliavin, I. (1964). *Institution of Foster Family: A Century of Debate.* New York: Child Welfare League of America.

Zastrow, C. (2000). *Introduction to Social Work and Social Welfare.* Pacific Grove, CA: Brooks/Cole.

CHAPTER

2 The Changing Family

$\mathbf{A}$ family has traditionally begun when two people decide to join together for the purpose of sharing their futures and possibly bringing into the world or into their lives children whom they expect to raise. Throughout history, no one institution has had more impact on the forming of the values of the society than the family. Today, the family may look quite different than it did in previous generations. The model of the "intact nuclear household unit composed of a male breadwinner, his full-time homemaker wife, and their dependent children" (Walsh, 1993, 13) belongs, for the most part, to the past. Yet, the Census of 2000 indicated that only 24% of households in the United States were made up of two parents (male and female) and their mutual children. Modern families may consist of a single adult, multiple generations, heterosexual or homosexual couples, or a mosaic of color, values, and culturally diverse variations.

Numerous factors have contributed to drastic changes in the picture of the family of today. First, there has been a decline in early marriage, and second, especially in some racial and ethnic groups, a growing tendency not to marry

23

at all. Also, marriages often do not last, leading to single-parent families and blended families. The need for mothers to work often leaves increased responsibility for care to extended family members, especially grandparents. And the emergence of more and more same-sex couples also has an impact.

Today, a majority of children in the United States will be born outside of marriage, and will spend at least part of their childhoods with a single parent. A significant number of children will experience several changes in the composition of their family (Teachman et al., 2000).

Why has marriage—especially one-time marriage—become less of a way of life for Americans? Teachman and colleagues (2000) blame the changes on the rapid shift in the economic environment that faces families in the twenty-first century. Although employment opportunities have increased for young women, their male counterparts are plagued with more uncertain futures. This may often lead to delayed marriage while the woman pursues her career goals and resists taking on a less secure partner. Once married, the employment of both the husband and wife in a family has forced a renegotiation of long taken-for-granted family tasks, roles, and expectations. The failure to forge a workable arrangement often leads to divorce. For lower socioeconomic groups, new regulations about financial aid have also influenced family composition.

Nonetheless, there is hope for the American family. Family members are learning to make their own individual adjustments to the economic crises and to their own needs. For example, male partners may be seen in the role of primary caregiver more than in years past, and the leveling off of the divorce rate suggests that couples are successfully renegotiating the assignment of domestic duties. Single parents as well as lower socioeconomic groups continue to feel pressure, but some policy analysts also feel that the current tone in the administration is more pro-family. Hopefully, continued policy changes will reflect that optimism.

No matter how the family is defined or configured, some form of family is responsible for protecting children and imparting to them the mores of the society in which they live.

The Responsibilities and Rights of the Family

In a world of flux, it is expected that the family will provide the context for the procreation, enculturation (imparting of society's values), and protection of children. When we think of the concept of family, we usually think of a group of people who choose to live together, or at least have regular contact, for the purpose of performing specific functions (Crosson-Tower, 2002). These functions can be broken down into a series of responsibilities taken on by the family system. First, it is assumed that the family will be responsible for *procreation*. Although biologically, procreation may require a male and a female partner, it is not uncommon for these individuals to procreate but, for whatever reason, decide not to remain together to parent the child. Whatever the family unit involved, it is expected that the family will then be responsible for the *so-*

cialization of the child, helping him or her to learn to relate to other members of society, both peers and adults. Families are also expected to teach children the values of the society, the process of *enculturation*. By verbalizing to and modeling for children, the parental figures let them know what is deemed appropriate by the culture in which they live. In addition, families model appropriate gender-linked and cultural roles (Mason et al., 1998; Hess et al., 1993). Male children learn from their male caregivers just as females learn from their female caregivers what is relevant to their gender.

Families are expected to provide *protection* for their offspring, ensuring that these children are given as safe an environment as possible to grow into adulthood. Families also *provide both financial and emotional support* to their members. They are expected to *meet the child's other basic needs* such as food, shelter, clothing, and affection. Our culture also expects that the family will *provide for the child's medical and educational needs*. Finally, the family has the extremely important role of *interpreting the world to the child and the child to the world*. The following situation illustrates the interpretation of the child to the world.

CASE EXAMPLE

Franz

Franz is a 12-year-old child with severe handicaps, whose younger brothers protect and nurture him with diligence. Unable to speak, Franz uses a wooden board on which the alphabet is printed. To make his needs known, he has learned to point to the letters on the board and spell out his requests. At a very early age, each of his three younger brothers learned to read his words or understand the hand signals he uses. "It is not unusual," recounts his mother, "to see Franz talking to a stranger surrounded by his brothers who are eagerly interpreting. The children seem to find it a way of connecting that meets everyone's needs."

Families who meet the expectations society has of them are subsequently awarded the *right to privacy,* and they carry out their roles with a minimum of societal intervention. The functional family need only deal directly with society when it comes to the school and the medical community. It is the family that does not meet its obligations that comes to the attention of the services designed to provide a safety net for family functioning.

The Setting for Today's Family

It is not always easy for the family to meet its responsibilities, especially against the backdrop of the complexity of today's world. There are several major factors that affect family functioning and require accommodation on the part of each family system.

The *violence* that characterizes society today can significantly affect children and the family (see Chapter 4 for more discussion). Daily, children are exposed to violence in the streets as well as in the media. The events of September 11, 2001, have spawned feelings of vulnerability to terrorism. Family violence, too, is at an all-time high. Whether the violence is within the family or external to the family, it will have an impact on the functioning of the family unit.

Divorce continues to threaten the stability of the modern home. Although the divorce statistics appear to be leveling out to some extent, the reality is that many families still find themselves coping with the emotional and financial ramifications of this phenomenon. With it, divorce brings an increase in *single-parent households* while the supports available for these single parents continue to decrease (Mason et al., 1998; Downs et al., 1999). In addition, two-parent families, as well as single-parent families, find it necessary for the *caregivers to work outside the home,* requiring more alternative care for children.

Profile of Today's Family

The family is a complex system that constantly changes. Within the greater system are a series of subsystems. The *parent subsystem* is made up of caregivers who are responsible for making decisions and regulating the activities of the family unit. It is expected that parents will protect and nurture their children and teach them the values of the culture so that they might grow to take their places in society. To do this, parents not only provide verbal cues to proper behavior but also model the behavior and attitudes that are expected socially.

The *sibling subsystem* is composed of the children in a given family and provides an arena for trying out relationships with peers. Children have an opportunity to compete, fight, negotiate, and learn from each other so that they can eventually transfer these skills to peers outside of the family (Minuchin, 1981). In the healthy family, there are clear boundaries between the parental and sibling subsystems. Parents have specific roles and children have their roles as well. Family dysfunction can occur when these generational boundaries become compromised. The sexually abusive family is characterized by a blurring of generational boundaries. Here, the sexual relationship that is appropriate between adults crosses boundaries and involves the children. By the same token, generational boundaries must also be fluid enough to allow members to have appropriate interaction with each other. When boundaries are too rigid, children often feel abandoned and as if their parents are not available to them emotionally.

In addition to these two main subsystems, families are composed of a variety of other units. For example, all the males of a particular family comprise another subsystem, as do all the females. Extended families living together increase the possibilities for subsystem combinations. For instance, there may be grandparent subsystems.

A family system must also maintain boundaries with the outside world. If these boundaries are poorly defined, the family may lose its identity as a family. If they are too rigidly kept, the family becomes isolated from the world in which it operates.

Family Roles and Rules

Historically, family members have assumed a set of roles expected by society and an individualized set of roles dictated by the individual family. Often, these overlapped. For example, at one time the father figure in the home was expected to be the breadwinner, and the female figure had the role of maintaining the home. Most families accepted these roles and governed themselves according to them. Certainly, some families deviated, based on their own needs to achieve homeostasis. Today, there have ceased to be these clear-cut, societally prescribed roles, partially due to the economic need for both parents to work outside the home. Therefore, families are more apt to find their own way of taking care of the family tasks. For some, the mother is still the regulator of the household functioning while also maintaining a job outside. Still other families find ways to share the roles and tasks inherent in everyday life. The assignment of these roles can in itself create stressors. Increasingly, women are pointing to the need for parents to take on more equal responsibility for child rearing so they are not overtaxed in their roles as wife and mother. New generations are increasingly conscious of this need to share in maintaining a home, but not always sure how to put it in practice. The way in which the family deals with these issues may be largely based on the personality structure of the adults (Swanson, 1993).

Some families find that their ethnic orientation imposes roles on them that they find difficulty in maintaining. For example, some cultures still see the man as the head of household and the primary breadwinner. Yet, it may be easier for the woman to work outside the home. As a result, the male feels he is losing some of the respect previously given him.

The assignment of roles can be spoken or unspoken and is often quite complex. In addition, roles are not always functional. Children are sometimes cast into roles that do not benefit them in their healthy development. Parents who are themselves unable to accept responsibility and nurture may see their children as their caregivers, thus robbing children of their right to be taken care of and protected.

Roles are often supported by family rules. Rules are "repetitive patterns of interaction that family members develop with each other" (Crosson-Tower, 2002, 26). Rules are either spoken or unspoken and govern the way in which families communicate and perform. Rules that are unspoken in one family may be spoken in another. For example, in one family the females do the inside tasks, such as cleaning and cooking, while the men do the outside tasks, such as mowing the lawn. In some homes this is just understood while in others it is clearly stated.

Rules may also support or cover dysfunctional behavior. In an alcoholic family, it might be understood that family members stay out of Dad's way when he is drinking or make excuses for Mom when her drug problem impedes her functioning. In sexually abusive families, siblings often know not to communicate with each other. This may actually be something impressed on them by the perpetrator, who recognizes that the secret of his abuse is best kept if family members do not talk to each other about it. Rules dictate how family members will behave, feel, and think. Conflict with these rules can also create conflict within the family.

Communication Patterns

Communication within a family system often is at the root of how the family functions. Communication is not always on the surface nor do people always communicate through words. Gestures, postures, voice intonation, and facial expressions sometimes say more than the words spoken. Culture also has an impact on the way in which families communicate. Some ethnic populations use communication patterns that are hierarchical. Elders are respected (as in Asian cultures) and the young must listen and learn from them. Some families express their emotions freely, given their cultural heritage, while in others, the show of emotions denotes a lack of strength or self-control (Mass and Geaga-Rosenthal, 2000). Family rules differ from culture to culture. Many cultures see the father as the family head and his word is not to be disputed. In this case, rules such as "asking father before decisions are made" are paramount. In still other cultures, the mother may be in a pivotal position.

It is important for those working with particular cultural groups to be familiar with the mores and values of that group. Not to take the time to do so could result in an inability to help the family and could even insult them, as the following event illustrates.

CASE EXAMPLE

From a Muslim Perspective

A Muslim family was referred to a family service agency by their son's school when the boy had become too difficult for school personnel to handle. The family came reluctantly, the mother encased in her traditional garb, including a veil over the lower half of her face. Interested in knowing how the family was functioning, the worker, unfamiliar with Muslim custom, made eye contact with the mother and asked her how she felt about their child's acting out. The whole family's reaction was immediate and the worker quickly realized that he had somehow offended them. It was not until he talked with another worker that he learned the cultural error of making eye contact with a Muslim woman and not allowing her to go through her husband to communicate.

To be clearly effective, communication patterns in families must be clear and open. With added stress on the family system, effective communication can often get lost in the demands of everyday life. It is often incomplete or unclear communication that brings families to child welfare agencies.

Observation of the Family as a System

One highly effective method of looking at the family as a system with its roles, rules, and communication patterns is through the use of genograms. *Genograms* are a "schematic diagram of the family's relationship system, in the form of a genetic tree, usually including at least three generations" (Goldenberg and Goldenberg, 2000, 325). Specific symbols (see Figure 2.1) are used to represent family members and relationships between them. Anecdotal data can then be added.

One advantage of a genogram is that it can give both the helper and the family a quick and fairly comprehensive view of what is occurring in the family, what patterns are present, and how these are impacted by previous generations. Often, clients are helped to recognize that they are part of generations of dysfunction and that the patterns they now practice have been handed down from previous generations. When this becomes evident, individuals and families can more effectively strive to break these patterns for future generations.

The Hartowski family came to the attention of social services because Mr. Hartowski was sexually abusing his daughter. It is obvious from the genogram (see Figure 2.2) that child sexual abuse has been a part of several generations as well as other types of family dysfunction. From the overall view provided by a genogram, it would become clear that intervention is needed in this generation.

Watts-Jones (1997) cautions, however, that not all families fit neatly into a genogram. The kinship bonds of African American families, for example, make it difficult to use the classic biologically based genogram. Watts-Jones proposes a genogram for African Americans that takes into consideration kinship/functional ties.

Types of Families

The picture of family life differs greatly today. Acock and Demo (1994) studied 2,457 families to look at diversity and family well-being. Within this sample they identified four types of family configurations: First marriages (N = 1,085), Divorced (N = 677), Stepfamilies (N = 277), and Continuously single mothers

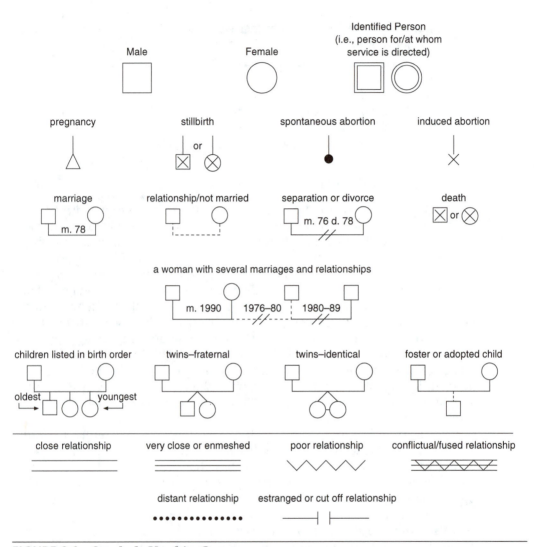

FIGURE 2.1   Symbols Used in Genograms

Source: From *Genograms in Family Assessment* by Monica McGoldrick and Randy Gerson. Copyright © 1985 by Monica McGoldrick and Randy Gerson. Used by permission of W. W. Norton & Company, Inc.

(N = 418) (51–52). The sample represented all income levels and included 255 African American, 1,367 white, 150 Hispanic mothers, and 26 mothers of other ethnic origins (64). African American children were more likely to come from single-parent households (42.7%), whereas only 3.9% of white children and 18.0% of Hispanic children have single parents. White children were more likely to be in first-married families (70.8%) or stepfamilies (11.1%). In contrast,

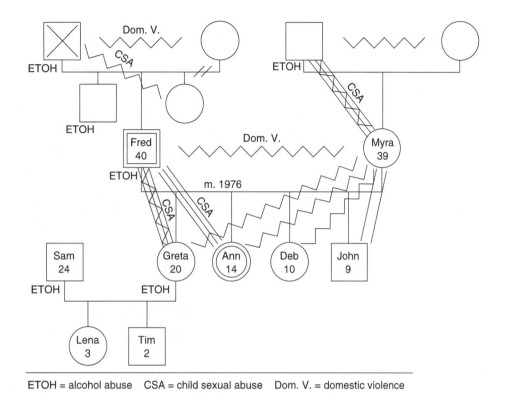

ETOH = alcohol abuse   CSA = child sexual abuse   Dom. V. = domestic violence

FIGURE 2.2   The Hartowski Family

only 31.8% of African American children are in first-married families and 5.1% in stepfamilies. Thus it is expected that 70% of white children and 94% of African American children will be part of other than a two-parent family system before their eighteenth birthdays (63).

Other authors (Hess et al., 1993; Walsh, 1993; Wells, 1991) divide the family into the two-parent–dual-wage earner family, the single-parent family, and the reconstituted family.

The *two-parent–dual-wage earner* family is the closest remnant of earlier family concepts. Here, two parents strive to raise their mutual children, but economic necessity has required the female parent to also enter the workforce. This family system grapples not only with common family demands but also with the time management and role assignment issues that are inherent in both parents being outside of the home for much of the time. It is the latter set of issues that have created the need for research and intervention and caused the family to seek help more often than any other. The pervading myth, despite the reality of today, is of father as breadwinner and mother as nurturer, and it is not uncommon for families to have difficulty adjusting these perceptions to meet their needs.

The *single-parent family* is usually headed by the mother (although fathers as single parents appear to be increasing as divorce laws attempt to cater to the best interest of the child) who tries to assume the role of both parents. The one-parent status of this family may have been created either by divorce, by death, or because the mother/parents chose not to marry.

The *reconstituted* or *blended family* refers to one in which there are two parents, one or both of whom have had children by another partner. These parents marry, bringing with them their respective families, which they then co-parent. They may also bring into the family children of their own. The definition of role, rules, and communication patterns for such families may be challenging. Each adult brings along at least two sets of role expectations (their family of origin and their first marriage/relationship) and the children may compare what they have been used to between their biological parents and what has developed with the new family system (McWhirter et al., 1998).

In addition to these family types, Walsh (1993) identifies several others: families by adoption (see Chapter 12) and gay and lesbian families.

CASE EXAMPLE

Rebecca and Denise

Rebecca and Denise have been partners for 10 years. After Rebecca's divorce, she was concerned about raising her two small children alone. Her early marriage had been the result of a pregnancy and had never been very happy. When she met Denise at work, she was very attracted to her. Their relationship eventually became intimate, and the two women had a commitment ceremony and settled down together to raise Rebecca's children.

Although gay and lesbian families have long been discounted as a viable family structure, there are an increasing number of them today (McWhirter et al., 1998; Mason et al., 1998). Laird (1993) comments that "'normalcy' [is] an idea located in the eye of the beholder" (283). Although some argue that being raised by two parents of the same sex does not provide children with adequate gender models, others point out that having two parents gives the child more adult role models. Many children grow up in single-parent families with a myriad of stresses placed on their sole parent. On the significance of families created by same-sex couples, Laird further comments:

Family theorists would do well to heed the lesbian and gay family, for it can teach us important things about other families, about gender relationships, about parenting, about adaptation to tensions in this society, and especially about strength and resilience. For in spite of the pervasive and profound stigmatization of gay life, gay men and lesbians are building stable and satisfying couple relationships and forming families that seem to be doing at least as well as other kinds of families in carrying out their sociologically defined family roles and tasks. (284)

In years past, families often consisted of multigenerations. Today there are a few *extended or intergenerational family systems,* often more likely among minority or newly immigrated families. Although the children of these groups have more adult models with whom to identify, they may also feel the pull of the greater society to become independent of their traditional cultures. This, in and of itself, can create stress within the family.

One family structure seen increasingly in today's society is *grandparents raising grandchildren.* There are numerous reasons (e.g., teen parents, career-oriented parents) why grandparents become the primary caregivers for their children's children.

Karpel and Strauss (1983) suggest that the family should be seen in several contexts:

The functional family, whose members share household tasks, activities, and child care;

The legal family, which is bound together by its legal structure and altered by divorce or the legal removal of children;

The family by perception, in which members see others as being part of the family (e.g., live-in partner, considered to be acting in the role of mate and second parent, compadres, and kinsfolk);

The biological family, which is held together by blood relationships;

The family of long-term commitments, in which long-term expectations encompassing trust, fairness, and loyalty are present. (as cited by Crosson-Tower, 2002, 23)

Obviously, some of these may overlap, but the framework provides an idea of how the family may see itself or be seen by others.

The Emotional Climate of Families

Each family functions differently depending not only on the composition of that family but also on the backgrounds, personalities, and past experiences of the members. Ideally, caregivers provide warmth, consistency, and stability for their children. In these families, children bond with their caregivers in a process called *attachment* (referred to in Chapter 1). Through the nurturance they receive and the process of attachment, children learn that they are lovable and the world is a friendly place to be. This also enables them to reach out beyond the microcosm that is their family and forge relationships with others. Unfortunately, not all children have the experience of being accepted, nurtured, and encouraged by their parents. Or, even if there is some nuturing, there is also a

TABLE 2.1 Continuum of Attachment

Secure	Anxious	Disorganized	Nonattached
• Comfortable with closeness and trust • Felt security • Vulnerability acceptable • Positive working model • Individuality/togetherness balanced	• Resists or ambivalent about closeness and trust • Moderately controlling and insecure • Negative working model (moderate) • Rejecting or clingy	• Unable to trust and be close • Lacks remorse • Aggressive and punitive control • Negative working model (severe) • Pseudoindependent	• Unable to form emotional connections • Lacks conscience • Predatory behaviors • Negative working model (severe) • Extreme narcissism

Source: Reprinted by special permission of the Child Welfare League of America from Levy, T., & Orlans, M. *Attachment, Trauma, and Healing: Understanding and Treating Attachment Disorder in Children and Families,* 1998, p. 94.

good deal of rigid control and restriction that often prevents the child from feeling good about himself or herself.

McWhirter and colleagues (1998) outline several types of child-rearing styles that may affect the emotional climate of a home (see Figure 2.3). Children will respond to these styles in various ways. Whereas the high support (Warmth) style would certainly encourage attachment and the low support (Hostility) tend to inhibit it, the other styles might be interpreted differently by individual children. For example, in the same family where a permissive atmosphere reigns, one child may develop independence while another rebels against the lack of rules.

Children who are not adequately and consistently nurtured by parents, due to the parents' own problems (often based on their own dysfunctional childhoods), may develop *attachment disruption* or *attachment disorder* (see Table 2.1) or the inability to respond to comfort, form relationships, or cope with stress (Levy and Orlans, 1998). As a result, they may develop conduct disorders, control problems, aggressive or withdrawn behaviors, or antisocial personalities (see Figure 2.4 for a more complete list of symptoms). It is such children who often come to the attention of the child welfare system.

How vital it becomes then that we understand the family, the supports it needs to properly nurture, and how we can help the children that the family has failed.

The Impact of Culture on Families

Families may have totally different roles, rules, and communication patterns depending on the culture in which they reside. The most statistically prevalent

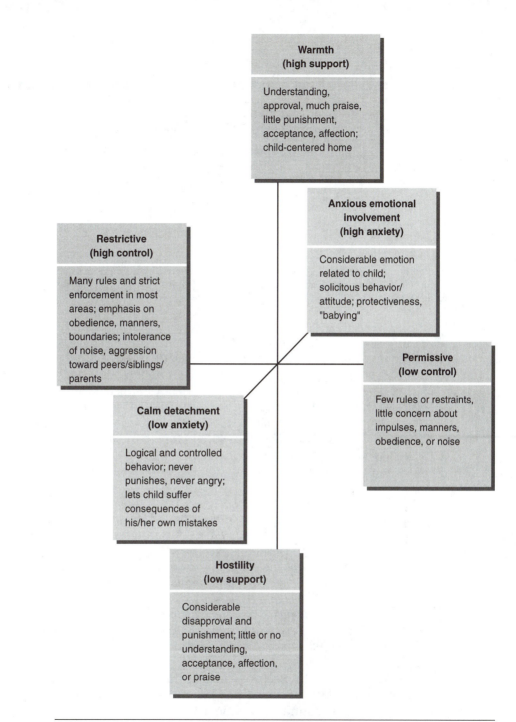

FIGURE 2.3 Dimensions of Child-Rearing Practices

Source: From *At-Risk Youth: A Comprehensive Response, 2nd edition,* by J. J. McWhirter, B. T. McWhirter, A. M. McWhirter, and E. E. McWhirter. © 1998. Reprinted with permission of Brooks/Cole, an imprint of the Wadsworth Group, a division of Thomson Learning. FAX 800-730-2215.

FIGURE 2.4   Characteristics of Children Experiencing Attachment Disorder

- Superficially engaging or "charming"
- Indiscriminately affectionate with strangers
- Lack of eye contact on parental terms
- Not affectionate or cuddly
- Destructive to self or others
- Cruel to animals
- Stealing
- Habitual lying about the obvious
- No impulse control
- Learning lags or difficulty
- Lack of cause and effect thinking
- Lack of a conscience
- Abnormal eating patterns
- Poor peer relationships
- Preoccupation with fire
- Persistent nonsense questions or incessant chatter
- Inappropriately demanding or clingy
- Abnormal speech
- Sexual acting out

Source: Reprinted by special permission of the Child Welfare League of America from Levy, T., & Orlans, M. *Attachment, Trauma, and Healing: Understanding and Treating Attachment Disorder in Children and Families,* 1998, p. 247.

cultures are discussed here, but the child welfare worker should become familiar with the variations present in his or her client population. For example, one can discuss generalized characteristics of Hispanic or Asian families, but within those two cultural groupings is a variety of individual orientations. Mexican families are not necessarily like Puerto Rican families, and Chinese families have different values from families whose origins are in India. Thus one should digest the generalizations but seek more detailed information as necessary.

How an individual family functions is influenced by several variables:

1. *The family's culture of origin;*
2. *The subgroup of that culture and its particular values (for example, cultures with caste systems may have different expectations of individuals depending on their castes);*
3. *The relationship of the culture or the subgroup to the wider culture in which it functions (prejudice and stigma play a role in how well families are able to integrate into the larger society);*
4. *Individual family member characteristics;*
5. *The family members' ability and strategies for adapting to the stresses of living in a family unit. (Crosson-Tower, 2002, 26)*

Leiberman (1990) reflects on the fact that, while other cultures value collectivism, the culture of the United States emphasizes individualism, two social values that he contrasts in some detail.

An individualistic culture is one where a person's social behavior is shaped primarily by personal goals and needs which do not necessarily overlap with the goals and needs of their in-group. Competition is stressed and cooperation is not. In contrast, in a collectivist culture the person's behavior is shaped primarily by the goals, needs, and values of the in-group, even when this involves giving up personal pursuits. These cultures tend to stress cooperation and avoid competition. There is also a high personal identification with the family and a sense of mutual obligation and responsibilities among extended family members. Personal sacrifices are expected on behalf of family welfare.... In individualistic cultures, people who sacrifice important personal goals for the sake of others may be considered masochistic, immature or overly dependent. ..} In a collective culture a person who fails to sacrifice personal goals for the welfare of others is often rebuked as selfish, disloyal, and untrustworthy. (107)

Because many families from collectivist cultures find this a difficult society into which to integrate, it must be assumed that at the root of the problem of an ethnically oriented minority family may be role confusion based on the differences between their cultures of origin and this one. Yet all families have at one time experienced the difficulties inherent in the fact that the United States is the "great melting pot" and therefore does not duplicate any one culture, including the Native American culture that settled it and the European cultures that colonized it.

Families with Anglo-European Roots

When considering culture, there is often no discussion of early immigrants with European heritage and how their values influenced the greater society of today. Such platitudes as "If you don't succeed, try, try again," "Where there's a will, there's a way," or "A penny saved is a penny earned" have become such an integral part of the thinking of so many people that we rarely stop to identify these sentiments as remnants of the philosophy of the early Anglo-European colonists (Hanson, 1998).

Reports of a rich, new world and disillusion with their native land brought early colonists from England, the Netherlands, Spain, Portugal, France, and Italy. They brought with them a desire to forge a new life and a set of values from their own lands. While they interacted with the Native people of their new land, they maintained their own traditions as they settled to hunt, farm, and trade. They possessed a pioneering spirit that was only enhanced by breaking from the rule of England in the 1700s. The westward expansion resulted from this desire to reach out and forge one's own way. With this need to settle and cope in the face of numerous odds came the strengthening of the rugged individualism that produced an undercurrent that still exists in many spheres today.

Values.   The values of those with European heritage tend to include independence, self-directedness, assertiveness, acquisition, equality, freedom, and self-help (Hanson, 1998). In his guide to the United States for foreigners, Althen (1988) suggests the following as representative of American values: (1) individualism and privacy; (2) equality; (3) informality; (4) the future and progress;

(5) goodness of humanity; (6) time; (7) achievement, action, work, and materialism; and (8) directedness and assertiveness (as cited in Hanson, 1998, 71).

The family is greatly affected by these values. Family *privacy*, for example, is a highly valued right among many individuals. It is expected that the family will be left to its own pursuits and allowed to raise its children as the parents see fit. Only when parents maltreat or fail to provide for their children is family sanctity threatened. Even then, some critics of current child welfare practices feel that agencies are too quick to intervene in family life.

Within the family context, everyone is encouraged to become an individual, and the sentiment is that all should be given the space, and in fact have the responsibility, to pursue what is best for their growth and enjoyment. Equality is valued and it is hoped that each individual will be given equal opportunity to achieve.

For many cultures, the American, as described by Althen, seems too informal to the point of being uncultured or uncouth. Slang, casual dress, and open discussions of almost any topic are the norm. The emphasis is on the future and what will happen tomorrow, as opposed to the historical or the happenings of today. Today is regarded in terms of how it will affect tomorrow (Hanson, 1998).

The tenor of communication and behavior is action oriented, direct, materialistic, and based on time constraints. Success is based on power and resources, especially money. Each individual is expected to do his or her best and is often thrown into the arena of fierce competition in which he or she is encouraged to flourish.

Communication Patterns.   Communication among those with European roots is usually relatively open and direct. Warmth toward others is expected, although there is a lack of the ritual characterizing many other cultures in the way people are met and dealt with. People are expected to be seen as equal and therefore they have an equal right to express themselves. Personal space is prized and many individuals expect about an arm's length in their physical closeness to others. There is not an expectation of a great deal of physical closeness such as hand-holding on the street or open displays of affection in public. It is polite to be on time and to keep one's commitments at all cost (Althen, 1988; Hanson, 1998).

The family interprets these norms of communication in different ways, depending on the influence from other cultural groups and the individual upbringing of the parents. For example, some families have little or no ritual in greeting or in their everyday lives; others have more. The Watson family greets relatives and friends with smiles and even handshakes, but it is not common to kiss or hug as a greeting. Their meals are taken informally and family members may come together at meals only if they happen to be there at the same time. The Whites, on the other hand, greet each other with a hug and a kiss, rarely a handshake. They make a practice of eating the evening meal together, and it is expected that each family member will be present unless otherwise arranged with Mrs. White.

Religion and Spirituality. Religion is seen as something that the individual has a right to espouse or not espouse. Because religion and one's spiritual beliefs are considered private, they are usually not discussed. It is also expected that there is a clear separation between church and state, giving rise to such issues as the cessation of prayer in public schools in many states.

The choice and practice of an organized religion is also up to the individual. Most families function within the framework of a Judeo-Christian belief system, with the majority ascribing to some type of Christianity. Although not everyone goes to church or synagogue, holidays that have religious origins, such as Christmas, Easter, and Chanukah, are celebrated by the majority of families (Hanson, 1998).

Families with Native American Roots

Native Americans have their roots in a time long before the European colonists arrived. Despite the changes brought on them over the years by immigrants, many Native American values and customs have survived and are actually seeing a revival as others become interested in the old world philosophy. Today, there are 400 distinct tribes, each with its own variation in customs and practices. Some Native Americans live on reservations and live as much within old traditions as possible, but many have been integrated into the larger society and may not be distinguishable from the general population. These families may practice a mix of their Native American rituals as well as hold the customs and beliefs of their non-Indian neighbors (Joe and Malach, 1998; Lum, 2002; Horejsi and Pablo, 1993). One of the stressors for Native Americans is learning to survive in two cultures (see Shaver, 1998). The variations in their ways of life and customs are influenced largely by their geographic regions as well as the impact of non-Indian people on particular tribes. There are, however, some generalizations that can be made about Native American cultures.

Values. For Native Americans the concept of *sharing* is an integral part of the community and their way of life. Individuals share freely with others even to the extent that child rearing is a shared and community experience. Children have the run of the community and each adult feels an obligation to interact freely with them through teaching, encouragement, or even discipline. Yet, learning among Native American children is largely experiential. For example, a child might be allowed to experience some minor harm (e.g., burning a finger to learn not to touch something hot) as a way of learning by experience (Crosson-Tower, 2002; Joe and Malach, 1998).

Native Americans also believe in a oneness with nature that dictates an acceptance of natural happenings and their impact on the individual. Thus, suffering at the hands of natural happenings becomes an integral part of growth (Crosson-Tower, 2002; Joe and Malach, 1998; Horejsi and Pablo, 1993; Thomason, 1993). Children are taught to have a respect for nature, natural events, and the land, and a harmony with Mother Earth is at the core of many rituals and ceremonies.

Native American families also teach that it is important to control one's emotions. It is not unusual for Native Americans to seem stoic or even aloof to members of other cultures in the face of stressful events. The family keeps to itself, as does the individual, practicing the noninterference that has characterized Indian peoples for centuries. The Native American's form of protest is silence or withdrawal. Such behavior may actually confuse those in the child welfare field who often mistake this behavior on the part of Native American parents as indifference (Crosson-Tower, 2002; Lum, 2002).

CASE EXAMPLE

The Graywings

The Graywing family had moved off the reservation several months earlier when the father took a job 50 miles from their reservation home. It was the first time in several generations that anyone from the Graywing family had lived off the reservation, and the mother and her four children were most uncomfortable with the idea, though this would never have been verbalized to anyone outside the family.

The Graywing children first came to the attention of the local child welfare agency when the youngest child, age 2, was found by a neighbor several blocks from the house. The child had been observed by another neighbor the previous day in an area even further away from the Graywing home. Talking about the events, the two women became concerned and felt that the agency should be notified.

When a social worker visited Mrs. Graywing, the mother seemed unconcerned. The next day, the neighbors again called the agency, saying that the same child had been seen on the railroad tracks. The worker again went to the house and, finding the Graywing children (ages 2, 3, and 5) alone, she took them into custody until the mother could be located. When the mother arrived home, she found a message from the worker, asking her to contact the agency immediately. Assuming that her children were somewhere in the neighborhood and resenting the agency intervention, the mother discarded the note and did not call. The agency assumed that the children had been abandoned and placed them in foster care. It was not until a worker familiar with Native American custom was brought in on the case that the issues were resolved and the children were returned to their parents.

Native Americans view time differently than many other cultures. To them time is a "rhythmic, circular pattern" (Ho, 1987, 71, as cited in Joe and Malach,

1998, 101). For this reason, such issues as developmental milestones are difficult to determine. Time is measured, not by the clock, but by the moon, the stars, and the seasons. Native Americans may also operate on their own time schedule, valuing congeniality more than rigidity, to the frustration of more punctual cultures or individuals (Joe and Malach, 1998).

Over the years, the values of the Native American have been greatly misinterpreted. In fact, there have been movements to alter that value system and force the Native American to conform to non-Indian values. Off-reservation boarding schools in the late 1800s were one attempt to separate Indian children and enculturate them into Anglo culture. These schools had a far-reaching impact on those who attended them, and have been much debated. Although today there may be more tolerance for ethnic diversity, Native American values may still come into conflict with those of other cultural orientations (Iglehart and Becerra, 2000).

Communication.   Because the Native American believes that each individual has his or her own right to dignity, each person is respected and revered. As a result, there is little hierarchical communication; rather, everyone is considered to be on the same level. Cooperation is also valued, and one tends to give in rather than compete.

Patience is also important to Native Americans, who believe that the universe is unfolding as it should. Although some outside the Indian culture view this ability to rest and wait as laziness, the Native American is comfortable with the recognition that what should happen will do so in due time.

Religion and Spirituality.   A new interest in Native American philosophy on the part of those outside the culture has made many people more familiar with the belief in the healing power of nature. The American Indian sees the need to remain in harmony with nature, and from this union will come a kind of harmony that is much valued. Ceremonies and rituals dedicated to the reverence for nature punctuate the Native American's daily life (Crosson-Tower, 2002).

When working with diverse populations, it is important to recognize their traditions. Familiarity with courtesies appropriate to each culture will help the child welfare worker dealing within various populations.

Families with African American Roots

The customs and traditions of the African American family have been part of this country since its early history. The majority of African Americans came from slave ancestors who were brought to this country in the 1700s and 1800s. A small number of Africans also came over as free but indentured servants who were seeking a new life. Once freed, southern slaves migrated north in search of more and better opportunities. These migrants were largely ignored and only some work in the settlement houses of the late 1800s furthered their integration into the mainstream culture (Willis, 1998).

During the 1900s, African Americans experienced much prejudice, and bitter controversy surrounded their integration into "white" areas. From school segregation and freedom marches to the efforts of the NAACP (National Association for the Advancement of Colored People) and other activist organizations, the African American has sought to be more fully accepted by others in American society (see Gadsden, 1999). Today, African Americans make up over 12% of the population of the United States (Willis, 1998; McGoldrick, 1993). Of the African American family's experience, McGoldrick (1993) comments:

> *We cannot understand the context of a Black family without looking at the context of the larger system: less access to medical care, housing, education, employment, political power, and a general sense of powerlessness, and of not belonging to the larger society. All these will have their impact on African-American families, even across class lines. They influence how parents raise their children—knowing they will be exposed to hatred and discrimination. (353)*

In addition to other stresses, the African American family is more likely than its white and Hispanic counterparts to experience poverty. About 29% of all African American families live below the poverty line, in contrast to only 8% of white families and 24% of Hispanic families (Willis, 1998, 129; Iglehart and Becerra, 1995, 26; McGoldrick, 1993, 353). In addition, African American families are most likely to live in inner cities amidst crime, unemployment, and other stresses. Infant mortality is twice as likely to occur among African American infants as it is among whites (Willis, 1998, 129). Amidst these realities, the African American family continues to persevere.

Values.   Values that have brought the African American through a myriad of stresses are reliance on each other and shared religious beliefs. Extended family and friends, often referred to as *kin,* provide mutual aid in a variety of situations, including such things as child care, financial aid, advice, and emotional support (Crosson-Tower, 2002; Willis, 1998; Prater, 2000). It is not uncommon for extended family or friends to take children whose parents are unable to care for them. Children are prized among African American cultures and their well-being is seen as the responsibility of the total family and even the community. Perhaps this strong sense of kinship originated in early tribal tradition and has been passed down through the centuries.

Within African American families, work is expected of all members. Today, it is African American women who are more able to enter the workforce and, because they are often single parents, the children are expected to assume a substantial amount of the household tasks (Crosson-Tower, 2002; Logan, 1996; Lum, 2002). The fact that African American children assume as much responsibility as they do has often been construed by white child welfare agencies as constituting neglect on the part of their parents. The reality, as is true for many minorities, is that African American parents recognize that it is only through hard work and perseverance that their children will survive in this world. This early training prepares their children for their later lot in life.

Because African Americans recognize that education can elevate one's status, they value educational opportunities. Elders are also seen as possessing knowledge that can be beneficial to the young, and oral tradition plays a large part in the African American culture (Willis, 1998).

Communication.   African American families are by nature closely knit. Children are given love and accepted into the family circle with warmth and understanding. Due to the emphasis on the extended family and friends, children move freely through the circle of adults and have a number of adult models with whom to identify. There is an emphasis on instilling in children a sense of pride in who they are. Communication is often abstract, and analogies are used to express feelings without explicitly identifying the feelings themselves. Rather than being out of touch with feelings, the African American family is very much in touch with feelings but has a characteristic manner of expressing them.

CASE EXAMPLE

Cora Lee

Cora Lee and her six children are a common sight at the Stafford Street School playground. The mother's loud, deep voice is often raised in hearty laughter as she watches her children in play. She frequently brings her mother or one of several aunts, who also encourage the children and chuckle about their antics. Despite the fact that the children remain largely independent of their mother, Cora Lee seems very much in tune with their feelings. A fall from the jungle gym usually results in the child being scooped up against his mother's big chest and hummed to while she continues to listen to her adult companions. In no time, the soothed child is off to play again with his siblings and peers.

Music often plays a part in the African American family's life. It is experienced rather than listened to and song may be used to sooth, to play, and to accompany work (Willis, 1998).

Religion and Spirituality.   Historically, the church has played a significant role in African American life. Religion and family are closely linked, and over the years the family has used its religious beliefs to protect it from the hostile white world. The church becomes a focal point, not only for emotional support, but also for socialization. Ministers are seen as teachers, counselors, spokesmen, and even kinsmen (Crosson-Tower, 2002).

The organized African church began in the late 1700s in Philadelphia. Known originally as the Free African Society, the movement eventually gave rise to the African Methodist Episcopal Church (AME). About the same time, New York City saw the development of the African Methodist Episcopal Zion (AMEZ). Over time, the Baptist churches began to attract African Americans in increasing numbers until today the Baptist churches represent a large percentage of the church-going population (Willis, 1998).

Whether associated with an organized church or not, the African American family holds a strong belief that "the Lord will provide." This assumption that life will unfold as it is meant to do may cause them to seem to those not familiar with African American philosophy as fatalistic or uninvolved in their own destiny. Nothing is further from the truth.

Families with Hispanic Roots

To say that a family is Hispanic does not fully explain the diversity of the Spanish-speaking peoples. The term *Hispanic* includes numerous cultures, each with its own traditions and values. Mexicans represent the largest number (62.3%) of Hispanics in the United States today, followed by Puerto Ricans (12.7%), Central and South Americans (11.5%), Cubans (5%), and other groups (8%) (Crosson-Tower, 2002, 29; Zuniga, 1998, 151–152).

Despite the cultural differences among these groups, it is possible to make some generalizations about families with Hispanic roots.

Values. The extended family plays a large part in the lives of the Hispanic community. In defining the extended family, however, one does not look at only blood relatives but also friends and anyone else who shares their living space. Godparents or sponsors (*padrinos*) play a major role in the lives of children. *Compadrazzo,* or the practice of using these compadres in a variety of ways, is integral to Hispanic life. Compadres, whether they be godparents, relatives, or close friends, maintain a close relationship with the children of the family, treating them almost as their own (Delgado, 2000; Leyendecker and Lamb, 1999; Zuniga, 1998).

The traditional Hispanic family believes in male supremacy, strict role delineations, and submissiveness on the part of the female. *Machismo,* or the male's sense of honor, courage, and responsibility to his family, is extremely important in the Hispanic family, but a much misunderstood concept in the outside world (Delgado, 2000). It is the father's role to keep the family together and to provide for them. The economic realities of the present may make it easier for the woman in a two-parent family to find work, making the man feel less powerful and placing extreme stress on the family as their adopted homeland tests their traditional views (Zuniga, 1998). This family tension may lead to aggression and possibly violence as the male's machismo is threatened. Today, some Hispanic families may also be headed by single females, changing the balance of power and the family's way of operating. Yet, as her male children grow, the mother may be more likely to recognize her sons' power than will mothers of some other cultures.

Also central to the value system of Hispanic families are the concepts of *dignidad, respecto,* and *personalismo. Dignidad* acknowledges the importance and worth of each individual. *Respecto* incorporates a hierarchical view of relationships in which elders must be respected and the young look to the older for decisions and teachings. *Personalismo* refers to the Hispanic reverence for individualized, warm, and close personal relationships. The feeling is that each individual deserves personal one-to-one attention, and large impersonal bureaucracies are usually avoided by Hispanics for this reason (Zuniga, 1998). Keeping these values in mind, workers dealing with the Hispanic family do best if they use a friendly, informal, but respectful manner that encourages trust on the part of the clients. Hispanic families need to see the helper as a professional whom they can respect, but one who does not look down on them or depersonalize them or their needs.

Communication.   The concept of *respecto* governs much of the communication between family members in the Hispanic family. Males and elders are given higher status and therefore communication tends to take place with these individuals in key positions. Traditional roles are adhered to and both genders have particular things that are expected of them.

Children are considered to validate a marriage in the Hispanic family and they tend to be pampered and overindulged. The parent-child relationship actually takes precedence over the marital relationship when the children are young. Male children are revered and daughters are protected. Hispanic mothers teach their sons that it is their role to protect and provide (Leyendecker and Lamb, 1999; Zuniga, 1998).

Strong negative emotions, such as anger and aggression, are not acceptable in the traditional Hispanic family. Family members maintain close emotional ties based on respect rather than the airing of personal grievances. For the Hispanic family, this tendency toward respecting and projecting congeniality toward others may cause them difficulty in the non-Hispanic world. Leiberman (1990) describes how Hispanic mothers may often agree graciously to appointments made by social workers, but then fail to keep them. It would be disrespectful to disagree.

Due to the fact that Hispanics are taught not to disagree or express negative emotions, they may turn stress inward and suffer from somatic ailments. Headaches, stomach aches, and other physical problems may indicate psychological distress (Derezotes and Snowden, 1990).

Religion and Spirituality.   Catholicism is the predominant religion of the Hispanic population and plays an extremely important part in family life. In the *barrio* (the Hispanic community), the church is the focal point for both social and inspirational events. Many families use *mandas* (a promise or offering asking for God's intervention) to call on their faith to direct their lives. Prayers to the Virgin Mary are also a common practice within Hispanic households (Zuniga, 1998).

Although it may seem contradictory to outsiders, Hispanic families also rely on folk healers to cure their ills and intervene for them. Delgado (2000) points out that Hispanics' strong reliance on and their belief in folk medicine make these practices especially effective.

Families with Asian Roots

Today, Asians are the fastest growing minority group in the United States. This growth seems to be a result of the Asian refugees and immigrants who have entered this country since the Immigration and Nationality Act Amendments in 1965 and the influx of people after the United States left Vietnam in 1975 (Chan, 1998). Although Asians and Asian Pacific Islanders are usually grouped together, there are probably more differences from culture to culture than in any other grouping. Asia encompasses China, Japan, Vietnam, Cambodia, Laos, India, Thailand, Burma, Malaysia, Singapore, the Philippines, Sri Lanka, Pakistan, and Korea, and each of these represents vastly different traditions and ways of life. In fact, so complex are these cultures that it would take volumes to consider many of them in any depth (Mass and Geaga-Rosenthal, 2000). Here, we can only consider Asian cultures in the most superficial manner.

Values.   Like the Hispanic family, the Asian family is one with clearly defined roles based on male dominance and a hierarchical structure. Although most Asian women are forced into the workforce, the family adheres to traditional gender roles (Kim and Kim, 1998). The older generation especially is revered. Parents command respect and must be obeyed. The family behaves as a unit, a closely knit group, and individuals are not expected to be autonomous. To do so would be a rejection of family values.

Shame plays a major role in dictating the behavior of adults and in disciplining and molding the behavior of children. Honor should be brought to the family at all cost, by doing one's best, behaving respectfully, and refraining from doing wrong. *Face* refers to the ability to hold one's head high, knowing that one has behaved honorably. Asians talk of *saving face,* or maintaining one's honor, as paramount to the family. Family honor is greatly valued and family members will go to great lengths to save face. Shame is used so much in child rearing that non-Asian agencies may question if this practice is emotionally abusive (Mass and Geaga-Rosenthal, 2000; Chan, 1998).

It would be unthinkable, for example, to sexually abuse children in Asian families, an attitude that makes the incidence of sexual abuse in this population extremely low. Such behavior would bring great dishonor to the family. In many types of Asian communities, the virginity of the female before her marriage is a high priority. The Vietnamese woman, for example, is expected to be a virgin when she marries, and the loss of her virginity may mean that she is prohibited from marrying (Mollica and Son, 1989). Similarly, daughters from Indian families are married whenever possible to someone who will improve their families' social status. The young woman is expected to come to her new husband pure and virginal. Thus, a father would not sexually abuse his daughter lest he endanger her (and his) chances of attaining a higher social status or caste. This too would dishonor the family.

Harmony is highly valued in some Asian families, especially when the family operates under a Confucian philosophy. The group is paramount, and the needs of the individual are secondary to the desires of the group. Self-esteem is dependent on how well one fits into and is accepted by the group and how well one avoids conflict with the group. Most Asians do not wish to stand out from others and will often take a seemingly benign or middle-of-the-road position to avoid being noticed as separate from the group (Mass and Geaga-Rosenthal, 2000; Yee et al., 1998).

Communication.   Because of the need to be part of the group and the value of harmony, communication among Asians brings with it a rigid set of rules. Since the elder is held in highest regard, communication begins at the top and filters down to others. One is not expected to be direct, as in Western cultures, but calm, respectful, and congenial. Thus, a "yes" from an Asian family member may not mean that he or she will do as requested, but only indicates that the person has heard you. It may also mean that he or she would not dishonor you by disagreeing. This cultural value is especially difficult for the non-Asian to comprehend and can cause problems between Asians and workers in Western agencies who are not familiar with this fine point (Chan, 1998; Lum, 2002).

Among themselves, Asian family members practice respect and recognize that honoring the family is paramount, because their self-esteem is based on how honorable each family member is. Further, the Asian is not likely to conflict with other family members, so intent is he or she on the protection of harmony.

Religion and Spirituality.   Religions among Asians differ greatly. Confucianism, Taoism, and Buddhism, as they are practiced in China and Korea, emphasize respect for one's ancestors, filial piety, and the avoidance of shame (Lum, 2002). Buddhism emphasizes "four noble truths": life is suffering; suffering exists because of people's overattachment to the world; suffering can be extinguished by giving up this attachment; and one does this by attending to one's views, speech, thoughts, and through meditation (Chan, 1998, 188). Confucianism has no specific doctrine other than a belief that people must be in harmony with the world and others in it. Taoism seeks to cultivate inner strength, selflessness, and harmony, and to stress being on the "path" toward spiritual truth. Koreans also practice Shamanism, although this is more prevalent in rural communities than in larger urban areas. Shamanism involves relationships among people, spirits, and the universe and how these interrelate in one's life (Chan, 1998).

Hinduism and Islam, which involve more of a moral code than actual worship of deities, are also practiced in some Asian countries. All of these Asian doctrines emphasize the concept of harmony with others and some form of fatalism or philosophical detachment. Possibly because of the fact that many

Asian cultures have been buffeted by a variety of political events beyond their control, many Asian peoples treat events as if they are inevitable. This means that the Asian family may be less likely to seek help from outside agencies as family members assume that the crisis they are experiencing is their "lot in life" and therefore must just be endured (Crosson-Tower, 2002; Ho, 1989).

Families with Middle Eastern Roots

The Middle East includes areas of Asia and Africa, which have distinct and different cultural orientations. These political states are usually identified as Iraq, Jordan, Saudi Arabia, Kuwait, Bahrain, Egypt, Sudan, Turkey, Iran, Oman, Yemen, and the United Arab Emirates (Sharifzadeh, 1998). These cultures are sometimes included with Asian groups, but to do so is to overgeneralize and do both types of cultures a grave disservice.

Immigration of people from the Middle East increased in the late 1800s when Arab tradesmen came to this country seeking new opportunities. From the 1890s to the 1930s, Armenians, who were being persecuted by the Turkish government, fled to the United States for sanctuary. Since that time there continues to be an influx of Middle Easterners seeking refuge from a variety of political events as well as in search of freedom and opportunity.

Values.   There is a marked difference between Middle Easterners who are educated and come from large urban areas and those from more rural settings. More highly educated people have more familiarity with Western culture and therefore an easier time assimilating in the United States. Many have learned English early and this also helps their integration into this culture.

The family is of primary importance in Middle Eastern cultures. Multiple generations, often as many as three generations, tend to live and work together. The family structure is patriarchal and the family adheres strongly to religious rules. The family values the collective achievement of its members and holds these achievements up in pride and as a form of identity. Those who have immigrated to the United States also try to bring kinsmen over and surround themselves with large families that provide support and encouragement. Having children is considered the essence of being. Boys are highly valued and the birth of a male child is a cause for celebration. Neglect of one's children is considered to be a serious violation in these cultures, and the internal sanctions for such parents are more threatening than those of a protective service agency (Sharifzadeh, 1998).

Communication.   Because Middle Eastern societies are patriarchal, the hierarchy of communication begins with the oldest males. Mothers are seen primarily as the nurturers of their children and their proximity to them is expected to be very close. Babies are usually kept in the same room, if not the same bed, as their mothers, and these mothers tend to be much more permissive with their children than their Western counterparts.

CASE EXAMPLE

Metah Halvanian

Metah Halvanian came to the attention of the protective service agency when the kindergarten her son attended reported that they were concerned that "there was something going on at home." The boy had few boundaries or inner controls and spoke of sleeping with his mother. When the worker investigated, she found an extremely devoted and overindulgent mother who was horrified that she had come to the attention of an agency. She openly told the agency that her 5-year-old son still slept in her bed as her husband worked long hours and she felt that it was better for the boy. As the mother and worker talked, the boy roamed freely about the house and interrupted frequently. It soon became obvious that he had as much, if not more, control than his mother. It took some time before the school guidance counselor, working with the family, was able to acclimate the child to the more structured school setting.

Individuation of children is an issue that may cause some problems for Middle Easterners as they attempt to integrate into their adopted culture. The emphasis on interdependence given to relationships may cause conflicts for children as they strive to acclimate to the Western school system (Sharifzadeh, 1998).

In communication, outsiders may find the Middle Easterner confusing. For example, a direct "no" is considered impolite. Instead, the Middle Easterner is likely to say "maybe" or a weak "yes," either of which can either indicate agreement or that he or she does not want to say no because that would be disrespectful. Some cultures of the Middle East also respect professionals to the point that it would be impolite to give the impression of being in conflict with a professional's opinion or recommendation. Therefore, the family may seem to comply when, in fact, they disagree. In addition, it is not acceptable to express one's own needs, and family members may actually deny that they want something (Sharifzadeh, 1998). It may require a worker who is familiar with the Middle Eastern culture to work successfully with a Middle Eastern family.

Religion and Spirituality. Religion to the Middle Easterner is not a private and personal issue. It occupies a central position socially, culturally, and politically. Islam was one of the earliest religions in the Middle East and continues to be the most widely practiced today. Judaism and Christianity are also part of the religious mosaic. The Eastern Orthodox and Catholic churches comprise the largest number of non-Muslims. Judaism is concentrated in Israel. Iran is also known for its populations of Bahais and Zoroastrians, now decreasing (Sharifzadeh, 1998). All of these faiths influence the customs of their followers and the way in which families carry on everyday life.

The Family Life Cycle

Like every other system, families change continuously. They also may follow somewhat predictable and definable life cycles. Carter and McGoldrick (1988, 18–19) suggest that middle-class Americans, for example, have six stages within their developmental cycle:

1. *Single young adults* who are charged with accepting emotional and financial responsibility as they leave their families of origin and become independent.

2. *The new couple* who commit to joining together to form their own family and in so doing rework their relationships with their own families of origin and friends.

3. *Families with young children* who must accept new members into the family system, decide how they will raise these children, and realign their own relationships, between themselves and with others, to accomplish this.

4. *Families with adolescents* who must increase their flexibility in order to allow their offspring to grow and begin to move away from the family. In addition, this may well be a time when the couple is asked to care for their own aging parents and readjust their relationship to do this.

5. *The couple who are launching children and moving on* must learn to accept the emancipation of their children and adjust to the impact that it has on their relationships; they may also be faced with the deaths of their own parents.

6. *Families in later life* must accept the change in generational roles, make room for grandchildren, maintain their own functioning as a couple, and continue to cope with the losses of family friends and perhaps each other.

Families who experience a breakdown caused by something such as death or divorce will probably not follow this developmental process. Herbert (1989, 109–111) outlines stages of transition that can be applied to families as well as individuals: immobilization, minimization of the experience, depression, testing, and, finally, finding meaning in the event. Families faced with acute stress may first be *immobilized*.

CASE EXAMPLE

Divorce in the Higgins Family

When Julia Higgins filed for divorce, the whole family, consisting of her husband and three children, seemed unable to respond. "It was as if we were all paralyzed," recounted Herb. "We had been having troubles but I couldn't believe it when I was served with papers. Neither could the girls, who were then ages 14, 16, and 19. I think they thought their mother had gone mad. They always thought we were so happy."

Families will often then *minimize the experience,* as the Higgins family did:

CASE EXAMPLE

Our daughters kept telling me "Don't worry about it, Dad! Mom will come to her senses. This is just a whim of hers." We all kept saying to ourselves that we didn't have to worry. Julia would realize that that was not what she wanted and drop the whole thing. But she didn't!

Once they realize that the crisis is real, families often *go into depression.*

CASE EXAMPLE

Once we realized that Julia really meant to leave, we all slumped into a kind of depression. We each appeared to be functioning okay, but there was this overtone of sadness and hopelessness. We bickered with each other and everyone seemed caught up in her or his own needs.

At some point, family members accept that the crisis is a reality and that they *must let go* of the concept of what they had hoped for, usually the idea of the happy, together family. There may be a period of testing when the family members strive to see if the new configuration is really what is wanted by all. This period is seen as a form of *testing.*

CASE EXAMPLE

There was a time, soon after I decided that the divorce was inevitable, that our children seemed to be trying to fix things up again. They would invite Julia and me places together, despite the fact that she had a new boyfriend. When Dianna, then age 20, got her first apartment, she invited Julia and me to dinner together. It was awkward, but we both love her, so we made the best of it. I finally had to talk to the kids and say that their mother and I would not get back together and they had to stay out of it. They finally got the message.

As the change completes itself, the family once again seeks homeostasis by *searching for the meaning* in the event. The Higgins girls spent long hours in discussion about what had driven their mother away. They talked about how their father had always made the decisions and that his need to control might have been a factor. And finally, each individual *internalizes the meanings* of the crisis, as does the family system.

Each of my daughters seemed to have a different idea of why Julia had divorced me. I know that they thought my immigrant father's old-world attitudes had made me into a bit of a tyrant too, but I think there was more to it than that. Each girl was also impacted differently by us being divorced. When they all eventually married, I could recognize in their choice of mates how they had interpreted what had happened in our family.

Families that experience the loss of a family member may join with other family units. Several years after the divorce, Herb Higgins remarried. His daughters, then ages 16, 18, and 22, had a difficult time with his decision. The two youngest, still living at home, found the adjustment challenging. Their new stepmother came to the union with four boys, ages 7, 9, 12, and 14. The girls feared that they would be placed in the role of babysitters. They also had comments about their stepmother's more permissive child-rearing standards. By the same token, their oldest stepbrother, used to being "the man of the house," resented being "bossed around" by two older girls. As is often common in blended families, the first several years were a challenge. For these families, the initial developmental task is to realign relationships so that the family can function relatively smoothly.

Culture, too, may have an impact on family development and change. Each culture has specific expectations of its members, and the family system is affected by these. There may also be variations depending on when a particular ethnic group immigrated to America (Lynch and Hanson, 1998; Walsh, 1993). For example, the way in which families from different cultures deal with specific developmental tasks of their children can differ greatly. For example, white children usually learn to dress themselves at age 3.7 years, African American children are 4 years old, and their Native American counterparts are only 2.8. Native American children are also allowed to stay alone in the evening earlier (9.2 years) than white children (14.4 years) and African American children (13.6). They also care for younger siblings at an earlier age (9.9 years for Native Americans; 13.1 years for whites; and 12.9 years for African Americans) (Joe and Malach, 1998, 104). Children from other immigrant cultures may be expected to tackle these tasks at earlier or later ages, depending on the values of the parents. These methods of dealing with children will affect the development of the entire family.

For the gay or lesbian family, the process of "coming out" to their families and friends may be construed as part of the family life cycle as well. When and how the parents disclose their lifestyle choice to individual families of origin impacts their intergenerational relationships. Parental experiences as children, who may have had to hide their true feelings from others, may result in families that strive to create different family rules and roles that influence how the family functions and develops (Laird, 1993).

Stresses on Families

Parental/Family Dysfunction

Chapter 1 discussed Kadushin and Martin's (1988) suggestion of a framework for ascertaining why families must seek help. They say that services are required when there are difficulties in parental functioning in the following areas: *unoccupied parental role,* usually through death, illness, imprisonment, mental illness, or abandonment; *parental incapacity* due to illness, ignorance, emotional immaturity, mental retardation, or substance abuse; *role rejection,* when a parent chooses to neglect, abandon, or abuse the child; *interrole conflict,* when there is conflict in the family about roles; *transition* issues, when a family is trying to cope with some type of transition, either developmental or environmental; and *child incapacity* issues, such as a family trying to cope with a child's disability. Several other specific issues will be discussed shortly.

Role Definition and Inequality

There has been much discussion about family roles in this era, when it is the norm in two-parent families for both parents to work outside the home. The dominant assumption, especially among higher socioeconomic groups, is that the father has assumed more in the way of house responsibilities to offset the stress on his partner of working and maintaining a home. The reality, based on a study of 2,457 mothers (Acock and Demo, 1994), appears different from what one might assume. These authors studied families in four categories: first-married (two-parent) families, divorced (single-parent) families, stepfamilies (reconstituted two-parent families), and continuously single families (in which the mother has had her children without being married and continues to remain so). A study of the distribution of household tasks found that mothers in all families do the household chores a disproportionate amount of the time: first married = 71.6%; divorced = 85.7%; stepfamily = 69.4%; continuously single = 84.4% (77). All mothers, regardless of the presence of a male partner, spent between 40 to 43 hours a week on household chores (79). Husbands performed between 6.2 to 7 hours on household tasks, excluding car maintenance, outdoor work, and driving (82). The amount of work done by children was also negligible. These data indicated that there was little difference in this division of labor whether women were in their first marriage or whether they had remarried. In addition, there appeared to be little reduction in the time spent on household tasks when the women worked outside of the home. Acock and Demo see the wife's perception that she is doing most of the work, contrasted with her husband's perception that he is contributing significantly, if not equally, as a major strain in family relations.

Parent/Child Relations

As the American family is threatened by economic strain and divorce, relations between parents and their children have come into increasing focus. As parents feel more stressed, they have less energy, time, and patience to give to their children (McWhirter et al., 1998). Rules and roles become more flexible and even less well defined to cope with the changing demands on the family structure. Mothers in one study (Acock and Demo, 1994) complained that they had less time with their children, more disagreements, less enjoyable times with their spouses, and less involvement in their children's schools, sports, and other activities than their parents did with them (120).

Stepparent relationships are another issue that many families point to as stressful. Reconstituted families are faced with the joining of two families, both with different sets of rules and expectations. As the parents strive to negotiate their own relationship, parental roles may come into conflict. Who will discipline whose children is often a bone of contention. Who controls the family decisions and who does what tasks in the house create other areas in which negotiation is necessary. Not all families are able to weather these storms of adjustment successfully.

Another issue of parent/child conflict may confront the newly immigrated family. Parents who hold cultural expectations of their children that differ from what is expected of American children may discover that, as their children become integrated into the school system and form relationships with peers, they are influenced by a new set of values.

CASE EXAMPLE

Conflict in a Vietnamese Family

A family recently immigrated from Vietnam expected that their teenage daughter would respect the traditions under which she grew up. It was anticipated by the family that she would not see boys alone and would wait until the family believed that she should be allowed to have contact with the opposite sex. But the boys in her high school class found her attractive and appealing and were soon asking her to go out with them. Knowing her parents' feelings, she at first refused. But it was also important to her to fit in with her new friends and they all seemed to be dating. She began to see boys after school and to sneak out of the house when her parents were not aware. When her father discovered what his daughter had been doing, he was extremely upset and felt that the family had lost face.

Disability

It is certainly obvious when discussing stresses placed on families that disability or illness on the part of the parent creates stress for the family. What many of us do not realize is how much stress the disability of a child within the family can place on the family system. The following older teen explained about living with his sister who was born with spina bifida:

CASE EXAMPLE

Deborah

The birth of Deborah changed our family's whole life. When she was first born Mom and Dad spent a lot of time in the hospital. We were left with grandparents and other relatives. We weren't neglected. Mom and Dad tried to explain to us and spend time with us but their priority had to be Deb. Even after she came home things were never the same. She always had to be the center of attention. She had so much medication and had seizures. We all learned to go into a "crisis mode." That meant that when she was in crisis and Mom and Dad had to be there for her, we kids learned to be very self-sufficient. One of my brothers really resented her though and that was hard for all of us. I think the stress destroyed my parent's relationship too because after about ten years they got divorced.

Families with special needs children learn to accommodate in a variety of ways, but often not without some type of support or outside intervention.

When Families Need Help

Kadushin and Martin (1988) divide the services provided for families into three categories: supportive services, supplementary services, and substitute services. *Supportive services* refer to home-based services that help the family to perform its role in the care, protection, and nurturing of its children. They strive to use the family's own strength to empower them to help themselves. Such services might include counseling, early intervention, and protective services. The last category might be confusing, as one often thinks of protective services as removing children from their parents. In reality, separation of children from parents is the last resort. The first goal of protective services is to discover and enhance parental strengths to help the parents cope and not abuse or neglect their children. Only when this is not possible are other interventions used. *Supplementary services* are used when the parent/child relationship has begun to be impaired or needs additional help. Financial assistance, daycare, and homemaker services are examples of supplementary programs. *Substitute services* are used as a last resort. These services substitute the care that the family of origin is not able to provide either temporarily or permanently. Such services are adoption, foster care, and residential treatment.

Although this is one way to categorize services, some find that it is inadequate. Services may actually overlap or parts of service provision can be categorized in different ways. Services may also be divided into categories, depending on who provides them. There are public agencies under state, federal, or country governments, voluntary nonprofit agencies supported by community funds, private for-profit agencies supported by client fees, and industrially sponsored agencies (Kadushin and Martin, 1988).

How services to families are categorized is not as crucial as how well the families' needs are met by these services. It is vital in the study of child welfare services that the potential professional be familiar with the wide range of services available and how these can be used to benefit clients. The most important aspect of helping is to empower. Empowerment enables families not only to solve today's problems but to gain insight in facing the problems of tomorrow.

Trends

When looking at the trends for something as woven into our thinking as the family, it is difficult to predict the future. One can only look at current trends with the expectation that they may continue.

Economic Stressors

It is evident that the family will continue to feel the stress that our current economic situation enhances. Family members will continue to be faced with the challenge of how to meet family needs while both parents work (Kim and Kim, 1998) or, in the case of single-parent families, when the only adult must work outside the home. Parents will continue to be faced with the necessity of finding adequate daycare arrangements in a market that is already overstressed. Both husbands and wives will need to find creative ways to negotiate with employers over such issues as maternity–paternity leave, flex time, and shared vacations. Families will continue the struggle of making decreasing paychecks meet the demands of increasing prices.

How these factors affect family dynamics will prove interesting. Already there is speculation and research on the influence that the working mother has on the mother/child dyad (Moorehouse, 1993). For example, although Moorehouse found that mothers who work had a stronger and more positive association with their older children, this author expressed some concern about the attachment of infants, who experienced prolonged hours of nonmaternal care (269). Studies related to fathers who assumed more caregiving roles as a result of their wives' employment showed mixed results. On one hand, researchers felt that these fathers formed closer ties with their children, while still another study pointed to the fact that in this sample fathers who cared for children on a regular basis were more irritable toward them and demonstrated more marital dissatisfaction (Moorehouse, 1993). Certainly the effects on children of their parents' working warrant further investigation.

The Optional Status of Marriage

In the twenty-first century, marriage has become an option rather than an expectation in the lives of most young adults. Increasingly, couples choose either to live together or merely date while bringing a child into the world. If this relationship terminates, as is often the case, given the lack of expectation of permanence, children often become the total responsibility of their mothers. In addition, the model for permanence and negotiation to sustain a relationship is absent. Some would argue that this is preferable to the past when children may have been trapped in loveless and conflict-ridden marriages because the expectation was that one would remain married. The fact remains that the lack of permanence of today's relationships can also take its toll on children.

The Vanishing Father

A trend of somewhat serious concern is the fact that fathers as a whole are assuming a different role in their children's lives. At one time, the father was the head of the house, the primary breadwinner, and only a part-time support in his wife's child rearing, but divorce and single parenthood has changed the position of fathers in today's society. Perusal of a fast-food restaurant on a typical Saturday will attest to the fact that fathers are more likely to see their children on a limited basis and engage in activities that are less likely to contribute to their overall care. The introduction of the stepfather does not change this picture but rather complicates it. Now children are thrust into two or more roles with men who, although assuming a fathering role, are doing so on a limited basis.

In addition to the impact of divorce on children's relationship with their fathers, more women are opting to become pregnant with the anticipation that the biological father of the child will not remain a part of the child's immediate home environment. Thus, we move more and more toward a matriarchal society in which women have the primary role for full-time parenting.

Blended Families

When we look at the previously mentioned trends, it is easy to recognize that the majority of children in the United States will not reside with both their biological parents for the entirety of their childhood (Teachman et al., 2000). As the circle of divorce widens and people remarry, more and more families will be blended together. Some parents choose the company of same-sex partners to help with the raising of their children. Inherent in this process of blending is a myriad of complex attitudes, emotions, and tasks. Not only will the new parental subsystem need to find its own balance but each adult will also need to forge a working relationship with each child, whether that child be his or her own or the new spouse's. Problems such as who will discipline whom, who is responsible for meeting the needs of whom, and a variety of other issues will be of increasing focus in the lives of tomorrow's families (see Mason et al., 1998; Herbert, 2002).

Resolution of Childhood Conflicts

A paramount need, met not necessarily by the family, but rather by society as a result of the family, will be services to resolve the residual effects of family conflict. Divorce and family instability have a profound effect on children, who grow into adulthood with resulting scars that may make it difficult for them to form their own families. Thus, we in the helping professions are increasingly recognizing the importance of providing an opportunity for teens and adults to understand the role their families played in the emotional conflicts that create problems for them. Granted, family dysfunction has always been with us and many young adults have sought to make sense of traumatic childhoods. But as we recognize more fully the impact of family unrest on children's development, services and resources seem more vital.

Currently, groups dedicated to understanding family dysfunction, books on the subject, and therapists who specialize in helping adults to "make peace with the past" strive to meet this need.

Changes in Family Control

At one time, the family could rely on controlling its own functioning. Only if members demonstrated gross inadequacies did societal institutions intervene. Often children were totally under the influence of the family until they went to school and then the family still exerted the major influence. Today that has changed. One of the most obvious factors in the decline of family control is in the case of divorce. Courts are now in the position of deciding with whom the children will reside and the amount of contact they will have with the non-custodial parent. Parents' freedom is significantly curtailed and their privacy is no longer sacred. The "best interests of the child" may be something that society rather than the parent is responsible for protecting.

Divorce is not the only factor affecting the family's ability to control its own functioning. As the traditional family disintegrates, and with it the supports provided by multiple adults, family members find themselves seeking outside help. Over half of all single-parent families have sought out some type of societal support, whether it be income maintenance, daycare, legal assistance, or counseling (Aerts, 1993). It does not look as though this trend toward the subversion of family functioning by outside sources will subside in the future.

Families have long been the framework on which our society is based. As the picture of the family changes, the way that we help families will also need to change. As we review the services that currently exist, it is important to keep in mind how these trends will affect the family of tomorrow and the needs that they will have for services.

Summary

The family provides the basic foundation for individuals in this and other societies. The functions of the family are procreation, socialization, enculturation, and protection. In addition, families provide financial and emotional support, meet the child's basic needs as well as providing for medical and educational needs, and serve to interpret the world to the child and the child to the world. Today's family must cope with a variety of barriers to functioning. Violence, both societal and intrafamilial, and the increase of divorce are two major factors.

The family is a system composed of a group of subsystems, each interrelated. This system operates through a series of roles and rules that govern how the family regulates itself and relates to the outside world. Communication refers to the manner in which family members relate to others within the family system as well as the outside world. Families may be two-parent, single-parent, reconstituted, or blended, or may be children with a parent who has chosen never to marry.

Culture plays a large role in the way families operate. The African American, Hispanic, Asian, Native American, and Middle Eastern groups are all comprised of smaller cultures, each with its own values, patterns of communication, and spiritual beliefs.

Every family, no matter the cultural background, has a life cycle from the time the parents first come together until their deaths. Each member of the family is affected by developmental milestones even after the adult children begin their own nuclear families.

The major stresses on today's families are role definition and inequality, a variety of problems in parent/child relations, and limitation in the family's ability to cope with the disability of one of its members. The future of family life in this country appears to be influenced by the continued economic stressors on families, the likelihood that many couples will never marry, the fact that the role of the father is changing dramatically, the role of blended families, the resolution of childhood conflicts, and the fact that families do not have as much control over their own functioning and resources as did their predecessors. How the family as a system will meet these challenges remains to be seen.

EXPLORATION QUESTIONS

1. What are the primary responsibilities of a family?
2. What are the influences that negatively affect the family in today's world?
3. What are family rules and what part do they play in a family's functioning?
4. What are genograms and why are they useful in studying families?
5. Cite six types of families.
6. What are the primary values of the family with European roots?
7. What are the values of the Native American family?
8. What are the values of the African American family?
9. What are the values of the Hispanic family?
10. What are the values of the Asian family?
11. What are the values of the Middle Eastern family?
12. What are the major stresses on the family today?
13. What appear to be the trends for tomorrow's family?

REFERENCES

Acock, A. C., & Demo, D. H. (1994). *Family Diversity and Well-Being.* Thousand Oaks, CA: Sage.

Aerts, E. (1993). "Bringing the Institution Back In" (3–41). In Cowan et al. (Eds.), *Family, Self, and Society.* Hillsdale, NJ: Lawrence Erlbaum.

Althen, G. (1988). *American Ways: A Guide for Foreigners in the United States.* Yarmouth, ME: Intercultural Press.

Carter, B., & McGoldrick, M. (1988). *The Changing Family Life Cycle: A Framework for Family Therapy.* Boston: Allyn and Bacon.

Chan, S. (1998). "Families with Asian Roots" (181–257). In E. W. Lynch & M. J. Hanson (Eds.), *Developing Cross-Cultural Competence: A Guide for Working with Children and Their Families.* Baltimore, MD: Paul H. Brooks.

Chow, J. (1999). "Multiservice Centers in Chinese American Communities: Practice Principles and Challenges," *Social Work,* 44(1), 70–81.

Crosson-Tower, C. (2002). *Understanding Child Abuse and Neglect.* Boston: Allyn and Bacon.

Delgado, R. (2000). "Generalist Child Welfare and Hispanic Families" (130–156). In N. Cohen (Ed.), *Child Welfare: A Multicultural Perspective.* Boston: Allyn and Bacon.

Derezotes, D. S., & Snowden, L. R. (1990). "Cultural Factors in the Intervention of Child Maltreatment," *Child and Adolescent Social Work,* 7(2), 161–175.

Downs, S. W., Moore, E., McFadden, E. J., & Costin, L. B. (1999). *Child Welfare and Family Services.* Boston: Allyn and Bacon.

Freeman, D. S. (1992). *Multigenerational Family Therapy.* New York: Haworth Press.

Gadsden, V. L. (1999). "Black Families in Intergenerational and Cultural Perspective" (221–246). In M. E. Lamb et al. (Eds.), *Parenting and Child Development in Nontraditional Families.* Mahwah, NJ: Lawrence Erlbaum.

Goldenberg, I., & Goldenberg, H. (2000). *Family Therapy.* Belmont, CA: Brooks/Cole.

Hanson, M. J. (1998). "Families with Anglo-European Roots" (65–84). In E. W. Lynch & M. J. Hanson, (Eds.), *Developing Cross-Cultural Competence: A Guide for Working with Children and Their Families.* Baltimore, MD: Paul H. Brooks.

Herbert, M. (2002). *Working with Children, Adolescents, and Their Families.* Chicago: Lyceum.

Hess, B. B., Markson, E. W., & Stein, P. J. (1993). *Sociology.* New York: Macmillan.

Ho, M. K. (1987). *Family Therapy with Ethnic Minorities.* Beverly Hills, CA: Sage.

Horejsi, C., and Pablo, J. (1993). "Traditional Native American Cultures and Contemporary U.S. Society: A Comparison," *Human Services in the Rural Environment,* 16(3), 24–27.

Hutter, M. (1991). *The Family Experience*. New York: Macmillan.

Iglehart, A. P., & Becerra, R. M. (2000). *Social Services and the Ethnic Community*. Boston: Allyn and Bacon.

Joe, J. R., & Malach, R. S. (1998). "Families with Native American Roots" (89–119). In E. W. Lynch & M. J. Hanson (Eds.), *Developing Cross-Cultural Competence: A Guide for Working with Children and Their Families*. Baltimore, MD: Paul H. Brooks.

Johnston, J. R. (1993). "Family Transitions and Children's Functioning: The Case of Parental Conflict and Divorce" (197–234). In Cowan et al. (Eds.), *Family, Self, and Society*. Hillsdale, NJ: Lawrence Erlbaum.

Kadushin, A., & Martin, J. A. (1988). *Child Welfare Services*. New York: Macmillan.

Karpel, M., & Strauss, E. S. (1983). *Family Evaluation*. New York: Gardner Press.

Kim, K. C., & Kim, S. (1998). "Family and Work Roles of Korean Immigrants in the United States" (225–242). In H. McCubbin et al. (Eds.), *Resiliency in Native American and Immigrant Families*. Thousand Oaks, CA: Sage.

Laird, J. (1993). "Gay and Lesbian Families" (282–328). In F. Walsh (Ed.), *Normal Family Processes*. New York: Guilford Press.

Leiberman, A. F. (1990). "Culturally Sensitive Intervention with Children and Families," *Child and Adolescent Social Work*, 7(2), 101–119.

Levy, T., & Orlans, M. (1998). *Attachment Trauma and Healing: Understanding and Tracking Attachment Disorder in Children and Families*. Washington, DC: Child Welfare League of America.

Leyendecker, B., & Lamb, M. E. (1999). "Latino Families" (247–262). In M. E. Lamb et al. (Eds.), *Parenting and Child Development in Nontraditional Families*. Mahwah, NJ: Lawrence Erlbaum.

Logan, S. L. (1996). *Black Families*. Boulder, CO: Westview Press.

Lum, D. (2002). *Culturally Competent Practice*. Belmont, CA: Wadsworth.

Lynch, E. W., & Hanson, M. J. (1998). *Developing Cross-Cultural Competence: A Guide for Working with Children and Their Families*. Baltimore, MD: Paul H. Brooks.

Mason, M. A., Skolnick, A., & Sugarman, S. D. (Eds.). (1998). *All Our Families: New Policies for a New Century*. New York: Oxford University Press.

Mass, A. I., & Geaga-Rosenthal, J. (2000). "Child Welfare: Asian Pacific Island Families" (107–129). In N. Cohen (Ed.), *Child Welfare: A Multicultural Perspective*. Boston: Allyn and Bacon.

McCowan, W. G., Johnson, J., & associates. (1993). *Therapy with Treatment Resistant Families*. New York: Haworth Press.

McGoldrick, M. (1993). "Ethnicity, Cultural Diversity, and Normality" (331–360). In F. Walsh (Ed.), *Normal Family Processes*. New York: Guilford Press.

McGoldrick, M., Gerson, R., & Shellenberger, S. (1999). *Genograms in Family Assessment*. New York: Norton.

McWhirter, J. J., McWhirter, B. T., McWhirter, A. M., & McWhirter, E. H. (1998). *At-Risk Youth: A Comprehensive Response*. Pacific Grove, CA: Brooks/Cole.

Minuchin, S. (1981). *Families and Family Therapy*. Cambridge, MA: Harvard University Press.

Mollica, R. F., & Son, L. (1989). "Cultural Dimensions in the Evaluation and Treatment of Sexual Trauma," *Psychiatric Clinics of North America*, 12(2), 363–379.

Moorehouse, M. J. (1993) "Work and Family Dynamics" (265–286). In P. A. Cowan et al. (Eds.), *Family, Self, and Society*. Hillsdale, NJ: Lawrence Erlbaum.

Pecora, P., Whittaker, J. K., Plotnick, R. D., Barth, R. P., and Maluccio, A. N. (2000). *The Child Welfare Challenge: Policy, Practice and Research*. New York: Aldine DeGruyter.

Prater, G. S. (2002). "Child Welfare and African American Families" (87–115). In N. Cohen (Ed.), *Child Welfare: A Multicultural Perspective*. Boston: Allyn and Bacon.

Sharifzadeh, V. S. (1998). "Families with Middle Eastern Roots" (319–351). In E. W. Lynch & M. J. Hanson (Eds.), *Developing Cross-Cultural Competence: A Guide for Working with Children and Their Families*. Baltimore, MD: Paul H. Brooks.

Shaver, L. D. (1998). "The Cultural Deprivation of an Oklahoma Cherokee Family" (80–99).

In D. Tanno et al. (Eds.), *Communication and Identity Across Cultures*. Thousand Oaks, CA: Sage.

Swanson, G. E. (1993). "The Structuring of Family Decision-Making: Personal and Societal Sources and Some Consequences for Children" (235–263). In Cowan et al. (Eds.), *Family, Self, and Society*. Hillsdale, NJ: Lawrence Erlbaum.

Teachman, J. D., Tedrow, L. M., and Crowder, K. D. (2000). "The Changing Demography of America's Families," *Journal of Marriage and Family,* 62(4), 123–136.

Thomason, T. C. (1993). "Counseling Native Americans: An Introduction for Non-Native American Counselors" (171–187). In D. R. Atkinson, G. Morton, & D. W. Sue (Eds.), *Counseling American Minorities: A Cross-Cultural Perspective*. Dubuque, IA: Brown and Benchmark.

Walsh, F. (Ed.). (1993). *Normal Family Processes*. New York: Guilford Press.

Watts-Jones, D. (1997). "Toward an African-American Genogram," *Family Process,* 36(4), 375–383.

Wells, R. V. (1991). "Demographic Change and Family Life in American History: Some Reflections" (43–62). In M. Hutter (Ed.), *The Family Experience*. New York: Macmillan.

Willis, W. (1998). "Families with African-American Roots" (121–150). In E. W. Lynch & M. J. Hanson (Eds.), *Developing Cross-Cultural Competence: A Guide for Working with Children and Their Families*. Baltimore, MD: Paul H. Brooks.

Yee, B. W., Huang, L. N., & Lew, A. (1998). "Families: Life-Span Socialization in a Cultural Context" (83–135). In L. C. Lee et al. (Eds.), *Handbook of Asian American Psychology*. Thousand Oaks, CA: Sage.

Zuniga, M. E. (1998). "Families with Latino Roots" (151–179). In E. W. Lynch & M. J. Hanson (Eds.), *Developing Cross-Cultural Competence: A Guide for Working with Children and Their Families*. Baltimore, MD: Paul H. Brooks.

CHAPTER

3 Children and Poverty

JUDY A. NOEL

DEE L. WHYTE

Childhood poverty relentlessly stalks its victims and affects every aspect of their lives. It triggers a deluge of problems for these children—hunger, homelessness, sickness, disabilities, violence, educational failure, too-early parenthood, and family stress are often the outcomes of child poverty. Perhaps cruelest of all, it even puts these children at higher risk of dying from birth defects, fires, and diseases.

Children continue to represent the largest group of poor in the United States. According to Children's Defense Fund statistics, 11.6 million children under 18 years of age, or one out of every six American children, lived below the poverty level in 2000. Although this number reflects a gradual decrease in the

63

number of poor children for the last seven years, more children live in poverty today than 30 years ago. Also, the proportion of children living in families where at least one parent worked is at an all-time high. (Children's Defense Fund, "Facts and FAQs"). This chapter will consider how poverty is determined by the federal government, the causes and consequences of child poverty, and the strategies needed to reduce the amount of child poverty in the United States. Although all of this information is important in order to understand the complexity of child poverty, it does not humanize the issue. As you review the facts, it is vital that you imagine how the lives of real children are affected by bearing the enormous burden of living in poverty.

CASE EXAMPLE

Brenda

Nine-year-old Brenda walked slowly home from her third-grade class. She was cold, she had a sore throat, and she was pretty sure she had a fever. She was sick and anxious to get home and lie down—even though home was a small drafty trailer. Actually, Brenda knew she was sick when she went to school this morning—but she went anyway because she would be sure to get breakfast at school. And as the morning wore on, Brenda felt even sicker, but decided to stay because then she would be able to eat the school lunch, which would probably be the last good meal she would have today. Brenda was shivering. She had on a sweater, but no coat. Her mother thought that she'd have enough money for a coat next month, but the weather had turned cold earlier than usual and Brenda was cold every day as she walked to and from school.

The tiny trailer was only slightly warmer inside than the weather outside. Brenda's mother hadn't been able to afford to have the gas tank filled for the trailer's heater yet, so Brenda turned on the electric oven and opened the oven door to warm up the room. She looked in the refrigerator and realized how wise she had been to stay long enough at school for lunch—there was only a small container of milk and a small bag of french fries that her mother had brought home from her job at a fast-food restaurant.

Brenda shivered under a blanket on the couch and tried to go to sleep. She knew sleep would help her get well, and she needed to try to get well fast. She remembered the last time she was sick and needed to go to see a doctor. Her mother's job didn't come with health insurance and so they waited until she was really sick and then they went to the emergency room at the hospital. Even though her mother didn't say anything to her, Brenda knew that the cost of the visit and the medicine she needed made her mother anxious and depressed. This time she would try to will herself to get better.

Children have not fared well in comparison to other vulnerable groups in U.S. society. For example, in 1996, 19.8% of children lived in poverty. The number of children living in extreme poverty (in households with an income less than half the federal poverty level, or less than about $6,250 for a family of three) actually grew from 8.5% in 1995 to 9.0 in 1996. In comparison, 11.3% of adults over the age of 18 were living in poverty during this time. Although government cash programs lifted 78% of otherwise poor elderly Americans (over age 65) out of poverty in 1996, government cash programs raised a mere 13% of children above the poverty line in the same year (Dahl, 1998). This reflects the dramatic reduction of elder poverty during the past 30 years due to growth in programs such as Social Security and Supplemental Security Income.

The number of children and adults living in poverty has declined during the past few years. In 2000, 11,633,000 children under age 18 (16.2%) were living in poverty compared with 10.8% of adults 18 years of age and over. However, the poverty rate for children under age 4 in the United States was 19.7% (Children's Defense Fund, "Census 2000 Supplementary Survey"). A later unpublished report by the CDC revealed that children living in full-time, year-round working families rose from 3.8 million in 1999 to 4.1 million in 2000. The decline in poverty rates for children are expected to be short-lived, however, due to the recent weakening economy, higher unemployment, and a decline in the safety net for children and their families (Children's Defense Fund, "Overall Child Poverty Rate").

Characteristics of Poor Children

Children are poor because they live in poor families. Just as all families are unique, with their own individual characteristics and histories, poor families have diverse backgrounds and life circumstances that cause them to live in poverty. Despite a commonly held perception that the heaviest concentrations of poor people live in large cities, more poor children actually live in suburban areas or rural areas.

> *It's hard to characterize the average American family, but even harder not to stereotype the poor. The popular conception that most poor families are black, inner-city welfare recipients is simply incorrect: "Ghetto Poverty" constitutes less than 10 percent of total U.S. poverty, according to Professor David Ellwood of Harvard's Kennedy School of Government. (Freedman, 1993, 32)*

Minority children are disproportionately at risk of growing up in poverty. Although minorities represent only one-third of all children under 6 years old, they represent the vast majority of poor children. In 2000, 28.0% of Hispanic children, 30.9% of black children, 13.0% of white children, and 14.5% of Asian and Pacific Islander children were poor. Even so, in terms of numbers of poor, non-Hispanic Caucasian children still outnumber poor African American and Hispanic children (Children's Defense Fund, "Census 2000 Supplementary Survey").

In 2000, families living in poverty had only slightly more children (2.3 children) compared with the average family (1.9 children) Children in single-parent families headed by women are at a much higher risk (39.8 percent) of being poor compared with those living in two-parent families (8.2 percent) (Children's Defense Fund, "Census 2000 Supplementary Survey").

Working alone will not lift children and their families out of poverty. In 2000, approximately three of four children (77%) lived with a family member who worked at least part of the year—an increase of 16% since 1993. Based on U.S. Census data for 2000, one out of three poor children (4.1 million) lived in a family where someone was employed full time during the year. This is the highest proportion of children living in "working poor" families in the 26 years for which the data exist (Children's Defense Fund, "Census 2000 Supplementary Survey"). As discussed later in this chapter, even with a robust economy and a modest increase in the minimum wage, employment no longer guarantees that a family will live above the poverty level.

Poverty Defined

What is poverty? Officially, _poverty_ is defined by the U.S. government in its "index of poverty." A poverty line is established as the means of separating those who are considered poor from those who are not. This measurement is important because it is used to compute whether people are eligible for many government programs (see Table 3.1).

To arrive at this estimate of a poverty line, the food budget thought to be the minimally adequate for a family's subsistence is "multiplied by 3 on the assumption that food should constitute one-third of a family's budget" (Karger & Stoesz, 2002, 118). Adjustments are then made for the number of children under age 18, family size, and the age of the head of the household. This method of defining poverty was first developed in 1963 when Mollie Orshansky of the Social Security Administration determined, as a baseline, the minimal diet necessary to survive. The first official poverty line was set for the year as $3,000 (Sidel, 1986). In 2001, a family of three (one parent and two children) had to make less than the poverty threshold of $14,269 in order to be considered poor by the Census Bureau. It is important to note that most poor families' incomes are usually far below the poverty threshold (U.S. Census Bureau, 2002).

Although the federal poverty line provides a useful tool for defining and measuring poverty, it is criticized on several accounts. Some believe that the criteria to determine the poverty level distorts the complexion of poverty by including only cash and not taking into consideration such in-kind resources as food stamps, housing assistance, tax credits, and medical problems. They claim that, if the noncash benefits poor families receive (which have expanded dramatically over the past 30 years) were included in the formula, there would

Table 3.1   **Poverty Thresholds for 2001 for Families with up to Five Persons, Including Children under 18 Years (Dollars)**

Size of Family Unit	Related Children under 18 Years				
	One	*Two*	*Three*	*Four*	*Five*
Two persons					
Householder under 65 years	12,207				
Householder 65 years and over	12,161				
Three persons	14,255	14,269			
Four persons	18,566	17,960	18,022		
Five persons	22,349	21,665	21,135	20,812	
Six persons	25,438	24,914	24,441	23,664	23,221
Seven persons	29,336	28,708	28,271	27,456	26,505
Eight persons	32,894	32,302	31,783	31,047	30,112
Nine persons or more	39,413	38,889	38,449	37,726	36,732

Source: U.S. Bureau of the Census, Current Population Survey.

be fewer people officially declared as living below the poverty level. Critics also point out that the poverty measure does not take into account assets such as a house. However, although it is true that using an assets test as well as an income test would decrease the number of poor, it is also true that more poor people have few assets.

Others believe that the index of poverty is outdated. It is based on the average expenditure of family income on food for three people 30 years ago, before the advent of more expensive processed and fast food, and calculated during a time when women were usually home all day to bake and cook meals from scratch. Further, they argue that the poverty level should be set in relationship to the status of others in contemporary society. These individuals, believing that poverty is best identified by comparing income groups within society, call for the development of a poverty standard that is equal to one-half of the median income (the midpoint in the range of family incomes, at which 50% of families have income about that point and the other 50% have less). When the poverty thresholds for a family were first adopted, they were roughly equal to what was then 50% of median family income. Since that time, the poverty level has dropped far below 50% of median income (Blong and Leyser, 1994). If this criterion were used, many more children would be living below the poverty line today.

Still others point out that the formula to compute the poverty line is outdated. They point out that American families now spend one-fifth of their income on food because of rising costs in other budget items such as housing and child care (DiNitto, 2000, 71).

The reality is that, no matter how poverty is computed, a large number of children are living in families unable to afford adequate food, shelter, medical care, and other basic necessities. As will be seen later in this chapter, the burden of living in poverty reduces a child's chances to grow up to be a healthy, well-adjusted, and contributing adult in our society and, at the same time, increases a child's chances of suffering the negative outcomes associated with growing up in poverty.

Why Children Live in Poverty

Why are a large number of children living in poverty in the United States? Why does almost one of every three American children experience at least one year of poverty before turning age 16? It is clear that the reasons are complex and interrelated, involving changes in our economic structure, the reconfiguration of society, as well as other factors, such as the individual characteristics of parents.

A major reason why so many children are living in poverty today is because *real wages have been falling for most Americans since 1973* (Coontz, 1995). This means that the value of wages in terms of buying power, what a family can actually purchase with a paycheck, has declined steadily for 30 years. Family historian Stephanie Coontz wrote the following about this long-term trend of income inequality in our country.

> *Most poverty...comes from our changing earnings structure, not from our changing family structure. Between 1969 and 1989 the number of young white men earning less than the poverty figure for a family of four rose from one in ten to almost one in four. For African American men the comparable figure rose from 26% to 37%; for Hispanics, for 25% to 40%. (9)*

The number of low-wage workers, or the "working poor," continues to expand, proving that work alone will not necessarily keep an individual or family out of poverty. We also know that the median income of young families with children plunged 35% between 1973 and 1992, after adjusting for inflation (Sherman, 1994).

A second factor in the explanation of high rates of poverty among children is that, as the real value of wages shrink, *more resources are going to a small number of people in our country.*

> *Even after taxes, the top 20% rake in 44% of total income (not counting capital gains from the sale of homes, wares, stocks, and bonds); the bottom 20% must get by on 3.9%. And this astonishingly small share includes the cash value of food stamps and other benefits for the poor! In fact, the top 1% of*

the population has as much income as the entire bottom 40%. (Coontz, 1995, 11)

Another reason for the high number of children living in poverty is that there has been *a decline in the real value of government assistance to families*. Until 1996, AFDC (Aid to Families with Dependent Children) was the major cash benefit for poor families. (In 1996, it was replaced by Temporary Assistance for Needy Families [TANF], which is discussed later in this chapter.) When AFDC was replaced with TANF, benefits from AFDC were worth less than 1975 benefits in every state, and the annual cost-of-living increases in food stamp benefits did not offset the loss.

Even so, many eligible families *do not use all services available to them*. This may be because they do not know they are eligible for assistance, because the administrative barriers are too cumbersome to overcome, or for other reasons, such as the placement of welfare offices in locations difficult to reach.

The *reconfiguration of families* in U.S. society also has contributed to the increase in childhood poverty. As the number of one-parent households grows, so does the chance that children will grow up in poverty. According to U.S. Census data for 2000, two of five children living in single-parent, female-headed families (39.8%) were living in poverty compared to 8.2% of children living in two-parent families in 2000. Additionally, the poverty rates for children living in minority, single-parent, female-headed households are higher compared with their white counterparts (DiNitto, 2000). This growing number of single-parent families is attributable both to increased divorce rates and to the tenfold increase since 1950 in the number of births outside marriage (Children's Defense Fund, "Census 2000 Supplementary Survey"). The *failure of absent parents to financially contribute to the support of their children* is seen as another major cause of child poverty today. This "gender-segregated division of labor" is often referred to *institutionalized sexism* (Heffernan et al., 1997). The vast majority of single-parent families (about 90%) are headed by women. Female-headed families often receive little or no financial help from the child's father. In 1999, only 35% of female-headed families received any child support or alimony during the year (Nelson, 2002).

The difficulties of a single-mother family are often compounded when the mother is a teen (see Chapter 10). In fact, we know that children born to unmarried teen mothers are more likely to drop out of school, give birth out of wedlock, divorce or separate, and be dependent on welfare. And when the mothers of these families do not complete high school, the children are 10 times more likely to be living in poverty by the ages 8 to 12 as children born to nonadolescent, married mothers with at least a high school education (Nelson, 2002).

Family poverty also is linked *to the level of education of the parents*. People without high school diplomas will earn only about 75% as much as high school graduates, and less than half of what college graduates are likely to make during their lifetimes (O'Hare, 1995). During the twenty-first century, economists believe that it will be increasingly more important for adults to have skills and technical knowledge in order to hold jobs that can support a family. Other *personal characteristics of parents,* such as mental retardation or emotional illness, can also increase the likelihood that families will live in poverty.

Advocates for children also believe that more children live in poverty each year because *children are too young to vote, lobby, and speak up for themselves.* They point to the dramatic reduction of poverty in elders in our country since the inception of AARP, which provides a vehicle for the elderly to lobby for improved living conditions. Children, on the other hand, must rely on others who are old enough to vote and lobby to speak out for them. Although there are several advocacy groups that work on behalf of children, they have not established the power base necessary to force policymakers to make the changes required to lift children out of poverty.

Consequences of Growing Up in Poverty

Regardless of the causes of poverty, increasing numbers of American children are growing up in environments that put them at high risk of adverse outcomes. Growing up in poverty places a child at a profound disadvantage and greatly lowers the chance that the child will mature into a well-adjusted, productive, and contributing member of society. Research today reveals that just about every part of a child's life is affected by poverty. Further, growing up in the adverse conditions created by poverty increases the chance that such children will cost the taxpayers more money as they will require more expensive publicly funded services throughout their lives.

CASE EXAMPLE

David

David's mother, Suzanne, was not quite 26 years old when she conceived him. He was the third of Suzanne's children; the other two were ages 2 and 5. David's father was a construction worker, making just slightly more than necessary to keep the family above the poverty level. The family constantly struggled to make ends meet and, no matter how hard they tried, never seemed to be able to save much money. They barely managed to rent a small house on the outskirts of a small city.

During the second month of Suzanne's pregnancy, her husband had a car accident and died after almost two weeks of hospitalization in intensive care. The little savings that they had accrued were quickly gone to pay for hospital bills and funeral expenses, and still there were bills left to be paid. Suzanne began to receive AFDC and tried to learn how to live even more frugally. She had been about 20 pounds overweight before her pregnancy, so she reasoned that dramatically reducing her food input would be both advantageous to her figure and help with her food budget. Suzanne managed to keep only two prenatal visits, as she could not afford a sitter to watch her other children, did not own a car, and lived miles from the health clinic.

Suzanne's son, David, was a low–birth-weight baby. He weighed only 4.9 pounds at birth and needed all of the special hospital and aftercare necessary for an infant born at low birth weight ($21,000). From the very beginning of his life, he was colicky, easily irritated, and seemed to his mother to always be awake and moving. David needed more attention and care than her other children and Suzanne began to resent her newest child. The stress of living in poverty and having a difficult child made it harder for Suzanne to nurture David. Just after his first birthday, Suzanne lost control and hit David harder than she ever had before. Despite her promises to herself to never lose control with David again, David increasingly suffered beatings from his mother.

David entered kindergarten at age 5 and his teachers quickly referred him for an evaluation. He was diagnosed as having severe learning disabilities and hyperactivity—conditions often associated with children born with a low birth weight. Although David was receiving special education services from the school system ($6,000 per year), he fell so far behind that he needed to repeat first grade (cost to repeat).

Meanwhile, David's mother found him harder to control at home as he got older and physically larger. She had made some attempts to work and get off AFDC, but could never make enough money to buy all of the necessities for her family and pay for health insurance. Also, it was hard to arrange for child care for David while she worked because he was so hard to manage. Eventually, Suzanne stayed on AFDC and became increasingly angry and resentful toward David.

David's third-grade teacher noticed several large bruises on both of David's arms and reported suspected child abuse to Child Protection Services. This agency conducted a thorough investigation and ordered a number of services for David and Suzanne, including counseling and after-school child care ($20,000). By now, however, David's siblings were adolescents who had also lived for years in poverty and were acting out their own anger and frustrations. The stresses on Suzanne continued to increase, as did the beatings on David.

When David was 10 years old, he was removed from his home and placed in a foster home for four years ($20,000). David had trouble getting along with his foster parents and was moved several times. When he was age 14, he rejoined his family. By then, David was an angry and frustrated adolescent who could not succeed at school or maintain healthy peer relationships. When he was age 16, he dropped out of school and decided to work full time. However, because he was a high school dropout with learning disabilities and poor reading skills, David could find only minimum-wage jobs. Soon he realized that the only way to make money was through a life of crime, and he began dealing drugs and breaking into houses. At age 18, David was caught and brought to trial and was found guilty. He served a 10-year jail sentence ($350,000). By the time David was 28 years old, he had consumed over $417,000 in publicly funded services, not to mention the cost of payments to his mother on AFDC.

David's story illustrates some of the human misery and economic cost of an early life spent in poverty. Poverty puts children at a higher risk for poor outcomes and increases life stressors that place heavy burdens on them as they travel through childhood. Further, the longer a child lives in poverty, the more impact it is likely to have on the child's development. Poverty is often present with other risk factors, such as low parental education or adolescent parents, making it difficult to judge how much of an effect poverty by itself makes on the life of a child. However, when research has held constant other factors that might lead to negative outcomes for children, sizable impacts remain that can only be attributed to poverty (Sherman, 1994). For many children such as David, the stress of living in poverty is greatly magnified as risk factors interact.

Life Stressor Factors

Living in poverty places extraordinary stress on families that can lead to isolation, tension, anger, and hopelessness. These families must worry about how to attain the basic necessities—food, clothing, medical care, and shelter—that other Americans take for granted. Further, poverty often forces them to live in inadequate and crowded housing, send their children to inferior schools, and be exposed to more crime and violence than nonpoor families.

Almost always the stressors of poverty interact and compound problems for poor children. Lisabeth Schoor discusses this phenomenon in her book *Within Our Reach* (1988).

> *The child in a poor family who is malnourished and living in an unheated apartment is more susceptible to ear infection; once the ear infection takes hold, inaccessible or inattentive health care may mean it will not be properly treated; hearing loss will do long-term damage to a child who needs all the help he can get to cope with a world more complicated than the world of most middle-class children. When this child enters school, his chances of being in an overcrowded classroom with an overwhelmed teacher further compromise his chances of successful learning. Thus risk factors join to shorten the odds of favorable long-term outcomes. (30)*

A growing body of scientific evidence reveals that the early brain development of the child is negatively affected by stressors often inherent with poverty, and that these deficits may not be reversible. Over the past 20 years, researchers have documented the effect of malnutrition on brain development. The Carnegie Corporation's report, *Starting Points: Meeting the Needs of our Youngest Children* (1994), emphasized this point.

> *We have long understood that factors other than genetic programming affect brain development. Nutrition is perhaps the most obvious example: we know that inadequate nutrition before birth and in the first years of life can so seriously interfere with brain development that it may lead to a host of neurological and behavioral disorders, including learning disabilities and mental retardation. (20)*

This report went on to say that brain development takes place more rapidly and extensively at an earlier age than scientists had previously thought.

> *Scientists are also learning that the brain is very vulnerable to environmental influences, making the environment a child lives in extremely important. Thus a baby that lives in a family that does not provide adequate stimulation and nurturance, or in a family living with the stresses of poverty, homelessness, or neglect experience changes in brain chemistry that make them more likely than others to be violent teenagers and adults. (Goleman, 1995)*

Complete reversal of the cognitive deficits of people raised in poor environments during infancy and childhood may not be possible.

Health and Health Care Factors

Poor Health Outcomes.   Poverty has a clear impact on the health conditions of children. Poor children are more likely to begin life at a disadvantage, as they are 1.2 to 2.2 times more likely to be born with a low birth weight (less than 2,5000 grams, or 5.5 pounds). In 1999, 301,183 babies born in the United States weighed less than 5.5 pounds. Low–birth-weight babies accounted for 7.6% of all births in 1999, which represented a 9% increase over the period from 1990 to 1999 (Nelson, 2002). Low–birth-weight babies are more likely to die in infancy, have a doubled risk of learning problems (such as learning disabilities, hyperactivity, emotional problems, and mental illness), have a significantly greater risk of neurodevelopmental problems (seizures, epilepsy, water on the brain, cerebral palsy, and mental retardation), and are at higher risk of losing their eyesight and hearing. Overall, poor children are three times more likely to suffer from fair or poor health and are much more likely to have health problems than nonpoor children.

No Health Insurance.   Another reason why poor children are at greater risk of poor health is that many poor families do not have health insurance. Employer-based insurance is the major source of insurance for children, yet the number of children covered by this benefit has decreased over the past two decades.

Employers are dropping coverage, ending coverage, or asking more from employee premiums for dependent coverage. This trend will greatly impact children in the future.

Uninsured children are less likely to have access to the medical and dental care services that they need to have a healthy start in life. A report from the Children's Defense Fund ("Key Facts: The Uninsured") found that, compared with children without health care, insured children are:

1. More than three times as likely to lack a regular source of health care
2. More than four times as likely to have delayed medical care because of cost
3. More than three times as likely to lack necessary dental care
4. More than twice as likely to go without needed prescription medications
5. More than twice as likely to go without eyeglasses

This same report also revealed that children of minority races were disproportionately represented among the uninsured, although the numbers were highest for white children. Of the 9.2 million children, 18 years of age and under, who were uninsured in 2000, 3.6 million (39.5%) were white, 3.3 million (35.3%) were Hispanic, 1.6 million (17.6) were black, 478,000 (5.2%) were Asian and Pacific Islander, and 221,000 (2.3%) were American Indian or Alaskan Native.

Some 90% of these children live in families with working parents. Many were eligible for Medicaid or the Children's Health Insurance Program (CHIP), which became effective in October of 1997 to benefit uninsured children, but were not taking advantages of these programs. It is possible that their families were either unaware of these programs or did not realize that their children were eligible. Lack of knowledge is the most likely explanation for low participation in CHIP, since enrollment increased dramatically from 1.3 million children in 2000 to 4.6 million children in 2001. More than 20 million children were enrolled in Medicaid in 1999; however, 5.8 million uninsured children are in families with incomes below 200 percent of the federal poverty level (Children's Defense Fund, "Key Facts: The Uninsured"). Some progress has been made in providing health care services to an increasing number of uninsured children through the combined efforts of the Medicaid program and CHIP, but many children are still without adequate medical care in the United States.

Poor Health Care. Lack of adequate health insurance means that poor children rely primarily on episodic health care. They often do not have routine "well checkups," but rely on emergency rooms and clinics for care when they are sick. Thus, the same physician does not see them each time to do a careful family history and to get a full picture of the child's needs. Around 20% of low-income children covered by Medicaid do not receive the federally mandated Early and Periodic Screening and Diagnostic Treatment (EPSDT) services at ages 12 and 24 months. The absence of a regular doctor also means that parents often do not receive information about preventive health care, such as immunizations, child-proofing their house, child safety seats, and balanced diets.

Nutritional Factors

Hunger and Malnutrition.   There are 31 million people in this country who are *food insecure,* defined as either hungry or not sure of when they will eat their next meal, according to a 1999 USDA study. Of these, 75% are women and children. Approximately 12 million children are food insecure and 10 million are malnurished (Karger and Stoesz, 2002). Parents describe the hungry child as 2 to 11 times more likely to experience fatigue, concentration problems, dizziness, irritability, frequent headaches and ear infections, unwanted weight loss, and frequent colds. An inadequate food supply causes other health problems, such as stunted growth (defined as being in the shortest 10% of children for their age), low birth weight, and iron-deficiency anemia (Sherman, 1994).

Anemia.   Iron-deficiency anemia is three to four times more prevalent in poor preschool children than it is in the general child population (Sherman, 1994). Anemia is the most common consequence of inadequate nutrition. Slow development in infants, inattentiveness, and conduct disorders have all be associated with iron deficiency.

Environmental Factors

Lead Poisoning.   Lead poisoning is one of the most serious environmental health hazards threatening children today. Statistics from the Centers for Disease Control and Prevention (CDC) estimate that approximately 900,000 children under the age of 5 currently have elevated blood-lead levels Although all children are at risk, those living in a low-income or minority family are at an increased risk. For example, African American children are five times more likely to be exposed to lead poisoning compared with white children. Lead contamination generally comes from lead-based paint found in older, inadequately maintained houses. Children living in these houses breathe the dust that forms after the paint deteriorates, and may eat the sweet-tasting paint chips. Repeated exposure may cause kidney damage, learning disabilities, developmental delays, and behavioral problems. Very high levels of lead in blood can cause seizures, coma, and even death.

Low-income children covered by Medicaid, the federal/state co-funded program designed to provide free or low-cost health care to children in families, are required by federal law to have a blood-lead screening at ages 12 and 24 months as part of the EPSDT program. However, only one of five children enrolled in Medicaid is screened for blood-lead levels in spite of the fact that this is a federal mandate and that these children are three times more likely to suffer from lead poisoning (Children's Defense Fund, "Lead Poisoning").

Inadequate Housing.   Poor children are more than three times as likely to live in inadequate and/or crowded housing, move around about twice as much as nonpoor children, and are more likely to go without heat or other utilities (Sherman, 1994; Ellwood, 1988; Sidel, 1986). In the past decade, homelessness has increased more among families with children than any other group. In fact, a 1997 survey conducted by the U.S. Conference of Mayors showed that families with children represent 36% of those in homeless shelters (Dahl, 1998).

Unsafe, Isolated Neighborhoods.   Poverty restricts a family's choices of neighborhoods where they can raise their children. Poor children are more likely to live in crowded, noisy, and crime-ridden neighborhoods. The lower quality of life in these neighborhoods means that poorer families have less access to good jobs, safe play areas and parks, and positive role models for their children (Sidel, 1986).

Increased Violence.   All of these factors contribute to increased life stressors for families raising their children in poverty. These stressors and inequalities can breed violence. Thus, poor children are more likely to live in neighborhoods with a high crime rate, and are more likely to experience violence firsthand.

> *Many social science disciplines, in addition to psychology, have firmly established that poverty and its contextual life circumstances are major determinants of violence.... Violence is most prevalent among the poor, regardless of race.... Few differences among the races are found in the rates of violence when people at the same income level are compared. But beyond mere income level, it is the socioeconomic inequality of the poor—their sense of relative deprivation and their lack of opportunity to ameliorate their life circumstances—that facilitates higher rates of violence.... Not only do the poor in America lack basic necessities, but they are aware that they do not have those things most other Americans have and that they lack other opportunities needed to obtain them in the future. Media depictions of other Americans, who are living the "good life" serve to compound the already untenable conditions of poverty with a heightened sense of deprivation. (Sherman, 1994, 38)*

Educational Factors

Lower Educational Outcomes.   Children brought up in poverty are much less likely to graduate high school and receive additional education or training, thereby making it more difficult to earn wages high enough to live above the poverty level as adults. For every year a child lives in poverty, the chance that he or she will fall behind in school increases by two full percentage points (Sherman, 1994).

Inadequate Schools.   Poor children cannot necessarily count on receiving a public education that will help them overcome the disadvantages they experience because they live in poverty, in part, because the richest school districts spend 56% more per student than do the poorest (Children's Defense Fund, "Key Facts about Education"). Although this additional funding does not guarantee a quality education, it certainly is a contributing factor. According to the National Academy of Sciences, the poorest children attend the poorest schools—schools that have fewer financial and material resources. Student achievement is found to be significantly lower (National Research Council, 1993).

Kozol's *Savage Inequalities* (1991) provides striking testimony to the lack of resources and attention to safety given to poor children in schools across the country today.

Recent Efforts to Fight Poverty

In recent years some of the antipoverty programs have changed dramatically, in large part because of the lengthy debate for AFDC. Implemented from 1935 to 1996, AFDC was a cash benefit program devised to assist poor families, financially, in the hope of giving them a push to become self-supporting. Critics argue that the program encouraged dependency and major work disincentives. After years of debate, the Personal Responsibility and Work Opportunity Reconciliation Act (PRWORA), passed in 1996, replaced AFDC with the Temporary Assistance for Needy Families (TANF) block grant.

Temporary Assistance for Needy Families (TANF)

Although AFDC was a federal entitlement program, TANF is a welfare to work program that leaves to individual states the question of whether to aid all qualifying families. The PRWORA requires recipients to work after two years, limits receipt of TANF benefits by any family with a member who has received aid as an adult for five years (a state can exempt up to 20% of its cases from this limit), requires unmarried parents under age 18 to live with an adult and stay in school to be eligible for benefits, makes poor legal immigrants ineligible for many forms of income assistance, and makes other major changes in antipoverty programs. States receive a fixed level of resources from the federal government for income support and work programs based on what they spend on these programs in 1994, with some opportunity for contingency funds if needs change. Each state can use state funds or waivers to extend benefits beyond time limits set by the federal law and they also can set shorter time limits.

It is still too early to understand the full impact of TANF. We do know that the number of families receiving TANF dropped 47% since the implementation of this program. However, the number of families on public assistance was decreasing even before the TANF legislation was passed due to a robust economy resulting in high employment during the 1990s. Available information on recipients who have left the program for employment suggest that 50 to 60% are employed in jobs that pay just above the minimum wage (Karger and Stoesz, 2002).

No data are being collected on the families who have been dropped from the TANF program, although it is speculated that many are living in poverty. Legislation regarding TANF was up for reauthorization in 2002. The Bush administration proposed that recipients put in 40 hours of work or training each week, including at least 24 hours on an actual job in comparison to the 30 hours of job-related activities including 20 hours of actual work. States also will be required to increase the percentages of welfare recipients in jobs or work-related activities from 50 to 70% over the next four years. The events of September 11, 2001, put the passing of this legislation on hold. If these changes *are* implemented during this time of a declining economy and increasing unemployment, it is likely that an increasing number of TANF recipients will be unable to meet the requirements and will be dropped from the program. The goal of reducing the number of recipients may be reached, but at the cost of an increasing number of families with children falling into poverty.

Earned Income Tax Credits (EITC)

Significant changes in Earned Income Tax Credits have occurred since 1993 that have benefited many poor working families. In fact, EITC is now the largest cash assistance program for families with children and lifts more children out of poverty than any other government program. The program allows families with children and low earnings to receive credits against their income tax. In 1996, the EITC provided an estimated $25 billion of assistance to 18.7 million low-income families (Behrman, 1997). As an example, in 1997, a family with two or more children that earned between $9,140 and $11,930 received a maximum EITC of $3,656. As wages increased, the credit diminished, and was phased out completely at $29,290. The value of EITC is adjusted for inflation each year. A few states have implemented similar earned income credit programs for state income taxes.

Child Tax Credit

In 1997, Congress passed a child tax credit that benefited families by allowing a $400 per child credit in 1998 and then a $500 per child credit in later years. This credit is computed before the Earned Income Tax Credit, and can be taken advantage of by two-parent families with incomes as high as $110,000 and single-parent families with incomes up to $75,000. Unfortunately, 20 million children in families with too little income to have a tax liability will not be helped by this tax credit (Dahl, 1998).

Supplemental Security Income (SSI)

Supplemental Security Income pays monthly cash benefits to people who are age 65 or older, or blind, or have a disability and who don't own much or have a lot of income. Children as well as adults can get benefits because of disability.

The federal government establishes eligibility for this program and provides a minimum benefit across all states. States may supplement the federal payments. The PRWORA restricted eligibility and made it more difficult for poor children with disabilities to qualify for SSI. By December of 1997, over 200,000 cases had been reviewed and about 135,000 children had their benefits cut off (Behrman, 1997).

Minimum Wage Increase

The federal minimum wage rose in 1997 to $5.15 per hour. Although this increase in the minimum wage is a step in the right direction, it still leaves full-time, year-round minimum wage employment at only 82% of the 1998 poverty level for a family of three (Dahl, 1998). Advocates are likely to continue to lobby for further increases in the minimum wage and for an automatic adjustment for inflation.

Child Health Insurance Program (CHIP)

The Child Health Insurance Program represents a landmark development for children's health. Effective October 1, 1997, it provides $48 billion over 10 years for children's health coverage. Medicaid expansions and state grants will enable as many as 5 million uninsured children who qualify to gain health insurance from this program at no or low cost.

A number of other programs—such as public housing (whereby poor families may receive aid for rent or have rents reduced), Women Infants and Children (WIC; providing prenatal care and supplemental food benefits for poor women and children), Head Start (early education and social start for young children), food stamps (benefit transfer card with which food can be purchased for less), and a variety of social services—also are available. The food stamp program was cut by $28 billion dollars when the TANF block grant became law—the equivalent of reducing the average food stamp benefit for 80 cents per person to 66 cents per person per meal (Super et al., 1996).

The Economics of Poverty

It makes sense in both humane and economic terms to make the changes necessary to raise children out of poverty. Adults who have grown up in poverty are more likely to require costly public assistance and programs, and they also earn less and produce less economic output.

The American labor force is projected to lose as much as $130 billion in future productive capacity—an amount more that twice the size of the U.S. annual trade deficit with Japan—for every year that 14.5 million American children continue to live in poverty. These costs will spill over to employers

*and consumers, making it harder for business to expand technology, train
workers, or produce a full range of high-quality products. (Sherman, 1997, 1)*

How much would we save in program costs if we could eliminate most
child poverty? Prevention experts estimate that the saving would be substantial. If we invested in programs now, we would need to find fewer programs
later on to address the outcomes of growing up in poverty. The extent of savings would be in direct proportion to the effectiveness of prevention programs.
In *From Cradle to Grave* (1993), Jonathan Freedman estimates that, even if only
a fraction of the programs were effective, they might save at least $15 to $60
billion each.

Reducing Child Poverty

*Mollie Orshansky, the creator of the Poverty Line, has retired from govern-
ment. She says, "Why don't we stop doing research on the right poverty number and do something about poverty?" (Freedman, 1993, 231–232)*

Indeed, why don't we do something? Are there steps our country can take
to reduce child poverty? Is it possible to dramatically lower the number of
avoidable consequences of modern society? Other industrialized nations with
fewer resources and similar economic and social problems have put public policies in place that ensure that children are protected and have a better chance
to reach their full potential. In fact, U.S. children are 2 times as likely to be
poor as Canadian children, 3 times as likely to be poor as British children, 4
times as likely to be poor as French children, and 7 to 13 times more likely to
be poor as German, Dutch, and Swedish children (Sherman, 1994). Lower levels of government assistance are usually attributed to the higher rate of child
poverty in the United States.

Attitudinal Changes

In order to make significant progress in lifting children out of poverty, our
country needs to undergo important underlying attitudinal shifts toward children as well as families and to implement important programs to address the
causes of poverty. These new attitudes about children and families will create
the public will to make the changes necessary to reduce child poverty.

First, Americans need to *value all our children*. Poor children, middle-class
children, and wealthy children—we must feel responsible for them all, and
not view them as "other people's children." If we do not make this important
attitudinal shift, we run the risk of more and more children growing up in poverty each year. Second, we need to *value the role of the family and the job of
parenting*. Our nation should view parents as the highest-priority job while
children are growing up. The family is the most important institution in shap-

ing the lives of children, and parents must be strengthened and supported in their job of raising and nurturing them. This means that we will need to take a two-generational approach to reducing poverty. Last, we need to *value and fund prevention programs,* and move away from our current crisis orientation that forces us to invest in more programs designed to deal with problems *after* the damage have been done. These three important attitudinal shifts will create the public and political will to eliminate child poverty. They will also lead us to understand that effective solutions must be two-generational, affecting both the child and the child's caregivers.

Complex Combination of Two-Generational Strategies

Just as the reasons why so many children and families live in poverty are complex and interwoven, so are the solutions needed to eliminate child poverty. As well as creating the public and political will to end child poverty and to fund family-friendly prevention programs, it will be necessary to implement a complex combination of strategies. To be truly effective, these must be two-generational and include income security as well as service and support programs. The following are the solutions to child poverty most often mentioned by experts.

1. *Understand the impact of TANF.* The new welfare should be rigorously evaluated to determine its impact on children and to ensure that it effectively treats the causes of poverty. Parents should have access to the resources necessary to work, such as transportation, child care, and training. Any changes implemented in the reauthorization of the TANF legislation need to be evaluated as well. As mentioned earlier, a reduction in the number of recipients may not reflect the number of people working and getting out of poverty. In several states, qualified TANF recipients are eligible for Individual Development Accounts (IDA) programs. These are savings accounts for low-income people that are matched by public or private funds at a ratio generally of 1 to 3 dollars for the down payment on a first home, home repairs, education, or the development or expansion of a microbusiness. The goal of IDA programs is to help low-income people develop the necessary assets to help them out of poverty and keep them out of poverty (Nelson, 2002). Preliminary results suggest that these programs, which were implemented in the late 1990s, have been relatively successful for those with incomes at or just above the poverty level. Although these programs have not proven to be successful for those whose incomes are well below the poverty level, further implementation of these programs in conjunction with TANF recipients should be considered and evaluated.

2. *Strengthen child-support enforcement.* States should vigorously implement provisions in the PRWORA Act of 1997 that requires them to operate programs to locate absent parents and take other measures to ensure that noncustodial parents bear financial responsibility for their offspring.

3. *Implement child-support assurance.* Even if they are contributing child support, noncustodial parents earning low wages cannot contribute enough to bring their children out of poverty. In order to protect all children, a national child-support assurance system should be put into place. This would guarantee reasonable levels of child support by the government if an absent parent cannot support the child above an established minimum, or if the parent avoids payment altogether. This method of assuring that children have adequate financial support has several advantages. The government would collect revenue from the absent parent; there would be no stigma attached to the program because the program would collect money for families from all income brackets; and it would not be considered public assistance and therefore would not prevent mothers from working.

4. *Increase the minimum wage.* The minimum wage should be increased so that working parents can earn enough to keep their family out of poverty. The cost of living fluctuates dramatically in various parts of the country. Since 1994, several cities have implemented a "living wage" that involves passing local ordinances requiring private businesses that benefit from public money to pay their employees a living wage, which most frequently is defined as being equivalent to the poverty line for a family of four. This approach to helping the "working poor" to get out and keep out of poverty needs to be considered and evaluated in the future (Karger and Stoesz, 2002).

5. *Create more jobs.* Public policies should be implemented (such as tax credits) that encourage job growth in the private sector. Government also can create additional jobs in the public sector that meet community needs.

6. *Invest in schools and training programs.* Experts project that occupations that require specialized education and training will grow the fastest in the future. Children should have an equal opportunity to receive a good education, regardless of the neighborhood in which they live. More Americans also must have access to job-training programs and higher education that will provide them with the marketable skills necessary to secure a job that pays adequate wages. A high school education alone no longer guarantees a living above the poverty level. The federal government should allow states to count training or education as an allowable work activity as part of the TANF program.

7. *Implement family-centered policies.* Flexible work schedules, family medical leaves, and assistance with quality child care, including after-school and summer child care, will make it easier for poor families to care for their children.

8. *Enact an Earned Income Tax Credit in all states.* These refundable credits should be available to families even if their earnings are too low to owe taxes.

9. *Prevent teen pregnancies.* Programs need to be expanded to discourage too-early childbearing, which dramatically increases the chance that the mother and child will live in poverty for an extended period of time.

10. *Implement health insurance for adults.* Poor adults, as well as poor children, need a program that assures quality health care. When a family is burdened by uncovered health care costs, it impacts all family members. Preventive health care, as well as treatment, should be funded.

11. *Implement adequate housing for families.* Families currently making minimum wages must pay more than half their wages for rent in most states. The government should make subsidies available to prevent homelessness and ease this economic pressure on families.

12. *Expand programs to support and strengthen families.* Parents who are supported in their caregiving role are better able to nurture their children, and these children have a better chance to grow up to be productive, contributing members of society. Research has demonstrated that programs such as parenting education, support groups, and home visiting are effective and produce positive, significant results for parents and their children.

13. *Ensure that emergency services are in place.* Emergency assistance programs that provide food, clothing, and shelter to families in time of crisis must be available and have adequate funding.

A Important Footnote

Advocates for poor children should remember that it is not necessary to implement all of these strategies at once (a daunting and unlikely task in any event). Prevention of poor outcomes for children is not an all-or-nothing proposition. Even removing some of the risk factors can increase a child's chances to avoid damaging outcomes (Schoor, 1988).

Finally, it is important to note that a child growing up in poverty is not necessarily doomed to failure. Indeed, stories abound in our country of people who grew up in adverse conditions who matured to become happy, successful, and contributing members of society. Sometimes these children are especially resilient, and often they have been lucky enough to have the encouragement of a parent, teacher, or some other adult in their community. However, even though it is sometimes possible to beat the odds and overcome the adverse conditions associated with poverty, it is simply unfair of us to place the relentless burden of poverty with its inherent risks on the most vulnerable in our society.

Summary

Children represent the largest population living in poverty in the United States today. The numbers have increased alarming over the last 20 years. Minority children make up a large percentage of this population. Other than this, it is difficult to draw an accurate picture of the "typical" poor family in spite of popular stereotypes.

Poverty is defined by the U.S. government in terms of the *poverty line*, a calculated formula that assesses a family's minimally adequate budget. Despite criticisms of this formula as being outdated and too restrictive, this mechanism is still used.

The increase in poverty among children can be attributed to several factors, including economic changes over the last few years, the reconfiguration of the family unit, the lack of use of services by families, the personal characteristics of parents, and the fact that children do not vote and so cannot lobby for themselves.

Children in poverty are subject to many life stressors, including a variety of health concerns, no health insurance, poor educational opportunities, inadequate housing, and increased violence, both at home and in the streets.

Currently, there are several programs to address the needs of poor children and their families. The most widely used of these was, until 1996, Aid to Families with Dependent Children (AFDC), the cash assistance program to families with young children who have been deprived of the support of one parent and who are income eligible. Due to the criticism that this program encouraged dependency and was a disincentive to work, the Personal Responsibility and Work Opportunity Reconciliation Act (PRWORA) was passed in 1996, replacing AFDC with Temporary Assistance for Needy Families (TANF). This is a welfare-to-work program that gives some autonomy to states to determine how benefits should be allotted. At this point, TANF appears to have been relatively successful in reducing the number of welfare recipients. Children or their parents may also receive Supplemental Security Income (SSI) if they are disabled or blind. And some low-income families with children may be eligible for Earned Income Tax Credit (EITC), which offsets the Social Security taxes on their wages. Child tax credit allows families tax credit for children based on their ages. Other programs such as food stamps, Women Infants and Children Program, Medicare, and Head Start also are available. Additionally, the increase in the minimum wage will benefit families, and the Child Health Insurance Program will enable more children to receive insurance coverage.

There has been much discussion about how we can reduce the incidence of poverty. Many feel that we need to value children more as well as supporting and strengthening the family. In addition, changes must be made in economic programs, schools, family-centered policies, housing, and emergency services. There are simple solutions that will change the increasing trend toward the juvenilization of poverty.

EXPLORATION QUESTIONS

1. How is *poverty* defined? How is the poverty line arrived at?
2. How would one characterize the child growing up in poverty?
3. What are the reasons for the increase in child poverty?
4. How did the effects of growing up in poverty most likely affect David's life?
5. What are the stressors under which children in poverty must live?
6. What are some of the programs available for poor children and their families today? What is provided by each?
7. What are some ways to reduce poverty among children?
8. What is meant by *two-generational strategies*?

REFERENCES

Behrman, R. (Ed.), (1997). *The Future of Children: Children and Poverty.* Los Altos, CA: Center for the Future of Children, The David and Louise Packard Foundation.

Blong, A. M., & Leyser, B. (1994). *Living at the Bottom: An Analysis of 1994 AFDC Benefit Levels.* New York: Center on Social Welfare Policy and Law.

Carnegie Corporation. (1994). *Starting Points: Meeting the Needs of Our Youngest Children,* New York: Author.

Children's Defense Fund. "Census 2000 Supplementary Survey: Poverty Status during Previous 12 Months, by Age." Every Child Deserves a Fair Start. Retrieved from the World Wide Web on June 28, 2000: http://childrensdefense.org/fs_poverty_statebystate.htm.

Children's Defense Fund. "Facts and FAQs" Every Child Deserves a Healthy Start. Retrieved from the World Wide Web on June 28, 2002: http://childrensdefense.org/.faurstart.faqs.htm.

Children's Defense Fund. "Key Facts: The Uninsured," Every Child Deserves a Healthy Start. Retrieved from the World Wide Web on June 28, 2002: www.childrensdefense.org/hs_kf_uninsured.php.

Children's Defense Fund. *Key Facts about Education.* Retrieved from the World Wide Web on June 28, 2002: http://www.childrensdefense.org/keyfacts_education.htm.

Children's Defense Fund. "Lead Poisoning: A Serious and Common Environmental Health Problem." Every Child Deserves a Healthy Start. Retrieved from the World Wide Web on June 28, 2002: www.childrensdefense.org/hs_tp_leadpois.php.

Children's Defense Fund. "Overall Child Poverty Rate Dropped in 2000 but Poverty Rose for Children in Full-Time Working Families. Retrieved from the World Wide Web on June 28, 2002: http://www.childrensdefense.org/release)10925.htm.

Coontz, S. (1995, March). "The American Family and the Nostalgia Trap." *Phi Beta Kappa.*

Dahl, K. (Ed.). (1998). *The State of America's Children Yearbook.* Washington, DC: The Children's Defense Fund.

DiNitto, D. M. (2000). *Social Welfare Policy: Politics and Public Welfare* (5th ed.). Boston: Allyn and Bacon.

Ellwood, D. T. (1988). *Poor Support: Poverty in the American Family.* New York: Basic Books.

Finlay, B. (Ed.). (1996). *The State of America's Children Yearbook.* Washington, DC: The Children's Defense Fund.

Freedman, J. (1993). *From Cradle to Grave: The Human Face of Poverty in America.* New York: Atheneum.

Goleman, D. (1995). "Early Violence Leaves Its Mark on the Brain," *New York Times,* October 3, p. 15.

Gustavsson, N. S., & Segal, E. A. (1994). *Critical Issues in Child Welfare.* Thousand Oaks, CA: Sage.

Heffernan, J., Shuttlesworth, G., & Ambrosino, R. (1997). *Social Work and Social Welfare.* Minneapolis/St. Paul: West Publishing.

Huston, A. C. (1991). *Children in Poverty: Child Development and Public Policy.* New York: Cambridge University Press.

Johnson, L. C., & Schwartz, C. L. (1991). *Social Welfare: A Response to Human Need.* Boston: Allyn and Bacon.

Jones, J. E. (1994). *Child Poverty: A Deficit that Goes Beyond Dollars.* New York: National Center for Children in Poverty.

Karger, H. J., & Stoesz, D. (2002). *American Social Welfare Policy: A Pluralist Approach* (4th ed.). Boston: Allyn and Bacon.

Kozol, J. (1991). *Savage Inequalities: Children in America's Schools.* New York: Crown.

National Commission on Children. (1991). *Beyond Rhetoric.* Washington, DC: U.S. Government Printing Office.

National Research Council, Commission on Behavioral and Social Sciences and Education. (1993). *Losing Generations: Adolescents in High Risk Settings.* Washington, DC: National Academy Press.

Nelson, D. W. (2002). *Kids Count Data Book.* Baltimore, MD: Annie C. Casey Foundation.

O'Hare, W. P. (1995). *Kids Count Data Book*. Baltimore, MD: Annie C. Casey Foundation.

Schoor, L. B. (1988). *Within Our Reach*. New York: Anchor Books.

Schoor, L. B. (1997). *Common Purpose: Strengthening Families and Neighborhoods to Rebuild America*. New York. Anchor Books.

Sherman, A. (1994). *Wasting America's Future: The Children's Defense Fund Report on the Costs of Child Poverty*. Boston: Beacon Press.

Sidel, R. (1986). *Women and Children Last: The Plight of Poor Women in Affluent America*. New York: Penguin Books.

Super, D., Parrott, S., Steinmetz, S., & Mann, C. (1996). *The New Welfare Law*. Washington, DC: Center on Budget and Policy Priorities.

U.S. Advisory Board on Child Abuse and Neglect. (1995). *A Nation's Shame: Fatal Child Abuse and Neglect in the United States*. Washington, DC: U.S. Government Printing Office.

U.S. Census Bureau. "Poverty 2001: January 22, 2002." Retrieved from the World Wide Web June 30, 2002: http://www.census.gov/jjes/poverty/threshld/thresh01.html.

Violence, Addiction, and Homelessness

Current Societal Problems and Their Impact on Children

◀ CHILD KILLED IN CROSSFIRE OF POLICE/GANG SHOOTOUT ▶

◀ DRUG ADDICTED MOTHER LEAVES NEWBORN IN TRASH CAN ▶

◀ HOMELESS PARENTS SEEK SHELTER IN ABANDONED CHURCH ▶

Newspaper headlines serve as painful reminders of the fact that the welfare of children is greatly influenced by the social problems plaguing the world today. As the numbers of homeless become startling, experts report that the fastest-growing population of homeless today are women and children. Increasingly, drug-addicted parents come to the attention of child welfare systems across the country. And all the while, the gunfire in our streets takes its toll not only on children but on the psyches of those who remain alive. Any exploration of the child welfare system must take into consideration the backdrop against which today's children live. This world is filled with many problems, but we will focus on three of the major issues that threaten the healthy development of many children: violence, addiction, and homelessness.

Children and Violence

It would seem that today, more than ever before, our children are exposed to violence on a daily basis. Kotlowitz (1991) observed the world of two brothers, Lafeyette and Pharaoh Rivers, as they fought to survive amidst the turbulence of their home in Henry Horner, a crime-ridden Chicago housing project. Gunfire was an all too familiar sound that caused their concerned mother to count her children for fear one of them would be the victim. Plagued by rival gangs, the young project dwellers were often caught in the middle of the violence perpetrated by them. Bird Leg, the 14-year-old friend of the Rivers brothers, was one such victim.

> *In the summer of 1986, while shooting dice with some friends he [Bird Leg] was approached by a man with a shotgun demanding his money, and Bird Leg, in his youthful defiance, ran. The man emptied a cartridge of buckshot into Bird Leg's shoulder. That incident added to the intensifying war between the gangs, [and] caused his mother to move her family into an apartment on the city's far north side. But, as is often the case when families move, Bird Leg and his brothers kept returning to Horner to visit friends. (45)*

Later that summer, Bird Leg was shot in the arm with buckshot while visiting his friends. The very next night, he returned to the project and, while watching his friends play basketball, he was taunted by a gang member. His sister begged him to take no heed and go into the building, but he sent her inside.

> *By the time she climbed the six floors to her cousin's apartment, a single pistol shot had echoed from below. Twenty-four-year-old Willie Elliott had stepped from between two parked cars and aimed a pistol at Bird Leg…. The bullet, which had hit him at point blank range, entered his chest and spiraled through his body like an out-of-control drill, lacerating his heart, lungs, spleen, and stomach. Bird Leg, struggling to breathe, collapsed beneath an old cottonwood, where, cooled by its shade, he died. (Kotlowitz, 1991, 46)*

So common are deaths in Henry Horner that a protocol has already been established: "When someone at Henry Horner is killed, mimeographed sheets go up in the buildings' hallways, giving details of the funeral" (Kotlowitz, 1991, 47).

War in the Streets

Life for the two boys of Henry Horner and their friends is not unlike the lives of many other children in the United States today. The Children's Defense Fund (CDF) (2002) reports that each day nine children will be killed by gunfire. A total of 3,365 children and teens were killed by gunfire in 1999. In fact, homicide is the number-one cause of death among Hispanic and African American youths and the third leading killer of white young people. It is not only adults who are killing our children. The majority of those in court for these crimes have never committed them before. Yet, there has been a 75% increase in juvenile arrests for violent crimes over the last decade. The Department of Justice predicts that arrests of 10- to 17-year-olds for violent crimes will double by the year 2010 if the trend continues. In 1997, there were about two million arrests of juveniles, making up close to 20% of total arrests. About one-third of these were for serious crimes (Siegel and Senna, 2000, 41). Of these, the rate of murder was slightly higher for black youths, whereas white youths were more likely to commit burglary, larceny, and arson. The majority of crimes committed by youths involve weapons, most often guns. The problem is of enough concern that President Clinton, at the end of 1995, cited juvenile crime by minors as the most serious crime problem at that time.

It is not only crimes against others that are of concern. The accessibility to guns has produced an increase in the suicide rate as well. In 2001, 1,078 young people committed suicide with a firearm (CDF, 2002). Although most of those who commit suicide are white, there has been an increase in the incidence of deaths among minority children as well (Siegal and Senna, 2000).

Influences on Youth Violence. In what context does violence in the streets occur? Certainly, as we become a more violent society, our children are increasingly aware of it. There is not a single news broadcast aired on television or radio that does not have at least one account of violence perpetrated against an individual or group. Fiction mirrors reality as prime-time shows feature a myriad of crimes and acts of violence; even situation comedies depict people being victimized by others, as though there were humor in it. Some critics of modern TV and movie entertainment suggest that violence depicted in the media actually increases violence by desensitizing us to it (Siegel and Senna, 2000).

The concern over promoting violence through the media is not new. As early as 1954, congressionally authorized studies looked at the influence of TV violence on human behavior. In 1968, a group of mothers in the Boston area, concerned over their children viewing too much violence and being influenced by certain commercials, founded Action for Children's Television (ACT) to try to influence what their children watched. By 1982, the National Institute of Mental Health had concluded that "excessive levels of television violence lead to aggressive, even violent behavior in children" (Kinnear, 1995, 24). Today, the typical American child watches 28 hours of TV per week and by the age of 18 will have seen 16,000 simulated murders and 200,000 acts of violence (CDF, 2002).

Why does TV violence promote violence in society? The most obvious answer is that when children see violent acts committed by heroes and villains alike, they tend to want to emulate them for the risk and the thrill. But critics tell us that the effects go beyond this simple explanation. Constant exposure to violence not only desensitizes individuals to the commission of it but increases the indifference one feels as the acts take place. This, in turn, decreases the ability to feel empathy with the victims. Psychoanalyst Denise Shrine feels that there are three elements found in the makeup of juvenile violent offenders: lack of respect, inability to understand or empathize with another person, and impatience (Siegel and Senna, 2000; Hoffman, 1996; Kinnear, 1995).

In addition to television, some experts also blame today's sports for the increase in violence among young people. Although sports are usually thought to be played for enjoyment and relaxation, an intense emphasis on winning can elevate competition to violent behavior. How many children observe hockey players club each other with sticks, football players use more force than necessary, and baseball players spit in the faces of umpires? Although there has always been some degree of highly charged emotions in sports events, the price tag placed on winning now creates an intense and even violent atmosphere (Hoffman, 1996; Kinnear, 1995).

Gangs on the Streets.   Gangs have been the subject of sociological and psychological study for decades. The musical classic *West Side Story* romanticized the violence of gang warfare, but the reality is not as appealing. Today, gangs are responsible for a great deal of the violence perpetrated against other teens. They exist not only in urban areas, but in suburban and rural areas as well. The National Youth Violence Prevention Resource Center (2000) estimates that there were as many as 840,500 gang members in the United States in 1999.

What constitutes a *gang?* A youth gang is a group of teens who band together for a variety of reasons, usually including a sense of belonging and protection (McWhirter et al., 1998). Miller (1980) proposes the following definition of gangs:

> *A youth gang is a self-formed association of peers, bound together by mutual interests, with identifiable leadership, well-developed lines of authority, and other organizational features, who act in concert to achieve a specific purpose or purposes which generally include the conduct of illegal activities and control over a particular territory, facility, or type of enterprise. (121)*

Other experts (see Morales and Sheafor, 2001) disagree with Miller's generalizations and describe four types of youth gangs: criminal gangs, conflict gangs, retreatist gangs, and cult/occult gangs. *Criminal gangs* are dedicated primarily to such illegal activities as theft, fencing stolen articles, and drug trafficking. *Conflict gangs* defend their turf against rival gangs. Their organization is often based on racial lines (e.g., Latino gangs, Asian gangs), and they often inhabit specific neighborhoods that then become their *turf.* Invading another gang's turf can result in gang warfare. *Retreatist gang* members dedicate themselves to getting "high" on a variety of drugs. They tend not to be involved with the drugs for financial gain, as criminal gangs are, but they retreat to use the drugs. *Cult* or *occult gang* members join with each other in devil worship or belief in some cult dogma. The Charles Manson family is one well-known cult gang. These gangs may or may not be involved in criminal activity or use drugs (Zastrow, 2000). Other authors suggest that gangs cannot be as clearly defined as to purpose and that their reasons for existing often include a variety of activities (Huff, 1990; Siegel and Senna, 2000).

Gangs offer youths a great deal in a time of family breakdown and social anonymity. In addition to a sense of belonging, gangs can offer status and a feeling of importance. This is especially true for ethnic groups who band together to cope with the stigma and discrimination of being in the minority. Gangs offer social situations and opportunities to take risks in the company of others who are also taking these risks. With the element of combined power, gangs, more than individuals, can exercise more power and have access to more resources.

CASE EXAMPLE

The Diablos

The Diablos were a Hispanic youth gang in an old, predominantly Italian neighborhood. Individually, the Mexican boys involved in the gang were not accepted by the old-time residents, but collectively they had made their mark. When the gang entered the local grocery store, the owner knew that it was easier to ignore their shoplifting of candy bars and soda than to repair the damage done when the gang members chose to retaliate because their shoplifting was prohibited. The store owner figured into his budget the loss of his merchandise, and the arrangement persisted for a number of years.

There is some debate as to how much of an increase in violence among gangs there has been over the years. It does seem clear, however, that the character of the violence has intensified. As this society becomes increasingly violent, so do the acts committed by gangs become more brutal and less comprehensible. More guns are involved and the rate of homicides has skyrocketed (Siegel and Senna, 2000). Many communities not previously affected by gang activity are finding that the gangs from nearby cities have moved into their area. Gang migration explains why many areas not previously plagued by gang activity now feel its impact. Gangs migrate because the drug markets are better or more open in new cities or because individual gang members may relocate and form new gangs (Siegel and Senna, 2000). Hispanic, African American, and white gangs are joined by Asian gangs. Los Angeles, for example, has become increasingly concerned about its Vietnamese gangs, in which over 1,000 Vietnamese youths were involved by the early 1990s. (Vigil and Yun, 1990). Vigil and Yun (1990) suggest that gangs of minority groups are based on their frustration with their inability to readily integrate into the dominant culture. Not only is English a major stumbling block for newly immigrated youths, but they often do not understand the cultural mores.

Traditionally, in Asian cultures, problems are handled by the family. But as youths find themselves trying to fit into new world traditions, they become increasingly at odds with the traditions of the family. Hence they look for belonging elsewhere and often find it with their peers, who are experiencing similar conflicts. In addition to belonging, Asian youths find that gangs can bring in money. As they remember the poverty that many of them experienced in their families of origin and observe their parents' financial struggles, because they lack the skills recognized in this new culture, and get caught up in the U.S. emphasis on financial success, it is not surprising that easy money would have an appeal. Auto theft, drug selling, and armed robbery provide quicker returns than hard work. Even the risks involved have an allure for teens. War is not foreign to them and many spent their early years absorbing the skills necessary to survive in a war-torn environment. Gang wars and the risks inherent in crime feel old and familiar (Vigil and Yun, 1990; McWhirter et al., 1998).

The role of girls in gangs has also evolved over the years (Molidor, 1996). Campbell (1990) suggests that the image of the female delinquent "has been depicted as isolated and inept; a pitiful figure trying to assuage her loneliness through brief, promiscuous liaisons with boys" (163). Early accounts of female gang involvement were based on the girls' dependence on male gang members. They were largely portrayed as sexual objects who were cajoled, tricked, or forced into sexual relations for the enjoyment of male gang members. Her status within the group was largely dependent on the relationship that she had with specific male members, although her allegiances and partners may have changed from time to time. In additional to sexual objects, girls may also have been used as lookouts, drinking partners, and weapon carriers (Campbell, 1990).

Moore and Hagedorn (2001) suggest that early descriptions of female gang members trivialized their role. New research indicates that females may have strong identities independent of male peers. They join gangs for reasons similar to their male counterparts (dysfunctional homes, poor economic conditions, and the need for a sense of belonging) and they too may be involved in violent or illegal acts. Female gangs tend more often to be African American or Hispanic.

Contemporary female gang members appear to be organized in one of three ways: as units functioning independently from male gang members; as regular members of "coed" gangs; and as auxiliary members of male gang groups. Unlike the boys, the girls are usually not pressured into joining a gang but rather do so as a result of friendships or network connections. These girls are responsible for their own affairs. They are usually closely knit as a sisterhood and resent the efforts of male gang members to interfere. Girls exert peer influence over the sexual behaviors of their sisters. They are also as likely as male members to engage in fights, violence, and illegal acts. Deschenes and Esbensen (1999) found that 78% of female gang members said they were involved in gang fights, 65% reported that they carried a gun, and 39% had attacked someone with it.

Autonomous girl gangs appear to be gaining more prominence. Membership in their own female-run gangs provides an even closer sisterhood and saves them from the exploitation they often experienced at the hands of male gang members, although some engaged in prostitution for financial gains.

Violence in Relationships

The violence among teens in dating relationships has increased in the last decade (Zastrow, 2000; Gray and Foshee, 1997; Carlson, 1996). Although much of the research has been done among the college student population, there is evidence that violence in relationships happens at younger and younger ages. Date or acquaintance rape appears to be related to specific attitudes and accepted behaviors among adolescents. The first attitude, still present despite the influence of the women's movement, is that girls should be submissive. Romance novels and popular television shows perpetrate the image that females desire to be overpowered sexually. In addition, the popular assumption that males cannot control their sexual urges adds fuel to the fire. When a girl "leads a boy on" sexually, the myth is that he has the "right" to continue the sexual encounter (Zastrow, 2000; Miller and Dyk, 1993).

The use of substances, especially alcohol, also has an influence on aggression between adolescents. Not only does alcohol lower inhibition, which might otherwise prevent both sexual and aggressive behavior, but it can also be used as a rationalization for the occurrence of the aggression.

In addition to sexual violence, teens are now more likely to physically abuse each other by slapping, pushing, and grabbing in relationships. Contrary to popular opinion, studies have shown that females are more likely than men to aggress against their partners, but less apt to cause severe harm when they do (Riggs, 1993). Female aggression was viewed less negatively, however, than that of their male counterparts. Acting out aggressively was often based on jealousy or the inability to successfully negotiate disagreements.

Why is there more violence in peer relationships? Some feel that because dating is an opportunity to rehearse later marital roles, the increase in domestic violence has an impact on the current rate of dating violence (Gray and Foshee, 1997; Falchikov, 1996). In addition, the predisposition in this culture to use violence instead of negotiation is mirrored in intimate and peer relationships.

Peer mediation in schools is one technique that appears to be having some impact on the incidence of peer violence (Zastrow, 2000).

The School as a War Zone

On Thursday, March 26, 1998, two boys, Mitchell Johnson and Andrew Golden of Jonesboro, Arkansas,…dressed in camouflage garb, stole a van, filled it with a tent, a sleeping bag, tools, food, and enormous quantities of ammunition and stolen weapons. Thus equipped, they drove to nearby Westside Middle School, where they set off the fire alarm…waited for students and teachers to emerge, then unleashed a fusillade. Four little girls and a teacher were killed. Ten other children and a teacher were wounded…. One hundred thirty-four spent shells were found at the crime scene. (Kellerman, 1999, 1–2)

While the nation remained horrified at the reality of two young boys so brutally murdering and wounding teachers and schoolmates, an Oregon youth, two months later, sprayed a school cafeteria with bullets and killed 2 students and wounded 22 others. Experts searched for answers. Schools instituted more stringent security measures. Concerned parents wondered if it could happen again. And then on April 20, 1999, in the worst incident to date, Eric Harris and Dylan Klebold, calling themselves members of a group self-titled the "Trenchcoat Mafia," went on a shooting spree that was to kill at least 12 students and one teacher and wound 24 others at a Littleton, Colorado, high school. The boys would then commit suicide (Siegel and Senna, 2000).

What has been the cause of the violence perpetrated by these and other by teenagers between the ages of 12 and 18? Some blame the drug problem in the nation. Others point fingers at the lax discipline and lack of standards in schools today. And still other experts insist that the degree of violence within our schools is merely a reflection of the pathology present within the society as a whole.

What is to be done to protect our children? Across the country, administrators have instituted a variety of strategies. In addition to better security measures, many schools have developed programs to train students in self-protection and make them more able to spot classmates who may be crying for help. Teaching life skills training to enhance self-esteem has also been felt to have some success. Peer mediation efforts to teach students to settle their differences in nonviolent ways have also been developed through many schools (Siegel and Senna, 2000).

It is too early to determine if our efforts have worked in preventing another serious school tragedy. Can any effort really be successful when students see all around them violence and destruction?

The Home as a War Zone

Many of us think of home as a place of safety. However, for the 3.3 million children between the ages of 3 and 17 who witness domestic violence (CDF,

2002), the home is far from a safe place. In addition, these children are at significantly greater risk of being harmed themselves either as part of the abuser's wrath or accidentally.

Spouse abuse has been tolerated for many years. The implications of this type of violence for not only the spouse, but the children as well, was most dramatically exemplified in the case of Nicole Brown-Simpson and her well-known abusive husband and sports figure, O. J. Simpson. The 1994 trial of Simpson for the murder of his former wife brought to light the fact that battered wives often seek help on numerous occasions before the violence ceases or the wife is dead. Shelters for battered wives also report that women leave and return to their husbands numerous times before they are able to break the bond between them. Although men can also be battered, males as batterers tend to do more harm. Studies show that nearly 11% of males who batter their wives end up murdering them (Zastrow, 2000; Dutton, 1995).

Men batter their wives for a variety of reasons. Many share the stereotyped view of women as permissive individuals who should do their bidding. When the woman resists, the man cannot tolerate it. Most have poor self-images and having power over another enhances their own esteem. The cycle of violence is well known. When a spouse batters, he usually escalates from verbal assaults, such as finding fault and name-calling, to actual physical aggression. Following the beating episode, he is usually guilty and contrite, often apologizing and "trying to make it up" to the victim. It is this inconsistency that causes many women to assume things will be better and to remain in the relationship. In addition, battered women often come from backgrounds in which abuse was the norm. Violence in their marriages seems all too familiar to them. But, seemingly paradoxically, the familiar gives comfort. Women may also be financially dependent on their husbands. And, trained by society to be the peacemakers, women often strive for harmony rather than confront the impossibility of their situations (Zastrow, 2000; Dutton, 1995).

It is the effect, not only on the victim but also on her children, that concerns child welfare experts. From watching their mothers, battered children learn that this is an acceptable way to treat women (Cummings, 1998; Falchikov, 1996). Some children identify with the aggressor, a less threatening stance than becoming a victim themselves. This may put them at risk to abuse when they later become involved in intimate relationships. This may also cause them to criticize the victim or even abuse her when they become older and stronger. Other children identify with the victim, feeling fearful, withdrawn, and depressed. Children from families fraught with domestic violence grow up to exhibit low self-esteem, depression, developmental delays, acute anxiety, rage, conduct disorders, chronic fear and rage, self-blame, and heightened suicide risks, and are more prone to be violent toward others. These children learn poor boundaries and how to use deceptiveness, lying, and cheating as protection. These behaviors often spill over into their dealings with others, especially at school (Crosson-Tower, 2002; Cummings, 1998).

CASE EXAMPLE

The Cordovas

The Cordovas were typical of the family in which violence is the norm. Will Cordova, trained as a military police officer, expected that his family would respect him. With a history of violence in his own parents' home, Cordova had had no other model. Tess Cordova, his wife, had also grown up in an abusive household, but when Will showered her with attention between his bouts of anger and abuse, she came to believe that she had married a good man who, just occasionally, was "a bit demanding." The Cordova children, Matt, age 10, and Belle, age 7, cowered in the corner when their father began to shout and hit his wife. But soon Belle, always her father's pet, saw that siding with her father against her mother met with more approval from her powerful parent and earned her special attention. When Will was out of the house, Belle began to criticize Tess and eventually began to hit her as well. Matt, on the other hand, felt protective of his mother, but was too fearful to oppose his father. It was not until he was age 15 that Matt found the gun with which his father had threatened his mother and shot his father. Although Will was not seriously injured, the incident served to cause the family finally to seek help.

For a discussion of the *abuse of children,* see Chapter 7. Although obvious aggression toward children is easily labeled as child abuse, Graziano (1994) suggests that there is a phenomenon he calls "subabuse," which cannot be as readily characterized as abusive, but is nonetheless harmful. *Subabuse* includes acts of violence that do not reach the proportions of being categorized as abuse. These include various forms of corporeal punishment such as spanking, whipping, and hitting. He suggests that these seemingly acceptable forms of child rearing may also convey to children that violence is condoned and cause them to replicate this behavior with their own children. Graziano urges researchers to continue to study the effects of subabusive behavior on children.

Parent abuse is also exemplified in the Cordova scenario. When children observe a parent being abused by another, they will often identify with the aggressor and adopt the battering behavior themselves. *Elder abuse* occurs when an adult child batters his or her elderly parent, grandparent, aunt, or other elder. For children, this can also have an impact. When the child sees a weaker person being subjected to abuse, that child may either identify and feel threatened or take on the aggressive behavior as well. Even if a child adopts neither of these stances, witnessing the abuse of an elder can have a significant effect on the child's relations with the family or view of interpersonal relationships.

The home should be the child's haven of safety. When violence permeates the home environment, the effects on children cannot help but be significant.

Children and Substance Abuse

Interwoven in the mosaic of violence are the statistics about the increase of substance use and abuse among not only adults but children and adolescents as well. The dimension of substance use and abuse as it affects children can be seen on two levels: the effects of addicted parents and addicted children.

Addicted Parents

In the United States today, substance abuse has become an alarming reality. When parents abuse drugs or alcohol the impact on their children is profound. Over 13 million children live with a parent who has used illicit and addictive drugs in the last year (CWLA, 2002). The use of drugs and alcohol can greatly diminish one's parenting ability. Substance-abusing parents can neglect, emotionally and physically abuse, sexually abuse, and even abandon their children, not to mention present a model of individuals who cannot control their own lives. The correlation between substance abuse and family violence is significant (Kelly, 1998; CWLA, 2002). In addition, research on the children of alcoholics indicates that there is a biological risk for alcoholism passed from parents to children (Robinson and Rhoden, 1998). Also, mothers addicted to both drugs and/or alcohol may well pass the effects on to their newborns.

Addicted parents come from all socioeconomic levels, but it is often the additional factor of poverty that brings them to the attention of child welfare agencies. Parents at higher income levels are often able to pay for outside child care when their addiction prohibits them from parenting adequately. How many prominent community figures have been stopped for driving under the influence but have not been referred to children's services for neglecting or endangering their children?

Fetal Alcohol Syndrome.   Studies done on infants born to alcoholic mothers point to the possibility that alcohol abuse during pregnancy can leave the child with fetal alcohol syndrome (FAS) or fetal alcohol effects (FAE). *Fetal alcohol syndrome* involves a variety of physical and psychological defects in children, including low intelligence or mental retardation, physical abnormalities (including characteristic facial features), hyperactivity, impaired development, and failure to accurately distinguish cause and effect (Zastrow, 2000; Baer et al., 1993). These symptoms result from the fact that when a pregnant woman drinks, the alcohol crosses the placenta, creating in the fetus the blood alcohol levels present in the mother. Such babies are also more likely to be born prematurely, have low birth weight and neurological defects, and become extremely irritable. The greater the amount of alcohol the pregnant woman drinks, the greater her chance of producing a baby with FAS. Studies indicate that five drinks or more at a given time produce a 10% chance that the baby will have FAS. Even an ounce a day can result in a 10% chance, whereas two ounces results in a 20% possibility, and so on (Zastrow, 2000). The difficulty is not only in the effects on the infant, but drinking alcohol may also affect the mother's ability to deal with her child.

CASE EXAMPLE

Ellen

Ellen drank heavily during her pregnancy. She and her live-in boyfriend, Greg, had been drinking partners before her pregnancy and her fear was that she would lose him if she did not go out drinking with him. Their relationship had been a fairly satisfying one until she became pregnant, but now Greg's annoyance about her getting pregnant was putting pressure on their interactions. Barbie was born prematurely and weighed only four pounds. She had "a funny little face" with her eyes far apart. Her first few weeks were spent in the neonatal intensive care unit with her anxious parents looking on. When they were not with her, however, they would drink to drown their fears and upset. Ellen had heard that she should not drink during pregnancy and she blamed Barbie's sickly first weeks on herself. When the infant finally did come home she was fussy and ate often. Ellen was exhausted and Greg soon grew tired of the routine. Barbie's poor muscle tone and constant crying sent Ellen to the clinic in tears. When the clinic diagnosed a heart defect, Ellen could not be consoled. She cried constantly and drank continuously. Greg left them, and a neighbor, hearing the baby's cries and finding Ellen drunk and asleep as she had many times before, called the protective services agency.

For Ellen, the reality of her drinking manifested in Barbie's fetal alcohol syndrome greatly affected her ability to parent and made her want to drink more to escape her problems.

Fetal alcohol effects (FAE) are less dramatic symptoms and may indicate that the mother ingested less alcohol or that, for some reason, the child escaped the full effects of the alcohol (Baer et al., 1993).

Due to the high incidence of FAS and FAE, a federal law was passed in 1989 that mandated manufacturers to put warnings on the labels of alcohol products that they can adversely affect fetuses. Yet, the responsibility still remains in the hands of the mother to protect her unborn infant. This may change in the future, as some child welfare advocates, as well as lawmakers, feel that abusing substances—drugs as well as alcohol—during pregnancy should be considered a form of child abuse.

Effects of Parental Drug/Alcohol Addiction on Newborns and Infants. Statistics tell us that the number of babies exposed to crack or cocaine ranges from 30,000 to 158,000 each year. The number of marijuana-exposed infants is estimated to be more than 611,000. Over 43,500 newborns' mothers have used hallucinogens, 92,400 have used stimulants, and 38,300 have used sedatives. An estimated 2.6 million infants have been exposed to their mothers' use of alcohol (Schmittroth, 1994). Although not all of the mothers using alcohol abused the substance, the effects of alcohol on the development of the human brain have been documented (Rivinus, 1991).

Drugs and alcohol not only affect children in utero but they can have a significant effect on the newborn infant. Nurses in neonatal facilities can describe the heart-wrenching experience of watching newborns go through withdrawal symptoms from the drugs or alcohol that were present in their first environment—the mother's body. The effects of such withdrawal are still being researched. There is evidence that some types of drugs leave long-term effects, whereas others exit the system within hours or days (Rivinus, 1991; Zastrow, 2000). For example, babies born to mothers who are addicted to crack cocaine experience significant effects at birth.

> *Cocaine causes the blood vessels in a pregnant woman to constrict, thus reducing the vital flow of oxygen and other nutrients to the fetus. Because fetal cells multiply swiftly in the first months, an embryo deprived of proper blood supply by the mother's early and continuous use of cocaine is likely to suffer an adverse cognitive impact. At birth such babies may look quite normal, but they are likely to be undersized, and the circumference of their heads tends to be unusually small—a trait associated with lower IQ scores. Only the most intensive care after birth will give these babies a fighting chance to have a "normal" life. (Zastrow, 2000, 247)*

So-called "crack babies" can have a myriad of deformities from which they will never recover, and they require extensive treatment and a variety of services to survive.

Children whose parents are addicted to other narcotics may go through withdrawal soon after birth. Withdrawal symptoms often include chills, severe cramping, sweating, nervousness, vomiting, dilated pupils, respiratory problems, and muscle aches. Hallucinogens can cause genetic damage in children that, in the case of the female whose eggs for a lifetime are present at birth, may cause abnormalities for the next generation (Zastrow, 2000).

In addition to the chemical aspects of parental substance abuse, parents who abuse drugs or alcohol are less able to care for their infants. Children whose parents are chemically addicted may have difficulty bonding, as the care they receive may be inconsistent. Their basic needs may not be met in infancy while their parents pursue their habit. As they grow older, they may become the caregivers for younger siblings and take on the role of *parentified child* (the child who meets adults' needs) (Rivinus, 1991).

CASE EXAMPLE

Marcy

At 7 years old, Marcy became her mother's caregiver. Early in the morning, she would awaken to find that her mother had already given herself a shot of heroin and was drifting in her own world of fantasy. Marcy would bathe her, try to get her to eat, and prepare for her own day. She got herself off to school and got herself dinner in the evening with food that a neighbor brought in. Only rarely was her mother not "strung out." If she tried to "kick the habit," she would become very sick and Marcy would take care of her. It was the only life Marcy knew.

Marcy is not unlike many children of addicted parents. When Marcy's mother began to prostitute to support her habit, the child was exposed to a variety of men and sexual acts. It was not surprising that, at age 9, she was sexually abused by one of her mother's johns.

Frustrations inherent in caring for babies can lead to further substance abuse, feeling overwhelmed, resenting the baby, abusing or neglecting the child, or withdrawing from the parenting experience altogether (Levoy et al., 1991). Many young women are totally unprepared for motherhood. Especially if she comes from a substance-abusing family, the mother may have no healthy models of parenting to follow. Her hormone imbalance after childbirth may make her emotions volatile, and the chemical effects of her abuse during pregnancy may create a fussy baby who further challenges her.

Addicted Parents and Preschool Children. Toddlers need to explore their world but have a safe place to which to return. Substance-abusing parents may not be able to provide the consistency and nurturance that translates into a "safe harbor" for their toddlers. The child who is just about to enter school has already begun to engage in internal dialogues about his or her view of the environment and the ability to cope with it. Inconsistency and a parent who is out of control or constantly criticized by the other parent for addicted behavior does not provide the safety or the modeling to help the young child develop the internal controls to cope with the environment. The child who has two drug/alcohol-addicted parents has even fewer resources with which to work. This ability to put his or her experiences into perspective becomes affected and his or her reality testing is impaired (Krestan and Bepko, 1993; Levoy et al., 1991).

Addicted Parents and Older Children and Adolescents. A child whose reality testing is impaired will have difficulty accepting and abiding by rules, and will not have the skills necessary for learning. His or her peer relations may also be impaired. Being a parentified child is not uncommon, and it is likely that he or she will be diagnosed in school as learning disabled, hyperactive, acting out, or even having a borderline personality. Because domestic violence and child abuse and neglect are strongly correlated with substance abuse, the child may also carry the scars of these problems as well (see Chapter 7). Sleepiness in class may belie the fact that the child has had little sleep as he or she hears drunken parents fight or cringes in bed wondering when she or he will next be physically or sexually abused (Crosson-Tower, 2002; Levoy et al., 1991).

For adolescence, a major developmental task is the consolidation of identity, which involves planning for the future and separating from the family of origin. It is difficult to complete these tasks effectively when besieged by the family problems brought on by substance abuse. The adolescent may also have developed survival skills that are not necessarily functional in other parts of his or her life (Winfree and Bernat, 1998; Levoy et al., 1991).

CASE EXAMPLE

Callie

Callie was the eternal caregiver. She had learned early in the home of two drug-addicted parents that to stay out of the way, unless one or the other parent needed something, was the best course of action. As her parents began to deteriorate, she took on more and more responsibility. It was actually due to her ability to cover up their addiction that the school and the protective agency did not recognize the full extent of the problem. In school, she was described as "bossy." "Callie is a real manipulator," said one teacher, "and she often antagonizes others by her need to be in control all the time. In addition, when the other children do something they should not, she is always there to 'clean up' after them. We used to think she just wanted so much to be helpful and liked but it seems like more than that. She really doesn't seem to care if she's liked. It just seems like a compulsion to do 'everything for everybody.'"

Practicing Alcoholic/Addicted Parent (PAAP) Syndrome. The children of addicted parents are seen in many social agencies for a variety of reasons. The alcoholism/addiction of their parents creates in them a wide number of symptoms, some physiological, some emotional, and some perceptual. Jesse (1989) summarizes these problems as (1) perceptual (e.g., "tunes out" or doesn't hear information properly); (2) cognitive (e.g., gets distracted or doesn't remember well); (3) affective (e.g., flat affect or, conversely, overreaction); (4) motor (e.g., hyperactivity or coordination problems); (5) social (e.g., poor peer or sibling relationships); (6) motivational (e.g., apathetic or, conversely, driven or compulsive); (7) self-development/regulation (e.g., gets fragmented under stress, poor self-esteem, poor ability to care for self); and

(8) stress barrier (e.g., somatic complaints, sleep problems, tension, easily distracted, enuresis/encopresis) (150).

Children of Addicted Parents and the AIDS Epidemic.   In the year 1998, 8,461
children under the age of 13 became victims of AIDS (acquired immune deficiency syndrome) and 1,875 tested positive for HIV (human immunodefi-
ciency virus). Of these, 91% were exposed by their mothers. Of the 10,998
women infected with AIDS in 1998, 62% were African American, 19% were
Hispanic, and 18% were white (CDC, 1999).

There are two ways in which children of chemically dependent parents are
affected by the HIV/AIDS epidemic: as bystanders watching their parents who
are victims of the disease and through contracting the disease either at birth or
from an infected parent. Parents may have contracted the disease themselves
either through intravenous drug use (from the small amount of blood left in
shared needles) or sexual contact with someone who was infected. There are
also a small group of people who developed the disease as a result of a transfu-
sion in the early years when the testing of blood was not as yet perfected.

The virus known as AIDS was first brought to light in the early 1980s when
it appeared to be affecting primarily homosexual men and intravenous drug users. Now the virus has become a household word and has affected millions of
people. The epidemic appears to be increasing among ethnic minorities and
women. Today, AIDS is the leading cause of death among Hispanic and African
American children (Forsyth, 1995). The disease is spread through the sharing of
blood from one person to another as well as through sexual contact. Although
most parents do not have sexual contact with their children (except in the case
of sexual abuse), they may come in contact with their children's blood and vice
versa. Breast milk is also thought to transmit the virus. HIV-positive mothers
face not only living with their infection but the guilt of what they have inflicted
on their children (Marcenko and Samost, 1999). Unlike adults, for whom the
onset of AIDS can take time, children tend to develop symptoms very quickly.
Of children exposed at birth, 70% will develop symptoms by about one year and
17% of those will die within the first year (Forsyth, 1995, 26).

Contracting the AIDS virus in utero means that the infection in the mother's
system has crossed the placenta. The virus attacks the white blood cells in the
baby's system and impedes the development of the baby's immune system.
The immune system is activated by what are called T cells or sometimes
"helper cells." These vital cells impede the reproduction of unhealthy cells
that might harm the body. The AIDS virus attacks the T cells to give itself an
opportunity to reproduce. Once weakened, the T cells are incapable of doing
their work and the AIDS cells become stronger. When babies are born, they
first have B cells, small cells that are present for only the first few days of birth.
When the AIDS virus attacks the B cells, the immune system is weakened.
When, several days after birth, the T cells begin to develop, they may already
be impeded in their strength and growth. The baby may then be said to be HIV
positive when tests for AIDS come up positive. It is possible for some babies'

immune systems to recover, however, and the baby who is diagnosed positive at birth, later has shaken off the virus. For other babies, the damage has been done, and they often die within the first year. Death is not actually from AIDS, but rather from other infections that take hold as a result of an inefficient or inactive immune system. For example, PCP (pneumocystis carinii pneumonia) is a frequent killer of individuals with AIDS (McCarroll, 1988).

Contracting AIDS in childhood is less likely but certainly possible. There are an increasing number of children who contract the virus because they were sexually abused by someone with AIDS.

Effects in Later Life of Having a Substance-Abusing Parent. Some children of addicted parents are not strangers to sexual and physical abuse, violence, and being used to carry or buy drugs or alcohol. Many of these develop a variety of survival strategies that protect them against a world that has not treated them kindly. They may hoard, lie, steal, and physically assault others as they imitate what they have seen. Seeing their parents' addicted behavior, they may decide to try drugs or alcohol for themselves. Others react in the opposite way and become almost phobic about not using substances. Many carry the scars of their parents' addictions into later life.

Seixas and Youcha (1985) talk about the "hangovers from childhood" and identify them as the need to control, denial of feelings, the lack of trust, guilt, fears or difficulty with intimacy, depression or sadness, "black and white" thinking, an excessive need to please, and an exaggerated sense of responsibility (47ff). These traits may cause the adult children of substance-abusing parents (ACOSAP) to have problems in their intimate relationships, difficulty finding, keeping, or enjoying a job, and regulating their lives in general. It is not uncommon for ACOSAPs to turn to chemical dependency as a way of escaping or coping with their feelings of inadequacy or lack of control. In addition, there is much research to suggest that the chemical predisposition adds to the emotional need to become drug dependent (Zastrow, 2000; Baer et al., 1993; Levoy et al., 1991; Rivinus, 1991; Seixas and Youcha, 1985).

Addicted Children and Adolescents

According to the Substance Abuse and Mental Health Services Administration (2002), 9.7 million adolescents (ages 12 to 20), drink alcohol on a regular basis. Of these, 6.6 million are binge drinkers and 2.1 million are heavy drinkers. Males (21.3% of the age group) were slightly more likely to binge drink than their female counterparts (15.9%). White youths (21.4%) led the number of binge drinkers, followed by Native Americans (20.3%). Although adolescents are seen as the primary users of all types of substances, the fact is that children are using all types of drugs at younger and younger ages. The drugs of choice tend to be marijuana and inhalants. A smaller number of youths also use cocaine, hallucinogens, sedatives, and stimulants. Some drugs are of more concern than

others. For example, although the drug Ecstasy has concerned the public because of the frequency of overdoses (1,742 reported emergency room visits in
2000), a relatively newer drug, GHB (gamma hydroxybutyrate), now plagues the
Drug Enforcement Administration and was responsible for 2,482 known overdoses (reported to emergency rooms) in 2000 (Leinwand, 2002).

Siegel and Senna (2000) suggest an upsurge in drug use since 1997 after a
brief period of stabilization between 1996 and 1997. The most recent studies
now report that we may be coming into another period of stabilization (404).
Although these statistics apply to adolescents, the rates of drug and alcohol
use among younger children has been only anecdotal. Yet teens or adults who
drink or use drugs often report beginning at a very early age, and more recent
studies disclose that children in eighth grade may still have illicit drug involvement (Siegel and Senna, 2000; Winfree and Bernat, 1998).

CASE EXAMPLE

Dominic

Dominic began drinking alcohol when he was 8 years old. "My friend's
old man used to buy us six packs," he reports. "He thought it was a riot
to see us get wasted [drunk]. We used to try and hold our liquor just to
get at him. Then over the years we could drink a lot more." His drug habit
began soon after. A neighbor offered him a bag of marijuana and later got
him hooked on cocaine so he could "study better." By age 15, Dominic
had a serious drug and alcohol problem.

Although some children become addicted to drugs at birth as a result of
their mothers' addiction, many become addicted later as children. Johnson
(1992) found that 12.3% of children began their alcohol use as early as the
fourth grade, 8.95% in the fifth, 15.5% in the sixth, 20.2% in the seventh, and
12.4% in the eighth grade. The seventh grade saw a higher incidence in the
beginning of marijuana, cocaine, and hallucinogen use than any other grade
(134). It is also clear from studies that many children do not perceive that the
use of drugs or alcohol will be addictive or harmful to them. For example, only
58% of Johnson's sample felt that having two to five drinks per weekend
would put them at risk for becoming alcohol-dependent (176).

What causes children and adolescents to become chemically dependent?
Rhodes and Jason (1988), in speaking of young children, cite social isolation
as a factor that can predispose them to addiction to substances. These authors
also suggest that poor self-concept may lead both young and older children to
find compensation through drugs. Certainly, these factors also play a role in
the substance abuse of adolescents, but there are other important factors as
well (see Siegel and Senna, 2000).

For adolescents, a number of developmental tasks as well as societal influences affect their likelihood of becoming dependent on drugs or alcohol. Developmentally, teens are going through a great many changes. The peer group becomes increasingly important as adolescents strive for autonomy from authority figures. Thus *they rebel against the attitudes of their elders,* paradoxically mirroring the behavior they may have observed.

CASE EXAMPLE

Jan

Jan's parents were both alcoholics during her younger years. When she was 6 years old, her father was laid off and forced to attend an alcohol rehabilitation program before he could be reinstated. He began to attend AA and put pressure on his wife to become sober. Finally, when Jan was age 9, her mother too started her recovery. During the early part of her teens, Jan watched both her parents conscientiously attend AA meetings and work hard at their sobriety. This effort was combined with their lectures to their daughter about the evils of alcohol and how she should never drink lest she become addicted. Jan promised that she would not drink, but was constantly frustrated by the taunts of her peers. She convinced herself that a few smokes of pot would feel good and would not betray her promise to her parents. But the more they nagged against drinking, the more involved she became in drugs, first pot and later cocaine. By age 17, Jan was as addicted to drugs as her mother had been alcohol-dependent at that age.

Even teens whose parents do not themselves have a substance abuse problem may find themselves becoming involved with substances as a way of asserting their independence.

One thing that adds to teens' perceptions that using substances makes them more important is *the influence of the media.* The prominent message on television and in the movies is that substances are fun and give one a macho or powerful appearance. Even the efforts made by drug prevention programs do not serve to obliterate these strong subliminal messages (Siegel and Senna, 2000; Gullotta et al., 1994; Rhodes and Jason, 1988; Towers, 1987).

Adolescents are also *influenced by their peers,* many of whom use substances. Some studies conclude that teens actually select their peers depending on the amount of drug use they find comfortable (Muisener, 1994; Rhodes and Jason, 1988). Preoccupation with acceptance by others is paramount in the teen years and if one's peers choose to do drugs, the other teens feel compelled to go along (Botvin et al., 1995; Towers, 1987). For some, their peer group is the gang and the gang may be involved in taking or selling drugs (Siegel and Senna, 2000; Botvin et al., 1995; Glick and Moore, 1990).

Drugs and alcohol also become *antidotes for the pain and stress of growing up.* Minority children who face discrimination on a daily basis, the children of the poor, and children from dysfunctional homes soon learn that a "high" is more pleasurable than dealing with the realities of their lives. Besides major life crises, all manner of issues can be stressful for the vulnerable adolescent, from failing a test in school, being shunned by a member of the opposite sex, moving to a new town or school, to having one's parents go back to work (Towers, 1987).

And finally, many adolescents are *attracted to the thrill and risk* of taking drugs. For those under the legal drinking age, alcohol is illegal. And illegal drugs, especially marijuana, cocaine, crack, and hallucinogens, are the substances most likely used by youths. With all these chemicals, there is a risk to getting them, possessing them, and sharing them. There may also be a profit motive if the teen sells them to others.

CASE EXAMPLE

Sean

At age 9, Sean started taking one beer at a time out of his father's supply and selling it to a teen down the street. He next experimented with taking two and drinking one himself. When a friend asked to share with him, Sean suggested that he would sell half the can for 25 cents. As he grew older, his friends were able to get alcohol themselves and his trade lost its appeal. When a local drug dealer suggested to 13-year-old Sean that he sell bags of drugs, the boy agreed. By this time, it felt good to have his own money. He reasoned that the market for his product had dried up, so he needed another one.

Society's emphasis on chemicals is obvious: There are television ads for every type of substance to heal or alleviate every type of condition. From this, teens learn that substances can have a miraculous effect. This, combined with the culture's need for the "quick fix" and the emphasis on power and control, conveys the message that if substances help in these areas, they are well worth the risks (Resnik, 1990).

Effects and Treatment of Adolescent Drug Abuse

Adolescents who are chemically dependent are usually experiencing problems in many aspects of their lives. Research indicates that these problems occur in the following areas: attendance and discipline difficulties in school; withdrawal and conflict from the family; fights or withdrawal from the peer group; stealing; absenteeism; decreased participation in school- or work-related activities; and anxiety, injury, accidents, or suicidal ideation that affect their health. As an adolescent's addiction progresses, a variety of factors influence the addiction pattern and therefore the type of treatment that will be most effective. Influencing factors are such environmental variables as drug availability, drug cost, and the models (other teens or adults) who also use drugs/alcohol. In addition, the teen's own personality characteristics, such as family history, and the youth's personal traits and developmental issues will also be important (McWhirter et al., 1998; Brown, 1993).

Less attention has been paid to the definition of types of treatment needed for adolescents than has been given to assessing and documenting the problem of adolescent substance abuse. Part of this problem is related to the fact that there has been little differentiation between the treatment needs of adolescents versus adults when adolescents are at a significantly different developmental level or levels (Rickel and Becker-Lausen, 1994). Treating adolescent abuse also involves telling parents that their son or daughter has a problem—a fact that many parents prefer not to face.

Towers (1987) cites three types of treatments used with adolescents: (1) drug-free, (2) detoxification, and (3) maintenance. *Drug-free treatment* refers to counseling the teen, without the use of medications. This is often used when the addiction is not so far advanced that the individual is unable to abstain himself or herself. When the dependence has reached the point of chemical addiction, *detoxification* may be necessary. Detoxification is often undertaken in the same units that house adults. Increasingly, however, there is a recognition of the need for specialized services due to the inexperience of teen substance abusers. *Maintenance* refers to the use of some type of medication, such as methadone, and is usually employed only with long-term addicts.

Due to the recognition of the increased problem with adolescent substance addiction, treatment programs designed specifically for this population have increased in the last few years. Some are conducted on an outpatient basis and others require a stay in an inpatient type of setting. Self-help groups such as Alcoholics Anonymous are expanding their programs to adolescent services. Siegel and Senna (2000) stress the importance of "multi-systematic treatment," which looks at the family and seeks to make changes there.

Because of concern with the magnitude of the problem of substance abuse among young people, programs have been developed across the country that seek to provide primary prevention. For example, the DARE program has instituted a new component known as "DARE to Be You" (DTBY), which targets 2- to 5-year-olds in high-risk families. The program strives to enhance parent/child interaction and in this manner contribute to later youth resiliency that will hopefully allow these children to resist the temptation of drugs (Miller-Heyl et al., 1998). Another prevention project, called the "Nee-Kon Project," is designed to provide early intervention services for the Native American children of one Head Start center in Oklahoma. By helping these young children to bond with the school and the adults in their lives, it is felt that their adjustment to their world will be more effective, their self-esteem better, and their need to turn to drugs later reduced (Laquer, 1998). Schools, too, recognize the need for early intervention if the substance abuse problem among youth is to be addressed.

Whether the substance abuse problem is with the parent or with the child or adolescent himself or herself, the issues are significant. Much additional research and attention will be needed in the years to come to combat the problems in this area.

Homeless Families

It is not surprising that the issue of homelessness would be housed in a chapter dealing with violence and substance abuse. Both affect homelessness just as homelessness influences the use of substances and violence. Although in 1980 the number of children who were homeless was relatively small, the fastest growing population of the homeless today is women and children.

What constitutes homelessness? According to the National Coalition for the Homeless (1999), individuals are considered to be *homeless* when they lack a fixed, regular and adequate place to spend the nights. Although the common myth is that the homeless live "on the streets," this is not the case for the majority of homeless individuals and families. Homeless families, children, and youths may be sharing housing with others (called the *marginally homeless*) due to loss of housing or economic hardship or are living in trailers, cars, campgrounds, or hotels/motels. Homelessness also includes children and youths who live, either alone or with families, in parks or other public places not designed to be a residence. Some families may also live in shelters designed to temporarily house those who have no permanent residence.

It is difficult to count the homeless due to the transience of their lives, but the National Coalition for the Homeless (1999) suggests that 40% of those who are considered to be homeless are families with children. These proportions might actually be larger in rural areas. Surveying 30 U.S. cities, the U.S. Conference of Mayors (1998) found that homelessness among this population increased by 15% between 1997 and 1998. Unfortunately, 32% of the requests for shelter for these families had to be denied. Most of the cities surveyed also predicted an increase in the number over the next few years.

Causes of Homelessness

Much speculation has focused on why the homeless problem is worse now than in years past. One possible explanation has to do with the complexity of life today. Families are faced with greater risk of poverty as well as such issues as limited housing and unemployment. There are several causal factors for homelessness among families. First, the current economy places numerous families below the poverty level and constantly at risk for becoming homeless. Even receiving both TANF and food stamps puts families well below the poverty level. In fact, the mean income of families who become homeless is 46% of the poverty line (National Coalition for the Homeless, 1999). In addition, housing has become a significant problem. Gentrification and condominium conversion mean that there is less low to moderate income housing. Between 1997 and 1999 there was a net loss of more than 300,000 housing units that might have been occupied by families (National Coalition for the Homeless, 1999). And the economic constraints on families mean that many families would be unable to pay for housing if they could find it. A recent study of 564 homeless families in New York City found that homelessness was resolved by the provision of subsidized housing (Shin, 1997).

Some families become homeless due to the substance abuse or mental illness of parental figures. When a parent is supporting a significant drug habit, there is often little money available for rent. And for some, homelessness has been passed down from a previous generation that never found roots.

Homeless Families and Children

According to the National Coalition for the Homeless (1999), 2% of American children will experience homelessness in the course of a year, and 40% of these will be under 5 years of age. Of these, 35% are residing in shelters, and the remainder stay temporarily with others or in cars, campgrounds, and motels. Although the requests for emergency stays in family shelters have increased every year since 1985, 52% of these requests cannot be met.

It is not unusual for homeless families to spend their time moving from place to place—first perhaps the home of one relative or friend and then on to the home of another. If one interviewed a family spending the night in a shelter, one might well find that they had already exhausted the hospitality of friends and relatives. "We lived with my sister for a couple of months," one shelter dweller explained, "but she didn't like having her husband come in later and find me on the couch. And then their landlord found out my kids and me were living there and he hit the roof. He told my sister that he'd kick them out unless we left. So..." she shrugged in apparent resignation to her plight.

Homeless families can be divided into several categories: (1) those who are victims of economic hardship (2) mothers leaving abusive relationships, (3) substance-abusing parents, and (4) long-term homeless. Those who are *victims of economic hardship* may be mothers receiving TANF, but can still not qualify for housing. These women usually have less than a high school education, have few if any job skills, and depend on welfare as a way of life. Some move from crisis to crisis and have never learned the tasks of independence, like paying rent regularly. When they are no longer able to receive assistance under the new welfare reform provisions, they may fall into homelessness.

It is not just individual mothers who suffer from economic hardship. Some couples find that neither can make a sufficient income to keep the family housed. Some become unemployed and have few resources.

CASE EXAMPLE

The Winstons

The Winstons were both 30 years old and had four children. Bob Winston had been employed by a large factory that had "downsized," laying off over 50% of its employees, including Bob. Gloria had not been employed since the children were born and had always expected that Bob would support her. She had never finished high school and was severely dyslexic, making it difficult for her to read or write. When Bob lost his job, the couple quickly found that they were unable to keep their apartment. Although Gloria tried to work as a waitress, her poor reading and writing skills made it difficult for her to decipher menus and take orders; after two days, she was fired. This so damaged her already poor self-concept that she adamantly refused to try to get another job. Bob, too, had difficulties. He was a recovering alcoholic who had managed to stay sober for 10 years. Now his lack of a high school education gave him few opportunities to find work and he began to drink once more. Thus, Gloria found herself sometimes with Bob and sometimes without (when he was on a binge), moving from one shelter to another. For a time, they stayed in a welfare hotel. Because they had no permanent address, they could not apply for welfare even if Bob, always a proud man, had agreed to it. They also stayed with Bob's brother and his family with six children. But the tensions of two families and 10 children caused the brother's wife to terminate this arrangement.

It is not uncommon for parents in this group to have little education and inadequate job skills. When they lose their employment, they find that they have few options.

Mothers leaving relationships may or may not have been married to their partners. Some leave because they are battered; others leave because the relationship has broken down. Most of these women have depended on their male partners to support them and now they, with their children, find themselves without support or a place to stay. These mothers usually worked prior to the birth of their first children but became full-time parents after that.

CASE EXAMPLE

Frankie and George

Frankie had lived with George for six years, during which time they had had two children together, Yari, age 6, and Freda, age 4. From the time that the couple moved in together, George had begun to beat Frankie. At first, the beatings occurred only every six months or so. After such violence, George was very contrite and assured Frankie that he would never do it again. But over the years the beatings increased in both frequency and severity. Frankie left George to stay with friends but always returned when he found her and apologized. But when Yari accidentally stepped in front of a blow meant for her, Frankie took her children and vowed that she had left for good. Having exhausted the goodwill of friends and having no idea where else to go, Frankie and the children went from shelter to shelter.

The *long-term homeless* are often mothers who were homeless as adolescents and know little of life that does not include homelessness. They are usually from severely abusive backgrounds and may have lived on the street for a period as youths. Some had tried to subsist through prostitution. Now, as parents, they find that there is more involved than just looking out for themselves.

CASE EXAMPLE

Kay

Kay was a victim of severe physical and sexual abuse while she was growing up. Her father beat her, then raped her, and then beat her again. Her mother, also a victim of similar abuse, left her father on numerous occasions. When she did, she and the children moved from shelter to shelter until they once more returned to him. At age 15, Kay ran away and lived with several other teens on the streets for several months. When one of the girls started earning money prostituting herself, Kay saw this as a way of eating regularly without stealing and approached the pimp for whom her friend worked. The pimp readily took in the attractive girl and, for several more months, she worked for him. But when he began to beat her, Kay decided she had had enough. She took the money from her last john and hopped a bus to a distant city. There she once again lived on the streets until she met a man who took her in. She thought she had found someone who cared for her and when, three days after her seventeenth birthday, she realized that she was pregnant, Kay enthusiastically told him. His response was to hit her hard in the stomach; the blow sent her to a local hospital. She did not lose the baby as he had intended, but was placed in a home for unwed and parenting teens. Kay remained here until her baby was 9 months old. Then she ran away and spent the next months going from shelter to shelter.

Poverty is shared by all types of homeless families. This has often led to homelessness, the duration of which depended on variables such as age, job skills, number of children, and personal resourcefulness. Bassuk (1992) adds that the families of origin of homeless families were characterized by disruption and dysfunction. In 12% of the cases of Bassuk's sample there was mental illness in the family of origin, death of a parent in 20% of the situations, and divorce in 49%, and over 33% reported being physically abused (259). Seltser and Miller (1993) chronicle many stories that exemplify these statistics in their discussion of the homeless families of Los Angeles.

What enables families to escape from homelessness? Although Shin (1997) believes that homelessness could be alleviated by more subsidized housing, in interviews, 89 homeless shelter providers in North Carolina and Georgia reported that it was the mother's attitudes and motivation that enabled the family to secure housing. It was the lack of social supports and the difficulties that families had with relationships that were most likely to lengthen their time at being homeless (Lindsey, 1998).

Effect of Homelessness on Children

What are the implications for children who are part of a homeless family? Several studies suggest that the children of the homeless *feel hopeless and out of control of their lives.* They may become *preoccupied with worry,* often to the point of *developing physical symptoms* (Tower & White, 1989; Hart-Shegos, 1999).

CASE EXAMPLE

Timothy

Timothy was an extremely nervous child, reported the staff of the shelter. Each time his family returned to the facility, he looked more tired but was more anxious and active. He developed a skin condition that he scratched until it became raw. He would often pick at the sores until they bled. He chewed his nails until there was nothing left. It was not long before the shelter staff became quite concerned about his health.

Children who endure homelessness often *learn survival skills that are not beneficial in other settings.* For example, some children become experts at finding and hoarding bits of food when living on the streets. But when this type of behavior is exhibited in school, teachers generally respond by sending such children to the principal.

Homeless children may also *feel that they must take care of their parents.* In reality, they may have developed better survival skills than the adults who are supposed to care for them. Tower and White (1989) describe just such a child and his parent.

> *Jane Hart was suffering from acute hypothermia and pneumonia when she was brought to the emergency room of the local hospital by a neighborhood worker and the police. The police were called more to restrain eleven-year-old Darren than to help the medics with his mother. Residents of a dumpster, mother and son had been homeless for several months. When Jane became ill, Darren had cared for her, bringing food he found in trash cans. When the weather became cold, he scavenged for rags and newspapers to cover them. Finally Darren stole a blanket. The store owner who observed the theft notified a local service center. "I thought that a kid who would steal a blanket must really need it. Most kids would steal something they could sell," the storekeeper told an outreach worker. From the merchant's description, the worker found Darren and his ailing mother. So fiercely protective was the boy of his parent that police were summoned to help. (19)*

A life of moving from place to place and of poverty means that most children are *poorly nourished* and may have *poor hygiene* as well. Dietary limitations can create a child who is *listless and withdrawn* or, conversely, this lifestyle of inconsistency and poor diet can give rise to *hyperactivity* and *hostile behavior* (Solarz, 1992; Tower and White, 1989; Hart-Shegos, 1999).

One significant challenge in working with homeless children is meeting their educational needs. Since homeless families often move from area to area, it is often difficult for children to attend school. Even when they do, studies have found that children who move frequently score lower on standardized test scores, require between four to six months to catch up with their classmates, and suffer psychologically, socially, and academically (Bassuk, 1992; Tower and White, 1989, Hart-Shegos, 1999). Moving during the high school years decreases the likelihood of graduation and increases the possibility of dropping out of school (National Coalition for the Homeless, 1999). Another problem is that the records must be sent from previous schools. By the time the records can be secured, the family has usually moved on (Polakow, 1998).

Out of concern over these issues, the McKinney-Vento Homeless Assistance Act was enacted in 1987 and reauthorized in 1990, 1994, and 2002 after an assessment of proven practices from across the United States. The current provisions, effective July 1, 2002, provide homeless children and youths with the ability to stay in their original school or enroll in any public school and have transportation to that school. In addition, there is training for school personnel in how to provide services to the homeless child, outreach and information provided to parents, liaisons trained in homelessness to provide advocacy and assistance to children and their families, and provision to keep records that may be easily accessed if the child moves to another school (National Coalition for the Homeless, 1999). Through these steps, it is hoped that homeless children and youths can receive the education available to other children.

Homeless and Runaway Youths

Youths may become homeless due to family dysfunction, or because of the economic instability or homelessness of their families. Others may leave, seeking financial independence or adventure, only to discover that supporting one's self is not as easy as they had imagined. The National Runaway Switchboard (a hotline for teens) (2001) reports that some youths become homeless as a result of being forced out by disillusioned or angry parents. These are frequently referred to as *push-outs*. Of those who called the Hotline in 2001, the youngest was 10 years old, with the largest number between ages 14 (11.1%) and 17 (26.7%) (with 17.9% at age 15 and 24.2% at age 16) (2). Of the youths studied, 42.4% blamed family dynamics for their leaving home, and 14.2% said that they were influenced by peers. Some 7.6% were involved with Youth Services, 7.2% were having difficulty in school, 6.4% blamed mental illness, and 4.6% attributed their status to alcohol or drug abuse (NRS, 2001, 2).

Adolescence can be an exceptionally difficult time when young people are eager to be on their own but unprepared for the issues that they must face.

CASE EXAMPLE

Georgette

Georgette felt totally controlled by her overbearing parents. Her father's drinking, and her mother's denial of it, angered and confused her. In addition, her parents expected her to do much of the work around the house while her mother worked. Georgette felt she did not have the freedom experienced by her peers. She found this stifling and ran to a friend's house, intending to stay until she could get a bus ticket. The friend's parents called Georgette's parents and she hastily got her ticket and prepared to leave. But the bus was delayed and she ended up sleeping in the station. The next morning, a group of youths that she knew slightly from school found her and invited her to go with them to a city several hours away. The boys drank for the entire trip and by the time they arrived in the city, Georgette was anxious to get away from their drunken suggestions. Saying that she had to go to the bathroom, they stopped at a fast-food place. Georgette exited through another door and ran until she was sure that the other youths were no longer aware of her whereabouts.

When the small amount of money she had brought with her was gone, Georgette found herself searching trash cans for food. It was not long before she was approached by a well-dressed man who offered her a place to stay "with some other girls like you." Little did the naive teen realize that as she went with him to the promised apartment, she had just become initiated into a life of prostitution. The offer of drugs, seduction, and later blackmail would ensure that she had little choice but to comply with the wishes of her new "manager."

Life for homeless and runaway youths is far from idyllic. Prostitution, drugs, and abuse may figure prominently in a life on the streets. The luckier ones may find shelter or become involved in programs for homeless and runaway youths.

Changing View of Runaway and Homeless Youths

Since early in our country's history, youths who ran from their homes were frowned upon, without giving much consideration to whether they had cause. Reform schools, the first of which began in Massachusetts in 1847, were filled with youths whose only "crime" was that they ran away. The juvenile court, first established in Chicago in 1899, saw numerous children and adolescents who were brought in for running from their homes. But in the 1950s and 1960s, child welfare advocates began to talk about how runaways were not like delinquent offenders and should not be subjected to the same punishments. In 1963, the New York Family Court Act established a new category for runaways, designating them as "in need of service." Further, this act acknowledged not only that these youths may have run for a reason, but that the only reason that they were coming before the court was their status as minors. By 1974, the Federal Juvenile Justice and Delinquency Prevention Act was passed, which decriminalized "status offenses" as applied to runaways, as well as truants and children whose parents found them difficult to handle (Rothman, 1991). In 1980, a Youth Development Bureau study identified several categories of runaway and homeless youth: *runaways,* who leave home without parental permission; *push-outs,* who leave home with parental encouragement; *throwaways,* who leave with parental approval and often pressure; and *noncrisis youths,* who are living in a problematic situation but not intending to leave. The study also identified 42% of the sample to be runaways, 28% push-outs and throwaways, and 20% noncrisis youths. The majority of the youths studied were white (72%), with 16% African American and 6% Hispanic (Rothman, 1991, 20).

Today, experts indicate that there are significant changes in the types of youths they are seeing. Runaway and homeless youths today tend to be younger, more representative of minorities, more emotionally disturbed, from more dysfunctional families, and more likely to have been abused or neglected (Siegel and Senna, 2000).

Problems and Solutions
for Runaway/Homeless Youths

Conditions for runaway/homeless youths are not ideal. Many report ailments such as sexually transmitted diseases, drug and alcohol dependence, malnourishment, and other significant health problems. In a California study, 52% of the sample were drug-abusing, 51% abused alcohol, 42% had psychiatric problems, 25% had significant health problems, and 9% were pregnant (Rothman, 1991, 77). Interestingly enough, the highest percentage of a Los Angeles sample (86%) were seeking job training and placement as a solution to their problem of being homeless (80). This might indicate that running away for many youths is the only response they know to an impossible situation. It may also be a transitional step between living at home and attempting to become a functional adult.

Meeting the needs of homeless youths may require a variety of creative innovations. Petry and Avent (1992) report on a 100-bed rehabilitation center in Los Angeles that is dedicated to helping homeless youths. Stepping Stone, which has been operating for over a decade, sees more than 1,250 youths between 7 and 17 years old (the majority are between 15 to 17 years old) each year. Of these, about 44% report family violence as the cause for their coming to the program. Over 50% of these youths have already dropped out of school, whereas an estimated 90% are "bright" and capable of schoolwork (300). The youths stay for 14 days, during which they receive counseling, life skills training, and attempted family reunification services. Approximately 94% of the residents have eventually been reunited with their families.

In addition to shelters, which unfortunately are not numerous enough, various social service agencies offer such resources as food, clothing and shelter, counseling, family counseling, health services, substance abuse services, and vocational services.

Homelessness, whether it affects families or youths, continues to be a significant problem in our culture today. Many feel that the solution lies not only in alleviating the societal problems (e.g., housing, unemployment, etc.) that cause homelessness but also in strengthening families so that children do not find it necessary to leave home and become homeless.

Summary

Daily, we are reminded of the problems that face our children and youths today. Three of the most obvious problems are violence, substance abuse, and homelessness.

Increasingly, children are exposed to violence on the streets and in their homes. Some feel that the media and the violence in sporting activities play a large role in both desensitizing and normalizing violent behavior. One manifestation of violence—gangs—has become a significant problem today. Some experts break gangs into four categories: criminal gangs that are involved with criminal activities; conflict gangs, dedicated to protecting their territory; retreatist gangs, the members of which "retreat" to do drugs; and cult gangs, which are involved in cultist activities. Gangs offer youths a sense of belonging, a feeling of purpose, and often the thrill of risk taking.

Relationships too have become violent for many teens. These abusive relationships often carry over into the home environment, creating men who physically and sexually abuse wives. This battering, in turn, has an effect on the children by making them fearful and guilty as well as causing them to repeat the cycle of abuse.

Children are affected by substance abuse in two ways: when they watch their parents abuse substances and when the children themselves become substance abusers. Children whose parents abuse alcohol or drugs may suffer physiological symptoms such as fetal alcohol syndrome or fetal alcohol effects, or from withdrawal at birth from some kind of drug. These chemicals can leave children with permanent impairments. In addition, children whose parents are chemically dependent are affected psychologically and may end up becoming caregivers of both their addicted parents and younger siblings and having later psychological scars. Some children also contract HIV from substance-abusing parents.

Chemically dependent children are often attempting to cope with lives that are less than satisfying. Still others become addicted as a result of peer influences. The thrill of a "quick fix," often perpetrated by the media, is another allure of drug taking. For these youths, there are often limited treatment resources, although the number of such services appears to be increasing.

Homelessness, often interrelated with substance abuse and violence, is a phenomenon that affects many families today. In fact, families are the fastest growing homeless population. Families may be homeless because of unemployment, because a mother and her children are leaving an abusive relationship, because a parent is on aid and cannot afford to keep housing, or because the parents have been homeless in adolescence and have difficulty finding another way of life. Homelessness affects the children by making them feel hopeless and powerless, causing them to care for their parents and affecting their health, both physical and emotional.

Youths may also become homeless by either running away from home, often as a result of severe family dysfunction, or by being encouraged to leave by their parents. Young people are more likely to spend time on the streets than are families. They may also spend time with friends or in shelters. There are minimal programs for homeless youth and this is an area where more work needs to be done.

EXPLORATION QUESTIONS

1. What factors influence the amount of violence among youths today?
2. What are the four types of gangs and what are their functions?
3. Why are more Asian youths becoming involved in gangs?
4. Why is there more violence in peer relationships today?
5. How does abuse in the home affect children?
6. What is fetal alcohol syndrome? What causes it and what are its effects?
7. How does parental substance abuse affect children at different ages?

8. How might children contract AIDS?
9. What causes children to become chemically dependent? What types of problems does it cause for them?
10. What causes homelessness?
11. Why do families become homeless? What is meant by the term *marginally homeless?*
12. What effects does homelessness have on children?
13. Why do youths become homeless?

REFERENCES

Baer, J. S., Marlatt, G. A., & McMahon, R. J. (Eds.). (1993). *Addictive Behaviors across the Lifespan: Prevention, Treatment and Policy Issues.* Newbury Park, CA: Sage.

Bassuk, E. L. (1992). "Women and Children without Shelter" (257–272). In M. J. Robertson & M. Greenblatt (Eds.), *Homelessness: A National Perspective.* New York: Plenum.

Blau, J. (2002). *The Visible Poor: Homelessness in the United States.* New York: Oxford University Press.

Botvin, G. J., Schinke, S., & Orlandi, M. A. (Eds.). (1995). *Drug Prevention with Multiethnic Youth.* Thousand Oaks, CA: Sage.

Brown, R. (Ed.). (1994). *Children in Crisis.* New York: H. W. Wilson.

Brown, S. A. (1993). "Recovery Patterns in Adolescent Substance Abuse" (161–183). In J. S. Baer, G. A. Marlatt, & R. J. McMahon (Eds.), *Addictive Behaviors across the Lifespan: Prevention, Treatment and Policy Issues.* Newbury Park, CA: Sage.

Campbell, A. (1990). "Female Participation in Gangs" (163–182). In R. C. Huff (Ed.), *Gangs in America.* Newbury Park, CA: Sage.

Carlson, B. E. (1996). "Dating Violence: Student Beliefs about Consequences," *Journal of Interpersonal Violence,* 11(1), 3–18.

Center for Disease Control and Prevention (CDC) HIV/AIDS Surveillance Report. (1999). *Year-End Edition.* Atlanta, Ga: CDC.

Child Welfare League of America. (2002). Retrieved from http://www.cwla.org/programs/chemical.

Children's Defense Fund. (2002). Retrieved from http://www.childrensdefense.org.

Crosson-Tower, C. (2002). *Understanding Child Abuse and Neglect.* Boston: Allyn and Bacon.

Cummings, E. M. (1998). "Stress and Coping Approaches and Research: The Impact of Marital Conflict on Children" (31–50). In B. R. Rossman & M. S. Rosenberg (Eds.), *Multiple Victimization of Children: Conceptual, Developmental, Research, and Treatment Issues.* New York: Haworth.

Curry, G. D. (1998). "Female Gang Involvement," *Journal of Research in Crime and Delinquency,* 35, 100–119.

Deschenes, E. P., and Esbensen, F. (1999). "Violence in Gangs: Gender Differences in Perceptions and Behavior," *Journal of Quantitative Criminology,* 15, 63–96.

Dutton, D. G. (1995). *The Domestic Assault of Women.* Boston: Allyn and Bacon.

Falchikov, N. (1996). "Adolescent Attitudes to Abuse of Women," *Journal of Interpersonal Violence,* 11(3), 391–409.

Forsyth, B. W. C. (1995). "A Pandemic Out of Control: The Epidemiology of AIDS" (19–31). In S. Geballe, J. Gruedel, & W. Andiman (Eds.), *Forgotten Children of the AIDS Epidemic.* New Haven: Yale University Press.

Geballe, S., Gruedel, J., & Andiman, W. (Eds.). (1995). *Forgotten Children of the AIDS Epidemic.* New Haven: Yale University Press.

Glick, R., & Moore, J. (Eds.). (1990). *Drugs in Hispanic Communities.* New Brunswick, NJ: Rutgers.

Goodchilds, J., Zelliman, G. L., Johnson, P. B., & Giarusso, R. (1988). "Adolescents and Their Perception of Sexual Interaction" (245–270). In A. W. Burgess (Ed.), *Rape and Sexual Assault,* vol. 2. New York: Garland.

Gray, H. M., & Foshee, V. (1997). "Adolescent Dating Violence," *Journal of Interpersonal Violence,* 12, 126–141.

Graziano, A. M. (1994). "Why We Should Study Subabusive Violence against Children," *Journal of Interpersonal Violence, 9*(3), 412–419.

Gullota, T. P., Adams, G. R., & Montemayor, R. (Eds.). (1994). *Substance Misuse in Adolescence.* Thousand Oaks, CA: Sage.

Hart-Shegos, E. (1999). *Homelessness and Its Effects on Children.* Minneapolis: Family Housing Fund.

Herzberger, S. D., & Hall, J. A. (1993). "Children's Evaluations of Retaliatory Aggression against Siblings and Friends," *Journal of Interpersonal Violence, 8*(1), 77–93.

Hoffman, A. M. (Ed.). (1996). *Schools, Violence and Society.* Westport, CT: Praeger.

Huff, C. R. (Ed.). (1990). *Gangs in America.* Newbury Park, CA: Sage.

Jesse, R. C. (1989). *Children in Recovery.* New York: W. W. Norton.

Johnson, J. L. (1991). "Forgotten No Longer: An Overview of Research on Children of Chemically Dependent Parents" (29–54). In T. M. Rivinus (Ed.), *Children of Chemically Dependent Parents.* New York: Brunner/Mazel.

Johnson, L. D. (1992). "Incidence of Use for Various Types of Drugs by Grade: Eighth Graders 1992" (134). In *National Survey Results on Drug Use from the Monitoring the Future Study, 1975–1992,* vol. 1. Secondary School Students, University of Michigan, Institute for Social Research.

Kadushin, A., & Martin, J. A. (1988) *Child Welfare Services.* New York: Macmillan.

Kandel, D. B. (1995). "Ethnic Differences in Drug Use" (81–104). In G. J. Botvin, S. Schinke, & M. A. Orlandi (Eds.), *Drug Prevention with Multiethnic Youth.* Thousand Oaks, CA: Sage.

Kellerman, J. (1999). *Savage Spawn.* New York: Ballantine.

Kelly, S. (1998). "Stress and Coping Behaviors of Substance-Abusing Mothers," *Journal of the Society of Pediatric Nurses, 3*(3), 103–110.

Kinnear, K. L. (1995). *Violent Children.* Santa Barbara, CA: ABC-CLIO.

Kotlowitz, A. (1991). *There Are No Children Here.* New York: Doubleday.

Kozol, J. (1988). *Rachel and Her Children.* New York: Crown.

Krestan, J., & Bepko, C. (1993). "On Lies, Secrets, and Silence: The Multiple Levels of Denial in Addictive Families." In E. Imber-Black (Ed.), *Secrets in Families and Family Therapy.* New York: Norton.

Laquer, B. (1998). "The Nee-Kon Project: Designing and Implementing Prevention Strategies for Young Native American Children," *Drugs and Society, 12*(1–2), 23–37.

Leinwand, D. (2002). "Emergence of GBH as a Recreational Drug," *USA Today.* Retrieved at http://www.coaf.org/research/news.htm.

Levoy, D., Rivinus, T. M., Matzko, M., & McGuire, J. (1991). "Children in Search of a Diagnosis: Chronic Trauma Disorder of Childhood" (153–170). In T. M. Rivinus (Ed.), *Children of Chemically Dependent Parents.* New York: Brunner/Mazel.

Lindsey, E. W. (1998). "Service Provider's Perception of Factors That Help or Hinder Homeless Families," *Families in Society, 79*(2), 160–172.

Marcenko, M. O., & Samost, L. (1999). "Living with HIV/AIDS: The Voices of HIV-Positive Mothers," *Social Work, 44*(1), 36–45.

Maxson, C. L., & Klein, M. W. (1990). "Street Gang Violence: Twice as Great, or Half as Great?" (71–100). In R. C. Huff (Ed.), *Gangs in America.* Newbury Park, CA: Sage.

McCarroll, T. (1988). *Morning Glory Babies: Children with AIDS and the Celebration of Life.* New York: St. Martin's Press.

McChesney, K. Y. (1992). "Homeless Families: Four Patterns of Poverty" (245–256). In M. J. Robertson & M. Greenblatt (Eds.), *Homelessness: A National Perspective.* New York: Plenum.

McWhirter, J. J., McWhirter, B. T., McWhirter, A. M., & McWhirter, E. H. (1998). *At-Risk Youth: A Comprehensive Response.* Pacific Grove, CA: Brooks/Cole.

Miller, B. C., & Dyk, P. A. H. (1993). "Sexuality" (95–123). In P. H. Tolan & B. J. Cohler (Eds.), *Handbook of Clinical Research and Practice with Adolescents.* New York: John Wiley and Sons.

Miller, W. B. (1980). "Gangs, Groups and Serious Youth Crime" (120–127). In D. Schichor & D. Kelly (Eds.), *Critical Issues in Juvenile*

Delinqency. Lexington, MA: Lexington Books.

Miller-Heyl, J., MacPhee, D., & Fritz, J. (1998). "DARE to Be You: A Family-Support, Early Intervention Program," *Journal of Primary Prevention,* 18(3), 257–285.

Molidor, C. E. (1996). "Female Gang Members: A Profile of Aggression and Victimization," *Social Work,* 41(3), 251–257.

Moore, J., and Hegedorn R. (2001). "Female Gangs: A Focus on Research," *Juvenile Justice Bulletin.* Rockville, MD: Juvenile Justice Clearinghouse.

Morales, A., (1989). "Urban Gang Violence" (433–368). In A. Morales & B. Schaefor (Eds.), *Social Work: A Profession of Many Faces.* Boston: Allyn and Bacon.

Morse, G. A. (1992). "Causes of Homelessness" (3–17). In M. J. Robertson & M. Greenblatt (Eds.), *Homelessness: A National Perspective.* New York: Plenum.

Muisener, P. P. (1994). *Understanding and Treating Adolescent Substance Abuse.* Thousand Oaks, CA: Sage.

National Coalition for the Homeless. (1999). Retrieved from http://www.nationalhomeless.org

National Runaway Switchboard. (2001). Retrieved at http:www.nrscrisisline.org/2001stat.asp.

National Youth Violence Prevention Resource Center. (2000). *Youth Violence Statistics.* Retrieved at http://www.safeyouth.org.

Nellis, M. (1980). *The Female Fix.* Boston: Houghton Mifflin.

Olday, D., & Wesley, B. (1988). "Dating Violence: A Comparison of High School and College Subsamples, " *Free Inquiry in Creative Sociology,* 16, 183–190.

Oleske, J. (1990). "The Medical Management of Pediatric AIDS: Intervening on Behalf of Children and Families" (27–40). In G. Anderson (Ed.), *Courage to Care: Responding to the Crisis of Children with AIDS.* Washington, DC: Child Welfare League of America.

Petry, S., & Avent, H. (1992). "Stepping Stone: A Haven for Displaced Youths" (299–305). In M. J. Robertson & M. Greenblatt (Eds.), *Homelessness: A National Perspective.* New York: Plenum.

Polakow, V. (1998). "Homeless Children and Their Families" (3–22). In S. Brooks et al. (Eds.), *Invisible Children in the Society and Its Schools.* Mahwah, NJ: Lawrence Erlbaum.

Resnik, H. (1990). *Youth and Drugs: Society's Mixed Messages.* Rockville, MD: Office for Substance Abuse Prevention, U.S. Department of Health and Human Services.

Rhodes, J. E., & Jason, L. A. (1988). *Preventing Substance Abuse among Children and Adolescents.* New York: Pergamon Press.

Rickel, A. U., & Becker-Lausen, E. (1994). "Treating the Adolescent Drug Misuser" (175–200). In T. P. Gullota, G. R. Adams, & R. Montemayor (Eds.), *Substance Misuse in Adolescence.* Thousand Oaks, CA: Sage.

Riggs, D. S. (1993). "Relationship Problems and Dating Aggression," *Journal of Interpersonal Violence,* 8(1), 8–35.

Rivinus, T. M. (Ed.). (1991). *Children of Chemically Dependent Parents.* New York: Brunner/Mazel.

Robinson, B. E., & Rhoden, J. L. (1998). *Working with Children of Alcoholics.* Thousand Oaks, CA: Sage.

Rothman, J. (1991). *Runaway and Homeless Youth.* New York: Longman.

Schmittroth, L. (Ed.). (1994). *Statistical Record of Children.* Detroit: Gale Research.

Seixas, J. S., & Youcha, G. (1985). *Children of Alcoholism.* New York: Crown.

Seltser, B. J., & Miller, D. E. (1993). *Homeless Families.* Chicago: University of Chicago Press.

Shin, M. (1997). "Family Homelessness: State or Trait," *American Journal of Community Psychology,* 25(6), 755–769.

Siegel, L. J., & Senna, J. J. (2000). *Juvenile Delinquency: Theory, Practice and Law.* Belmont, CA: Wadsworth.

Solarz, A. L. (1992). "To Be Young and Homeless" (275–286). In M. J. Robertson & M. Greenblatt (Eds.), *Homelessness: A National Perspective.* New York: Plenum.

Substance Abuse and Mental Health Services Administration (SAMSHA). (2002). *National Household Survey on Drug Abuse.* Washington DC: Dept. of Health and Human Services.

Terr, L. (1990). *Too Scared to Cry: Psychic Trauma in Childhood.* New York: Harper & Row.

Tower, C. C., & White, D. J. (1989). *Homeless Students*. Washington, DC: National Education Association.

Towers, R. L. (1987). *How Schools Can Combat Student Drug and Alcohol Abuse*. Washington, DC: National Education Association.

U.S. Conference of Mayors. (1998). *A Status Report on Hunger and Homelessness in America's Cities: 1998*. Washington, D.C.: Author.

U.S. Government Accounting Office, Report to Congressional Committees. (1989). *Children and Youths: About 68,000 Homeless and 186,000 in Shared Housing at Any Given Time*. Washington, DC: U.S. Government Printing Office.

Vigil, J. D., & Yun, S. C. (1990). "Vietnamese Youth Gangs in Southern California" (146–182). In R. C. Huff (Ed.), *Gangs in America*. Newbury Park, CA: Sage.

Winfree, L. T., & Bernat, F. P. (1998). "Social Learning, Self-Control and Substance Abuse by Eighth Grade Students," *Journal of Drug Issues*, 28(2), 539–558.

Zastrow, C. (2000). *Introduction to Social Work and Social Welfare*. Pacific Grove, CA: Brooks/Cole.

5 Serving the Developing Child

Daycare and School-Based Services

MARY ANN HANLEY

DENISE A. O'CONNELL

ELAINE FRANCIS

MAUREEN C. MOOREHOUSE

MATTHEW D. PORTER

Daycare: Serving Infants and Preschool Children

When we think of daycare as a service for children, we often imagine the family of two wage earners or the single parent who must seek alternative care of their children during working hours. Historically, children were cared for in their own homes or by relatives, but as women are pressed increasingly into the workforce and the demands of employment take parents away from their extended families, child care at a center or at the hands of strangers or friends becomes more the rule than the exception.

Daycare not only meets the needs of working parents; many see the preschool care of children as a method of enhancing development. Programs such as Head Start were actually designed to give economically disadvantaged children that extra developmental and educational boost that would enable them to begin school at the same level as their more privileged peers. And for some overwhelmed or overburdened parents, daycare provides a respite for both parent and child. The United States, however, is the only industrial nation that has no national policies or standards for the welfare of young children and their families.

Family Needs

In many families, particularly single-parent families, economic necessity requires that parents seek daycare for their children. In some cases, parents choose day care for the positive effects that the socialization with other children can have.

Daycare is necessary for the children of many families in crisis. The children need a safe, nurturing place in which they can thrive (Wasik, 1998). Often, parents, too, need respite from their child-rearing duties. Parents of children with special needs also use daycare. Their needs encompass a wide range of disabilities, requiring a wide variation of attention, and parents often need respite from the demands of raising them. Many daycare providers have special skills in working with these children.

For many, if not most, parents, the cost of daycare is a major consideration. Although quality is important to all, it is of no use if parents cannot afford it. For poorer families, securing adequate daycare may be a financial impossibility (McWhirter et al., 1998).

As we consider the needs of parents for daycare, we must also consider the kinds of services provided. Do we strive for quality, assuming that there will be costs for the families, or is afford ability, in order to ensure universal opportunity, the most important issue (Scarr, 1998)? Solutions, whether financial or otherwise, need to be found in order to protect the well-being and development of the nation's children.

A Brief History of Daycare Provision

Daycare for children began as an economically based need. Historically, mothers who were pressed into work, whether in the fields or later in factories, depended on their female relatives for child care. But in 1828, the first daycare center was opened in Boston to serve those mothers who sought to escape poverty by working outside the home. The purpose of this center was not only to provide a safe place for children but also to provide them with a "religious and moral foundation" (Reeves, 1992). The federal government made its first real commitment to child care in 1933, when Roosevelt's Federal Emergency Relief Act and Work Progress Administration (WPA) provided funds to establish day nurseries and nursery schools to establish employment for preschool teachers. These programs tended to be housed in public schools. By 1937, about 40,000 children were enrolled on WPA-funded child care programs. Although these benefited children and parents, their purpose was more the employment of teachers than serving children (Reeves, 1992).

When women became increasingly a part of the war effort in the early 1940s, Public Law 137, known as the Latham Act, allotted funding for the support of child care centers in defense plants employing women. Working mothers, and therefore the provision of daycare for their children, became culturally sanctioned (Scarr, 1998). The eventual 3,102 centers served close to 600,000 children. Perhaps stimulated by these efforts, Kaiser Industries was the first large employer to institute employer-sponsored daycare for its workers (Reeves, 1992).

After the war, governmental supports for daycare were withdrawn and "mothers were told to go home to make way in the workplace for returning veterans" (Scarr, 1998, 96). But economic recession and a new independence drove women back into the workplace in increasing numbers, until, by 1995, 62% of mothers with children under age 6 were employed (Hofferth, 1996).

In the meantime, child care advocates became concerned about children who were economically disadvantaged and who needed additional stimulation to keep up with their peers. Thus, in 1964, Project Head Start was instituted to serve such children (see later explanation of Head Start services today), adding another dimension to the provision of daycare services.

Examining the Goals of Daycare Provision

Previously, we identified four reasons why parents or social agencies might place children in daycare: (1) to provide a safe alternative environment while parents work, (2) to provide disadvantaged children with an extra social and educational boost to ready them for school, (3) to create a therapeutic respite for parents who may have abused or neglected children in the past, and (4) to create a respite for parents with special needs children. Let us explore each of these in turn.

Working Parents and What Is Best for Children. Today, in most two-parent families, both parents are employed outside the home. Add the startling increase in single-parent families, and the need for quality child care programs becomes more and more apparent. But as they consider how they will choose the providers for their children's care, most parents feel ill-prepared. This may account for the abundance of articles in many magazines that offer basic advice on choosing a daycare provider. Parents know that they want their provider to be reliable and trustworthy as well as the best match for their child, but they are often unsure of how these qualities should be measured. Many parents find daycare through word of mouth from friends or relatives. Such connections raise the parents' trust, without merit. Neugebauer (1995), in his evaluation of the national daycare scene for the *Child Care Information Exchange,* commented that although parents value the quality of daycare that their children are receiving, they often have no idea how to measure quality. Compared with the impressions of trained observers who felt that specific settings were adequate to mediocre, the parents whose children were cared for in these settings rated them much higher. Since most parents cannot recognize quality, they do not demand it, and therefore programs supported by parents' fees have no impetus for providing a higher-quality service, even if at a higher cost.

The dilemma of the cost versus quality care issue is not lost on parents and professionals. Parents often pay a large percentage of their net income on child care and want the best they can afford. Yet, the study indicates that it costs substantially more to produce better results.

Working parents are given information regarding child care from a variety of sources, and the decision as to where their child will go is often a very difficult and unsettling one. For those families who cannot afford any daycare, it is that much more problematical. Head Start was developed to help these families.

Giving Children an Educational and Developmental Head Start. As part of the War on Poverty in the 1960s, child advocates began taking a closer look at the readiness of low-income and culturally disadvantaged children to keep up with their peers as they entered the school setting. Head Start, instituted in 1964 as the first federally funded childhood education program since World War II for low-income families, was designed as a comprehensive child care model that provides educational opportunities for the child, social support for the family, and health and nutritional services that assist each child to reach his or her full potential (Siegel and Senna, 2000; Cromwell, 1994).

Beyond the provision of quality educational services, Head Start has other unique qualities. Social service workers conduct home visits to support each family and are in a position to assist in a crisis. Head Start was one of the first programs to mandate that children with special needs be fully included in the classroom setting, and a percentage of each center's enrollment is set aside for them. Another important aspect is that Head Start is designed to provide job training for low-income parents at the center where their child attends. Many current Head Start teachers were parents of Head Start children. Ironically, the jobs that parents are trained for are some of the lowest-paying professional jobs in our society.

Head Start has evolved into a multidimensional program that includes full-day programs, at-home programs, and summer care. Despite the political changes since the early 1960s, Head Start has increased its funding and is a vital part of our educational system. Today, there are 36,000 Head Start classrooms that serve 800,000 children and their families. From a service with an allotment of $96,000,000 in 1965, Head Start is predicted to require an investment of $8 billion in this century (Siegel and Senna, 2000). Many feel that the results of this service to children and families are well worth the expenditures.

When Parenting Becomes Overwhelming: Need for Respite.   Every year, numerous children are abused and neglected by their parents (see Chapter 7). Some parents, from abusive or neglectful backgrounds themselves, are ill-equipped to parent their own children effectively. Yet, with sufficient treatment and support, many can learn these parenting skills. It is in these situations that social services agencies providing child protection may use daycare of children as part of the treatment plan (Wasik, 1998).

Although welfare reform has changed the type of arrangements that can be made by social agencies, daycare services for parents remains a useful way to allow parents the emotional space to prepare themselves to better care for their children.

Parenting the Child with Special Needs: A Special Kind of Care.   The families of children with special needs face significant challenges in their role as parents. Children who are seen as "different" endure isolation, teasing, and stares while their parents stand by feeling helpless to make the road easier for them. Early child care can provide a setting for children with special needs that can be safe and supportive and can partner the parents in their attempts to encourage these children to discover their strengths and interests. Competent providers may also offer a strong support to parents by building trust and focusing on the positive. Since the federal Individuals with Disability Education Act requires states to provide public education for special needs children ages 3 to 21, it seems logical that many more parents will now be seeking out daycare as well as early intervention services.

When a child enters a daycare program, teachers and administrators also act as the first line of action in identifying children with special needs. State laws require a physical examination and immunization before entering the program. In addition, some states require a developmental history that the parent must fill out, and this is added to the child's record.

One role of daycare personnel is to provide pertinent information regarding their observation of the child's behavior at the center. Another important function is to act as an advocate for the child and the family. Meeting with public school teachers, doctors, administrators, and others can be intimidating for parents. Daycare staff are usually people the parents know and trust, and having these people in the room may lessen the parents' anxieties.

Not every child care center can provide for children with special needs. If the special needs are beyond the scope and skills of the center, then the appropriate course of action is to make a referral.

Types of Daycare

When daycare is mentioned, various ideas and concepts may come to mind. Most children under the age of 5 are cared for in their own homes or in the home of a relative or family daycare provider. Others may be provided for in center-based programs.

At-Home Care. Many children are cared for in their own homes by relatives, such as grandparents, aunts, or uncles who have the time or interest to care for the children. Another variation is the shared care concept in which one parent stays at home with related children from a single extended family. In some cases, there is money exchanged for child care services, and usually the rate of pay is considerably lower than that of a commercial daycare center.

The issue of grandparents as primary caregivers is currently under scrutiny. Young and energetic grandparents may well wish to look after the "baby" on an occasional basis. However, there may be a physical cost to the process. The energy required to look after an active toddler may be too much for some.

In families with many resources, the use of a professional nanny may best serve their needs. There are numerous agencies that supply nannies; some families find someone themselves who serves in this capacity. Nannies are usually paid a salary, provided with room and board, and given Social Security benefits and appropriate free time.

Family Day Care. In many states there is a legal requirement that, if you take care of someone else's child in your home, you must be licensed by the state. Most states limit the number of children allowed in the home to not more than six, including the caregiver's own children and only two children can be under the age of 2. One of the concerns regarding this model of care is that the care of children is usually left to one person, and if the provider is ill or unable to separate personal/family concerns from the provision of care, the quality of care may be unacceptable. In all other models there are at least two adults present and, if one of them is unable to provide quality care, then the other adult is able to cover the needs of the children.

Some states allow up to 12 children in a home if there is an approved assistant, though other licensing requirements apply regardless of size. It is important to refer to the state law regarding the allowable size and scope when researching the requirements of each area.

In some larger communities there are systems of family daycare homes. The system coordinator works closely with each provider through telephone contact and/or at-home visits. The system provides benefits, such as vacations, sick time coverage, training, and access to government funding sources. The advantage of this model is that the provider is not isolated from other adults, and emergency situations can be handled efficiently. The provider pays a percentage of the tuitions collected for this service to the organization that has set up the system.

Nursery Schools and Other Half-Day Programs.   One type of program, called a *parent cooperative nursery school,* has been in existence since the early 1920s. These were formed largely because parents' recognized that children benefited from social and educational experiences obtained before entering school. They also recognized that costs to families could be reduced if each family shared the experience. Although professional teachers are employed, the duties of assisting the teacher, handling the finances, purchasing supplies, and other duties related to the program's operation fall to a parent board. There is usually a rotation of jobs, with new families taking over from outgoing ones.

Many churches have worked with interested teachers and families to open half-day *church-sponsored programs* for preschool children (ages 3 to 5). When most mothers stayed home, those who could afford it sent their children to these facilities two or three days a week, believing that this extra time away from home helped prepare the children for the kindergarten experience. Nursery schools exist today in limited numbers due to increasing demands for full-time daycare.

Lab schools are sometimes offered in colleges or universities. These schools provide the opportunity for students to learn about child care while actually also providing this service for the community. These programs combine community relations' efforts with a living laboratory for education and psychology departments. Parents who choose such programs know that college students as well as professional teachers will be interacting with their children. The opportunity to go beyond the textbook and learn from actual living subjects is an attractive feature for the college or university student. These programs usually charge a nominal tuition and are often subsidized by the college.

Full-Day Programs.   Every daycare center is a unique entity that serves the community and its families. Most daycare programs serve children ages 3 to 6 with a combination of educational, social, recreational, physical, and other developmentally appropriate experiences. Infants and toddlers may be served in separate rooms with specially trained staff. There is a myth that daycare is just a babysitting service or that children watch TV or are just entertained. In reality, a quality daycare center is run by professionally trained people whose backgrounds and training are often equivalent to that of their public school counterparts. A daycare center may be the culmination of one individual's dream to own his or her own program or it may be part of a chain of centers that stretch from coast to coast.

There are two types of centers: the for-profit program and the nonprofit program. A *for-profit program* is run like any other business, whereas a *nonprofit program* is not owned by an individual or partnership but has a board of directors that guides the program, hires the director, and sets polices. The misconception here is that it does not make money. Every program must cover all its expenses in order to survive. The nonprofit program doesn't pay sales or property taxes but must pay its staff. The for-profit program pays all expenses, and, if it is successful, will return a portion of any profits to the investors. A quality program provides quality services regardless of its organization.

Montessori Schools.   The Montessori movement was begun by Maria Montessori (1870–1952), a medical doctor who opened the first "Children's House" in a Rome, Italy, slum in 1907. Throughout her work with children, Montessori had been faced with many who were considered "uneducable." Montessori discovered that children's developmental education is affected by the considered use of natural materials and a form of self-education. She designed an educational system based on exploration, orientation, order, imagination, manipulation, repetition, precision, control of error leading to perfection, and communication (Lillard, 1996). The children were taught a variety of skills, including hygiene, good work habits, and manners. The philosophy of the Montessori approach to education

> *combines freedom with responsibility, high standards of academic excellence, social awareness and moral development, and a vision of humanity and accomplishment that inspires children to take their place in their communities, when the time comes, as responsible, contributing adults. (xxi)*

In recent years, Montessori education has expanded beyond the traditional preschool base and offers programs for the infant/toddler years as well as children of elementary age. The Montessori approach is sometimes practiced in state-supported charter schools and in the Head Start program. The demand for a well-formulated, developmentally appropriate method of education has enabled the Montessori method to spread into communities throughout our country and around the world.

Private Kindergartens.   Many child care programs have developed an alternative to the public school model for children five to six years of age. The private kindergarten in most cases will have a much smaller staff-to-child ratio than is found in the public school and the program may be the logical extension of services for families that need a full day education program.

Day Nurseries.   Day nurseries have the longest history of early childhood services in the United States. Since the mid-1800s, day nurseries have served the inner-city family. Their focus on the "whole child" is based on the belief that in order to give each child the opportunity to fully develop, the family must be involved. Day nurseries are the forerunners of the Head Start multiservice, family-involved model of care. In most major cities there are some variations of the day nursery program (Cromwell, 1994).

Early Childhood Programs in Public Schools.   In public school systems across the country there is a new focus on the young child. In part, this effort is the result of the poor preparation that many children displayed when entering kindergarten. The wide disparity between children who have attended an educationally based preschool program and those who have spent little time with other children and adults is a much debated issue. There is also a recognition that by age 5 or 6, the child is already well on the way to the development of lifelong moral, social, and educational values, and children who have not had prekindergarten training may be at a disadvantage. In addition, in many public school kindergartens there is a large staff-to-child ratio, with one teacher and 26 to 29 children and perhaps one aide. This does not give the child new to the school experience enough attention from adults during this crucial adjustment period. Further, children need constant care: The typical public school schedule of vacation, staff development, and assorted holidays may create service gaps in the typical public school-based program. Most public school early childhood programs are half-day and may not be a viable option for working parents, who might otherwise enroll in this low-cost alternative to daycare. New variations in the public schools include contracted after-school programs and, in some cases, daycare programs operated by the public school system itself.

Teachers' Cooperatives.   Another model of care is the result of a collaborative effort on the part of early childhood professional teachers who band together to divide the workloads of teaching and administration. The "profits" are divided between the members, and the hiring of new staff is also done in a collaborative fashion.

Employer-Sponsored Daycare.   In recent years, some large employers have offered daycare services to their employees. Although this effort encompasses only a small fraction of U.S. business, the publicity surrounding the establishment of this type of employee benefit may be conducive to more and more businesses providing daycare facilities.

School-Based Programs

There is a universal acceptance that children attend school for the purpose of acquiring an education. Most parents expect that their children will do well and acquire at least a high school diploma. The program that schools primarily provide for all students is an education. *Education,* traditionally, is defined as the *learning of knowledge.* This learning takes place in the classroom with the teacher as the primary facilitator.

Children who face challenges in academic, social, and emotional development require programs and services beyond those that a classroom teacher has the skills or time to provide. The second half of this chapter will delineate those services that are usually available to all students, as well as services provided to students with disabilities. The "ideal" in programs and services is described, with the obstacles outlined whenever relevant.

Philosophy of Education

One's beliefs about schools and the mission they should fulfill serve as guiding forces in the development of "schools of excellence." Before discussing the programs a school should provide, it is necessary to consider the mission of schools in general. Research on learning processes has significantly changed the thinking on education and the approaches to teaching. There are several major assumptions on teaching children and how they learn that guide school services.

Children Learn in Different Ways.   A great deal of research has been conducted that considers the various learning styles of children and adults. Today, based on the evidence of this research, we know that each child brings to the learning situation a unique way of processing information. Some learn visually; others learn by listening. Some require a structured, sequential approach to learning; others feel constrained by this approach and need opportunities to think randomly before forming concepts. Some students have disabilities that require modifications in typical instruction or in expectations that will allow them to be successful. It is clear that the challenge of teachers is to recognize their students' learning styles and needs and to teach in ways that allow each individual to succeed. To accomplish this task, a teacher needs also to recognize his or her own preferred teaching style.

Children Learn Best When They Learn Together.   Considering the diverse needs and learning styles of students in schools, an easy solution might appear to be to group students with similar issues together in homogeneous settings. Such an approach has historically been utilized with students who have disabilities. It was not uncommon to find separate classes for students with disabilities. The failure of this approach has been in the damage to the self-image of students who are labeled as being "different," as well as in the limitations of opportunity to access the general curriculum and achieve their potential.

Today, the practice in education in general, and special education in particular, is to educate all students together in the regular classroom, and in their neighborhood schools, whenever possible. This concept is called the *least restrictive environment* (20 U.S.C., section 1412 [5] [B]). This removes many of the restrictions placed on students who have learning needs that, in the past, prevented them from being assigned to regular classrooms. With effective teaching strategies and the support that leads to individualized learning, all students can successfully learn together. As we consider services to children, we will find that more and more of these services are being provided in the regular classroom.

We Must Teach the Whole Child.   Schools should be holistic in their approach, addressing both the academic and the social/emotional needs of students, recognizing that all children can learn. Students should receive a strong academic foundation that provides them with the basic skills and critical thinking necessary to be productive citizens. A child's self-esteem and emotional growth have to be strong in order for that child to be successful. Thus, an effective school is as concerned with how a child feels about test scores as it is with the test scores themselves.

In our society, children's views of themselves are often defined by their performance in school. When meeting a family member or friend, a child is most often asked, "How's school?" Parents compare notes on their children's performance in school, remarking with awe on children who are singled out for honors. Students with learning problems often only feel different or inferior when they are in school. Teachers, counselors, and other school staff must recognize the challenges students face in school and at home and provide the support and encouragement that is necessary for optimum learning to occur.

Schools are in business primarily to meet the academic needs of students. As we consider those needs, most of us think of the "regular" academic program that is provided in the classroom, with the classroom teacher as the central figure. However, sometimes children and adolescents have needs that extend beyond those that the classroom teacher can address. If a student is experiencing great stress in his or her life, academic needs are a secondary focus in that child's life and grades may suffer. For this reason, schools offer not only basic academic work but also support services to ensure that all students, and particularly students with disabilities or problems that hamper achievement, will have the resources to help them deal successfully with the school environment. The next section describes support programs that are offered to help meet students' academic, social, and emotional needs.

Student Support Programs: Addressing Academic, Social, and Emotional Needs

Student support programs vary in breadth and content from one school district to another across the nation (Cormany, 1999). Historically, the program model for student support services involves a developmental approach that impacts all students at level one to greater restriction aimed at serving fewer students at level three. An individual student may actually benefit from the programs existing at all levels. This traditional model has the *guidance program* as the foundation, with *health, psychological, social work, and other intervention* at level two, and *special education instruction* at level three. Defining the student support program provides a challenge in itself, as it may include any program beyond that of the regular curriculum. For example, some school districts include attendance, bilingual education, early childhood education, federal, food services, and even transportation as part of the student support program. We will limit our discussion to the programs of guidance, counseling and psychological services, health, and special education. All personnel in these areas work to help remove the barriers to the learning process and to assist children in growing academically, socially, and emotionally. Growth in all three of these areas is important and speaks to the need for services to be available to positively affect the learning of all children. It is appropriate that the recent reauthorization of the Elementary and Secondary Education Act is entitled "No Child Left Behind Act of 2001" (Hickok, 2002). This legislation redefines the federal role in K–12 education and has as its goal the closing of the achievement gap between disadvantaged and minority students and their peers. Although the act focuses on academic and accountability measures, it also speaks to the need for student support programs and the inclusion of parents as partners in each child's education.

A staff person who provides this support may vary as to title, but generally includes school counselors, special education teachers, social workers, mental health workers, school psychologists, and school nurses. Different states may use dissimilar titles and use unlike credentialing standards. Professional organizations try to clarify roles. In 1998, one such organization, the American School Counselor Association, attempted such an explanation in a position paper; however, duplications of role functions continue to exist. Whatever the title, all of the identified job functions fall under the structure of *pupil personnel services* or an acronym. No matter what the label, the positions require that the individual performing the job needs to have a high level of self-understanding and mastery over feelings, thoughts, and actions.

Guidance Program.   There are many models for a comprehensive guidance program. Many of us think of guidance as it pertains to academic counseling.

CASE EXAMPLE

Sara

Sara knew that she wanted to attend college but had no idea where she wanted to go or what she would choose for a major. She approached her school counselor, who talked with her about her options. He asked Sara about the environments in which she learned the best and then demonstrated the use of the school's college search computer. After Sara had an opportunity to used the program during several study periods, she and the counselor discussed the selections Sara had made considering the likelihood of her acceptance in each. They then reviewed affordability and explored financial aid options. They then downloaded college catalogues and applications. The counselor then suggested that Sara speak with her parents and they all meet together.

There are several components to a comprehensive guidance program. *Career development* was the area that introduced guidance into the schools nearly a century ago. Today, this important feature of every middle and high school guidance program has been improved and expanded. The exploration of careers is not exclusive to in-school activities. Now, cooperation is sought with communities so that partnerships with businesses provide experiential learning for students through internships, shadowing experiences, summer employment, and other work-related opportunities (Staley and Carey, 1997).

Curriculum is an aspect of guidance that may take place in a classroom or in large or small group settings. Relevant material is presented in modules or units centered on topics pertinent to the specific group. For example, an elementary program might have a presentation on interpersonal skills presented in a small group, whereas a ninth-grade class might have a school-to-work assembly. School staff might also present materials on diversity, conflict resolution, human sexuality, family issues, or alcohol and drugs.

Individual planning helps students to develop short- and long-term goals for themselves, recognize their values, abilities, and aptitudes, or progress toward an identified career. The school counselor guides a student through this process, often in collaboration with the parents.

Responsive services (Starr and Gyspers, 1997) refer to such services as personal counseling, crisis intervention, consultation, and referral for other resources in the community. These services may be provided to students either individually or in small groups, where the counselor listens to their problems and helps them explore possible solutions. Groups are often favored for support, as developmentally peers play an important role in the lives of students—especially adolescents. Studies have shown that group work is effective in increasing academic achievement, school attendance, self-esteem, and more positive attitudes toward school (Borders and Drury, 1992). Individual counseling is needed when problems are very personal, complex, or serious, when many resources are required to deal with the problem, or when students seem unable to make good use of a small group.

Working with families of students is another function of responsive services. This is critical for the elementary school student, as the student has limited self determination over his life. Elementary school counselors spend much of their time helping families work on issues that may affect their children's school progress and/or the children's social and emotional growth. Family work is currently considered to be one of the major emphases in school counseling (Paisley and Borders, 1995). Referring a student and his or her families for more extensive counseling when necessary is a function of counselors at any level, as is consulting with the student's teachers and others working with the student and family.

There remains controversy regarding the provision of counseling services in schools. Those involved in providing and setting policy regarding services to children in school disagree as to who, within the school, should provide counseling, or if schools should offer personal counseling at all. Some professionals believe that school counselors are not qualified, by virtue of their training, to provide personal counseling. These critics contend that all counseling, except that related to education and career planning, should be referred to another professional, either within the school setting (social worker, mental health counselor, or psychologist) or associated with an outside agency. Others feel that this service is a necessary role of the school counselor for several reasons. First, parents may agree to have their children seen by a counselor at school but, due to their biases about psychological services, would hesitate to seek the services of a counseling agency. Second, children of parents who are financially unable to afford counseling outside the school or whose insurance does not cover such services may not be able to receive personal counseling unless the school provides it. And, third, issues of access are removed, as counseling is provided on site.

Counseling and guidance are direct services to students and are included in any good program. School counselors usually provide most of these services. However, teachers and other staff may do guidance work, and social workers, school psychologists, or mental health workers often provide more in-depth, long-term counseling services for students who have serious difficulties.

Intervention Programs: Social Work, School Psychology, and Nursing

<hr>

CASE EXAMPLE

Carlos

When Carlos began missing a great deal of school, his teacher was concerned. He first consulted with the school nurse to ascertain if Carlos had any medical problems. The nurse made a home visit and learned that Carlos's mother was quite ill and that Carlos was afraid that if he went to school, his mother would die while he was gone. The nurse also learned that Carlos had missed a lot of school prior to his mother's illness and had repeated the first grade. The nurse reported this back to Carlos's teacher. Together, they decided to make a referral to the school social worker and the school psychologist for follow-up. The social worker was able to offer intensive counseling to Carlos, so he could deal with his fears, rather than referring him to a community mental health center. The school psychologist evaluated Carlos's academic skills and determined that Carlos needed the services of the bilingual language therapist.

<hr>

Counseling and Case Management Services.   Social work or mental health counseling, when available in a school setting, includes working with students who have attendance problems, who are in trouble with authorities, or who need intensive counseling/therapy on specific difficulties. It also involves working with students who have behavioral problems or with those whose home environment does not provide enough help for them to develop in the major areas of their lives (social, emotional, academic, and physical). It includes arranging referrals for additional services (within and outside of the school) for some and monitoring equal opportunity and fair treatment for all students. There may be a need to deal with child abuse issues, domestic violence problems, and other violent behavior, sometimes with students who are victims and other times with students who are perpetrators. When social workers or mental health counselors are part of the school staff, they usually work with a small group of students who have been identified as having one or more of the above problems and who need a great deal of individual attention. Often, there is a need to coordinate counseling efforts with services provided by outside agencies. A crucial element of any student service plan involves working closely with the family.

Collaborative Consultation.   Collaborative consultation is a major function in helping students develop academically, often by working on social or emotional issues that hamper academic achievement. School counselors, social workers, psychologists, and nurses consult with teachers and parents primarily, but also with administrators, community representatives, and students. Collaborative consultation recognizes that each party brings knowledge to the conversation, and service focuses on classroom achievement or behavior. Sometimes working with the teacher to provide intervention strategies is more effective than long individual sessions with the student. These professionals can also help parents with overall strategies in parenting or may give concrete advice on how to handle a specific situation. Administrators may wish to work with counselors in designing an individual student's program, as well as with broader school programs. Professionals at the school are needed to link school/community programs. And, finally, students look to counselors for information on such things as peer mediation or interpersonal relationships.

There is a "well-established and interdisciplinary knowledge and research base on consultation that has been developed in the fields of guidance and counseling, special education, educational psychology and organizational development" (West and Idol, 1993, 678). By approaching consulting issues from a collaborative perspective, we help promote the team approach to problem solving. It is increasingly important for schools to move in this direction.

Assessment Services.   Assessment services are for all students, insofar as they monitor academic growth or offer insights into vocational interests and career direction. The assessment process may include formal or informal test results, observations or reports from parents or professionals, and/or student self-assessments. Typical tests or inventories would be measures of basic skills, achievement tests in subject areas, and inventories reporting general career interest areas. Social and emotional growth is not usually measured for the majority of students; however, students, like Carlos in the earlier case example, are referred to the school psychologist for evaluation because of possible problems.

Interpreting results to students, parents, teachers, and other appropriate staff is a part of assessment services—it may well be the most important one! The basis for test scores is not completely understood by most laypeople. School personnel need to explain the limitations and ramifications of test results so that students and their parents can utilize the results effectively. Assessment reports need to be jargon free and understood by those expected to offer support, such as teachers and parents. The changing demographics of the student population, particularly in urban areas, necessitates that the school psychologist have familiarity with nondiscriminatory assessment tools. Since few test instruments are culture free and nonlanguage specific, it requires continual education on the part of school psychologists regarding the interpretation of test results. This makes it even more important that a team approach to diagnostic work is used to enable the development of realistic and effective service plans.

Testing and assessment for disabilities—whether physical, academic, or social/emotional—are available only to those students who have been referred by teachers, parents, or other school personnel for evaluation. Various staff members are involved in this. School psychologists assess intelligence, academic potential, and emotional needs; counselors and/or teachers test for academic achievement and perhaps for social skills; and the school nurse (or a physician consultant) will test for physical or health problems. When additional services for the child or adolescent are being considered, it is important to hear from parents and, when feasible, from the students themselves.

If the test results demonstrate that the student has a special need, an individual treatment or educational program is required, spelling out in specific terms the services that the student will need. Programs are developed using the results of tests and other evaluations, parents' wishes, teachers and counselors or psychologists' recommendations, and, if appropriate, input from the student. An individualized education program (IEP) is developed by a team of people, including the special education teacher, the regular classroom teacher, the school counselor, and the social worker; the parents contribute their knowledge as well. The school psychologist and other involved professionals from outside the school (e.g., a physician) may be included in this planning. It is important that all assessment practices are aimed toward creating interventions that strengthen students' capabilities and build systems' abilities to improve education outcomes for all students (Ysseldyke, 2001).

Health Services.   The role of the nurse or other health professional in the school is varied. Some health professionals assist children who need medication or other medical procedures, such as changing bandages, monitoring catheters, or other health-related issues. In some schools, the regular sight and hearing evaluations are done by in-house staff.

Health services are important at all levels of schooling. There is an increase in the incidence of students diagnosed with attention deficit/hyperactivity disorder, and these students may require medication to help them keep their behavior under control (Hardman et al., 1999). Students need to have information regarding possible pregnancy, sexually transmitted diseases (especially AIDS), and child care. The school nurse is usually the person providing these services. The increase in substance abuse, violent behavior, and medically involved children in schools has led to an increased demand for health services. In both elementary and secondary schools, students may have classes on health or hygiene topics, which the nurse or other health professional teaches. School nurses are also available for consultation and help with health-related problems.

Services for Children with Disabilities.   Before discussing the services provided to students with disabilities, it is important to define what constitutes a disability. A *disability* refers to an inability to perform as other students do because of an impairment in sensory, physical, cognitive or other areas of functioning (Gargiulo, 2003). These disabilities are identified as mental retardation, learning disabilities, behavioral disorders, speech and/or language impairment, visual impairments, hearing impairments, physical disabilities, and health impairments. Historically, students who are considered gifted and talented have also been included due to the fact that they may also need modifications in their instruction to learn effectively.

Each of the types of issues just identified refers to students who have similar characteristics. It is important, however, not to overgeneralize about any disability or need. Each child should be considered an individual with unique characteristics and needs.

Special Education Legislation.   Special education services have become such an integral and accepted part of our educational systems that it is difficult to imagine that students with special needs might have ever been excluded from these services or from school. Prior to 1975, that was, in fact, the case. Many students with special needs were not identified. Many who were identified were excluded from school programs, especially those with significant disabilities. Public school programs for students with special needs were in separate classrooms, or, in many cases, separate buildings.

In 1975, federal law PL 94-142 was passed to ensure that free and appropriate educational services are provided to children with special needs. In 1990, PL 94-142 was amended by PL 101-476, which, among other things, changed the name of the legislation to the Individuals with Disabilities Education Act, or IDEA. Some of the guiding principles include the entitlement of all children to a free and appropriate education ("zero reject"), nondiscriminatory evaluation, the provision of an appropriate education in the least restrictive environment, parental participation, and the application of due process rights.

One of the major components of this federal legislation is the concept of the individualized educational program. The *IEP* is an educational document that outlines a description of the child's current level of performance, the specific special education and related services to be provided, and the child's annual goals and short-term objectives. It also delineates when services are to begin, how long they are expected to last, and how the school district will determine whether the goals and objectives are being achieved. As discussed earlier, the IEP is developed by an educational *team,* which is always comprised of the parents and educational personnel, including the general and special education teachers. It may also include specialists such as the school psychologist or speech therapist, depending on the student's disability and needs.

The Continuum of Services.   Once a child has been identified as having a special need, a range of services can be provided. These include regular education classes with consultation with special education personnel, separate special education classes that are utilized on a full- and part-time basis, special day and residential schools, and home and hospital instruction. Placement in any of these programs is the decision of the IEP team and is based on the unique learning needs of each student.

The 105th Congress passed a comprehensive revision (reauthorization) to IDEA in 1997. This restructuring of IDEA resulted in revised definitions and several key components, including funding, discipline, and student access to the general curriculum that must be reflected in the development of the IEP. At the present time, the groundwork for reform and reauthorization of IDEA is being laid. The House Education Reform Subcommittee intends to concentrate on accountability measures that mirror those envisioned by the "No Child Left Behind Act" in an effort to increase the effectiveness of the federal special education program.

A Team Approach: Parents and Professionals as Partners

In order to achieve the goals of academic, career, social, and emotional growth for all students, it is imperative for school personnel to work together, as well as with parents and the community. There is an increasing recognition of the need for a team approach to helping children and adolescents (Davis and Garrett, 1998; Murphy, DeEsch, and Strein, 1998; Poncec, Poggi, and Dickel, 1998; Dittmer, Dyck, and Thurston, 1993). The full-service community school approach articulated since the 1980s holds promise for the provision of better services at less cost, and now has a body of research to substantiate the premise (American Youth Policy Reform, 2001). This approach also has an after-school component that lends itself to offering support to children with social, emotional, and health needs, yet not taking these children away from instructional time (Dryfoos and Maguire, 2002).

Although they are not usually considered to be "personnel," parents play an important role in their child's education. Parents who support their child's efforts in school are helping to promote their child's social, emotional, and academic growth. Parents who are uninterested or inattentive to their child's schoolwork are communicating that neither an education nor the child is valued.

For a student to succeed in school, just as in daycare, it is imperative that parents and school personnel work together. If a child has a learning problem, strategies need to be developed that can be implemented at home and at school. If a child has met with great success on a project in school, recognition from parents and teachers should be provided (Powell and Graham, 1996).

Often, schools and parents may not be working in concert with each other. Through misconceptions or miscommunication, distrust may grow between parents and school staff (Turnbull et al., 1993). As an example, when a student who is truant is called into the office with his or her parent(s) to discuss the matter, the school may feel that the parents are in part to blame for their child's misbehavior. The assumption may be that the parent has not done an adequate job in disciplining the child. The parents may, perhaps because of their own negative experiences at school, be very reluctant to attend this meeting. They may feel they are to be blamed for their child's conduct or that the school personnel are not doing a sufficient job of making the school a welcoming place for their child. Many assumptions may be in place before the meeting begins, none of which may be accurate.

School personnel need to work to provide an environment that provides understanding and support for parents who may be facing many challenges in raising their children. A message must be sent from school to home that parents play an important role in the educational process and that they are valued members of the educational team. Teams are more effective when all members feel that their opinions and ideas are valued.

Controversial Issues and Dilemmas in the Provision of Services

A number of issues, arguments, and disagreements are reflected in the delivery of the services presented in this chapter. They relate to what the goals for children/students are and what services should therefore be provided, who provides which services, and what is the best way to provide them. There are also issues of cost and professional ethics, as well as a growing concern about school violence.

Daycare: The Dilemma of Quality versus Affordability. Is daycare an option or a right? As more programs are developed that see daycare for children as a vital service for parents and children of poor and disadvantaged families, and as the need for daycare nationally becomes greater, the dilemma of quality versus affordability becomes an issue. Quality, most experts agree, involves a safe, supportive environment that stimulates children appropriately and enhances their physical, emotional, social, and intellectual development (Scarr, 1998). Experts also postulate that the better-trained caregiver is equipped to be more appropriately sensitive and responsive. In addition, the lower the child/caregiver ratio, the more attention can be given to children. But trained caregivers and a low child-to-adult ratio require money. Better pay attracts more highly trained daycare providers, and the more staff, the greater expenditures on salaries will be necessary.

Scarr (1998) suggests that a two-tier system is developing: "A higher quality one for both affluent and the poor who get public support for child care, and a lower quality one for middle- and lower-income working families, who cannot pay for high-quality care" (105). Her suggestion is to institute more public support for child care so that quality services can be made available to any working family. Scarr and many other experts agree that maintaining quality daycare at affordable prices will greatly affect the future of our nation's children.

Who Provides Services in Schools and How Should They Be Provided?   With increasing specialization in the roles of teachers and counselors, it is sometimes difficult to determine who will provide services and where the services will be provided. Repeatedly stressed in this chapter has been the need to address students' academic, social, and emotional growth as the intertwined areas of development to be addressed by schools. One cannot easily separate one area from another. Teachers often find themselves in the role of counselor, and school counselors certainly provide instruction, often to full classes of students. For the child with serious emotional problems, should there be counseling in school, or would he or she best be served by a community agency? Who will assume the cost of services? How can all aspects of a child's services be integrated and coordinated? The challenge to provide services in a coordinated manner, meeting the needs of the child throughout the day, is and will continue to be a great challenge facing schools.

What Is the Ethical Responsibility of Professionals?   Ethics in professional practice is always an issue. We need to protect the interests of the child, including confidentiality. However, there are times when confidentiality is not in the best interest of the child or circumstances dictate that action must be taken. One example would be the child's disclosure that he or she threatened harm to self or others; professionals must inform appropriate others in such a case (Isaacs, 1997). Also, if a professional in the school suspects child abuse or neglect, he or she is legally mandated to report that suspicion to authorities. Professional organizations have codes of ethics that guide their respective disciplines. In addition, support services personnel have an ethical responsibility to be aware of relevant state and federal laws, as well as school district policies. There is sometimes a conflict as to the right to privileged communication. For example, a school counselor may hold state licensure as a psychologist. The license allows for privileged communication. However, in the school setting, the license is not required. Licensure as a school counselor does not provide the counselor with the right to privileged communication.

How Will Schools Deal with Violent Behavior of Students?   Children today live in a more complex and a more dangerous world than in the past. Students who act in unsafe ways (bringing weapons to school, causing harm to themselves or others, bringing drugs to school and/or selling drugs) challenge the educational system. Often, these are students who are victims of environmental or social problems they have encountered, or they may be suffering from serious mental illness. Although the rights of all students must be protected, these students are also in need of services. Schools and our society face a tremendous challenge in ensuring safe environments while meeting the needs of everyone in their community (Murphy, DeEsch, and Strein, 1998).

The rash of high-profile violence in our nation's schools has prompted educators to investigate a variety of new approaches to dealing with issues. School districts have implemented a number of protocols unheard of 10 years ago. Many districts combine these procedures in the form of a manual and conduct annual trainings on the contents. These manuals usually contain district and school crisis response plans, bomb threat evacuation procedures, 911 communication protocol, a hospital disaster plan, threat protocol (including assessment procedures), critical incident stress debriefing information, resource guide for coping with death in the school, resource directories of school administrators and community responders, child abuse and neglect policy and procedures, and emergency health issues. Although some student behavior necessitates "punishment" and court action, all such behavior brings with it the need for intervention strategies. The ideal is not to have to do either but to have in place prevention programs.

Student support personnel are in the forefront when dealing with potential/actual school violence, because they are the school personnel who have the greatest knowledge and skills to effectively deal with such behavioral issues. Even though this is the case, not all student support staff has the necessary training to become "debriefers" or assessors of the likelihood of a student to carry out a threat. Ongoing professional development is critical. Issues are raised regarding job function priorities, as this expanded area of need takes time. If we as a society are to effectuate a climate of peace, then prevention strategies must impact on all students. Successful research-based strategies already exist for replication.

Helping Mobile Students: Who Are They and Whose Job Is It to Respond to the Issue? We live in a mobile society. Families and children move their residences frequently as parents move up the career ladder. Educated parents prepare their children for such moves and have myriad safety nets in place to make the transition as smooth as possible with the least amount of social and emotional trauma for their children. This is clearly not the type of mobility that raises the issue for educators. The mobility that places students in jeopardy is one that most seriously impacts urban areas and occurs when poor families are dislocated for negative reasons. Because housing issues are so prevalent, it is critical that the public housing authority and department of human or social services work closely with the school to deal with this problem. Other community allies need to be juvenile justice authorities, homeless shelter staff, social service and mental health agencies, and child and adolescent recreational administrators. Each public and private institution needs to assess its own practices to determine if their procedures contribute to student mobility. They also need to implement actions that will help the student adjust to a new school. One urban school system went so far as having a social worker write, illustrate, and publish a book to help those students with their feelings about moving in the middle of the night with their belongings in trash bags (Belliveau, 1997).

Overidentification Issues and the Need for Change.   The Individuals with Disabilities Education Act mandates that all students with disabilities receive a free and appropriate public education in the least restrictive environment. Although successful in opening up educational opportunities for students with disabilities, this law has had an unintended negative impact as well (Horn & Tynan, 2001). The fact that the increases in need for special education has skyrocketed to 6.1 million students (up 65%) over the past 25 years is concerning. Of particular concern is the overrepresentation of minority students (specifically African American) in this student population (Hehir, 2002). In addition, there is evidence to suggest that African American students are inappropriately identified and often served in the most restrictive settings (Hehir, 2002). Several actions to address this issue include the strengthening of general education programs, strategies, and professional development initiatives; the examination of school climate issues; the augmentation of prereferral intervention processes in an effort to increase efficacy; the encouragement of active family involvement; full funding of IDEA; and increased district monitoring and support. The overrepresentation of minority students in special education is concerning on both legal and ethical levels. The need to ensure that only students who are justifiably in need of special education receive such services cannot be overstated.

Trends in the Provision of Educational Services

Delivery of Services within Daycare.   Daycare is a service that has no national standards, no observable leadership, and, consequently, no power at present to effect meaningful change. Although there is a delivery of service system that provides a wide range of care for many children, there is still no guarantee of care for all children. With all this in mind, children will hopefully be cared for by dedicated, if underpaid and underappreciated, providers.

As we look toward the continuation of the twenty-first century, several trends emerge. There will be a need for more centers to service the increasing numbers of childbearing women in the workplace. Public school systems will be compelled to become more involved in the provision of care for young children. Further, there may be an increase in multigenerational models, where elders and young children are served by the same facility while helping each other.

We have long recognized that the lack of national standards can actually put children at risk. It seems only a matter of time before the federal government will develop national guidelines for the provision of daycare services. Standardization may enable an increase in the quality of services in many centers and raise pay throughout the system, which may in turn attract better and more skilled staff.

Delivery of Services within the School.   For many reasons, schools are being asked to provide increased services for their students. Students who in the past may have been referred out for assessment, services, or their entire education are more likely today to be assessed, serviced, and educated in their local schools. This puts more burden on school staff, who must be prepared to help these students. Schools need to hire well-trained professionals and they need to provide in-service education for their present staffs. The pressure to provide more and more services comes largely from three sources: (1) the changing health care reimbursement system, (2) the financial crunch many schools are facing that forces them to find ways to avoid expensive contracted services, and (3) the increasingly complex and violent society that puts so many more pressures on students.

More Programs to Address Children "at Promise."   Some children live in homes where drug use, abuse, and emotional trauma take place on a daily basis. Oftentimes, children living in the poorer areas come to school lacking the nourishment to perform effectively. Schools are seeing their roles expanded beyond the classroom to provide programs to meet the physical and emotional needs of children (Keys, Bernak, and Lockhart, 1998). However, care must be taken, as research on resilient children indicates that there exist large individual differences among children exposed to risk and stress. These differences translate into the need for a broad range of intervention strategies to foster resiliency (Henderson and Milstein, 1996). Why "resiliency"? This question is akin to asking why "wellness" rather than "illness." *Resiliency* is the ability to bounce back from adversity. Research has proven that of the number of individuals who display so-called risk factors at birth, most become productive adults. Studying what makes the difference is a challenge to educators and mental health workers to focus on strengths rather than deficits and to build into programs and services the proven protective factors that build resiliency.

Health Care Issues.   What some call the "overmedication of our children" bring many students to school on some form of medication, whether for attention deficit/hyperactivity disorder (ADHD) or some other problem. For students who are taking medication, school staff must learn about the side effects and the appropriate responses to negative reactions. In many cases, effective classroom strategies are sufficient to address a behavioral problem (Hardman, Drew, and Egan, 1999).

Because of teenage pregnancy, schools have become the center for human sexuality education. Students are receiving more in-depth and, at times, controversial instruction on sexual development, contraception, and pregnancy care; condoms are being offered to students in some schools. Daycare for the children of teenage mothers is also offered as well as parenting programs for the young parents. AIDS education has become another major part of the school curriculum.

The proliferation of school-based health centers exacerbates these concerns as personnel provide physical and mental health services to students who do not report to the school administration. Medical codes of conduct may in fact clash with school policy on such issues as pregnancy testing, the reporting of minor-age girls who are pregnant under the child abuse mandate, distribution of birth control, parental notification, and so on. Further student support staff and agency staff may view each other as stepping into each other's turf and may question the credentials of each for the functions they perform. Bringing agencies together to support students and their families may be difficult, but it is not an insurmountable task. The clear delineation of roles and policies and procedures is a given, with the benefit to students making it worthwhile. Healthy children learn better! These issues bring new challenges to the role of schools and will continue to be subject of controversy.

Counseling and Guidance Emphasis on Developmental Issues.   The emphasis in comprehensive counseling and guidance programs today is a developmental one, based on such theorists as Erikson, Piaget, Kohlberg, Gilligan, Loevinger, Dupont, Hunt, and Selman (Borders and Drury, 1992; Paisley and Peace, 1995). Of 41 states that replied to a survey on the subject, 24 reported that they had developed models that reflected a developmental approach. These findings suggest that comprehensive counseling and guidance programs are gaining momentum (Sink and MacDonald, 1998). Counselors, or whoever is planning classroom activities, present students with information and challenges that relate to their developmental level. Guidance units for adolescents, for instance, might deal with identity issues; for older elementary students, one might plan programs that teach practical skills. The goal is to help students better understand what they are experiencing and to aid them in coping with the challenges that accompany growth.

> *Developmental school counseling programs are intentional, educational experiences specifically designed to encourage the development of more complex meaning-making structures. Outcomes associated with such movement would include more complex structures for processing experience and higher levels of cognitive, ethical, and interpersonal maturity. (Paisley and Peace, 1995, 92)*

The National Standards for School Counseling Programs (Campbell and Dahir, 1997) suggests standards for student development in three areas: academic, career, and personal/social. The *academic* goals relate to helping the student become a more effective learner. In *career development,* the goals include learning to relate personal skills and interests to the world of work. Counselors working in the *personal/social area* aid students in understanding and appreciating themselves and others, including families. Further, the counselors promote responsible citizenship and effective goal setting and decision making.

Planning for Diversity in the Student Body.   We are becoming more aware of how diverse our society really is, and how this diversity is likely to become more pronounced as we continue in the twenty-first century. Schools have had to deal with many issues related to the multiplicity of cultures from which their students come, often before state and federal funding sources have provided funds for programs to meet these needs. On the issue of language alone, there is an ongoing debate about the teaching of English as a second language or as the only language taught. We also have a long-standing and continuing debate on how best to deal with the issue of racism and ethnicity. We have seen evidence of how lack of sensitivity to race and gender lead to bias in teaching.

Including students with a variety of individual needs in the regular classroom is a relatively new model for meeting the needs of this population. We are currently trying to find ways to meet the needs of gay and lesbian youth, who suffer discrimination both in and outside the schools. School professionals need to learn skills to work effectively with a diverse and multicultural school population (Arrendondo, 1999).

It is also incumbent on school district administrators to recognize the importance of diverse role models for students and to hire staff with this in mind. A diverse student population needs a diverse school staff, as do their families. A by-product of such diversity also is that it assists in the breaking down of staff prejudices as they observe the professionalism of their peers. The richness of the cultures creates a daily learning experience for adults as well as for students. It is also critical that support staff reflect the student diversity. Perhaps more than their fellow educators, support staff has the most contact with families. It is understandable that the comfort level increases when parents are able to speak with someone who knows their first language and culture.

Toward More Inclusive Programs.   More and more, schools are considering ways that they can serve all children in the regular classroom. This philosophy is being advanced through legislation at the state and national levels and litigation, with several cases being won in the courts, that will allow students with disabilities to participate fully in the regular classroom with support. At issue is the amount of support (which can be costly) school systems must provide before placing a child in a separate classroom. A concern for some is the appropriateness of the curriculum in the regular classroom for students with disabilities. Proponents of inclusion suggest that curriculum modifications can be made and that the most important lifelong benefit is that the student with a disability has membership in the community of the school and thus has a sense of belonging.

Accountability.   A major trend in national and state policies over the past few years has been toward student achievement and school district accountability. This includes the testing of children and of teachers, and the necessity for proving success in support services as well as in teaching. School personnel are increasing their efforts in research to demonstrate approaches that are effective. A review of research in school counseling, for instance, has shown tentative support for career planning, group counseling, social skill training activities, and peer counseling (Whiston and Sexton, 1998). Since academic achievement is a major goal for support services, it is important to measure the academic results of various interventions. There is much work to be done in the area of accountability, and school personnel need to learn techniques for evaluating their work (Scruggs, Wasielewski, and Ash, 1999; Granello and Granello, 1998; Gillies, 1993).

Summary

The need for daycare is growing in our society. The number of working mothers, whether in two- or one-parent families, the growing need for placements for abused or neglected children, and the need for respite care for parents raising a child with disabilities—all are putting a burden on the existing daycare services. Although there are a number of different models available, there is a national need for more and better services.

Schools face many challenges in meeting the needs of a diverse student population. Societal problems place pressures on students that were not experienced by previous generations. Student safety is a major concern. Programs beyond the actual teaching of basic subjects are necessary to enable students to build resiliency and to become full members of society. To achieve this goal, an array of programs and interventions must be available to impact the total child and family. To accomplish this task, the resources of the school and community must be joined in partnership with the child and family in a respectful collaboration for success and in a concerted effort to make certain that "no child will be left behind."

EXPLORATION QUESTIONS

1. Everyone talks about quality daycare. What are the critical components of *quality*?
2. Compare and contrast the delivery of service components in daycare. Why do we need so many types of care?
3. What are your state standards for professional daycare? Do you feel that they protect the best interest of children and families? If so, how? If not, why?
4. How has the role of schools changed in recent years?
5. How have the laws changed in the last 20 years to provide more appropriate education for students with disabilities?
6. What does *inclusion* mean? What ramifications does it have for teachers? For students with and without special needs?
7. What is the recent trend in school guidance programs and what are the implications of this trend?
8. What should professionals be doing to address violence in the schools?
9. Describe the roles of the various personnel in schools.
10. In what ways do counseling services and special education services overlap?

REFERENCES

American Youth Policy Reform (2001). *Is the Concept of Full-Service Community Schools Ready for the Federal Support Question?* http://www.aypf.org/formbrief2001/fb030901/html.

Arredondo, P. (1999). "Multicultural Counseling Competencies as Tools to Address Oppression and Racism," *Journal of Counseling & Development, 77,* 102–108.

Belliveau, H. (1997). *Mikey's World.* Worcester Public Schools, Worcester, MA.

Borders, L., & Drury, S. (1992). "Comprehensive School Counseling Program: A Review for Policy Makers and Practitioners," *The Journal of Counseling and Development, 70,* 487–498.

Campbell, C., & Dahir, C. (1997). *The National Standards for School Counseling Programs.* Alexandria, VA: American School Counselor Association.

Cormany, R. B. (1999). *Administering Pupil Services in the Third Millennium.* Boston: National Association of Pupil Services Administrators.

Cromwell, E. S. (1994). *Quality Child Care.* Boston: Allyn and Bacon.

Davis, K. & Garrett, M. (1998). "Bridging the Gap between School Counselors and Teachers: A Proactive Approach," *Professional School Counseling, 1*(5), 54–55.

Dittmer, Dyck, & Thurston, L. P. (1993). *Consultation, Collaboration and Teamwork for Students with Special Needs.* Boston: Allyn and Bacon

Dryfoos, J. G., & Maguire, S. (2002). *Inside Full Service Community Schools.* Thousand Oaks, CA: Corwin Press.

Education for All Handicapped Children Act (EHA). (1975). 20 U.S.C. sections 1400 et seq. and amendments.

Galen, M. (1995). "Honey, We're Cheating the Kids," *Business Week,* 38.

Gargiulo, R. (2003). *Special Education in Contemporary Society: An Introduction to Exceptionality.* Belmont, CA: Wadsworth/Thomson Learning.

Gillies, R. (1993). "Action Research in School Counseling," *The School Counselor, 41,* 69–72.

Granello, P., & Granello, D. (1998). "Training Counseling Students to Use Outcome Research," *Counselor Education and Supervision, 37,* 224–237.

Hardman, M. L., Drew, C. J., & Egan, M. W. (1999). *Human Exceptionality: Society, School, and Family* (6th ed.). Boston: Allyn and Bacon.

Hehir, T. (2002). "Over-identification Issues within IDEA and the Need for Reform," *Urban Perspectives, 7*(1), 2–14.

Henderson, N., & Milstein, M. (1996). *Resiliency in Schools.* Thousand Oaks, CA: Corwin Press.

Hickok, E. W. (2002). *Testimony Before Congress on Implementation of No Child Left Behind Act.* Retrieved June 24, 2002, from White House website: http://www.ed.gov/PressReleases/04-2002/04232002.html.

Hofferth, S. (1996). "Child Care in the United States Today," *The Future of Children, 6*(2), 41–61.

Horn, W., & Tynan, D. (2001). "Revamping Special Education," *The Public Interest, 7,* 36–53.

Is the Concept of Full Service Community Schools Ready for Federal Support? Retrieved June 16, 2002, from American Youth Policy Forum website: http://www.aypf.org/forumbriefs/2001/fb030901.html.

Isaacs, M. (1997). "The Duty to Warn and Protect: Tarasoff and the Elementary School Counselor," *Elementary School Guidance & Counseling, 31,* 326–342.

Keys, S., Bernak, F., & Lockhart, E. (1998). "Transforming School Counseling to Serve the Mental Health Needs of At-Risk Youth," *Journal of Counseling & Development, 76,* 381–388.

Lawrence, G. (1996). *People Types and Tiger Stripes.* Gainesville, FL: Center for Applications of Psychological Type.

Lillard, P. P. (1996). *Montessori Today.* New York: Schocken Books.

McWhirter, J. J., McWhirter, B. T., McWhirter, A. M., & McWhirter, E. H. (1998). *At-Risk Youth: A Comprehensive Response.* Pacific Grove, CA: Brooks/Cole.

Murphy, J., DeEsch, J., & Strein, W. (1998). "School Counselors and School Psychologist: Partners in Student Services," *Professional School Counseling, 2*(2), 85–87.

Neugebauer, R. (1995). *Cost and Quality Study Findings Unveiled.* Redmond, WA: Child Care Information Exchange.

Paisley, P., & Borders, L. (1995). "School Counseling: An Evolving Specialty," *Journal of Counseling and Development, 74,* 150–153.

Paisley, P., & Peace, S. (1995). "Development Principles: A Framework for School Guidance Programs," *Elementary School Counselor,* 85–93.

Poncec, D., Poggi, J., & Dickel, C. (1998). "Unity: Developing Relationships between School and Community Counselors," *Professional School Counseling, 2*(2), 95–102.

Powell, T. H., & Graham, P. L. (1996). *Parent-Professional Participation in Improving the Implementation of the Individual with Disabilities Education Act: Making Schools Work for All of America's Children* (Suppl., 603–628). Washington, DC: National Council on Disability.

Reeves, D. L. (1992). *Child Care Handbook: A Reference Handbook.* Santa Barbara, CA: ABC-CLIO.

Role of the Professional School Counselor, The. Retrieved June 16, 2002, from American School Counselor Association website: http://www.schoolcounselor.org/content.cfm.

Scarr, S. (1998). "American Child Care Today," *American Psychologist, 53*(2), 95–108.

School-Based Health Centers Continue Strong Expansion Across the U.S. National Survey Finds. Retrieved June 16, 2002, from George Washington University, Center for Health and Health Care in Schools website: http://www.healthinschools.org/press/PR00002.asp.

School Social Work Association of America. (n.d.). Retrieved June 16, 2002, from http://sswa.org/about.html.

Scruggs, M., Wasielewski, R., & Ash, M. (1999). "Comprehensive Evaluation of a K–12 Counseling Program," *Professional School Counseling, 2*(3), 244–247.

Siegel, L. J., & Senna, J. J. (2000). *Juvenile Delinquency.* Belmont, CA: Wadsworth.

Sink, C., & MacDonald, G. (1998). "The Status of Comprehensive Guidance and Counseling in the United States," *Professional School Counseling, 2*(2), 88–94.

Smith, C., & Maurer, F. (1995). *Community Health Nursing: Theory and Practice.* Philadelphia: Saunders.

Staley, W., & Carey, A. (1997). "The Role of School Counselors in Facilitating a Quality Twenty-First Century Workforce," *The School Counselor, 44,* 377–383.

Starr, M. F., & Gyspers, N. C. (1997). *Missouri Comprehensive Guidance: A Model for Program Development, Implementation and Evaluation.* Jefferson City, MO: Missouri Department of Elementary and Secondary Education.

Turnbull, A., Patterson, J., Behr, S., Murphy, D., Marguis, D., & Blue-Banning, M. (1993). *Cognitive Coping, Families and Disability.* Baltimore, MD: Brookes.

Turnbull, A., & Turnbull, R. (1990). *Families, Professionals and Partnerships.* Columbus, OH: Merrill.

United States Department of Education. (1997). "To Assure the Free and Appropriate Education of All Children with Disabilities," *19th Annual Report to Congress on the Implementation of the Education for All Handicapped Children Act.* Washington, DC: U.S. Government Printing Office.

Wasik, B. H. (1998). "Implications for Child Abuse and Neglect Interventions" (519–541). In J. R. Lutzker et al. (Eds.), *Handbook of Child Abuse and Research Treatment.* New York: Plenum.

West, J., & Idol, L. (1993). "The Counselor as Consultant in the Collaborative School, *Journal of Counseling and Development, 71,* 678–683.

Whiston, S., & Sexton, T. (1998). "A Review of School Counseling Outcome Research: Implications for Practice," *Journal of Counseling and Development, 76,* 412–426.

Ysseldyke, J. (2001). "Reflections on a Research Career: Generalizations for 25 Years of Research on Assessment and Instructional Decision Making." *Exceptional Children, 67*(3), 295–309.

6 Counseling for Families and Children

LLOYD T. WILLIAMS

Counseling is certainly inherent in all types of child welfare services, such as foster care, adoption, or protective services. Sometimes, however, as a part of coping with specific issues, families or children are referred to agencies whose primary service is that of counseling. These agencies might be family service centers, child guidance clinics, mental health centers, or even private therapists, such as psychiatric social workers, psychologists, mental health counselors, psychologists, or others trained in the field. This chapter addresses counseling as a specific psychotherapeutic service and how families are served by this service.

What Is Counseling?

Counseling is a process of interaction between human beings, the goal of which is to improve the quality of life for those being counseled. Counselors act on behalf of their clients in such a way as to facilitate adjustment to self-discovery, healing, and positive change. Since all human beings, including those in the counseling professions, struggle throughout their lives with personal problems, emotional wounds, nagging anxieties, and self-limiting fears, it is important to understand that counseling is a contractual process. It is an agreement between people that, in a designated place at a designated time, certain roles will be assumed.

The role of counselor is taken on by a person who, for the duration of each counseling session, puts aside his or her own life challenges, and attends to the needs of others. The role of the people being counseled is assumed by those who, for the duration of each session, put aside the ways in which their lives are successful and satisfying to look instead at aspects of life that are painful or disappointing. Ideally, in the process of taking up these roles, both counselor and counseled deepen their experience of life.

Basic Assumptions

At the core of the counseling professions, certain basic assumptions are operative:

1. Human beings, by nature, strive toward wholeness. This striving occurs across every level: physically, mentally, emotionally, and spiritually. By "wholeness" is meant more than problem-free happiness. Wholeness implies an integrity of being that embraces fragmentation, tension, and conflict as ingredients crucial to the process of growth and the enjoyment of life.

2. Central to psychological health and well-being is the ability to make meaning out of one's life experience.

3. In the search for wholeness and meaning, people create or encounter obstacles in their path. These obstacles can be external or internal.

External obstacles include people, things, situations, or events that act on us, or appear to act on us, from outside ourselves. For example, a child, adolescent, or adult may be substantially set back in his or her development by injuries sustained in an automobile accident. A person's goals may be thwarted in some significant way by the deliberate interference of other people with opposing values. Illness may strike at an inopportune time. Or perhaps one's efforts in a particular endeavor do not get the hoped-for results because a family crisis occurs at a critical moment. Whatever the particular circumstances, external factors seem to play a deciding role.

Internal obstacles include conflicts and complexes, fears, inhibitions, hang-ups, limiting belief systems, and maladaptive thought and behavior patterns. Ultimately, these obstacles are often much more difficult to come to terms with precisely because they operate within us and tend to be rooted in formative childhood experiences.

4. Finally, in almost every model of counseling it is assumed that change is possible. Human beings can learn to think, feel, and behave in different ways. The birth that brings us into this world and the death that ultimately leads us out of it are mirrored throughout life in real and equally profound experiences of death and rebirth wherein old ways of being are left behind, making way for the unfolding of new possibilities.

When a Family Might Seek Counseling

Referral System

Families generally come to a counseling agency either by way of a self-referral or via a referral made by an outside agent. Self-referred families recognize that a problem exists that needs attention and that is more than the family can cope with on its own. Such circumstances include difficulties that continue to cause distress despite the family's attempts to respond to them, as well as crisis situations that occur without warning and overwhelm family resources. Some families familiar with counseling, who have had successful past counseling experiences, also seek counseling services as a preventive measure, hoping thereby to address problems in their early stages, before things become more serious.

Examples of problems for which a family might refer itself for counseling cover the gamut of possible difficulties: A child or teenager may be noticeably depressed, without meaningful friendships, performing poorly in school, or have recurring thoughts of suicide. A mother or father may struggle with depression, with adverse consequences for the children. A family member may suffer with a serious mental or physical illness, with stressful repercussions for the rest of the family. A trauma may have occurred, such as a rape, murder, automobile accident, sexual molestation, or incident of domestic violence, leaving the family devastated and needing support and assistance.

Family dynamics such as marital strife often create ongoing tensions within the home, with children acting out the conflict in negative ways. Divorce issues can throw a family into crisis, creating a situation that calls for containment and direction. Stepfamily issues are another stumbling block for many families: Children frequently resent the intrusion of a "stranger" into their lives when their divorced mother or father remarries. If the new partner has children of her or his own, the picture is further complicated and stress may intensify. Substance abuse is a common focus for counseling services also, a parent's or a child's drug or alcohol use often causing considerable disruption and/or dysfunction within the family.

For children and adolescents, behavior problems often motivate a family to seek outside intervention. Temper tantrums, oppositional and defiant behaviors at home or at school, hyperactivity, aggressive interactions with peers, and general disregard for family and/or community rules and expectations are among the many concerns presented by parents during an initial counseling session. For younger children, separation anxiety (excessive distress whenever out of sight of primary parenting figures), prolonged toilet training problems, inability to relate positively with other children, unexplained obsessions and/ or compulsions, aggressive or cruel behavior toward animals, prolonged thumb-sucking, excessive whining or clinging behaviors, as well as various developmental delays or complications are also regularly brought to counseling professionals as areas calling for assistance.

These listed examples by no means exhaust the many reasons families choose to refer themselves for counseling. Indeed, the important point is to underscore the enormous variety of situations for which counseling may offer families a means of support during difficult times. It should also be noted that counseling services can be employed by families to provide family members with a vehicle for self-exploration, to support them through demanding developmental phases, such as adolescence or midlife, or simply to assist them in the ongoing process of learning about themselves and making sense of their lives.

Referrals by Outside Agencies.   For many families, counseling services are arranged as a result of pressures or recommendations coming from outside the family circle. Families unable or unwilling to respond to the needs of a troubled child or adolescent often find themselves contacted by school personnel, police officers, or other local authorities about their youngster's behavior. In the case of child neglect or abuse, child protection organizations are empowered by the state to mandate counseling for families as part of comprehensive service plans implemented to protect victimized children or children at risk (Crosson-Tower, 2002). For delinquent youths, the juvenile court system frequently recommends or orders counseling as a condition for avoiding more serious legal consequences, especially in the case of first-time minor offenders.

Families coming to counseling agencies via outside referrals frequently present exactly the same kind of core issues as do self-referred families, but problems have often reached a more critical stage, involve a more serious degree of intensity, have led to legal proceedings, and/or have come to the attention of child protective service agencies. Examples might include the following situations:

1. A teenage boy and his family are referred to counseling by the juvenile court following an incident at school in which the boy pulled a knife on another student.

2. A family is referred to counseling by the treatment team of a hospital mental health unit following a suicide attempt by an adolescent girl. The father and his long-term girlfriend have made plans to marry and they fear that this may have contributed to the daughter's attempt.

3. A 6-year-old child is in temporary foster care because of substantiated physical abuse charges against her father. The parents are required to begin family counseling as a condition for having their child returned to their home.

4. Repeated school suspensions for aggressive behavior, chronic truancy, and recent threats made to peers about gang retaliation result in a family meeting arranged at school. At this meeting, school personnel make it clear to the parent(s) that if their 13-year-old son's behavior does not improve immediately, placement in a more restrictive educational setting will be recommended. The parents are referred to a local counseling center to get help for the boy.

5. Teachers discover marijuana in the desk of an 11-year-old girl. Inquiry results in the child's disclosure that her mother and her mother's "boyfriend" frequently allow her to smoke pot with them. The disclosure is reported to the local authorities. An investigation is conducted, and the family is referred for counseling as part of a service plan put into place to protect the child.

The specific circumstances that compel a person, agency, or social institution to recommend, pressure, or require a family to seek counseling services are virtually infinite in variety. The important point is that many families find themselves in counseling, at least initially, not because they recognized a situation needing attention, but because someone outside the family recognized it for them.

Attitudes about Receiving Counseling

Self-Referred Clients

Families who take it upon themselves to seek out services in response to recognized needs tend to approach counseling with positive expectations, or at least with an open mind toward the possibility of change. The fact that a problem or area of distress motivates a family to self-refer implies that at least some degree of denial has already been worked through. A certain readiness exists to look the problem in the eye and to grapple with it. The counselor is viewed as someone who has the training and experience to be of assistance to the family, someone with whom the family can cooperate for its own benefit.

Clients Referred from Outside Agencies

For children and parents directed to counseling services by outside agencies, attitudes toward counseling run the range from cooperative and appreciative to cautious and suspicious, to resentful, resistant, and even hostile. Although it is risky to make generalizations, it is safe to say that children and/or families *mandated* to go to counseling by outside sources often adopt a defensive attitude, at least initially.

CASE EXAMPLE

The Baxter Family

The Baxter family was referred to counseling by a child protective service agency as a prerequisite for being reunited with their 13-year-old daughter, Tonya, following eight months of placement in a foster home. Tonya had been removed from her parents' home after a school gym teacher noticed and reported bruises on her back and legs. An investigation uncovered a history of physical beatings given to Tonya by her father whenever she disobeyed family rules. Tonya and her mother showed up at the first meeting, explaining to the counselor that Mr. Baxter refused to come with them because, in his words, "I don't need people sticking their noses into my personal business." When, several meetings later, the father succumbed to pressure and attended his first session, he told the counselor, "If you think you're going to tell me not to hit my kids when they have it coming, I'll tell you right now this whole therapy thing isn't going to go too far."

The defense mechanism of "denial" is often operative for families brought to counseling via outside referring agents. If a family is not actively seeking help for itself or one of its members in response to a recognized need, it frequently means the need itself, or the severity of it, is being denied. In essence, the family chooses "ignorance" as a way of coping. When outside interests pressure the family to confront a problem, a degree of resistance is expectable.

Attitudes about Having a Problem

Most families bring to counseling a degree of anxiety about having a problem in the first place, and especially about giving an outsider (the counselor) detailed information about personal issues. Particularly for first-time consumers, but for people with previous experience in counseling as well, the idea of talking to a therapist produces anxiety because it implies vulnerability and exposure. The tender, not-so-successful areas of life may be revealed. A tremendous pressure exists in Western industrialized society to present oneself to the outside world in as positive a light as possible, as successful, happy, healthy, autonomous human beings in control of life. Conflicts, inhibitions, hang-ups, fears, insecurities, traumas, habits, addictions, pain, weakness, mistakes, failures, dysfunction, and so on, are viewed as undesirable. Instead of being valued as potential and powerful teachers, such "shadow" areas of life are seen as shameful (Cederstrom, 2002). To let down the mask that is presented outwardly so that the inner, more private world can be explored raises anxiety and directly influences the attitude families have about seeing a counselor.

"Therapy Is for Crazy People."   The still common opinion that therapy is for "crazy" people inhibits many from considering counseling as a possible means of assistance during times of crisis or enduring family distress. Again, the stigma related to getting help in this particular form reflects the pervasive idea that having problems is not acceptable. In a society that places supreme value on productivity and autonomy, not being able to produce solutions to problems without outside help places one in the same camp as "crazy" people because it implies breakdown and dependence.

CASE EXAMPLE

Henderson and Son

Mr. Henderson scheduled three intake appointments for his 8-year-old son, Michael, at a local youth guidance center. Each appointment came and went, with Mr. Henderson and his son failing to show up at the designated hour. Follow-up calls made by the counselor to the home resulted in explanations about transportation problems, scheduling conflicts, illness, and other extenuating circumstances. After the third "no-show," Mr. Henderson called to ask if the counselor could come to his home for the meetings. After careful questioning, the counselor learned that Mr. Henderson was troubled by the fact that the guidance center was located on the same grounds as the local state hospital. "We're not crazy," he told the counselor. "We're just looking for some help with a normal problem."

"What Will the Neighbors Think?"   Preoccupation with the opinions of others is, for some populations, an anxiety related to counseling. It is somehow assumed (usually erroneously) that the neighbors (whether these be literally neighbors or "other people" in general) have no problems and that therefore one's own difficulties make one less by comparison. Being less in the eyes of others is a matter of shame for many families because it leads to a perceived diminishment of self.

CASE EXAMPLE

Location Can Be Everything

Evan Johnston, Ph.D., opened a private practice for counseling in a small quiet town in Connecticut. In spite of extensive outreach to the community, Dr. Johnston's services were used by very few people in the area. Commenting on this disappointing situation to a friend one day, Dr.

Johnston was told, "Evan, the reason you're not getting business is that your office is right in the downtown area. Everybody knows everybody in this town, and no one wants to be seen turning into your driveway, with that big sign in front telling the whole world that it's a Family Counseling Center." When Dr. Johnston later moved his office to a less public location in the same community, with no sign publicizing the type of services offered, business developed steadily.

"It's His (or Her) Problem, Not Mine."   An attitude frequently observed in family therapy is the stance that "it's *his* (or *her*) problem, not mine." The so-called identified patient (e.g., an acting-out son or daughter) is the problem and the rest of the family is fine. Parents can sometimes be stubbornly insistent that they have nothing to do with a child's distress. A defensive attitude is presented, nourished by a fear that blame may be attributed to the parents. Fear of blame has to be defended against only to the degree that parents believe it is not OK for them to be less than perfect.

"We Have a Problem, You Fix It."   Some parents come to counseling with the attitude, "Here is the problem; now you fix it." This attitude provides adult caregivers with a measure of distance from the discomfort they feel about having a child who is experiencing problems. If the child can be dropped off at the therapist's office to be fixed, parents can more easily maintain the fantasy that they are not responsible for their children's circumstances. When a car breaks down, it is taken to a garage, left for a period of time in a professional's skillful hands, and repaired. Parents with child-related problems often act as if they wish their difficulties could similarly be given over to someone else's skillful expertise to be resolved.

CASE EXAMPLE

But It's Jacob's Problem!

Jacob's mother brought her 14-year-old son to counseling because he was depressed, failing school, and giving her a hard time at home. After three sessions talking with Jacob, it became clear to the counselor that the boy received limited structure, encouragement, or direction at home from either his mother or his stepfather, and that the parents had significant problems of their own that were affecting Jacob negatively. With Jacob's permission, the counselor called his mother and suggested that the next several meetings include her and Jacob's stepfather. The mother agreed, but proceeded to miss every meeting subsequently scheduled. Sending Jake to counseling by himself was never a problem. Involving herself was obviously too threatening, because it implied that she might have something to do with the difficulties Jacob was experiencing.

To approach a child's unhappiness responsibly means parents must be open to the possibility that they play a part in that unhappiness. It requires parents to cut through their own denial, to look at ways in which they might be contributing to their child's distress, and to accept the fact that time, effort, and a willingness to change themselves may be required if difficulties are to be overcome.

Ethnic and Cross-Cultural Considerations

Cross-cultural counseling with children and families—that is, counseling situations where one or more members of the family hold strongly to cultural values and traditions significantly different from those held by the counselor—present unique challenges to the counseling process. Working with an ethnically diverse clientele requires a counselor to be sensitive to cultural differences, respectful of unfamiliar customs, and open to perspectives of life quite different from his or her own. Beyond sensitivity and open-mindedness, active study and comprehensive knowledge of different cultures, together with specialized skills in counseling, are demanded of counselors who are engaged primarily in cross-cultural work (Wilson and Stith, 1998; Poterotto et al., 2001).

Attitudes toward counseling vary notably between ethnic groups, with strong beliefs and subtle differences in values complicating and coloring each individual case. Although the subject of cross-cultural counseling is a vast and complex topic that can only be briefly mentioned in the present context, it is hoped that some examples may serve to give the student an appreciation for the many kinds of issues involved.

CASE EXAMPLES

The Dega Family

The Dega family, of Jamaican origin, was referred to counseling by a state child protection agency following the placement of the family's 16-year-old son, Matthew, in a foster home due to substantiated physical abuse. Mr. and Mrs. Dega came to the first meeting furious, humiliated, and determined to make it quite clear to the counselor that they resented the intrusion of outsiders into their private affairs. As counseling proceeded, the counselor learned that, in Jamaica, families settle their problems internally, without professional intervention. Such intervention is felt to be invasive, offensive, and unnecessary. In addition, the parents and grandmother of the family were outraged that a practice of child discipline common and accepted in their native country was viewed as "abusive" in the United States.

The Yamiko Family

The Yamiko family came to counseling for help with problems centering on the defiant behavior of teenaged children. Mr. and Mrs. Yamiko held to traditional Japanese values in which the authority of parents was never openly challenged by the children. The adolescents in the family (James, David, and Irene), raised in the United States since early childhood, were rebellious, directly confrontational, and angry that their parents did not understand their need for independence, self-expression, and peer acceptance. The parents looked to the counselor for back-up, fully expecting that their values would be reinforced during counseling sessions.

These two examples present situations occurring in the United States in which therapists with North American values work with families from other cultures. It should be recognized, however, that *cross-cultural counseling* "refers to any counseling relationship in which two or more of the participants are culturally different" (Atkinson, 2002). The same kind of issues that must be attended to when a white counselor from the United States works with an African family from Nigeria are present and in need of sensitivity when an African, Puerto Rican, Japanese, or Haitian counselor works with an American family from Boston. (Very similar kinds of concerns are involved when a hearing counselor works with a family that has deaf family members, when a gay or lesbian counselor works with a family valuing a heterosexual lifestyle, or when a counselor from the Jewish faith works with a Catholic family.) In all cases, respect for difference (in attitude, orientation, belief system, and behavior) must underpin the counseling endeavor if effective work is to be accomplished.

Changing Attitudes about Counseling

Beginning in the late 1960s and gaining increased momentum throughout the 1970s, a notable development could be observed in the United States relative to the mainstream public's attitude toward psychotherapy. Among other factors, the influence of mind-altering drugs, the political unrest of the times, and the impact of the Vietnam War turned the attention of individuals, and the nation, inward. Self-reflection and self-exploration became primary interests. An entire generation of concerned and thoughtful individuals began delving into the workings of the human mind, with an emphasis on personal development, and psychological and spiritual growth. The stigma of psychotherapy, which once caused people to be ashamed to see a therapist, began to shift toward an appreciation of "inner work" as a vehicle for positive change, a pathway to self-knowledge, a catalyst for the realization of human potential.

In the 1980s and 1990s, emphasis on individual self-exploration in psychotherapy was challenged on the grounds that preoccupation with strictly personal growth, unbalanced by equal time and effort given to local and global needs, contributes to the birth, intensification, and tenacity of problems on the collective level. As an increasingly connected and globally more sophisticated world community progresses through the new millennium, changing attitudes toward counseling will no doubt continue to reflect the complex dynamics of internal and external developments on the micro- and macrolevels.

Medical Model versus Holistic Model

As increasing numbers of individuals from mainstream society began to value psychotherapeutic and counseling services as valid means for personal growth, the traditional medical model of mental health also began to evolve. The old hierarchy of "helpless sick patient" treated by "powerful healthy doctor" could not maintain itself in the face of an expanding consciousness about the nature of health in general. "Health" came to be understood as operating along a continuum, the positive end of which moved into the arena of human potential and knew no limits. The traditional medical view of mental health as a condition free of categorized psychological symptoms was supplemented by a more holistic understanding of health that began to challenge the equation "symptomless = healthy" (Shannon, 2002).

The holistic model opened up the entire investigation of mind/body integrity, and posed the questions, "Are symptoms necessarily bad? Could symptoms be seen as communications, as motivators for change, lessons, or as flags for conditions needing attention below the level of manifest sign? Could symptoms sometimes simply be part of an individual's life, adding color and hue, individuality and peculiarity to one's experience?"

Emphasis on the "whole person" has led to careful consideration of such factors as the quality and depth of a person's relationships with others, the extent to which one's creativity is free to express itself, the effectiveness of one's communications, the degree of meaningfulness that operates in one's life, one's relationship to death, and to such concepts as God, spirituality, joy, purpose, and so on. Whereas the medical model tended to view human beings primarily in terms of pathologies to be cured, the holistic model called attention to human beings as evolving selves challenged by life and life's circumstances to stretch themselves toward ever more expansive ways of being. From this perspective, the doctor/patient relationship becomes more a matter of role rather than a statement about relative health. Even when a clear and marked discrepancy exists between level of functioning of doctor and patient, the holistic view understands that both are engaged by life with possibilities for becoming increasingly whole, however differently that wholeness may express itself (Cassidy, 1994; Dossey, 1994; LeShan, 1992).

The Impact of Feminism

A growing and significant movement within the field of psychology calls attention to issues of gender, questioning assumptions and core beliefs about human nature that have historically been proposed and developed predominantly by male thinkers. The supremacy of traditional masculine values—such as autonomy, detachment, productivity, and rationality—is now being challenged by feminist theorists who wish to achieve a more balanced understanding by emphasizing the importance of relatedness, involvement, stillness, and feeling (Gilligan, 1993).

As the impact of such thinking permeates the culture, changes can be observed in prevailing attitudes toward counseling. Increasingly, men come to counseling actively seeking to better understand problems of intimacy and relationship in their lives. The ability to adequately express feelings and to communicate on deep levels is also a more commonly heard goal. Counseling itself, as a context for openly and directly expressing one's inner thoughts and feelings, is arguably less threatening today for men than it was 40 years ago, due in large part to the contributions of feminist thought (Zastrow, 2000).

As feminist concepts and analyses continue to be developed and refined, and as men specifically and the culture in general absorb and respond to these new understandings, it is likely that the counseling professions will continue to see a gradual evolution in consciousness on the part of men and women, boys and girls, and adolescent youths. That this evolution has already begun is affirmed by the notable changes observable in societal attitudes toward rape, domestic violence and battering, incest, workaholism, child support, fathering, sexual orientation, gender roles, and intimacy.

Types of Counseling

The Professions

Psychiatry.   Psychiatrists are medical doctors who specialize in treating pathologies of the mind and emotions. Training requirements include medical school, residency in psychiatric medicine, and licensure by the medical community. Psychiatrists are the only counseling professionals who can legally prescribe psychotropic medications (i.e., medications that act on mental processes) for their patients. Although there is an enormous variety in the actual work that psychiatrists do—including in-depth short- and long-term psychotherapy/counseling with individuals, couples, families, and groups—a significant number of psychiatrists work in their practices primarily to prescribe and monitor the effect of psychotropic drugs. Due to the length, demand, and cost of their training, psychiatrists are generally the highest-paid workers within the counseling field.

Psychology.   Training to be a clinical psychologist includes graduate study for a master's and doctorate degree in psychology, clinically supervised internship, and licensure by the American Psychological Association. Psychologists receive extensive training in administering, scoring, and interpreting the full battery of recognized psychological tests. Because these tests are often requested by schools, courts, hospitals, clinics, and other institutions, some psychologists are able to make testing the core practice of their careers. Most psychologists do a combination of testing and psychotherapy (counseling) with clients, but some prefer to concentrate on the counseling aspect of treatment, and opt for doing as little testing as possible. Like psychiatry, there is a great variety in the work that psychologists can do, the areas of expertise they can specialize in, and the settings in which they can practice.

Social Work.   Training in clinical social work includes two years of graduate study toward the completion of an MSW (Master of Social Work) degree. Graduate study requires both classroom work and field placement internship for on-the-job experience. Licensure for social work involves two years of full-time postgraduate employment under the direct supervision of a licensed social worker, and the passing of a nationally standardized board examination. Although psychiatric training includes a focus on medication, and psychologists are trained to do testing, clinical social work training places an emphasis on understanding the psychological/emotional struggle of individuals and groups within the context of the greater social environment. As with the other two professions, social work is a versatile field, offering a wide variety of opportunities for employment, including private practice.

Mental Health Counseling.   To work professionally as a mental health counselor, graduate study is required for a master's degree in counseling. In addition, a documented two-year period of full-time clinically supervised postgraduate work experience is required as a prerequisite for taking the certification examination. In most states, master's-level mental health counselors are not permitted to take third-party reimbursement for services rendered. This means they can work in certain clinical settings, but cannot do private practice.

Art Therapy.   To work as a certified art therapist, a person must complete a master's-level degree in art therapy and an internship in a recognized and approved clinical setting. Art therapists, like mental health counselors, are working diligently at present to have their profession recognized and licensed under state regulation. Art therapists work in private practice, in clinics, and in hospitals.

Settings

The counseling professions are carried out in a great variety of settings, each environment defining its own parameters for the work accomplished, and each exerting influence on the precise nature of the counseling process. Counseling with children and families is done in schools, outpatient clinics, private practice offices, inpatient hospital units, local parishes, synagogues, mosques, residential treatment programs, the juvenile courts, detox centers, prisons, half-way houses, homeless shelters, private homes, on the street, and on the phone, to name just some of the possibilities.

The Counseling Process

Assessment, Differential Diagnosis, and Treatment Planning

All types of counseling services involve a process of assessment, diagnosis, and treatment planning, whether this process is conducted formally or informally. When a child or family comes to treatment, the counselor must evaluate a multitude of factors to ascertain the nature of the presenting concerns so that therapeutic work can be effective.

Assessment. The assessment process involves taking a thorough history of the child or family, a history that generally includes, but is not limited to, the following:

1. Names and ages of involved persons
2. Description of the presenting concern(s)
3. Precipitating factors
4. Why coming to treatment now?
5. Strengths and weaknesses
6. Genogram (family "map"—see Chapter 2)
7. Developmental history
8. Medical history
9. Psychiatric history
10. School and learning history
11. Work history
12. Depth and duration of family and peer relationships
13. Previous counseling experience
14. Suicide history, if any: attempts, statements, gestures
15. Abuse/trauma history: physical, sexual, emotional, ritual, and so on
16. Substance abuse history
17. Criminal/legal history
18. Extended family history: ethnic/cultural factors, abuse history, mental illness, physical illness, substance abuse, learning disability, criminality, and so on
19. Mental status exam
20. Initial hypotheses

Differential Diagnosis. Based on the nature and specific details of the information gathered during the assessment process, a tentative diagnosis is formulated.

Whether done formally/medically, or informally, skillful diagnosis is a critically important factor in counseling work, and one that directly guides the direction and course of treatment.

If a family brings a child in for counseling, for example, because of depressed mood, the counselor needs to diagnose whether the problem is related to organic factors, circumstantial events (e.g., death of a loved one, birth of a sibling, or peer conflicts), or perhaps parental expectations that are unrealistic for the child's developmental stage of life.

A teenage boy brought to treatment due to oppositional behavior at home and at school may be acting out frustration related to a learning disability, expressing anger over marital tension between his mother and father, reacting to his own ingestion of alcohol or drugs, or perhaps simply responding to his parents' and teachers' inability to set and maintain firm limits.

In all cases, misdiagnosis can lead to ineffective treatment or actual harm done to the client. Accurately assessing and diagnosing the problem, and its context, leads directly to appropriate treatment planning.

Treatment Planning.   Once the counselor has completed an initial assessment and made a tentative diagnosis, a plan of intervention may be made and implemented. In true practice, assessment, diagnosis, and treatment planning all work together in an ongoing process, each affecting and modifying the other as the work proceeds. Treatment planning includes decisions about the following questions: (1) Who, specifically, is going to be the primary recipient of therapeutic services and in what modality? (2) What are the goals of treatment? (3) What approaches are going to be used in treatment to reach those goals effectively (e.g., cognitive, behavioral, psychodynamic, psychopharmacological, substance abuse detox, strategic family therapy, play therapy, expressive therapy)? (4) What specific interventions will be made? (5) Should the counselor ideally be a man, a woman, or a co-therapist team? (6) What collateral parties, if any, must be involved? (7) Will the counseling likely be short or long term?

Modalities

Individual Therapy.   Individual therapy is the treatment of choice when difficulties a child or family is having are assessed to be best treated by working one-on-one with a particular family member. Case examples may serve to illustrate some of the considerations involved when counseling is recommended for a single individual.

CASE EXAMPLE

Anna

Eight-year-old Anna is brought to counseling for deep depression related to unresolved grief over the unexpected death of a beloved grandmother.

Anna's family's attempts to help her understand and integrate the loss, including work in family therapy sessions, have not been sufficient to help Anna move through her grief. Individual therapy is recommended.

Family Therapy.   Family counseling is a treatment modality often recommended when children or teenagers are having difficulty in some aspect of their lives; family dynamics frequently lie at the core of problematic behaviors. A referral for family therapy is made when a child's struggles are understood to be primarily reflective of the family context within which those struggles arise and develop. Counseling a youngster individually may not be indicated when the child lives day to day within a family environment that is itself full of tension and conflict, especially when that conflict calls forth and supports the continuance of the child's symptoms (Nichols and Schwartz, 2000).

CASE EXAMPLE

Toby

Toby, a 10-year-old boy, is referred out for counseling by the residential treatment center in which he resides. Because he is soon to be returned home, it is felt that his mother and father should be seen with him. They are concerned that his defiant, oppositional behaviors will resume when he comes home. A careful assessment brings to light intense marital conflict with the child caught in the middle of tensions between his mother and father. Further family therapy is recommended, to help the family sort out and appropriately attend to its various levels of discord. As Toby's parents become increasingly committed to working out their own problems, concurrently working with Toby on behavior issues, the boy's difficulties diminish notably in intensity, and reintegration into his home seems more promising.

Marital Therapy.   Couples therapy is often indicated whenever conflict between primary partners is determined to be a key element underlying child-related difficulties or family dysfunction. In the example of Toby, initial family sessions might well be replaced or supplemented with marital work for the parents. It is not an uncommon therapeutic experience to see a child's problematic behaviors decrease or disappear, without direct intervention, after the mother and father successfully begin to address and resolve conflict between themselves.

Group Therapy.   Many psychological and emotional issues have been found to be effectively approached within a group therapy format. In spite of the wide variety and types of therapy groups available, the healing experience common to group work is the support given and received by people struggling with similar life challenges. The group context—with time, care, and skillful facilitation—can reduce isolation and stigma, increase connection and depth of relationship, and provide for an environment conducive to the working through of sensitive issues. For children and families, groups can also offer straightforward information and education.

Case Management/Advocacy.   Counseling services for children and families often require substantial collaborative work with key personnel outside the family circle. It is frequently necessary to speak with teachers, school adjustment counselors, school principals, family doctors, juvenile court officials, police officers, protective child care workers, lawyers, group residence staff, hospital intake workers, inpatient psychiatric staff, public assistance workers, landlords, employers, and other counselors/therapists, to mention just a few of the possibilities. To manage a difficult and complicated case successfully, and to advocate effectively for the best interests of a child or family, a counselor must be ready and able to network with the key figures and institutions involved. In this area, particularly, issues of confidentiality must be handled with great care and attention. It should also be mentioned that the end goal of all advocacy work (and, ideally, all counseling work in general) is to empower the family, not to do things for them that they can do, or learn to do, for themselves.

Technique, Schools of Thought, Theoretical Approaches.   For the student intern or beginning counselor sitting with a troubled child or distressed family, a degree of anxiety and confusion is perhaps inevitable when faced with the questions, "What do I do, and how do I do it?" A profusion of techniques and theoretical approaches available for study and practice is complicated further by ongoing research and development in the field, refining and modifying established theories, and giving rise to new discoveries, approaches, and methods. To make matters more confusing, controversy enlivens the counseling professions, with differences of opinion often feverishly debated between proponents of opposing schools of thought.

Developing skill as a counselor involves many factors over and beyond formal academic training and practice experience. The counselor's personality style, belief system, assumptions about change, personal history, and experiences of healing all play an integral role. Perhaps unlike any other field, artistry as a counselor demands work on oneself, in addition to and as a counterpart to work with other people. When an individual of any age, or a family, comes to counseling for assistance with some kind of troublesome life dilemma, a counselor's efforts are given considerable power by the extent to which he or she has honestly grappled with his or her own problems in life. Because human development entails transformations and challenges throughout life that are universal to people everywhere, inevitably the issues brought to counseling by a family, sooner or later, are going to touch on some issue the counselor knows from his or her own experience.

With time, training, practice, and the deepening of one's own personal life experience, a particular style of working as a counselor evolves, with techniques and specific methods pulling together around the counselor's history, personality, interests, and natural talents. For most counselors, this is a process that unfolds slowly, and brings together the meeting ground between helping others and developing oneself. A well-known Jungian analyst and pastoral counselor was once asked what he thought about Freudian dream interpretation. He replied, "If you are reasonably competent, love what you do, have a genuine passion for it, and believe in it because of your own experience, then you are going to do good work regardless of what approach you use."

The Experience of Counseling

Consumer Perspective

What is it like to be in counseling? Does counseling help? The success of the counseling experience, and the degree of satisfaction derived from it by children and families, is conditioned by several key factors.

Counselor/Client Chemistry.   Counseling entails a relationship between human beings. Like all human relationships, personal chemistry plays a role in determining the depth and intensity of connection between people. Having the "right" chemistry between counselor and the child and/or family favors the establishment of trust and greatly facilitates the work in progress.

Timing.   Timing is an important element when it comes to counseling because it implies a certain readiness for the work involved. Issues, life dilemmas, and personal challenges tend to energize as time passes, with a certain critical tension often building before people make the decision to seek professional assistance. Life circumstances also play a role when it comes to readiness, events oftentimes occurring in response to which people turn to the counseling professions. The "right" timing favors the counseling process because internal tension and/or external life circumstances present optimal opportunity and motivation for change.

Attitude and Expectation.   A child's or family's attitude toward counseling, and the nature of their expectations, often have a direct impact on the degree of success experienced. An open and cooperative attitude, combined with positive and realistic expectations about change, favor success and client satisfaction.

Level of Functioning.   *Level of functioning* is a phrase that refers to internal and external resources available to a child or family, including physiological, cognitive, emotional, social, and economic factors. A relatively high level of functioning favors a positive experience in counseling because individuals and families are able to more quickly and effectively use the support, direction, information, and specific tools provided through the counseling endeavor.

Counselor Skill.   As in all professions, a continuum exists among counselors in skill level, energy, creativity, dedication to the work, passion for the profession, and willingness to "go the extra mile." Well-trained, experienced, skillful, and dedicated counselors contribute in a major way to the likelihood that a child or family will have a productive and satisfying experience in counseling.

Benefits.   Perhaps the best way to consider the experience of being in counseling, and the benefits derived from the process, is to listen to the words of children and families who have used counseling services for themselves.

Varied Reactions to Counseling

1. "I felt like someone really listened to me, like my words were not only heard, but what I meant and what I felt were understood and somebody cared."—Fifteen-year-old girl in individual outpatient therapy while in foster care

2. "It's great to have someone on my side, for once. I feel like I've got someone in my corner, like when my dad comes at me with one of his criticisms, I don't have to struggle with it all by myself. It's also great because my counselor makes my father listen to me. If Dad interrupts me, my counselor cuts him off and asks him to let me finish. He also does the same to me when I want to interrupt my dad. He makes me try to see things from different perspectives."—Fifteen-year-old boy in family counseling

3. "I like going there. I get to play with the toys. Sometimes Mommy plays too. Mrs. Peterson [counselor] told my daddy he couldn't hit my mommy any more. I never saw Daddy cry before."—Seven-year-old girl in individual play therapy and family counseling

As these comments illustrate, counseling is an experience that can include being carefully listened to, having one's feelings accurately reflected and validated, having one's emotions contained, receiving information, being constructively challenged and confronted, receiving support, giving support, being coached, learning new skills, expressing one's feelings, communicating effectively, and discovering new things about oneself.

Professional Perspective

What is it like being a counselor? For the vast majority of people who work as professionals within the counseling fields, the direct person-to-person aspect of the work can be immensely rewarding and challenging, though not without its own unique frustrations and aggravations. Requirements of the job that involve work only tangentially related to direct service are often those that are experienced most negatively. An honest appraisal of counseling as a profession reveals both positive and negative considerations.

Negative Aspects of Counseling as a Career. Counseling has several negative aspects that may offset the positive.

Burnout. Professional "burnout" is a common occurrence in the counseling professions due to a variety of factors. Working with psychological trauma, emotional crisis, relational dysfunction, substance abuse, domestic violence, behavior and conduct problems, depression, family conflict, and the gamut of difficulties daily presented to workers in the counseling fields can be an emotionally draining experience. In many settings, counselors are expected to work directly with a large number of cases on a weekly basis, and to keep track of even more via case management and paperwork requirements. Problems often feel overwhelming, and endless, and unsolvable (Zastrow, 2000).

Multiproblem Families. When poverty, lack of education, substance abuse, domestic violence, out-of-control children, delinquent adolescents, depression, and other difficulties all combine to overwhelm a single family and cause problems in the community, workers in the counseling field are often called in to help. Working with such families can be a particularly frustrating experience for counselors, especially when, on top of everything else, families are hostile to outside intervention. Internal (psychological/emotional) and external (money, friendships/support network, opportunities) resources are often so limited in such families that counseling seems an inadequate and ineffective response.

Failure. All counselors experience numerous cases in which the best of efforts results in little or no positive change. Particularly when working with children and teens, efforts made with little noticeable results can be a discouraging experience.

Paperwork. Increasingly, third-party payers (insurance programs) are becoming more and more stringent in their requirements, demanding substantial record-keeping procedures relative to accounting and clinical review (Moline et al., 1998). The business/financial component of the counseling professions requires time, careful management, and frequent adjustment to third-party policy changes. The paperwork involved, in addition to the demands of the therapeutic work itself, can often lead to extra hours and the feeling that "catching up" is an impossibility.

Liability. Counseling professionals are often summoned to court to testify in cases involving their clients. The legalities and ethical parameters of client confidentiality can add stress to already demanding work. Written court reports are often required. In addition, careful documentation of counseling sessions and other case-related communications can be requested for review.

Income.   Although counseling professionals with highly successful private practices and/or high-level administrative positions can earn substantial incomes, earnings as a human service provider generally fall far short of those possible in the business world. Counseling professionals often feel frustrated that the value and difficulty of their work is not recognized or rewarded on a level commensurate with the importance of the services provided.

Ethical Dilemmas.   Counselors, on a regular basis, find themselves in the middle of situations that present ethical dilemmas relative to decision making. It is not uncommon, for example, for a counselor's input to result in children being taken away from their parents. What this feels like for the counselor, for the parents, and for the child, and the long-term effect it has on the family, are all factors that counselors must grapple with in the course of doing their job. A variety of decision-making choices present themselves to counselors that directly and profoundly influence the lives of the children and families with whom they work. Making these decisions, and living with their consequences, pull counselors into the middle of ethical questions that have no easy answers.

Positive Aspects of Counseling as a Career.   Counseling is a field in which burdensome elements of the work must be weighed in contrast to elements that are deeply rewarding. Counselors are known not only to complain about the demands of their profession, but also to sing its praises.

Counselors Speak about Their Work
1. "What I love about my work is the opportunity it gives me to make some small positive difference in the lives of my young clients. The greatest resource any society has is its children. It is a great blessing to be able to assist the development of young people and to beneficially influence the home environments in which they are raised. Also, I enjoy being part of the process of change for families."—Social worker in a community family counseling center
2. "You know, it's a chance to contribute something positive to the world. These kids are sent to me expecting more adult discussion and direction. Instead, they find a person and a space where they feel safe to express who they are, how they feel, what they think. There is a lot of pressure on children to conform. Kids have to meet expectations and standards, follow rules, do assignments in school, control their behavior, and so on. All of this is good and necessary. But children also need to be respected and valued as children, to let themselves go, to be creative and spontaneous in the way that only children can be. I try to provide a setting in which they can do this."—School counselor and art therapist
3. "I am always moved by what children communicate to us if we just learn to understand their language. They are profoundly wise, and will almost always tell us what they need, or point us in the right direction. We only

need to listen to them, and tune into the symbolic and metaphorical meaning of their behavior, artwork, play fantasies, and symptoms."—School psychologist

Counseling as a profession is full of rewards and frustrations. As in all professions, it is the dynamic tension between what is inspiring in the work and what is discouraging that keeps the field alive, creative, and growing.

Trends in Counseling Services

At the beginning of a new millenium, powerful forces from within and without the counseling professions are pushing and pulling the field in new directions, challenging counselors in every setting to respond creatively. The successes and failures of this response will largely shape the possibilities and parameters for counseling in the future. A brief overview of the most influential of these forces must include consideration of the significant external and internal forces at work.

External Forces

Economic Factors.   A variety of economic factors influence counseling today.

Deficit Reduction.   National policy is immersed in efforts to reduce the federal deficit. As efforts toward this end unfold, funding is being cut or substantially reduced for a multitude of programs. After-school programs for children and teens, community daycare, sports and the arts in the public schools, summer work programs for adolescents, city and town recreation programs, special programs for minority and underprivileged youth, community health care clinics, and many other projects that rely on state and federal support are finding they must drastically scale down their operations or close their doors due to lack of money. As this trend continues, overburdened families, bored and frustrated youth, lack of adult supervision and direction for teenagers, and increasingly limited opportunities for lower-income families all contribute to an intensification of already pressing societal crises. It is to the ongoing repercussions of national budget cutting that counselors in most settings will inevitably have to respond, at the same time as they must contend with vanishing resources for their own efforts in this regard (Keigher, 1994).

National Health Care Crisis.   The escalating cost of health care provision has prompted a revolution in the insurance industry, with major changes occurring over the last two decades and continuing unabated at present. As market pressures and dollar efficiency increasingly guide and determine the delivery of care, one notable trend is that more and more people appear to be getting less and less in terms of services in the area of mental health. Of particular concern to professionals in the counseling fields, third-party reimbursement for mental health care services has seen the rise of large "managed care" companies.

The managed care industry, unlike traditional commercial insurance companies, seeks to intervene directly in the provision of mental health care services to consumers by providers, efficiently managing and thereby limiting the expenditure of dollars. Although a heated debate rages currently as to the pros and cons of managed care, the appearance and influence of these companies has unquestionably resulted in dramatic changes in the way many counselors do and think about their work.

Managed care favors brief, in the present, goal-oriented, solution-focused, behavior- and symptom-directed psychotherapy. A major shift away from long-term depth work in counseling is promoted. Self-exploration, in-depth childhood trauma processing for adults, long-term relationship building between counselor and client, transference- and countertransference-based therapies, existential and/or spiritual questing, and all other nonspecific, non-symptom, or present behavior-related concerns and approaches are discouraged. The managed care industry asserts that it does not pass judgment as to whether such approaches are valid or useful, but decisive policy has been implemented that vigorously resists paying for them (Behrman, 1998; Bagarozzi, 1995; Mone, 1994), creating a severe restriction as to what many third-party reimbursors are willing to cover under mental health benefits.

Social Factors.   Social ramifications follow directly from decisions pertaining to money. The social welfare system is perhaps the best example of this relationship. No one argues against changes in the welfare system. What changes, how to implement them, and what to do about poverty and all its related social ills remain a quandary for those currently wrestling with the problem. Unquestionably, overwhelmed, broken, impoverished, and chaotic families and their children show up in schools, counseling centers, hospitals, courts, residential treatment programs, detox centers, 12-step programs, homeless shelters, battered women's groups, sexual offender programs, and so on. Certainly, wealthier, less burdened, intact, and higher functioning families can show up in the same places, but lack of resources is arguably a predisposing element for family dysfunction and mental/emotional disturbance.

As economic decisions on the federal, state, and municipal levels continue to affect lower-income families negatively, phenomena such as single-mother households, fatherless adolescents, teenage pregnancy, child and adolescent suicide, juvenile delinquency, substance abuse, domestic violence, violence by children and teens against other children and teens, gang involvement, the high school dropout rate, and child neglect/abuse continue to increase. When these trends are combined with the trend toward managed care, brief therapy, and restricted mental health care dollars, counseling efforts begin to feel increasingly like Band-Aid responses taped over conditions calling for more radical treatment.

Political Factors.   Politics inevitably enters the picture whenever major economic decisions are made. Based on allocation of resources, it appears clear that political leaders do not place families, women, or children high on the list of national priorities, especially those who are uneducated, poor, and non-white. A conservative trend in government lobbies diligently for legislation that slashes funding for social programs, deregulates environmental protection, and places the interests of corporations and wealthy Americans over those of other citizens. Native Americans, African Americans, Hispanics, other minority groups, and the poor find themselves ill-equipped to access the same opportunities taken for granted by more prosperous and privileged segments of the population. Policy-making at the macro level does not seek to remedy this discrepancy in any meaningful way, as the distribution of funds reflects. Rhetoric from politicians, liberal and conservative alike, speaks of cracking down on crime and violence without so much as a passing comment about unequal access to resources or opportunities for advancement.

Internal Forces

Notwithstanding the somewhat discouraging trends touched upon above, from within the counseling professions some notable and exciting developments can be discerned.

Mind-Body Connection.   Within the counseling community, beginning back before the 1960s, but gaining increasing steam from the 1960s onward, a fringe group of practitioners has incorporated into their work techniques based on a holistic understanding of mind-body integrity. In recent years, massage therapies, bioenergetics, Rolfing, therapeutic touch, breath work, meditation, relaxation and visualization techniques, and a host of other methods that have historically been looked down on by mainstream counseling professionals have gained greater acceptance. Eastern meditation practice, yoga, deep breathing, and visualization exercises are now standard fare at many hospitals and clinics working with stress, phobias, panic disorders, chronic pain, depression, and other conditions. As the medical and scientific communities slowly, and often begrudgingly, show cautious approval of such approaches, the general public has gained greater exposure to them as well, with considerable benefit for many people, including children and families.

Spirituality.   Hand in hand with a deeper understanding and appreciation for the body-mind connection, many counselors have begun to reassert the place of psyche (soul) in psychological work, no longer so sharply distinguishing between psychotherapy, "soul making," or spirituality (Moore, 2002). If a pattern of thought can actually create a problematic physical condition that in turn changes or modifies thinking, such that the physical symptom begins also to heal, it is difficult not to wonder at the inherent intelligence of such a system, or to speculate as to the possibility of some purpose or intention behind symptoms.

Questions of meaning, purpose, intention, and healing lead naturally to wondering about human potential. As counselors employ meditation techniques in their practice, this, too, opens a door to spiritual experience, to the experience of being part of something greater than, but inclusive of, human life. As medicine, physical science, and psychology explore the human psyche, it is perhaps inevitable that the mind-body connection will be mirrored by an equally profound connection between psyche, soul, and spirit.

Evolving Frontiers in Theory and Practice

The counseling professions rest on a dynamic interplay between theory and practice whereby the understanding of mental health grows and deepens over time. Research, experience, and scholarship all contribute to this process of discovery and refinement. Exciting developments in the following areas, among many others, are worthy of note and further study.

- *Attachment theory.* Increasingly, the counseling professions are presented with children suffering from the complex and disturbing effects of early abuse and neglect. The experience of such early trauma appears in many cases to negatively alter the very formation of personality and development of the psyche. Attachment theory seeks to understand what happens when the natural and normal bonding between children and caring adults is disrupted in infancy, with an eye toward effective treatment for these most traumatized children (Goldberg, 2000).
- *Constructivism in psychotherapy.* The constructivist movement is playing an increasingly significant role in the shaping of psychotherapeutic theory and practice. Viewed from a constructivist perspective, human beings are understood to organize their experience and behavior based on meanings that are *constructed,* not given (Neimeyer, 1999).
- *Narrative therapy.* A constructivist approach to understanding human problems and struggle can be seen in terms of the stories people develop over time about themselves and others, about the world and "the way things are." Counseling seeks to open the door to a consideration of alternative stories (Payne, 2000).

Ethical Considerations in Counseling

Counselors can, in subtle and dramatic ways, directly influence the lives of the children and families with whom they work. Counseling professionals are seen as experts, knowledgeable about psychology, development, and behavior, experienced in intervention, and qualified to give guidance. As such, they are entrusted with private and highly personal information. Their opinions, comments, and perspectives are taken seriously by clients, by courts of law, and by child protection agencies. Their suggestions, direct or implied, are often followed. Such a position inevitably involves questions of ethics, because authority and influence can have serious repercussions in the lives of those it touches. The following areas of ethical concern include those that are well-known stumbling blocks of the trade, as well as more controversial categories presented as food for thought for interested students.

Confidentiality

Counselors receive information daily about the private lives of children and families. Some of this information can be disturbing. How the information is handled, with whom it is shared, and what decisions follow from it do not always have simple, clear-cut answers.

If a 16-year-old boy develops a trusting relationship with his individual counselor, and finally shares with the counselor that he has been experimenting with marijuana, alcohol, and LSD on the weekends with some of his friends, should the counselor necessarily notify the boy's parents?

If the single mother of three young children confides to her counselor that she has, on a couple of recent occasions, left the house at night for two hours while the children were asleep, does the counselor report her to the local authorities for child neglect?

What is the ethical duty of a counselor who hears from a teenager that a friend who is HIV-positive is regularly having unsafe sex with uninformed partners?

When parents from a minority culture innocently reveal to their counselor a routine child discipline technique that is common and accepted by the culture but judged to be excessive and too punitive from the American perspective, should the parents be reported to a child protection agency?

If a client reveals to her counselor that she committed a serious but non-lethal crime, does the counselor report her to the authorities?

These confidentiality dilemmas, and countless others, come up daily in the practices of counselors in many different professions. In spite of careful parameters set forth by civil law and professional codes of ethics, many situations arise for counselors in the course of their work that fall between the lines of established protocols, and/or force a decision about what is acceptable by the profession and what is not. In these numerous cases, counselors sometimes have to struggle to come to their own conclusions, make their own decisions, and respond to the consequences (Crosson-Tower, 2002).

The Dilemma of Diagnosis

Formal, medical diagnosis for mental/emotional problems entails assigning a recognized medical label to a carefully assessed profile of human behavior. Labels such as *attention deficit disorder, borderline personality disorder, bi-polar disorder, conduct disorder,* or even *major depression,* often carry with them negative social implications for the people so categorized.

Aside from the more obvious ethical questions pertaining to misdiagnosis, the entire issue of labeling people is one worthy of careful consideration. What will the person diagnosed be told about the diagnosis? What does the diagnosis mean to that person and/or to the family? Who else will have access to records where that diagnosis is made? What will the diagnosis mean to *those* people?

One readily observable danger of using diagnostic labels is the tendency to lose track of individual human beings in favor of medical categories of disorder. "My borderline client," "my conduct disordered kid," "my PTSD boy," "the ADD group," "my group of heroin addicts," and so on are commonly heard terms used by practitioners in reference to counseled individuals. When, and by what process, does a person, with a personal name, an identity, a developed personality, thoughts, feelings, hopes, and fears become a "heroin addict" or a "borderline"? Does such a process insulate counselors from the problems that are brought to them? Does it protect them from seeing their own human condition reflected in their clients' lives? Does it set up and maintain a hierarchy between counselor and those being counseled?

Training

In notable contrast to the training of psychiatrists, psychoanalysts, Jungian analysts, and other established professions that require neophyte practitioners to go through a prolonged in-depth form of psychotherapy as a critical part of their formal training, many professions, including social work, mental health counseling, and psychology, make no such demand of their trainees. What are the ethical implications for professionals who engage their clients in a process they themselves have not experienced? Is it even possible to competently guide a child or family through a psychotherapeutic process if one has never gone through such a process oneself?

Value System Differences

One of the most common types of ethical dilemmas, perhaps especially for beginning or student counselors, arises when working with families who hold to value systems markedly different from their own. For example, how does one work with a family whose religious beliefs prohibit their adolescent children from dancing, going to movies, or wearing the latest teenage fashions? If these prohibitions are at the root of parent–child conflict, and if the parents' belief system allows no room for compromise, how does a counselor proceed? If the counselor's belief system is closer in substance to the adolescent's in this case, how is collusion with the child against the parents, subtle or overt, avoided?

For counselors working with cases involving cross-cultural issues, value system conflicts can complicate and/or inhibit the therapeutic work. To take one example, families from certain ethnic backgrounds do not value direct and open communication among family members. Private thoughts and feelings are considered just that, private. If a counselor trained in the United States and raised in a very open and expressive family environment pressures a minority family to be self-revealing and openly communicative, what are the ethical considerations involved when this pressure results in significant psychological distress for the family?

Counselor/Client Boundaries

A long-standing and well recognized ethical stumbling block for the counseling professions concerns "doctor/patient" boundaries. Counselors listen to highly personal life stories on a daily basis. Transference and countertransference dynamics, whereby the intimate nature of therapeutic work triggers family of origin issues for both counselor and client, can sometimes lead to a misplacement of feelings. A counselor who was himself abused by an alcoholic father may find himself wanting to *be* a father for an adolescent client who himself lives with an abusive and alcoholic parent. Instead of working to help the boy and his father come closer together, the counselor unconsciously allies himself with the son against the father. The counselor's deep personal feelings, relative to his own father, get mixed up in his professional work.

Writings on transference/countertransference dynamics, sexual attraction between doctor and patient, boundary confusion between counselor and counseled, and the related ramifications for both professionals and their clients abound in the psychological literature. Though the subject is too complex to consider at length in the present context, it is important for students to understand that boundary issues exist, with important and serious ethical implications.

Power

Professional counselors are generally seen by their clients as experts, with all the authority brought by higher education, advanced training, and long-term direct experience. When the position of "expert" interfaces with the vulnerability of families in distress, dynamics of power often enter into the therapeutic process. A counselor's thoughts, feelings, suggestions, innuendos, admonitions, warnings, and praises can carry tremendous influence with children and families in crisis (Wilson and Stith, 1998; Courtois, 1988).

When perceived power differentials are great, the possibility that such influence will be misused, or received in an unintended way, needs to be recognized. Take, for example, an adolescent who tells her counselor that she feels uncomfortable when her father kisses her. She may decompensate quickly if the counselor prematurely suggests intentional sexual impropriety on the part of the father. For the adolescent, the fact that the counselor mentions such a possibility means it must be true because the counselor *knows*. Because counseling involves working with children and families at varying levels of cognitive functioning, developmental maturity, and emotional stability, counselors must be acutely aware of the power their statements and actions carry if they are to avoid misunderstandings with potentially grave consequences.

Counseling as a Healing Art versus the Business of Mental Health

Productivity Requirements.   As the counseling professions have had to re-spond to market conditions, national economic policy, health care reform, and other fiscal realities, ethical questions around the interface of money and therapy have proliferated. In most outpatient child and family counseling cen-ters, where third-party reimbursement covers a substantial portion of the op-erational expenses of the clinic, counselors have "productivity" requirements. This means that each counselor is required to see a given number of children or families each week, as prerequisite to receiving his or her salary.

When quantity of clients becomes a financially driven issue for counselors, there are inevitable implications for the quality of care, as well as ethical dilem-mas for counselors who must "make their numbers" each week. This becomes increasingly problematic as productivity requirements and counselor caseloads expand. Meeting one's productivity requirement can too easily become an unstated goal of therapeutic work. Into the pool of factors determining length of treatment can occasionally enter the question of how many hours a coun-selor needs to satisfy productivity requirements for a given week. With many mental health clinics incorporating "incentive policies," whereby a counselor is rewarded, financially, for clients seen over and above the productivity re-quirement, and penalized financially for being below productivity, counselors are pressured to consider quantity as a motivating force in their work.

Linking Diagnosis to Length of Treatment.   With the advent of managed care, some third-party reimbursers have begun to categorize diagnoses, allowing more sessions for certain types of disorders than for others. Again, this poses eth-ical questions for the practitioner. If it is assessed that a given family needs more counseling, over and above the number of sessions allowed by the insurance company for the stated diagnosis, one way around the problem would be to change the diagnosis. If the original diagnosis more accurately describes the family's situation, the counselor is in an ethical dilemma: Does the practitioner tell the family he or she can no longer work with them unless they wish to pay for sessions with their own money, or does the practitioner change to a less ac-curate diagnosis that enables work to continue under third-party coverage?

Clients without Insurance.   Federal and state deficit reduction measures over the past two decades have gone hand in hand with the virtual disappearance of "free care dollars." Many counseling centers no longer have the financial support to see even a limited number of clients who cannot pay, or who can-not pay much. No ability to pay translates into no services provided. This equation poses ethical questions for all the counseling professions.

Out-of-pocket fee-setting scales also can be challenged on ethical grounds. For families with no insurance coverage, fees are often set by counseling facil-ities at levels tied to family income, with a minimum payment policy in place.

Families who cannot meet the minimum payment are often out of luck, no matter how badly they need services. The demands and realities of keeping a counseling center financially solvent frequently mean preferential treatment for families with insurance coverage and/or independent resources.

Money Management versus Confidentiality. Tighter management of mental health care dollars has been accompanied by increasing intrusiveness on the part of third-party payers. In contrast to traditional commercial insurance company reimbursement, which simply requires a medically recognized diagnosis for a given problem, managed care companies now ask for details about presenting concerns. A written description of problems and goals and a specific treatment plan are routinely required. Additionally, if a particular managed care review board does not feel a counselor's written request for authorized sessions is justified, the counselor may be required to discuss the case in greater detail with a company representative on the phone. Such practice continues to be hotly contested by many on the grounds that it violates consumers' rights to confidentiality.

With insurance companies on line and engaged in extensive computer processing of records and files, and with the "information superhighway" a reality linking computer databases within a colossal internationally plugged-in information network, questions about who has access to what kind of information suggest possibilities with disturbing implications.

Band-Aids versus Commitment to Social Change

For many counselors, especially those who work for agencies serving lower-income families, an area for sober reflection in the arena of professional ethics involves the relationship between problems faced by children in the United States and societal conditions that directly or indirectly contribute to the creation and maintenance of those problems. For these counselors, therapeutic work with the microrealities of families in distress must constantly be evaluated against the macrorealities of societal structures. If national priorities do not appear to place a high value on children, women, the plight of the poor, education, or equal opportunity to resources for all citizens, what becomes the ethical response of professionals who earn an income counseling the disenfranchised? Do middle-class professional counselors benefit from the same hierarchy of priorities that keep them supplied with a steady and inexhaustible clientele? What kind of political action commitment might be ethically demanded of those who counsel?

Summary

Counseling is an interactive process that seeks to facilitate positive change for those being counseled. That such change is possible is an assumption central to the counseling professions. Families come to counseling either by way of self-referral or via a referral made by an outside agency. Self-referred families actively look for professional attention in response to recognized problems or potentially problematic situations. In contrast, families referred to counseling by outside parties have often failed to notice or to respond adequately to difficulties experienced by family members.

Attitudes toward receiving counseling vary widely among individuals and between cultures and tend to mirror an individual's or culture's feelings about having a problem in the first place. For many, societal pressures to present a strong and positive face to the outside world conflict with the need in counseling to openly acknowledge and talk about painful and disappointing aspects of life. Instead of being valued as potential teachers, these "shadow" areas of life are frequently hidden, judged as shameful, or denied.

Counseling with families and children involves a process of assessment, diagnosis, treatment planning, and intervention. Intervention takes place within distinct modalities: individual, family, marital, and/or group therapy. Case management and advocacy work often accompany and support counseling sessions. The goal of all counseling modalities is to enable families and individuals to successfully manage and respond to the many demands and challenges of life.

Developing skill as a counselor demands work on oneself, in addition to and as a counterpart to work with other people. In addition to self-exploration, counseling as a profession involves complex questions of ethics, because counselors are often perceived by their clients to be in positions of considerable power and influence. Issues concerning confidentiality, client/counselor boundaries, medical diagnosis, value system differences, parental rights, child protection, money, insurance, poverty, discrimination, and the inequities of social institutions present counselors with ethical dilemmas that have no easy answers.

At present, domestic policy-making in the United States is being shaped largely by efforts to reduce the federal deficit. Economic pressures radically influence policy decisions affecting the delivery of services to families and children. In an effort to cut government spending, many programs designed to aid and support families have been curtailed or eliminated. At the same time, a crisis in national health care has seen the rise of large managed care companies determined to limit the expenditure of dollars significantly paid to professional providers for the provision of mental health services. As pervasive belt-tightening decisions continue to be made, lower income families suffer the consequences increasingly, with serious repercussions for the counseling professions and for the society as a whole.

EXPLORATION QUESTIONS

1. What is meant by *counseling?* What are some basic assumptions of counseling?
2. Cite some situations in which a family might seek counseling.

3. What attitudes might people have about receiving counseling?
4. What should a counselor consider when working with people from different ethnic or cultural backgrounds?
5. What is the difference between the medical model and the holistic model of counseling?
6. How has the feminist movement influenced counseling?
7. What is meant by *assessment?* By *differential diagnosis?* By *treatment planning?*
8. What are some different treatment modalities?
9. What factors can influence the success or failure of the counseling experience?
10. What are some of the negative aspects of counseling as a career?
11. How does the current political climate in the United States affect the future of the counseling profession?
12. What is meant by the term *managed care?*
13. What are some of the ethical dilemmas a counselor might face?

REFERENCES

Atkinson, D. (2002). *Counseling American Minorities.* New York: McGraw-Hill.

Bagarozzi, D. A. (1995). "Evaluation, Accountability and Clinical Expertise in Managed Mental Health Care: Basic Consideration for the Practice of Family Social Work," *Journal of Family Social Work,* 1(2), 101–116.

Behrman, R. E. (Ed.). (1998). "Children and Managed Health Care," *The Future of Children,* 8(2), 4–151.

Budd, M. A. (1992). "New Possibilities for the Practice of Medicine," *Advances,* 8(1), 7–16.

Cassidy, C. M. (1994). "Unraveling the Ball of String: Reality, Paradigms, and the Study of alternative Medicine," *Advances,* 10(1), 5–31.

Cederstrom, L. (2002). *Jungian Archetypes in 20th Century Women's Fiction: The Persona, the Shadow, the Animus, and the Self.* Lewiston, NY: Edwin Mellen Press.

Courtois, C. (1988). *Healing the Incest Wound.* New York: Norton.

Crosson-Tower, C. (2002). *Understanding Child Abuse and Neglect.* Boston: Allyn and Bacon.

Dossey, L. (1994). "Antonovsky's Perspective May Not go Far Enough," *Advances,* 10(3), 13–15.

Ford, D. Y. (1997). "Counseling Middle-Class African-Americans" (81–107). In C. Lee et al. (Eds.), *Multicultural Issues in Counseling: New Approaches to Diversity:* Alexandria, VA: American Counseling Association.

Gilligan, C. (1993). *In a Different Voice: Psychological Theory and Women's Development.* Cambridge: Harvard University Press.

Goldberg, S. (2000). *Attachment and Development.* London: Edward Arnold.

Keigher, S. M. (1994). "The Morning after Deficit Reduction: The Poverty of U.S. Maternal and Child Health Policy," *Health and Social Work,* 19(2), 143–147.

LeShan, L. (1992). "Creating a Climate for Self-Healing: The Principles of Modern Psychosomatic Medicine," *Advances,* 8(4), 20–27.

Moline, M. E., Williams, G. T., & Austin, K. M. (1998). *Documenting Psychotherapy: Essentials for Mental Health Practitioners.* Thousand Oaks, CA: Sage.

Mone, L. C. (1994). "Managed Care Cost Effectiveness: Fantasy or Reality?" *International Journal of Group Psychotherapy,* 44(4), 437–448.

Moore, T. (2002). The Soul's Religion: Cultivating a Profoundly Spiritual Way of Life. New York: HarperCollins.

Neimeyer, R. A. (1999). *Constructivism in Psychotherapy.* Washington, DC: American Psychological Association

Nichols, M. P., & Schwartz, R. C. (2000). *Family Therapy: Concepts and Methods* (5th ed.). Boston: Allyn and Bacon.

Payne, M. (2000). *Narrative Therapy: An Introduction for Counselors.* Thousand Oaks, CA: Sage.

Ponterotto, J. G., Casas, J. M., Suzuki, L. A., & Alexander, C. M. (Eds.). (2001). *Handbook of Multicultural Counseling*. Thousand Oaks, CA: Sage.

Shannon, S. (2002). *Handbook of Complementary and Alternative Therapies in Mental Health*. San Diego, CA: Academic Press.

Wilson, L. L., & Stith, S. M. (1998). "Culturally Sensitive Therapy with Black Clients" (116– 126). In D. Atkinson et al. (Eds.), *Counseling Minorities*. Boston: McGraw-Hill.

Zastrow, C. (1984). "Understanding and Preventing Burn-Out," *British Journal of Social Work*, 14(2), 141–155.

Zastrow, C. (2000). *Introduction to Social Work and Social Welfare*. Pacific Grove, CA: Brooks/Cole.

7 Protecting Children When Families Cannot

Child Abuse and Neglect

Historical View

Societal Role of Children

The historical overview in Chapter 1 acquainted us with the fact that the concept of childhood is recent and that children were previously considered the property of parents and were dependent on those adults. Parents were free to kill children, sell them into slavery, maim them, or abandon them. They might even be used in sacrifices as in the biblical account of Abraham's intent to sacrifice his son, Isaac. DeMause (1995–96) reports that acheological findings of an abundance of skeletons of infants and toddlers suggest that child murder and sacrifice were all too common. The much-quoted biblical passage that charges parents to "withhold not correction from the child for if thou beatest him with the rod he shall not die; thou shalt beat him with the rod and deliver his soul from Hell" (Proverbs 23:13–14) is often still paraphrased as "spare the rod and spoil the child" in support of corporal punishment of children.

The circumstances of the parents dictated the circumstances of their children. Poor parents, subject to almshouses, went there with their children—who often suffered neglect and even death. In the United States, children who arrived as immigrants worked alongside their parents and did much to shape this country. African American children came originally as slaves who were at the mercy of not only their parents but also their masters. It was not unusual for them to be beaten or separated from their families according to the needs of those who owned them. Asian and Pacific Island children may have fared somewhat better. Their parents' cultural values ensured that these children were absorbed into and protected by the family, when in fact the family was able to do this. Hispanic and Native American children too had the benefit of the family or the greater community. The fact that families also were not well treated impacted the children (Crosson-Tower, 2002).

By the late 1800s, some children from poor families found placement in so-called *orphan asylums,* a misnomer, as many of these children still had at least one living family member. Conditions in these institutions varied, but incidences of physical and sexual abuse are well documented (Smith, 1995). Even if these orphanages had not been settings in which maltreatment could be hidden from the eyes of the public, children suffered from being institutionalized.

Child Neglect throughout History

Neglect is a concept alluded to rather than fully discussed in historical contexts. Early images of neglect conjure up street waifs, cold, hungry, and destitute. To sustain themselves, these children resorted to theft, begging, and loitering, to the annoyance of the upper-class passersby. In fact, such scenes were a contributing factor to the child-saving movement. In reality, such children reflected the social conditions of their time, when poverty was largely unaddressed.

Swift (1995) contends that it was the mother at whom fingers were pointed for the neglect of these children. Rarely, she says, was the father's role considered. These mothers were felt to be "morally wanting," and often it was assumed that they were under the influence of alcohol or guilty of "loose living." Early case records describe these mothers as "mentally limited" and immature. Rarely were circumstances other than their own ineptitude given weight. For example, Swift (1995) recounts that in one case of wife abuse the mother was described as "self-centered, does not think of the children, complains constantly, and takes no responsibility for the house" (82).

Only recently have such societal issues as poverty and housing been considered. Yet, even today, individual characteristics of maternal figures are seen as the primary reason why their children are neglected (Swift, 1995), despite assertions by some experts that neglect results from a complex matrix of society personal, and systemwide inadequacies (Garbarino and Collins, 1999).

Child Labor and Maltreatment

Childhood, as we know it, is a relatively new concept. Children of previous centuries were expected to be as useful as their parents. Many parents sought to ensure their children's future through a practice known as *indenture:* apprenticing children to tradesmen or masters to learn a trade. Indenture began when the child was quite young and lasted into adolescence or early adulthood. Although it was seemingly a good way to learn a future vocation, reports tell us that masters were not always benevolent and that some children suffered from a variety of abuses.

As the industrial revolution dawned, children began to find employment in factories. They were expected to work long and hard, often beyond their endurance. Child advocates became concerned about the abuses to children in the work-force and voiced these concerns about the need for reform. One such critic was Jane Addams of Chicago's Hull House. Hull House, a settlement house established in the Chicago slums on the model of New York's Toynbee Hall, strove to help immigrants integrate into their new society. Economic need found immigrant children working in factories along with their parents, but without the strength or endurance of their elders. Often the conditions under which they worked were also dangerous. These conditions became a special concern of Jane Addams. She recounts these concerns in her memoirs, *Twenty Years at Hull House:*

> During the…winter three boys from the Hull House club were injured at one machine in a neighborhood factory for lack of a guard which would have cost but a few dollars. When the injury of one of these boys resulted in death, we felt quite sure that the owners would share our horror and remorse, and that they would do everything possible to prevent the reoccurrence of such a tragedy. To our surprise they did nothing whatever, and I made my first acquaintance then with those pathetic documents signed by the parents of working

children, that they will make no claim for damages resulting from "careless-ness." (Addams, 1910, 148)

Although the staff of Hull House fought valiantly for the rights of children, it would be some years before laws protecting children from unfair labor practices would be passed. Some families were actually dependent for their survival on the income brought in by their children. Thus poverty must be viewed as an important contributor to early child labor.

Sexual Mores and Abuses

Children have been sexually exploited throughout history, though the definition of sexual exploitation has changed. In ancient times, female children especially were seen as the property of the father, who could do with them what he chose. A daughter was something that could be used for barter to gain lands, money, and prestige. Such practices are still evident in some parts of the world. Betrothal might also be sealed through intercourse if the father, and tradition should dictate. Daughters given in betrothal or marriage might be as young as 12 years. Other girls entered the convent at as young an age as 9, sometimes to later be used sexually by the monks associated with the convent (Rush, 1992).

DeMause (1991, 1995–96) reports that mothers often masturbated their sons to increase penis size or handed them over to other adult men to be indoctrinated into sexuality. For example, the ancient Greeks are known to have practiced *pederasty,* the use of young boys by adult men. Families of these boys might seek out a wealthy benefactor to whom they would offer their son for sexual training and pleasure. The rationale was that such practices turned boys into better warriors and prepared them more effectively for adult life (Rush, 1992; deMause, 1995). But the sexual use of children, sanctioned by and large by society, has continued to occur into modern times.

One often thinks of the Victorian era as staid and proper. On the surface, Western society frowned on sexuality; masturbation was considered a precursor to insanity, promiscuity, and even death; and women saw sexual behavior in the marital bed as an odious duty they had to perform. Yet, the sexual abuse of children flourished. Child pornography and prostitution were the alternatives sought by men who felt they could not prevail on their wives. Slave owners in the southern United States sought their sexual pleasures by "breaking in" their young slave girls at ages 11, 12, 13, and even younger (Jackson, 2000).

The Victorian era also was the setting of a debate over sexual abuse that would be written about until the end of the twentieth century. Sigmund Freud, the father of modern psychoanalysis, found that many of his female patients reported that they had been sexually molested by fathers, uncles, and brothers. Fleetingly, he considered the magnitude of the incidence of incest that the reports must represent. Yet, soon after disclosure, the women would flee treatment or recant their allegations. (Modern therapists now see this practice as typical of survivors of incest.) For this reason and because he found little sympathy or precedent for this thinking in the medical community of his day, Freud eventually dismissed the women's reports as the "hysterical symptoms [which] are derived from fantasies and not from real occurrences" (Freud, 1966, 584). Critics would later criticize Freud for not having developed his early theories, which might have provided help for survivors who would not be fully believed until late in the twentieth century.

Although in Western culture, sexuality seems like an adult activity and one in which we should not involve children, deMause (1995–96) believes that the practice of sexually using children continues today in many other parts of the world.

Efforts to Control Child Abuse

Sagatun and Edwards (1995) suggest that two reform movements, the Refuge Movement and the Child Saver Movement, influenced the exposure of children to abuse in the nineteenth and twentieth centuries. The Refuge Movement began in the early 1800s by seeking to remove children from the almshouses, and place them in institutions designed for their care. Unfortunately, the conditions in these refuge houses often rivaled those of the almshouses, and children rarely fared better than they might have if left with their parents. Abuse and neglect were rampant at the hands of overworked staff and other residents. In 1838, a Pennsylvania court also set a precedent by removing children from the custody of their parents, thus establishing a practice that would continue until today (Sagatun and Edwards, 1995; deMause, 1995–96). There is some question as to whether the early practices of the Refuge Movement were designed to protect children or to keep them away from the rest of society. However, in 1874, a case in New York City would change the history of helping children.

Mary Ellen Wilson lived with Francis and Mary Connelly and was the daughter of Mary Connelly's first husband. It was not uncommon for neighbors to see the poorly clad figure of the 8-year-old shivering, locked out in the December cold. But it was her cries as she was beaten with a leather strap that made one neighbor alert a neighborhood church worker, Etta Wheeler. After getting no help from the police, Wheeler finally turned to the Society for the Prevention of Cruelty to Animals and its director Henry Burgh, arguing that animals had more protection than little Mary Ellen. Whether Burgh acted on behalf of the SPCA or as a private citizen is unclear but history does record that the case was prosecuted by Burgh's good friend, attorney Elbridge Gerry. From this trial and the controversy surrounding it came the Society for the Prevention of Cruelty to Children in early 1875. From New York City, the SPCC spread to other major cities as the first agency designed to intervene on behalf of abused and neglected children (Crosson-Tower, 2002). By 1881, the SPCC was given authorization to make investigations and place magistrates in courts to protect the rights of children. At that time, the purpose of the society was not only to protect children but to prosecute their abusive parents (Sagatun and Edwards, 1995). Today, as we understand more about the psychology of those who become abusive, the trend is toward the protection of children and the rehabilitation of their parents.

The Child Saver Movement was founded chiefly by middle- and upper-class women whose aim it was to protect children from abuse, at the same time influencing child labor practices and legal practices affecting children. It was these efforts that gave rise to the founding of the juvenile court system through the Juvenile Court Act of 1899 (Sagatun and Edwards, 1995). (See Chapter 9 for more detail.) The juvenile court system is the primary legal entity that deals with child abuse and neglect. The use of this system will be discussed later in this chapter.

Another significant milestone in the protection of children from maltreatment was the work of C. Henry Kempe and his colleagues. In the late 1940s, Columbia University radiologist John Caffey led his colleagues in the recognition that multiple unexplained and often improperly healed fractures in children could be indicative of abuse by their caregivers. As Caffey made his theory better known through medical conferences and writings, Kempe, then chairman of the Department of Pediatrics at the University of Colorado Medical School, began his own study of the phenomenon. In a subsequent article providing the early definition of child abuse, Kempe coined the term *the battered-child syndrome,* which he and his colleagues defined as "a clinical condition in young children who have received severe physical abuse, generally from a parent or foster parent" (Kempe et al., 1962, 17). Clearer definition of this phenomenon brought it to the attention of a variety of professionals who sought to intervene through their own disciplines. By 1972, the National Center for the Prevention of Child Abuse and Neglect was established, through financial aid from the University of Colorado Medical Center, for the purpose of research and the sponsorship of training programs in the area of child abuse and neglect. In 1974, 100 years after Mary Ellen Wilson endured the beating of her caregivers, the Child Abuse Prevention and Treatment Act (PL 93-247) was passed. This act established the National Center on Child Abuse and Neglect (NCCAN), which would administer funding for a variety of programs and research to help abused and neglected children. Since that time, great strides have been made in the interest of maltreated children. In 1980, Congress passed the Adoption Assistance and Child Welfare Act (PL 96-272), which was designed to discourage long placements in foster care and to encourage permanency planning for all dependent children, including those who were abused and neglected in their own homes. And in 1986, the Child Abuse Victims' Rights Act was passed to improve investigation, court intervention training, victim protection, and treatment for maltreated children. Finally, improvements in record-keeping and more stringent penalties for offenders were mandated by the Child Protection and Penalties Enhancement Act of 1990.

Over the years, child protection has been the focus of much controversy and the subject of extensive research. Although some say that the upsurge of societal violence and the higher incidence of drug abuse has caused figures to escalate, the reality is that, with heightened awareness on the part of professionals and the general public alike, there is a much higher percentage of recognition and reporting. This trend, one hopes, can only serve to aid families in getting the help they need. It is up to future professionals to ensure that help meets the best interests of children.

Maltreatment Defined

Child abuse and neglect fall into specific categories with different symptoms and often different etiologies. The four categories most often used are *physical abuse, physical neglect, sexual abuse,* and *emotional or psychological abuse.* Some authors break down neglect into physical neglect, emotional neglect, educational neglect, and medical neglect.

Physical Abuse

The physical abuse of children can be defined as a *nonaccidental injury inflicted on a child.* The abuse is usually at the hands of a caregiver but can be perpetrated by another adult or, in some cases, an older child. Some protection agencies add the proviso that the abuse needs to have caused disfigurement, impairment of physical health, loss or impairment of a bodily organ, or substantial risk of death (Stein, 1998).

In the consideration of what constitutes physical abuse, two dilemmas arise. The first is related to cultural context. Some cultures have customs or practices that child protection would consider abusive. For example, some Vietnamese families, in a ritual called *cao gio,* rub their children with a coin heated to the point that it leaves burn marks. It is an intentional act, but designed, in that culture, to cure a variety of ills. Do the good intentions of the parents therefore exempt this practice from being considered abusive? Similarly, the use of corporal punishment is sanctioned in many Hispanic cultures, but is seen as abusive in this culture when it becomes excessive. Some child protection advocates adopt the "when in Rome do as the Romans do" attitude that says that minorities must abide by the laws of the culture in which they now reside. One Puerto Rican social worker, working in a predominantly Hispanic section of New York City, vehemently disagreed: "Yes, there are laws," he said, "but those laws were made by Anglos. Is it fair to deprive new immigrants of everything, including their customs? Maybe the laws should be changed!" The reality is that, if a child is reported as being harmed for whatever reason, a child protection agency will usually investigate. If the reason is one of culture, this will be considered. Fontes (2002), in speaking of Hispanic families using harsh discipline, suggests that understanding the cultural values and approaching the family in a nonblaming way will go a long way toward gaining cooperation.

Another dilemma for society is: What constitutes discipline and how is that differentiated from abuse? The physical punishment of children as a form of discipline has been practiced extensively throughout history in the United States. Although more recently many parents are seeking alternatives to physical punishment in the raising of their children, there is still a significant number of parents who hit as a way to discipline. Some argue that what separates this type of discipline from abuse is a matter of degree. If bruises are left on the child and those bruises last for a prolonged period, the act is considered abusive.

Symptoms.   Children who have been physically abused display a variety of symptoms. Bruises are frequently what come to mind when one thinks of abuse, and indeed these constitute the most frequent symptoms. Children may acquire bruises over time and one can often discern this when the bruises are at different stages of healing. For example, on lighter skins, when bruises are first made they are usually red in color, but turn blue about 6 to 12 hours later. During the next 12 to 24 hours the site will become blackish purple, eventually taking on a greenish tint in 6 days and healing to a pale green or yellow by 5 to 10 days. Thus a child who is observed to have bruises in various stages of healing may have been abused on different occasions (Crosson-Tower, 2002; Hobbs and Wynne, 2001).

Bruises may also be in the shape of objects such as ropes, cords, belt buckles, or coat hangers, indicating that the child has been hit with force using one of these instruments. Bruises that are inflicted on areas of the body that are less likely to sustain accidental injuries are also suspect (e.g., the face and head, upper arms, back, upper legs, and genitalia). Certainly it is possible for a child to be bruised by accident, but if there is an unusual quality to the bruise, poor supervision and abuse should be considered.

Another classic abuse symptom is the burn. Infants and small children may be especially vulnerable to being burned in the heat (literally) of a parent's anger. Burns may be inflicted by cigarettes, pokers, irons, scalding liquids, heating grates, or radiators. Abuse burns often appear on such unusual places as the palms of the hands, soles of the feet, abdomen, or genitals (Hobbs and Wynne, 2001).

Fractures are one of the recognizable signs, to the medical community, of abuse. From Caffey's early work (mentioned earlier) to the present, physicians are especially vigilant for signs of certain types of fractures. For example, a spiral break is particularly indicative of abuse. A parent who, in his or her anger, grabs a child and twists the leg or arm, may cause this type of break. Previously untreated fractures, which can be detected by X rays of the calcium deposits surrounding these improperly healed breaks, suggest a situation in which the parent was hesitant to seek medical treatment. When healthy children receive a fracture, there is swelling and pain, which usually prompts the parent to seek medical advice. But a parent who has inflicted the trauma may feel hesitant to do so. Head injuries or skull fractures are especially dangerous. In addition, blood can collect around the surface of the brain, causing a condition known as a subdural hematoma. Children experiencing this injury may vomit, have seizures, lose consciousness, or even die.

Physical indicators are not the only clues to abuse. Children will often act out their cries for help in their behaviors. As infants, children cry as a way to communicate with the world. Different cries mean different things. But a baby who has learned through being abused that the world is a threatening place may develop a shrill undifferentiated cry. As abused children become older, their development may not progress as it should. They may be slow to reach milestones in social and physical development. The school years may find them unable to concentrate or doing poorly without the necessary energy to learn. On the other hand, some abused children throw themselves into school as a way of coping with an unhappy homelife. This child is the chronic over-achiever, the child to whom a grade of B seems like the end of the world.

Some abused children shrink from contact and withdraw into themselves. Some wet the bed or soil themselves in their anxiety. Still others fight their world by becoming pugnacious or acting out in other ways. The source of the behaviors of many delinquent children is a background of abuse. Children who have experienced abuse may also be physically hurtful toward others, especially younger children or animals. Some run away in a desperate attempt to escape their pain (see Table 7.1). There are as many ways for children to cry out for help as there are individual children, and every symptom here may not spell abuse by itself. It is the cluster of symptoms that gives one cause for suspicion.

Profile of the Abuser.   Who physically abuses children? Hurting a child seems so foreign to many of us that we question how any parent could be capable of such harm. Yet, everyone has the potential, under certain circumstances, to harm another—and especially a child. Parents who abuse may feel over-whelmed and depressed or angry with their own lives. Most people discover that it is possible to feel out of control. When one is out of control, anything can happen. It depends on how hard one is pushed.

In addition to poor control or anger, many abusive parents have never had their own needs met. They may not have been parented by stable, caring indi-viduals who knew how to model good parenting. If they were abused, they may assume that that is how one raises children. They may be bitter about the alco-holism that racked their childhoods or the inconsistency that moved them from place to place. Most abusive parents do not intend to hurt their children. Granted, there are a few who have been so damaged by their life experiences that they strike out to hurt others, but luckily they are in the minority.

The self-esteem of many abusive parents is dependent on their children's behavior. If their children "look good," they feel like good parents. When their children misbehave, these parents often see themselves as failures. Some par-ents see their children as people who can nurture them when their own parents did not. And there are parents who were raised with corporal punishment and are only repeating the patterns with their children that they learned in their own childhood homes.

Fortunately, there are only a few parents who, caught up in their rage over their own unmet needs, abuse their children sadistically. These parents may

TABLE 7.1   Physical and Behavioral Indicators of Child Abuse and Neglect: Clues to Look for in Detection

Type of Child Abuse/Neglect	Physical Indicators	Behavioral Indicators
PHYSICAL ABUSE	Unexplained bruises and welts: • on face, lips, mouth • on torso, back, buttocks, thighs • in various stages of healing • clustered, forming regular patterns • reflecting shape of article used to inflict (electric cord, belt buckle) • on several different surface areas • regularly appear after absence, weekend, or vacation • human bite marks • bald spots Unexplained burns: • cigar, cigarette burns, especially on soles, palms, back, or buttocks • immersion burns (sock-like, glove-like, doughnut-shaped on buttocks or genitalia) • patterned like electric burner, iron, etc. • rope burns on arms, legs, neck, or torso Unexplained fractures: • to skull, nose, facial structure • in various stages of healing • multiple or spiral fractures Unexplained lacerations or abrasions: • to mouth, lips, gums, eyes • to external genitalia	Wary of adult contacts Apprehensive when other children cry Behavioral extremes: • aggressiveness, or • withdrawal • overly compliant Afraid to go home Reports injury by parents Exhibits anxiety about normal activities, e.g., napping Complains of soreness and moves awkwardly Destructive to self and others Early to school or stays late as if afraid to go home Accident prone Wears clothing that covers body when not appropriate Chronic runaway (especially adolescents) Cannot tolerate physical contact or touch
PHYSICAL NEGLECT	Consistent hunger, poor hygiene, inappropriate dress Consistent lack of supervision, especially in dangerous activities or long periods Unattended physical problems or medical needs Abandonment Lice Distended stomach, emaciated	Begging, stealing food Constant fatigue, listlessness or falling asleep States there is no caretaker at home Frequent school absence or tardiness Destructive, pugnacious School dropout (adolescents) Early emancipation from family (adolescents)

TABLE 7.1 *Continued*

Type of Child Abuse/Neglect	Physical Indicators	Behavioral Indicators
SEXUAL ABUSE	Difficulty in walking or sitting	Unwilling to participate in certain physical activities
	Torn, stained, or bloody underclothing	Sudden drop in school performance
	Pain or itching in genital area	Withdrawal, fantasy or unusually infantile behavior
	Bruises or bleeding in external genitalia, vaginal or anal areas	Crying with no provocation
	Venereal disease	Bizarre, sophisticated, or unusual sexual behavior or knowledge
	Frequent urinary or yeast infections	Anorexia (especially adolescents)
	Frequent unexplained sore throats	Sexually provocative
		Poor peer relationships
		Reports sexual assault by caretaker
		Fear of or seductiveness toward males
		Suicide attempts (especially adolescents)
		Chronic runaway
		Early pregnancies
EMOTIONAL MALTREATMENT	Speech disorders	Habit disorders (sucking, biting, rocking, etc.)
	Lags in physical development	Conduct disorders (antisocial, destructive, etc.)
	Failure to thrive (especially in infants)	Neurotic traits (sleep disorders, inhibition of play)
	Asthma, severe allergies, or ulcers	Behavioral extremes: • compliant, passive • aggressive, demanding
	Substance abuse	Overly adaptive behavior: • inappropriately adult • inappropriately infantile
		Developmental lags (mental, emotional)
		Delinquent behavior (especially adolescents)

Source: Some material previously appeared in *Child Abuse and Neglect* by Cynthia Crosson. Copyright 1984. Washington, DC: National Education Association. Reprinted by permission of the NEA Professional Library.

get high on the power they feel from hurting others, sometimes even to the point of killing them. Obviously, the prognosis for this type of abuser is poor.

Another type of abuse, known as Munchausen-by-proxy, has gained more attention in the last few years. *Munchausen-by-proxy* is found predominantly in mothers of young children and is a variation of Munchausen syndrome, which affects adults. Adult Munchausen involves an adult who is so desperately in need of attention that she or he induces some form of medical condition so as to necessitate a hospital stay. The patient then basks in the attention of hospital staff while proving a very demanding patient. The psychological community has concluded that this syndrome is based on the internalized rage felt by the patient toward parents by whom he or she feels abandoned emotionally (Eminson et al., 2000).

Munchausen-by-proxy is a syndrome manifested predominantly by mothers, though a few rare cases of fathers suffering from the condition have been recorded. These mothers, who may have been Munchausen patients themselves, appear to be caring and concerned about their hospitalized children, almost to a fault. The children come to the attention of the medical community for a variety of reasons and the etiology of their condition is often not discovered until well into their hospital stay. The mothers provide a picture of a concerned parent who is always involved in the resolution of the child's health problem. At the same time this mother may have induced severe vomiting by giving the child large doses of ipecac, produced diarrhea by administering phenolphthalein, interfered with the blood sugar level or contaminated the blood by injecting insulin or fecal matter, or even smothered the child to simulate Sudden Infant Death Syndrome or respiratory problems (Parnell and Day, 1998; Eminson et al., 2000).

It is difficult to understand this type of pathology, but experts now say that it is based on the mother's need to establish a close and collegial, albeit dependent, relationship with the physician. Her extreme need for this fantasized relationship with someone she sees as symbolically powerful distorts her perception of the harm she is doing to her child. Recognition of this syndrome as a form of child abuse is too new to have the benefit of any longitudinal studies but the residual effects on victims who survive.

Physical Neglect

The concept of neglect differs from culture to culture. In general, it is the role of parents to meet the physical and emotional needs of their offspring. These needs usually encompass shelter, food, clothing, medical care, educational needs, protection, and supervision and moral guidance. The manner in which they are met may differ, but failure to meet these basic human needs in some acceptable manner constitutes neglect. Polansky and colleagues (1975) expand this definition further:

> *Child neglect may be defined as a condition in which a caretaker responsible for the child either deliberately or by extraordinary inattentiveness permits*

the child to experience available suffering and/or fails to provide one or more of the ingredients generally deemed essential for developing a person's phys-ical, intellectual and emotional capacities. (5)

Cowen (1999) breaks neglect into various types: *abandonment,* when par-ents desert their children on a temporary or permanent basis; *educational neglect,* when parents fail to see that their children attend school on a regular basis or provide an approved alternate educational plan; *emotional neglect,* when parents are psychologically unavailable to their children; *health care neglect,* when par-ents do not provide preventative care or adequate care during illness or injury; *nutritional neglect,* when parents' failure to provide age-appropriate food and liq-uids results in poor growth, starvation, dehydration, or failure to thrive; *phys-ical neglect,* which involves the failure to provide safe and hygienic housing; and *supervision neglect,* when children are not protected by their parents from dangerous situations.

Various cultures interpret the definition of neglect in different ways. For ex-ample, protection and supervision in the Native American culture is a commu-nity rather than an individual responsibility. A parent in such a culture would feel comfortable letting even a fairly young child out of his or her sight because of the knowledge that the neighbors will not let harm come to the child. In other cultures, it is the role of the extended family to assume supervision. Dubowitz and Klockner (1998), in their study of how neglect was defined across cultures, found that the definition differed only slightly among white and Afri-can American caregivers. These authors do comment, however, that a "clear def-inition of neglect is sorely needed to help guide research, understanding, clinical practice, and policy and program development of this problem" (235).

Symptoms.   Although it may be difficult to be clear in all situations, protec-tive services must have some guidelines to determine what symptoms to look for in children. Practice and research have developed a list of symptoms that can be found in children who are deemed neglected.

Neglected children may demonstrate consistent hunger and even malnu-trition. Very young infants who have been neglected may withdraw from their environment and waste away, demonstrating a syndrome known as Nonor-ganic Failure to Thrive (NFTT). Older children may also become listless and have little energy. They may not be appropriately clothed to protect them dur-ing cold weather. They may be dirty, with body odor and lice, although the lat-ter is highly contagious and does not always suggest neglect. Neglected children often demonstrate unattended physical or medical problems.

CASE EXAMPLE

George and Tag

George's teeth were badly decayed. He and his 3-year-old brother, Tag, were often left alone and subsisted on the snacks that 8-year-old George could beg or steal from the package store near their apartment. Their mother, a heroin addict, had tried numerous times to "kick her habit" but to no avail. An "aunt" watched George and Tag while their mother attended rehabilitation programs, but when the mother came home they were once again left to her inconsistent care. Tag had developed a cough, possibly due to the fact that his light clothes offered little protection against the weather. It was not until George's sporadic school attendance was noticed that the family came to the attention of protective services.

Like George, children who are victims of neglect may steal either to get food or because they have learned not to trust that their next meal will be there when they need it. Neglected children are often tired and listless. Developmentally, they are usually significantly delayed, lacking the stimulation, consistency, and encouragement that has benefited other children. Some neglected children fail to bond with their inattentive caregivers and may demonstrate attachment disorder.

Many neglectful parents do not value education for their children. Or if they do feel that school is important, they lack the ability to get them there consistently. For this reason, school attendance may be sporadic. In later years, the adolescent drops out of school because school says little to him or her about the struggles of life.

Neglectful Parents.   Parents who neglect were often neglected themselves as children. For them, it is a learned way of life. Their childhoods have produced in them nothing but anger and indifference. Their adult lives are dedicated to meeting the needs that were not met for them as they were growing up.

CASE EXAMPLE

Eulalia

Eulalia is a slight woman with a quiet, indifferent manner. She seems oblivious to the bits of food on the cluttered table, the flies coming in from the broken windows, the stench of urine, and the children fighting and screaming in the background. She puffs absentmindedly on a cigarette, hardly seeming to hear as the social worker explains about the complaint they have received about her children's vandalism of a local school. Eulalia has learned to tune it all out. She has heard it before.

Pregnant at age 13, Eulalia followed her itinerant boyfriend to the city where she now resides. There was nothing for her at home. The middle child of 10 children, Eulalia had tired of taking care of the younger ones and being beaten up by the older ones while her parents were away working as field hands. There had been little to eat and less to do at home, and she longed to be on her own. But after dumping her with friends, her boyfriend left her, pregnant again. She drifted from relationship to relationship, each promising her some stability. But now Eulalia, at 21-one-years old and with five children, has an apartment in a run-down housing development. She is too involved in the goings-on of the neighborhood to find time for the children. Even if she did, she would not know how to mother them adequately. Don't children just raise themselves? That is what happened in her family.

For Eulalia, life held little meaning. For her children, life would not be much different without intervention.

Throughout the years it has been mothers who have been described when the discussion of neglectful parents has emerged. Polansky and colleagues (1975, 1991) have created the best known profile of neglectful mothers. They defended their one-gender profile by pointing out that fathers were usually unavailable in neglectful households. Swift (1995) suggests that abandonment on the part of these fathers is the ultimate neglect.

Polansky and colleagues studied neglectful mothers in both urban and rural settings and categorized them into five types:

1. The *apathetic futile mother* demonstrates little or no affect to the point of seeming numb. Burdened by her own unmet needs, she has little energy and finds that nothing is worth doing. Why put diapers on the baby when he will only get them wet? Why do dishes when they will only be dirty again? It is difficult to reach her, as her thinking is very concrete and she communicates on only the most basic level, referred to by Polansky and colleagues (1991) as verbal inaccessibility. Her seeming depression is infectious, and social workers describe this mother as a very difficult client with whom to work.

2. The *impulse-ridden mother* is impulsive and inconsistent. She may have the energy to meet life expectations, but it is instead directed toward defiance, restlessness, and manipulation. She cannot tolerate stress and frustration. This is the mother who has never learned inner controls and who is therefore not capable of performing the tasks required by consistent mothering.

3. The *mother in reactive depression* is one who is responding to life circumstances by giving up rather than fighting. She is intensely depressed or overwhelmed by grief.

CASE EXAMPLE

Leanna

Leanna had been a fairly consistent mother with her first child. She found her second more difficult but she settled into the task of mothering nonetheless. She took pride in her parenting and saw her children as important extensions of herself. Her young husband, too, found parenthood to his liking. The couple managed to weather several financial and emotional storms in their early marriage, but their future promised to be bright.

One hot summer day, Leanna took 3-year-old Sam and 2-year-old Jessie to the beach. She had hardly looked away when she noticed that Sam was gone. Frantically she searched for him, screaming for others to help. He was found caught between two rocks, face down in the water. Efforts to revive him were fruitless and Leanna became hysterical. Once calmed, she slipped into an almost catatonic depression. No amount of coaxing by her husband or professionals could bring her out of her passiveness. She was hospitalized and put on antidepressants. Her husband, feeling that the drugs were making her worse, insisted she be taken off them. "She'll be okay," he assured. "Her brother was drowned when he was a baby too. It's just too much for her." But Leanna never fully emerged from her depression. She could not care for her remaining child, a fact that her concerned husband denied. Again and again he would return home to find that his wife had not moved from her bed. His own immaturity and frustration finally drove him away and Leanna was left alone until protective services finally intervened.

---

4. The *mother who is mentally retarded* may neglect her children, but not all mentally retarded mothers do so. When these mothers do neglect, it is usually because they lack the necessary supports to compensate for their own impaired functioning.

5. The *mother who is psychotic* may be hampered in her ability to parent by her thought disturbances, severe anxiety, withdrawal, or bizarre behavior.

Despite long reliance on the research by Polansky and colleagues, newer studies seek to understand neglect in order to combat what is a chronic and generational treatment issues. Crittenden (1999) suggests that neglect has to do with the processing of information. Neglectful mothers have difficulty processing both cognitively (thinking) or affectively (feeling). She fits these mothers into several categories: Mothers who practice *disorganized neglect* live from crisis to crisis, feeling (affective) rather than problem solving (cognitive). Their children learn that crisis is a way of life and may actually use extremes of emotion to manipulate their parents and, later, others. In *emotional neglect,* caregivers process cognitively, but the feeling seems to be diminished or absent. These parents appear to their children as cold and uncaring or emotionally unavailable. Children may feel rejected and withdraw, often adopting this diminished affect themselves. This type of neglect may be seen at all socioeconomic levels. And finally, families demonstrating *depressed neglect* guard against expressing both affect and cognition. For them, nothing is worth doing and they, too, become withdrawn and lacking in emotion.

All of these categories produce families who, for whatever reason, are unable to meet the needs of their children. Many lack the insight into their own actions that is required in order to use the help they might be given. It should also be noted that although neglect spans all socioeconomic levels, it is the lower socioeconomic groups that tend to be identified. This may be because higher groups have the resources to mask their neglect of their children. By the same token, it is often assumed that minorities make up a higher proportion of neglectful parents. This, too, is untrue, although it is often the minority parents who are reported.

Sexual Abuse

Sexual abuse refers to "contact with a child where the child is being used for sexual stimulation by the other person" (Sagatun and Edwards, 1995). It is assumed that the abuser is older than the child and therefore has more power and resources. Due to this difference in power, it is believed that the child is enticed, cajoled, entrapped, threatened, or forced into the abuse. The abuse is progressive, beginning from the least intrusive behaviors, such as observation, or exposure, to more intrusive behaviors, such as actual penile or rectal penetration. During this progression, the abuser gauges the reactions of the child and grooms her or him for further abuse. In addition to being touched sexually or being compelled to touch the abuser, sexual abuse also includes in its definition the use of a child in the production of pornography or encouraging the child to view pornography or other sexual acts (Stein, 1998).

Types of Sexual Abuse.   Sexual abuse may be divided into several categories: incest or familial abuse; extrafamilial molestation; exploitation through pornography, prostitution, sex rings, or cults; and abuse within institutions.

Experts in the area of *incest* caution that most children are abused by family members rather than strangers, as was once supposed. In fact, an estimated 60 to 70% of all abuse is perpetrated within the family (Faller, 1990). Abusers might be fathers, older siblings, mothers (although less common), or stepfathers. Finkelhor (1984) suggests that girls who have stepfathers are statistically more likely to be sexually abused even if the abuse is not perpetrated by the stepfather. The most common type of incest is usually thought to be between father and daughter, although new studies suggest that older siblings perpetrate much more abuse than was previously assumed (Wiehe and Herring, 1997).

Incestuous relationships within families have usually gone on for years before they stop or are discovered. The sexual contact has progressed from seemingly benign tickling or observing the child in the bath to more obvious sexual activities such as mutual masturbation or vaginal or rectal intercourse. Children have usually been compelled to secrecy by admonishments ranging from

"This is our special relationship and no one would understand or believe you" to "They will send me (or you) away if you tell." Sometimes children are threatened or physically hurt to prevent them from telling.

The perpetrator in an incestuous situation usually lacks the social and communication skills to negotiate an effective relationship with another adult—in this case, his wife. In father/daughter incest, he therefore seeks a nonconflictual partner and finds this in his daughter. In his child he finds someone over whom he can feel power in order to mold her into a sexual partner. This father, a master at denial and manipulation, can rationalize away the inappropriateness and illegality of this arrangement, often telling himself and his daughter that he is "teaching" her lessons for later life (Hanson et al., 1994).

Extrafamilial abuse is abuse that is perpetrated outside the immediate family. This can be by a friend, an acquaintance, or a stranger. Although it is a common myth that most abuse is perpetrated by strangers, children are more often abused by someone they know. Children may be abused individually or become part of *prostitution rings*. In these, children are bribed, blackmailed, or forced to participate in sexual acts for money. The money is then kept by those who have involved them. Or some sex rings are dedicated to the production of *child pornography*. These groups create photos, films, and videos that are then sold at a significant profit.

Over the last decade, one form of extrafamilial abuse has become of special concern. The Internet has made the engagement of children for *sexual exploitation* extremely easy. Today, an abuser has a wider geographical range of children that he or she might engage in sexual activity, and has better access to them than ever before. Perpetrators can contact children who are under the seemingly watchful eyes of parents, stimulate them and desensitize them through pornography, engage them in discussions, and even arrange meetings with them for sexual activities. Many abusers pose as children or teens themselves in order to "chat" more convincingly with unsuspecting victims.

McLaughlin (2000) suggests the term *technophilia* to refer to those who use cyberspace to engage in the sexual exploitation of children. Perpetrators may collect child pornography over the Internet; produce their own, often through using pictures of real children; or "chat" with children for the purpose of engaging them in sexual activity either through online discussions or by arranging to meet them.

Although there is consensus among child abuse experts that the use of the Internet by perpetrators is a risk for children (Foley, 2002), the general public often argues that the dissemination of pornography is part of their right to free speech. Although the 1996 Child Pornography Prevention Act outlawed the production or sharing of child pornography over the Internet, the 2002 overturn of that ban by the Supreme Court gave rise to much discussion (Jeffrey, 2002). According to that Court decision, virtual pornography (images of children in sexual acts or poses) cannot be equated with actual pictures and therefore is not banned under the 1996 law. This splitting of legal hairs concerns those experts who recognize that child pornography, even in fantasy form, helps stimulate the sexual abuser (Foley, 2002).

In addition to finding their victims on the Internet, perpetrators have other methods of finding children. Sometimes the perpetrator has a bond with the parent, such as in the case of a family friend. Or the parent may need services from the perpetrator, such as a daycare provider. Parents may not be supervising closely and the child wanders off or is home alone, or parents may be otherwise occupied (Crosson-Tower, 2002). For example, one survivor recounted that she used to help her mother in the family bookstore. A customer used to come in and ask her (the child) for certain books. Invariably they would be on top shelves. While her mother waited on customers, the child would go in search of the books, followed by the customer. "The first time he put his hand up my skirt when I was on the stepladder, I was very surprised. I jumped down but he smiled and I thought it must have been my imagination." The stranger continued to fondle the child over the next few weeks. He threatened that if she told her mother she would never work in the store again. Liking her job, the girl kept quiet. "Finally, he just stopped coming in," she continued, "but I was afraid that he would and the job lost much of its enjoyment for me."

In the last few years, increased attention has been given to the abuse of children in *cults*. In these instances, the perpetrators are usually multiple and the techniques used to confuse the victim often render her or his story suspect by anyone she or he tells. As more and more of these cases emerge, clinicians seek answers as to how to deal with them. Hayden's *Ghost Girl* (1992), the story of a special education teacher faced with a child who chooses elective mutism as a way to cope with the abuse, gives an excellent portrayal of the dilemma of the professional faced with the prospect of the cult-abused child.

Institutional abuse has gained increased attention over the last few years. Daycare centers and child care institutions provide an excellent opportunity for a perpetrator to have access to children. One of the most publicized daycare cases was in Manhattan Beach, California, where the McMartin trials stimulated numerous legal proceedings and much debate. Such situations have inspired institutions to screen staff more effectively and to take precautions so that staff do not have many opportunities to be alone with children.

Symptoms.   Sexually abused children demonstrate a variety of symptoms, some of which may also be associated with other types of problems. Physically, sexual abuse may not always be visible. When children do have physical symptoms they take the form of rectal or vaginal tears, urinary tract or yeast infections, and burns or bruises in the genital or rectal area. Children may also have sexually transmitted diseases such as gonorrhea, syphilis, genital warts, herpes, chlamydia, and AIDS, as these can be contracted only through contact with infected mucous membranes.

Behaviorally, sexually abused children may seem secretive or withdrawn. Their school work may suffer or, conversely, they may see school as the only safe place in which they can excel. They may suffer mood swings, cry without provocation, or engage in such self-injurious behavior as bulimia, anorexia, maiming or cutting, or suicide attempts. Some sexually abused youths use drugs or alcohol to dull the pain. These behaviors can also be indicative of non-sexual disorders and must be seen as possible indicators rather than definite signs. By the same token, not all sexually abused children demonstrate symptoms. Conte and Berliner (1988) found that 20% of the children studied did not manifest observable symptoms of their abuse. When there are no symptoms, it usually means that either the reaction is delayed or the child has repressed the material to the point that he or she is unable to feel it (Faller, 1990).

There are a few symptoms that in and of themselves point strongly to the fact that the child has been sexually abused. It is not unusual for molested children to act out their inappropriate sexual knowledge in their behavior by sexually molesting younger children. Usually this acting out will demonstrate knowledge that they would not normally have. Chronic and compulsive masturbation too can be indicative of a disturbance of a sexual nature. Older children may become extremely promiscuous. These types of sexual acting out, as well as behaviors such as fire-setting and mutilation of animals, should always raise one's suspicions about the presence of sexual abuse.

Perpetrators.   There are three predominant theories about what motivates someone to sexually abuse a child: the Groth typology, the Addiction Theory, and the Precondition Model.

A. Nicholas Groth, a psychologist working with incarcerated offenders, first created the fixated/regressed typology, known as the *Groth typology.* He contended that offenders could be separated into two categories: *fixated,* or those who were emotionally "stuck" in childhood with respect to their sexual interests, and *regressed,* those whose sexual interests reverted back to childhood due to the stresses of their life in the adult world.

The fixated offender is primarily interested in male children and he comes down to the child's level in his engagement of that child. His primary orientation is toward children and he has little interest sexually in age-mates. His first sexual offense is premeditated and there is a compulsive nature to his acts. This is a man who is not motivated by stress nor is he probably under the influence of drugs or alcohol. Instead he is someone who demonstrates a socio-sexual immaturity and has failed to resolve his life issues (Groth, 1979).

The regressed offender, on the other hand, is someone who may appear to function fairly well as an adult. In reality he finds that his adult life is too conflictual, especially his relations with peers. He therefore turns to a nonconflictual female partner in a female child with whom he has a sexual relationship. In the process he elevates this child to the level of an adult by treating her like one. Although he may continue to participate in peer relationships, perhaps even sexually, he depends on the child to feel powerful. He may be under a great deal of stress and his first offense is often impulsive in nature. This is the father who goes a bit too far in washing his daughter's genitals or the grandfather who ends up fondling his granddaughter when she sits on his lap. Neither may have planned the event initially, but after the first incident they may engineer circumstances to give them the opportunity to abuse again. This man may also use or abuse substances, but these are not the cause of his behavior. Rather, he uses them as an excuse to abuse children (Groth, 1979).

The problem with Groth's typology is that offenders do not always fit neatly into one category or another. Carnes (2002) suggests that sexual abuse is an addiction (sometimes referred to as *Addiction Theory*). In this addiction, the addict develops a faulty belief system that leads to impaired thinking. As part of this thinking, he denies, rationalizes, and blames others for his actions and thoughts. He becomes preoccupied with his fantasies and ritualizes his behavior. Therefore, the offender who uses one strategy on a child will probably continue that strategy with others. Finally, his behavior becomes compulsive and he feels that he has to abuse children. Some child sexual abusers feel despair afterwards and some do not. Again, not all offenders fit neatly into the addiction category.

Probably the most widely used theory today is that of Finkelhor's *Precondition Model*. Finkelhor (1984) theorizes that in order for the sexual abuse of a child to happen, four factors must be operating: (1) the perpetrator must be motivated to abuse, (2) the internal inhibitors that would tell most people not to abuse would not be working, (3) the external inhibitors that normally protect children would not be in place, and (4) the child's resistance would not be sufficiently strong (see Table 7.2).

Motivation to sexually abuse involves three components. First, the perpetrator must feel an *emotional congruence toward children*. This is more than a simple attraction to or desire to be with children. Rather, it is based on a pathological phenomenon in which being around children satisfies the perpetrator's emotional needs. He may feel this way because he needs to feel power over someone, because his own emotional development is arrested, or because of some childhood trauma that he feels compelled to reenact. Second, the perpetrator is *sexually aroused by children*. Once again, it may be a childhood trauma that is the root of this response. Or he may have grown up observing another's sexual involvement with children. For example, research tells us that an increasing number of brothers of victims in families in which father/daughter incest is present are modeling the behaviors of their fathers by themselves abusing their sisters or, later in life, their own children. Some sexual abuse perpetrators are aroused by child pornography, often misinterpreting the behavior of children as sexual and therefore inviting sexual contact. Finally, perpetrators are motivated to turn to children because their own *normal outlets for sexual expression are blocked*. Blockage may be a result of marital problems, inadequate social skills, fear of adult females, or some previous traumatic sexual experience with an adult (Finkelhor, 1984).

Most of us have an internal voice that lets us know that certain behavior is unacceptable. These *internal inhibitors are not operating efficiently* for sexual abuse perpetrators. They may be hampered by the influence of alcohol, senility, an impulse disorder, or psychosis. More likely, perpetrators have not developed

TABLE 7.2 Preconditions for Sexual Abuse

	Level of Explanation	
	Individual	*Social/Cultural*
Precondition I: Factors Related to Motivation to Sexually Abuse		
Emotional congruence	Arrested emotional development Need to feel powerful and controlling Reenactment of childhood trauma to undo the hurt Narcissistic identification with self as a young child	Masculine requirement to be dominant and powerful in sexual relationships
Sexual arousal	Childhood sexual experience that was traumatic or strongly conditioning Modeling of sexual interest in children by someone else Misattribution of arousal cues Biologic abnormality	Child pornography Erotic portrayal of children in advertising Male tendency to sexualize all emotional needs
Blockage	Oedipal conflict Castration anxiety Fear of adult females Traumatic sexual experience with adult Inadequate social skills Marital problems	Repressive norms about masturbation and extramarital sex
Precondition II: Factors Predisposing to Overcoming Internal Inhibitors	Alcohol Psychosis Impulse disorder Senility Failure of incest inhibition mechanism in family dynamics	Social toleration of sexual interest in children Weak criminal sanctions against offenders Ideology of patriarchal prerogatives for fathers Social toleration for deviance committed while intoxicated Child pornography Male inability to identify with needs of children
Precondition III: Factors Predisposing to Overcoming External Inhibitions	Mother who is absent or ill Mother who is not close to or protective of child Mother who is dominated or abused by father Social isolation of family Unusual opportunities to be alone with child Lack of supervision of child Unusual sleeping or rooming conditions	Lack of social supports for mother Barriers to women's equality Erosion of social networks Ideology of family sanctity
Predisposition IV: Factors Predisposing to Overcoming Child's Resistance	Child who is emotionally insecure or deprived Child who lacks knowledge about sexual abuse Situation of unusual trust between child and offender Coercion	Unavailability of sex education for children Social powerlessness of children

Source: Reprinted with the permission of The Free Press, an imprint of Simon & Schuster Adult Publishing Group, from *Child Sexual Abuse* by David Finkelhor. Copyright © 1984 by David Finkelhor.

these internal voices because they have seen sexual abuse in their own child-hood. From a societal perspective, they may also not be compelled to develop internal inhibitors. With the availability of child pornography and the fact that our culture tolerates advertising that presents children in a seductive manner, the individual with a shaky set of inner controls finds little reason not to be in-terested in children. Further, most perpetrators know that intoxication pro-vides an excellent excuse for a wide variety of deviant behaviors. And while patriarchy is still accepted, incestuous fathers feel justified in their abuse of their daughters (Finkelhor, 1984).

There are also external inhibitors that can protect children, but when these *external inhibitors are not operating,* children are placed at risk. External in-hibitors are those things that keep a child safe or rob a perpetrator of the op-portunity to abuse. For example, mothers are often in key roles to protect their children. When mothers are absent or unavailable either physically or emo-tionally or are dominated by an abusive husband, they may not be able to pro-tect their children. Many mothers lack social supports. The societal concept of family sanctity, although functional for the autonomy of a healthy family sys-tem, leaves the abusive family isolated and the children at risk for the contin-uation of abuse (Finkelhor, 1984).

Finally, in order to abuse a child, the perpetrator must *overcome the child's resistance.* Children who are emotionally needy or who are unaware of the po-tential for being sexually abused are usually easier targets. Society's view of children as powerless individuals with few rights renders them especially vul-nerable to being victims (Finkelhor, 1984).

The correlation between abuse in childhood and perpetration in adulthood is well known. We also know that not all sexual abuse perpetrators had sexual abuse in their backgrounds, nor do all who were sexually abused as children become abusive as adults. What then predisposes an individual to become a perpetrator? Gilgun (1990) studied sexual abusers and a control group of non-abusive men in an effort to determine why some men abuse and some do not. She found that there were differences in four areas. First, the perpetrators were more likely to have had childhood problems in the areas of *confidant relation-ships,* having few confidants and feeling isolated from and excluded by others. Second, abusers also differed in the area of *sexuality.* Most abusers began mas-turbation prior to the age of 12 and used it to maintain their equilibrium. Fur-ther, they reported repetitive, coercive sexual fantasies. The control group masturbated later in adolescence and used the act to release tension. They also had peer-related (e.g., imagining appropriate sexual acts with peers) and non-coercive fantasies.

Third, Gilgun found that the *families of abusers were characterized by domestic violence and child maltreatment.* Those who had not been abused themselves had watched the abuse of siblings or their mothers. Finally, the *peer relationships* of offenders were more likely to be centered around antisocial activities that equated masculinity with power and sexual conquest. There is an increasing amount of material pointing to the fact that children who are denied secure attachment lose the ability to relate to others in a secure manner. This inability to attain intimacy and empathize with the feelings of others may create an individual who becomes abusive (Freeman-Longo and Blanchard, 1998).

Most of the research done on perpetrators refers to males. Does this mean that women do not abuse children? Unfortunately, this is not the case. Women, too, have been found to be abusive, often in larger numbers than we realize. In 1984, Finkelhor postulated that women were not as often abusive because of their enculturation. Our culture taught them to prefer older and stronger partners, whereas men learned to look for smaller and weaker partners; women are more closely aligned with nurturing and therefore more capable of relating to the whole child; women are less likely than men to sexualize affection, and, because women themselves have for centuries been victimized, they are more likely to empathize with the victim and therefore less likely to put others in a victim role.

Since this theory that somewhat exonerated women as perpetrators, reports of female abusers have increased. Little research has been published on female offenders. Mathews and colleagues (1990) felt that women were motivated to abuse for several reasons: (1) they were repeating the abuse they had experienced themselves as children; (2) they were going along with the abuse perpetrated by their male partners; (3) they were seeking closeness, affection, attention, or acceptance from their victims; (4) they were displacing anger, a need for power, or feelings of rejection onto their victims; or (5) they saw children as safe targets for their displaced feelings.

Kaufman and associates (1995) compared the motivations and other factors between perpetration by male and female offenders. They found that females were more likely than male offenders to engage in abuse with another perpetrator, thus supporting Mathews's hypothesis that women act as accomplices in the abuse. Males and females just as often use threats, pornographic materials, and coercion to compel their victims, but women are more prone to use devices or foreign objects in the abusive act. There was little difference in the genders in regard to their relationship to the victim and the location of the abuse, although 31% of the females (compared to only 8% of the males) were the teachers or baby-sitters of the victims (Kaufman et al., 1995, 331). Despite the similarities in the methods of male and female offenders, Kaufman and colleagues postulated that the motivations were different. These authors felt that men more often abused for sexual satisfaction, whereas women abused to meet such nonsexual needs such as emotional gratification.

Over the last few years an increasing amount of attention has been given to juvenile offenders, or children who sexually abuse younger children (see Masson and Erooga, 1999). We know that almost all of these children have themselves been victims of sexual abuse. Many children are what Gil and Johnson (1993) term "reactive" and cannot necessarily be classified as children who will be abusers in the future, provided they receive treatment. In fact, it is difficult to tell, except in retrospect, those children who will abuse later and who will not. It is doubly important, then, that intervention be undertaken early to try to ensure that some of the juvenile offenders do not go on to become adult abusers.

Events over the last decade have also brought to our attention the prevalence of child sexual abuse by authority figures outside the home: teachers, coaches, daycare providers, and even the clergy (Crosson-Tower, 2002). Sexual abuse within churches especially rocked the confidence of the public in church leaders and has the potential to bring about major changes. In fact, the Roman Catholic Church dedicated the Conference of Catholic Bishops in June of 2002 to seeking to understand and respond to the crisis of discovering that a number of its clergy had been accused of abusing children. Out of this meeting came "The Charter for the Protection of Children and Young People" (United States Conference of Catholic Bishops, 2002), which outlined the steps that would be taken by the Church to respond to the crisis and react to future allegations of sexual abuse by clergy.

Why might clergy sexually abuse children? Ministers, priests, or rabbis who are abusive might well fit within any of the previously mentioned typologies. Crosson-Tower (2002) suggests that it is not as much that clergy are abusive as it is that individuals who have the potential to be abusive are attracted to life in the church. She postulates that the best way to look at the question of motivation among clergy is "to consider what religious life offers and how it fits into the needs of a perpetrator" (191). She goes on to point out that the respect and unquestioned authority given to clergy would appeal to the insecure potential perpetrator. The trust and sanction of the community, along with the nurturing and protection of both the "mother church" and the church members, add to the attraction and give clergy the opportunity to be alone with their victims. And, for some, life as a celibate gives them a reason for not becoming involved sexually with peers. (See Crosson-Tower, 2002, for more in-depth discussion.)

Other Family Members in Incestuous Families.   The nonabusive parent in an incestuous family is often held partially responsible for the abuse. Some authors feel that, instead of blaming the nonabusive parent (usually the mother) for not knowing about the abuse, we should support her efforts to intervene once she does know. Yet, not all mothers feel able to intervene.

Johnson (1992) categorizes mothers in father/daughter incest situations as the *collusive mother* or one who is withdrawn, cold, or psychologically absent and who pushes her daughter into her own role in the family; the *powerless mother,* who feels victimized, powerless, defeated, and unable to protect herself, let alone her child; and the *protective mother,* who does provide protection once she learns of the abuse. Many theorists now contend that the mother should not be blamed for the abuse within her family. She is already the victim of the societal expectation that women are responsible for maintaining family balance. Often devoid of adequate nurturing in their own backgrounds, these mothers are usually ill-equipped for this task. They are often either financially or emotionally dependent on their perpetrator husbands and are therefore unable to perceive that they have choices (Peterson et al., 1993).

CASE EXAMPLE

Nora

Nora grew up the youngest of 10 children. Her next oldest sibling was 10 years old when she was born, and her mother made it clear that she had not planned on Nora's birth. As a child, Nora was withdrawn and her siblings nicknamed her, with some derision, "the mouse." When, at age 5, one of her uncles began to sexually abuse her, Nora told no one. She was sure no one would believe her. Nora drifted through school with few friends. In high school, a boy, Jake, began to ask her out, and she was immediately enthralled with him. He seemed to be everything she wanted. When he told her that his family had had problems, too, Nora felt even closer to him. They were married when they graduated from high school and Jake went to work at the local mill. Their son, Tim, was born within the year. From his birth Nora knew that there was something wrong. When the doctors told her that he had Down syndrome, she was not surprised. Jake, on the other hand, was very upset and refused to believe that their son would not be normal. He urged Nora to have another child, which they soon did. This girl's birth was followed by the births of two more girls. In the meantime, Nora strived to care for Tim, but Jake virtually ignored their son. He chided Nora for coddling him and making a baby of him. Nora felt angry that Jake could not see how much Tim needed her. She withdrew more and more from her husband and her other children.

Sally, her third child, was 8 years old when a social worker came to the house and said that Sally had told her teacher that her father was sexually abusing her. Nora was horrified and accused Sally of lies until the oldest daughter confirmed that she, too, had been sexually abused by her father.

Nora, plagued by her own insecurities, was ill-equipped to handle the needs of her family. Despite the care she gave her son, her daughters described her as cold and unavailable. She was, however, eventually able to believe her daughters and stood by them as the family sought help from the social service system.

The nonabused siblings in the incestuous family are often forgotten as the family copes with the crisis of disclosure. Yet, they, too, are in crisis. The boys in a father/daughter incest family may perceive that there is something amiss but may also be too fearful either to face the situation or to intervene. They often do not recognize that, as children, it is not their place to intervene. They may instead feel very guilty. Many male siblings handle their guilt by either total denial or by what is referred to as *identification with the aggressor*. These children, too fearful to oppose their abusive father, join in the abuse either by targeting their sister, by abusing other children, or by molesting their own children when they become adults (Crosson-Tower, 2002). Sisters in situations of father/son or mother/son incest often appear either to be unaware or to deny that the abuse is occurring.

When a father abuses one son or one daughter, the other siblings of the same sex, who are old enough to suspect the sexual abuse, may wonder why they were not "chosen." One sibling explains: "I knew Dad was after my younger sister. It was not that I wanted to be abused, too; I didn't. But Dad and my sister seemed awfully close and I really resented it. Dad had actually approached me a year or so before. I thought he was kidding and laughed at him. He was hurt and never bothered me again. Then when I saw him being so chummy with my kid sister, I was at first horrified and then jealous, as awful as that may sound." For other siblings, recognition that abuse is occurring is too threatening a concept with which to deal. Instead, they live with the cloud of family dysfunction hanging over their heads. Some survivors feel that it was actually as difficult for their siblings as it was for them (Tower, 1988).

Emotional or Psychological Abuse

Emotional abuse refers to undermining the self-esteem of a child, or humiliating, belittling, rejecting, isolating, or terrorizing a child. Some authors suggest that the term *emotional abuse* be amended to *psychological abuse,* as this type of abuse is a pattern of psychically destructive behavior (Binggeli and Hart, 2001). Although psychological abuse is an integral part of neglect and physical and sexual abuse, it is one type of assault that can also stand alone.

CASE EXAMPLE

Sandy

Sandy remembers that he felt that his parents never had time for him. They both worked and Sandy was what was commonly referred to as a latch-key child. Sandy didn't really mind. He actually liked being alone better than having anyone else at home. When they were at home, they always yelled at him. Nothing he did seemed to please them. "You are so stupid!" his father told him. "Can't you ever learn?" his mother screamed. But the punishments were the worst. Sandy dared not tell them if he was fond of something. He knew that it would mean that that thing would be gone. At the first infringement, he knew that his father would destroy anything that Sandy loved. Like the baseball cards he had saved for over a year. He loved their shiny pictures. He had some that were quite rare. But one day he had not cleaned his room fast enough and his father had burned the cards. "This will make a man out of you!" his father had said. "No," Sandy thought, "It will just make me hate you more."

The definition of *emotional/psychological abuse* is sometimes complicated by cultural variations. For example, many Asian families use shame to socialize their children to do what is expected of them (Mass and Yap, 2002). Shame may be seen as belittling a child in other cultures. And some Native American and African American families employ the cultural equivalent of the "bogeyman" to frighten children into compliance. Such practices are construed by others as terrorizing children.

Symptoms. Emotionally or psychologically abused children demonstrate a variety of different behaviors. Burdened by low self-esteem, they may belittle themselves or engage in self-destructive behaviors either passively, through using drugs or alcohol, or actively through suicide attempts or eating disorders (O'Hagan, 1993; Binggeli and Hart, 2001). Some exhibit physical symptoms, such as headaches, asthma, ulcers, hyperactivity, or hypochondria. Children may withdraw or they may fight back by being openly aggressive.

Abusive Parents. Parents who abuse their children psychologically are often disillusioned with their own lives. They may be frustrated by unmet needs and unfulfilled expectations. In response, they lash out at the most vulnerable of their family members—their children (O'Hagan, 1993). Some parents abuse drugs or alcohol and some have learned their abusive patterns at the hands of their own parents.

Today, in an era when the incidence of divorce is extremely high, children sometimes suffer. Some children become symbols of one parent to the other and are emotionally battered by that person. Even well-meaning parents, embittered by divorce proceedings, can forget that the child should not be compelled to take sides, and that criticizing the child's other parent reflects on the child.

Finally, some adolescents who are ill-prepared for and overwhelmed by parenthood may find themselves emotionally abusing their children.

CASE EXAMPLE

Dinah

Dinah had had no idea how demanding a baby could be. She found that she was unable to do any of the things she enjoyed. The baby cried and cried until Dinah wanted to cry too. "Shut up, you stupid little jerk!" she found herself screaming. It wasn't long before her frustration made itself known to her infant daughter, who cringed when her mother touched her.

Reporting Child Maltreatment

As a result of the 1974 Child Abuse Prevention and Treatment Act, every state in the United States requires that instances of child abuse and neglect be reported to the state's child protective agency. Some states name specific *mandated reporters*—that is, individuals who, in their professional capacity, are obligated to report suspected abuse. For example, the law in Massachusetts lists certain professionals—such as physicians, dentists, social workers, police, educators, and most recently, clergy—who are considered mandated reporters. Other states are more general in their requirements, dictating that any individual must report. In addition, state laws indicate *to whom the report should be made* (child protective services, police, etc.); *under what conditions the report should be made* (suspicion, reasonable cause to believe, etc.); *the time period during which the report must be investigated by the child protection agency* (between 2 hours to 30 days, depending on the state and the degree of emergency of the situation); *the action taken if a mandated reporter does not report* (anything from imprisonment to a fine); and *the type of immunity provided to mandated reporters who do report* (Crosson-Tower, 2002).

The question always arises: Does a reporter have to give his or her name? It is always helpful for an agency to know the identity of the reporter. This enables the worker to contact the reporter for additional information. In states where there is a penalty for not reporting abuse, the mandated reporter who reports anonymously may not be protected from the penalty if his or her identity is unknown. The reporter who identifies himself or herself in good faith cannot be held liable.

Intake

Once the report has been made to a child protection agency, by phone and sometimes in writing, the situation is screened. Most agencies use a risk factor formula. They determine, by looking at certain factors, how much danger the child is in. For example, a situation in which there is alcohol involved, in which there has been a previous report of abuse, and in which the child is especially young might be considered a higher risk than a situation in which the child is older, the abuse has never been reported before, and the parents are substance-free. The intake social worker will look at patterns in the risk factors rather than just one variable. If the intake worker feels that there is sufficient indication that there was abuse and the child is at further risk, the case will usually be substantiated or screened into the system (see Figure 7.1). If there are concerns about the family functioning or services the family needs, but the case is not appropriate for protective services, a referral will be made to a more appropriate agency. For example, a family might need counseling or require assistance with housing issues and would be directed to someone who could help them. Although not the procedure in the past, more and more children's protective agencies are

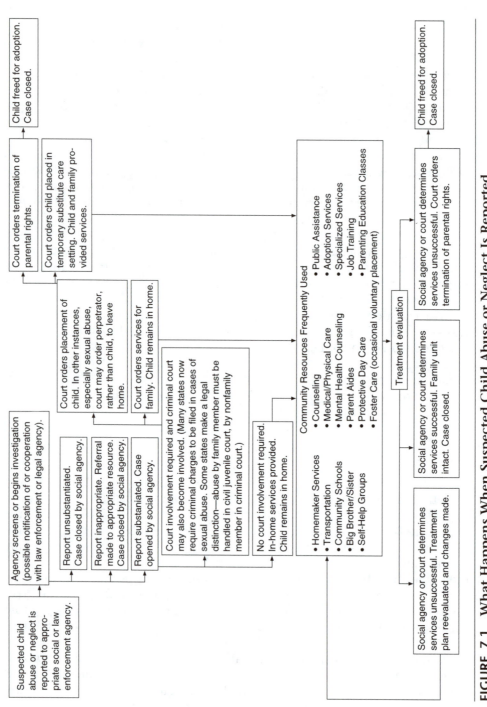

FIGURE 7.1 What Happens When Suspected Child Abuse or Neglect Is Reported

Source: Some material previously appeared in *NEA Training Package for Teachers,* 1984. Washington, DC: National Education Association. Reprinted by permission of the NEA Professional Library.

screening in situations of domestic violence. Although a child might not have been hit in a violent home, witnessing a parent being hit has significant impact.

CASE EXAMPLE

The Farmer Family

For the Farmer children, watching their mother being battered was a way of life. The call that there was yet another bout of abuse by Mr. Farmer came in to children's protective services from a concerned neighbor. She had called the police earlier in the week, but was concerned that "nothing had been done." Ironically, the CPS office had received a call earlier that day from Gail Farmer's first-grade teacher, who was concerned that the girl was being sexually abused. After considering the reports, the intake worker, in conference with his supervisor, felt that there was enough evidence to screen in the report.

Assessment

If a case is screened in by the intake worker or team, the next step is diagnostic assessment or investigation. The assessment worker uses this time to gather pertinent data through interviews, previous reports, or piecing together facts to determine if the maltreatment has in fact occurred and how serious the risk is for the child for future maltreatment (Myers et al., 2001).

CASE EXAMPLE

Once the report had been screened in, a worker was sent to the Farmer home. Because there was a potential for violence on Mr. Farmer's part, the police accompanied the worker. Had Mr. Farmer still been in the act of abusing his wife, he might have been removed by the police. He was not, however, at home. Mrs. Farmer was badly bruised and three-year-old Laura and five-year-old Jake were cowering in a corner. The worker talked with the mother, encouraged her to seek medical attention, and also talked with the children. Mrs. Farmer tearfully recounted that she suspected that her husband had sexually abused at least Gail if not Laura, but she had been too frightened of him to tell anyone. Now, she agreed to go to a shelter until plans could be made for her and her children.

Now it was the role of the assessment worker to gather additional information. Toward this end, she spoke with Gail's teacher, interviewed Gail at school, and talked with the concerned neighbor. Further, she checked with the police department and found that, although there had been other complaints of abusive behavior, Mr. Farmer had never been arrested. She also discovered that he had a drinking problem that seemed to have become worse since he was laid off his last job. For this assessment worker, the Farmer case began to evolve into a readable pattern that told her that the children were in danger.

As in this case, law-enforcement officers may be involved from the onset. Most states encourage or mandate law-enforcement involvement in cases of domestic violence, sexual abuse, or very serious injury. It is the primary role of officers to conduct criminal investigations, remove children, or offer protection for social workers in volatile situations.

Cooperation between a variety of agencies dealing with protective situations is crucial. Toward this end, some states have established child advocacy centers. Such centers are multidimensional, providing, often under one roof, such services as social service and criminal investigation, legal intervention, counseling, case management, and other treatment needs. Instead of being taken from place to place and seen by a wide variety of people, children are seen for validation of the abuse, counseling about court involvement, and treatment in one area by fewer professionals.

Once the assessment worker creates a picture of the family through facts and impressions gleaned from those involved in the case, she or he determines whether the family needs additional intervention or service. Some agencies require the formation of a treatment plan, which is a blueprint of the problems manifested by the family, the services they need, and the services that can be provided by the agency (Myers et al., 2001).

CASE EXAMPLE

The assessment worker on the Farmer case concluded that the children as well as Mrs. Farmer continued to be in danger. She learned that Mr. Farmer did work steadily and, when he was not drinking, was amenable to help. Initially, he did not admit that he had sexually abused Gail or Laura, but when questioned by the police, he finally broke down and admitted the abuse. The police referred the case to the District Attorney's office pending prosecution for sexual abuse. The assessment worker realized, however, that this father would soon be released on bail, leaving his wife and children again vulnerable. She encouraged Mrs. Farmer, who after her husband's arrest had returned home, to seek a restraining order against him. This she agreed to do.

Case Management and Treatment

The Farmer case was then transferred to a case manager who would work with the family and oversee the provision of service to them.

who involved

CASE EXAMPLE

Provision of service for the Farmers involved support for Mrs. Farmer and her children, legal aid, job training for this mother, and finding daycare services while she trained or worked. In the meantime, the case manager kept in contact with the District Attorney's office to determine what was happening with Mr. Farmer. It was finally decided that Mr. Farmer would be put on probation while he sought treatment for his alcoholism and attended group and individual treatment for sexual offenders. His supervised visits with his children were also monitored by the protective agency.

The case manager's role differs from agency to agency. In some agencies, the case manager is no more than a referral person who coordinates the various services provided. Other agencies expect their case managers to have clinical skills with which they can provide supportive counseling. The term *treatment* can refer to any service, from counseling to contracting with another agency for the provision of some service. The services provided can be medical services, legal services, daycare, remedial help, parent aids, counseling, substance abuse treatment, or a variety of others (Crosson-Tower, 2002).

Of course, not all cases assessed by protective services continue to be serviced by the agency. It is certainly possible for the case to be closed as a result of inconclusive evidence or the recognition that the situation was not as serious as was first assumed. Maltreatment may be unsubstantiated at this time and the case closed.

Court Intervention in Protective Cases

Chapter 9 will discuss the court system in depth. For the purposes of our discussion of protective services cases, it is important to know how a situation might become involved with the court system.

Child protection cases might become involved in either the civil or criminal court or sometimes with both. The difference between the two courts is that the civil court, usually the juvenile or family division, is designed to protect children when parents are either abusing them or are not able to care for them. The emphasis is not on the guilt or innocence of the parents but rather on how the children can be protected from further harm. Criminal court, on the other hand, seeks to prove that someone, usually the abuser, is guilty "beyond a reasonable doubt." Whereas the children and their needs are paramount in juvenile court, criminal court considers only proving whether the offender is at fault (Davidson, 1997).

In both types of courts, everyone involved (children and parents) are entitled to "due process rights," which include:

1. The right to formal notice of the hearing
2. The right to legal counsel
3. The right to a hearing in which evidence is presented
4. The right to present a defense and cross-examine witnesses.

Juvenile or Civil Court

A protective services case might become involved with the juvenile or family division of the civil court system at any point in its progress through social services. When a situation is first reported to protective services, the intake worker makes a determination of whether the parents will work with the agency. If they seem to be amenable, the CPS may investigate and provide services without court involvement. However, if the parents are unwilling to cooperate with the investigation or treatment plan, and/or the children are in imminent danger, court involvement might be sought. Sometimes it appears that the parents will cooperate, but further along in the investigation this cooperation ceases. An investigative social worker or even a case manager might feel it necessary to involve the juvenile court. A few states automatically refer cases to the juvenile court. This, they feel, gives them more control over protecting the children. If, during the investigation, the children appear to be in immediate danger, they can be removed without going back to court.

CASE EXAMPLE

Initially, Mrs. Farmer agreed to work with CPS while it completed its investigation. The worker was confident that Mr. Farmer was of no threat to her due to the restraining order, which she believed he would respect. But as time went on, she became lonely and contacted Mr. Farmer herself. She begged him to come home. Knowing that continuing with his treatment meant staying out of jail, Mr. Farmer at first refused her requests. The worker soon learned, however, that the couple was meeting secretly, often in the company of the children. When confronted with this, Mrs. Farmer became angry and said that she would not stop seeing her husband. She began missing appointments with her social worker and the worker became concerned that the children were again being placed at risk. The decision was then made to file a petition on the children's behalf in juvenile court.

Filing a petition necessitates that a social worker, or other concerned party, sign a petition on behalf of the children. The petition is reviewed, usually by the clerk of court, to determine if there is enough evidence to go forward. A hearing may be scheduled to review evidence and determine what will be required. (See Chapter 9 for a more in-depth explanation.) Involvement of the juvenile court ceases when either the conditions set down by the court are met or there is insufficient evidence to continue.

Criminal Court

Criminal court involvement is sought most often when the parent is found to be criminally negligent or neglectful; when the parent has severely injured a child physically or killed a child; or when a parent has sexually abused a child. Criminal negligence is exemplified in the following case.

CASE EXAMPLE

Roxanne

Roxanne was a 25-year-old woman who had been prostituting for the last 10 years. She had had a variety of different "business managers," or pimps, several of whom had fathered her three children. Her children, now ages 3, 2, and 3 months, were left in the next room while she "entertained" her clients. She also drank heavily and had used various drugs. She often left her children alone while she went out to get new supplies. The 3-year-old had taken to wandering down the hall while Roxanne was out. The neighbors complained. The next time Roxanne went out, she tied the child to a chair and the 2-year-old in his crib. In her absence a grossly overloaded electrical socket caught on fire. The fire department was summoned and they found the children alone. By the time the children were rescued, the 2- and 3-year-olds were badly burned and the baby had died of smoke inhalation. Roxanne was charged with criminal neglect.

Some parents abuse their children to the point of severe injury or even death.

CASE EXAMPLE

Jeremy

Four-year-old Jeremy's father had high standards for his children. He expected them to mind him immediately and would not tolerate any "fresh talk." Jeremy, an active child, taxed his father's minimal patience. On several occasions, his father struck him with such force that he left bruises. Neighbors noticed the bruises but could not believe that a "nice family like Jeremy's" could have caused them. One particular night Jeremy talked back to his father. Angered by an especially bad day at work and a fight with Jeremy's mother, the irate father slapped his son hard in the head. The blow sent the small body into the wall and left the child unconscious. Frantic, his mother rushed him to the hospital. The child was diagnosed with a subdural hematoma (blood collecting on the brain) and brain damage. The boy lapsed into a coma and died soon after admission. His father was charged with his death.

In the earlier Farmer case, Mr. Farmer was charged with sexual abuse. In that situation the court agreed to put Mr. Farmer on probation while he attended treatment. When he violated probation by seeing his wife and children secretly, he was eventually incarcerated.

Criminal procedures differ depending on the court. In some instances, agreements are made between the parties (called *plea bargaining*) to minimize the charges, sometimes allowing the accused, like Mr. Farmer, to become involved in treatment instead of being incarcerated. Obviously, the accused is hoping for the "best deal" and it may require vigilance to insure that the children's interests are not neglected as this "deal" is being made.

Criminal court does provide leverage in dealing with the offender. Because power is an issue, especially for violent offenders and sexual abusers, such leverage may be what is needed. For the children and family, however, involvement in criminal court can seem to permeate their lives.

The Effect of Court Involvement on Children

When children are abused and neglected the damage can be profound. One hopes that the intervention will be swift and competent. Unfortunately, that is not always the case. Court involvement can seem like one more assault to traumatized children. How children are able to cope with court procedures depends largely on the type of support systems available to them. Victim witness advocates now provide families with the support they need to survive the legal process. *Guardians ad litem* (discussed in Chapter 9) are often assigned to children to protect their interests. Fortunately, many more attorneys and judges assigned to juvenile and criminal court cases involving children are becoming aware of the need to shelter them from additional trauma (Crosson-Tower, 2002).

An interesting approach to protecting the psyches of children in court cases was described in the book *Unspeakable Acts,* by Jan Hollingsworth. Hollingsworth (1986) writes of the so-called Country Walk Case in Miami, Florida, in which a group of children were sexually abused by the owners of the baby-sitting service their parents used. So traumatized were the children that child psychologists Joe and Laurie Braga were called in to help both parents and children deal with the court process. The case set a precedent for the protection of children in such situations.

The Role of the Protective Services Worker

A protective services worker might provide one or more of a variety of services. It is the role of this individual, along with the agency employing him or her, to provide protection for children but also to seek family preservation whenever possible. A child's family is the best place for him or her if that family is able to meet the child's basic needs and protect him or her. For new workers, especially, it sometimes feels like a child would be better off removed from a family that is less than ideal. But separation is another form of trauma for children. Thus, the decision to remove must be considered with great care (Myers et al., 2001).

The role of the child protection worker depends on the particular agency in which he or she is employed, and perhaps on the regulations of that state. Child protection agencies are usually run by the state or county and are therefore influenced by the political climate. "Every time there's a new governor, things change a bit," explained one protective services worker. "Sometimes we find ourselves trying to protect our clients' best interests amidst these changes."

Some workers are assigned to intake, which means that they screen cases as they come in. This can be a high-stress role, as referrals often peak at certain times of the year. For example, the holidays seem to correlate with more reports of abuse as parents and children both become more stressed as the contrast between the pain they are feeling and the happiness they perceive that everyone else is feeling becomes more pronounced. Intake requires that one think quickly and not be afraid to be assertive in situations in which it is necessary. Both intake and assessment require that a worker be creative in discovering information and skilled in putting that information together. These roles do not allow the worker to form long-term relationships with clients.

The role of ongoing worker or case manager does allow one to get to know clients. Workers learn to support clients and help them capitalize on their strengths rather than their weaknesses. It can be a challenging and frustrating job, as clients may not be able to maintain their growth, and watching them slip back into old patterns sometimes makes one wonder why the effort was made in the first place. Moved from place to place, many of these children and parents lack the ability to form healthy relationships without considerable time, patience, and consistency. But there are success stories, too, and these tend to sustain one in protective services work.

Richards, in his *Tender Mercies: Inside the World of a Child Abuse Investigator* (1999), provides an excellent view of the joys and frustrations of protective services work. He captures the essence of protective work when he says:

> *I'm not supposed to take the cases home with me; I'm not supposed to get emotionally involved. Yet there are people's lives I touch that touch me right back. Now and then a case rears up that I can't stop thinking about, coiling itself around me like a boa, refusing to let go, squeezing me until I stagger. For these cases especially, I go the extra yard and make sacrifices*

because I see the potential for positive change on my hands, and I know that I can make a difference that may still be felt long after I'm gone. (4)

Crosson-Tower's *From the Eye of the Storm: The Experiences of a Child Welfare Worker* (2003) provides similar insight into the day-to-day role of a social worker in protective services.

CASE EXAMPLE

Reflections of an Abused Child: Consumer Perspective

When I was asked to write this for a book to be read by potential social workers, I wondered what I could possibly say. But when I thought more about it, I realized that I had a great deal to say.

I was the oldest of five kids and the only girl. Sometimes I think my mother had me just so she would have someone to take care of us, because that is what I did from as early as I can remember. Someone once asked me if I was neglected as a child. Neglect? How does one define that? Did we have enough to eat? No. Did anyone care about us? No. Did we have what kids need to grow up emotionally healthy? No. If that's neglect, I guess I was but I never really thought about it. I was too busy surviving.

We had a lot of contact with the social service system—some good, some not so good. My father left us when I was 3 years old. I never asked who was the father of my youngest three brothers. I am not sure my mother knows. She had a lot of boyfriends when I was younger. She worked as a waitress in a bar and she often brought guys home. They would just sort of move in. Some were great and I liked them. But some were creeps. Like Jasper, who used to beat my mother and me and tell my little brothers that that was what men did to women. And another guy, I can't even remember his name, who messed with me sexually until my mother found out and kicked him out.

I can't really blame my mother, I guess. I think she was always look-ing for someone to love her. She got pregnant with me at age 15. I think she hoped I would love her. But I found out when I had my baby at age 16 that babies aren't like that right away.

Right after Jasper beat me up, I was 10 I think, a social worker started coming to our house. It really scared my mother. She did love us and was afraid we would be taken away. The social worker said that Jasper had to leave and my mother had to see her on a regular basis. So for a while she did. But then one weekend, my mom took off with Harry (I think that was his name), a guy she met at work. I was 11 and she left me with the other kids. The next thing I know, the social worker came and told us we were abandoned and had to go to a foster home. They put me and my oldest brother in one home and the three littlest ones in another. That really upset me because I worried about them. I was so used to taking care of them. I cried and cried and the foster mother thought I "wasn't adjusting to foster care." So then they put me in a group home for girls. That was okay, I guess, but I still missed the other kids. My mom used to visit and we'd cry together. Finally she must have convinced them she could take care of us because we all went back home again.

That lasted for a few years. When I was 15 years old, my brother, who was 13, stole our landlord's car. The guy pressed charges and my brother went to court. He ended up in a home for "delinquent kids" and my mother got real upset. She took off again and we all went to juvenile court. Again, we ended up in foster homes. I was in six, because by this time I was really mad at the whole deal. I dated this guy while I was at one home and got pregnant. So they put me in another home where the foster mother was great. She helped me through my pregnancy and showed me how to take care of the baby. I stayed there until I was 18 years old.

Now my son and I live on our own. He's 5 and I'm 20. I work at a diner but I don't take guys home with me like my mom did. I haven't seen her for years. I don't know where my younger brothers are, but I see my oldest brother once in a while. I still call my last foster home my home. I don't know what I would do without Pam (my foster mother).

What would I say to people who are going to be social workers? Maybe I'd say "Be careful not to judge." My mom did the best she could and I still love her. She didn't have the breaks I had. She thought men would solve her problems. And I'd say "Listen to kids. We know what's happening and we'll tell you if you listen." I had a couple of good social workers. I've actually thought of going to college to be one. Wouldn't that be something? If I became a social worker?

Future of Protective Services

As resources become more limited and children continue to be abused and neglected, there is a need to consider how to improve existing services or develop new paradigms for services in the future.

Narrowing of Services

Waldfogel (1998) discusses the need for "narrowing" the services provided by CPS. Such a move would dictate that CPS take only the most severe cases of abuse and neglect, while filtering less serious situations into other services or agencies. Currently, CPS is mandated to protect the child, but the national emphasis on strengthening families means that the role of CPS becomes a mixture of family preservation, as well as maltreatment screening and investigation. These multiple activities are not always compatible.

There has already been a move to narrow services in some states. For example, the abundance of reported cases have meant that some CPS agencies will screen in only the most severe situations. Some have developed risk management matrixes to ensure consistency of service among cases. Agencies have also made greater use of kinship placements, encouraging extended family members to take some of the responsibility.

Waldfogel (1998, 143–147) suggests that CPS services could best be implemented in the future by (1) customizing CPS response to families, (2) developing community-based child protection, and (3) promoting a larger role for informal and natural helpers.

Customized Response and the Necessity of Training.   "Starting where the client is" has traditionally been a tenant of social work practice, yet in protective services, the worker, overwhelmed perhaps by the magnitude of the job, sometimes finds himself or herself approaching families who abuse or neglect their children in a similar manner. The policies of agencies in fact perpetuate this tendency. Attention must be given not only to changing agency policy but also to the staff that will serve clients. The hiring of social workers must be attended to as never before. Agencies that develop screening procedures to assess suitability for the field (e.g., protective services workers come from a variety of different educational backgrounds) will reap the benefits of better service. Assessing and providing services to families on an individual basis required workers who are more effectively trained in casework skills and challenges for administrators to ensure that such training is available.

Once they are hired by the agency, new workers can receive anywhere from a day to a week of initial training. Many agencies feel that on-the-job training is the best teacher, leaving new and inexperienced workers at a loss when they first enter the field. Adequate training, not only initially but periodically, is vital to the worker's appropriate services to families.

One way to achieve such advanced training is to require universities and colleges to become more involved in skill-based protective training. In addition to casework skills, educational institutions should provide instruction in community analysis, cultural competence, political systems, and the workings of local, state, and federal government so that they might use this knowledge to advocate individually for clients.

Community-Based Child Protection.   It is vital that agencies work together to serve protective service families and those who have the potential to come to the attention of CPS. If CPS screens for the most serious cases, some families will be left without the service that they need. Some of these consumers might be served by other agencies. In addition, agencies providing similar services are recognizing the need to prevent duplication and the need to communicate with each other in order to enhance services to families.

Waldfogel (1998) suggests that collaboration between agencies in the interest of customized services will require crossing boundaries between the public and private sectors. She points out that the barriers to these boundaries are many and that implementation of such a plan will necessitate creative responses.

Agencies might also take on different roles in the total picture. For example, strengthening prevention efforts within communities might mean that individuals who might have eventually come to the attention of CPS receive services before this need arises. Prevention programs instituted in schools and agencies have been found to be successful in limiting the amount of later abuse. Early intervention programs provide parents with the skills they need so that they are able to improve their child-rearing standards.

The future must also see built-in evaluation of services to families. The current child protection system is not effectively serving families or protecting children. A new paradigm must look at how services would be evaluated. This must necessitate provisions and funds for ongoing research on the efficacy of service.

Encouraging Informal and Natural Helpers.   Part of customized service for families should be assessing and using the network of informal and natural helpers that are in place. For example, individuals within the community, church groups, and civic associations are often in the position to be of help. Also, just because caregivers in a family have abused or neglected their children does not mean that their extended family members either condone or practice this maltreatment. Not only will involving extended family members possibly provide additional resources for the care and protection of children, but the abusive family might enjoy a new-found reliance on, acceptance by, or intimacy with other family members.

The use of informal and natural helpers will admittedly require both commitment and training from the agency. And the burden of identifying such available resources will fall upon the social worker. However, providing encouragement and training to these community and family members, while helping them see themselves as part of the team, may serve to lessen the mistrust that plagues CPS in the greater community. Only through such cooperation and trust can families be effectively served.

Summary

Historically, children were seen as the property of their parents. Practices such as infanticide and the sexual misuse of children were a painful part of early history. Children often worked and suffered along with poverty-stricken parents. Significant relief of these conditions did not come until late in the nineteenth century when Mary Ellen, a neglected and abused child in New York City, prompted intervention and gave rise to the first child protection agency. In 1974, the Child Abuse Prevention and Treatment Act shaped the services to maltreated children that we know today.

Maltreatment can be divided into four categories: physical abuse, physical neglect, sexual abuse, and emotional or psychological abuse. Each of these categories has a separate set of symptoms and etiology. Perpetrators of each type of abuse do so for a variety of reasons.

When child abuse and neglect is detected, it must be reported to the child protection unit of the local social service agency. This agency screens and assesses the case and determines if additional services are needed. Treatment, in the form of services, counseling, or other resources, may be offered to families. In some instances, child protective services will seek out court intervention through either the juvenile (civil), criminal, or probate court.

Although we have come a long way in the provision of services to abused and neglected children, much can still be done. The streamlining or unification of services, improvement in staff training, and increased prevention services are just a few of the innovations needed.

It is difficult to determine the direction in which this new political era will take the provision of services to maltreated children. Only by understanding the impact that abuse and neglect have on children and their families can we hope to work in the best interests of all concerned.

EXPLORATION QUESTIONS

1. Throughout history how have children been perceived? What examples of this view do we have?
2. Who was Mary Ellen? What impact did she have on the history of helping abused children?
3. What two reform movements influenced the response to abused and neglected children in the last two centuries?
4. What are the three types of child maltreatment?
5. What are the symptoms of physical abuse? Why do people physically abuse children?
6. What are the symptoms of neglect? What are the typologies of neglectful families? Why are mothers the ones primarily studied in neglectful situations?
7. What are the symptoms of sexual abuse? What are the types of sexual abuse?
8. What three typologies explain sexual abusers? What characterizes each type?
9. What happens when a case of abuse or neglect is reported? Draw a diagram of the process involved.
10. What three types of court services might be involved in maltreatment? How?

REFERENCES

Addams, J. (1910). *Twenty Years at Hull House.* New York: Signet.

Binggeli, N. J. & Hart, S. N. (2001). *Psychological Maltreatment of Children.* Thousand Oaks, CA: Sage.

Carnes, P. (2002). *Out of the Shadows: Understanding Sexual Addiction.* Minneapolis: CompCare.

Casanova, M. (2002). "The History of Pornography on the Internet," *Journal of Sex Education and Therapy,* 25(4), 245–252.

Conte, J., & Berliner, L. (1988). "The Impact of Sexual Abuse." In L. Walker (Ed.), *Handbook on Sexual Abuse of Children*. New York: Guilford Press.

Cowen, P. S. (1999). "Child Neglect: Injuries of Omission," *Pediatric Nursing,* 25(4), 401–416.

Crittenden, P. (1999). *"Child Neglect: Causes and Contributors,"* (47–68). In H. Dubowitz, (Ed.), *Neglected Children: Research, Practice and Policy*. Thousand Oaks, CA: Sage.

Crosson-Tower, C. (2002). *Understanding Child Abuse and Neglect*. Boston: Allyn and Bacon.

Crosson-Tower, C. (2003). *From the Eye of the Storm: The Experiences of a Child Welfare Worker*. Boston: Allyn and Bacon.

Davidson, H. A. (1997). "Courts and Child Maltreatment" (482–499). In M. E. Helfer, R. S. Kempe, & R. D. Krugmen (Eds.), *The Battered Child*. Chicago: University of Chicago Press.

Dawson, K., & Berry, M. (2002). "Engaging Families in Child Welfare Services: An Evidence Based Approach to Best Practice," *Child Welfare,* 87(2), 293–318.

deMause, L. (1991). "The Universality of Incest," *Journal of Psychohistory,* 19, 123–164.

deMause, L. (1995). *The History of Childhood: The Untold History of Childhood*. New York: Peter Bedrick.

deMause, L. (1995–96). "The History of Child Abuse," *Spirit of Change Magazine,* 28–34.

Dubowitz, H., & Klockner, A. (1998). "Community and Professional Definitions of Child Neglect," *Child Maltreatment,* 3(3), 235–244.

Eminson, M., Postlethwaite, R. J., & Eminson, D. M. (2000). *Munchausen by Proxy Abuse: A Practical Approach*. Woburn, MA: Butterworth, Heinemann.

Faller, K. C. (1990). *Understanding Child Sexual Maltreatment*. Newbury Park, CA: Sage.

Finkelhor, D. (1984). *Child Sexual Abuse*. New York: Free Press.

Foley, T. P. (2002). "Forensic Assessment of Internet Child Pornography Offenders." In B. K. Schwartz (Eds.), *The Sex Offender* (vol. IV). Kingston, NJ: Civic Research Institute.

Fontes, L. A. (2002). "Child Discipline and Physical Abuse in Immigrant Latino Families," *Journal of Counseling and Development,* 80(1), 31–41.

Freeman-Longo, R. E., & Blanchard, G. T. (1998). *Sexual Abuse in America: Epidemic of the 21st Century*. Brandon, VT: Safer Society Press.

Freud, S. (1966). *The Complete Introductory Letters of Psychoanalysis*. New York: Norton.

Garbarino, J., & Collins, C. C. (1999). "Child Neglect: The Family with the Whole in the Middle" (1–23). In H. Dubowitz (Ed.), *Neglected Children: Research, Practice and Policy*. Thousands Oaks, CA: Sage.

Gil, E., & Johnson, T. C. (1993). *Sexualized Children*. Rockville, MD: Launch Press.

Gilgun, J. F. (1990). "Factors Mediating the Effects of Child Maltreatment" (177–190). In M. Hunter (Ed.), *The Sexually Abused Male,* (vol. I). New York: Lexington Press.

Groth, A. N. (1979). *Men Who Rape*. New York: Plenum Press.

Hanson, R. F., Lipovsky, J. A., & Saunders, B. E. (1994). "Characteristics of Fathers in Incest Families," *Journal or Interpersonal Violence,* 9(2), 155–169.

Hayden, T. (1992). *Ghost Girl*. New York: Basic Books.

Hobbs C., & Wynne, J. M. (2001). *Physical Signs of Child Abuse*. Philadelphia: W. B. Saunders.

Hollingsworth, J. (1986). *Unspeakable Acts*. New York: Congdon and Weed.

Jackson, L. (2000). *Child Sexual Abuse in Victorian England*. London: Rutledge.

Jeffrey, T. R. (2002). "Justice Kennedy Supports 'Good' Child Pornography," *Human Events,* 58(15), 8.

Johnson, J. T. (1992). *Mothers of Incest Survivors*. Bloomington: Indiana University Press.

Kadushin, A., & Martin, J. A. (1988). *Child Welfare Services*. New York: Macmillan.

Kaufman, K. L., Wallace, A. M., Johnson, C. F., & Reeder, M. L. (1995). "Comparing Female and Male Perpetrators' Modus Operandi,'" *Journal of Interpersonal Violence,* 10(3), 322–333.

Kempe, C. H., Silverman, F., Steele, B., Droegemueller, W., & Silver, H. (1962). "The Battered-Child Syndrome," *Journal of the American Medical Association,* 181, 17–24.

Laviola, M. (1992). "Effects of Older Brother–Younger Sister Incest." *Child Abuse and Neglect,* 16(3), 409–421.

Levine, M., & Levine, A. (1992). *Helping Children: A Social History.* New York: Oxford University Press.

Mass, A. I., & Yap, J. (2002). "Child Welfare: Asian Pacific Island Families." In N. Cohen (Ed.), *Child Welfare: A Multicultural Perspective.* Boston: Allyn and Bacon.

Masson, H. C., & Erooga, M. (Eds.). (1999). *Children and Young People Who Sexually Abuse Others.* London: Rutledge.

Mathews, R., Mathews, J., & Speltz, K. (1990). "Female Sexual Offenders" (pp. 275–293). In M. Hunter (Ed.), *The Sexually Abused Male (*vol. I). New York: Lexington Books.

McLaughlin, J. F. (2000). "Cyber Child Sexual Offender Typology," *Knight Stick,* 51, 47–51.

Myers, E. B., Hendrix, C. T., Berliner, L., Jenny, C., Briere, J., & Reid, T. (2001). *The APSAC Handbook on Child Maltreatment.* Westlake Village, CA: APSAC.

O'Hagan, K. (1993). *Emotional and Psychological Abuse of Children.* Toronto: University of Toronto Press.

Parnell, T. F., & Day, D. O. (1998). *Munchausen by Proxy: Misunderstood Child Abuse.* Thousand Oaks, CA: Sage.

Pecora, P., Whittaker, J. K., Maluccio, A. N., & Barth, R. P. (2000). *The Child Welfare Challenge: Policy, Practice and Research.* New York: Aldine deGruyter.

Peterson, R. F., Basta, S. M., & Dykstra, T. A. (1993). "Mothers of Molested Children: Some Comparisons of Personality Characteristics," *Child Abuse and Neglect,* 17(3), 409–418.

Polansky, N. A., Chalmers, M. A., Buttenwieser, E., & Williams, D. P. (1991). *Damaged Parents: An Anatomy of Child Neglect.* Chicago: University of Chicago Press.

Polansky, N. F., Holly, C., & Polansky, N. A. (1975). *Profiles of Neglect: A Survey of the Department of Health, Education and Welfare.* Washington, DC: Department of Health Education and Welfare.

Richards, K. (1999). *Tender Mercies: Inside the World of a Child Abuse Investigator.* Chicago and Washington, DC: Noble Press and The Child Welfare League of America.

Rush, F. (1992). *The Best Kept Secret: Sexual Abuse of Children.* New York: McGraw-Hill.

Sagatun, I. J., & Edwards, L. P. (1995). *Child Abuse and the Legal System.* Chicago: Nelson Hall.

Schreier, H. A. (1992). "The Prevention of Mothering: Munchausen Syndrome by Proxy," *Bulletin of the Menninger Clinic,* 56(4), 421–237.

Smith, E. (1995). "Bring Back the Orphanages? What Policymakers of Today Can Learn from the Past," *Child Welfare,* 74(1), 115–142.

Stein, T. (1998). *Child Welfare and the Law.* New York: Longman.

Swift, K. (1995). "An Outrage to Common Decency: Historical Perspectives on Child Neglect," *Child Welfare,* 74(1), 71–91.

Tower, C. C. (1984). *NEA Training Package in Child Abuse and Neglect for Teachers.* Washington, DC: National Education Association.

Tower, C. C. (1988). *Secret Scars.* New York: Viking/Penguin.

United States Conferences of Catholic Bishops. (2002). *Charter for the Protection of Children and Young People.* Washington, DC: Author.

Waldfogel, J. (1998). *The Future of Child Protection.* Cambridge, MA: Harvard Univ. Press.

Wiehe, V. R., and Herring, T. (1997). *Sibling Abuse: Hidden Physical, Emotional, and Sexual Trauma.* Thousand Oaks, CA: Sage.

8 Family Preservation or Child Placement?

Serving the Child's Best Interests

Ask most people about where a child should be raised and the answer would probably be the same—in a family. Families are the basic unit that provides nurturance, offers protection to the child, and passes on the values of the culture (see Chapter 2). We also know from research over the years that removing a child from his or her family of birth can cause separation trauma. Therefore, strengthening the birth family is the initial goal that has been adopted by child protection agencies across the country. But how do we accomplish this often challenging goal and by what means? And when do we decide that the child's best interests would be better served by admitting that his or her birth family may never be able to meet the child's needs? The decision of when to remove children from their homes is not an easy one to make and has a myriad of political, social, emotional, and casework implications.

This chapter will consider the family-based services movement, primarily from the perspective of family preservation. In this context, we will consider some of the programs that have been part of that movement: the success of family preservation and when family services must give way to child placement.

Brief History of Family-Based Services

Families are so much a part of our daily lives that we cannot imagine being without them. When we think of families, many of us still have the image of the idealized family portrayed for years on televisions. Today, the Ozzie and Harriets, Ward and Junes (*Leave It to Beaver*) and James and Margarets (*Father Knows Best*) have ceased to exist. Our current families have a much more complex world before them and a greater challenge to meet the needs of their children (Hewlett et al., 1999; Coontz, 1998). For many children, families do not meet the needs that are expected. Being a parent is probably one of the most important jobs one can undertake, and yet, it is one that comes with no training manual. In addition, the stresses on parents and families today are significant. Some experts fear that the negative indicators for child well-being will continue to increase in the next years (McCronsky and Meezan, 1998). Even the healthiest of families needs support. Many find it in their natural and relational support systems, such as extended family, friends, church, neighborhood, and community. For other families, these systems either do not exist or have not been fully developed, making families feel isolated and mistrustful of society. It is often these families that come to the attention of the social service system.

Berry (1997) divides the history of services to protect children and later to meet family needs into several categories: almshouses and charities, scientific philanthropy; settlement house influence, mothers' pensions, and public child welfare services.

Almhouses and Charities

Chapter 1 discusses the fate of children whose parents were poor or could not care for them. Adults were dependent on either the charity of their communities or placement in publicly supported institutions—almshouses or workhouses. Children were at the mercy of the system that dealt with their parents, often ending up in almshouses, those much written about institutions for the poor. There, the plight of children did not differ significantly from that of the adults, who were considered to be the dregs of society and stigmatized as lazy and unworthy (Schene, 1998). The very young often stayed with their parents, but the older children might be indentured to learn a trade. In short, the method of dealing with the poor in the early history of this country taxed the resources of those who could or would provide for them, while demeaning the socioeconomically deprived for their need to take such charity. The strain of such an arrangement soon became the subject of controversy.

Scientific Philanthropy

Critics of the conditions of almshouses argued that children should not be subjected to the fate of their parents. Because poor parents were seen as undeserving, the prevailing sentiment was that children should be "rescued" from them. Charles Loring Brace blamed parents who drank, abused their children, neglected them, drove them out, or were financially unable to care for them for the fact that many of their children ended up on the street or in public facilities like orphanages. This, in turn, caused problems for the rest of society. As he explained, "All the neglect and bad education and evil example of the poor class tend to form other, who as they mature, swell the ranks of ruffians and criminals. So, at length, a great multitude of ignorant, untrained, passionate, irreligious boys and young men are formed, who become the 'dangerous class' of our city" (Brace, 1872, 28). The solution of the day for Brace and other like-minded people was to enlist the help of benevolent societies and churches to "save the children" by finding them more suitable homes away from the negative influences of the cities (see also Chapter 12).

Brace's philosophy of removing children and finding homes that would care for them, often in exchange for helping on the farm or around the house, was that of the Charity Organization Societies (COS). These organizations that centered within the larger cities sought to serve the poor in a variety of ways. Emphasizing hard work and personal initiative, these groups felt that the poor could be encouraged through a "friendly" approach to give up their dependence on charity and almshouses and to work to make their own way. These agencies also attempted to coordinate services in the communities so that those who benefited from them were truly needy and deserving. Thus, it fell upon the COS workers to develop knowledge of the needs and motivations of families and the ability to investigate and assess these needs, taking a more scientific approach than had been done in the past (Berry, 1997).

Settlement House Influence

The settlement house movement (also discussed in Chapter 1) had a great influence on family-based services. In fact, neighborhood centers and the current family preservation initiatives find their roots in the work of settlement houses that served the poor and immigrants in many large cities. The basic philosophy of the movement was the importance of identifying, appreciating, and building on the strengths of individuals and families. These strengths could be defined through " the democratic ideal of participation by all" (Berry, 1997, 6). The settlement workers not only got to know families but they also discovered the resources of the communities in which these families lived. By matching the needs of the families with the potential benefits available in the community, the family's stress could be ameliorated or eliminated and they would become less dependent on formal and institutional services (Berry, 1997; Altstein and McCoy, 2000).

Mothers' Pensions

The field research done by the settlement workers went a long way toward the understanding of the effects of poverty. It also became evident that it was mothers who shouldered the burden of poverty as they attempted to care for their children. The controversy over whether to give mothers a pension to help them more ably provide for their children brought into conflict the ideologies of the Charity Organization Society's and the settlement houses. Despite the heated debate, mothers' pensions became a reality by the end of the first decade of the 1900s, but these were administered mostly on the local level. In order to become eligible for such public funds, a mother must be "a proper person, physically mentally and morally fit to bring up her children" (Berry, 1997, 9). The granting of such pensions and the determination of eligibility shifted the focus of child rearing away from a woman's individual need to care for her children and gave pensioned mothers an obligation. Mothers were henceforth being supported by the community in order to serve society by caring for their children. In this role, a woman must be worthy of the support of the public (Leff, 1973; Berry, 1997).

From the "friendly visitors" sent out by settlement houses to support and assist, the visits to family homes now became required as a monitoring of a mother's worthiness to continue to receive her pension. Some workers still offered a sympathetic and helping hand; others took their role more as an administrative one and saw fit to punish "moral transgressions" such as the presence of an unauthorized man in the house or the maltreatment of children (Leff, 1973).

Public Child Welfare Services

Given the explanation of mothers' pensions and the requirements for eligibility, it is not surprising that such careful scrutiny into child-rearing practices would meet with the practice of removing children who were not fortunate enough to have mothers who met the requirements. At one time, the placements of children in other homes was primarily for orphans, but now mothers could have their children removed for being "unfit" (Clement, 1978). The definition of unfit depended largely on the discretion of the home visitor who, not too surprisingly, was not always welcome in homes. Once a child was removed from the home, it fell to the mother to prove that she was morally fit in order that her child might be returned. The mentality of expecting mothers to prove their worthiness to "earn" their child's return continued well into the history of child welfare practice. A social worker who began her career in the 1960s commented: "I used to feel badly for some of the moms from whom we had removed children. Many of the mothers were so distraught that they had lost their children that they had little energy to do anything. And there we were, the social service agency, saying to her, 'You can have your kids back if you meet this condition and that condition.' It was a lot to ask from folks who probably hadn't had great childhoods themselves."

The Child Abuse Prevention and Treatment Act (CAPTA) of 1974 mandated the reporting of child maltreatment and added additional emphasis to the concept of "saving" children. The children rather than their families were the targets of treatment programs (Courtney, 1998). Increased investigations to determine if there was maltreatment in turn led to an increased number of removals and children placed in foster care. Despite the allotment of additional funds to states through Title XX of the Social Security Act, 75% of these funds in the late 1970s were still being used for foster care services instead of to strengthen or preserve families By 1977, over 500,000 children were living in foster care, with little attempt to work with their birth families. In addition, the average stay in care had lengthened to almost two and a half years (Shyne and Schroeder, 1978; Burt and Pittman, 1985; MacDonald, 1994; Altstein and McCoy, 2000).

The Emerging Concept of Permanency Planning

Two areas of research would help change the focus of child welfare practice. The first was spearheaded by the work of John Bowlby, who found that children who did not have the advantage of a consistent caregiver failed to develop healthy attachments that would carry them through later life. From this research, experts began to point to the practice of removing children from their birth families, suggesting that separation would have a significant negative influence on these children's development.

In the late 1950s and early 1960s, there was also an extensive movement to study the efficacy of foster care. The results of several studies suggested that not only were birth families not given sufficient services to support them in their parenting, but children, once removed and placed in foster care, often existed in limbo, drifting ambiguously with no clear picture of what their future would bring. Little attempt was made to connect them with their birth families, and there was equally as little emphasis on placement in a permanent adoptive home. For example, Allan Gruber (1973) and associates found that in Massachusetts, 83% of the children in foster care had never had a trial visit with their birth families and 31% of these parents had never seen a social worker.

From this research, the concept of *permanency planning* emerged. Proponents of this concept argued that children had a right to a permanent arrangement as soon as possible in order to lesson the trauma caused to them and to ensure their normal development in the future. The first avenue to gain permanency for children was clearly to offer better services to their own families and hopefully prevent the necessity for seeking other placements. Fanshel and Shin (1973) comment, "Service to parents of children in placement is the manifest and blatant area of failure in service delivery that one can find as one reviews the foster care phenomenon" (486).

   The trend now became to keep children out of foster care whenever possible, an idea that was strengthened by the redefinition of child welfare services through the Adoption Assistance and Child Welfare Act (PL 96-272) in 1980. This act stipulated that "reasonable efforts" should be made to work with birth parents around keeping their children in the home. If the family was unable to care for the child, another permanent option, such as adoption or long-term foster care, should be sought (Altstein and McCoy, 2000). "Reasonable efforts" were defined as having three elements: (1) an accurate case assessment, (2) means to determine if a specific service was needed in specific cases, and (3) documentation of all activity involved in providing these services (Berry, 1997). But some social workers and agencies feared that children would be harmed by keeping them in dysfunctional homes any longer than necessary. And, would these services really be effective? As a result of this questioning, as well as the lack of community resources and supports, the provision of services based on "reasonable efforts" was inconsistent from agency to agency and state to state. Foster care statistics remained high and family advocates complained that families were not being given a chance.

   The failure of PL 96-272 to fully meet the needs of children and their families brought about speculation about what other steps might be taken. In 1990, legislation was introduced to Congress that would strengthen the role of families in children's lives. But the Family Preservation legislation of 1990, 1991, and 1992 became surrounded with controversy and was defeated. In response, the National Commission on Children, an influential body of children's advocates, published the report *Beyond Rhetoric: A New American Agenda for Children and Families* (1991). Influenced by this report, the Omnibus Reconciliation Act of 1993, containing the Family Preservation and Family Support Act (PL 103-66), was passed. Public Law 103-66 contained many of the recommendations discussed in the previous legislation on family preservation as well as being influenced by the suggestions of the National Commission on Children. This act more clearly indicated support for children returning to or being kept with families whenever possible. After years of debate, there was now a mandate to look first to a child's birth family before removing him or her from the home (Berry, 1997).

Demonstrating Effectiveness of Family-Based Services

Even before the passage of legislation, there were moves to explore the efficacy of family-based services. The 1970s saw several demonstration projects that sought to meet the goal of preventing the need for children to be placed outside of their homes. The *Alameda Project* in California in 1974–75 studied 428 children and families, assigning 227 children to the experimental group and 201 children to the control group. Those in the targeted (experimental group) population received intensive services from two designated workers—a county worker assigned to provide service for both the child and his or her parents and a worker assigned by the project whose role it was to serve the child's biological parents. Through written contracts, tracking, and reinforcers, the families in this group were encouraged to mobilize in order to keep or be reunited with their children. The results were that 79% of the children in the experimental group were kept out of foster care compared to only 40% of the control group (Stein et al., 1978).

The *Oregon Project,* a product of the Oregon Department of Human Resources and the Regional Research Institute for Human Services at Portland State University School of Social Work, sought to free children from long-term foster care placement by working with their families. By the completion of the study, 66% of the children involved had been placed in permanent settings, with 26% of these returned to their birth families and 40% in adoptive homes (Pike, 1978; Lahti et al., 1978).

The HOMEBUILDERS Project was initiated in Tacoma, Washington, with the receipt of a grant from the National Institute of Mental Health. The project sought to work with particularly disturbed and dysfunctional families, giving them intensive services for a six-week period. During the treatment, families were provided with 24-hour coverage by social workers with extensive in-home services. By the end of 16 months of the initial project, workers found that 97% of the children served had avoided institutional placement (Kinney and Haapala, 1994). Although the finding were limited in scope, the model became particularly popular in the 1980s (Berry, 1997).

Although differing in scope, intensity, and outcome, these early family-based projects provided the impetus for further efforts in the area of family preservation.

Types of Family-Based Services

Family-based services target the family and see the client as the total family system. These services are all encompassing and multidisciplinary. Some experts point to a continuum of family-based services from least intense to most comprehensive. Such services can also be divided into two categories: family support and family preservation.

Family Support Services

Family support services are designed to prevent crises and problems that might interfere with healthy child rearing. As a result, they are provided to families *before* a crisis occurs. These voluntary services are often sought out by families themselves (Altstein and McCoy, 2000).

Individual models of family support can differ widely. Some services are homebased, whereas others are offered at centers. All, however, are designed to offer programs that prevent family stress, provide education, and promote family unity and health. The goals of individual programs are often dependent on the missions of the agencies that sponsor the programs. But whatever these goals may be, the services are based on a strengths model that encourages families to feel more competent and acknowledges their right to self-determination. Workers often have supportive and even collegial relationships with families (Kagan and Weissbourd, 1994). There is an assumption that parents want the best for their children, but a recognition that life can be complex and that parents can be taxed by the multitude of demands placed on them.

What types of programs could be considered family support services? One well-known example of family support efforts is the Healthy Start Program in Hawaii. This multidimensional program was designed to educate and support families, enhance their coping skills, and promote positive parent/child relationships in order to promote healthy development for their children. Services are offered to families of newborns who are felt by hospital personnel to be at risk. These children are followed by paraprofessionals until they are about 5 years old or enter school. During this time, the families have access to a variety of services as they need them, including home visiting, assistance with housing, respite or daycare, medical support, counseling for substance abuse or domestic violence, and nutritional support through the WIC (Women Infants and Children Program (Breakley and Pratt, 1991; Earle, 1995).

Braekley and Pratt (1991) outline the following components of the Healthy Start Program:

1. Systematic hospital screening to identify high-risk families
2. Homed-based visiting in order to
   - gain the trust of the family
   - develop a therapeutic relationship with the family
   - be watchful for early signs of abuse or neglect
   - model effective parenting
   - be aware of the child's needs
   - provide concrete services to the family
3. Awareness of how the family defines itself (e.g., mother's boyfriend may be actively involved) and be inclusive of these members
4. Tailor the services to the individual family's needs (16–19)

Duggan and Windham (2000) studied 734 families involved with the Healthy Start Program. They concluded that the model had altered slightly since it inceptions, but the the work, although challenging, was successful.

Other family support programs may not target the same age group or be as comprehensive. For example, some child care programs provide services for the parents as well in order to enhance their abilities to respond effectively to their children. "Our neighborhood center," explained one social worker, "had been offering after-school care for elementary school children. We are a low-income, ethnically diverse area. When some concerns came up about the care the children were receiving, we decided to expand our services. We wrote a grant that enabled us to hire several home visitors and provide a series of classes and support services for parents. We also hooked up with a variety of social services in the area, from family planning to the literacy volunteers and the local TANF office. Through these contacts, we were able to help our parents get the services they needed. Eventually, we hope to be able to establish a teen center and enlist the help of the teens to care for younger children while we teach them about child development."

Although there are programs that service families who have older children, the consensus is that providing support services to families when children are young multiplies the chances for healthy development.

prevention

Family Preservation Services   *vs. family support*

Family preservation services differ from family support services in that they are usually mandatory and are used when crisis is imminent or has already occurred. Families receiving these services are at risk of having their children removed or have already had them removed and are seeking reunification. Such services are provided in the home (Altstein and McCoy, 2000).

Theories That Underlie Family Preservation.   McCoy (in Alstein and McCoy, 2000) points out that family preservation services draw heavily from several theoretical bases: crisis intervention theory, family systems theory, social learning theory, ecological theory, attachment theory, and functional theory. The *crisis intervention theory* helps one to understand the behavior of families who need preservation services. In crisis, one's defenses are down, one feels vulnerable and in a state of disequilibrium. It is at this time that family members may be open to trying new behaviors. As a system, the family is a complex network of roles, and each has its own methods of communicating (see Chapter 2), however dysfunctional this communication may appear to be. Understanding *family systems theory* enables workers to know where and how to intervene (Barth, 1990).

Family preservation is about enabling families to change their behaviors from those that are dysfunctional to those that will promote family stability and healthy child rearing. *Social learning theory* involves the examination of expectations and cognitions and the ways in which behavior can be changed. Interventions that include problem solving, role playing, and behavior modification—elements inherent in social learning theory—may all be used in these family services, and many family preservation models rely heavily on such techniques (Barth, 1990; Altstein and McCoy, 2000).

The *ecological theory* brings to the attention of those working with families the environmental influences from which it is impossible to escape. The environment may demand more than the family is able to accomplish and the resulting mismatch creates problems. By understanding the impact of environment, workers can help plug the family into the supports that will compensate for their deficits (Barth, 1990; Berry, 1997; Alstein and McCoy, 2000).

The final two theories that influence family preservations have been noted only recently. *Attachment theory*, although preceding the emphasis on family preservation, has more recently began to be recognized as an important influence in the development of children, especially those who face separation from their families of birth. Children must develop healthy attachments to their earliest caregivers in order to form relationships later in life. When this early bonding does not go well as a result of inconsistent or abusive parenting, these children will be adversely affected. Separation from parents may also have a negative impact on child development. And finally, *functional theory*, basic to social work practice, emphasizes the importance of self-determination and client empowerment. Only when families become a part of their own change process will these changes have the chance to be lasting ones. This theory urges workers to make use of a client's strengths and abilities to accomplish change (Altstein and McCoy, 2000).

The Characteristics of Family Preservation Services. Although family preservation services may differ not only in scope but also in intensity, there are some fundamental points of commonality among them. First, the *whole family becomes the client* and must be treated within its own environment. Second, family preservation services are based on a *strengths perspective*. The strengths of the family are assessed and the *goals of treatment are set by the family* in ways that will enhance their strengths. Next, the *treatment relationship becomes a partnership* between the worker and the family, who work together on the family's behalf. And finally, family preservation services are provided to the *family in the home or within the community*. By definition, these type of services are provided in time of crisis, but tend to be *short term and intensive*. During the time that they are being provided, a great deal is expected of the worker in terms of time and energy (Berry, 1997, 76–80).

Models of Family Preservation Services. McCoy (in Alstein and McCoy, 2000) explains that family preservation services can be divided into two different categories: rehabilitative and intensive. *Rehabilitative* services target families that might be at risk for removal of their children if some changes are not made. The goal here is to help the family through parent education, anger management training, behavior modification, or other techniques that will help them provide a safer and less dysfunction environment for their children.

CASE EXAMPLE

The Johns Family

Entering the Johns family's apartment brought to mind a carnival. The noise and choas of the home was almost overwhelming. Mrs. Johns's love of unusual "junk" dictated furnishings that were neither functional nor attractive, though they *were* colorful. The myriad of smells, not all of them pleasing, assaulted the nose as soon as the front door was opened. The five children were undisciplined and did pretty much what they wanted. This had resulted in complaints from the neighbors, not only about the children but also about the garbage that literally flowed out the back door into the halls below. The older children's erratic attendance and dirty, unkempt appearances had prompted a report for neglect from the concerned school. Mrs. Johns was a single mother, at least at the moment. Reports were that an array of men had been in residence at different times.

Despite the chaos that was the Johns home and the neglect of the children, ages 2 to 12, it became clear to the worker that Mrs. Johns loved her children and was concerned about them. Her neglect was more a result of her inability to problem solve or prioritize, combined with the fact that she had had no parenting models in her dysfunctional childhood. She was an excellent candidate for the services of an agency that provided family preservation services. After several months of visits three times a week from a social worker, regular visits from a homemaker and parenting classes, Mrs. Johns was able to improve both her housekeeping and her parenting so that the child protection agency agreed that her children need not be removed.

Intensive services (sometimes referred to as *intensive family-based services* or *IFBS*) are provided to families where placement could be imminent or when re-unification of the family and children is planned. Help is provided by a worker who carries only one or two cases at a time. The worker sees the family between 4 and 20 hours a week and is on call at all times (Fraser et al., 1997; Alstein and McCoy, 2000). If there is any question of danger to the children who are still in the home, they are removed (Hagedorn, 1995; Walton et. al., 2001).

Types of Service Provision in Family Preservation.   For the purpose of research, the services provided to families are divided into two categories: hard and soft services. *Hard services* refer to concrete resources, such as food, housing, furniture, and so on. Concrete resources are provided for several reasons. First, it is difficult for families to concentrate on improving communication, parenting, and other interpersonal skills when they are concerned about their basic needs or stressed by their physical environment (Berry, 1997). Second, research (see Kinney and Haapala, 1994; Berry, 1997; Alstein and McCoy, 2000) tells us that families can be more effectively engaged when they can see tangible proof that the worker is concerned for their welfare. As one client put it after she received assistance from a worker in furnishing her once bare apartment, "I can hear you talking better when I am sitting in this comfortable chair."

Finally, research (Lindsey, 1991; Berry, 1997) has indicated that the decision to place children in foster care may actually be influenced by the worker's perception of the child's physical environment as well as the economic stability of the family. Often, improving the physical setting and the financial resources that a family has will not only improve their self-concept and willingness to cooperate but it may also give workers hope that further improvements are possible.

Soft services refer to services that the worker provides to engage the family and to give them hope that they might improve their lives (Berry, 1997). Listening, empathizing, understanding, and supporting families by establishing a bond between worker and families and lays the groundwork for goal setting. Workers may also model effective communication and parenting skills so that family members might understand what is expected of them.

Berry (1997) suggests that enabling services are also necessary. These services help families provide linkages with other informal supports that will be there for them when the worker terminates with the family. Enabling work also empowers families so that they are able to find their own services in the future.

Whatever type of service that is provided, the bottom line is that it empowers the family and allows the members to have input in their own treatment.

Kinship Care: Family Preservation or Child Placement?

Kinship care is a concept that dates back to well before the coming of child welfare services. Usually, the arrangement had been an informal one where aunts, uncles, grandparents, and older siblings cared for children when their parents could not do so (Walton et al., 2001). This arrangement is beneficial for children because it allows them to stay with relatives that they already know and trust, thus diminishing the effects of separation from their parents. In addition, children can maintain their family connections, culture, and family history, which in turn positively influences their identity and self-esteem (Wilson and Chipungu, 1996; Hegar and Scannapieco, 1999; Walton et al., 2001). In 1997, with the passing of the Adoption and Safe Families Act, which stipulates that extended family placement should be considered, what was once an informal arrangement became the first option explored by child welfare workers when a child is in need of out-of-home care. The number of grandparents raising children today, for example, is significant. In fact, kinship care in all of its forms is the fasting-growing type of out-of-home care (Alstein and McCoy, 2000). Altstein (in Alstein and McCoy, 2000) suggests that, in addition to the need to comply with federal standards established by the Adoption and Safe Families Act, kinship care has become popular among states because it is less costly to maintain a family on financial assistance than to place a child in foster care.

The question then arises, Is kinship care a form of family preservation or a type of foster care? The answer is that it is both, and it will be discussed further in Chapter 11. It is difficult to distinguish when kinship care is seen as family preservation and when it is seen as foster care. Some clinicians have made the distinction based on several factors: Who initiated the arrangement and is the kinship home being furnished with foster care payments to care for the child?

CASE EXAMPLE

Sara Jackson

Sara Jackson's mother, Nadine, was 14 years old when Sara was born. Nadine was one of seven children herself, and her mother tried to convince her to place the child for adoption. Nadine refused and insisted that she would care for Sara in her mother's home—an arrangement to which the mother, Mrs. Jackson, finally reluctantly agreed. She also consented to watch Sara while Nadine attended school. The arrangement continued until Nadine was almost 16 years old, at which time she became involved with a 25-year-old man. Mrs. Jackson tried to convince her daughter that this was not a good match, but Nadine insisted that as long as she (Nadine) cared for Sara, her mother had no right to interfere in her life. The dispute finally came to a head and Nadine quit school and moved into an apartment with her boyfriend and Sara.

Mrs. Jackson had no contact with her daughter, though she received sporadic reports from a neighbor with whom Nadine still kept in touch. The neighbor reported that Nadine was drinking. Mrs. Jackson wondered what she could do for her granddaughter, but before she had a chance to act, she accidentally met Nadine in a mall. Sara was dirty and thin and Nadine was obviously drunk. After trying to talk with her, Mrs. Jackson concluded that there was little that she could do. It did not surprise her, however, when the neighbor soon reported that protective services had removed Sara from Nadine, who had subsequently left home with a new boyfriend.

Mrs. Jackson contacted child protective services and requested to have Sara placed with her. Concerned about this grandmother's own housekeeping standards, the agency was reluctant to comply. They finally agreed to make the placement if Mrs. Jackson would agree to the services of a social worker.

For the Jackson family, the services offered by the agency were seen as family preservation. Hegar and Scannapieco (1999) respond to the question of how kinship is defined by suggesting that kinship as foster placement is when it is ordered by the court, while all other kinship arrangements constitute family preservation efforts.

Who provides kinship care? According to a study done by the Casey Foundation in 1994 (LeProhn and Pecora, 1994), most kinship caregivers were either grandmothers (54%) or aunts (38%), with most being in financial stress themselves. These caregivers also tended to be less educated and older than traditional foster parents.

The effectiveness of kinship care for children is debated by some. Alstein (in Alstein and McCoy, 2000) contends that kinship care leaves children in limbo. Since kin caregivers usually have no interest in adoption, feeling that the child is already in the family, the child's legal status remains in question. In addition, these caregivers have no obligation to continue the care of the child until his or her majority.

As kinship care becomes a more widely used option, there is a move toward studying these homes as kinship foster homes. In this way, more services and training can be offered to kin caregivers, and there will be a better defined arrangement for the children in kinship homes.

Family Preservation Worker

One of the most important determinations of success in family preservation programs is how they are administered (Dylla, 1997). Staff has a crucial role in ensuring that families become empowered and can continue to maintain the changes that they make. Like most child welfare workers, these workers require education and experience, but some researchers found that none of these variables guaranteed a skillful family preservation worker (Kinney and Haapala, 1994). Agencies do find that some experience and knowledge in crisis intervention and family systems is important, but there is also a need for specific personal characteristics (Dylla, 1997). There may not be that much consensus on the particular qualities needed by workers, but rather someone who has the ability to "provide therapeutic as well as case management services in work situations that are demanding, stressful, unstructured, unpredictable, and potentially dangerous" (Dylla, 1997, 108). Dylla goes on to suggest that workers in family preservation must

> *exhibit external characteristics such as a sense of humor, resourcefulness, co-operativeness, adventurousness, a pleasant and positive attitude, and a warm personality.... Workers are expected to be team players, and to hold values that are consonant with the philosophy of family preservation. Workers who exude internal characteristics such as courage, autonomy, comfort with ambiguity, tolerance for differences, good judgment, common sense, conscientiousness, and pride in their work are preferred, as well as work who set high standards for themselves. (108)*

There is no question that work in family preservation is demanding and taxes one's energies. Rick found that 18 months of such work was enough: "I loved the work at first. I was employed by a pilot project that provided intensive family services to at-risk families. We had one client (family) at a time and we worked intensively with them for six to eight weeks. By that time, it was assumed that they would have learned how to take better care of themselves and we could move on to another family. I was hired because I speak Spanish. The families I served had so many problems—not just that they were at risk for abusing their children. In two of the families I had, the kids were the only ones who spoke English. This gave them incredible power over their families and I think that was part of the problem. Most of the families were great to work with. It was the community that was tough. I saw a lot of prejudice and a lot of broken promises. I got to be very cynical about getting help in a community. And the degree of problems that these families had began to really depress me. I worked with one family twice—a year apart. It wasn't that we hadn't made progress the first time, but a new crisis came up.

"By the end of a year and a half and working with seven families, I couldn't take it anymore. I was always at a state of heightened awareness, waiting for the phone to ring at any hour of the night or day. Then I would get really involved with these folks and they were all I could think about. I had no social life—no life really except my work. It can be rewarding work, but it is very taxing too."

Dylla (1997) emphasizes the importance of training to enhance the effectiveness of the family preservation worker. Training should cover the philosophy of family-based services and family preservation in specific, technical skills needed (e.g., mediation, role playing, modeling, active listening, etc.), and specific types of techniques and therapeutic options (e.g., behavior modification). Also helpful are training in community analysis, advocacy, and other ways that might help one to impact the environment (111–112).

It is vital that family preservation workers are supervised competently. When one provides services on a round-the-clock basis, it is often necessary to have the support and consultation of another uninvolved professional (Kinney and Haapala, 1994; Dylla, 1997).

Some programs reflect the belief that the intensive services expected of workers are too much for an individual. For this reason, some have employed teams. A team, instead of a single worker, may be assigned to a family so that the workers are called on to join together in providing the services. Although the opportunity for the division of labor is helpful, and families have an additional role model, agencies are aware that the benefits can be outweighed by the negatives if the team is not well matched (Dylla, 1997). A poorly communicating team may actually defeat its own efforts as they strive to enhance communication and cooperation within the family.

Preserve the Family or Place the Child?

The debate about the efficacy of family preservation continues to be addressed by practitioners as well as researchers in the field of child welfare. In *Does Family Preservation Serve a Child's Best Interests?* Alstein and McCoy (2000) demonstrate how fundamental the controversy has become to the practice of social work.

Berry (1997) suggests that there are some basic reasons why families should be preserved. First, she says, *keeping families together* is more humane. Not only are children traumatized by separation, but relationships are damaged, often hampering family members in building healthy later relationships with others. Second, services aimed at families can and should be *more efficient,* using less in social service dollars. Foster care, on the other hand, can be expensive. And finally, such services can be *more effective.* Personal problems are often a result of poor communication. Teaching families to communicate will not only enhance their functioning but it will also improve the members' ability to forge other relationships. Family members can learn to support one another, and through this, children are helped to develop that in crisis one does not just give up (50–51).

Kelly and Blythe (2000) comment that "family preservation services seemed to hold much promise for the child welfare field, and for the lives of families and children. Unfortunately, this promise has never been fully realized throughout the United States" (29). These authors suggest that states attempted to implement family preservation services in a vacuum with little technical support. Models have mutated to the point that some are no longer well designed. The stigma—for being poor, minorities, drug addicted, single parents—attached to many of the families who could receive family preservation services, when colored by the media, has also served to diminish the amount of public funds available for the implementation of these programs. Critics of family preservation have influenced the passing of legislation that would further support family preservation plans. In short, Kelly and Blythe (2000) argue,

> *Any one of these factors—the media backlash, Congressional skepticism, the disarray with the child welfare community, lack of funding or questions about the efficacy of the models would have proved a formidable foe to the implementation of family preservation as a natural strategy. Taken together, these factors proved to be nearly fatal to family preservation. (33)*

Heneghan and Horwitz (1996) urge policymakers to remember that family preservation is not a panacea. It does not work for all families. Assuming that it will work with any family at risk is to invite possible failure and put children in danger of maltreatment.

Altstein (in Altstein and McCoy, 2000) does not feel that family preservation programs have met their goal of reducing or eliminating the likelihood of children being placed in foster care. He suggests that this is because the families at whom these services are directed are those with the most "dysfunctional, severe and even pathologic" (61) difficulties. These families often come with generations' worth of histories of involvement with the mental health and social welfare agencies.

Perhaps what concerns Altstein most about the continuing use of family preservation models is the lack of data to support their efficacy.

> *Effectiveness is demonstrated through classic experimental design where two similar groups (of families) are assembled, with one receiving this case family preservation intervention and the other receiving traditional interven-*

tion(s) and no services. At the end of a given period, both groups are examined to determine whether predicted results were achieved…. A review of the literature revealed that practically no definitive data exist suggesting that family preservation works, that indeed these efforts actually made a real difference in the lives of families and prevented a child's removal from the home. (Alstein and McCoy, 2000, 64)

This author goes on to remark,

Given the fanfare and funding surrounding these [family preservation] programs, it is curious that so little evaluation appears. What the lack of data says to this reviewer is that perhaps we are dealing with what may be the sacred cows of the human service (social work) establishment and its political allies, who are not keen for these approaches to be "put to the (real world) test." (71)

Altstein's bias leans toward the termination of parental rights and the more permanent solution of adoption placement as a method of preventing children's lengthily stay in foster care.

Berry (1997) argues that evaluation research has failed "because workers have not understood the value of research" (161) and researchers have misunderstood how complex family preservation programs really are.

The debate about the efficacy of family preservation promises to continue, sometimes heatedly. In the meantime, child welfare agencies must make "reasonable efforts" to return the children to or keep them with their birth parents. At the same time, they must also abide by the dictates of the Adoption and Safe Families Act, which requires them to initiate termination of parental rights once a child has remained in foster care for 15 of the last 22 months.

Shaping the Future of Family-Based Services

It becomes clear that for family preservation services to continue, there must be some provisions to increase the efficacy of service provision. Altstein (in Alststein and McCoy, 2000) expresses concern about the effect that TANF will have on the implementation of family preservation. Temporary Assisstance for Needy Families requires that families must leave public assistance after 60 months (see Chapter 3). Granted, states have the right to define some recipients as "hardship" cases, making them exempt from the cut-off after this time. But only 20% of a state's cases can be deemed hardship, leaving a significant number that must comply to the limitations of the program. Employment is seen as a necessity under the new provisions. What, then, happens to single mothers who reach the limit of their TANF benefits and cannot be considered "hardship" cases? Will these previously marginally stable families, faced with one more stressor, be able to meet the challenge?

McCoy (in Altstein and McCoy, 2000) suggests that we not criticize the existing family preservation programs as much as seek to refocus and restructure child welfare services in general. She comments,

> *Instead of blaming programs or policies for problems, we need to look at the entire system of child welfare services and identify needed changes. We must acknowledge that the system has not always protected the children or found ways to help families provide for the well-being of their children, or, when necessary, found appropriate placements for children. In many cases, failure to implement programs, lack of sufficient resources to effectively support the programs and families, and/or inadequate resources to train workers in conducting good assessments to determine which children are at risk of harm may have led to negative outcomes, not the programs themselves. (51)*

Kelly and Blythe (2000) argue that improving family preservation is worth the effort. They also suggest that family preservation must be reintroduced to courts and that court personnel must be reeducated to look at the strengths of parents rather than the deficits. These authors and others outline specific changes that must be made if family preservation services are to survive and achieve their worthy goals.

Screening of At-Risk Clients

As we evaluate family preservation efforts, it becomes clear that some clients can benefit more from these services than others. Screening must involve careful assessments of family strengths and ability to utilize services (Berry, 1997; Kelly and Blythe, 2000; Walton et al., 2001). If the focus of such services centers on self-determination, the potential for healthy child rearing, and the family's ability to develop into a functional and healthy unit, families should be sought with this potential. At the same time, programs must guard against accepting families because their potential for development will ensure a positive statistic for evaluation purposes. Although some of these families may look like ideal candidates, they may, in fact, not be those who most need family preservation services (Berry, 1997; Daro and Harding, 1999). In addition, no matter how confident a worker may be on the potential of a family to be preserved, the safety of the child is paramount. Knowing when to protect the child as opposed to continuing to keep the child in a home is vital.

Selection and Training of Workers

As previously mentioned, the attitude and skill of the worker can greatly affect the outcome of family preservation with a given family. Yet, to date, there is no definitive research indicating what the educational or experience requirements of such workers should be. Most successful programs find that workers benefit most from some experience in working with families, especially in the areas of crisis intervention, family therapy, parent training, and case management (Kinney and Haapala, 1994; Berry, 1997). Whether these workers require specific academic degrees is still being debated. What does seem to be helpful is for these professionals be knowledgeable in some traditional clinical skills such as communication, active listening, and so on, as well as some concrete skills such as household management and budgeting (Berry, 1997).

Training of workers who deliver family preservation services is an equally vital component as screening for those who have an aptitude for such work. Without adequate training in a variety of areas, these workers cannot be effective (see earlier section on Family Preservation Worker).

Supervision and Consultation

Dylla (1997) contends that supervision is another vital aspect of family preservation services. She suggest that family preservation supervisors "should supervise in nontraditional ways" (113). Since workers must serve families beyond the normal work day, supervisors must exhibit the flexibility to be available at whatever time they are needed. They must model good communication skills, provide support, confront when necessary, and have knowledge of and access to resources that might be of use to the worker (Dylla, 1997; Walton et al., 2001). As workers are asked to recognize and develop the family's strengths, so must a supervisor mirror this for his or her workers. Family preservation is a demanding and sometimes isolating job. An effective supervisor can go a long way to prevent the burnout of his or her workers.

Operationalism of Program Design Goals

A program that involves clients may appear to be successful, but in order to prove that success, one must know how it is defined. The most effective way to know if the goal has been reached and to demonstrate this positive outcome is to use behavioral objectives. Early family preservation programs sought to keep children from being placed in foster care, but did not narrow their goals sufficiently. Operationalizing a programs goals would result in a series of measurable behavioral tasks that a family would be able to do at the completion of a specific time period. Such concrete goals not only enable more careful and reliable evaluation but they also provide a family with tasks that they can recognize that they have completed.

Building Community Supports

Families who require family preservation services are often isolated from their communities, who may have seen them merely as consumers of vital and much in demand resources. There is a great need to educate communities in the values of family preservation. Community members must come to see the strengths that can be tapped in families rather than their deficits. This will require networking and relationship building between agencies, families, and the greater community (Berry, 1997). Kelly and Blythe (2000) suggest the need to engage the media in positive portrayal of families. They also stress the importance of involving legislators and national organizations in the effort to promote such services.

Evaluation and Research

As discussed earlier, the paucity of credible research and evaluation of family preservation programs provides one of the most significant threats to the expansions of such services. Berry (1997) cautions that it is important not only to discover whether a program worked but also *how* it worked. Much more needs to be known about what services are the most effective and what families are best suited to use them. Obtaining this knowledge will require a variety of types of evaluations, many using specific behavioral measures.

Although many in the child welfare field believe that family preservation is the best alternative for children, some, as we have discussed earlier, question whether emphasis on keeping the family together is in the best interests of the child. Only through careful research and evaluations over time will we discover the most developmentally sound answer for the children who come to the attention of the child welfare system.

Summary

Families are basic to the raising of children. Yet these families cannot always meet their children's needs. Knowing when to preserve the family or when to place the child has been an issue that has created a significant amount of debate in the field of child welfare. More recently, there has been an emphasis on family-based services to strengthen families in order to help them provide a nurturing environment for their children.

In the early history of the United States, children in poor and often dysfunctional families joined their families in almshouses or, if older, were indentured to learn a trade. They were at the mercy of and dependent on the charity of the more economically advantaged in society. As critics began to complain about the treatment of children in almshouses and as national values became more reflective of the work ethic, children began to be placed with families to work and be provided for. Latter, the settlements were to influence services to children.

By the early 1900s, mothers' pensions were provided for poverty-stricken mothers to care for their children. But there were strings attached to these allotments. A recipient was required to be of good moral character, and not being so might mean that not only did a mother lose her pension but she might also lose her children. Investigation to assess her character were the early forerunners of assessment visits in child protection.

It soon became obvious in the 1950s and 60s that not only were more and more children being placed in foster care, but they remained there for longer periods of time. The Adoption Assistance and Child Welfare Act of 1980 and the Family Preservation and Family Support Act of 1993 were designed to attempt to provide permanency for children while first assessing the family for its potential to be helped to keep or be reunited with their children.

Family-based services can be divided into two types: family support services and family preservation services. Family support services are used to support and strengthen families so that they can better meet the needs of their children. Family preservation services are provided in times of crisis when removal seems imminent or when children are scheduled to be reunited with their families. Family preservation services can be either rehabilitative or intensive, differing mostly in the amount of time the worker spends with the family. Family preservation services are grounded in several theories: crisis intervention theory, family systems theory, ecological theory, attachment theory, and functional theory. Services may be either "hard" services (food, housing, furniture, etc.) or "soft" services, which refer to the intangible attention the worker gives to the family (listening, understanding, helping with problem solving, etc.). Kinship care may also be a form of family preservation service as well as a type of foster care.

The worker is an important part of successful family intervention. Although selection and training are vital, a worker must also have specific personal characteristics and some experience in working with families.

Some feel that family preservation has been an important and effective part of child welfare. Critics feel that there is a concern that efforts to preserve the family will actually put children at risk. It seems clear that there is not sufficient research to settle the argument conclusively. Proponents for the continuation of family preservation services call for increased training of workers, careful program design, better supervision, community support, and more intensive evaluation to determine if family preservation services are in the best interests of the child.

EXPLORATION QUESTIONS

1. Trace the history of responding to children of poor and/or dysfunctional families.
2. What is meant by *scientific philanthropy?*
3. How did child welfare assessment visits originate?
4. What two acts influenced the provision of family-based services? How?
5. Name several significant projects in the early family preservation services movement. What was their success rate?
6. What are the types of family-based services? How do they differ? Cite an example of each.
7. What six theories underlie family preservation? How does each apply?
8. What are the two models of family preservation services? How do they differ?
9. What are the types of services (categories) in family preservation?

10. What does a family preservation worker need to have?
11. What are the criticisms leveled against family preservation services?
12. What must shape the future of family preservation?

REFERENCES

Altstein, H., & McCoy, R. (2000). *Does Family Preservation Serve a Child's Best Interests?* Washington, DC: Georgetown University Press.

Barth, R. P. (1990). "Theories Guiding Home-Based Intensive Family Preservation Services." In J. K. Whittaker, J. Kinney, E. M. Tracy, & C. Booth (Eds.), *Reaching High Risk Families: Intensive Family Preservation in Human Services.* New York: Aldine deGuyter.

Berry, M. (1997). *Families at Risk: Issues in Family Preservation Services.* Columbia: University of South Carolina Press.

Brace, C. L. (1872). *The Dangerous Classes of New York, and Twenty Years' Work among Them.* New York: Wynkoop and Hallenbeck.

Breakley, G., & Pratt, B. (1991). "Healthy Growth for Hawaii's 'Healthy Start,'" *Zero to Three,* 9(4), 16–22.

Burt, M. R., & Pittman, K. J. (1985). *Testing the Social Safety Net.* Washington, DC: Urban Institute Press.

Clement, P. F. (1978). "Families in Foster Care: Philadelphia in the Late Nineteenth Century," *Social Services Review,* 53, 406–420.

Coontz, S. (1998). *The Way We Really Are: Coming to Terms with America's Changing Families.* New York: Basic Books.

Courtney, M. E. (1998). "The Costs of Child Protection in the Context of Welfare Reform," *The Future of Children: Protecting Children From Abuse and Neglect,* 8(1), 88–105. Los Altos, CA: The David and Lucille Packard Foundation.

Daro, D., & Harding, K. (1999). "Healthy Families in America: Using Research to Enhance Practice," *The Future of Children: Protecting Children From Abuse and Neglect,* 9(1). Los Altos, CA: The David and Lucille Packard Foundation.

Duggan, A., & Windham, A. (2000). "Hawaii's Healthy Start of Home Visiting for At-Risk Families: Evaluation of Family Identification, Family Engagement, and Service Delivery," *Pediatrics,* 105(1), 250–260.

Dylla, D. J. C. (1997). "Administrative and Organizational Issues" (106–128). In M. Berry (Ed.), *Families at Risk: Issues in Family Preservation Services.* Columbia: University of South Carolina Press.

Earle, R. (1995). *Helping to Prevent Child Abuse and Future Criminal Consequences: Hawaii's Healthy Start.* Washington, DC: U.S. Department of Justice.

Fanshel, D., & Shinn, E. (1973). *Children in Foster Care: A Longitudinal Investigation.* New York: Columbia University Press.

Fraser, M., Nelson, K., & Rivard, J. (1997). "Effectiveness of Family Preservation Services," *Social Work Research,* 21(2), 138–153.

Gruber, A. (1973). *Foster Home Care in Massachusetts.* Boston: Governor's Commission on Adoption and Foster Care.

Hagedorn, J. M. (1995). *Forsaking Our Children: Bureaucracy and Reform in the Child Welfare System.* Chicago: Lake View Press.

Hegar, R. I., & Scannapieco, M. (Eds.). (1999). *Kinship Foster Care: Policy, Practice and Research.* New York: Oxford University Press.

Heneghan, A. M., & Horowitz, S. M. (1996). "Evaluating Intensive Family Preservation Programs: A Methodological Review," *Pediatrics,* 97(4), 535–543.

Hewlett, S., West, C., & West, E. (1999). *The War Against Parents.* New York: Mariner Books.

Kagan, S. L., & Weissbourd, B. (Eds.). (1994). *Putting Families First—America's Family Support Movement and the Challenge of Change.* San Francisco: Jossey-Bass.

Kelly, S., & Blythe, B. (2000). "Family Preservation: A Potential Not Yet Realized," *Child Welfare,* 79(1), 29–43.

Kinney, J. M., & Haapala, D. A. (1994). "Preserving Families through the Homebuilders

Program," *Building Bridges: Supporting Families across Social Service Systems,* 13(1&2). Chicago: Family Resource Coalition.

Lahti, J., Green, K., Emlen, A., Zadney, J., Clarkson, Q. C., Keuhnel, M., & Casciato, J. (1978). *A Follow-Up Study of the Oregon Project.* Portland: Regional Research Institute for Human Services, Portland State University.

Leff, M. (1973). "Consensus for Reform: The Mother's Pension Movement in a Progressive Era," *Social Service Review,* 47, 397–417.

LeProhn, N., & Pecora, P. (1994). *Summary of the Casey Foster Parent Study.* Seattle: The Casey Program, Research Department.

Lindsey, D. (1991). "Factors Affecting the Foster Care Placement Decision: An Analysis of National Survey Data," *American Journal of Orthopsychiatry,* 61(2), 272–283.

MacDonald, H. (1994). "The Ideology of 'Family Preservation,'" *Public Interest,* Spring, 45–60.

McCronsky, J., & Meezan, W. (1998). "Family Preservation Services: Approaches and Effectiveness," *The Future of Children: Protecting Children From Abuse and Neglect,* 8(1). Los Altos, CA: The David and Lucille Packard Foundation.

National Commission on Children. (1991). *Beyond Rhetoric: A New American Agenda for Children and Families.* Washington, DC: National Commission on Children.

Nelson, K., & Allen, M. (1995). "Family Centered Social Services: Moving Toward System Change." In P. Adams & K. Nelson (Eds.), *Reinventing Human Services: Community and Family Centered Practice.* New York: Aldine de Guyter.

Pike, V. (1978). "Permanent Families for Foster Children: The Oregon Project," *Children Today,* 5, 22–25.

Schene, P. A. (1998). "Past, Present and Future Roles of Child Protection Services," *The Future of Children,* 8, 23–38. Los Altos, CA: The David and Lucille Packard Foundation.

Shyne, A. W., & Schroeder, A. G. (1978). *National Study of Social Services to Children and Their Families.* Washington, DC: Children's Bureau.

Stein, T. J., Gambrill, E. D., & Wiltse, K. T. (1978). *Children in Foster Homes: Achieving Community Care.* New York: Praeger.

Walton, E., Mannes, M., & Sandau-Beckler, P. (2001). *Balancing Family-Centered Services and Child Well-Being.* New York: Columbia University Press.

Wilson, D. B., & Chipungu, S. S. (1996). "Introduction: Special Issue on Kinship Care," *Child Welfare,* 75, 387–395.

9 Court Services on Behalf of Children

JUDY A. NOEL

What is it that hampers the effectiveness of the function and operation of the juvenile court today. The problem is one basic to most large social institutions. It is that juvenile courts are continually given more duties and responsibilities than resources with which to perform those duties and responsibilities. Often, social institutions are abused simply because they exist. The juvenile court is a perfect example. It has to bow to the capricious nature of those who wish to use it. Thus its autonomy has been gravely undermined, and it is held in low esteem by judges, lawyers, and other professionals in the corrections field.

—C. E. Simonsen

The juvenile court is the primary part of the judicial system that serves children and their families today. Although some cases involving the abuse or custody of children are seen in criminal or probate court, it is the juvenile or family court that, by design, protects the best interests of minor children. Court services are provided in the context of the civil court, because the emphasis is on protection and rehabilitation rather than on proving guilt or innocence, as is required in a criminal court. In reality, juvenile courts are expected not only to orchestrate rehabilitation for wayward youths, but also to protect society from them (Simonsen, 1991). In addition, juvenile courts are given the task of protecting children whose parents cannot adequately do so. It is no wonder that the system is hard-pressed to perform these conflicting obligations in a manner that pleases everyone involved.

How juvenile court services are offered varies throughout the United States. In some areas, a specialized juvenile court provides services to alleged delinquent, dependent, and neglected and abused children. Additional needs that children may have for court intervention are provided through courts of jurisdiction and municipal courts. Other communities have established more extensive services through a family court system. In addition to the services provided in juvenile courts, family courts may also be involved in custody cases due to divorce, child support, paternity cases, and all situations concerning minors that require court intervention.

The function and structure of court services are established through legislation. Although all must be in compliance with federal legislation, court services in each state are controlled by state statutes. The result has been major differences in the implementation of court services to juveniles.

Historical Perspective

Specialized court services to meet the needs of children are a relatively new phenomenon in the United States. Until the early twentieth century, juveniles who committed crimes were treated too severely, as adults, or too leniently in the criminal justice system (Elrod and Ryder, 1999). Societal values supported the ultimate authority of parents, particularly fathers, over children. Dependency issues, including abuse and neglect, were deemed private issues and not public concerns.

Several events beginning in the first half of the nineteenth century have been identified as precipitating the development of separate court services for juveniles. The first of these is the combined impact of immigration, industrialization, and urbanization. This time period is characterized by unprecedented immigration from Europe. Many early immigrants worked as apprentices. Eventually, apprentice programs were not able to absorb this rapidly growing new labor supply. This, and periodic recessions, resulted in poverty and high rates of unemployment.

Strangely enough, in this social climate, one of the first cases in which a court ruling made reference to what was best for a child occurred. In 1813, the case of *Commonwealth v. Addicks and wife* involved a custody dispute between the biological parents of two minor children. The father considered the mother's behavior to be immoral, and he wanted the custody of the children. Although the court recognized that the mother's behavior was "highly improper," the children were being well cared for and well educated. The court's decision to leave the children in the custody of the mother against the father's objections was made based on the best interests of the children (Stein, 1991, 27).

In most instances, poor, dependent children were placed in almshouses or poorhouses if they were too ill or too young to work. Older, able-bodied dependent children were placed in workhouses. Those who committed minor offenses were placed in community asylums or homes, and those involved in serious crimes received the same punishment as adults—imprisonment and sometimes death (Siegel, 2002; Siegel and Senna, 2000; Simonsen, 1991).

As industrialization and urbanization accelerated, so did the number of destitute children. Young children were left to care for themselves because their parents did not want to take care of them, could not afford to support them, or were unable to supervise them while they worked long hours. Many children resorted to committing petty crimes to survive on city streets. The increasing number of destitute and delinquent children could no longer be ignored, which led to the child saving movement, the second event preceding the development of a juvenile court system (Siegel, 2002; Siegel and Senna, 2000).

The Child Savers

The *child savers* were primarily middle-class women interested in providing care for neglected and delinquent children and protecting society from their activities. For the first time, services specifically intended to meet the needs of children were developed, including shelter homes, educational opportunities, and social activities. The child savers were instrumental in developing governmental control over parental authority by promoting legislation that gave states legal jurisdiction to "control and protect" children (Siegel, 2002; Siegel and Senna, 2000).

An outcome of these legislative efforts was the establishment of specialized institutions, houses of refuge, in several states for the placement of delinquent and uncontrollable children. The purpose of these institutions, which were privately funded and publicly supported, was to prevent future poverty and crime by separating these children from their undesirable environments, including their natural parents, and reforming them through training and a "family-like" environment (Siegel, 2002; Siegel and Senna, 2000).

Reform School Movement

The reform school movement was another effort leading to the development of a juvenile court system in the United States. During the mid-1800s, the child savers used their influence on local and state governments to develop institutions exclusively for delinquent and homeless children. The first of these state-supported reform schools opened in Massachusetts in 1848 and others were established in several states soon after (Siegel, 2002; Siegel and Senna, 2000; Binder et al., 1997).

Opposition to houses of refuge and reform schools to protect neglected and delinquent children continued to grow throughout the mid-nineteenth century. Charles Brace, a minister and social reformer, developed an alternative to institutionalization in houses of refuge or reform schools. Under the auspice of the Children's Aid Society, which he helped to establish, delinquent and dependent urban youths were sent on what became known as *the orphan trains* and placed with rural farm families in the West who wanted additional children to help with the chores. Brace's thought, it appears, was for moral reform as well as the provision of homes for children. In one of his much publicized speeches, Brace quoted one of the New York City newsboys he placed in the western United States addressing others of his kind:

> *Do you want to be newsboys always, and show blacks, and timber merchants in a small way selling matches? If ye do you'll stay in New York, but if you don't you'll go West and begin to be farmers, for the beginning of a farmer, my boys, is the making of a Congressman, and a President. (Simonsen, 1991, 22)*

This practice of "placing-out," the forerunner of foster home placement, was highly criticized and eventually was discontinued. One major objection was raised by the Catholic Church. Urban children, who were predominantly Catholic, were often placed in rural Protestant homes where they were unable to actively participate in their religion. Others objected on the basis that the failure to complete extensive home studies would result in the exploitation of children. Some institutions protested because they were being deprived of child labor. Despite these critics, later research did suggest that, for the most part, these placements were successful.

The Concept of *Parens Patriae*

The concept of *parens patriae* was the final development leading to the creation of the juvenile court. *Parens patriae* was a term that originated in English common law and assumed that children could be made "wards of the state." In the United States, the philosophy of *parens patriae* was extended to houses of refuge, giving them complete parental control over both delinquent and dependent children committed to these institutions by *Ex Parte Crouse* (1838) and *Commonwealth v. Fisher* (1905). At the same time, stronger objections were being made about the commitment of children under the doctrine of *parens patriae* without due process of law. This concern was reflected in the *O'Connell v. Turner* court case, which restricted admissions to only those children who had committed delinquent acts (Siegel and Senna, 2000).

The Emergence of the Juvenile Court

Several child savers and early social workers involved in the settlement house movement had a significant influence in the development of court services for juveniles. Jane Addams, who founded Hull House during the late 1800s, Julia Lathrop, and several other residents of this settlement house used their political influence to develop and implement the legislation, establishing the first juvenile court in Chicago on April 2, 1899. Their concerns involved inadequate treatment in institutions for delinquent and dependent children and the placement of delinquent children with adults in jails and prisons (Siegel and Senna, 2000; Downs et al., 1996; Dziech and Schudson, 1991).

These proponents of separating juveniles from the adult court system believed that the rationale for this move was threefold:

> *(1) Children committed crimes not from a sense of evil or malice, but rather from a sense of need. A child's crime was an expression of pain, a signal that something was not right with the individual or family. The child needed help, not criminal court punishment. (2) Children suffering from abuse or neglect might have to be removed from the family, an action that required special procedures to evaluate the circumstances of the family and the needs of the child in order to balance their respective rights. (3) Those responsible for decisions about delinquent, abused, or neglected children should have the special inclination and expertise needed to understand the young. (Dziech and Schudson, 1991, 25)*

The initial legislation establishing the juvenile court, the Juvenile Court Act, made clear distinctions between delinquent and dependent children, although both groups came under the jurisdiction of the juvenile court. It established a specific court for juveniles, provided for a juvenile probation system, permitted the commitment of children to institutions under the control of state laws, and established juvenile delinquency as a legal concept (Siegel, 2002; Siegel and Senna, 2000; Simonsen, 1991).

The purpose of the newly formed juvenile court was to prevent crime and rehabilitate the juvenile offenders. The philosophy of the court stressed the best interests of the child (Stein, 1991). Because treatment rather than punishment was the focus of this specialized court, the need for protection of constitutional rights was minimized. The functions of juvenile court judges and probation officers were to identify problems and provide the necessary individualized treatment in a benevolent manner. Attorneys were not provided, hearsay evidence was admissible, trial by jury and the right to an appeal were often not available, and only a preponderance of evidence was needed for a conviction (Siegel, 2002; Siegel and Senna, 2000; Binder et al., 1997).

Incorrigibility and truancy from school had come under the jurisdiction of the juvenile court in many states by 1920. In addition to probation officers, new professions were created to provide treatment services for both delinquent and nondelinquent children who came under the jurisdiction of the juvenile courts, including social workers, sociologists, criminologists, and psychologists. Once established, the specialized court services for juveniles spread across the country, and by 1925, juvenile courts had been established in all but two states. By 1945, the last two states—Maine and Wyoming—had also added juvenile courts. Today there are over 2,700 juvenile courts, with many dissimilarities, in the United States (Siegel, 2002; Siegel and Senna, 2000; Simonsen, 1991). During the 1960s, legislation was passed to establish the first family court in New York. The broader focus of this court includes not only delinquent, dependent, and neglected children but paternity, adoption, and child support cases as well.

One set of issues dealt with by the newly established family court were children who ran away, were truant from school, or were difficult for their parents to manage. These "offenses" were soon identified as problematic only because the offenders were underage or had the "status" of children. Thus, they became known as *status offenses,* and a new set of criteria under the term Person in Need of Supervision (PINS) was developed to address the needs of the families involved. States addressed these issues differently, even adopting different names such as Children in Need of Services (CHINS), Minors in Need of Services (MINS), and Families in Need of Services (FINS). These new categories necessitated that family and juvenile courts increase the social services available to meet the needs of the growing numbers of nondelinquent status offenders (Siegel, 2002; Siegel and Senna, 2000).

Although family courts have received support by the American Bar Association and the National Council on Crime and Delinquency, they have not been a growing force in the provision of court services to juveniles and their families. Resistance to change by juvenile court staff and judges and the massive litigation involved have been identified as possible reasons for the limited growth of family courts (Downs et al., 1996).

Several events occurred during the 1960s that influenced a change in the direction of the juvenile court system. Long-term concerns about the informal juvenile court processes, particularly the constitutional rights of children in the judicial system, came to a head in several U.S. Supreme Court decisions beginning in the mid-1960s (Siegel and Senna, 2000). These are *Kent v. United States* (1966), *In re Gault* (1967), and *In re Winship* (1970).

Not all Supreme Court decisions in the 1970s reinstituted the due process rights guaranteed to adults. In a 1971 ruling, the Court ruled in *McKeiver v. Pennsylvania* that juveniles do not have a constitutional right to a jury trial (Stein, 1991). In recent years, rehabilitation has continued to be the primary focus of the juvenile courts, whereas more recent Supreme Court decisions have required that these activities take place within the context of due process more so than in the past (Siegel and Senna, 2000; Binder et al., 1997).

Federal legislation enacted in the 1970s and early 1980s also reflected growing recognition of abused and neglected children. In addition, these statutes influenced the types of services to be provided by child welfare agencies for these children.

In 1974, the Child Abuse Prevention and Treatment Act was passed, establishing a National Center on Child Abuse and Neglect as well as providing federal funds for the demonstration programs on the prevention, identification, and treatment of child abuse and neglect. In an attempt to strengthen statutes in this area, states had to provide for

1. *The reporting of known or suspected instances of child abuse;*
2. *Investigations of reports of child abuse or neglect, including procedures for protecting children if abuse or neglect are found;*
3. *The confidentiality of all records concerning child abuse and neglect;*
4. *A guardian ad litem to represent the child in any court proceedings;*
5. *Public education on child abuse and neglect; and*
6. *Immunity for persons who report in good faith. (Stein, 1991, 44)*

This legislation was amended by Congress in 1984 to require reports of suspected abuse or neglect of children in state custody, including foster home and residential care settings as well as institutions.

The move toward family reunification and away from long-term foster care was evident in the enactment of the Adoption Assistance and Child Welfare Act, also known as the *permanency planning legislation.* This federal legislation did not designate the implementation of specific reunification services, but it did stipulate that (1) reasonable efforts be made to reunify children with their biological parents; (2) specific, written case plans for reunification are required; (3) periodic case reviews and an 18-month dispositional review must be done; and (4) due process safeguards for parents must be in place (Stein, 1991). This legislation was further strengthened in 1997 by the passage of the Adoption and Safe Families Act, which limits the permanency planning for children in care to a maximum of 12 months form entry into the system or when the child spends 12 out of 18 months in out-of-home care (Midgley et al., 2002).

Today juvenile courts continue to develop and function in accordance with state statutes within the due process guidelines established by earlier U.S. Supreme Court decisions. Variation in state laws has resulted in court services being delivered in several diverse organizational structures. Most often, juvenile courts are part of a lower court (district court, city court, recorder's court) with jurisdiction limited to delinquency issues. A growing number of states are establishing juvenile courts at the highest court of general trial jurisdiction. Some have a statewide independent juvenile court system, and others provide juvenile court services as part of a larger family court system (Siegel and Senna, 2000).

Situations Warranting Juvenile Court Intervention

Since court services are established by state legislatures, statutes involving juvenile court practices and procedures are far from standardized. The age range of juvenile court jurisdiction varies from 16 years of age and under to 18 years of age and under in the United States (Siegel, 2002; Siegel and Senna, 2000). At one time, gender influenced the age range for jurisdiction under the juvenile courts, with a lower maximum age for males than females. This practice was discontinued in the 1970s after being found unconstitutional (Binder et al., 1997). Delinquency, dependency, abuse, and neglect are defined somewhat differently in state statutes, as well. Even so, there are many commonalities in the types of situations that come under the jurisdiction of court services to juveniles. Simonsen (1991) breaks the services provided by juvenile courts into two categories: deed, when a child has committed an act requiring court intervention, and need, when a child is in need of the court's protection.

Delinquency

CASE EXAMPLE

Darryl

Darryl was 14 years old when he and two friends stole a car. The car, a flashy late-model sports car, had been parked outside a local bar each evening for the last several weeks. "The guy will be too sloshed to even know we took it!" joked Ralph, age 16, when they discussed the plan to steal it. "It'll buy us some great grass," added Willie, age 15. Darryl couldn't believe how easy it was when they finally wired the car and took off. Had Ralph not tried to see how fast it could go and been stopped by the police, the boys might have gotten the car to the drug dealer who had promised his juvenile customers free drugs if they brought him cars. Instead, the three boys found themselves in juvenile court.

Delinquency, one aspect of court services to children, generally is defined as the violation of any federal, state, or local law and involves behavior that would be considered a crime if committed by an adult. State statutes do vary on how individual cases are handled. For instance, severity of offense and the age of the offender generally determine whether a case is even heard in juvenile court. Often distinctions are made between misdemeanors and felonies committed by those under and over the ages of 15 and 16. Minor offenses (i.e., loitering, vagrancy) may or may not come under the jurisdiction of the juvenile court. There are also variations in how traffic violations are handled. In some instances, these cases are heard in traffic court while the juvenile court has jurisdiction in others (Downs et al., 1996).

Statutes in most states allow for the waiver of jurisdiction from juvenile court to criminal court. The seriousness of the crime and the age of the offender at the time the crime was committed are factors in this decision. In all cases, the protection granted by the U.S. Supreme Court in *Kent v. United States* must be taken into consideration before a waiver to adult court takes place (Downs et al., 1996).

Status Offenses

CASE EXAMPLE

Guido

When 15-year-old Guido had missed 10 days of school in the first month, the school became concerned. The school counselor contacted his mother only to discover that she had no idea of her son's whereabouts. "He's gone days at a time!" she admitted tearfully. "I don't know what to do with him." After numerous efforts to reach Guido in the past, the school felt it was time to file a CHINS petition in juvenile court, identifying him as a status offender.

Status offenses—which often include running away from home, truancy from school, sexual misconduct, uncontrollable behavior, curfew violation, and the use of substances such as drugs or alcohol—often come under the jurisdiction of court services to children. These offenses are illegal only because the child has not reached the status of adulthood. There is much debate about the way in which status offenders should be dealt with.

In the original legislation establishing a juvenile court, there was no separation between delinquency and status offenses. During the 1960s and 1970s, concern about the frequent long-term incarceration of status offenders in the place of treatment prompted the passage of the Juvenile Justice and Delinquency Prevention Act of 1974. Under this legislation, federal funds were made available for states that provided separate detention facilities for adults and juveniles. Secure detention could not be used for status offenders until 1980, when this legislation was amended to allow secure detention of status offenders if a valid court order was violated (Sagatun and Edwards, 1995).

A few remaining states continue to define status offenses as delinquent behavior. Statutes in four states incorporate status offenses under the classification of abuse, neglect, or dependency (Binder et al., 1997). The others have developed a separate category for status offenses, generally called PINS, MINS, JINS, CHINS (as discussed earlier), and Families with Service Needs (FWSN).

Including status offenses under the jurisdiction of the juvenile court was controversial even before the legislation establishing this court was enacted, and it continues to be a controversial issue today. Opposition has been based on the constitutionality of the vague terms used in the statutes to define status offenses and the misuse this may lead to in the court system. Court cases challenging the constitutionality of juvenile court jurisdiction over status offenses have been defeated based on the premise that the implementation of these statutes are in the best interest of the child. Those who support the continued involvement of the court in status offenses do so on the basis that, without these legal protections, many children and their families will not get the services needed to prevent future problems (Siegel, 2002; Siegel and Senna, 2000; Binder et al., 1997; Simonsen, 1991).

In recent years, federal legislation has been enacted mandating the separation of status offenders from delinquents in detention facilities (Siegel and Senna, 2000; Binder et al., 1997). The American Psychiatric Association has recommended that courts also establish services for nondelinquency offenders. The reality is that status offenses continue to be a perplexing problem for both the courts and social service agencies.

Dependency, Abuse, and Neglect

CASE EXAMPLE

A Case of Neglect

Amber (age 5), Arthur (age 2), and Candy (age 9 months) were found in a condemned factory building where their mother had set up housekeeping. The children were dirty and, from what the police could discover from Amber, they had been alone for several days. Baby Candy was severely dehydrated and the other children had apparently survived on chocolate bars and potato chips. They were taken to the hospital and then to a foster home. In the meantime, the social worker assigned to their case filed a petition on their behalf in juvenile court.

Children who have been neglected or abused come under the jurisdiction of court services for juveniles. Some state statutes classify and define dependency, abuse, and neglect separately. In others, either dependency is classified with abuse and neglect or abuse and neglect are categorized under dependency. Generally, children are defined as dependent if their guardians cannot or are not providing adequate care. Dependency may occur in cases of abandonment, when both parents are deceased, or when both parents are incarcerated for extended periods of time. A finding of dependency, the termination of parental rights, and the transfer of guardianship must occur to free a child for adoption. The number of children who are classified as dependent may significantly increase in the future as more children outlive both parents who die from AIDS.

Definitions of abuse and neglect differ somewhat from state to state (see Chapter 7). In general, neglect involves the failure of parents, guardians, and caretakers to adequately provide for or protect a child through acts of omission. Such behaviors commonly include failure to provide necessary physical care, supervision, a proper home environment, adequate food and clothing, basic medical care, financial support, and education as prescribed by law. Abandonment by guardians or caretakers and the failure to provide a safe environment for a child are frequently defined as neglect in the statutes (Crosson-Tower, 2002). In contrast, the definition of abuse involves the use of nonaccidental physical force by a parent, guardian, or caretaker.

Related Situations Involving Court Intervention

Several other situations involving the legal status or rights of children and/or their parents often come under the jurisdiction of court services to children. Included are termination of parental rights, paternity determinations, child support, adoption, appointment of a *guardian ad litem,* determination of legal status, granting of legal custody of a minor for purposes of institutional placement, and domestic violence matters (Stein, 1991).

Factors Influencing Court Intervention

CASE EXAMPLE

A Concerned Officer

Winston LeBlanc was a newly assigned police officer in a gang-ridden area of the city. A fairly young foot patrolman, LeBlanc tried to develop a rapport with the gang members. He became particularly fond of Chico, a 15-year-old youth who LeBlanc was hopeful could finish high school and leave the area. The officer was angered when an arrest following a robbery brought in Chico among the group of boys involved. Still convinced that the boy could be helped, LeBlanc testified in juvenile court on Chico's behalf.

Other factors affect whether court intervention will take place and, if so, the type of action initiated. The police have considerable authority in determining court action because most juvenile court referrals for delinquency are made by them, whereas status offense complaints generally are made by parents to the police. State statutes provide only vague guidelines for interaction between police and juveniles. Results of studies suggest that the severity of the offense, the frequency of delinquent behavior, prior arrest records, community attitudes toward the behavior, and the behavior of juveniles in interaction with the police also are decisive factors in determining what action will be taken by the police (Binder et al., 1997; Simonsen, 1991). However, the tendency for police to make subjective decisions from a parental rather than a law enforcement perspective is supported in findings of recent studies, which show that status offenders are more likely to be detained and referred to juvenile court than delinquents, and girls are more likely to be detained than boys (Cheney-Lind, 1988). Thus, many status offenders initially may enter the court system mislabeled as delinquents (Binder et al., 1997).

Once a case has been referred to the court for action, a lawyer representing the child, the parents, or the court may determine if the statutory definitions of dependency, neglect, or delinquency have been adequately met (Duquette, 1990).

Judges also have an influence on determining court action in juvenile cases. Ideally their actions must be based on statutory definitions. However, legislation often is worded in general terms, which leaves considerable interpretive discretion (Dziech and Schudson, 1991).

The Rights of Juveniles

The rights of those involved with the juvenile court system have been much debated over the years. Three cases were most influential in establishing rights for children in court. In 1966, *Kent v. United States* established uniform procedures for waiving children from juvenile court to adult court. *In re Gault* (1967) reinstated many of the constitutional rights children lost with the development of the juvenile court system, including:

1. *The right to notice of charges in time to prepare for trial;*
2. *The right to counsel;*
3. *The right to confront and cross-examine the accusers;*
4. *Privilege against self-incrimination, at least in court. (Simonsen, 1991, 257)*

In re Winship (1970) established that evidence in delinquency cases in juvenile courts must meet the more stringent criterion of beyond a reasonable doubt rather than the lesser test of preponderance of evidence or clear and convincing evidence, required in most courts throughout the country (Siegel, 2002; Siegel and Senna, 2000).

Since these landmark cases, other rights have been given to youths in juvenile court settings. Today, youths brought before the court for delinquency have these additional rights:

5. *The right to a judicial hearing;*
6. *The right to proof beyond a reasonable doubt that they are guilty. (Simonsen, 1991, 260–261)*

Although there is no legal requirement for a trial by jury in juvenile court, an advisory jury is an available option that is rarely used.

Advocating for Children

Sometimes in the court process, it is necessary for an advocate to be appointed to protect the rights and interests of the children involved. Although advocates were originally appointed in cases where there was money or property at stake, the practice now may be to protect the psychological as well as financial interests of children (Duquette, 1990). The Child Abuse and Neglect Prevention and Treatment Act of 1974 required that states appoint a *guardian ad litem* or special advocate to represent children in abuse and neglect proceedings. The advocate could be an attorney or another professional trained to assume this role. Advocates are also used in situations where the child is a delinquent (Crosson-Tower, 2002).

In 1977, Seattle established its special court advocate program under the name of CASA (court-appointed special advocates) using trained volunteers to act on behalf of children in court cases. About the same time, a similar program began in Minnesota. Court-appointed special advocates are strongly recommended in state children's codes and, today, there are over 200 local CASA chapters in every state (Crosson-Tower, 2002; Ridell, 1998).

The concept of child advocacy in court arose from the fact that attorneys did not always feel comfortable being the sole representatives of children's interests. Many did not feel adequately trained in child welfare issues and welcomed another voice.

How the advocate—whether a CASA volunteer, an attorney appointed as *guardian ad litem* (GAL), or someone from another advocacy model—serves the child differs from state to state. For the most part, advocates attempt to see the situation in light of the best interests of their clients. They may interview the child, do home visits, or generally assess what is the best plan for the child. Many advocates also provide guidance or preparation to their young clients about what will happen in court proceedings.

For the most part, victim/witness or child advocacy programs have been successful, but some attorneys still have questions about the use of volunteers who are expected, after a brief training, to function effectively in the court setting. Volunteers, on the other hand, often complain that they are not taken seriously enough. The fact remains that court advocacy is important for children, both victims and offenders, and seems likely to continue (Crosson-Tower, 2002).

Juvenile Court Process and Procedures

Juvenile court processes and procedures are implemented based on state statutes that vary across the United States, although they must be within the boundaries of federal legislated guidelines. Even so, the process generally includes an intake stage (initial screening process), an adjudication stage (fact-finding process), and a disposition stage (decision making) (Downs et al., 1996, 381–383; Stein, 1991, 29).

Intake Stage

The intake stage involves the screening of cases to eliminate those that do not require court action from those that do early in the process (Duquette, 1990). Intake procedures may be initiated in several ways, depending on the circumstances. In cases of alleged delinquency or status offenses, it may begin when a minor child is taken into custody by the police, or when a parent or someone in the community files a complaint about the minor's behavior (Binder et al., 1997).

Dependency or neglect and abuse situations generally begin with a petition being filed on behalf of a minor child due to the inability of a parent, guardian, or caregiver to provide proper care, failure to provide adequate care or protection, or intentional injury of a child. A petition may be filed by the police, social workers, representatives of other community institutions (e.g., school personnel, daycare staff, medical staff), neighbors, relatives, or anyone suspecting child abuse or neglect.

Whatever the initial intervention, the juvenile probation department usually becomes involved. It is often the probation officer who decides what route the case will take. This preadjudication assessment may determine whether the child continues in the judicial process. Among the options available at this point are:

- *Referral to another jurisdiction.* When the juvenile lives somewhere other than the court in which the petition or complaint is filed, the case may be transferred to the court in that jurisdiction.
- *Referral to a social service agency.* When a probation officer feels that another social agency can adequately deal with the case instead of having the child involved with the court.
- *Counseling and dismissal.* When the probation officer deems that brief counseling rather than lengthy court involvement will remedy the problem.
- *Informal supervision.* When the probation officer, with the consent of the parent(s), determines that supervision under probation without further court intervention is justified (Simonsen, 1991, 196–197).
- *Informal adjustment agreement.* When restitution for damages is made;
- *Waiver.* When states have exclusive or original jurisdiction, a transfer of the case to adult court for trial may occur under certain circumstances (Clement, 1997, 134–142).

Adjudication Stage

If the case does proceed, fact finding is the primary goal of the adjudication stage. The initial phase of the adjudication stage begins with the filing of a complaint or petition that provides information about the allegations and requests of a particular finding from the court. Complaints are reviewed to establish the authority of the court by statute to intervene and to determine if the facts sufficiently support the allegations (delinquent, dependent, neglected, status offender), and then a decision is made either for dismissal or for further action by the court. Additional information may be provided by a variety of outside sources to assist the court in making a determination in this phase. When the decision is to involve the court further, a social study, the final phase of the adjudication stage, is ordered and a dispositional hearing is scheduled.

The purpose of the social study is to provide evaluations and factual information for consideration by the court during the dispositional phase. Probation staff or social workers assigned to the juvenile court, protective services, or other social agencies generally are responsible for completing the social study (Clement, 1997; Duquette, 1990).

Disposition Stage

Information provided in the social study is used to determine an appropriate treatment plan for the child. Although there are variations on a state-by-state basis, this stage of the process is limited by federal requirements that mandate that the best interests of the child be met in the least restrictive environment (Downs et al., 1996; Stein, 1991).

In the disposition stage, if a minor child is found to be delinquent, a status offender, dependent, neglected, or abused, a plan is devised. When the delinquent or status offense behavior is a first offense and of a minor nature, the case may be closed with no further court action. If found to be delinquent or a status offender, the child may be permitted by the court to remain at home on probation under the supervision of the court. A child found to be neglected or abused may remain at home under the supervision of a social service agency.

Finally, the court may decide that placement outside of the home for a child found to be a status offender, delinquent, dependent, neglected, or abused is justified. This decision has the most serious consequences for the child and his or her parents. Depending on the circumstances, the purpose of placement may be for adoption, protection, treatment, or rehabilitation. Out-of-home placements often include foster homes, adoptive homes (permanent placement), group homes, residential treatment institutions, or correctional institutions (state training schools). When placement out of the home is the decision of the court, the disposition stage often includes the process of transferring custody or guardianship of the child (Binder et al., 1997).

The Role of the Social Worker and the Court

To be effective in any role associated with the juvenile court, social workers must be knowledgeable about the federal and state statutes. These statutes provide the guidelines for practice. For example, statutes define if a child is abused, neglected, dependent, or delinquent. They determine if the court should intervene, outline the processes and procedures to be followed, and detail what interventions can be used.

Social workers are involved in obtaining and organizing evidence for the juvenile court. In the role of investigator, the social worker may interview the parents, the child, other relatives, and collateral resources, including school personnel, medical staff, and police. Evaluation by psychiatrists or psychologists may be requested. At the intake stage, this information is used in screening cases to determine if court involvement is necessary. During the dispositional stage, the material, presented in the form of a social history, will assist the court in developing a treatment plan for the child. Those involved primarily in the investigative role may be employed by law enforcement agencies, child welfare agencies, or family and juvenile courts (Johnson, 1995).

Historically, social workers have provided direct services for children with problems and their families. Child welfare workers have supervised children found to be dependent, neglected, or abused in their own homes or in foster homes, as directed by the court. Social workers employed by community agencies or by the court have counseled minors needing rehabilitation or experiencing mental health problems as a consequence of parental abuse or neglect.

Occasionally, those with a social work background are employed as juvenile probation or parole officers. Roles of probation and parole officers are similar in that the goal is rehabilitation and prevention. The purpose of probation is to prevent incarceration in a juvenile correctional institution, whereas the goal of parole is to prevent the return to an institution.

It is not uncommon for social workers to provide testimony in court. Child welfare workers are called on to describe indications of abuse and neglect as well as home environments that they judge to be below standards of safety and cleanliness, in the course of working with children and their families. Social workers with a master's degree and experience now qualify as expert witnesses and frequently are called on to testify in divorce cases involving contested child custody, child abuse and neglect cases, termination of parental rights situations, and delinquency cases (Crosson-Tower, 2002; Downs et al., 1996). Recently the role of the social worker has been expanded to include assessing a defendant's mental state and competency to stand trial.

Consumer Perspective

Britta was 15 years old when she became involved with the juvenile court. She lived with her mother, who found her increasingly difficult to handle.

CASE EXAMPLE

Britta's Story

My father left when I was really little. I don't even remember him. We lived with my Mom's dad for awhile. He was really old and would do things like forget where he was and wander around. I kind of had to watch him a lot. It was a pain. When he died, it was almost a relief, you know. I mean, that sounds awful but it was. I thought, "Okay, now we'll be okay." But then my Mom started seeing this guy and he moved in with us. He was a real jerk. He used to beat her up. She didn't think I knew that. She'd hide the bruises and stuff, but I did. So I used to stay out a lot. My Mom got on my case about that. Then I met Renardo. He was cool. He did pot and crack and got me using the stuff. I sold a little for him, but was afraid to do that too much. My friend Angie got in big trouble selling and I didn't want to.

When I was high, my Mom would hassle me and it bugged me. We got into a few real screaming matches. When we did, I would cut out and go stay with Renardo. He was 24 and had this apartment with some other guys. He had his mattress on the floor and we'd sleep there. It was fun, sort of like camping inside. But one day my Mom had her creepy boyfriend follow me. I mean, can you believe it! He followed me! He found out where I was and my Mom really lit into me about that. I was skipping school too and she got really mad. I told her what did she expect with her boyfriend beating her. I couldn't take it. She cried and said that she'd get rid of him and she did. But she still hassled me and I stayed out more and more. Renardo wanted me to run away, but I really didn't want to.

My Mom went to a counselor and the guy told her to go to court and take out this thing called a CHINS on me. It's what parents do I guess when they just can't handle their kids. The next thing I know I get dragged into juvenile court. There's a judge and a lawyer and a bunch of people working for the court. This lady, a probation officer, was "assigned to our case" as they put it and told me I had to come see her. It kind of scared me a little bit. I mean here was this big deal in court, like I had a record or something. Renardo said it was no big deal. It was then that he told me he'd done time. I didn't like that. Being in jail didn't seem like where I wanted to be. He said that I was getting to be a wimp and he kind of disappeared. He just didn't come around anymore.

The court also made me see a social worker at the Department of Social Services. She was nice and I liked her. We made up a plan. I had to go to school and I couldn't do drugs and I couldn't run away. That was okay for a while but then one night my Mom and I had a big fight. I blew up and left the house. I had no place to go so I just walked. Then the next thing I know, the police picked me up!! I couldn't believe it. I figured they'd take me home but they took me to this detention center. There were kids there who had done all kinds of stuff. I was afraid they'd beat me up and I just stayed in bed. They kept me there all night. The next day they took me back to court. My Mom was there and the judge told me that if I did that again they'd put me in a foster home. Angie was in a foster home and she hated it! I said "No way!"

So for the next year I saw my social worker and I went to this after-school group for kids who had done the stuff that I did. My Mom and I went to a counselor too. I knew that if I pulled anything, she'd take me back to court. I didn't want that!

Now I am almost seventeen and we're doing okay I guess. I met this guy at school who is really nice to me. It's just easier not to hassle my Mom and not get hassled. I think that if I hadn't gotten involved with the court, I might be in bigger trouble. It kind of woke me up!

Fortunately for Britta, court intervention was early enough to make a difference. There are others for whom the system does not work as well. It is not uncommon for such juveniles to be seen later in the adult criminal system.

Alternative Approaches to Court Intervention

Even before the first juvenile court was established in Illinois in 1899, there was controversy over the loss of due process in juvenile court proceedings and concern about the legitimacy of court intervention, particularly in status offense cases. Rapid growth in the number of juveniles entering the juvenile justice system and discontent with the court throughout the years has resulted in the development of an alternative to judicial intervention—diversion.

Diversion

Concerns about the constitutionality of juvenile court jurisdiction in status offenses and the failure of many states to carry out the federal mandate separating alleged delinquents from nondelinquents have prompted the development of diversion programs. The purpose of these programs is to involve status offenders and their families in relevant community services and divert them from the juvenile court system (Siegel and Senna, 2000; Binder et al., 1997).

The Office of Juvenile Justice and Delinquency Prevention has defined *diversion* as "a process by which youth who would otherwise be adjudicated are referred out of the juvenile justice system sometime after apprehension and prior to adjudication" (DeAngelo, 1988). The primary goal of diversion is to direct referrals from the attention of the juvenile court and link status offenders and first offenders with a variety of community-based services. A secondary goal is to reduce the stigma caused by court involvement, and a third is to free the courts to focus on the increasing number of serious juvenile cases requiring attention (Siegel and Senna, 2000).

Services offered through diversion programs are not standardized and vary considerably in different communities. In some areas, individual, group, and/or family therapy by psychologists or social workers is provided through private, not-for-profit, community-based organizations as opposed to traditional mental health agencies. Others offer alternative school programs, recreational programs, job counseling, training, and placement. Some have a community service component that requires juveniles to "volunteer" to work a designated number of hours in a service agency. These services generally are offered through traditional, public or nonprofit agencies that have extended their services to include diversion programs or by nonprofit community-based organizations that have been developed to meet a specific need in a given community (Siegel, 2002; Siegel and Senna, 2000).

Research on the effectiveness of diversion programs in circumventing juvenile court involvement is inconclusive at this time. Some studies have shown a decrease in court appearances of status offenders referred to diversion programs in comparison to those referred to juvenile court (Stewart et al., 1986), whereas others have found no difference between the two groups (Gensheimer et al., 1986).

Treatment of Juvenile Offenders

Traditionally, young offenders have been ordered by the court to undergo some type of treatment. These treatment approaches have ranged from individual counseling and group counseling, to placement in settings where milieu therapy—or regulation of one's total environment—has sought to rehabilitate them (see Chapter 13). Some programs stressed education and job-related activities, as well as therapy, in an attempt to positively prepare juvenile offenders for a noncrime-oriented future. For a child who is not that deeply into crime, these programs may work. However, for the more serious offenders, with some exceptions, these approaches were not wholly effective in meeting their goals.

More recently, several alternatives have been tried to determine if they could be successful with the more serious offenders. One approach, referred to as the Violent Juvenile Offender Program (VJO), places youths in very structured, secure environments that are sufficiently small that the youths receive a good deal of attention. Gradually the offenders are worked back into the community, with continued supervision.

Wilderness programs have demonstrated some success as an alternative to traditional measures to deter and prevent delinquent behavior. Developed in Chicago in the 1930s, the idea of placing offenders in forestry camps in remote settings has been refined by several organizations. Today, the goal of these programs is to use the environment and a small staff/student ratio to help young people who have demonstrated delinquent behavior at home, in school, and/or in the community to develop appropriate social skills, self-control, and a sense of self-worth. Results of studies on these programs are mixed, but there are some preliminary indications that they may have a positive effect on reducing recidivism (Siegel, 2002).

Boot camps are another alternative for dealing with juvenile offenders. These programs focus on self-esteem building, discipline through rigorous physical conditioning, and academic and vocational education. Mirroring adult military boot camps, the experience is meant to be a shock-value experience that will instill discipline, cooperation, and teamwork. The studies done on the efficacy of such programs also have demonstrated mixed results. Despite this, they currently exist in more than thirty states (Siegel, 2002; Siegel and Senna, 2000).

It appears to be too early to measure the success of these alternative methods of treatment. Many child advocates insist that, to deter juvenile crime, we must begin at the level of primary prevention. The fact remains that we must also become inventive in dealing with the youths *already* in the juvenile justice system.

Trends

Should There Be a Separate Juvenile Court?

The concern of some people about the guarantees of due process through the juvenile court, an issue since this court was established, continues today. For many who believe that this court has not met the goals of protection and rehabilitation, the solution is to do away with the juvenile court system completely. Although this has been a relatively strong movement at times, it does not seem feasible in light of several Supreme Court decisions since the 1960s reaffirming due process protection within the context of a specialized court system for juveniles (e.g., *Kent v. United States, In re Gault,* and *In re Winship*). Developing national guidelines that assure due process procedures are implemented in a standardized way throughout the country may be a more satisfactory solution.

Should Status Offenders Come under the Jurisdiction of the Juvenile Court?

Much concern has been voiced over whether there should be a separate bureaucracy to handle status offenses. Critics of the current procedures argue that intervention through juvenile court relegates these youths to the same status as their delinquent counterparts. Some argue that status offenders are more likely to be older children who are reacting to being abused or neglected and should not be treated as if the fault is with them. By the same token, many feel that it is the family who should be responsible for children's misbehavior. Does giving this task to the courts weaken the family's already dwindling power?

To compound this argument, Downs and colleagues (1996) point to research that suggests that status offenders are, in fact, "more similar than different from delinquent youth" (97). Although the delinquent behavior in which status offenders appear to be involved is not usually as serious as the quality of crimes committed by their delinquent counterparts, the fact remains that this research disproves the idea that status offenders are merely older dependent children.

What Should Be Done with Serious Offenders?

As the violence in our society continues, the crimes committed by youth are becoming more and more serious. In 1999, of the 14 million arrests made in the United States, about 19% were juveniles. Of the youths arrested, 28% had committed serious crimes (Siegel, 2002, 25). Heide (1993), in her study of children who killed their parents, found that 1 in 11 of all family murders involve children killing family members. There are indications that the rate has risen. Of those studied by Heide, a significant number of the children were under age 18 at the time of the crime (531, 541). Fox and Zavitz (1998, as cited in Siegel and Senna, 2000) reported that close to 20% of all murders are committed by youths who are ages 14 through 17 (43). The fact that an increased number of these serious offenders are under the influence of one or more drugs compounds the implications for treatment.

In the past, a small number of juveniles who had committed serious crimes were bound over to be tried as adults. The increase in such crimes has resulted in tougher laws and federal funds for new programs that target these young offenders for surveillance (i.e., Florida's Serious Habitual Offender Community Action Program) (McNeese, 1998).

Summary

The role of the juvenile court is a complex one. The services provided by these courts evolved as people began to realize that the offenses of children did not warrant the same treatment as those of adults. In addition, some parents could not adequately care for their children, and so it fell to the legal system to make provisions for them. The juvenile court emerged largely under the influence of the settlement houses, most notably Hull House in Chicago, and the first juvenile court was established there on April 2, 1899. Once established, the concept spread, and by the early 1900s, all but two states had juvenile courts. The last two had established such a system by 1945. The subject of the rights that juveniles are entitled to has been debated for some time. The case of *In re Gault* did much to establish a firm set of guidelines.

There are three types of situations that would bring a youth before the juvenile court: delinquency, a status offense, or being dependent, abused, or neglected. Delinquents commit crimes that might also be committed by adults: assault, robbery, theft, drug dealing or possession, murder, and so forth. Status offenders are those who have been accused of running away from home, being truant from school, exhibiting sexual misconduct, violating curfew, using substances, or exhibiting uncontrollable behavior. These are acts or behaviors that would not be seen in court if the individual had reached the status of adulthood. Abused or neglected children may come before the juvenile court so that plans can be made to insure their welfare.

When a child enters the juvenile court system in intake, he or she is often screened by the probation department. The probation officer has a great deal of influence about what happens next. The child may then proceed to adjudication, which is basically a fact-finding stage. The disposition determines what type of services will be offered to the juvenile and, possibly, the family. It is possible that, instead of being seen in court, the child might become part of a diversion program and be referred to services in agencies other than the court with the hope of preventing further court intervention.

Today several questions plague those professionals involved with the juvenile court system: Should there be a separate juvenile court? Should status offenders continue to be seen along with delinquents in the juvenile court system? What provisions should be made for the increasing number of juveniles committing serious crimes? These are questions that will probably be debated well into this century.

EXPLORATION QUESTIONS

1. What is the role of the juvenile court?
2. How did court services for children become specialized?
3. What is meant by the *child savers?*
4. What are family courts?
5. What influence did the 1974 Child Abuse Prevention and Treatment Act have on the juvenile justice system? What did it mandate?
6. What is meant by *parens patriae?* Where did the term originate?
7. What did the Juvenile Court Act mandate?
8. What situations might warrant juvenile court intervention?
9. What are status offenders?
10. What are the rights of juveniles when they become involved with the juvenile court system?
11. Outline the juvenile court process.
12. What is the role of the social worker in the juvenile court?
13. What are the trends in the juvenile court system today?

REFERENCES

Ardovini-Brooker, J., & Walker, L. (2000). "Juvenile Boot Camps and the Reclamation of Our Youth: Some Food for Thought," *Juvenile and Family Court Journal, 51,* 12–28.

Bernard, T. (1999). "Juvenile Crime and the Transformation of Juvenile Justice: Is There a Juvenile Crime Wave?" *Justice Quarterly,* 16, 335–356.

Binder, A., Gees, B., & Bruce, D. (1997). *Juvenile Delinquency: Historical, Cultural and Legal.* Cincinnati, OH: Anderson.

Briar-Lawson, K., & Drews, J. (2000). "Children and Family Welfare Policies and Services: Current Issues and Historical Antecedents" (157–174). In J. Midgley, M. B. Tracy, & M. Livermore, (Eds.), *The Handbook of Social Policy.* Thousand Oaks, CA: Sage.

Cheney-Lind, M. (1988). "Girls in Jail," *Crime & Delinquency,* 54, 151–168.

Clement, M. (1997). *The Juvenile Justice System: Law and Process.* Boston: Butterworth-Heinemann.

Crosson-Tower, C. (2002). *Understanding Child Abuse and Neglect* (5th ed.). Boston: Allyn and Bacon.

DeAngelo, A. J. (1988). "Diversion Programs in the Juvenile Justice System: An Alternative

Method of Treatment for Juvenile Offenders," *Juvenile & Family Court Journal, 39,* 21–28.

Downs, S. W., Costin, L. B., & McFadden, E. J. (1996). *Child Welfare and Family Services* (5th ed.). New York: Longman.

Duquette, D. N. (1990). *Advocating for the Child in Protection Proceedings.* Lexington, MA: Lexington Books.

Dziech, B. W., & Schudson, C. B. (1991). *On Trial: America's Courts and Their Treatment of Sexually Abused Children.* Boston: Beacon Press.

Elrod, P., & Ryder, R. S. (1999). *Juvenile Justice: A Social, Historical, and Legal Perspective.* Gaithersburg, MD: Aspen.

FBI. (2001). *Crime in the U.S.: Uniform Crime Reports, 2000.* Washington, DC: U.S. Government Printing Office.

Fox, J. A. & Zavitz, M. (1998). *Homicide Trends in the U.S.* Washington, DC: Bureau of Juvenile Statistics.

Gensheimer, L. K., Meyer, J. P., Gottschalk, R., & Davidson, W. S. (1986). "Diverting Youth from the Juvenile Justice System: A Meta-Analysis of Intervention Efficacy" (39–57). In S. J. Apter & A. Goldstein (Eds.), *Youth Violence: Problems and Prospects.* Elmsford, NY: Pergamon.

Heide, K. M. (1993). "Parents Who Killed and the Children Who Kill Them," *Journal of Interpersonal Violence,* 8 (4), 531–544.

Johnson, H. W. (1995). "Criminal and Juvenile Justice" (199–222). In H. W. Johnson (Ed.), *The Social Services: An Introduction* (4th ed.). Itasca, IL: F. E. Peacock.

Kids Count Data Book. (2002). Baltimore, MD: The Annie E. Casey Foundation.

McNeese, C. A. (1998). "Juvenile Justice Policy: Current Trends and Twenty-First Century Issues" (21–39). In A. R. Roberts (Ed.), *Juvenile Justice: Policies, Programs, and Services* (2nd ed.). Chicago: Nelson Hall.

Midgley, J., Tracy M. B., & Livermore, M. (Eds.). (2000). *The Handbook of Social Policy.* Thousand Oaks, CA: Sage.

Riddell, S. (1998). "CASA: Child's Voice in Court," *Juvenile and Family Justice Today, 7,* 13–14.

Sagatun, I. J., & Edwards, L. P. (1995). *Child Abuse and the Legal System.* Chicago: Nelson Hall.

Siegel, L. J. (2002). *Juvenile Delinquency: The Core.* Belmont, CA: Wadsworth/Thomson Learning.

Siegel, L. J., & Senna, J. J. (2000). *Juvenile Delinquency: Theory, Practice, and Law.* Belmont, CA: Wadsworth/Thomson Learning.

Simonsen, C. E. (1991). *Juvenile Justice in America.* New York: Macmillan.

Stein, T. (1991). *Child Welfare and the Law.* New York: Longman.

Stewart, J. J., Vockell, E. L., & Ray, R. E. (1986). "Decreasing Court Appearances of Juvenile Status Offenders," *Social Casework,* 67, 74–79.

10 Teenage Pregnancy and Parenting

LYNNE KELLNER

Shannon, a 16-year-old high school junior, and her 1-year-old son live with her 22-year-old boyfriend and her mother. Her mother looks after the baby while Shannon attends high school. Immediately upon returning home, she assumes full responsibility for the baby, since her mother and boyfriend both work evenings. Shannon arranged with her guidance counselor to enter a half-day job-training program while condensing her academics into the other half; however, she has not attended the program in 9 of the past 10 days. "Why would Shannon pass up this opportunity to improve her income potential?" the counselor asks in frustration.

Raising a child to adulthood has become increasingly complicated and expensive in our technologically advanced world. Children tend to remain at home longer as they complete their educations to enter an ever-more competitive work world. Inflation makes it harder for young adults to become self-supporting. No wonder Shannon's guidance counselor thinks that acquiring job skills is giving her "the best chance" at self-sufficiency. Shannon, however, is struggling with the adolescent developmental issues foreshortened by her pregnancy. Peer contact, with its frivolous concerns and moments of forgetting her responsibilities, satisfies needs that are separate from her those of her child.

The emergence of adolescent pregnancy as a national social problem in the 1960s focused on the following: the psychological and financial inability of teen parents to care for their children; the foreshortening of adolescent development, including decreased career and economic options for parenting teens; the economic consequences for the country in supporting children of unwed mothers; and the absence of fathers in the lives of children. This chapter will review and analyze these concerns and assumptions, place adolescent pregnancy in a historical context, review current research to enhance our understanding, identify risk factors, and highlight key intervention strategies.

Definition of Terms

Children having children is a popular term to describe adolescent pregnancy; however, this term will not be used. Despite its catchiness, it simplifies a very complicated phenomenon. Determining when adolescence ends is no simple feat in today's society. Using traditional responsibilities of adulthood—such as establishing a career, buying a home, and marrying and raising a family— many psychologists now extend adolescence into the mid-twenties; however, such a definition is based on middle-class values. Pearce (1993) notes that pregnancy prevention programs based on middle-class values often negate the experiences of poor and minority adolescents when they "do not affirm the positive impulse underlying early sexuality and motherhood: the desire to achieve or gain recognized adult status" (48).

When teen parents are viewed as children, intervention strategies can take a patronizing tone. If the intention is to empower teens to assume responsible parenting, the "children having children" perspective is counterproductive. Luker (1996) suggests that this perspective denies the teen mother "the status of full personhood, exempting her from the obligations of being a moral actor held accountable for the choices she makes" (4).

For the purposes of this chapter, age groupings established by the Department of Health and Human Services (Martin et al., 2002) will be used to distinguish between three sets of teenagers: young teens (ages 10 to 14), middle teens (ages 15 to 17), and older teens (ages 18 and 19).

Historical Perspective

Teen pregnancy has been construed differently since our country was first settled. Many have preconceptions of the early Americans as moralistic and repressive. Think of Nathaniel Hawthorne's *The Scarlet Letter,* in which Hester Prynne, bearing the minister's love-child, is publicly humiliated and sentenced to wear a scarlet *A* (for adulterous) across her bosom. Harari and Vinovskis (1993) clarify that the colonists reserved condemnation for adultery and actually tolerated premarital sexual activity as long as any offspring were legitimatized through marriage. Luker (1996) estimates that 10% of brides in colonial Massachusetts and as much as one-third in the Chesapeake Bay colony married pregnant (17). Colonists feared that younger parents, who were not "fit," would not be able to provide for their children, who would then become a social and economic burden to the community.

The technological advances of the mid-nineteenth century made it possible to produce flexible rubber products, including condoms and vaginal diaphragms. As a by-product of the surgical advances ushered in by the Civil War, abortions became surgical procedures rather than herbal inductions. Women took charge of ending their own pregnancies, often dangerously, with buttonhooks. Many physicians were horrified that wealthy, well-educated, and "moral" women were choosing not to have children or carry pregnancies to term. Wealthier women had access to birth control, but poorer women did not. Physicians, arguing that the class-based differences in birth control practice would bring on "racial suicide," led the battle cry to outlaw abortion (Luker, 1996). The emphasis on pregnancy prevention as desirable for the lower socioeconomic class, however, has continued into public thought today.

Whereas previous generations resolved the problem of out-of-wedlock pregnancies by "shot-gun weddings," by the late nineteenth century, homes for unwed mothers provided shelter, medical care, and a moral education (Harari & Vinovskis, 1993). As the number of young pregnant women living in group homes increased, researchers began to study the effects of illegitimacy. In 1914, the newly established Children's Bureau concluded that babies born to unmarried mothers had a three-times higher mortality rate than those of married couples. Concerns that teen mothers were "too young" physically to bear healthy babies emerged. Of additional concern, one-third of children born out of wedlock received public assistance (Luker, 1998, 22). As the twentieth century began, teenage and premarital pregnancy became the domain of the professional social worker.

G. Stanley Hall's 1904 book, *Adolescence: Its Psychology and Its Relations to Physiology, Anthropology, Sociology, Sex, Crime, Religion and Education,* established adolescence as a unique time of turbulence and continuing immaturity while teens strove toward adulthood. Although not children, teens were seen as incapable of full adult responsibilities, including child rearing. However, when the nation entered World War II, many older teens were forced into adult roles. After young men returned from the war and young women returned from their military-supporting jobs, they continued with "adult development" by marrying and starting families. Post–World War II "baby boom" teen birthrates peaked at 96.3 per 1,000 women in 1957 (Ventura et al., 2001, 1). Although many older teens had children, since most were married, this did not pose a problem in the national consciousness.

In the 1960s, public policy emphasized the economic impact of teen, particularly unmarried, pregnancy. In the National Fertility Survey of 1965 (as cited in Campbell, 1968), 34% of poor people reported unwanted pregnancies, compared to 15% of those more financially stable. Politicians argued that those least able to provide for families were having the most children; 55% of all women receiving welfare first became mothers as teenagers (Alan Guttmacher Institute, 1999, 3). The rising rates of federal assistance, coupled with an eight-times higher birthrate to unmarried poor women than nonpoor women, created a climate in which teen mothers were blamed for taxing the national economy.

In 1969, over 70% of Americans disapproved of premarital sexual relations, but by 1973, the American public was evenly divided in its acceptance, an astounding shift in such a short time (Luker, 1996). When the birth control pill was introduced in 1960, contraception became less intrusive. Concurrently, leaders in the women's movement affirmed women as sexual beings, thus making it easier for teen women to say "yes" to sex, or perhaps more realistically, made it harder to say "no" to their partners. In 1973, *Roe v. Wade* legalized abortion and made terminating unwanted pregnancies safe and legal.

Stemming back to the 1960s, economic support, education, job training, and developmental opportunities for their young children through ventures such as Head Start (see Chapter 5) were provided to teen mothers to help stop the "cycle of poverty" in future generations. During the 1980s, a new belief emerged that teen pregnancy could be reduced by "*eliminating* economic support as an incentive for nonmarital childbearing and by enforcing work among welfare mothers" (Harris, 1996, 2). During this same period, welfare benefits actually decreased in real dollars at the same time that most teen mothers choose not to marry. Luker (1996) comments that

> although incentives certainly affect behavior, they do so in a moral and social context that shapes how people interpret those incentives. For all women—rich and poor, teenage and older—decisions regarding childbearing and marriage have a great deal to do with feelings, values, beliefs, and commitments. (177)

It is simplistic to think that teens choose to bear children so they can receive federal assistance that keeps them below the poverty line.

Through the 1960s, pregnant students were forced to withdraw from high school. In 1971, a Massachusetts pregnant honor student, frustrated that home tutoring was not as challenging as school, sued the school system on the grounds that her right to attend regular classes had been violated (*Ordway v. Hargraves*, 1971). The school argued that it had banned her to protect her health, that the school environment was too dangerous for a pregnant teen. This perspective was typical of policies that ostracized pregnant teens for fear that they would negatively influence peers. The court ruled that the school had acted illegally by expelling a student due to pregnancy. This case drew national attention to the rights of young pregnant women, and shifted the focus from a moralistic one to a practical one on educational equality (Kiester,

1972). Only four years later, Title IX mandated that public schools educate pregnant teens (Luker, 1996, 121).

When Senator Edward Kennedy proposed the National School-Age Mother and Child Health Act of 1975, it plummeted teenage pregnancy into the national consciousness. Although the bill did not pass, and pregnancy rates have generally declined since 1940, teen pregnancy is now firmly established as a social problem.

Through the Eyes of Society: Myths Revisited

Welfare Mothers

Popular opinion holds that teen parents risk living in poverty due to disrupted educations and dead-end jobs, but growing evidence suggests that many young parents were poor *before* they became parents. Poverty itself is a risk factor for adolescent parenthood. Hotz and colleagues (1997) distinguish between temporary and permanent effects of early child rearing. Having more childbearing years ahead of them, teenage mothers tend to have more children over their lifespans and often spend more time single parenting (permanent effects), but economic effects appear more temporary. Over the long run, Hotz and colleagues found that teenage motherhood appears

> to alter only the timing *of events and activities over the mother's lifetime. For example, we find that although teenage mothers have lower labor-market earnings in their late teens and early 20s compared to what they would have earned had they postponed their childbearing, they actually earn more money in their late 20s and in their 30s than if they had delayed childbearing. (70)*

Medical Concerns

Because teens have more complications in pregnancy than do older women, many argue that teens are not ready physiologically to bear children. The research elucidates the roles of poverty, lack of education, and poor health care decisions on the poor outcomes of teen pregnancies. Many teens delay or avoid prenatal care, as they deny their pregnancies, fear or do not know of resources, or are unable to pay for services. In 2000, only 69.1% of teen mothers received first trimester prenatal care, in contrast to 77.8% of mothers ages 20 to 24, and 86.2% of mothers ages 25 to 29. Of concern, 7.1% of mothers from ages 15 to 19, and 16.3% of mothers under age 15, received prenatal care only in the third trimester, if at all (Martin et al., 2002, 64). Smoking is correlated with low birth weight, miscarriage, infant mortality and compromised postnatal development; pregnant teens are more likely to smoke than older mothers (Martin et al., 12). Teen mothers have high rates of maternal anemia, diabetes, hypertension (equally prevalent in mothers ages 40 to 54) and eclampsia, a potentially life-threatening condition in which the placenta prematurely dislodges from the uterine wall (Martin et al., 57).

Development of the Children

Do medical complications in many teen pregnancies result in later developmental difficulties for the offspring? Research has yielded mixed results, often complicated by the choice of comparison group and the length of the studies. Comparisons to children of mothers 20 to 24 years old revealed moderate negative differences. However, when compared to mothers 25 years or older, children of teen mothers had more learning disabilities, poorer school performance and higher rates of grade retention, increased run away behaviors, behavior problems at home and at school, delinquency, and psychological problems (Moore et al., 1997).

In the early 1960s, Furstenberg began studying 296 children of teen mothers. At the 17-year follow-up, Furstenberg and associates (1987) reported that many had severe academic problems and had repeated a grade. When studied three years later, Furstenberg and colleagues (1993) found that mediating factors, such as the mother's marital history and time spent in poverty, had a greater impact than the mother's age at birth. Children of mothers who provided financial and emotional stability performed well at school and eventually entered the work world successfully.

The impact of a teen's emotional immaturity as a parent is harder to assess. Some teens welcome the challenge of parenthood, whereas others feel overwhelmed and are impatient with their children. One consequence of parental frustration and lack of parenting skills is increased child abuse and neglect (see Chapter 8).

Demographics

Each year, more than 900,000 adolescents become pregnant; and about 500,000 women ages from 15 to 19 give birth (Ventura et al., 2001, 21) (see Figure 10.1). As previously stated, teen birthrates peaked during the post–World War II "baby boom," then dropped for two decades only to raise again from 1986 to 1991.

Over the past decade, birthrates for teens have fallen (see Table 10.1). In 1999 and 2000, the birthrates for the youngest mothers reached a 30-year low of 0.9 per 1,000 girls, a 35.7% decrease since 1991. Rates for middle teens fell from 38.7 to 27.5 per 1,000 women, a 28.9% decrease since 1991. Birthrates for the oldest teens fell 15.8% from 94.4 to 79.5 per 1,000 women in 2000 (Ventura et al., 2001, 3–4).

The steepest drop in teen birthrates in the 1990s was for African Americans, declining 31.4% from 115.5 per 1,000 women in 1991 to 79.2 in 2000. Hispanic teenagers had the highest birthrate of 94.4 in 2000. Asian or Pacific

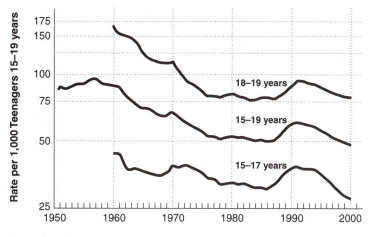

Notes: Data for 2000 are preliminary. Rates are plotted on a log scale.

FIGURE 10.1 **Birthrates for Teenagers by Age:
United States, 1950–2000**

Source: Ventura et al. (2001).

Islander teens have consistently had the lowest birthrate: 21.8 births per 1,000
women in 2000. Birthrates for non-Hispanic white teens dropped 24.4% to
32.8 births per 1,000. Native American teen births fell 20.1% to 67.9 per 1,000
(Ventura et al., 2001, 4, 11) (see Table 10.2).

Ventura and colleagues (2001) suggest multiple factors for the recent decline in teen births. Public concern has led to a greater availability of prevention programs, and teens are more willing to access them. The number of
sexually active high school students decreased 8% from 1991 to 1999 (Ventura
et al., 2000, 21); however, sexual activity among children under age 13 has
increased 15% since 1997 (Terry and Manlove, 2000, as cited in National
Campaign, 2002a, 3). Contraceptive use among adolescents is increasing. The

TABLE 10.1 **Birthrates for Teenagers by Age:
United States, 1991 and 2000 (Rates
are reported per 1,000 women)**

Age	1991	2000	Percent Change
10–14	1.4	0.9	–35.7
15–17	38.7	27.5	–28.9
18–19	94.4	79.5	–15.8

Source: Ventura et al. (2001).

TABLE 10.2 Comparison of Birthrates for Teenagers by Ethnicity: United States, 1991 and 2000 (Rates per 1,000 women)

Ethnicity	1991	2000	Percent Difference
Total	62.1	48.7	–21.6
White Total	52.8	43.9	–16.9
White Non-Hispanic	43.4	32.8	–24.4
Black	115.5	79.2	–31.4
Native-American	85.0	67.9	–20.1
Asian/Pacific Islander	27.4	21.8	–20.4
Hispanic (any race)	106.7	94.4	–11.5

Source: Ventura et al. (2001).

introduction of injectable and implant contraceptives for women, which are longer lasting and less intrusive, many also account for the decline in pregnancy rates. The economic stability of the 1990s allowed teens greater educational and career opportunities, thus encouraging them to delay parenthood. Despite declining birthrates, the United States has the highest teenage birthrate of all developed countries: 48.5 per 1,000 teen women. Japan has the lowest teen birthrate at 4.3 per 1,000 women (Ventura et al., 2001, 7, 20).

Some 33.2% of all babies born in 2000 were to unmarried mothers; 83% of teen mothers were single. Younger teens are less likely to marry: 96.5% of mothers under age 15 remained single, followed by mothers ages 15 to 19 (78.8%), and 49.5% of mothers ages 20 to 24 (Martin et al., 2002, 46). With growing acceptance of out-of-wedlock parenthood, many do not feel the pressure of previous generations to marry. Many young mothers consider the weak earning power of potential husbands in deciding to stay single.

Teens at Risk

Many correlations exist between teenage pregnancy and socioeconomic status, parents' educational level, family structure, previous history of sexual abuse, age, and cognitive and developmental levels.

Family Function

Hogan and colleagues (2000) analyzed the impact of changes in family composition from 1985 to 1995 on adolescent sexuality. Since one in two marriages end in divorce, single mothers are often forced into full-time employment.

Mothers who do not work outside the home declined from 37 to 24% (1422). Increasingly, teens experience changing, perhaps unstable, family living situations; young women navigating between two families increased from 32 to 43%, and those experiencing three or more living situations increased from 16 to 24% (1422). The researchers found that adolescent girls who do not live with both parents are 30% more likely to be sexually active than teens living with both parents (1423). Supervision often becomes more relaxed, perhaps due to the practical limitations placed on parental time, or to how well children are at "playing parents off of one another," particularly when there is discord. Adolescents' behaviors often embody implicit family messages, and parents in flux often convey confusing messages about family structure and values.

CASE EXAMPLE

Mark

Mark, age 16, has had to make many decisions on his own since his parents separated 10 years ago. He lives with his father and three older siblings; his mother maintains regular contact. Mark has learned which parent to ask when he wants something, and often "guilt trips" each into giving him money or allowing him privileges. Now his older brother is getting married, and Mark knows that his father disapproves of the early marriage as well as feeling anger and sorrow over his failed marriage. Mark tells his Dad that he will not go to the engagement party, that he has "a hot date." Given his ambivalence over the party, his Dad finds it hard to convince Mark that he needs to attend. Mark stays home with Bethany, his 15-year-old girlfriend. As they get closer to sexual intercourse, she asks if his Dad is coming home. Mark assures her that his Dad will not "find them," and adds, "My Dad practically knows what we're doing anyway. He's cool!"

Miller and associates (2001) found that when parents are supportive and maintain warm and close relationships with their teens, teens delay or reduce sexual contact. Generally, consistent parental supervision helps lower rates of teen pregnancy; however, overly strict supervision or intrusive parenting appears to have the opposite effect. For the teen rebelling against tyrannical parents, pregnancy may be a way to establish independence, to assert adult identity, or to spite parents.

Socioeconomic Status

According to Sally Ann, age 16, mother of 1-year-old-daughter, "None of us is ever going to get a real good job. They're not for us, those real good jobs! If you're real smart, maybe you could stay in school, and go to college, and then you could get yourself one of these 'plum jobs' I hear folks talking about. But none of them are out there, around here, for any of us" (Coles, 1997, 62–63).

Teenagers from families with higher parental education levels and socio-economic status delay sexual intercourse and use contraception more often (Hogan et al., 2000; Miller et al., 2001). When middle-class teens conceive, anticipating greater opportunities, they are more likely to abort than teens from less-educated, poorer families (Bulow & Meller, 1998). For young women from disadvantaged families, a child can be a motivating force to "get her life together," or to have a goal. Luker reflects that "having a baby can give a young woman permission to be assertive and motivated on her baby's behalf when she has trouble mustering these qualities for herself" (182).

Sucoff and Upchurch (1998) question whether racial homogeneity in communities impacts teen pregnancy rates. They compared teen pregnancy rates of African Americans from neighborhoods varying in socioeconomic status (from below the poverty line to middle class); two were segregated, one racially mixed, and one predominately white. Adjusting for socioeconomic status (SES), racial segregation was found more significant than SES. The researchers concluded, "The shared experience of social isolation in segregated black neighborhoods may engender norms sanctioning (or at least not proscribing) premarital adolescent childbearing" (582).

Previous Sexual Abuse and Date Rape

Many young women raised in households without adult males do not view men as nurturing. As mothers, they tend *not* to expect their male partners to contribute financially or emotionally. Harris (1996) found that girls raised without caring, responsible father figures were prone to sexual abuse and date rape. Once victimized, teens often lack the skills to protect themselves. Boyer and Fine (1992) sampled 535 teen women with sexual abuse histories; 44% reported subsequent rapes and 11% of those became pregnant. Estimates of the prevalence sexual coercion of teen women ranged from 42 to 74% (Abma et al., 1998; Alan Guttmacher Institute, 1994; Moore et al., 1989). The 13- and 14-year-olds were most vulnerable, and often their perpetrators were considerably older.

CASE EXAMPLE

Maritza

Maritza's stepfather sexually abused her when she was 9 and 10 years old. When her mother learned of the abuse, she had her husband leave immediately and brought Maritza to a counselor. Maritza responded well to treatment, and as a young adolescent, did well in school and had a circle of friends she could trust. When she was 15 years old, a church youth group leader sexually assaulted her younger brother, Pedro. This new family crisis revived the old issues of trust for Maritza. Much to her mother's horror, Maritza began to put herself in vulnerable situations. For instance, when a male neighbor, Juan, in his early twenties, dropped by, she entered the living room to talk to him wearing only her underwear. Juan, uncomfortable with the situation, immediately left the home.

Maritza began making provocative comments to older boys on the streets. When her mother confronted her, Maritza said that she "knew the boys," and that they "wouldn't do anything." Maritza's placing herself in vulnerable positions seemed inconsistent with her good judgment of the last few years. Her therapist wondered if Maritza was "testing the waters," placing herself in potentially vulnerable situations, only to hope that if she was not further victimized, it would proof that the world was "safe." Unfortunately, the neighborhood boys began to think of her as "loose," and one night at a party she was raped.

Educational Goals

Career aspirations and teacher encouragement help prevent teenage pregnancy. Enrollment in college preparatory courses, and its inherent goals, is a preventive factor. Only half as many college-bound students become pregnant as those not planning on college (Upchurch & McCarthy, 1990). Berlin and Sum (1988) found that reading levels predict the likelihood of teen pregnancy. On a basic skills test, teen women scoring in the bottom 5th percentile were 38 times more likely to conceive than their peers with more solid skills. Significantly, none of the teens scoring in the 95th percentile had a child.

Age

Younger teens often exhibit numerous behavioral problems before conception, including school behavior problems, smoking, drinking, illicit drug use, and having intercourse before age 13 (and earlier within relationships). These symptoms are consistent with a diagnosis of a conduct disorder. Perhaps the sexual activity and choice of older partners is part of the behavioral disorder. After becoming pregnant, they are more likely to drop out of school to marry or live with their much older partners (Lamb et al., 1986; Rickert et al., 1997).

How Teens Make Decisions about Fertility and Child Rearing

Teens view the costs and benefits of sexual activity and contraception differently than adults do. Adolescents, typically risk-takers, often believe they are invulnerable to adversity, including unplanned pregnancy. Lowenstein and

Furstenberg (1991) found that the vast majority of sexually active teenagers (ranging from 99% of 14-year-olds to 77% of 18-year-olds) believed that the "best age" for first intercourse was to be *older* than they were at first intercourse, regardless of age. This suggests that sexually active teens find themselves in situations they are not emotionally or cognitively ready to handle.

Stevens-Simon and associates (2001) found that most sexually active teenagers will deny plans to conceive when asked directly; they suggest, rather, asking the teen if she intends to remain *nonpregnant*. Once declaring the intention to remain nonpregnant, a teen can anticipate factors that might interfere and then problem solve. Possible discussions topics include willingness to use contraceptives, misconceptions about fertility, false beliefs that sexual contact with "just friends" (not considered "lovemaking") cannot lead to parenthood, and hopes that parenthood will foster adult status in the community.

Many teenagers report that they did not consciously decide to have sexual relations, but it "just happened." Teen women often do not plan for intercourse because it is inconsistent with their self-images. Planning for intercourse implies that they are willing partners, which goes against societal messages that "good girls" do not seek out sex. As relationships become established, young women are more comfortable publicly seeking contraceptive services.

Adolescents are concerned with what they *believe* their peers are doing or thinking. Lowenstein and Furstenberg (1991) found that teens who believed their peers are sexually active were significantly more likely to experiment sexually. Whether their peers truly were sexually active is immaterial; however, the perception of others guides their actions. Adolescents take their cues on contraceptive use from their peers, as well. Schinke (1998) found that when youths thought their peers viewed condom use positively, they were significantly more likely to use condoms themselves.

Teens are less willing to use contraception when they believe it will interfere with sexual pleasure, or will be too expensive or inconvenient to acquire (Lowenstein & Furstenberg, 1991). Effective contraceptive use requires a comfort with one's body; younger adolescents have not had time to adjust to raging hormones and changing body images. Not surprisingly, contraception use increases with age. Only 21% of 14-year-olds used contraceptives at first intercourse, compared to 64% of 18-year-olds. Understanding the risks of HIV transmission increases contraceptive use; Santelli and colleagues (1997) found that adolescents educated about HIV were more likely to use condoms.

Parental attitudes regarding sexuality and early parenthood impact adolescents more than most parents realize. Moore and associates (1986) found that when mothers were comfortable and willing to talk about sexuality, it positively influenced their daughters' comfort with their own sexuality and use of birth control. Adolescents who thought their mothers accepted early pre-marital parenthood were more likely to bring a pregnancy to term; teen women usually considered their mothers' attitudes over those of the fathers of their babies (Williams, 1991). Adler and Tschann (1993) asked teens how opinions of family and friends would impact a hypothetical situation in which they became pregnant within the coming year. Significant cultural differences emerged: African American and Hispanic teens perceived those close to them as opposed to abortion, whereas white teens perceived others as supporting an abortion. Asian teenagers' responses fell in the middle.

> *And I thank God for the baby, every morning when I look at him, because he's all I've got, and he's a good baby. With him, I can try to do things right, so he'll be different from others: he can grow up to be somebody, and not be hurting people, doing them in. You raise a child—and you have a second chance, you know. (Beth, age 16, cited in Coles, 1997, 127)*

Geronimus (1997) found that poor African Americans families often convey messages, implicitly or directly, encouraging teen parenthood. Comparing mortality rates of middle-class whites to highly impoverished African Americans in Harlem and Chicago, Geronimus found those in the poor communities had significantly shorter lifespans than whites and those more affluent. From this culturally sensitive perspective, teen parenthood is a practical way to ensure that the older generation will have the opportunity to grandparent and that the young will have the benefit of their nurturance.

Some adolescents have sex to "get a message" to their parents. Williams (1991) extensively interviewed 30 African American teen mothers from Boston. She observed that the "adolescents often replaced extracurricular activities and sports with early sexual exploration and behavior designed to get the attention of parents" (61). These teens risk normal developmental tasks by running away, having sex, or getting in trouble at school or at home to attract attention to their sense of isolation.

CASE EXAMPLE

Alicia

Alicia, age 14, lives with her 30-year-old mother, Sharon, four younger siblings, and her mother's partner (father of the youngest two children). Alicia has been intermittently running away from home for the last year and is failing eighth grade despite her above-average intelligence. Sharon often expresses intolerance at Alicia's normal adolescent frustrations, thinking, "After all, I never had to worry about going out or clothes or schoolwork. I had Alicia to worry about."

Alicia is sexually active with her 18-year-old boyfriend, Brent; they plan to marry when Alicia graduates high school. One night after another screaming argument with her mother, Alicia is grounded "for the rest of her life"; Alicia and Brent had planned to go out. Atypically, rather than leaving, Alicia sits at the kitchen table with the three condoms she had stored away. She blows each up like a balloon and draws faces on them and shows them to her mother.

As Alicia "bumps up" against her mother developmentally, they are more and more angry at one another. Her mother has little patience for the "normal" crisis of adolescence; her development was foreshortened when she had to care for a baby. Alicia has not experienced her mother as protective or nurturing, and many of her behavioral problems serve to draw her mother into a more involved role. Although seldom admitting it, Alicia would like her mother to take a more authoritative role and "to be a mother."

Fathers

CASE EXAMPLE

Bruce

Bruce, age 17, is the father of Korinna, 18 months old, and Rickie, a newborn. Last year, Bruce dropped out of school to take an apprenticeship at his uncle's automotive repair shop. Never having much patience, Bruce did not take directions well. Three months later, his uncle asked him to leave.

When Bruce's girlfriend, Hannah, became pregnant the first time, her parents tried unsuccessfully to convince her to break off the relationship. Hannah had planned to place the baby for adoption. But once Korinna was born, and her parents held their first grandchild, she and her family decided to raise the child. Bruce visited Hannah and the baby each day, but relations with Hannah's parents were strained. Bruce resented that Hannah's mother thought she knew more about the baby than he did. He boasted of the work that he could get, the income he could make to support Hannah and the baby, but remained unemployed except for occasional work through "Day-Temps." Hannah dreamed of having her own apartment with Bruce and the baby, but there was no way.

On two occasions, to prove themselves "worthy parents" to Hannah's family, they "took off" with the baby for a few days. Hannah's parents were worried sick; the young couple had little money and did not say where they were going. Both Bruce and Hannah continued to want to spend time with their friends, who alternately enjoyed the baby and felt confined by her presence.

When Korinna was 9 months old, Hannah became pregnant again, and she and Bruce decided to marry. Hannah's parents hoped that the engagement meant that they were both maturing. Bruce looked harder for work this time, but there were few jobs for those with his low level of skills and low frustration tolerance. When Rickie was born, Bruce was especially proud to have fathered a son. He spoke of his intentions to "be there" for his son, to provide for his family, but day by day his certainty that he could do so decreased. As it became harder to maintain that he could support his children, he began to have one-night stands.

Early parenthood, stressful for many, can be particularly difficult for young fathers struggling for economic independence and identity formation. Elster and Panzarine (1983) found that teen fathers had four sets of concerns: vocational and educational (school disruption, and financial and job security); health of mother and baby (including labor and delivery); parenthood; and relationships (problems with partner and her parents, with friends, and worries that new fatherhood would affect the affiliation with his church). Often, these young fathers are "marginalized" by their partners' families, thus making it difficult to participate in parenting.

Like adolescent mothers, teen fathers often have histories of poor academic performance. Teen fathers averaged from 0.9 to 2.5 years less education than those delaying fatherhood, with the greatest difference being among whites. African American teen fathers completed their education more often than other races: 74.3% received their high school diplomas or General Equivalency Diplomas (GED) compared to 59.3% of white teen fathers and 48.8% of teen fathers of other races (Pirog-Good, 1996).

In recent decades, supporting a family has become more difficult as the U.S. economy has moved more to skilled jobs requiring advanced education. Teen fathers typically have not completed their educations; but the impact on their earning potential is not always immediate. Until their mid-twenties, there is no significant difference in incomes between early fathers and those who waited until after age 20. However, by age 29, whites who had been teen parents earned approximately one-third less than peers who delayed paternity, and African Americans who parented as teens earned less than half that of peers who delayed parenthood (Pirog-Good, 1996, 244, 250).

Adult males father more than half the babies born to adolescents. High school mothers had partners averaging 4.2 years their senior, but middle school mothers had partners averaging 6.7 years older (Males & Chew, 1996). The younger the mother, the more likely her partner will be significantly older. Males (1995) found that 11- to 12-year-old mothers reported fathers averaging 9.8 years older. Agurcia and colleagues (2001) found that teen mothers with partners at least five years older are less likely to continue schooling or pursue careers and often become pregnant again soon. Older males tend to be more involved in child care, to provide economically for their families, and to treat their partners more respectfully. Adolescent mothers with older partners receive less emotional or financial support from their families, who often assume that an older father will be more mature and stable.

CASE EXAMPLE

A Teen's View: Angelica

Bobby and I were going out almost a year. I thought we were serious, that he really loved me. So when he asked to have sex, I said okay, except for trying to hide it from my mother. Then I got pregnant. He pulled out, so I didn't think it could happen, especially so soon. I told Bobby, and he tried to avoid me. Always had something to do, somewhere to go. I told him we had to talk, finally he did. And he wanted me to have an abortion. But, I couldn't. No, it's wrong. I didn't plan to have Kyle, but I really love him.

But, it sure has changed things. I go to group [expressive arts group] and I have to leave early so I can get home for Kyle. My mom watches him, but she has to go to bed early to get up for work. The other girls talk about clothes and boyfriends and school…I used to hate school, used to say I hated school anyway…. But I sure miss it now. Funny thing is, now that I'm not really in school [attends GED classes] I want to be there. I want to do good and get a job. Now that I'm around a kid all day, I want to be a pediatric nurse. Never thought I'd want that. But it's hard to find time to study. I'm tired at the end of the day. I'm glad I have the play-group at the Y(MCA) to see other moms. Sometimes it's hard for them too. But I do love Kyle. I just wish Bobby would come over more. Last Saturday I did my hair and had a new dress and waited and waited for him. I was so angry; he didn't call. He finally came, but it was too late to go out…. I have to be up at six with the baby.

When Angelica learned she was pregnant, she went to the health counselor at school, who was there under a grant, since her school had one of the highest teen pregnancy rates in the state. The counselor informed Angelica that she would need to live with her mother or another adult relative in order to receive welfare benefits. She had hoped to live with 19-year-old Bobby, but never found a way to discuss it with him. Angelica disliked the idea of daycare, so she did not see how she could continue school.

When Angelica gave birth, her mother was with her. Bobby came to the hospital the next day, but did not visit for another month. Her mother taught her how to care for an infant. The counselor helped her find a Saturday GED class; her mother cared for the baby when she went to classes. During the week, she was so tired that it was hard to study. One day, she dropped by the Teen Center, even though she did not feel that she "fit in" there, but she wanted desperately to be around kids her age. The Teen Center director invited her to an expressive arts program for adolescent girls. Delighted with the idea, she joined immediately, even though she was the only parent in the program.

This satisfied Angelica's need to be with peers, even though she still misses shopping with her friends, going to parties, going to sports games at the high school, and just "hanging out."

Her mother helps with child care as well as supports her emotionally. Angelica longs for some commitment from Bobby but knows it's a dream. Every few weeks, he visits but doesn't show much interest in the baby. Although Bobby is mandated to pay child support, he seldom does. Sometimes, Angelica is so angry, she thinks she never wants to see him again, but feels that would be unfair to their son. She receives WIC, which helps pay for food. As the baby sleeps through the night, Angelica is able to study. She starts to plan for her future without counting on Bobby and hopes to attend a nursing school close to home so that her mother can help care for Kyle while she pursues a career.

For in-depth interviews of pregnant and parenting teens, the reader is referred to *The Youngest Parents: Teenage Pregnancy as It Shapes Lives* by Robert Coles (1997), which portrays teens from Washington, DC, North Carolina, West Virginia, New York City, Baltimore, California, New Mexico, and Boston. Teens vary in ethnic and racial backgrounds, and both rural and urban teens are represented. Two photo essays of teen parents and their children provide glimpses of their vast emotional experiences.

Services: Primary Prevention

With more than half of high school students reporting previous intercourse, and 38% currently sexually active (Dryfoos, 1998, 28), there is a dire need to disseminate appropriate information. Primary prevention programs, aimed at preventing sexual activity and/or pregnancy, vary in format, philosophy, and success rates (Kirby, 2001).

Programs Focusing on Sexual Antecedents

Sexual antecedents include decisions around abstinence, sexual activity, and contraception.

Abstinence: "Just Say No!" In 1996, federal law allocated $85 million per year for abstinence-based sex education programs (Kirby, 2001, 7). Historically, religious organizations have urged abstinence and provided moral instruction, youth-centered activities, and a sense of community for teens. Their importance to teens, even though they rarely attend formal religious services as they get older, remains strong. Whitehead and colleagues (2001) found that teen girls often site religious or moral reasons for not engaging in premarital sex.

Differences on whether abstinence should be the only intervention, and the role of morality teaching, have resulted in a divide between efforts of religious and public health organizations. Along with the emphasis placed on abstinence by the Clinton administration, the newly created Bush White House Office of Faith Based and Community Initiatives is likely to help bridge this "divide between 'faith talk' and 'public health talk'" (Whitehead et al., 2001, 1).

Arnold and associates (1999) found that the effectiveness of abstinence programs increased when key ideas and values were reinforced through the added support of parents, job opportunities for teens, and media campaigns spreading the message that abstinence is "cool." On the whole, the effectiveness of abstinence-only programs is mixed; however, research is scarce. It is hoped that we will understand these programs better after the completion of a well-designed federally funded study currently underway (Kirby, 2001).

Sex and HIV Education Programs for Teens and Their Families. Sex education programs vary considerably in length (from less than 10 hours to more than 40) and in curriculum. Programs provide information and emphasize skills building and values clarification; some incorporate peer education, expressive therapy projects, computer-assisted instruction, and conferences for youths and their parents. Role playing, in which students practice skills such as saying "no" to sexual advances, or going to buy condoms, increases their effectiveness (Franklin and Corcoran, 2000). St. Lawrence (1993) found that teen men and women, when presented with the same factual material on contraception, recall specifics differently. She recommends that sex education classes be tailored and taught separately for each gender.

Parents are often uncomfortable talking with their teens about sexuality and birth control, but they underestimate their influence. In a national survey, "teens cited parents more than any other source as having the *most* influence over their sexual decision-making" (National Campaign, 2001, 2). The continual presence of parenting magazine articles on discussing sex with one's teen speaks to the need that parents feel for learning ways to increase such communication (Simanski, 1998). Some school districts host forums for parents; although participation seems to temporarily increase communication between teens and their parents, long-term effects are not clear (Kirby, 2001, 9).

Programs Providing Contraceptive Access. Three types of programs provide access to contraceptive services: community/family planning clinics, school-based health clinics, and school-linked clinics (in which schools establish working relationships with area clinics). Kirby (2001) found that one-on-one counseling, incorporating clear messages about sex and condom/contraceptive use is key to the success of these programs. Clear messages about abstinence and/or contraception and the personal touch of individual or group counseling are essential.

Baltimore, a city with a high rate of adolescent pregnancy, ran a successful program for junior and senior high school students. School-based services included classroom lectures, informal discussion groups, and individual counseling; social workers and medical personnel provided group and individual counseling and reproductive health services at a nearby clinic. The program significantly decreased teen pregnancy rates. Students were more likely to seek contraceptive services *before* first intercourse, in contrast to teens who typically seek clinic services *after* becoming sexually active (Zabin et al., 1996).

Communitywide Initiatives.   Media campaigns informing the public about teen pregnancy and available services are increasing. Some provide sex education for teens and forums for parents. These initiatives are most effective when they are continuous, thus allowing communities to reach each group of youngsters as they reach the age of possible sexual activity. When programs end, the use of contraception decreases and teen pregnancies increases (Kirby, 2001, 12). Perhaps the lack of personal contact also limits their effectiveness.

Programs Focusing on Nonsexual Antecedents

Programs focusing on nonsexual antecedents target risk factors, such as school failure and societal disadvantages, help young people develop skills and confidence and to broaden their horizons.

Early Childhood Programs.   Preschool programs, such as Head Start (see Chapter 5) provide structured learning experiences to help young children overcome the disadvantages of poverty linked to teen pregnancy. Some programs intervene at younger ages. The Abecedarian Project, sponsored by the University of North Carolina, provided low-income families with full-time, high-quality child care from infancy to age 5. When compared to a control group at ages 12, 15, and 21, the Abecedarian Project graduates had higher reading and math scores in the primary grades, had their first children later, completed more education, and were more likely to attend four-year colleges ("Carolina Abecedarian Project," 2002).

Youth Development Programs for Adolescents.   Youth development programs provide volunteer opportunities for teens to participate in society in meaningful ways and develop decision-making skills. The Teen Outreach Program, a collaborative project between local Junior Leagues and schools nationally, combines community service with a school-based educational component, including values clarification, communication skills, handling family stress, developmental issues, and understanding a parent's perspective. Students in grades 7 through 12 typically volunteer as aides in hospitals or nursing homes, help organize walkathons, or tutor. Middle school students particularly enjoy the developing sense of autonomy fostered through the volunteerism. Older students, who have had other experiences that foster autonomy, find the classroom component more fruitful. Over a seven-year consecutive stretch, this program has reduced teen pregnancy rates, academic failure, and dropout rates from 15 to 50% when matched with comparison groups (Allen et al., 1994).

Programs Focusing on Sexual and Nonsexual Antecedents

Comprehensive programs are based on two premises: that adolescents with hopes for the future delay parenthood, and that intervening in more than one realm of the teen's life is more effective than treating only one.

The Adolescent Pregnancy Prevention Program, sponsored by the Children's Aid Society, was started by Dr. Michael Carrera in 1984 for 13- to 15-year-old girls from Harlem. Due to its exceptional success, the program has been replicated at other sites in New York City and across the country. Teens participate in five activities (job club and career awareness; academic assessment, tutoring, and college admissions assistance; performing arts workshops; a family life and sex education curriculum; and sports instruction). Reproductive health services and mental health counseling are available. Teens meet daily after school and on Saturdays; in the summer, they work while maintaining contact with the program. A three-year evaluation across seven cities yielded impressive results: 49% less pregnancies and 46% less births compared to a control group ("Children's Aid Society," 2001). New York City teens were given an added incentive: Those who completed the program and high school were guaranteed admission to Hunter College with a full tuition subsidy (Dryfoos, 1998, 126).

Evaluating Primary Prevention Programs

Walter (2001) found that effective prevention programs are research based and theory driven; provide comprehensive services, including family, peer, media, and community influences; begin in the primary grades and are reinforced later; embody a developmental framework; include interactive learning exercises; are ethnically and culturally sensitive; and provide intensive staff training to ensure program quality.

Since sociodemographics impact how youths and their families view the benefits and risks of unintended pregnancy (Schinke, 1998), tailoring programs to target populations increases effectiveness. Adolescents assess the trade-offs of young parenthood versus careers and educational opportunities within a particular "culture." A program in Durham, North Carolina, "A Journey Toward Womanhood," provides a four-stage culturally specific group program for African American women (Dixon et al., 2000):

1. *Reaching for Success (weeks 1–4).* The group explores the role of cultural issues, the media, and historical factors on one's identity as a woman.
2. *Developing Inner Health for Outer Beauty (weeks 5–7).* Members learn about self-care, including nutrition, exercise, and healthy relationships; a local teen parent shares her experiences and struggles with the group.
3. *Finesse, Dignity, and Pride (week 8).* Participants develop job interviewing and communication skills through role playing and actual experiences; a culturally related field trip encourages group cohesion.

4. *Tools for Survival (weeks 10–13).* Each participant makes a unique cultural garment to reflect her identity; the group hosts a luncheon for parents and friends, learns how to manage money, and how to job hunt.

Program participants were one-third less likely to have unprotected intercourse or to conceive than a control group. The program's effectiveness appears to stem from the cultural pride inherent in the Afrocentric approach and the small group format.

Services: Secondary Intervention

About a quarter of teen mothers have their second child within two years of the first (National Campaign, 2002a, 5). Secondary prevention targets second unwanted pregnancies and provides supportive services to parenting teens and their children. Adolescent parents, particularly those in poverty, often need multiple services to ensure the financial and emotional stability of their families. School-based programs, vocational skills training, life skills training, health care, child care, counseling and case management, and GED classes address the many needs of adolescent parents.

Teen Parents and Their Families

Of the nearly 159 million children nationally, 5.6 million live with grandparents. Grandparents are the primary caregivers of 2.35 million children; in a third of the cases, grandparents are the primary caregivers for five or more years (U.S. Census Bureau, 2002). When parenting teens live with their parents, both babies and their mothers benefited. Oyserman and colleagues (1993) found that when grandmothers help with child care, teens experience less conflict in their roles as mothers and respond more positively to their babies. Although grandfathers interacted, their contact helped the babies become more compliant with family expectations and increased their emotional stability. Whereas the babies had two female attachment figures (mother and grandmother), grandfathers typically provided the sole adult male figure in the home—a role that seems key.

Keeping Fathers Involved

Helping teen fathers succeed in the cultural role of breadwinner helps keep them involved. In neighborhoods where the majority of men are unemployed, 45% of households consist of single mothers and their children. However, in neighborhoods where 80% or more of the men are employed at least half the year, single mothers head only 14% of the households (Annie E. Casey Foundation, 1995, 7). When a man is able to provide for his offspring, he is more likely to have frequent contact with them. Young mothers involve fathers more who contribute financially.

Three types of services foster young fathers' economic stability: job training and placement, education assistance, and mentoring (Governor's Advisory, 1998). The federally funded Parents' Fair Share project, started in 1992, helps noncustodial young parents (usually fathers) obtain secure employment at livable wages; it also offers parent education and peer support groups. This program has been successful in helping poorly educated and minimally skilled fathers to find work. Once employed, they paid more toward child support than a control group (The Challenge, 2001).

The Boston-based Comprehensive School-Age Parenting Program (CSAPP), in addition to providing academic assistance, offers college preparation and career exploration, counseling and outreach, linkages to health care services, and parenting skills groups ("Volunteer Opportunities," 2002). An impressive 90% of the participants remain in or graduate high school each year (Governor's Advisory, 1998, 41).

The Mentoring Project in Phoenix, Arizona, has been replicated in other parts of the country. Older men established in their careers volunteer to mentor young fathers as they develop goals and implement a step-by-step plan for employment. Often, this is the first time that the young fathers have positive relationships with adult males in authority positions. A caseworker helps the fathers access educational benefits and other services. Of the 120 participants in the Phoenix program, 73% obtained jobs, compared to 48% of a control group, and 71% strengthened their relationships with their children, compared to 41% of the control group (City of Phoenix, 2002).

Child Care

Teen mothers are hesitant to let nonfamily members care for their children; many are uncertain how to judge child care settings and unsure how to assert themselves with nonfamilial providers. One Georgia school ran an innovative program; while teens attended classes, their babies were cared for in a school-based daycare staffed by the teens' mothers or other caregivers (Ripple, 1994). Young mothers enjoyed visiting their babies during school hours. Grandmothers who otherwise would have stayed home to care for their grandchildren became employed; all the mothers completed high school.

Parenting Programs

Programs for teen mothers and their children, sometimes called "Teen-Tot Programs," have three goals: (1) preventing repeat pregnancies while teen mothers complete their educations, (2) improving the health of both mother and child, and (3) improving parenting skills (Akinbami et al., 2001). Programs are typically held in schools or in hospital clinics. Akinbami and colleagues reviewed four programs. Compared to control groups, all reported decreased subsequent pregnancies 12 to 26 months later and improved child health. Educational completion rates varied; no programs reported improvement in care-giving skills, such as the use of infant car seats.

Residential Programs

Although established for young women unable to live with their families due to abuse or substance abuse in the home, many teens enter "Second Chance" homes for other reasons, including being in conflict with parents; needing a place to live after parents, learning of the pregnancy, insist they leave; living in homes too small to accommodate a baby; or wanting their own apartments.

Massachusetts developed a network of programs, called Teen Living Programs (TLP), to help teen mothers develop parenting and self-sufficiency skills. Collins and associates (2000) interviewed 199 former and current TLP residents in all 22 programs and found mixed results. Although outcomes related to educational goals, health and safety of mothers and their babies, and decreasing reliance on public assistance were favorable, employment and improved housing after discharge outcomes were not. About a quarter were pregnant again within two years. Employed teens did only marginally better financially than those on public assistance. Particularly disturbing, 16% reported homelessness after discharge from the TLP; and 14% reported that they were in violent relationships. Collins and colleagues suggest that stronger case management upon discharge is necessary to solidify gains made while in the program.

Trends in Teen Pregnancy Prevention

Legislative Initiatives

Under the Personal Responsibility and Work Opportunity Reconciliation Act of 1996, teen pregnancy was targeted as a way of reducing entitlement benefits. Consequently, the Department of Health and Human Services initiated a National Strategy to Prevent Teen Pregnancy, which incorporated five guiding principles: (1) mentoring by parents and other adults; (2) emphasizing abstinence and personal responsibility; (3) providing access to college and careers for teens so they see reasons for remaining in school; (4) creating partnerships within the community to address teen pregnancy; and (5) committing to a sustained effort to reach the goals (U.S. Dept. of Health, 1998, 1).

Under Welfare Reform, mothers under age 18 are required to live with their parents or other adult relative, and to remain in school in order to receive benefits. The five states producing the biggest declines in teen birth rates receive an "illegitimacy bonus"; additional funding is available to states providing abstinence programs. Increased efforts are mandated to establish paternity and to enforce child support payments. States have the authority to spend federal funds as they choose, provided they meet the basic goals of the Welfare Reform Act (Sawhill, 2000).

Philosophical Shifts

Decades after the sexual revolution and shifts in family structure, many parents are again willing to set stricter expectations. Public policy has also become more conservative. In the 1960s and 70s, intervention focused on preventing future hardship and a second (or third) generation of pregnant teens; today's efforts focus on providing opportunities and changes in attitudes about the future for today's teens *before* they have children. Many interventions are broad based and include educational, social, and vocational opportunities as well as helping at-risk teens develop goals and hopes for their futures. Despite fiscal realities, there is a growing consensus that interventions spread over longer time periods are more effective.

The Media

"T.V. makes kids think that having sex before marriage is something that everybody does, and is the right thing" (National Campaign, 2002b). Many criticize the media for showing indiscriminate sexuality. Sampling four weeks each year from 1989 to 1999, the Parents Television Council (2000) found that sexual material on television increased threefold. In recent years, however, the media has occasionally addressed teen sexuality in an informed and serious manner. On May 8, 2002, the first National Day to Prevent Teen Pregnancy, many of the national networks aired programs sensitively addressing teen pregnancy, including Ricki Lake, ABC Daytime, Channel One Network, Frontline FOX, and MTV (National Campaign, 2002b).

Popular culture presents some thoughtful scenes concerning teenage sexuality and pregnancy. In the 2002 movie *Crossroads,* Britney Spears plays a young woman able to say "no" at virtually the last minute. The Spears' character, Lucy, has agreed to have sex with her friend/lab partner on the eve of their high school graduation; they believe they are the only virgins left in their class. They rent a motel room and begin to have sex. Almost undressed, Lucy decides that she wants to wait for someone she loves rather than "doing it" because everyone else is. Her frustrated lab partner honors her wishes.

The Internet is a source of information for teens on sexuality and early parenthood. The National Campaign (2002a, 6) found that adolescents use the Internet to obtain health information more than they do to chat, shop, or download music. The National Campaign hosts an extensive website (www.teenpregnancy.org) to inform teens; they can take a quiz on sexual knowledge (popular activity of teen websurfers) or read what other teens say about how they make decisions, the impact of the media, the realities of early parenting, and related topics.

Summary

Teenage pregnancy and parenthood is a multifaceted issue; understanding teens as they grapple with their decisions regarding sexuality and parenthood involves understanding their perceptions of themselves and their assessments of the opportunities that await them. The more opportunities a teen perceives as available in the near and distant future, the more likely she or he is to delay parenthood. Teenagers, particularly younger ones, are not accustomed to thinking of themselves as sexual beings; taking responsibility for the consequences of sexual activity means acknowledging a host of new and conflicting feelings, negotiating with a sexual partner, and determining one's values regarding premarital intercourse and parenting in light of family beliefs.

Teen pregnancy prevention programs have many foci. Sex education and/or abstinence programs teach teens the risks of sexual activity and provide factual information. More effective ones integrate skills building and value clarification. More comprehensive programs address individual or family disadvantages and societal dysfunctions such as poor academic achievement, growing up in poverty and/or single-parent homes, lack of health care services, and lack of vocational opportunities. Many poor teens do not see themselves as "giving up much" by beginning parenthood.

Teen mothers, now required to live with their parents under Welfare Reform, receive the benefits of having their mothers help care for their children. Those who cannot live with their families can move into residential programs in which they receive housing, child care instruction, support, case management, and other needed services. Young mothers receiving welfare need to complete high school as well. Various programs exist to help young parents develop a myriad of skills; increasingly these programs also help young fathers.

EXPLORATION QUESTIONS

1. How do economic and class factors affect the options available to parenting teens?
2. How have attitudes changed about the causes of teen pregnancy and the sources of support we *should* offer teen parents?
3. What factors have contributed to a decline in teen pregnancy rates in the last 10 years?
4. How does continued involvement on the part of the father benefit both the teen mother and the baby?
5. What factors contribute to the unusually high rate of births to teen mothers in our country compared to the other industrialized countries?
6. What factors comprise a good prevention program?
7. If you were to design a program for pregnant and parenting teen, what would it look like?

REFERENCES

Abma, J. C., Driscoll, A., & Moore, K. (1998). "Young Women's Degree of Control over First Intercourse: An Exploratory Analysis," *Family Planning Perspectives, 30,* 12–18.

Adler, N. E., & Tschann, J. (1993). "Conscious and Preconscious Motivation for Pregnancy Among Female Adolescents" (144–158). In A. Lawson & D. L. Rhode (Eds.), *The Politics of Pregnancy.* New Haven, CT: Yale University Press.

Agurcia, C. A., Rickert, V. I., Berenson, A. B, Volk, R. J., & Wiemann, C. M. (2001). "The Behavioral Risks and Life Circumstances of Adolescent Mothers Involved with Older Adult Partners," *Archives of Pediatric and Adolescent Medicine,* 155(7), 822–830.

Akinbami, L. J., Cheng, T. L., & Kornfeld, D. (2001). "A Review of Teen-Tot Programs: Comprehensive Clinical Care for Young Parents and Their Children," *Adolescence,* 36(142), 381–393.

Alan Guttmacher Institute. (1994). *Sex and America's Teenagers.* New York: Author.

Alan Guttmacher Institute. (1995). "Teenage Pregnancy and the Welfare Reform Debate." Retrieved June 19, 2002, from http://www.agi-usa.org/pubs/ib5.html.

Alan Guttmacher Institute. (1999). "Facts in Brief: Teen Sex and Pregnancy." Retrieved June 18, 2002, from www.agi-usa.org/pubs/fb_teen_sex.html.

Allen, J. P., Kuperminc, G., Philliber, S., & Herre, K. (1994). "Programmatic prevention of Adolescent Problem Behaviors: The Role of Autonomy, Relatedness, and Volunteer Service in the Teen Outreach Program," *American Journal of Community Psychology,* 22(5), 617–638.

Annie E. Casey Foundation. (1995). *Kids Count Data Book: State Profiles of Child Well-Being.* Baltimore, MD: Author.

Arnold, E. M., Smith, T. E., Harrison, D. F., & Springer, D. W. (1999). "The Effects of an Abstinence-Based Sex Education Program on Middle School Students' Knowledge and Beliefs," *Research on Social Work Practice,* 9(1), 10–24.

Berlin, G., & Sum, A. (1988). *Toward a More Perfect Union: Basic Skills, Poor Families, and Our Economic Future.* New York: Ford Foundation.

Boyer, D., & Fine, D. (1992). "Sexual Abuse as a Factor in Adolescent Pregnancy and Child Maltreatment," *Family Planning Perspectives,* 24, 4–11, 19.

Bulow, P. J., & Meller, P. J. (1998). "Predicting Teenage Girls' Sexual Activity and Contraception Use: An Application of Matching Law," *Journal of Community Psychology,* 26(6), 581–596.

Campbell, A. (1968). "The Role of Family Planning in the Reduction of Poverty," *Journal of Marriage and the Family,* 30, 236–245.

"Carolina Abecedarian Project." (2002). University of North Carolina. Retrieved June 24, 2002, from www.fpg.unc.edu/'abc/.

"Challenge of Helping Low-Income Families Support Their Children, The." (2001). *Lessons from Parents* from www.mdrc.org/reports2001/pfs.

Children's Aid Society. (2001). "Striking Breakthrough in Teen Pregnancy Prevention Substantiated by New Scientific Evaluation." Retrieved June 27, 2002, from www.childrensaidsociety.org/388/?art=8287&pg=0.

City of Phoenix. (2002). "Step-Up Young Fathers Program." Retrieved June 24, 2002, from www.acf.dhhs.gov/programs/cse/rpt/fth/fth_b.htm.

Coles, R., with Coles, R. E., Coles, D. A., & Coles, M. H. (1997). *The Youngest Parents: Teenage Pregnancy as It Shapes Lives.* New York: W. W. Norton.

Collins, M. E., Stevens, J. W., & Lane, T. S. (2000). "Teenage Parents and Welfare Reform: Findings from a Survey of Teenagers Affected by Living Requirements," *Social Work,* 45(4), 327–338.

Dixon, A. C., Schoonmaker, C. T., & Philliber, W. W. (2000). "A Journey toward Womanhood: Effects of an Afrocentric Approach to Pregnancy Prevention among African-American Adolescent Females," *Adolescence,* 35(139), 425–429.

Dryfoos, J. G. (1998). *Safe Passage: Making It through Adolescence in a Risky Society.* New York: Oxford University Press.

Elster, A. B., & Panzarine, S. (1983). "Teenage Fathers: Stresses during Gestation and Early Parenthood," *Clinical Pediatrics,* 22(10), 700–703.

Franklin, C., & Corcoran, J. (2000). "Preventing Adolescent Pregnancy: A Review of Programs and Practices," *Social Work,* 45, 41–52.

Furstenberg, F. F., Brooks-Gunn, J., & Morgan, S. P. (1987). "Adolescent Mothers and Their Children in Later Life," *Family Planning Perspectives,* 19(4), 142–151.

Furstenberg, F. F., Hughes, M. E., & Brooks-Gunne, J. (1993). "The Next Generation: The Children of Teenage Mothers Grow Up" (113–135). In *Early Parenthood and the Coming of Age in the 1990s* (113–135). New Brunswick, NJ: Rutgers University Press.

Geronimus, A. T. (1997). "Teenage Childbearing and Person Responsibility: An Alternative View," *Political Science Quarterly,* 112(3), 405–433.

Governor's Advisory Commission on Responsible Fatherhood and Family Support. (1998). *Dads Make a Difference: Action for Responsible Fatherhood.* Boston: Author.

Hall, G. S. (1905). *Adolescence: Its Psychology and Its Relationship to Physiology, Anthropology, Sociology, Sex, Crime, Religion and Education.* New York: Appleton.

Harari, S. E., & Vinovskis, M. (1993). "Adolescent Sexuality, Pregnancy, and Childbearing in the Past" (23–45). In A. Lawson & D. L. Rhode (Eds.), *The Politics of Pregnancy.* New Haven, CT: Yale University Press.

Harris, I. B. (1996). *Children in Jeopardy: Can We Break the Cycle of Poverty?* New Haven, CT: Yale University Press.

Hofferth, S. L. (1987). "Social and Economic Consequences of Teenage Childbearing." In S. L. Hofferth & C. D. Hayes (Eds.), *Risking the Future* (123–144). Washington, DC: National Academy Press.

Hogan, D. P., Sun, R., & Cornwell, G. T. (2000). "Sexual and Fertility Behaviors of American Females Aged 15–19 Years: 1985, 1990, and 1995," *American Journal of Public Health,* 90(9), 1421–4125.

Hotz, V. J., McElroy, S. W., & Sanders, S. G. (1997). "The Impacts of Teenage Childrearing on the Mothers and the Consequences of Those Impacts for Government" (55–94). In R. A. Maynard (Ed.), *Kids Having Kids: Economic Costs and Social Consequences of Teen Pregnancy.* Washington, DC: Urban Institute Press.

Kiester, E. (1972, June). "The Bitter Lesson Too Many of Our Schools Are Teaching Pregnant Teenagers." *Today's Health,* 56.

Kirby, D. (2001). *Emerging Answers: Research Findings on Programs to Reduce Teen Pregnancy.* Washington, DC: National Campaign to Prevent Teen Pregnancy.

Kirby, D., Short, L., Collins, J., Rugg, D., Kolbe, L., Howard, M., Miller, B., Sonenstein, F., & Zabin, L. S. (1994). "School-Based Programs to Reduce Sexual Risk Behaviors: A Review of Effectiveness," *Public Health Reports,* 109, 339–360.

Kiselica, M. S., & Sturmer, P. (1993). "Is Society Giving Teenage Fathers a Mixed Message?" *Youth and Society,* 24(4), 487–501.

Lamb, M. E., Elster, A. B., & Tavare, J. (1986). "Behavioral Profiles of Adolescent Mothers and Partners with Varying Intracouple Age Differences," *Journal of Adolescent Research,* 1, 399–408.

Lowenstein, G., & Furstenberg, F. F. (1991). "Is Teenage Sexual Behavior Rational?" *Journal of Applied Social Psychology,* 21(12), 957–986.

Luker, K. (1996). *Dubious Conceptions: The Politics of Teenage Pregnancy.* Cambridge, MA: Harvard University Press.

Males, M. (1995). "Adult Involvement in Teenage Childbearing and STD," *Lancet,* 346, 64–65.

Males, M., & Chew, K. S. Y. (1996). "The Ages of Fathers in California Adolescent Births, 1993," *American Journal of Public Health,* 86, 565–568.

Martin, J. A., Hamilton, B. E., Ventura, S. J., Menacher, F., & Park, M. M. (2002). *Births: Final Data for 2000. National Vital Statistics Reports* (Vol. 50, no. 5). Hyattsville, MD: National Center for Health Statistics.

Miller, B. C., Benson, B., & Galbraith, K. A. (2001). "Family Relationships and Adolescent

Pregnancy Risk: A Research Synthesis," *Developmental Review,* 21(1), 1–38.

Moore, K. A., Morrison, D. R., & Greene, A. D. (1997). "Effects on the Children Born to Adolescent Mothers" (14–180). In R. A. Maynard (Ed.), *Kids Having Kids: Economic Costs and Social Consequences of Teen Pregnancy.* Washington, DC: Urban Institute Press.

Moore, K. A., Nord, C. W., & Peterson, J. L. (1989). "Nonvoluntary Sexual Activity among Adolescents," *Family Planning Perspectives,* 21, 110–114.

Moore, K. A., Peterson, J. D., & Furstenberg, F. F., Jr. (1986). "Sex Education and Sexual Experience among Adolescents," *American Journal of Public Health* (Brief), 75 (11), 1331–1332.

National Campaign to Prevent Teenage Pregnancy. (2001). *Halfway There: A Prescription for Continued Progress in Preventing Teen Pregnancy.* Washington, DC: Author.

National Campaign to Prevent Teenage Pregnancy. (2002a). "Not Just Another Single Issue: Teen Pregnancy Prevention's Link to Other Critical Social Issues." Retrieved June 19, 2002, from www.teenpregnancy.org.

National Campaign to Prevent Teenage Pregnancy. (2002b). "Now Showing." Retrieved June 19, 2002, from www.teenpregnancy.org/media/nowshowing.asj.

Oyserman, D., Radin, N., & Benn, R. (1993). "Dynamics in a Three-Generational Family: Teens, Grandparents, and Babies," *Developmental Psychology,* 29(3), 594–572.

Parents Television Council. (2000). "What a Difference a Decade Makes" from www.parentstv.org/main/publications/reports/decadestudy/exsummary.asp.

Pearce, D. M. (1993). "'Children Having Children': Teenage Pregnancy and Public Policy from the Woman's Perspective" (46–58). In A. Lawson & D. L. Rhode (Eds.), *The Politics of Pregnancy.* New Haven, CT: Yale University Press.

Pirog-Good, M. A. (1996). "The Education and Labor Market Outcomes of Adolescent Fathers," *Youth and Society,* 28(2), 236–262.

Rickert, V. I., Wiemann, C. M., & Berenson, A. B. (1997). "Health Risk Behaviors among Pregnant Adolescents with Older Partners," *Archives of Pediatric and Adolescent Medicine,* 151(3), 276–280.

Ripple, R. P. (1994). "Intergenerational Education: Breaking the Downward Achievement Spiral of Teen Mothers," *Clearing House,* 67(3), 143–145.

St. Lawrence, J. S. (1993). "African-American Adolescents' Knowledge, Health-Related Attitudes, Sexual Behavior, and Contraceptive Decisions: Implications for the Prevention of Adolescent HIV Infection," *Journal of Consulting and Clinical Psychology,* 61(1), 104–112.

Santelli, J. S., Warren, C. W., Lowry, R., Sogolow, E., Collins, J., Kann, L., Kaufmann, R. B., & Celentano, D. D. (1997). "The Use of Condoms with Other Contraceptive Methods among Young Men and Women," *Family Planning Perspectives,* 29(6), 261–267.

Sawhill, I. V. (2000). "Welfare Reform and Reducing Teen Pregnancy," *Public Interest,* 40–48.

Schinke, S. P. (1998). "Preventing Teenage Pregnancy: Translating Research Knowledge," *Journal of Human Behavior in the Social Environment,* 1(1), 53–66.

Simanski, J. W. (1998). "The Birds and the Bees: An Analysis of Advice to Parents through the Popular Press," *Adolescence,* 33(129), 33–46.

Stevens-Simon, C., Beach, R. K., & Klerman, L. V. (2001). "To Be Rather Than Not to Be— That Is the Problem with the Questions We Ask Adolescents about Their Childrearing Intentions," *Archives on Pediatrics and Adolescent Medicine,* 155, 1298–1300.

Sucoff, C. A., & Upchurch, D. M. (1998). "Neighborhood Context and the Risk of Childbearing among Metropolitan Black Adolescents," *American Sociological Review,* 63, 571–585.

Upchurch, D. M., & McCarthy, J. F. (1990). "The Timing of a First Birth and High School Completion, *American Sociological Review,* 55, 224–234.

U.S. Census Bureau. (2002). "Profiles of Selected Social Characteristics: 2000." Retrieved June 30, 2002, from http://factfinder.census.

gov/servlet/QTTable?ds_name=ACS_C2SS_
EST_G00_QT02&_lang=en.

U.S. Department of Health and Human Services. (1998). "A National Strategy to Prevent Teen Pregnancy: Annual Report 1997–98." Retrieved March 21, 2001, from http://aspe.hhs.gov/hsp/teen/97-98rpt.htm.

Ventura, S. J., Mathews T. J., & Hamilton, B. E. (2001). "Births to Teenagers in the United States, 1940–2000," *National Vital Statistics Reports* (Vol. 49, no. 10). Hyattsville, MD: National Center for Health Statistics.

Ventura, S. J., Mosher, W. D., Curtin, S. C., Abma, J. C., Henshaw, S., & The Alan Guttmacher Institute. (2000). *Trends in Pregnancies and Pregnancy Rates by Outcome: Estimates for the United States, 1976–96* (Series 21, no. 31). Hyattsville, MD: National Center for Health Statistics.

"Volunteer Opportunities-Greater Boston." (2002). Retrieved June 28, 2002, from www.volunteersolutions.org/boston/volunteer/agency/one_165960.html.

Walter, H. J. (2001). "School-Based Prevention of Problem Behaviors," *Child and Adolescent Psychiatric Clinics of North America,* Special Issue, 10(1), 117–127.

Whitehead, B. D., Wilcox, B. L., Rotosky, S. S., Randall, B., & Wright, M. L. C. (2001). *Keeping the Faith: The Role of Religion and Faith Communities in Preventing Teen Pregnancy.* Washington, DC: National Campaign to Prevent Teen Pregnancy.

Williams, C. W. (1991). *Black Teenage Mothers: Pregnancy and Child Rearing from Their Perspective.* Lexington, MA: Lexington Books.

Zabin, L. S., Hirsch, M. B., Smith, E. A., Street, R., & Hardy, J. B. (1996). "Evaluation of a Pregnancy Prevention Program for Urban Teenagers," *Family Planning Perspectives,* 18(3), 119–126.

11 Children in Family Foster Care

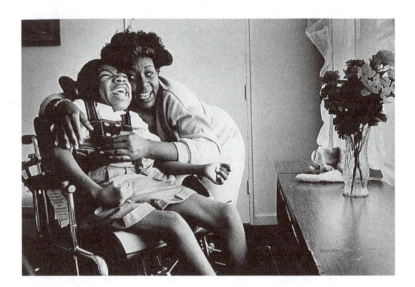

Riki was 6 years old when her father abandoned the family. Even at that age, Riki knew that her father sold drugs and that he had had to leave before the police found him. Her mother, an addict, was usually too strung out to care for her daughter. A younger child had died several years earlier and it was only because the family fled that Riki had not been removed by Child Protective Services (CPS). Mother and daughter drifted from place to place until they found themselves in the home of a man her mother knew. Riki begged to go to school and finally they agreed to send her. But the school recognized that the child was ill-kept and poorly fed. They became concerned that she was overtired and that she had lice. The school's report to the CPS initiated an investigation and resulted in Riki's removal from her home. At age 6½ , Riki found herself in a new home—a foster home—with three new siblings and a mother and father who appeared to care about her. Although she missed her mother, it was kind of nice to be warm in her own bed instead of wondering where they would sleep or where the next meal would come from.

Child welfare advocates attest to the fact that the best environment for a child, especially a young one, who cannot be maintained in his or her own home, is another family setting. Although some children cannot tolerate a family atmosphere once their own has failed them, many do well in family foster care.

History of Family Foster Care

Early Beginnings

To better understand foster care today, we need to look at the origins of the foster care system. From ancient times, it was expected that children would be attached to and part of a family. Without a family, children became a problem to society. If these children could not be taken in by relatives, another solution had to be found. Indenture was a popular method of providing for children, but it was not always a solution, especially with very young children who were not of an age to work. Institutions such as almshouses were often the solution for poor children, much to the detriment of their health and safety.

In the early 1800s, Charles Loring Brace became concerned about the children abandoned in institutions and on the streets of New York. In 1853, he and a group of New York City clergymen founded the New York Children's Aid Society, designed to advocate for and solve the problem of dependent children. Brace initiated a program of transporting children from the city to farm families in the middle United States. His plan involved sending small groups of children—40 to 100 per trip—by train accompanied by "agents" (nurses and social workers) to preselected spots in the rural Midwest. These children, who soon became known as "train orphans," would be greeted at the train station by families interested in caring for them. Later, churches became involved and would preselect families before the trains arrived. This practice, called *placing out,* lasted well into the 1920s (Cook, 1995; Hacsi, 1995).

Other agencies besides Brace's adopted the practice of placing out. One woman, abandoned at the New York Foundling's Hospital in the early 1920s, recounts her experience as part of an orphan train:

> *By the time I rode the train out to Nebraska, in 1923, you knew where you were going to. I was 22 months old and wore a sign with my birth name on it and the name of the family who expected me. Years earlier, my parents told*

me later, children used to be dropped off at stations and lined up for people to pick up which one they wanted.

My Mother and Father told me that a priest had announced in church some months before that an orphan train was coming. If anyone wanted a child, they were to tell the priest. My folks had lost six of their own children and had a boy of 19. To them, a girl sounded ideal. We arrived all dressed in white. I later learned that the clothes were made of bed sheets. A nurse handed me to my new parents and that was that.

For some children, the experience was a positive one. Some were adopted while others remained in an early form of foster care. From 1853 to 1929, 31,081 children were placed in families through the orphan trains (Thurston, 1930, 121).

Support for the concept of foster care became stronger in the 1890s when Homer Folks, also of New York City, extolled the virtues and importance of family life for children. It was Charles Britwell of the Children's Aid Society of Boston who instituted the concept of supervised boarding homes instead of orphan asylums. These homes were initially developed with the idea of rescuing "good" children from "bad" parents. Initially it took no more than a willingness to do so for parents to foster children. Not until the 1930s were foster parents assessed for their suitability for caring for children (Carp, 1998; Holody, 1998).

Early foster homes did not expect payment for the children they housed. Agencies advocating foster care argued that payment for foster care might cause them to take children for money rather than goodwill. Later, however, in the early 1900s, the practice of paying foster parents evolved. It wasn't until the twentieth century that the government became involved in regulating and administering the foster care system (Hacsi, 1995).

Over the years, foster care became an increasingly acceptable method of caring for children whose parents were unable to do so. Voluntary placement by parents, who recognized their inabilities or who sought a place for their children while they underwent a period of treatment or looking for employment or housing, became more widely practiced. Infants awaiting adoption were often placed in foster homes pending their placement.

Foster Care in Recent Years

After World War II, the complexion of foster care changed considerably. With the advent of more resources within the community, families who had placed their children while they recovered from illness, received treatments, or solved financial problems were less dependent on foster care. Increasingly, newborn infants were placed in adoptive homes directly from the hospital. With the advent of the Aid to Families with Dependent Children (AFDC) program, impoverished families who might have previously had to place children in asylums or homes were able to maintain them at home. By the 1950s, more of the children not residing in their own homes were in foster care rather than institutions. These figures increased until the late 1960s, when three times as many children in care were in foster homes. Subsequent amendments to the Social Security Act made more federal monies available to support the practice of foster care (Holody, 1998; Hacsi, 1995).

By the 1970s, the trend in child welfare became *permanency planning* (see Chapter 8). The move toward permanency planning was the result of several studies that found that children placed in foster care remained there, in virtual limbo, for years.

With the emphasis on permanency planning, the mandate of child welfare agencies was to ensure that a child who could not remain at home was placed with a permanent family as soon as possible. But continued research brought attention to the effect that separation had on children. The Indian Child Welfare Act in 1978 and Adoption Assistance and Child Welfare Act of 1980 both sought to place emphasis first on the preservation of the child's biological family. *Family preservation* became the new phrase in the practice of child welfare. Now efforts were made to save the family unit with a variety of services and resources so that the children would not be subjected to the pain of separation. It soon became obvious that, with the advent of such problems as drug addiction, homelessness, and HIV/AIDS, it was not always possible to save the original family unit. By the 1990s, the numbers of children placed in foster care began to increase again.

Today, the emphasis is on family continuity or attempting to strengthen or preserve the family unit while recognizing that foster care may be a necessary alternative. Increasingly, there has also been an effort to assess the availability of kinship care, or the placing of children with the relatives of their natural parents. This practice may also serve to acknowledge and preserve important cultural connections for the children. However, we must see foster care as only one option in the effort to protect the best interests of the children in our society.

The Nature of Foster Care Today

At the end of 1999, approximately 581,000 children lived in out-of-home care, including foster care, kinship care, or residential care. Of these, 274,100 were placed in licensed nonrelative foster homes (U.S. Department of Health and Human Services, 2001).

The intent of foster care is to offer children care within a family environment when their own homes are temporarily unable to do so. When their own extended family is not able to provide a home for them, foster care is the next option. Foster care is meant to provide the following:

- Temporary emergency care of a child
- Relief for a parent when he or she cannot manage stress
- Time for a parent to solve problems (e.g., housing, addiction, illness)
- A different home experience or protection for a child (in case of abuse, neglect, or extreme instability)

- Care until institutional treatment is available
- Care until release for adoption, or adoption, is approved

The National Commission on Family Foster Care (NCFFC, 1991) suggests that family foster care must fulfill five critical tasks:

1. *Protecting and nurturing infants, children and youth;*
2. *Ameliorating developmental delays and meeting social, emotional, and medical needs resulting from physical abuse, sexual abuse, neglect, maltreatment, exposure to alcohol and other drugs, and HIV infection;*
3. *Enhancing positive self-esteem, family relationships, and cultural and ethnic identity;*
4. *Developing and implementing a plan for permanence; and*
5. *Educating and socializing children and youth toward successful transitions to young adult life, relationships, and responsibilities. (36)*

Foster care may be voluntary or at the request of the parent. This written agreement between the parent and the agency may be terminated on either's request. In most instances, however, foster care is mandated by the situation involved, whether it be the parents' abuse or neglect of children or another type of inability to care for them.

Types of Foster Homes

There are several types of nonrelative foster homes, designated by their various functions: crisis or emergency foster homes, family boarding homes, small group homes, and specialized foster homes. Some states use homes interchangeably, whereas others clearly define the role of the home for one particular service.

The *crisis home* is designed to accept children at any time—day or night—and to keep them for a limited amount of time while other arrangements are being made. For example, children who have been abandoned may be placed in a home temporarily while their parents are found. Or parents who must undergo short-term medical or rehabilitation treatment may require an emergency home for their children. In some situations, the risk of severe abuse necessitates that children be placed on a short-term basis until protective services workers can diffuse the situation. Foster parents who operate emergency homes may require specialized skills. Sometimes this short respite care is used for diagnostic purposes, and it is important that foster parents have a keen awareness of crisis intervention skills. Not all foster parents are trained in these skills, however, and it may actually make their jobs more difficult. Crisis homes, like all foster homes, are paid for the care of children. Sometimes the rate reflects their crisis status or the specialized training some foster parents have received. In other states these foster parents are paid at the same rate as long-term boarding homes.

Family boarding homes are committed to taking children for longer periods— months or even years. Foster parents are expected to work as part of the therapeutic team overseeing the needs of the children in their care. For this, they are usually paid according to the numbers and ages of the children in their care. The amount differs from state to state. In addition, children usually receive a clothing allowance and some kind of medical benefits such as Medicaid. A *small group home* is a family that takes small groups of children—often siblings or adolescents. The home may be administered like a boarding home or a specialized foster home.

An emerging concept in the area of foster care is the *specialized foster home.* Such homes are set up to deal specifically with certain populations of children or for one or two particular children. For example, some foster parents have skills in dealing with adolescents, or with sexually abused children, or with children who are HIV-positive. As a specialized home, these parents take only these types of children. The number of children in the home usually depends on the need as well as the particular population. Theoretically, these specialized foster parents are better trained, receive more support, and are better paid than the average foster home.

The term *specialized* can also refer to foster parents who are screened by the placement agency and have been approved for a specific child or children. For example, if an adolescent runs away to the home of a friend, the friend's parents might be screened by the agency involved in the case as potential foster parents for this child. Or a teacher who befriends a child who must be placed outside of his or her home might request approval as a special foster home.

Kinship care is another type of fostering arrangement that reflects the increasing awareness that the trauma of placement may be minimized if children can be placed with extended family members. Kinship care refers to the caring for children by a relative, close family friend, godparents, or other tribe or clan member when the children's parents are unable to perform this task (Hegar and Scannapieco, 1999). Popular in the African American community for centuries, this practice has now become an option for other cultures as well. An exploratory study of kinship homes in New York City in 1996 found that only 10% were African American, whereas 70% were white protestant (Gebel, 1996, 5). In addition to continuity, kinship placements offer children an opportunity to remain within their own cultural/ethnic group. These homes are also less likely than nonrelated placements to be disrupted, and they are more likely to keep the children until they reach majority. An estimated 88% of children in kinship care left to live on their own, compared with 1% who returned to their parents and 10% who were placed for adoption, contrasted with 42% of the children in nonrelated homes who left for independent living, 14% who returned to their parents, and 38% who were placed in adoptive homes (NCFFC, 1991).

The purpose of kinship homes differs slightly from traditional foster homes. Although most foster homes provide substitute care, kinship placements also allow for some degree of family preservation when the children are kept with relatives (Hegar and Scannapieco, 1999).

Although kinship care has become increasingly popular, some child advocates are concerned that the quality of care in these untrained homes be maintained. Answering these concerns, the Child Welfare League Kinship Care Policy and Practice Committee (CWLA, 1994) recommended that several factors be considered in the assessment of such homes:

1. *The nature and quality of the relationship between the child and the relative;*
2. *The ability and the desire of the kinship parent to protect the child from further abuse and maltreatment;*
3. *The safety of the kinship home and the ability of the kin to provide a nurturing environment for the child;*
4. *The willingness of the kinship family to accept the child into the home;*
5. *The ability of the kinship parent to meet the developmental needs of the child;*
6. *The nature and quality of the relationship between the birth parent and the relative, including the birth parent's preference about placement of the child with kin;*
7. *Any family dynamics in the kinship home related to the abuse or neglect of the child;*
8. *The presence of alcohol or other drug involvement in the kinship home. (44–45)*

Increasingly, there is a move toward licensing kinship homes, raising the question of whether the same standards should be applied to these homes as to other types of foster homes (see Hegar and Scannapieco, 1999).

Foster homes are funded in a variety of ways. The majority of foster homes are state or countyfunded, either directly or through contracts. Most state or county protective services agencies maintain a number of foster homes that they study, approve, pay, and supervise. In other instances, privately funded agencies approve foster homes that they agree to let state agencies use for a contracted fee.

Reasons Children Come into Foster Care

Today, most of the children who come into foster care have parents who are not able to care for them for one reason or another. At one time, however, it was not unusual for children to be placed when their parents had died.

In other instances, one parent died and the other felt too overwhelmed to take on the role of parenting. One former foster child has this story to tell:

> *We were very, very poor. My mother, who was very small, was told not to have more children after her first five. She had a bad heart. But she continued to have them feeling that it was her duty as a good Catholic. She had five more, but during the birth of the last one, she had a heart attack. My father was left with ten children. He became an alcoholic and put us all into foster care, but he would never release us, so we just grew up in foster homes.*

Today, more effort would be expended to help children find relatives who could assume their care.

A large number of children come into care because they are *abused or neglected.* Chapter 7 outlines in depth how children are placed in foster homes as a result of abuse and neglect. Usually foster care serves as a way to protect them from continued abuse. In some instances, they will return to their parents. In others, they will be released for and placed for adoption. Children who come into care as a result of maltreatment often exhibit behavior that is reactive to their abuse. Increasingly, foster parents are trained to recognize and help them with a variety of reactions and disturbances. Sometimes the abuse cannot be clearly pinpointed but it becomes obvious that the child's home is dysfunctional, such as in the following:

> *I saw my mother really torn between two men. She'd married one but she still loved her ex-husband. She used to flip back and forth between them. I was 15 and desperate for stability. I had a boyfriend and was an honor student in school. But when we began all these moves, sometimes six times a month, my school work began to suffer. If my school records were anywhere, they were in the mail. I wanted to run away. I thought of suicide. I finally attempted it and the school called Protective Services. They knew I was really unhappy with all the moves. Because my mother was into drugs and alcohol, they put me in a foster home. It was really better. I had stability and I got to finish school.*

Increasingly, families are being seen with histories of *domestic violence.* When a parent is being battered, the children often suffer as well. While agencies first attempt to work with the family to stop the violence, it is often impossible. If the battered parent will not leave, the children are sometimes removed and placed in foster care to protect them.

Substance abuse is a phenomenon that destroys many families today. Children of substance-abusing parents may come into care voluntarily or through court mandate. Some parents recognize their need for drug rehabilitation and request voluntary foster care while in a program, or children may be addicted to drugs and automatically taken into care as a result. For many other families, substance abuse results in their maltreatment of their children. Child welfare systems are reporting an increase of 50 to 80% in the number of substance-abusing (mostly drugs) parents on social workers' caseloads (Solomon, 1990, 24). Many of these children will end up being placed in foster homes.

Physical and mental illnesses are often a factor in the families of children who come into foster care. Parents who find themselves facing operations and who have no other resources may request foster care.

CASE EXAMPLE

Doreen

Doreen discovered that she had uterine cancer, but that the prognosis was good if she could be operated on immediately. She had no family in the area and no friends able to care for her daughter. She requested that her daughter be placed in foster care while she had her operation and got back on her feet.

Such a request would be considered carefully. Being placed in the home of strangers could compound a young child's trauma in the face of a parent's illness. If children are placed too early or too often, they may fail to attach to their caregivers (Levy and Orlans, 1998). Because one of a child's most profound fears is abandonment, and separation can have a profound effect on children, all avenues other than placement must be explored. In Doreen's case, foster care was the only alternative, but sensitive preparation of the child enabled the plan to work.

Throughout the years, mental illness has had a more significant impact on the need to place children in foster homes than physical illness. Although mentally ill parents still need placement for their children during periods of acute crisis, there have been changes in the provision of long-term mental health services that have had an impact on how long children remain in care. Prior to the 1970s, the chronically mentally ill were treated in institutionalized settings. Today, with the implementation of community-based treatment, whereby people live in the community and are seen on an outpatient basis with counseling and support, more mentally ill parents care for their own children.

Today, some children are given up for foster care or adoption due to *their own physical or mental problems*. Increasingly, children who are HIV-positive are coming into foster care. Their parents, usually with AIDS themselves, are either unable to care for them or feel that they would have a better chance in placement. Coping with children with particular disabilities, such as cerebral palsy, mental retardation, brain damage, attention deficit disorder, or autism, may be beyond the skills of some parents. As a result, these children may be placed in foster care.

Mothers or single fathers who are incarcerated may also have a right to have their children in foster care. Usually, other relatives are sought who can assume this responsibility, but if no one is available, foster care may be the answer.

Over the years, children have sometimes been placed in foster care due to their parents' *inability to provide adequate housing*. Fortunately, this practice is now discouraged due to the reports of several studies that found that, under subsidized housing, the monthly rental assistance for a family of four is about $482 (although it varies from state to state) (U.S. Department of Housing and Urban Development, 1999), while the monthly foster care maintenance payment for just one child ranges from $356 for 2-year-olds to $431 for children of age 16 (APWA, 1998). In addition, it is better for children to remain with their own families whenever possible. For this reason, social service agencies now make a concerted effort to find housing for intact families rather than placing children in foster care.

Finally, foster care may be an *interim arrangement* while a child awaits an adoptive home or placement in a residential setting. Either parents wanting to give up their children for adoption may need a period to decide if this is the right course or an agency may need time to find the appropriate home. By the same token, children who are slated to be placed in a residence may find that there are no beds open at a given time, or that the agency placing them needs time to find the appropriate setting. In these situations, a child may be placed in foster care for days, weeks, or even months.

Foster Parents

Foster parenting is not the relatively uncomplicated task that it once was. Today, it is expected that foster parents will be part of the therapeutic team involved in children's lives. This task requires new responsibilities and brings with it many stressors. Agencies differ in their recruitment, training, and involvement of foster parents, but some standards can be found throughout the field.

Recruitment

Foster parents are recruited to their job in a variety of ways. Public service announcements, newspaper ads, television spots, and personal contacts represent some methods. Which means are most effective is a much-debated question.

A Minnesota study found that the media was an extremely effective tool for recruiting. Through a series of public service announcements and newspaper ads, the agency studied received more foster parent applicants than by the use of any other method. Television public service announcements seemed to yield an especially high number of much-needed African American applicants (Moore et al., 1988). One problem with media recruitment is that many of the applicants who respond may not actually have the necessary qualities to become foster parents. One recruiter remarked, "The media often appeals to the soft-hearted, and a soft heart doesn't help one through the real world of foster parenting. Foster parents must mix caring for kids with realistic expectations of kids who are often reacting to tough lives. They must also refine their parenting skills beyond those expected of most parents." Critics of the Minnesota method argued that the agency wasted valuable time screening out inappropriate homes. Yet, the results of the study did prove that the number of acceptable foster homes increased significantly (Moore et al., 1988).

Some agencies use trained foster parents to recruit others. Initially, these recruiters began in their own neighborhoods. Each recruiter was helped to develop a unique plan designed for his or her own environment. Agency social workers provided support, coordination, and supervision. As an additional incentive, the foster parent recruiters may be paid for each family they recruit. Agencies using recruiters encourage them to evaluate agency policy. For example, if applicants dropped out of the process of being studied because of some restrictive agency policy, the recruiter was asked to report it. The agency will then try to remedy this situation. Throughout the process of application and selection to become foster parents, these recruits are followed closely by agency social workers.

Terpstra (personal communication, 1990), foster care specialist for the Bureau for Children, commented regarding recruitment "In the long haul, the most effective recruitment is foster parents who are satisfied with agency services. This is often apart from any specific recruitment effort: word of mouth reports tend to be viewed as most credible."

Why do people want to become foster parents? Reasons vary from the altruistic motivation of identifying with unhappy children and wanting to provide a community service, to the more individual motivations of wanting to continue to parent or wanting a playmate for their own children. Increasingly, agencies are encouraging potential foster parents to assess their own motivations and determine how realistic they are.

In predicting the success of parents' ability to provide foster care, several authors (Fine, 1993; Walsh and Walsh, 1990) found that successful foster parents had a sincere liking for children and a strong sense of themselves and their own abilities, and were able to put up with a variety of behaviors from children that some other homes might find difficult to tolerate.

The shortage of foster homes, particularly for specific ethnic groups, necessitates that agencies look closer at recruiting foster homes from the children's own families or informal networks, referred to earlier as *kinship care*. In the past, there was some resistance to the extensive use of kinship care for several reasons. First, if natural parents abused or neglected a child, their relatives may also behave in similar ways. Yet, what drives one individual to abuse may not affect his kin in the same manner. A second issue is that children's relatives might be less easy to locate, thus requiring more social worker energy for recruitment. Yet, using relatives can be more beneficial for the child.

A third issue that tended to make agencies less likely to use informal support systems is the fact that parents considered for a particular child are less likely to see themselves as working for an agency. They are less aware of child welfare policies and may seem less interested in cooperating with agencies in the interest of the child. These same characteristics make the home a more natural atmosphere for the child, but may present difficulties for social workers who expect to have total cooperation from the foster parents.

There are significant advantages to kinship care, however. Placement with known relatives causes less trauma for children. Whereas unrelated foster homes have a median duration for one child of 6.5 months, kinship homes tend to last (median) 10.5 months. Certainly, homes studied for specific children have a greater commitment to those children, perhaps lessening the feelings of isolation described by many former foster children. It may be likely that these homes might also maintain the tie more closely with natural parents (Hegar and Scannapieco, 1999).

There are trade-offs for the advantages of kinship care from the standpoint of both the kin caregivers and the agency. If kin agree to take on the role of formal foster parenting for an agency, they will undoubtedly lose some of their autonomy—including compliance with state regulations governing sleeping arrangements, discipline methods, and other family matters. The financial benefits they receive may not compensate for their loss of privacy, the need to attend trainings, and the necessity of having home visits by social work staff (Hegar and Scannapieco, 1999). Agencies interested in giving children the advantages that kinship care can provide must exercise more ingenuity. Not only must the child's informal networks be explored for potential homes, but these parents must be studied, trained, and supervised with the understanding that they may only be foster homes for a single child rather than the many children taken by professional foster homes. Yet the result—the child's well-being—would seem worth the effort. In this time of scarcity of foster homes, this approach is also a way of increasing foster care resources.

Homestudy and Training

Once recruited, potential foster parents undergo a lengthy process of screening, selection, and training, known as a *homestudy*. At one time, this homestudy was an individual affair between the foster parents and the social worker, known as a *homefinder* or *family resource specialist*. Now, however, most agencies favor a group approach. One reason for this is that the current emphasis is on foster parents as part of a team that strives to ensure that the child is provided with the best plan possible. *A Blueprint for Fostering Infants, Children, and Youths in the Nineties* (National Commission on Family Foster Care, 1991) was the Child Welfare League of America's effort to outline the new role of foster parents as team members. With this new emphasis came revised training for potential foster parents. These trainings are based on a variety of models.

The Model Approach to Partnerships in Parenting (MAPP) has been adopted in numerous states and combines screening with intensive training for future foster parents. One Massachusetts family resource worker described their program: "Our training is completed in ten sessions. We explain to our group participants at the onset that foster parents need three things: certain information, attitudes, and skills that will enable them to be good at their job. Some people develop the attitudes and skills as they go through life and bring them to the group. Other people will learn them through the ten weeks of the group process. We, as facilitators, reserve the right to discuss with the applicants at the end of training whether we feel that they have the information, attitudes, and skills that our agency has found are needed by foster parents."

Similar curricula are used by other states or agencies as part of their training efforts.

Whatever model the agency uses, through a combination of providing information, role-play, exercises, and discussion, it encourages applicants to explore their attitudes toward discipline, natural parents, loss and separation, how their own children might react to sharing their parents, the behaviors exhibited by children in foster care, and a variety of other topics relevant to parenting a foster child successfully. Participants also discuss feelings about their own upbringing, and how their pasts, or realizations about their pasts, help or hinder them in their role as parents. The social workers visit the families in their homes to determine how their thinking has evolved.

Not all applicants who begin the training finish. Some learn that foster parenting is not what they had hoped for. Others drop out for other reasons, such as the following: "I dropped out of the homestudy because I learned that I had a great deal of emotional housecleaning to do before I could be comfortable parenting someone else's kids. When I applied to be a foster parent I imagined saving poor little kids from abusing parents. Now I realize that part of a foster parent's job is to work with those same parents and I am not sure I could do that."

In addition to being studied, trained, and selected, foster parents must be licensed. Many states include the licensing process as a part of the homestudy. Other states have an independent process. Basically, a license will mean that the family and their home have passed specific requirements, such as fire safety, health safety, cleanliness, and so forth. Potential foster parents are expected to have a physical exam and also to undergo a criminal records check. It is certainly possible for a family to meet licensing criteria, but not be approved by a homefinder because of their emotional instability or lack of readiness. The reverse is also possible.

Although the preceding is the typical plan for recruiting, screening, and training foster parents, agencies recognize the need for flexibility, given the diverse cultural differences in the children in foster care today and the families who apply to take them in as foster children. The importance of training workers to understand ethnic and cultural variations so as not to fit families into a particular mindset cannot be understated.

Once foster parents have been approved to take children, their file is kept until a child needs such a home. The amount of matching done between child needs and foster parent characteristics differs from state to state, but studies show that the more these factors are taken into consideration, the more successful the placement. Given the shortage of foster homes, however, foster parents are often asked to take children who do not fit the age-range or type of child they feel equipped to handle. This may not be beneficial for the child or the foster parents.

Placement and Follow-Up

When a child needs a particular type of foster home, the foster family is approached about taking him or her. The placement process can take as much as a week but more likely happens very quickly. "When I go into court on a particular abuse case," said one social worker, "I know that I may need to place the child immediately after the hearing. I line up a home that will be ready to take the child. It doesn't give the foster family much time to prepare but that is the way the system works."

Once children are in foster placement, they are visited on a regular basis by an agency social worker to provide support and monitor the placement. Foster families provide ongoing care and may also be responsible for such extras as transportation to medical appointments, therapy visits, or even visits with the child's parents. If parents are allowed to visit in the foster home, the foster parents may also supervise these arrangements. Further, foster families are included in periodic case conferences to assess the progress of the child and the family. For these services, they are paid a small foster care allowance and often a sum for clothing for the children in their care.

Although it is the foster mother who usually shoulders the major part of the responsibility for caregiving and dealing with the social service agency, the role of the foster father cannot be underestimated. The support he provides his wife can make a real difference in the success of the care. If foster children are truly to be part of the family, their involvement with the foster father is equally as important as their involvement with the mother.

The inclusion of foster parents on the therapeutic team is a continually evolving concept. At one time foster parents were seen as mere caregivers, but they are now expected to be part of the child's treatment. Some agencies, such as the Casey Foundation, use highly trained foster parents for intense thera-peutic services. Other agencies provide ongoing training and even special cer-tification for foster parents. Certified foster parents receive higher rates of payment for their services and describe feeling more competent and able to handle the problems presented by their charges.

Stresses of Being a Foster Parent

Foster parenting comes with many stressors. First and foremost is the fact that foster care is designed to be temporary. Thus, foster parents are asked to love children in their care but then to *be ready to let them go.* How well they have been able to handle the losses in their own lives may determine how successful they are at letting go and preparing their foster children for return home or adoptive placement.

Foster parents are also asked to *handle a variety of behaviors* exhibited by the children who come into their care. These children may be withdrawn, be de-structive, abuse others, set fires, or act out in a variety of ways. Foster parents are expected to consider the underlying causes as opposed to just reacting to the be-havior. In the crunch of everyday activities, this may not always be easy. It is also not unusual for children whose early relationships have been problematic or traumatically terminated to have experienced disrupted attachment. These chil-dren may now have difficulty forming any type of new relationships.

It may be a challenge for the foster parents to *provide foster care while still con-sidering the needs of their own family members.* The foster parents' own children may not always understand the needs of the children in care. Or they may mimic behaviors that their parents do not appreciate. Foster couples find that they need to pay careful attention to their own relationships lest the stresses of having foster children alienate them from one another. Dedicated foster parents tell us that none of these tasks are easy and that they must be constantly aware of the dynamics of their own families.

It is also not easy to have one's parenting techniques under constant scrutiny. Providing care for someone else's child under agency supervision may make people feel that *they are constantly under observation.* In addition, each social worker has his or her own method of supervision, and foster parents sometimes feel that they cannot please anyone. More experienced foster parents learn to develop a personal style that will help them weather the *turnover of social work staff.*

In addition to agency scrutiny, foster parents may feel that they are being criticized by the natural parents. But this too must be understood. As one foster mother commented, "It must not be an easy thing to have your children taken away from you. It's like a judgment that says "You weren't a good enough parent." So, if you see someone else taking care of your children, it is just human nature to want to find fault with them. I try to understand how hurt these parents must feel and it helps when I feel criticized by them."

Visits by natural parents may not always be easy on foster parents. Not only can foster parents feel criticized, but they may have to deal with birth parents who abuse alcohol or drugs. Or the visit by a natural parent may send the foster child into crisis. Foster mothers often describe the conflict felt by foster children about separation from their parents and the reactions exhibited by children after each visit. Once again, foster parents are expected to understand these problems and deal effectively with natural parents.

Foster Parents as Part of the Team

With the number of profoundly disturbed children coming into foster care, more and more is expected of foster parents. Many states require foster parents to seek out or participate in ongoing training. Foster parents are often asked to observe, monitor, and record the behavior of the children in their care. They are asked to participate in foster care reviews not only as advocates for their foster children but also as professionals with vital pieces of information to contribute to an overall assessment of the child(ren).

It is not unusual for foster parents to be asked to help natural parents by providing role models or aiding them in the understanding of their children or such parenting skills as behavior management, discipline, and the management of challenging health care issues.

CASE EXAMPLE

Demetrius

Demetrius was a 5-year-old child whose medical problems necessitated that he have a colostomy. The bag that collected his urine had to be changed regularly and the medical incision cleaned properly. Although well meaning, Demetrius's mother had failed to complete these procedures properly. In fact, she was totally overwhelmed by the magnitude of his care. Feeling unable to cope after a drinking binge, she left her child with a neighbor and disappeared. After a week, she missed him and felt very guilty for having abandoned him. She called the neighbor who told her that she had had no idea how to care for the child's medical needs and had taken him to the hospital and explained that his mother had abandoned him. The hospital called CPS and Demetrius was placed in a foster home with a foster mother who was a nurse.

After talking with the boy's mother, CPS became convinced that she could care for her child if educated to do so. Thus, for the next three months, the mother visited the foster home and received intensive training from the foster mother on how to care for Demetrius.

In this situation, it was the skill of the foster mother that provided the needed therapeutic intervention that allowed Demetrius to eventually return home.

As foster parents become more involved as members of the therapeutic team, there is more pressure on agencies to change the attitudes that formerly saw these parents as merely caregivers of children. There is also an increased emphasis on more intensive training opportunities.

Birth Parents with Children in Foster Care

The characteristics of parents whose children are in foster care are included in various chapters throughout this text. When we are caught up in protecting children form maltreatment and improper care, it is not always easy to recognize the impact that placement has on the birth parents.

Attitudes and Reactions

Our society communicates the message that anyone can parent. Having children is something that most people expect to be able to do. There are no directions provided for the important role of parent, and unless individuals have had role models in their own parents, they may have no concept of what parenting is all about. Yet, this lack of knowledge can remain a carefully hidden secret until society, in the guise of CPS, intervenes and removes the children because they are being inadequately parented. Or, in some cases, parents are forced to place their children because life circumstances interfere with their ability to parent. Imagine the resentment, no matter how aware you may be of your inabilities, should your children require the care of someone else, often a stranger. Parents often go through a variety of feelings. The first may be *shock*.

Although some may protest that it should be obvious to some parents why they lost their children, the feelings are not diminished. "When my kids were taken away," says one parent, "I just couldn't believe it. I knew I had been drinking a lot and I know I left them alone overnight, but I still loved them. It's just that no one ever told me that it would be so tough to take care of kids! As I sat in that apartment after they were gone, I just stared at the walls. I kept thinking I heard them. No, it wasn't them—just the unbearable silence. I hated myself then. I hated the drinking and drugging. I hated everything. But I missed my kids!"

When parents come out of the shock, they may feel *resentful and angry.* These feelings are often masks for their *feelings of failure* because they have not been able to do what, it seems to them, every other parent in the world does—care for their children. This may lead to *feelings of inadequacy* that may manifest themselves in a variety of ways (Plumer, 1992; Rutter, 1989). The manner in which parents demonstrate these feelings of inadequacy may differ. Some parents eat more, drink or drug more, or act out in other ways.

There may also be cultural reasons for how they react. For example, some cultures become extremely hostile and threatening. Still others protest with silence.

CASE EXAMPLE

Poppi

Poppi was a 34-year-old African American mother whose children were removed after she neglected them. Although she sincerely loved her children, her drinking had created problems for her in caring for them. When they were removed, she was very angry and depressed. The social workers told her that there were numerous things she had to do to have them returned. Feeling that she could never please what she referred to as "them nigger hatin' child stealers," Poppi refused to respond to phone calls or attempts on the part of CPS workers to visit her. Unfortunately, this was interpreted by the workers as this mother's lack of interest in her children.

Many natural parents get stuck in the anger stage. It is easier to be angry than to acknowledge the hurt. Unfortunately, some social workers react to the angry behavior rather than recognize the feeling beneath it. Parental rights may actually be terminated if the parents cannot move beyond the anger stage and the desire to strike out long enough to cooperate with the agency. It is often forgotten that people who lose their children due to their inability to effectively parent have usually faced failure, betrayal, and disappointment throughout their lives. The coping patterns they have developed may not seem appropriate, but for some the anger or withdrawal has enabled them to survive.

Parents who give up their anger often go into *despair.* They become depressed and unmotivated. Nothing seems worth doing. For some, there may also be *feelings of relief* that there are no children at home to force them to do daily tasks. Some parents reach out to social workers or foster parents. But many, from troubled backgrounds themselves, cannot trust others to this degree and turn inward. Again, their lack of energy and motivation is often interpreted by social service personnel as a lack of caring.

Due to feelings of inadequacy, some parents search for ways in which the present caregivers are also inadequate. Birth parents who visit their children in foster homes may look for ways to criticize foster parents. It may be difficult for the foster parent to remain sympathetic to the loss the birth parents have experienced, but for the child's sake, it is important that relations remain harmonious.

Certainly, some birth parents are able to adjust to their children's placement in foster care and can work in cooperation with the agency involved to secure the return of their children.

Rights and Responsibilities of Birth Parents

While their children are in foster care, and especially if the plan is reunification of the family, birth parents are encouraged to visit their children. Traditionally, these visits have taken place in the foster home, although they may also be arranged at the agency. Some parents describe it as being very difficult to see their children for brief periods of time and then having to leave them again. As one parent put it:

> *You see your child in a home situation where everything is apparently orderly and calm, and, quite often, materially superior to anything you are going to be able to offer them, and you wonder why the hell you are bothering to rock the boat...maybe it would be better to leave your child there. It would be a lot less upsetting for everyone involved if you just drop out of the picture. (McAdams, 1972)*

But therapeutically it may be better for children to maintain contact with their birth parents than to cut all ties. Studies also show that children do better in foster care and are less likely to be damaged by separation if they are able to maintain contact with their natural parents.

In reality, natural parents should be considered as an integral part of the foster care team for several reasons: First, their involvement with the foster home helps the child's adjustment. Second, natural parent involvement may be therapeutic to these parents as well. Through modeling the parenting skills of the foster parents, they may recognize what their children need. And finally, if the children return home, the ongoing contact maintained between birth parents and children may smooth the return.

Certainly, not all natural parents end up being reunited with their children, nor should all continue to be involved with their children. But the fact is that natural parents who are encouraged to be involved with their children, while still held accountable, tend to make more effective progress toward reorganizing their lives and having their children returned.

What is meant by *parental involvement?* Parental involvement can refer to minimal contact of parents with their children in foster care. On the other end of the continuum is a more active role that may involve participation in goal setting, attending conferences and reviews concerning their children, and visiting and even caring for the children at the foster home or during extended home visits.

Natural parents are actually entitled to certain rights while their children are in foster care. Unless parental rights are terminated by the court, parents have a right to see the treatment plan (an outline of what is expected from them and what the agency will provide to them) and to attend all court hearings concerning their children. Whether parents exercise these rights depends on several issues, not the least of which is whether they have been informed by the agency of what these rights are. And even if parents are informed of their rights, they are not always able to act on them. Some parents are so angry that they refuse to cooperate, whereas others feel that nothing they do will make any difference.

When Children Return Home

Removing one individual from a family constellation shifts the balance of that family. Because a family is a system and all systems seek homeostasis, the family may rebalance itself without the missing member(s). Thus, when a child returns to a natural family, the transition may not always be smooth no matter how much it was anticipated by parents or children. Children will test limits. They will expect the old patterns to continue to exist and are confused when they do not. Parents who worked hard on their own issues may find that the added stress of the child's return brings up those issues again.

It is often careful reunification planning and implementation that makes the difference between a child's ability to reintegrate into the home and his or her returning to foster care.

Children in Foster Care

Feelings about Placement and Separation

When children are placed in foster care, they may not understand what is happening to them. For children, separation evokes many different feelings. For most, there are *feelings of sadness*. No matter what the experiences they have had there, most children want to be at home. They may also feel *lonely and abandoned*. They may feel that they are unlovable, and if their parents "didn't want them," they wonder if anyone ever will. Feeling that they are somehow to blame for being taken from their parents, children often *feel guilty*. They wonder how they could have been so bad that their parents wanted to "get rid of them." Even if children are removed because of abuse or neglect, they may feel that their parents wanted them sent away (Stahl, 1990).

CASE EXAMPLE

Nicole

Nicole was 5 years old when she came into foster care. At age 12, she was still in a foster home, although she had been in seven since she first entered care. At first, her mother had visited but this had been short-lived. When Nicole talked about her life, she expressed resentment toward her parents for "dumping her." In reality, she had been removed from her mother's care due to severe neglect. Nicole also demonstrated what some foster children do—*hostility.* She was very angry and spat her words as she described how she felt about her mother.

The reality of being without birth families causes some children to *feel fear.* They wonder who will care for them and where they will live. And some children *feel shame*—shame at being a foster child; shame at having parents who, seemingly unlike other people's parents, cannot take care of them. And like their birth parents', children's feelings are often experienced in phases—shock, protest, despair, and detachment (Plumer, 1992).

Being with one's own parents seems like such a fundamental part of childhood that foster children begin to *wonder why they are different from other children.* But it is too threatening to attribute the blame to adults; the result is that children *internalize the guilt.* As one teen put it: "I used to lie in bed in my foster home and think about every lousy thing I had ever done when I was with my parents. It never occurred to me that the fact that both of my parents were drug addicts could have been the cause of my placement. I was convinced that if I had been good enough, they would have kept me." This feeling of being different and unworthy causes foster children to *devalue themselves.* For each child, these feelings of inferiority are expressed differently. Some children become withdrawn, compliant, and even self-abusive or suicidal; others act out in anger. A few are able to question the injustice of the fact that for their parents' problems they, the children, must leave home. Even if the child is able to recognize the injustice, there is not always a good explanation provided to them.

Some children may feel, in addition to the hurt and anger, a sense of *sadness.* A former foster child described this sadness in her life: "I think I did a lot of crying that people never knew about. I suppose I was scared. I never let my mother see me cry when she visited. I always felt that I had to be strong for her. I knew that she hadn't wanted us taken away but she just couldn't kick her problems long enough to take care of her kids. I cried alone in bed at night and just wished sometimes that the world would end."

Not only are children separated from their parents but they may also be separated from their siblings as well. For many who are taken into care with their siblings, their overwhelming desire is to protect younger brothers and sisters.

It is not unusual for older siblings to care for younger ones in dysfunctional families. Separation from each other may increase the impact of separation on both siblings. The caregiving role has given the older child a sense of purpose and even a feeling of some degree of control. This separation robs the older child of not just the home but of the responsible role he or she may have needed. Separation of siblings may also make the younger child feel more vulnerable and alone. Certainly there are exceptions, but for the most part, when siblings can be placed together, it may ease their transitions.

Feelings about Natural Parents

The ability of foster children to attach to their new caregivers is often related not only to their previous experiences with natural parents and how they separated from them but also to their contact and relationship with these parents while they are in foster care (Levy and Orlans, 1998). Although it might seem that the less contact with natural parents, the better the child's ability to adjust, this is not the case. In addition, the attempt of foster parents or agency personnel, however well-meaning, to discredit natural parents makes placement more difficult for the child. When foster parents convey that they do not approve of natural parents, it sets up conflicting loyalties for the child. As one former foster child explained, "My parents were part of me. I guess I knew that they would never get me back, but I needed closure, I guess. At first they visited and then they didn't, but it helped me to adjust. My foster parents were great about the visits. That was good because no matter what my parents had done to me, I cared about them. If anyone had knocked them, I would have felt that they were knocking me."

Some children, hurt by abuse at the hands of their birth parents, are angry and do not want contact. Although this is usually respected, the child may deal with this issue in later life.

Feelings about Foster Parents

The feelings that foster children have about their foster parents are varied. Some are hampered from their experiences at home so that they are unable to trust and bond with others. For them, the foster parents may seem like a threat or perhaps just someone else who has the potential of letting them down. Some learn from their foster families how to trust again. For young children, foster care may represent the first consistent care they have experienced.

Certainly the chemistry that affects any type of relationship is important in the bond or lack thereof between foster parents and foster children. Children who have had an abundance of foster homes recount that some "felt right" and some did not. Today foster parents are trained to understand what their charges are experiencing in the hope that the relationship can be as strong as possible.

Life in Foster Care

What is it like for a child who is residing in a home that was totally strange to him or her at placement? A former foster child recounted: "Every family has different rules—not just the spoken ones like when to come in at night or who takes out the trash. It's the unspoken rules that are hardest. For example, it may not seem like a big deal, but everyone sets the table somewhat differently. That shouldn't matter, but when you're new in the home and you're asked to set the table and you do it wrong, it can seem monumental. Like you have failed when you are really trying to fit in and please these people. It may sound silly, but when you don't have a home you can really call your own, it is important to fit in."

It is not only family rules, routines, and relationships that may be difficult for a foster child. There continues to be stigma attached to being "in care," and foster children can feel it profoundly. In school, children often feel like the "foster kids" and may perceive a separation from their classmates. They may also recognize that foster care is designed to be a temporary arrangement and wonder when they will be asked to move again. It is small wonder why permanency planning has been considered to be an important move in the provision of services to children (Plumer, 1992).

Leaving Foster Care

Children leave foster care for a variety of reasons. For some, their parents are able to readjust their lives and welcome their children home. Some foster children who are not able to adjust to a foster home move to institutions designed to cope with behavior that the foster home could not handle. But some children, though fewer in number in recent years, "age out" of foster care by turning age 18. There may be provisions for continuing the support of a child if he or she seeks more education or has a physical or mental disability, but for others, 18 is the cutoff age. After this, it remains the choice of the foster parents and the child as to how and if the relationship will continue.

When we think of living on our own, rarely do we consider all the implications of this independence. Our complex society mandates that we have specific skills and resources. Usually, children are prepared for independence by their parents, who then maintain ties with them to help them along the way. How many people can honestly say that they have not called their parents for extra money, for advice on budgeting, career choices, or moves, or for child care? For many people, their first apartment is furnished by excess or cast-off furniture, eating utensils, and dishes from the family household. But foster children do not have this luxury, nor have they been able to watch parents balance the checkbook or make everyday decisions. The responsibility for their emancipation education rests in the hands of their legal "parents," the state or county agency. Thus, programs have been set up to enable these foster children to develop the skills they need to leave care.

Canada's concerns for youths leaving care are much like those in the United States. In 1988, newly emancipated foster youth, Brian Raychaba, expressed his concerns for his Canadian peers in his book, *To Be on Our Own with No Direction from Home* (1988). The report, done for the National Youth in Care Network, was a culmination of Raychaba's research on youths who had recently left foster care. Raychaba pointed out that youths leaving care not only need practical information but they also require help in addressing their own personal needs. Abuse may have been part of their experience either prior to or during foster care, resulting in residual scars. Their years in foster care may have failed to address these issues and even possibly augmented them. When faced with emancipation, these issues of emotional conflict do not disappear.

Although preparation for leaving care is usually considered to be an orientation to independent living, Raychaba's study clearly attested to the fact that foster youths need a whole range of services. He recommends that a full assessment be made of the psychological, emotional, and health-related needs of each foster child about to leave care. Once these needs are identified, they can be more adequately addressed. The youths in Raychaba's study also felt the need for a "mentor" to follow them after care. Raychaba suggested that "after-care workers" or alumnae workers be created to carry a caseload of youths who are out of care but who are still resolving issues to help them to live more independently. The financial feasibility of such a plan might make it difficult to undertake, but it is clear that agencies need to pay even more attention to the needs of children who become independent after being in foster care.

Until not too long ago, the emancipation of youths from foster care was informal. During the Ninety-Ninth Congress, states were mandated under Title IV-E Foster Care Program to provide transitional living programs for foster children 16 years and older who were "aging out" of the foster care system. In June of 1999, additional legislation, the Foster Care Independence Act, was passed and doubled the funds previously available under Title IV-E. These funds increased from $1,000 to $10,000 the amount that foster children are allowed to have in savings or other assets while still being eligible for foster care. Further, the legislation enables states to provide funds for room and board and to extend Medicaid coverage for medical/mental health services to youths who are ages 18 to 21, have left foster care, and are living on their own. Training must also be provided to help foster parents, group care staff, and social workers to transition these youths into independent living (CWLA, 1999). Such steps to improve the future of foster children are much applauded by child welfare advocates.

The Role of the Foster Care Social Worker

> *Being a foster care caseworker demands intelligence, fairness, good judgment, empathy, and determination. The job entails being responsible for the safety of foster children, being the target of angry or bewildered biological parents, consoling confused or anxious children, and handling the demands and irritations of foster parents.... Endless reams of paperwork accompany all tasks. (Hubbell, 1981, 110)*

The description of the foster care worker has not changed much since Hubbell's description in 1981, except perhaps that the endless paperwork is now done on computer in many agencies. The foster care social worker enters the child's life during a troubled, volatile period and must assess the situation with understanding and expertise. Often, this worker makes the recommendation that leads to the decision to place a child in foster care. It may be that the foster care worker follows the child through foster care until either the child returns home or is placed for adoption or the worker leaves the unit or the agency. The latter often happens first. Every day, a social worker may witness pain and loss. And every day, the decision that the worker must make alone or in conjunction with his or her supervisor must be covered by an immense paper (or computer) trail of forms to document that decision. It is not surprising that workers can feel overwhelmed.

What exactly does a foster care worker's job entail? There are at least two and often three types of workers involved in foster care. The first, usually referred to as a *homefinder* or *family resource specialist,* recruits and assesses foster parents for approval (see the previous section on homestudy). Often, homefinders keep in touch with approved parents until they receive children. Sometimes these workers perform a supportive role to ensure some degree of continuity for the foster parents. The average day for a homefinder might be filled with group meetings with foster parents, home visits, case recording, or supportive counseling with foster parents. Group meetings necessitate a good deal of preparation, supervision, and consultation, which also takes time.

The foster care caseworker is responsible for *case management.* Some agencies use their protective services workers to monitor the homes in which they place children. Other agencies use protective services workers (see Chapter 7) to do intake and the placement of children and then transfer the case to a foster care worker for ongoing case management. While larger agencies use a variety of workers in various roles, smaller agencies might require a social worker to follow a case from start to finish. Both these models of service have advantages. Although fewer workers may provide more consistency and continuity of services, having multiple workers allows for specialization and fresher, more objective viewpoints.

The day of the case manager varies greatly, depending on what is happening in individual cases. One day might involve fairly leisurely, routine visits to foster homes or to schools to monitor a child's progress. Another day might be punctuated with the problems generated by a disrupted foster home or a foster child who has run away or acted out in some other way. Plans that have been made for a day might change with the needs of the children and the foster home.

Caseworkers work not only with natural parents and foster parents but also with foster children. One particularly difficult task is helping children sort out the feelings about the people in their lives. No matter what they have suffered in their natural homes, children have feelings for their parents. The social worker must be skilled in listening to children's feelings and in allowing them their ambivalence without being judgmental. Children must know that their parents' problems predated them. They must also be helped to deal with their disappointments when the hopes they have about being with their parents are not realized. One social worker stated, "It used to kill me every time we arranged for Jody's mother to visit her. The foster mother would get Jody all ready. I would prepare her emotionally for the visit and then we'd wait—and wait. Most of the time the mother never came. But we never knew, because sometimes she would come full of smiles and gifts and promises. But when she didn't come, I could feel Jody's pain. It hurt her so much that it hurt me too. So we'd talk about the hurt. No matter how angry I was at her mother, right then I had to remember that Jody loved her and that she was an important part of Jody's life."

Children may also feel torn by divided loyalties—loyalty on one hand to the parents they love and, on the other hand, to the foster parents with whom they live. It is the worker's role to accept that confusion and help children recognize that there is room for both in their lives.

Leaving a foster home or moving from one home to another can be a traumatic event for which children must be prepared. Not only must the foster care worker arrange for the logistical elements of any move, the children, foster parents, and often natural parents must also be prepared. Each individual must be helped to deal with the impending loss and guided through the grieving process following it. Counseling children around the time of the move becomes more intense and a social worker involved in several moves at one time can be constantly on call. If the children go to another foster home, the adjustment must be carefully monitored. If children return to their natural parents, supervision may be necessary to ensure that the reunification will be successful. And of course, every move must be documented by reams of paperwork. Forms authorize the payment of foster parents. Forms keep track of the children through the system. Forms open cases and close cases. As one social worker put it, "I felt as though I couldn't even breathe unless I did it in triplicate!"

Another important aspect of the role of the foster care worker, which often gets overlooked, is the need to do grief counseling with foster parents. Losing children to which one has become attached is not an easy task. In the past, agencies have not always recognized the need for foster parents to process their grief. Yet, the inability to grieve makes for difficulty with the next child and can hasten burnout for foster parents. Social workers now realize that it is important to do visits following the departure of children to enable foster parents to adjust.

Although not always an easy role, the job of the foster care case manager can have a great many rewards. Watching children gain stability and direction for their lives can be energizing. Seeing a child return home because of the effective casework done by the agency gives the worker a sense of accomplishment.

Yvonne Barry Cataldi, currently a professor in the field of Human Services, shares her experience of what it was like to be in foster care:

> I was a young adult, approximately 26 old, when I read my file and learned that I had been placed in foster care when I was 3 years old. This was quite a surprise to me. I remembered being in elementary school and being in foster care but nothing younger than that. Unfortunately, I also have no memory of a lot of the experience. I think that many foster children who have been in more

than one placement lose pieces of their memories. We often don't know things like what illnesses we had, what schools we went to, whether we were with our siblings or not. We wondered what had really happened to our parents. And little questions made us think. When did we lose the first tooth? Did anyone save it? Did we ever take music lessons or play sports? Were we good at some things? I have no answers to those questions. Most children have the oral tradition of their families to fill in gaps. I did not. I didn't even remember the names of the foster families who had sheltered me. Sometimes I recall faces, but I don't know if those faces had any significance in my life. Most of the time I felt like a "yoyo," repeatedly having to leave home and then come back.

I remember not wanting to go home sometimes and at other times wanting to return to my parents. These feelings often had more to do with the foster family I was with than my parents. When I was with the family who washed my sister's mouth out with soap, I wanted to return home. Often we were expected to be playmates for the foster parents' children even if we didn't like them. We had to adapt to the different ways people did things. I was told that I should feel "at home" when I didn't even know where the bathroom or the kitchen was. Sometimes it wasn't clear to me where I was expected to sleep. It certainly didn't feel like home and by the time it did, I was returned to my parents once again. No one ever asked me what I wanted. It just happened.

I do recall that the placements I was fondest of were the ones in which I was placed with other foster children, like in group foster homes. I finally felt like I fit in. There were others in the same boat and I felt that I fared well. The toughest placement was when I was separated from my sister because neither home had two beds available. I felt a tremendous loss being away from her. I was 13 and she was 12 and that was the last time we would ever be together. She died of cancer when she was 18 years old.

I finally did have a set of foster parents in a group home who are still in my life today. Their acceptance and compassion and understanding gave me a view of what family life really could be. I regarded their son as my "brother." When my mother was again discharged from the hospital, a worker finally asked me if I wanted to return. I said no. I liked where I was.

My sister and I talked about how unstable living with our mother was. When we finally had an opportunity to make some choices about where we lived, we were able to benefit from placement. It allowed us to begin to develop the skills we needed in order to become responsible, productive adults. I know that living with my family was not good for me, but parts of my experience in foster care had negatives, too. Once I had some choice, my view of foster care changed and I believe that I felt more positive about it.

The Future of Foster Care

The future trends in the provision of foster care services are influenced largely by the political climate in which those services will be provided.

Political Influences

Policies related to foster care are based primarily on four major laws enacted by Congress in the last 25 or so years. The Child Abuse Prevention and Treatment Act (PL 93-247), passed in 1974, changed the provision of services for children who were abused or neglected. In so doing, it influenced how alternative home care was provided for them. The Indian Child Welfare Act (PL 95-608) of 1978 mandated that more concern be given to the placement of Native American children when foster care was the only alternative. The Adoption Assistance and Child Welfare Act (PL 96-272) in 1980 and the Adoption and Safe Families Act of 1997 gave increased emphasis to the need to consider permanency planning for all children who come to the attention of the social service system. Finally, The Independent Living Initiative of 1986 (PL 99-272) and the Foster Care Independence Act of 1999 amended Title IV-E of the Social Security Act in such a way that youths leaving foster care would be given increased attention and support. With each of these laws came significant changes in the way foster care was provided.

There is still considerable political debate focused on the termination of parental rights when abuse or neglect is an issue (see Chapter 8). Some states have streamlined court procedures to free children for permanent placements in a more timely manner. Others have mandated time frames that allow parents only a certain amount of time to rearrange their lives and resume the care of their children. Critics say that change for many of these parents is a long-term goal and the expectation that it can be accomplished in a short period is unrealistic. Still others, especially among former foster children, argue that the only way for children to lead healthy lives is to separate them earlier from dysfunctional families and place them in permanent, consistent environments.

Trends

Numerous trends and alterations in child welfare policy appear to be affecting the provision of foster care services.

Permanency Planning and Family Preservation. Although, at one time, the only apparent options for permanency for a child were family reunification or adoption, new alternatives are now being considered. For example, there is now more extensive exploration of the child's extended family as a potential placement alternative. Kinship care, mentioned in Chapter 8, is a viable plan for children whose parents cannot care for them but who can find a home with relatives, godparents, or close family friends. This trend may have gained strength from minority families who are connected with their own culture and extended families and who, in the past, have solved child care problems within their own familial circle. As increased stressors have been put on these families, however, and they begin to look to the dominant culture to solve more of their problems, *formalized* kinship agreements may become more effective.

In addition to kinship care or placement with relatives, the nature of adoption has also changed. Instead of the closed adoptions of the past, they may now be arranged according to the needs of the child. Open adoption, in which the child maintains contact with either the birth parents and/or the foster parents, provides children with more consistency while still offering permanence. Subsidized adoptions by adoptive or foster parents provide children whose medical or emotional needs, and the financial obligation inherent in meeting these needs, may formerly have precluded their ability to be adopted, to find stable homes.

Finally, permanent foster homes or guardianship arrangements make it possible for many children to have more consistency in their lives. Such arrangements might not have been sanctioned in the past, but today there is more of an emphasis on the needs of the children. By the same token, more efforts are made in the area of family preservation (see Chapter 8). Programs provide more intensive services to help natural families be able to care for their children. At the same time, families are being held more accountable so that children can be offered permanency at as young an age as possible.

Training and Professionalization of Foster Parents.   Although foster parents have, for some time, been seen as members of the child's therapeutic team, it was clear that some agencies merely paid lip service to this concept. As foster parents have developed more of a voice on their own behalf, through such organizations as the National Foster Parent Association, and handling of the problems of the children coming into care have required more skill, foster parents have become more involved in training and areas of therapeutic intervention. Some agencies actually see foster parents as agency employees and treat them as such, but the concept of the professionalization of foster parents is defined differently by each agency and each organization.

Although some programs, such as the Annie E. Casey Family Program out of Washington, do an excellent job of providing the respect and training that foster parents feel they need to accomplish their tasks, many public agencies still lag behind. Possibly as a result, or perhaps due to other economic factors, there is a serious lack of foster parents. Increasing the number of foster homes available as well as keeping those already committed will require that agencies take a serious look at how foster parents fit into the scheme of therapeutic intervention for children.

Attention to Special Populations in Foster Care.   Over the years, the type of children placed in foster care has changed. As drug addiction becomes more prevalent (see Chapter 4), more children will be placed into care because of their parents' inability to overcome their addiction sufficiently to care for them. Many of these children will be born addicted to substances themselves, and many will live with the aftereffects of the addiction of their parents to alcohol or drugs. In addition, there are an increasing number of children born of HIV-positive mothers who may or may not be HIV-positive themselves in years to come. The care of all of these types of children requires special knowledge and skills. Currently, most agencies have instituted training for both foster parents and staff to aid them in the handling of these issues. Agencies will be called on more and more in the future to find creative solutions to the provision of services to such children. Not only education, but other support services, such as grief counseling for foster parents who have an AIDS baby die while in their care, are vital to meeting these needs.

Another population that is becoming more visible in foster care is a growing number of gay and lesbian youths. Increasingly, foster parents and foster care workers are requiring training to understand the complex issues and feelings faced by gay and lesbian youths. A few agencies on the West Coast provide homes specifically for gay and lesbian young people (Ricketts, 1991). Although this gives the foster children support and validation for their feelings, it does not always insulate them from the sentiments of the larger society. As more homosexual youths feel comfortable in identifying themselves, agencies will be pressed to respond more to their needs.

More Complex Demands of Foster Care Provision.   No longer the relatively simple service provided for dependent children, the provision of foster care now demands attention to a myriad of cultural, community, and family-based issues. The skill of the social worker dealing with foster children must be more finely honed. As well as a case manager, a counselor, and a broker, the worker must also be an advocate for both foster children and their caregivers. Their knowledge must be more specialized, including knowledge of cultural variations, HIV awareness, knowledge of drug issues, and a variety of other specialties. Foster parents, too, cannot be merely caregivers, but must also be able to deal with the complexity of the children who come into their care.

The provision of foster care is also affected by managed care regulations. Funding is dependent on meeting specific criteria and those providing care must be able to meet the needs of children while remaining within the guidelines set down by outside funding sources. This is not always an easy task.

Inherent in the changes in the provision of foster care is the necessity to ensure that the care given to dependent children is of quality. It will be increasingly necessary to consider the best interests of the child. Such assistance as protecting children from maltreatment in care and ensuring effective services for reunification along with termination of parental rights when necessary will provide a more therapeutic environment for foster children. Increased emphasis must be given to preparing children to leave care both to return home and, especially, to become independent.

For many children, family foster care is a necessity. Although there are some who feel that a return to the concept of orphanages would better serve children, there is a sufficient amount of research that attests to the fact that a family environment, if healthy and sensitive to a child's needs, provides more for dependent children than an institutional environment. Our challenge as practitioners is to create the healthy environments that can be the most effective in helping children become functioning adults.

Summary

Family foster care has long been a method of providing dependent children with a nurturing environment. The origins of the placement of children with families seems to have been when apprentices, while learning their trades, were sheltered in the households of their masters. Later, in the late nineteenth century, Charles Loring Brace sent children, via orphan trains, to the midwestern United States to be fostered or adopted. Eventually, foster parents were expected to undergo scrutiny to be surrogate parents for children, and in the early 1900s they began to be paid for this service.

Today, foster care is influenced largely by the concept of permanency planning, providing the best possible nurturing for children while moving toward the goal of a permanent environment for them. Although more emphasis is now placed on family preservation, which requires more concentrated attempts to salvage the family structure, there is growing recognition that, if this plan fails, children must be provided with alternatives that help to ensure their stability and protection.

There are several different types of foster homes, including *crisis homes* for short-term emergency placements, *family boarding homes* for longer periods of substitute care, *small group homes,* which provide care for several children in the same home, and *specialized homes* that provide care for certain individual children or certain types of children. *Kinship care,* or the provision of care by the child's extended family members, is an increasingly popular alternative, especially among minority populations who, before their integration into the larger society, solved many of their child care needs informally, within their own culture. Kinship homes have the advantage of providing consistency for children in that the kinship parents may already be known to them and may also share the children's cultural values.

Children come into foster care for a variety of reasons. Some have been *maltreated by their parents* and foster care is seen as a method of protecting them from further abuse or neglect. Some children come from families in which there is *domestic violence or substance abuse,* preventing the continuation of their care by their parents. *Parents who are physically or mentally ill* may also place their children, or these children may be removed from them due to their inability to provide for their care. *Incarcerated parents* may require placement for their children until they are released or until another plan can be devised for the children's care. Finally, foster care may be used as an *interim arrangement* while a child awaits placement in an adoptive home.

Foster parents are recruited or become foster parents because they want to provide a service, because they want to continue to parent, or as a result of other personal experiences. Minority families are less likely to come forward, except in kinship situations, but there is more need for such homes. Potential foster parents undergo a screening/training process called a homestudy. This is usually accomplished in groups and is often based on the NOVA model, which provides an eight to twelve week intensive program that exposes the applicants to a variety of topics inherent in foster care. Once they have finished this process, children can be placed in the home and supervised by foster care social workers.

It is not always easy to have one's child placed in foster care. Birth parents often feel that they have failed in a role—that of parenting—that society expects anyone to be able to do. As a result of separation, they may go through several stages, from denial, anger, and despair, to eventual acceptance, in an attempt to cope with their dilemma. Research now tells us that how effectively these parents are helped to adjust to the placement and to work with the agency and the foster parents may determine how successful the placement will be for their children.

Children who are placed in care may have feelings about separation that mirror those of their parents. They may feel guilt, shame, fear, hostility, isolation, and sadness. They may want to return to their parents while feeling abandoned and resentful toward them. Life in foster care may also be punctuated with a variety of conflicting feelings that are not always dealt with while children are in care and may surface for them in later years.

When children leave foster care, it may be to return home, to be placed for adoption, or to live on their own. The writings of former foster children tell us that there is a need to improve the services provided for children who go from care to independence. Not only do they need physical and logistical supports, but they may be dealing with a variety of emotional issues that hamper their ability to live comfortably as autonomous adults. Increasingly agencies are creating programs to offer these necessary supports.

The role of the foster care worker is one that requires patience, flexibility, and stamina. One never knows exactly what a daily schedule could encompass. From routine foster home visits, supervised visits for birth parents, and attendance at school review meetings to dealing with a variety of emergency situations, the foster care worker does his or her best to keep in touch with children and foster parents and meet the needs of both, often while working with birth parents as well. It is not surprising that the turnover in such a profession is high.

Today, the provision of foster care is influenced by several trends. The balance between family preservation and permanency planning for children puts increasing pressure on agencies, courts, and child advocacy groups to devise better ways to serve the best interests of children. There is an increasing emphasis on the need to train foster parents and include them more effectively as integral members of the therapeutic team. There is also a need to redesign some foster care services to meet the needs of special segments of the child population now coming into care, such as children who have been exposed to substance abuse, children who are HIV-positive, or youths who are gay or lesbian. And finally, there is a need to fine-tune or reconceptualize the structure of foster care in a variety of ways so that the children who are in need of this vital service can be best served.

EXPLORATION QUESTIONS

1. Who was Charles Loring Brace and what was his contribution to the history of foster care?
2. What two concepts most influence the provision of family foster care today?
3. What is it expected that foster care will provide?
4. Cite the different types of foster homes and explain each one.
5. What is kinship care? What are the advantages and why has it become so popular?
6. Cite the reasons that children come into foster care.
7. What is the process one must go through to become a foster parent?
8. What are the stresses inherent in being a foster parent?
9. How might birth parents feel about having their children placed in foster care? How might they express these feelings?
10. What feelings do children have about separation and placement? About their natural parents? About being in foster care?
11. What are the needs of a child leaving foster care to go out on his or her own?
12. What trends influence the future of the provision of foster care?

REFERENCES

American Public Welfare Association. (1998). *APWA Survey of 1996 Family Foster Care Maintenance Payment Rates.* Washington, DC: APWA.

Barth, R. P. (1989). "Programs for Independent Living." In J. Aldgate, A. Maluccio, & C. Reeves (Eds.), *Adolescents in Foster Care.* Chicago: Lyceum Books.

Berrick, J., Barth, R., & Needell, B. (1993). "A Comparison of Kinship Foster Homes and Family Foster Homes." In R. P. Barth, J. D. Berrick, & N. Gilbert (Eds.), *Child Welfare Research Review.* New York: Columbia University Press.

Carp, E. W. (1998). *Family Matters.* Cambridge, MA: Harvard University Press.

Child Welfare League of America (CWLA). (1989). "Children's Legislative Agenda 1989." Washington, DC: Author.

Child Welfare League of America (CWLA). (1994). "Kinship Care: A Natural Bridge." Washington, DC: Author.

Child Welfare League of America (CWLA). (1998). *State Agency Survey.* Washington, DC: Author.

Child Welfare League of America (CWLA). (1999). "CWLA Applauds New Legislation That Will Provide Help for Teens Leaving Foster Care." Washington, DC: Author.

Cook, J. F. (1995). "A History of Placing-Out: The Orphan Trains," *Child Welfare,* 74(1), 181–197.

Festinger, T. (1983). *No One Ever Asked Us: A Postscript to Foster Care.* New York: Columbia University Press.

Fine, P. (1993). *A Developmental Network Approach to Therapeutic Foster Care.* Washington, DC: Child Welfare League of America.

Gambrill, E., & Stein, T. J. (1994). *Controversial Issues in Child Welfare.* Boston: Allyn and Bacon.

Gebel, T. J. (1996). "Kinship Care and Non-Related Family Foster Care," *Child Welfare,* 75(1), 5–18.

Hacsi, T. (1995). "From Indenture to Family Foster Care: A Brief History of Child Placing," *Child Welfare,* 74(1), 162–180.

Hegar, R. L., & Scannapieco, M. (1999). *Kinship Foster Care.* New York: Oxford University Press.

Holody, R. (1998). "Children in Out-of-Home Placement" (135–153). In N. K. Phillips (Ed.), *Children in the Urban Environment.* Springfield, IL: Charles C. Thomas.

Hubbell, R. (1981). *Foster Care and Families: Conflicting Values and Policies*. Philadelphia: Temple University Press.

Leashore, B. R., McMurray, H. L., & Bailey, B. C. (1991). "Reuniting and Preserving African American Families." In J. E. Everett, S. S. Chipungu, & B. R. Leashore (Eds.), *Child Welfare: An Africentric Perspective*. New Brunswick, NJ: Rutgers University Press.

Levy, T., & Orlans, M. (1998). *Attachment, Trauma and Healing*. Washington, DC: Child Welfare League of America.

McAdams, P. (1972). "The Parent in the Shadows," *Child Welfare*, 51(1), 15–25.

Moore, B., Granpre, M., & Scoll, B. (1988). "Foster Home Recruitment: A Market Research Approach to Attracting and Licensing Applicants," *Child Welfare*, 67(2), 147–160.

National Black Child Development Institute. (1989). *Who Will Care When Parents Can't?* Washington, DC: Author.

National Commission on Family Foster Care (NCFFC). (1991). *A Blueprint for Fostering Infants, Children, and Youths in the 1990's*. Washington, DC: Child Welfare League of America.

Plumer, E. H. (1992). *When You Place a Child...* Springfield, IL: Charles C. Thomas.

Raychaba, B. (1988). *To Be on Our Own with No Direction from Home: A Report on the Special Needs of Youth Leaving the Care of the Child Welfare System*. Ottawa, Ontario: National Youth in Care Network.

Ricketts, W. (1991). *Lesbians and Gay Men as Foster Parents*. Portland, ME: University of Southern Maine, National Child Welfare Resource Center.

Rutter, B. (1989). *The Parent's Guide to Family Foster Care*. Washington, DC: Child Welfare League of America.

Solomon, R. (1990). "Substance Abusive Parents: A Challenge for Child Welfare Systems." In *1990 Abstract Compendium for the National Symposium on Child Victimization*. Washington, DC: Children's National Medical Center.

Stahl, P. M. (1990). *Children on Consignment*. Lexington, MA: Lexington Books.

Terpstra, J. (1987). "The Rich and Exacting Role of the Social Worker in Foster Care," *Child and Adolescent Social Work*, 4(3–4), 160–177.

Thurston, H. W. (1930). *The Dependent Child*. New York: Columbia University Press.

U.S. Department of Health and Human Services, Administration on Children, Families and Youth. (2001). Retrieved from http://www.acf.dhhs.gov/programs/.htm.

U.S. Department of Housing and Urban Development. (1999). *HUDFY 2000 Budget Summary*. Washington, DC: Author.

Walsh, J., & Walsh, R. (1990). *Quality Care for Tough Kids*. Washington, DC: Child Welfare League of America.

12 The Adoption of Children

What is adoption? A child brought into your home? A bigger family? A new brother or sister for an only child? Not so fast! Adoption is not just an event. Adoption is a lifelong process.

—L. Coleman, K. Tilbor, H. Hornby, and C. Boggis

Adoption has long been a method of providing children with both legal and emotional security. Through adoption, children find permanency and parents can nurture or increase their families. Adoptive parents provide substitute, societally sanctioned, long-term care when birth parents have been unable to assume their roles adequately. Through adoption, a new family is created—hopefully, one that can meet the needs of all those involved.

The History of Adoption

Adoption has not always been designed to meet the needs of *all* participants; rather, the practice was originally seen as a method of meeting the needs of the adoptive parents. Reasons for adopting children have varied from a desire to continue the family line or trade (especially through the male heirs), to provide for ancestor worship, to ensure additional workers, to maintain family wealth, to provide a solution for out-of-wedlock pregnancies, and to provide homes for homeless children.

Perhaps one of the best-known adoption stories was that of Moses, who was found in the bulrushes by the Pharaoh's daughter. Cognizant of the fact that he was a Hebrew child whose future was in jeopardy and being childless herself, the Pharaoh's daughter adopted Moses as her own son, thus ensuring his survival and (she thought) his future. Documentation supporting adoption can be found as early as 2285 B.C. in the Babylonian Code of Hammurabi (Carp, 1998).

Early Rome, Greece, and Egypt had formal adoption requirements. The motivation was primarily to ensure male heirs. Female children were not eligible for placement, and only men could do the actual adopting. The transaction was sealed with a judicial hearing (Howe, 1983). India and China used adoption as a formal method of providing male heirs. For Hindu men, a male child met the demands of religious ceremonials. For the Chinese family, an heir was expected to provide for the parents in their old age. In other early cultures, the adoption of children was more informally arranged.

European countries, throughout history, developed adoption practices based primarily on Roman law. In France, the Napoleonic Code most closely resembled Roman practices. England, a country with traditions based on blood lineage, found it more difficult to espouse the practice of adoption. In order to adopt, therefore, a family was required to seek a special act of Parliament. Only then could the adoptee be considered a legal heir. It was not until 1926 that England passed a statute that made adoption a viable option for any family (Carp, 1998; Smith and Miroff, 1987).

Much of early legislation in what was to become the United States was based on English common law. Because adoption was unknown in England, the new states were forced to devise their own standards; each did in its own way. There is some controversy about which state actually enacted the first legal statute. Whether we believe sources that cite this forerunner as Mississippi in 1846 (Sloan, 1988), Texas in 1850 (Cole, 1987), or Massachusetts in 1851 (Carp, 1998; Samuels, 1990), the fact remains that the Massachusetts statute was the closest to currently accepted philosophies. Both Texas and Mississippi statutes were geared more toward real estate transactions; through adoption, property could be legally passed on to the adoptee. Massachusetts law, on the other hand, provided for the "best interests of the child." The four components of the 1851 law that have remained to the present require that:

- *There be written consent by the child's biological parent;*
- *Both the adoptive mother and father join in the petition;*

- *A judge must decree that the adoption is "fit and proper";*
- *There be legal and complete severance of the relationship between biological parents and the child. (Kadushin and Martin, 1988)*

Although there are exceptions to and variations on these provisions in current adoption practice, the 1851 law still influences adoption policy today.

By 1929, all states in the United States had enacted some type of adoption legislation. Prior to this time, state legislatures continued to adopt legislation as individual cases came to their attention. As more procedures became formalized, standardization of adoption practice seemed imminent. Yet, in the late nineteenth century, states still interpreted their laws differently. For example, all that was required by federal law was the legal transfer of the child from the biological to adoptive parents, and the pronouncement by a judge that all was "fit and proper," but this did not protect children from abusive adoptive situations, and some states began to look more closely at adoptive applicants. Finally, in 1891, Michigan instituted a requirement that the judge investigate the adoptive home before finalizing the adoption. Later, agencies took over this task. A 1917 Minnesota law requiring detailed investigation by a social agency was copied in numerous other states by the late 1930s (Kadushin and Martin, 1988).

Where were the children while their fate was being debated by politicians and lawmakers? During the nineteenth and early twentieth centuries, most homeless children resided in orphanages. Some had been placed there by their unwed mothers or poor parents; others had been orphaned by death, substance abuse, poverty, or other problems. Some were destined to grow up as permanent orphans, whereas others—the younger and more appealing perhaps—would find themselves placed with adoptive parents.

The orphan trains (mentioned in Chapter 11) were also responsible for some adoptions. Although Charles Loring Brace's initial idea appeared to be to provide permanency for homeless children of all ages, some of the children sent to families in the western United States were eventually legally adopted. In 1859, close to 5,000 children had been placed "out West" (in both foster care and adoption) and 24,000 children had found homes nationwide (Brace, 1872).

Finally, in the early twentieth century, more emphasis was being placed on the "best interests of the child." Minnesota, in 1917, was the first state to mandate the sealing of birth records (Gitlin, 1987). Agencies began to assess adoptive couples more rigorously. In 1938, the Child Welfare League of America published the first set of standards for adoption practice. But adoption did not become a popular form of substitute care until the end of World War II, when homeless children were more visibly plentiful. The upsurge in the demand for children caused agencies to further reassess and redesign their policies.

By the 1950s, the demand for healthy white infants outweighed the availability of such children. African American and mixed racial infants were also available, but usually only African American couples were considered as adoptive parents for such children. However, the numbers of African American couples seeking to adopt from agencies was small, so agencies began to look at other types of adoptive arrangements—both interracial and international (Simon and Altstein, 2000).

In order to find suitable homes for all children, Ohio, in 1958, developed an adoption resource exchange that pooled statewide resources in search of homes. Other states followed, and in 1967, the Child Welfare League of America established the Adoption Resource Exchange of North America (ARENA) (Pecora et al., 2000).

The 1960s and 1970s saw a significant shift in the adoption picture. Agencies recognized that children who had once been considered unadoptable might also be placed. "Special needs" adoptions—defined as those involving older, African American, and disabled children—began to be seen as possibilities. For the first time, single parents were considered for otherwise "hard-to-place" children. Agencies began assessing couples in groups rather than just individually.

But as the adoption picture became more complex, more controversies arose. In 1972, the National Association of Black Social Workers took the stand that transracial placement was "a threat to the preservation of the black family" (Pecora et al., 2000). Why was more not being done to place these children within the African American community? they asked. Agencies were criticized for using white middle-class standards in their recruitment and assessment of minority adoptive applicants.

At the same time, researchers and reformers of the child care system found that children—many of whom were legally free for adoption (or could be with a minimum of work with their families)—were living in temporary foster care when they could have been given the permanency of adoption (Gruber, 1973). Foster families who were stimulating and providing well for children questioned why they could not adopt them. Although the practice of foster parents adopting had been discouraged in the past, in 1973, CWLA recognized the acceptability of this practice if the needs of the child would be best served.

Amidst the controversy over the placement of African American children in white homes, the Native American community began to question outside placement of its children. Largely in response to the fact that between 25 and 35% of Native American children were being placed in substitute care (foster care and adoption), the Indian Child Welfare Act of 1978 (PL 95-608) was passed. This legislation mandated that Native American children be kept within their community whenever possible in order to maintain connections with their own tribes (Cohen, 2000; Hollingsworth, 1998).

The numerous debates and controversies made it clear to child welfare advocates that more standardization of adoption practice had become necessary. In 1980, the passage of PL 96-272 became a milestone in substitute care history. This law made state adoption programs mandatory and provided federal matching monies for subsidized adoption. Adoption subsidy meant that families who were interested in adopting children with special needs, but were unable to do so financially, would be provided with funds to supplement the child's care. These payments could not exceed the amount that would be given to a foster family for the same child. To guide states in developing their own laws to govern subsidy payments, the federal government published the Model Act for the Adoption of Children with Special Needs (Kadushin and Martin, 1988).

PL 96-272, the Federal Adoption Assistance and Child Welfare Act of 1980, urged agencies to have as a priority "permanency planning" for every child. Agencies were encouraged to first strengthen the child's biological family. If this was not possible, agencies should place the child in an immediate long-term or permanent nurturing situation with caring adults—usually an adoptive home. And in 1997, the Adoption and Safe Families Act sought to provide even more impetus to the move to provide children with permanent homes as quickly as was feasible. Although the intent of these laws was beneficial for children, agencies argue that they do not always have the funds or resources to adhere to them.

Today, adoption agencies provide services for older children and children with special needs in greater numbers than infants.

Definitions and Assumptions

The purpose of adoption is to provide a permanent home for a child whose biological parents are unable or unwilling to provide that home. Today, we assume that, although the needs of the adoptive family are important, the adoption is primarily to provide a home for a child.

Adoption is a legally sanctioned arrangement. The Child Welfare League of America describes this legal agreement as "the method provided by law to establish the legal relationship of parent and child between persons who are not related by birth" (Child Welfare League of America, 1978, 11). It is in this legality that adoption differs from foster care. While foster care is seen as a temporary living arrangement, adoption substitutes adoptive parents for biological parents—giving them all the rights and privileges of biological parents.

Adoption is based on several assumptions or values:

1. A child has a right to grow up in the safe, nurturing environment of a family.
2. If the child's biological family cannot provide him or her with what he or she needs, the child has the right to a substitute family.
3. Adoption is the preferred type of substitute care because it provides legal sanction and permanency of the relationship.
4. Children should be placed for adoption as early as possible in order to provide as much consistency as possible.
5. Adoption is expected to be a lifelong experience for all the participants.
6. Adopted children are entitled to information about their birth, their biological family, genetic information, placements, and particulars about their adoption (Cole and Donley, 1990; Adamec and Pierce, 2000).

Types of Adoption

Adoptions may be divided into two types: related and unrelated. In *related* adoptions, the child has a preexisting blood tie to some member of his or her adoptive family. In other words, a stepfather might adopt his wife's child or a couple might adopt the child of their unmarried son or daughter. Or, in more recently recognized *kinship adoptions,* relatives of the birth parents may opt to care for and adopt a child (see Hegar and Scannapieco, 1999). Another recognized practice that can be seen as related adoption is created by *surrogate mothering.* The term *surrogate mothering,* created by Keane, an attorney in Michigan, refers to the agreement between a couple and a surrogate mother. The mother agrees, for a fee, to be artificially inseminated and impregnated by the adoptive father's sperm, to carry the baby, and then to relinquish the child to the sperm donor and his wife. Usually this couple will then legally adopt the child (Shanley, 2002). Although this practice seems relatively new, it has in fact been practiced since ancient times. Surrogate mothering appeared to be gaining momentum until two legal landmarks brought the practice under scrutiny. In 1988, Michigan, concerned that surrogate mothers might use this practice as a lucrative business, passed a law that limits the amount of money surrogates can receive. Further, the controversy and court battle over "Baby M" may have changed sentiments. Baby M's biological mother, Mary Beth Whitehead-Gould, was impregnated by the sperm of Stern and agreed that, once the child was born, to relinquish it to the Sterns. Once the baby had been born, however, Mrs. Whitehead-Gould decided that she wanted to keep the child. The result was the case Whitehead-Gould versus Stern, which received a lot of media coverage and gave rise to 70 bills in 27 state legislatures seeking to ban, regulate, or undertake research on surrogate parenting (Carp, 1998). Currently both the Child Welfare League of America and the National Committee for Adoption (a lobbying organization representing 145 nonprofit, private adoption agencies nationally) oppose the practice of surrogate parenting (Samuels, 1990).

Unrelated adoptions are what comes to mind most frequently when the word *adoption* arises. In this type of adoption, the child has no blood relation to the adoptive family. Most of these adoptions are *agency sponsored;* that is, the agency counsels and contracts with biological parents of the court to place the child, recruits and assesses the adoptive couple, places the child, and provides follow-up until or after the adoption is legalized.

By March 2000, there were 588,000 children in foster care and only 127,000 were free for adoption (AFCARS, 2001). For this reason, agencies sometimes sponsor *legal risk* adoptions. In these arrangements the agency has already petitioned the court to terminate the biological parents' rights. The expectation is that the court will agree and the child will be legally free for adoption. In the meantime, instead of placing the child in yet another foster home, the agency places the child with the family that hopes to legally adopt him or her. Because the courts usually take considerable time to process the termination of parental rights, this arrangement seems to be in the best interest of the child. The problem arises, however, when the biological parents contest the termination of their rights. In addition, adoptive couples often feel insecure until they know the child is legally free.

Another type of adoption that is fairly recent is what is known as a *special needs* adoption. Children who might be difficult to place are placed with families who have been assessed especially for them.

CASE EXAMPLE

Walter

Walter was a 2-year-old boy with Down syndrome. When it became necessary for Walter to be moved from the foster home where he had been from birth, the agency decided to place him in an adoptive home instead. The Brandts had had their children when they were young and now these children were grown and married. Mrs. Brandt, a teacher, and Mr. Brandt, a nurse, felt they could give love and a home to a special kind of child. The agency studied them for a special needs child and eventually placed Walter with them. The match was a good one and, until Walter's death 10 years later, the family provided consistency and love for him.

Currently, children with disabilities and older children are being placed with increasing frequency. Sometimes the placement of special needs children requires subsidized adoption (discussed earlier). Parents interested in adopting a child whose care necessitates extra costs (beyond those expected in raising a child) are given a subsidy to defer the extra expense. Thus, children who require expensive medication, medical procedures, or therapeutic services can still benefit from an adoptive home.

Single-parent adoptions, which gained popularity in the 1960s and 70s, are still in vogue today. The assumption is that although a child should be given the opportunity for a two-parent home, some children would be better suited to a single-parent family. For example, if a child had been severely abused by most of the men in her life, she would likely be distrustful of men and unable to bond with them. The agency would therefore seek a placement for this child with a mother in a fatherless home. Often, teenagers in particular do better with a one-parent figure rather than in a two-parent family. Some children require the undivided attention of the parent, leaving this person with little energy to maintain a healthy marital relationship.

When children of one race are placed with parents of another, the adoption is referred to as *transracial* or *interracial adoption.* Adoptive parents involved in these placements are guided in aiding children to understand and accept their own racial backgrounds. It is most common for children of African American or mixed parentage to be adopted by white families, although there continues to be much controversy around this practice (see Simon and Roorda, 2000). At one time, Native American children were also placed in the homes of white parents. The Indian Child Welfare Act of 1978 reserved the right of determining where an Indian child would be placed, with the hope and intention of placing him or her in a family of the tribe in which the biological parent was registered. Tribal governments try to place Indian children within their own Native American culture first.

International adoptions are those in which children are brought from other countries and placed with adoptive couples in the United States. The Holt Agency, founded in 1956, by Harry and Bertha Holt of Eugene, Oregon, to aid children of the Korean War, is responsible for the greatest number of international adoptions. Originally the agency brought over Korean war "orphans" who were in fact the American children of wives, lovers, prostitutes, and rape victims of servicemen. Later, Vietnamese children joined the ranks of children who needed permanent homes. Now, children are adopted from a variety of countries, led by China (4,690), Guatemala (1,609), Korea (1,776), Russia (4,200), and the Ukraine (1,246) (Holt International, 2002). In 2001, 19,137 visas were issued to children brought to the United States for the purpose of being adopted here (Holt International, 2002).

Register (1991) describes a 5-month-old child from Honduras whose mother gave him to a lawyer to place, a 7-year-old from Guatemala who was found on the streets, and a malnourished 4-pound baby placed by her young mother in an orphanage in India. All of these children were adopted by American families. As children become less available in the United States, many families seek out this type of adoption.

Independent adoption refers to placements of children with parents unrelated to them without going through an agency. Gibbs (2000) refers to these as *parent-identified adoptions* as opposed to *agency-assisted* placements. Downs and colleagues (2000) describe three types of independent placements:

1. Direct placements: *biological parents give their child to someone known to them;*
2. Intermediary placement not for profit: *the person who acts as an intermediary is well intentioned and the money exchanged is only for legal services or the mother's medical bills; the biological parent often knows the adoptive parents. Such adoptions are sometimes referred to as "gray market";*
3. Intermediary placement for profit: *often called "black market" adoption, these arrangements involve "selling" children for profit; the intermediary fee is as high as the participants will pay. The "service" may be connected with an abortion clinic and the intermediary is connected with mothers who have agreed to give up their child rather than abort. These placements are illegal and are outlawed in most states. (389)*

Even when adoptions are done independently, an agency may become involved. In many states the adoption cannot be legalized until an agency undertakes an adoptive home study.

Issues in Adoption Today

Today's adoption literature is dedicated to the discussion of several pertinent issues:

1. The decreasing numbers of children available for adoption
2. Changes in the types of children available for adoption
3. The controversy of agency versus independent adoption
4. Adoption disruptions and the need for follow-up
5. Openness in adoption
6. The effects of adoption on children and families (mental health implications)

Decreased Number of Adoptable Children

During the mid-1980s, the National Committee for Adoption (NCFA) estimated that there were 104,088 adoptions within the United States. Of these, 52,931 (or about 51%) were adoptions of children by family members (related adoptions). These family members may have been stepfathers, grandparents, uncles and aunts, or other concerned relatives. Unrelated adoptions (children placed with families usually unknown or unrelated to them) totaled 51,157 (about 49%). But if we compare data published in 1982 and in 1986, we discover that the numbers of children placed in 1982, 91,141, exceeded the numbers placed in 1986, 52,031 (NCFA, 1989). If we look further, there appears to be a pattern. The total number of adoptions (related and unrelated) increased in 1951 from 72,000 to an all-time high of 175,000 in 1970. From 1970, the rate of adoptions has fallen considerably and continues to do so (Kadushin and Martin, 1988). According to the Administration for Children and Families of the Children's Bureau there were an estimated 46,000 children adopted from the public foster care system in 1999 (AFCARS, 2001).

What accounts for this decline? Researchers attribute it to several factors. First, the increased acceptance of abortion, birth control, and the laws regarding these have influenced the numbers of children being born. Second, although teen pregnancy has gained more attention in recent years, more teens are actually keeping their babies. Increased societal acceptance of single parenthood may affect this decision. For example, although at one time a pregnant adolescent was forced to leave school, this is no longer the case. Birth fathers are also expected to be more involved in the adoption and decision-making process. A father's protestations over a mother's decision to place her child for adoption may influence a teen to keep her baby, whether out of concern for the father or because fighting him on her adoption decision would be too complex and overwhelming (Carp, 1998; Samuels, 1990).

The adoption story does not end for teens when their child is in its infancy, however. Often, these children are released by their parents when they are older, when the teen parent finds their care too great a task. Unfortunately, by this time the children are often abused, neglected, or have developed other problems. Their age may also be a deterrent to finding an adoptive placement easily.

African American teen mothers often do not place their children for adoption for cultural reasons (Hollingsworth, 1998). A high percentage of the children born to those teens are found living in their mother's family of origin (now often in a kinship placement). Hispanic and Asian women too may place their babies with extended family members.

Changes in Types of Children Available for Adoption

Although at one time the most adopted and adoptable child, the healthy white infant, was available, this is not the case today. The Administration for Children and Families (AFCARS, 2001, 9) reports that 45% of the children adopted through public agencies were black, non-Hispanic; 15% were Hispanic; 1% were Asian; and only 38% were white. Of these only 2% were under 1 year old, with 45% being 1 to 5 years, 36% in the 6- to 10-year range, and 15% who were between 11 and 15 years old. Despite the fact that it is the older or minority child who needs a home, not all couples are able to parent such a child.

Today, many children do not become available for adoption until they are older. Whether this can be attributed to more emphasis on family preservation or increased services for unwed parents, the fact remains that there appear to be more older children who have recently become available for adoption. Robinson (1998) points to the additional problems that adoptive parents of older children must face. She contends that many of these children suffer the residual effects of abuse and neglect. Many are attachment disordered, having difficulty forming any relationships (see also Levy and Orlans, 1998). And a significant number of these children, old enough at the time of separation to remember their parents, never properly complete their grieving process. All of these factors can lead to additional behavioral or psychiatric difficulties and the need for more intense services for the child and the adoptive family. In addition, many of the children—both old and young—have some type of special need, whether it be mental health or physical.

Some couples' hesitation in adopting older or special needs children may be related to the recognition of their own infertility. Studies indicate a correlation between a couple's comfort level with their infertility and their ability to accept adoption. Infertility is as much of a loss as a death in the family and some couples have never been helped to grieve. For them adoption may become a less than healthy replacement (Helwig and Ruthven, 1990). These couples feel the need to parent an infant to whom they could have given birth. According to experts, the rate of infertility is on the rise (Pavao, 1998; Register, 1991). As couples marry later, their fertility rate may decrease. Resolve, Inc., a national infertility education and advocacy network, reports that one in six of the couples in the United States are experiencing infertility. In the face of these statistics, it becomes increasingly important to help couples come to terms with infertility before they adopt. Although some childless couples want to parent, they may not want the extra responsibility of a special needs child (Register, 1991).

CASE EXAMPLE

Margie

Margie, a 43-year-old white social worker, and her husband finally concluded that the only recourse for their fertility problem was adoption. They approached several agencies about adopting an infant and, as they had expected, they were told that the wait could be from five to eight years. "They offered us special needs children but I wasn't ready for that," Margie admitted. "I work with abuse and neglect all day long and have for years. I've seen children maimed and their emotional growth retarded. After working with it all day long, I just couldn't cope with it at home."

Some couples believe that they are able to cope with special needs children, but after the adoption goes through, a couple will admit that it is more difficult than they imagined. "People must really know what they're getting into," says one such parent, "the doctors' visits, the bills, the attitudes of other people." Agencies cognizant of this fact are now beginning to better prepare adoptive parents for special needs children.

Controversy over Agency-Assisted versus Independent Adoptions

Each year, numbers of couples and single adults seek to adopt children without going through a public or private agency. Whether an intermediary is involved or the mother places with the couple, there are still numerous risks to all parties. If this is the case, why then do people seek out independent adoptions?

Currently, couples are being told by agencies that either they are not taking applications for healthy infants or the waiting period will be anywhere from five to eight years. On the other had, a study of independent adoptions found that of the 105 infants placed independently, two-thirds were already with their adoptive parents within 4 months of the parents' attempts to find the child. The remainder of the children in the study were with their new parents within 11 months of the parents' initial search (Register, 1991).

Rights of the Child. Despite the advantage of a short waiting time, there are also disadvantages for both the child and for the adoptive couple. First and foremost, independent placements do not protect the child's right to the best home possible. Because the only real eligibility criterion is that the couple can provide the necessary fee, there is no guarantee that they will be suitable parents. Granted, undergoing an agency homestudy does not guarantee that the parents will be ideal, but agencies put their years of experience into their decision about whether to approve an adoptive couple.

Today, agency homestudies not only assess the readiness of the applicant to parent through adoption, but they also provide valuable information and education for potential adoptive parents. The intensity of today's homestudies also aids parents in sorting out their feelings about whether adoption is in fact for them. Some applicants, after participating in the homestudy, have realized that adoption is not a suitable alternative to their particular needs. The time involved in the study and in waiting for the child, which every potential adoptive parent hates to consider, can actually contribute to the success of the adoption. As one adoptive mother recounts:

> *Sam and I knew when we were married at age 22 that I'd never be able to conceive. So shortly after we were married we approached agencies to adopt. What an eye opener! We had no idea it could take so long—up to six years they told us. We tried to find an independent adoption. We found a doctor who would arrange it for us. He knew a teenager who was due in two months. A week before the baby was due I panicked. Suddenly I realized it was too soon. We hadn't even been married a year. We'd had no time to gel as a couple, so I backed out. Sam was really angry. It actually drove us to counseling. Then we reapplied to the adoption agency. They had us complete a 10-week homestudy with four other couples. At those meetings we looked at a lot of stuff I'd never considered—like how we would discipline. Sam and I totally disagreed. More negotiations followed. We learned a lot about our differences as well as our similarities. After a series of home visits, we were approved. Then came the waiting. It seemed an eternity. But three years to the date that we applied, they called us about a baby girl. After I took the call, I just sat there and thought—"Yes, now I'm ready."*

No Follow-Up Services.   In addition to no education about adoption, parents who adopt independently receive no follow-up services. There will be no supportive social worker to answer their questions, suggest resources, or provide referrals. Increasingly, researchers are citing agency follow-up as one of the most significant contributions to a successful adoption experience.

No Assurance of Confidentiality.   Couples who adopt independently have little or no assurance that particulars about the adoption will be kept confidential. Neither intermediaries nor natural parents are necessarily bound to keep what is told to them confidential. In addition, biological parents may be given the name and address of adoptive parents and may in some cases feel justified in seeking them out. One couple recounts:

We adopted through an attorney. He told us the mother didn't want to have any contact with us. She didn't want our name and didn't want us to have hers. But a year later I was at the laundromat and overheard two women talking. One said, in conversation, "My niece had a baby a year ago and gave it to a foster couple over on Chestnut. I told her she should go look them up." That was us! I whisked my son out of there quickly and went home. I was petrified. Would the mother come? Would she want Aaron back? I was also extremely angry with the attorney who had arranged the adoption. He would have been the only one who could have told. Who else had he told?

Biological parents may agree to, or seek out, independent arrangements because they are reluctant to face the red tape and the perceived impersonal treatment afforded by an agency. They may also feel that they have more control over the people with whom their child will be placed. Yet their right for confidentiality may also be unprotected.

This biological mother who gave up her child through her doctor recounts her experiences:

He [the doctor] must have given the couple my name and address. I hadn't wanted that. The couple paid some of my medical bills and felt I owed them. They'd call up around holidays and tell me that the baby needed this or that. Hey, I was working two jobs just to get by. They sent some pictures, which was a nice thing to do, but it made it hurt more. I just wanted to forget. I'd done what I thought was best. Then I got involved with someone and before I could tell him about the baby, they did. He answered the phone one day when he was at my apartment and they told him my daughter needed something. I was really angry and hurt.

Insufficient Information about the Child.   Experience has taught agencies who place children for adoption that honesty ensures the best placements. When adoptive couples are told as much as possible about a child they are offered, they are more likely to be comfortable with their choice. Agencies give couples the right to refuse a particular child if that child does not seem right for them. On the other hand, in an independent placement couples are often told little about the child. In addition, they may fear that if they refuse a child offered them, another might not be available.

Legal Aspects of Adoption Are Not as Clear-Cut..   Agencies who place children for adoption either ensure that these children are legally free or inform the adoptive parents that this is a "legal risk" adoption—that is, the biological parents have not yet legally surrendered the child or the court has not yet terminated parental rights. In independent adoptions it is not always as clear-cut. If a biological mother places her own child in an adoptive home, she may have never legally surrendered her rights. If a couple is not cognizant of the legal procedures necessary, they may not realize this. Thus, at any point, the child's mother could reclaim her child. If any intermediary is involved there is still no guarantee that the adoption is free of legal risk.

No Counseling for Biological Mother or Adoptive Couple.   Agencies recognize that the decision to place one's child for adoption is not made lightly. Birth mothers often require counseling to sort out their feelings and feel comfortable with their decision. Mothers who place their own child usually have not had the opportunity for professional help with their decisions. This lack of professional support often leaves the mother in conflict and makes it more difficult for her to get on with her life. Adoptive couples also may need support and counseling. The adjustments that come with new parenthood can be great. When an agency is not involved, this help is not readily available. Recognizing that independent adoption is not agency-sanctioned, couples may also be reluctant to seek out counseling from any agency.

No Protection in Adoption Disruption.   When an agency places a child and, for whatever reasons, the placement is not successful, the agency will find another home for the child and provide counseling for both the child and the adoptive parents. Without agency involvement the disrupted adoption becomes even more problematic. Where does the child go if he or she cannot remain with the adoptive couple? Who will help the child and the parents cope with the loss and feelings of failure? Currently most states discourage or prohibit independent adoptions. In many instances, however, the penalties for violations are minimal.

Adoption Disruptions and the Need for Follow-Up

Each year approximately 10% of adoptions will be disrupted (Berry and Barth, 1990; Barth and Berry, 1988). The disruption statistics increase when an older child is placed for adoption. Berry and Barth (1990) reported that the adoptions of 22% of children between the ages of 12 and 14 will be disrupted, as will 26% of those where the children are 15 years and older.

Although placement assessment, education, and support are vital to a successful adoption, follow-up services are also crucial. Currently, agencies provide placement services to adoptive families for only short periods of time. For example, infants are usually followed for three months, whereas older children may be visited in their adoptive homes for up to a year; few agencies offer more extensive supervision. Yet, most experts agree that postplacement services are vitally important and should be available whenever needed, throughout the life of the family.

Lack of postplacement services can be an important factor in adoption disruption. While adoptions are most likely to fail when the child exhibits behavior problems, when the child is older, or when he or she has already had an interrupted adoption experience, adequate services once the child has been placed in the adoptive home can often prevent the adoption from ending. Increasingly, agencies are recognizing the importance of follow-up services. In reality, adoptive families receive fewer services than birth families despite the fact that they are parenting the child.

Openness in Adoption

Emerging in the late 1970s and continuing today, there is much controversy on how open the adoption process should be. The confidentiality of the past is no longer the norm in all cases. *Openness* refers to the amount of contact there is between the parties involved, but more specifically the birth and adoptive parents. There is a continuum of openness from the closed confidential arrangement of the past to the totally free interaction of birth parents and the adoptive family (Grotevant and McRoy, 1998). There has been little research to guide agencies in making choices about where their policies will fall along the openness continuum. To gain more insight, Grotevant and McRoy (1998) er gaged 720 participants recruited from 35 adoption agencies throughout the United States to assess their feeling and experiences around adoption openness. The sample included 190 adoptive mothers, 190 adoptive fathers, 171 adoptive children (ages 4 to 12 at the time of the interview), and 169 birth mothers (21). From their research, these authors concluded that many of the fears about openness are unfounded. Children do not have a more difficult time with divided loyalties, fully disclosed adoptions do not involve a confusion about parenting rights and responsibilities, and birth mothers who are allowed contact are able to resolve their feelings of loss more effectively than if they had been denied access to the child and the adoptive family. The contact and comfort between all parties allows more understanding as to the implications of adoption for each individual. The authors did suggest, however, that the degree of openness be decided on a case-to-case basis, and that agencies strive to act in the best interest of the parties involved. Carp (1998) argues for the openness of adoption records as well as of the adoption process itself. Such studies and arguments give agencies, birth parents, and adoptive parents a great deal to consider.

Effects of Adoption on Children

Typical of our society's desire for happy endings, we often think of postadoption life for families and children in a happily-ever-after context. In reality, family life is never without its adjustments. When the concept of adoption is added to the already delicate balance of familial relationships, problems may arise.

Therapists report that it is not uncommon for adopted children to question why their parents gave them up. Although some are told "your biological mother [parents] loved you and wanted the best for you, so she gave you up," this explanation does not necessarily quell the conflicts over being abandoned and rejected. Adoptees who struggle with these feelings may feel distrust and confusion.

Any loss creates the need for grieving. Even the individual placed as an infant recognizes that another mother, some shadowy figure of his or her thoughts, once carried him or her in her womb and gave that baby to others. Most adopted children are never given the opportunity to grieve this loss, however insubstantial it may appear to others. The result can be a profound and often deep-seated sense of sadness. When other losses occur in later life, they may be especially difficult to bear as they serve as reminders of the initial separation from birth parents. The individual may therefore provoke rejection from others as confirmation that he or she is still unlovable (Rosenberg, 2000; Helwig and Ruthven, 1990; Simon and Roorda, 2000).

In addition to potential conflicts related to adoption in general, particular populations of adopted children experience problems related to their own adoptions. For example, transracial adoptees who, cognizant of their African American or Asian origins, find themselves living in a white family may experience an identity crisis. "Who am I?" "What culture is mine?" are thoughts that plague some (Simon and Altstein, 2000; Patton, 2000). Older children may have been exposed to physical abuse, substance abuse, or domestic violence before they were adopted and be coping with the residual scars of these traumas. Or, adopted parents may know little of the children's background, leaving adoptees with vague, possibly distorted memories and no answers to questions about their origins. Adoptive children, assured that they were "chosen," may harbor feelings that they must live up to the expectations of those who have adopted them.

All of these issues translate into a variety of behaviors and attitudes. Although some adopted children exhibit problem behaviors for their parents, others express the fears and conflicts inherent in having difficulty with trust and therefore relationships. Others repress their conflicts, becoming the "perfect children" they feel that their parents wanted. The inner toll may be enormous. For some adopted children, it is counseling or the readiness of their adoptive parents to face issues openly and help them master developmental tasks that enables these children to cope with or resolve the conflicts of their adoptive status.

Adoptive Participants

Birth Parents

The Reasons behind the Decision.   Giving birth to a child does not guarantee the parent's ability to care for that child or to face the responsibilities of parenting fully. Such responsibilities, with the many sacrifices involved, may be overwhelming for the woman or man whose own needs have never been fully met. Some parents recognize this early and give up their children at birth. Others believe that they can parent, only to discover later that they are not able to meet the needs of either their children or themselves.

Not every parent gives up his or her child voluntarily. Those who abuse or neglect their children may have the decision to release them made for them by the social service or court system (see Chapter 7).

There are three ways that children become available for adoption:

- Their parents voluntarily relinquish custody.
- Their parents abandon them.
- The court terminates parental rights.

Voluntary Surrender.   Parents voluntarily surrender their children for a variety of reasons. When we think of birth parents who give up children, we often conjure up an image of the pregnant teen who cannot keep the baby due to her own immaturity, educational needs, or financial situation. In Chapter 11, Kellner reports that the highest percentage of pregnant teens is Hispanic followed by black and Native American. This does not necessarily mean that these teens will release their children for adoption, however. Cultural values have a significant impact on who surrenders children.

Unwed teens who decide on adoption may do so because they recognize their inexperience and inability to parent effectively. For example, Chandra was 14 years old when she became pregnant. Initially, she had decided that she would carry her baby to term and raise it herself. But she soon realized that her emotional supports at home were minimal and her options were few with a young child. Raised by an abusive, alcoholic mother, Chandra wanted better for her child.

It is not only the adolescent who gives up her child for adoption. For instance, Monica was 35 and separated from her husband when she realized that she was pregnant. Her career was thriving and rewarding and she could not imagine herself parenting at this stage of her life. Her strong religious belief made having an abortion out of the question. Instead, Monica took a leave of absence from her job, had the baby in another state, and placed her for adoption.

What of the biological father of the child who is given up for adoption? He, too, may be young and not ready for parenthood. Or he may not be in the position to parent this particular child. The father of Monica's baby was her husband, but he saw the pregnancy as Monica's attempt to reengage him in what had been a conflict-ridden marital relationship. He had children from a previous marriage and had no desire to support Monica's having this child.

Other fathers may be concerned, but not willing to share their parenting with the baby's mother. Some putative or biological fathers have asked for custody of children their mothers intended to release for adoption. Whether this request is granted depends on the father's prior involvement, his plan for the care of the child, and the laws in individual states. Some states require that the biological father also be involved in surrendering the child.

Parents who give up children for adoption do so because they realize that their lives cannot accommodate the responsibility. Adoption is not a decision that can be made lightly, nor is it one devoid of future conflicts. For some parents, parenting a particular child is something they do not feel able to do.

CASE EXAMPLE

Joshua

Joshua was born with many medical problems. His young mother, Janet, already had two other children, 3 and 4 years old. Joshua required frequent hospitalizations and consistent attention to giving him his medications. When his overwhelmed mother was unable to follow through with either medical appointments or the administration of his medicine, Joshua lapsed into a coma and was rushed to the hospital by a neighbor. Janet, frightened that Joshua would die and she would be blamed, took her other children and hid out for several weeks. The local social service agency took Joshua into custody when he was released from the hospital. Janet returned and, learning that her son was in foster care, angrily called the social worker involved in the case. After counseling to see if this mother was able to have Joshua returned to her, Janet was finally able to admit that her son's care was more than she could handle. She signed adoption releases and Joshua was eventually adopted by his foster parents.

Parents who voluntarily surrender their children do so by signing an *adoption surrender.* This legal document is a legally binding agreement by which parents give up their parental rights. To ensure that this document is legally binding, many states have stipulations that must be followed. For example, in many states, a mother cannot sign a surrender for a newborn until she has left the hospital. The rationale for this is that she should be free of medications that might confuse her and have some distance to be sure of her decision. There is also a trend toward encouraging birth parents to see their children at the hospital to determine if they are comfortable with their decision. Birth mothers, especially, who are ambivalent are given counseling to aid them in making a decision about relinquishing their child (Pavao, 1998; Samuels, 1990).

Currently, there is much more attention paid to birth fathers than in years passed. Numerous cases, such as *Stanley v. the State of Illinois* (1972) and *Lehr v. Robertson* (1983), brought attention to the rights of these fathers. As a result, the Supreme Court ruled that the rights of birth fathers must be protected when adoption is being considered (Gitlin, 1987). Some sources (Samuels, 1990; Brodzinsky and Schechter, 1990) feel that agencies' previous reluctance to consider the birth father was based on the stereotype about his lack of involvement. He was often thought to be an unworthy, uninvolved character who gave the mother little or no support and whose involvement was merely in the sexual encounter. In reality, many birth fathers are interested in and concerned, if not about the mother, at least with the child. In their study of African American adolescent fathers, Dallas and Chen (2002) discovered that their lack of resources was one of the primary reasons they may not have remained involved with their children.

Abandonment.   Parents who abandon their children may do so because they feel they have no other choice. A Hmong (a Laotian sect) baby was found in the back of a church. When the young mother was finally found, it was learned that she had been ostracized by her community and saw her only choice as abandoning her baby and killing herself.

Still other parents are so disturbed themselves or caught up in their own dysfunction that they have little time or energy for their children. The police in a large city were called to an address when neighbors were concerned that three children had been left alone. The children's parents had left town for several days on a "drug run" and had left the children alone. The children were taken into the custody of the local child welfare agency. When parents abandon their children and show no inclination to resume their care, the court steps in. Often the children are placed in foster homes and sometimes for adoption.

Termination of Parental Rights.   When parents cannot care for their children, either because they have abused or neglected them, are using substances that hinder their ability to care for the children, or are unable to protect their children, the juvenile court may intervene (see Chapter 9). Initially these children are usually placed in foster care. At one time, they may have remained in foster homes until they were age 18. But PL 96-272 (1980 and 1997) shifted the emphasis to permanency planning—finding the children a permanent home. Thus, more children brought into foster care due to their parents' inability to care for them effectively were freed for adoption by court action.

The issue of permanency planning raises several questions. The primary goal of child welfare agencies is family preservation. Therefore, when children come into foster care, agencies stress that services will be focused on reuniting the family. The reality is that a dearth of available workers in an agency, funds, and resources may mean that sufficient services are not available to reunite families quickly. In addition, change or rehabilitation is not an easy process. Thus, children may sometimes remain in foster care for an inordinate amount of time. Many of these children, already dealing with the scars of abuse and neglect, must also learn to adjust to living in a state of limbo. To reduce the trauma of children not knowing where they belong, many states have now mandated a time period during which biological parents are helped. If the parents are not able to demonstrate stability within this proscribed period, their rights as parents are legally terminated.

Some states require an additional process beyond the termination of parental rights to free a child for adoption. Instead the agency must then petition the court, usually probate, for the further termination of right for the purpose of adoption. This extra step may mean an additional period of time before the child can find permanency.

The Emotional Aspects of Losing One's Child.   Parents, especially those who voluntarily surrender their children, deal with the impact of this decision for many years to come. For many, their view of themselves is significantly changed. Plumer (1992) suggests that biological parents face the separation from their children with diverse feelings:

- *Feeling that they lack control.* Even parents who choose to place their children often feel that they had no choice. They may feel that others were telling them what to do, or that there was no other action open to them.
- *Feeling inadequate.* Our society assumes that parenting is something that anyone can do. To admit that one cannot parent often makes an individual feel ashamed, guilty, and a failure.
- *Feeling stigmatized by the community.* Because everyone "should be able to parent," someone who cannot is somehow "different" and may feel stigmatized by others.
- *Feeling that they would like to blame others.* It is often easier, when one is in pain, to assume that another caused it. "If the baby's father had been more supportive" or "If my parents had not abused me" are classic reasons parents may use to account for their separation from their children.
- *Feeling bitter or angry.* Birth parents, in their desire not to face separation, may project their feelings onto others, becoming bitter, angry, and sometimes abusive to those around them.
- *Feeling like they want to give up.* Losing a child is emotionally draining and, experienced with the preceding feelings, can seem overwhelming. Some parents do not feel they can cope. Some parents become childlike ("the agency can take care of everything for me"). Some become apathetic; some want to escape the pain though denial, or even suicide.

Other sources identify feelings of sadness, worry, nervousness, emptiness, anger, bitterness, and thankfulness. For birth fathers, the feelings were sadness, worry, thankfulness, nervousness, anger, and bitterness (Plumer, 1992).

Birth parents wonder what will become of their children. Will they be loved? Will the children wonder about them? Will the children be safe? The stereotype of parents who can easily forget the experience and go on with their lives is erroneous. Numerous studies have borne this out. Birth mothers have reported having disturbing dreams about giving up their babies and emotional reactions when seeing children who were about the age of those they had given up.

Services for Birth Parents.   Despite research attesting to the significant effect that giving up a child has on the birth parent, agencies do not always provide a sufficient amount of help for those parents. As one social worker explained, "We are a child welfare agency. Once a mother has given up her children, she is technically no longer eligible for services. We can counsel her for the period right after the placement, but then we have to close the case. It's policy. We just have to hope that she finds a counselor later who can help her grieve."

The problem is that many birth parents do not recognize that their problems or feelings are related to the loss of a child. Many find it easier to deny. So, if parents are able to get help with their grieving, those who work with birth parents suggest that they should be allowed the space, empathy, time, and expression necessary to come to terms with the loss. They also point out that rituals can play a large part in the passages of our lives. Part of the grieving process may be acknowledging the day of separation or some other way to accept that this has been part of one's experience. It is the individual who has been helped to put his or her life back in perspective who can go on with his or her life in a healthy manner.

Children Available for Adoption

At one time, there were basically three categories of adoptable children: healthy infants; special needs children, which included children who were older than age 3; and children from other countries. Now the picture has become a bit more complex. In addition to a few healthy infants of all races, there are numerous older children awaiting the chance for adoption. Of these, a large percentage were not released from their parents care until they were older. The Administration for Children and Families (AFCARS, 2001) estimates that only 28% of the children waiting for adoption were under 1 year of age, 41% were between ages 1 and 5, 24% were between ages 6 and 10, and 7% were between ages 11 and 15 (7). Many of these older children also have brothers and sisters, and agencies are faced with the decision about whether to place sibling groups together or separately. "The problems is," explained one adoption worker, "adoptive families often want children as young as possible. Some will take sibling groups that have very young children just because they want the little ones. In these cases, it is the older children that get the short end of the stick."

An attempt to assign categories for the children available for adoption today would probably include healthy infants; older children and sibling groups; children with medical or emotional problems; and children adopted from other countries. Admittedly, some of these categories may overlap.

Whether children are infants or older in age, there may also be cultural variables that come into play. For example, Native American children were placed predominantly with white couples until the 1978 Indian Child Welfare Act. This legislation gave tribes the authority to make placement decisions for their own children. Preference was given first to the child's extended family members, then to other tribal members or other Native Americans.

Today, there are numerous children available for adoption and they represent all racial groups. Whether these children are placed with same-race parents or are considered special needs may depend on their geographic area and the demographics of that area, as well as the types of parents who are seeking to adopt.

A recent study (Dave Thomas Foundation, 2002) polled Americans about the types of children they might consider adopting. Of those polled, 78% would want a healthy baby of the same race as themselves, 64% would consider a sibling with the oldest under 4 years, 40% would accept a child of a race other than their own, 25% would adopt a child who had been in foster care for several years, 14% could accept a child with medical problems, and 11% with behavioral problems (18). From these findings, one can deduce that the type of children available for adoption do not always meet the demand.

Healthy Infants.   Fewer and fewer healthy infants are available for adoption today. Despite the fact that adolescents have become sexually active at younger ages than in past decades, birth control and abortion are increasingly available. There has also been a trend toward young mothers keeping their babies. If these children do come to the social service system, it is usually at an older age and often as a result of abuse, neglect, or family dysfunction. The increased abuse of substances has also altered the picture of how many healthy infants are available. As more mothers abuse drugs and alcohol during pregnancy, more babies are born either addicted to drugs at birth or suffering from the effects of fetal alcohol syndrome (FAS). The demand for healthy infants has always outweighed the availability of such children, but today this especially true. It is not uncommon for a family requesting a baby to be told that they will wait between 5 and 10 years. Some agencies refuse to study couples waiting for babies and some applicants seek other sources, such as overseas or independent adoption.

Older Children and Sibling Groups.   Children who are not released for adoption until they are older than 3 years old may have a greater risk of having been abused or neglected, or having witnessed domestic violence or drug abuse (Robinson, 1998). Children who come into care at a later age do so either because their parents' rights have been terminated or because their birth parents have determined that they are unable to care for them for some reason.

CASE EXAMPLE

April

When April was a baby, her 16-year-old mother, Lara, found that parenting was a novelty. But by the time April was age 3, the responsibility weighed heavily on the young mother. Lara had a new boyfriend who drank heavily. When he wasn't beating Lara or April, he was taking them places they had never been before. Lara was jealous of his attention to April. She began leaving April home when they went out. During one two-day absence, a neighbor reported to the police that April was alone in the house. The police took April to a local child protection agency. Lara's inability to work consistently with the agency over the next year led to April's release for adoption.

Lara's inability to properly care for her child is not unlike other parents whose children become free for adoption at a later age. Most of these releases are involuntary. Only infrequently do parents recognize the need to help their children find permanency.

Children who have experienced dysfunctional homes bring with them not only feelings of loss but also scars from the pain they have experienced and witnessed. For them and their adoptive parents, the adjustments may be many.

Sibling Groups.   At one time, siblings who were free for adoption might have gone to different adoptive homes, perhaps not being allowed to maintain contact with each other. Increasingly, agencies are trying to keep family groups together whenever possible. This sometimes presents a challenge.

CASE EXAMPLE

The Russells

The Russell children were ages 3, 5, and 7 when the court terminated their birth parents' rights. Three-year-old Kit and 5-year-old Kerry were outgoing, responsive children who would adjust well to a new home. For 7-year-old Kim, life had been dedicated to taking care of her younger siblings. She had done this well, but it had taken its toll. Angry and sullen, Kim had no use for adults. They had betrayed her before and she would not trust them again. It would take Kim years before she would see her adoptive parents as anything but a threat.

Although sibling groups can be a challenge, some couples value the prospect of a ready-made family.

Children with Medical or Emotional Problems.   Children may have a variety of medical problems. The following are some examples.

- Addison was a perky 3-year-old African American child who was born deaf. His mother's drug use during pregnancy had sent him into withdrawal soon after birth. The doctors were initially somewhat guarded about his condition, but at age 3, Addison's only apparent problem was his deafness.

- Helen was shaken by her abusive father when she was an infant. The result was that both her retinas were detached. Although surgery had been tried, the results were less than the medical community had hoped for.
- Bobby was born HIV-positive. Soon after his birth, his mother and her boyfriend (Bobby's father) both died with AIDS. With no relatives willing to parent him, Bobby was placed for adoption. Some children with Bobby's diagnosis will test negative as they grow older. Others will continue to be positive for HIV and will eventually die.

Of all the medical issues, adopting an HIV-positive child is one of the newest and most uncertain. Families interested in providing a permanent home for these children must be prepared for the worst as well as the best. While there may be only a few physical adjustments to be made by a family parenting an HIV-positive child, the emotional issues are significant. There is still pronounced negative sentiment toward those who are HIV-positive. In addition, when parenting an HIV-positive child, common childhood illnesses become more significant and problematic.

Mental retardation can also present a challenge in children who are available for adoption. In some cases, it is possible to recognize the probability that a child will be mentally retarded or developmentally delayed, but there are other situations when this fact does not become apparent until the child has already been adopted. Agencies are increasingly recognizing the need for post-adoption support when such unforeseen problems arise.

Children with emotional or behavioral issues may be seen in children who are older or who have experienced dysfunctional family life prior to being released for adoption. Pain takes its toll on children and that pain becomes visible in children who act out their anger behaviorally. Multiple moves may also create attachment problems that impede children's ability to trust enough to risk new relationsip.

Children Adopted from Foreign Countries.   The adoption of children from other countries has been practiced formally for about 50 years. Since 1956, the Holt Agency has sought to place children from a variety of countries in adoptive homes in the United States. Although this was not the earliest attempt to place war orphans, it has been one of the most extensive. The numbers of children from the various countries cooperating in intercountry adoptions fluctuates from year to year. For example, although there was a very slight decrease in the children adopted from China (5,053 in 2000 compared to 4,681 in 2001), China still represents the highest number of children being placed. On the other hand, there has been a significant increase in the children who come from the Ukraine (659 in 2000 to 1,246 in 2001) as well as from Guatemala (1,518 to 1,609). Currently, a significant number of countries across the globe send children to be adopted in other countries.

Who are these children? Some of these children have been abandoned by overwhelmed parents whose poverty makes it impossible to care for them. In Dehli, India, for example, Dara was born with a deformed arm. Her mother often used the child to illicit sympathy when she brought her children with her to beg on the street. When the mother died, all the children were placed in a home and Dara was registered with an International adoption agency. As another example, military men left behind children who were not accepted by either of their races and were placed in orphanages or foster homes awaiting adoption. In countries where illegitimacy is a stigma, unwanted babies may be given up to hospitals or agencies in the hope that they will be adopted.

All of these children remained in an orphanage or a foster home until they could be placed with adoptive families. For many of these children, international adoption is their only hope for survival. Cultural taboos, such as illegitimacy, or economic conditions may make it impossible for them to remain in the countries of their birth. Because professionals feel that these children will face less stigmatization and have more resources available to them, agencies like Holt arrange for them to be adopted in North America and Western Europe.

Adoptive Applicants

Recruitment.   Recruitment is an important part of the adoption process. Although some applicants seek out adoption agencies, others may either not know where to start pursuing their interest in adopting or may not perceive that there is a need for agencies to find homes for children. Recruitment is especially important for special needs children. Sometimes, when potential applicants become aware of a particular child, they are more able to consider adoption. For example, a television network in Boston features a piece called "Wednesday's Child." Here, children who may have some special need are introduced as viewers watch them on the TV screen. Invitations to call in often generate numerous applicants and may result in finding an adoptive home for the child.

"One Church, One Child" is another example of a recruitment effort that has been successful. In 1979, a Chicago priest, Father George Clements, challenged the African American churches in Chicago to see that at least one member of each congregation adopted an African American child. Using slide presentations about specific children, the program was instituted by more than 50 churches and eventually supported by the federal government. Currently, over 20 states have some variation of this recruitment tool (Pecora et al., 2000). The North American Council on Adoptable Children offers newsletters that discuss how to recruit from different racial groups. They suggest that issues such as mistrust of government agencies, fears about the stigma attached to infertility in that culture, language barriers, and views of the greater community as unfriendly to minorities prevents many people from Hispanic,

African American, and Asian cultures from seeking to adopt through agencies (see http://www.nacac.org/newsletters).

Other innovative strategies have been implemented by corporations, newspapers, and civic groups, though undoubtedly more widespread recruitment should be done to place the children who are available.

Profile of Applicants.   Couples and individuals apply to adopt children for a variety of reasons. The traditional applicant is the couple who is not able to have children biologically.

CASE EXAMPLE

Sam and Melissa

Sam and Melissa married after both became established in their respective careers. In their early thirties, the couple decided to add children to their satisfying relationship. After several years, they became concerned about their fertility. Melissa originally sought help and underwent a series of fertility tests. Ruling out infertility for her, Melissa's physician suggested that Sam be seen. The results of preliminary tests revealed that, probably due to a childhood illness, Sam was infertile.

"It really upset him," Melissa recounts. "He was from a family of macho men and he felt that this made him less of a man. It took a year of counseling to convince him otherwise."

No matter who is the infertile partner, or even if no cause is discovered, couples often go through a grieving process. "You don't really question being able to have children," Melissa explains. "You just expect that you will."

Infertile couples experience not only disappointment but also anger and guilt. Often, they describe difficulties in their relationship with each other. But couples who do not adequately grieve their inability to have their own biological children may never fully accept an adopted child. They may have difficulty accepting their child's origins and be less able to discuss adoption openly with her or him (Robinson, 1998; Samuels, 1990). For this reason, during the screening process, most agencies discuss in depth the couple's feelings about their infertility.

Preferential applicants are those who choose, for whatever reason, to adopt. Some couples hope to complete an already existing family with a child of the opposite sex. The mother of three boys, Arlene had always wanted a girl. "I worked so hard at being comfortable being female," she recounts. "I felt that I wanted a daughter with whom I could share all this."

Other couples seek to adopt children from other cultures. Bus Wagner had been in India during the service. He knew of the plight of many poor children in that country, and had always hoped to adopt one. After having a biological child, he and his wife felt ready to take a child from India into their home.

Granted, not all couples who adopt foreign-born children have biological children. Many are unable to have their own families but prefer to adopt children who are unlike the children they might have had. Although some couples have altruistic goals for adopting internationally, others feel that children are available from other countries more quickly and at a younger age.

Some couples who decide to adopt may do so because they perceive that there is a need. Connie and George Adams had one biological child when they applied to adopt a disabled child. They had spent a good deal of time with Connie's Down syndrome sister and felt ready to parent such a child themselves.

The term *couples* may not always refer to heterosexual partners. Increasingly, gay and lesbian couples are seeking to adopt. States and agencies differ as to their policies regarding these couples. Over the last few decades, an increasing number of single people have also become adoptive parents.

Studies show that single adoptive parents are more likely to be women who have occupations and skills that lend themselves to understanding children's special issues. For example, nurses, social workers, and teachers are highly represented among single adoptive applicants. They usually have extended family backup and a high percent were raised themselves in single-parent homes (Feigelman and Silverman, 1983; Adamec and Pierce, 2000).

Foster parents are another relatively recent group of adoptive applicants. Although foster parents have always adopted some of their foster charges, the practice was not encouraged. "We used to call it the back door to adoption," recounts a social worker who worked with foster parents in the 1960s and 1970s. "If you wanted to adopt, we felt you should apply for adoption, not do foster care. But foster parents grow to love children in their care and the children become fond of them. Our old ideas weren't too realistic." Recent statistics indicate that 64% of the children adopted in 1999 through public agencies were adopted by their foster parents (AFCARS, 2001).

Today, people are still not encouraged to pursue adoption by becoming foster parents. The reality is that many of the children placed in foster care are not free for adoption. However, when a child becomes available for adoption whose foster parents have become attached, they are often given the option to adopt.

There are still pros and cons to this type of adoption. While the greatest advantage in undeniably the consistency for the child, foster parents who adopt must also consider the disadvantages. The foster parents' relationship with the biological parents will change if they adopt. Can all parties adjust to this? In addition, foster parents must consider whether they expect to continue fostering. If they do, can their adopted child be helped to feel secure when he or she sees other foster children leave the home? Although foster parent adoption is no longer discouraged, the child's bonding within the home, the length of the child's stay, and the availability of other potential adoptive homes are all considered before this kind of adoption is allowed.

An increasingly popular type of adoption is referred to as *kinship adoption*. Kinship arrangements (mentioned in Chapters 8 and 11) may vary in form. Rather than the relinquishment of all parental rights, some kinship alternatives offer a sharing of some rights while the adoptive kin maintains the legal authority under adoption. Hegar and Scannapieco (1999) argue that the increasing number of these arrangements make it mandatory that new legislation be proposed to outline that standards of this practice.

Adoptive Siblings.   One often forgotten part of the potential adoptive family is the couples' biological children. Potential siblings come in all ages, yet the wise couple will have explained their desire to adopt and be assured of some degree of enthusiasm and cooperation from their children. Biological children may be extremely worried about their contribution to the homestudy and the adoption placement. One anxious 4-year-old refused to come out of his room when the social worker came to visit the applicants' house. Finally, the worker overheard the child's response to his mother's pleas to appear. "If you think I'm going to come out and blow this whole deal, you're crazy!" The child, knowing how much his parents wanted this adoption, was convinced that his reservations would spoil their chances (see Crosson-Tower, 2003).

Biological children often wonder and express, either nonverbally or out loud, their concern that they are not enough for their parents. They may fear that the new child will receive all the parents' love and worry that they will be "left out." Children facing the arrival of any new sibling may have these fears, but the biological sibling may be much more aware of what his parents have been going through to get this new child. For this reason, most agencies encourage careful preparation of biological children.

The Adoptive Process

The Homestudy

A child has just become free for adoption, possibly through years of court appearances and/or counseling. In the meantime, the couple (or individual) who will eventually adopt this child have been going through a process themselves. Allison Kelly remarks:

> *When we initially decided to adopt, we called an adoption agency we had heard about. They invited us to an information meeting the next week. Here we met with 10 other couples who were interested in adopting, too. We learned what types of children were available for adoption, why they became available, and what we should expect if we adopted them. Some of these children came from rough home backgrounds and might have behavior problems. The logistics of the homestudy was also explained to us. After we left there, I was very excited but I also realized that things would not be as quick and easy as I had hoped.*

Early meetings of this type have several purposes. First, they acquaint applicants with agency requirements. They also ask applicants to consider their suitability related to the several other factors on which they will be judged.

- *Motivation.* Agencies are interested in applicants' reasons for wanting to adopt. If couples are unable to have children, have they explored infertility issues? Are they trying to replace a child they have lost? Agencies wonder if an applicant's altruistic desire to take children ignores the fact that real children have real problems. For example, it may seem commendable to a couple to take a child who was maltreated, but can they cope with the scars that may result from this maltreatment? Most agencies expect applicants to be consciously aware of their motivations (Pavao, 1998; Steinberg and Hallinan, 2000).
- *Stability of the relationship.* Couples who wish to adopt will be assessed with respect to their relationship as a couple. It is hoped that they have given their marriage/relationship a chance and that they do not hope that adopting a child will cement a faltering union.
- *Age.* Agencies usually consider applicants who are within normal child-rearing ages. Much also depends on the age of the child the applicants are considering. Couples in their forties, for example, may be studied for an older child, but they might not be considered for an infant. In situations where unmarried partners or gay/lesbian couples are considered, it is usually expected that the relationship is stable and of some duration.
- *Physical and emotional health.* Since the intent of adoption is to provide permanency and a healthy environment for children, the applicants' physical and emotional health is important to agencies. Required medical examinations explore the potential adopters' physical capability to care for children. Social workers also look for applicants who appear emotionally stable, are mature, have a good self-concept, and are able to meet a child's emotional needs.
- *Financial stability.* Taking a child into one's home requires sufficient income to accommodate the needs of another individual. Although subsidized adoption is available, these monies are earmarked for special circumstances. In general, applicants (or at least one member of a couple) must be employed and financially secure. Mothers who intend to work are asked about child care arrangements. Some agencies still lean toward at least one parent being the primary caregiver of the child.

Despite these requirements, agencies often find that they must be flexible, respecting cultural diversity and increasingly different family values and lifestyles.

Informational meetings may serve another purpose in addition to outlining agency requirements and informing applicants about the children who are available. For some, the meetings also generate self-selection. Potential adoptive parents who perceive that they do not meet agency criteria or discover that adoption does not meet their expectations may opt to discontinue the process.

After the informational meeting, Allison and Dan Kelly decided to continue in their quest to adopt and were invited to be part of a homestudy group that was to begin several months later. *Homestudy* is the term agencies use to describe the screening, education, and selection of adoptive couples and individuals. While at one time the norm was to study couples individually, home studies are now more likely to be done initially in groups. This allows applicants to gain support and learn from their peers. Allison Kelly describes the process:

> We met with five other couples with whom we became quite close. The groups met for a 10-week period, during which we were asked to explore our values and attitudes about such issues as biological parents, our infertility, disciplining children, and telling children they are adopted. Sometimes it was painful to look at our feelings. And sometimes it was funny. Danny and I discovered a lot about each other that we hadn't known after six years of marriage.

The model followed by the Kellys, called the Model Approach to Partnership in Parenting (M.A.P.P.), is currently used by numerous agencies because it has been found to strengthen high-risk placements (Barth and Berry, 1988).

Placement and Legalization

Once adoptive applications have been approved for placement, their names are kept on file until a particular child who fits the criteria they can accept is in need of a home. Depending on the age of the child, the placement process may be fairly swift or spread over a longer period of time to ensure proper adjustment on the part of all parties.

Time from actual placement to legalization differs once again. Agencies usually maintain contact with adoptive families for at least three months, although research indicates that the length of this supervised adjustment period is really not sufficient. Having a "ready-made" child placed in one's home is quite different from knowing the child from birth. The older the child, the more adjustment issues there may be.

Legalization through probate court may mean that the agency's contact with the new adoptive family will cease. The child's birth records are sealed and a new birth certificate is issued with the adoptive couple or individual shown as the parent(s).

Open Adoption.   Following their release for adoption, children's contacts with their birth parents terminate. Traditionally, this was felt to be best for all involved. Only then could children grieve properly for birth parents. This practice also allowed adoptive couples who were not entirely comfortable with their own infertility to deny that the child had ever had another family.

More recently, experts in adoption began to see that some children, especially those who were older when placed, needed continuity from the past.

Some actually feel that the secrecy of traditional adoptions denies children their rights (Grotevant and McRoy, 1998; Carp and Frankfeldt, 1997).

Open adoption describes what Siegel (1993) has called "a continuum of options" (16) enabling birth parents and adoptive parents to have contact or information about each other prior to and after adoption placement. At one end of the continuum, parents do not meet but exchange letters and photographs through an intermediary. In other adoptions, the parties not only meet but carry on relationships (e.g., adoptive parents become mentors for a young unmarried birth mother). Between these two extremes lies a variety of options. The underlying criterion, however, is the birth parents' ability to relinquish their claims and recognize the adoptive parents as the child's legal and emotional parents (Carp and Frankfeldt, 1997).

Siegel (1993) studied 21 adoptive couples who had participated in open adoptions. None of these individuals regretted the openness of their adoptions, but collectively they generated a list of advantages and disadvantages. The adoptive parents felt more in control over which birth parents they worked with. They were comforted to know that they interviewed birth mothers firsthand rather than having to rely on information given them secondhand by an agency. They could learn more about prenatal care and issues that might affect their children's future—for example, genetic risk factors, substance abuse, and so forth. These parents also felt more able to answer their children's questions about their histories and birth parents. Finally, it was comforting for the adoptive parents to know that the birth parents had given up their children willingly. They also felt it would be comforting for birth parents to know that their offspring had found good homes (Siegel, 1993).

The disadvantages cited by adoptive couples related more to their own comfort than to the welfare of children or birth parents. Several parents felt it would be difficult to tolerate the birth mother's pain over her loss. One mother recognized that her discomfort with her own infertility made it difficult for her to bond with another woman's child when she knew the woman. Couples who had mentored birth mothers during their pregnancy found it difficult to adjust once the child was born. Some parents felt the need to look especially competent as parents in front of the birth family. Finally, adoptive couples worried about meeting birth parents on the street or being expected to be more involved than they felt comfortable with (Siegel, 1993; Carp and Frankfeldt, 1997).

Most experts conclude that agencies should be more open in their adoption procedures. But open adoption, like other types of adoption, requires recognition that agencies must provide continued support, education, and counseling services.

Postlegalization Services

Services available to adoptive families following placement and legalization are both formal (agency based) and informal (parent generated).

Agency Services.   Many agencies, recognizing that adoption is a lifelong experience, make support groups and educational programs available. Developmental milestones (e.g., adolescence) are as difficult for adoptive families as any other parents, but the added issue of adoption makes the picture even more complex. Understanding these milestones through educational seminars may help adoptive parents anticipate and deal with them. Many agencies offer workshops on parenting techniques, parenting toddlers, parenting adolescents, or even helping older children separate, and may also provide libraries of films and books for those who are interested. Support groups of other adoptive couples who are experiencing similar issues may also fill a need for families. Social events and retreats are an additional form of support for both adoptive couples and children.

Agencies today report that a significant number of adoptive families and adoptees are returning to request record reviews. At one time families were given only a scant amount of information about their adopted children, but today agencies recognize that more information is necessary. Although agencies and state laws differ, many agencies, at a couple or adoptee's request, will review records and provide whatever additional health or background information is available that was not given at the time of the adoption.

Counseling is also a service that should be available for postadoption. Adopted children may have the same issues other children present in therapy—for example, poor school performance, acting out, oppositional behavior, and poor self-esteem. Not all adoptive families remain functional. Any of these eventualities may bring adoptive families to counseling. In addition several themes seem to be more prevalent among adoptive families:

- *Powerlessness.* Often the members of adoptive families feel powerless. The couple may bring with them their initial feelings of helplessness over not being able to have children. They may feel powerless in their relations with the agency involved. Adopted children often feel that they had no decision in their placement and feel powerless over their futures. All members may feel unable to deal with the early trauma the child experienced (Hartman and Laird, 1990).
- *The "bad seed" myth.* Hartman and Laird (1990) describe how parents often fear that the child's biological past may predestine him or her to respond in negative ways. Or families worry that the child's past experiences will be unalterable. These "ghosts" become a part of family secrecy and may lead to disfunction.
- *Adoptive issues.* Some families seek counseling to enable them to handle how to explain adoption to their children. Often those sessions bring up the parents' old uncertainties about adoption. Parents may also seek help when they perceive that their adopted children may search for birth parents (Pavao, 1998; Rosenberg, 2000; Hartman and Laird, 1990; Simon and Altstein, 2001).
- *Needing to be a perfect parent.* It is not uncommon for adoptive parents, who may have worked hard to become parents, to feel the need to be per-

fect in that role. Caught up in a sense of failure over not being able to have children themselves, these couples often seek reassurance that they are doing a good job (Hartman and Laird, 1990).

- *Identity issues.* Adoptees may seek counseling in an attempt to understand who they are and where they belong. They were born to one set of parents and are being raised by others. Children whose adoption has been the traditional, closed, secretive affair wonder about their histories. They may feel the need for loyalty to both birth and adoptive parents and wonder how to bridge the gap. This is especially true of nonwhite children placed in white families. Nonwhite children often identify with both cultures but may find it difficult to figure out where they feel comfortable (Pavoa, 1998; Rosenberg, 2000; Silverman and Feigelman, 1990; Simon and Altstein, 2001).

Telling the Child about Adoption.   There has been some controversy over the years as to how and when to tell a child that he or she is adopted. Although a few psychoanalytic theorists (Berger and Hodges, 1982; Wieder, 1977) contend that discussion of adoption before the resolution of the Oedipal Complex causes psychic damage to the child, most adoption resources recommend the use of the word *adoption* early in the child's life. Brodzinsky, Smith and Brodzinsky (1999) conclude that children's understanding of adoption grows over time. Before they are 6 years old, children can accept that they are adopted but do not comprehend the significance. Statements about having "two mommies" are so far out of their frames of reference that they mean little. By the time they are close to age 6, children begin to worry and focus on why they may have been given up. Between 8 and 11 years of age, children finally begin to understand the complex nature of adoption, with its losses and changes, and some children fantasize that birth parents will appear to claim them. By adolescence, children are more able to understand the legalities, rights, and responsibilities of adoption (Rosenberg, 2000; Samuels, 1990; Simon and Altstein, 2001).

In reality, not telling children they are adopted until after they are 5 years old can also have negative results. Not telling them forces adoptive parents into keeping a secret, and children may later resent not being told. In addition, children may inadvertently learn from someone else before parents tell them. Adopted Rob recounts:

> *When I was twelve, my aunt, who was drinking at the time, told me I was adopted. At first I didn't believe it. When I was finally convinced it was true, I was angry. Angry that my parents didn't tell me. I had a right to know. It made me wonder what else they hadn't told me and how much I could trust them.*

Parents who use the word *adoption* in a loving way early in the child's life help the child to become comfortable gradually. Adoptive parents who are not able to talk openly about adoption may have difficulty with the concept themselves. On the other hand, Samuels (1990) cautions against overemphasizing the issue of adoption, suggesting that belaboring the issue may also point to adoptive parents' discomfort. Open, honest, confident telling in age-appropriate ways appears to correlate with successful adoptions (Pavoa, 1998; Rosenberg, 2000; Simon and Altstein, 2001).

Some agencies currently provide "life books" to enable children to understand their histories. These books consist of pictures, letters, and narratives depicting the child's life from birth to adoption. The use of "life books" is often a way to help children understand how they came to be adopted. Children are curious about why they were given up. It is important not to imply inadequacy on the part of birth parents, as they are an integral part of children's perception of themselves. Children often fear that they contributed to being released for adoption by being intrinsically undesirable or misbehaving. Adoptive parents must assure adoptees that they were wanted by both sets of parents. Yet there is a delicate balance between describing as truthfully as necessary the circumstances of the birth parents' decision to give up their child and, at the same time, not portraying them as totally victimized.

There are several books out for children that aid adoptive parents in explaining adoption to their children, including *How I Was Adopted: Samantha's Story* (ages 4–8) (Wm. Morrow, 1995), *The Day We Met You* (4–8) (Alladin Books, 1997), and *A Koala for Katie, An Adoption Story* (9–12) (Albert Whitman, 1997).

Adoption Disruption

Not all adoptions are successful. About 10% of all placements will be unsuccessful or disrupted each year. Some families, though at risk for disruption, will either receive counseling or find other ways to avoid it. Often, however, families do *not* seek services or alternatives until it is too late.

Several factors put adoptive families at higher risk for disruption. The seeds that grow into failed adoption relationships may have been undetected during the initial homestudy, may have been recognized but not explored, or may not have been predictable.

CASE EXAMPLE

Roland and Bev

Roland and Bev Markham felt they had a good marriage. When it became apparent that a childhood illness had rendered Roland infertile, the couple dealt with the issue openly. Several years later, the Markhams were approved for adoption and eventually received a 3-month-old girl who was the picture of redheaded Bev. After several years of successful parenting, the Markhams asked for a second child. This time a black-eyed, black-haired Native American boy of 6 months, who looked very much like Roland, was placed in their home. A Native American himself, Roland initially welcomed this addition. The child had minor medical problems, but recognizing how well the Markhams had done with their daughter, the agency felt that this was an appropriate placement. Six months after the initial placement, it became obvious that the family was in trouble. Roland, always very involved with his daughter, could not bond with this male child. Sensing the rejection, the boy had become withdrawn. After counseling the couple, it became clear to the agency that this child must be removed. Roland had come to recognize that this child was too much of a reminder of his own sickly childhood in a culture that stressed strength in males. He had also been helped to realize that these memories brought up his unresolved anger and guilt over his infertility.

The risk for disruption is rooted in several areas. Certainly the adoptive parents' own issues may prevent them from being successful with adoption in general or with a specific child. The family balance may also be a factor. For example, a couple with older children may find that the family cannot sufficiently rebalance when a new child is added. This causes disharmony. Although, through counseling, some families can find solutions, others cannot and the result may be disruption.

The adopted child also brings issues with which a family may have difficulty dealing. The child's age, behavioral problems, number of previous placements, and past history can influence his or her integration into the household (Robinson, 1998; Rosenberg, 2000; Simon and Altstein, 2001). Children may never have resolved their conflict over loyalty to birth parents versus their adoptive parents. Some experience attachment disorder and have a great deal of difficulty with new relationships (Levy and Orlans, 1998). Experts suggest that the adoptive family's ability to handle destructive, aggressive behaviors (often the result of the child's abusive history or multiple moves) and the adequacy of the family's support system are also key factors.

Effective casework on the part of the placement agency is vital when the family is at risk for disruption, and indeed throughout the placement process. In her study of adopted children, Festinger (1986, 1990) found that continuity from the agency lowered the risk of disruption. Families who maintained the same social worker throughout the placement process, for example, were less likely to experience disruption. Helping families work out these issues is a difficult task, but a vital one in the adoption process.

The Role of the Adoption Worker

Adoption workers perform a variety of roles. In some agencies, workers specialize (e.g., home finding, recruitment, placement) while in other agencies workers vary their assignments. Stacia Fellows, who has been in adoption for close to 25 years, describes her experience:

When I first got out of school I worked for a large state agency, first as a placement worker. My role was to see children in foster homes and prepare them for adoption. Often I worked closely with their family worker, the social worker who was helping the family release the child for adoption. Once the child was legally free, I'd look for a couple or individual to meet the child's needs. I'd place the child and follow up with the family until the adoption was legalized. I still have families who keep in touch with me.

My role, once I transferred to home finding, was equally as satisfying. I ran group home studies for couples and singles and did a few individualized studies. I'd often become quite involved with these people. Their hopes for a family, so important to many of us, rested on my relationship and ultimate impression of them.

Years later I worked at a small private agency. For this agency, adoption was one service of many. We were less likely to see older children; more likely to have infants. As a worker, I worked with both children and couples. Although it was nice to see all sides of an adoption, I found specializing somehow easier.

The Search

The term *search* refers to adult adoptees' interest in finding information about themselves and about their biological parents, with the possible end of locating and meeting with them. As mentioned earlier, legal adoption results in the child's records being sealed, and they become available only to the child who, as an adult, requests access and then only if the court deems the request to be justifiable.

Supporters of the Search

Over the last few decades, several women have supported and made contributions to adoptees searching for their roots. In 1954, social worker Jean Paton, an adoptee herself, searched for and found her 69-year-old biological mother. She wrote of her experience, and founded an organization called Orphan Voyage. As an organization, Orphan Voyage gives support and guidance to adoptees. Paton lectured widely on adoption and advocated for a "reunion file" that would keep updated information on adoptees and biological parents. This file would then be available to help either party in the search (Coleman, 1988).

Florence Ladden Fisher, another pioneer of adoption searches, spent 20 years searching for her own parents. From overcoming barriers to the end of her successful search, Fisher said that she learned that everything based on her biological and genetic heritage was negative, whereas her adoptive experience was considered positive. Her eventual reunion with her birth parents helped her to resolve her own identity crisis and strengthened her belief that sealed records are an infringement on an adoptee's rights (Coleman, 1988). The writings of numerous authors have done much to support the need for adoptees to search.

Who Searches

In reality, fewer adoptees undertake a search than one might expect. Although there are few accurate statistics on how many adoptees actually search, females tend to be more likely to do so than males (Schechter and Bertocci, 1990). This may be, Smith and Miroff (1987) suggest, because women are trained by the culture to be more sensitive to feelings about identity issues. In addition to being female, most searchers are between ages 26 and 30 (Adamec & Pierce, 2000). Several other researchers have found that searchers are more likely than nonsearchers to have significant stressors in their lives as well as a weaker sense of identity and self-esteem (Feigelman and Silverman, 1983; Sobol and Cardiff, 1983). The search itself may be an attempt to fill what these adoptees perceive to be a void in their lives. Most adoptees are curious about their pasts but comparatively few search. African American adoptees are more likely to search than their white or Asian counterparts. Feigelman and Silverman (1983) estimated that, while 39% of African American adoptees will search, only 2% of whites and 14% of Koreans will (220). Those who search for birth parents may also have had more problematic relationships with adoptive parents (Stein and Hoopes, 1985; Sobol and Cardiff, 1983). Adoptive parents who are uncomfortable with the concept of adoption can actually impel their children to search. Yet, according to Feigelman and Silverman (1983), parents who support their adopted children's need for and efforts to search promote a closer and more positive relationship with these children.

Search Outcome

Of those adoptees who search, a fairly high percentage experience a favorable reunion. For many, having an opportunity to search gave them a more positive view of life in general. Arlene, for instance, was a college student when she began her search. She reports:

> *I think it was just the typical college student's questioning mind, rather than unreal disharmony in my adoptive family that made me want to find my biological parents.*
>
> *My search was actually fairly easy, probably because I knew the agency that had placed me. The social worker was still there. She located my natural mother and asked if she'd meet with me.*
>
> *I'm a carbon copy of my mother and it was such a shock to see her. I was so nervous at our meeting! But I guess she was, too. I learned that she was a college student when she had me, had gotten into drugs and had gotten pregnant. She actually was asked to leave school! Now she's in business and seems to have done well for herself.*

> *I don't regret finding her, or learning that my father was just a party date. I have no real desire to find him. I rarely see my biological mother now, but I feel more self-directed—like I know who I am. My parents had a tough time initially, but they're supportive. I feel more sympathetic now to what adopting meant to them."*

Data in the area of favorable reunions are collected primarily from cases in which birth parents have voluntarily relinquished children. The neglect and abuse underlying situations in which the court removes children may make for more problematic reunions.

What of the effect of adoptees' need to search for their biological parents? Many of those who have given up children for adoption (or had them taken away) rebuilt their lives, and they experience various emotions when a living memory of the past comes into these lives. Yet most birth parents are agreeable to a reunion once their children have requested it (Samuels, 1990). "I felt like it was the last chapter in a book I'd never finished," explained Elaine, a 40-year-old birth mother. "I knew I had a daughter. But I had no idea what had happened to her. Once I knew, I was content to let things rest. She was, too, and it worked out."

Sealed Records

It was the frustrations of both adoptees and birth parents that gave rise to organized search efforts. Orphan Voyage (mentioned earlier) aids adoptees in their searches. The Adoptees' Liberty Movement Association (ALMA), the inspiration of Florence Fisher, publishes a handbook giving advice to adoptees on how to search. Other organizations have become involved in the debate about sealed versus unsealed records. Although United Birth Parents (CUB) advocated opening sealed adoption records when a child reaches a certain age, the Association for the Protection of the Adoptive Triangle (APAP), composed mostly of adoptive parents, insists that records should remain closed. The Child Welfare League of America (CWLA), the primary standard-setting organization for children, still advocates the practice of sealing records (Schechter and Bertocci, 1990), although other factions (see Carp, 1998; Carp and Frankfeldt, 1997) argue that they should not be. Today, access to sealed adoption records can be obtained in most states only if the adoptee has "good cause" to petition the court for access. "Good cause" is not, however, adequately defined; in the past, matters of concern over genetic abnormalities, health, and contested inheritance have been considered. The subject of sealed versus unsealed records continues to be debated (Carp, 1998; Carp and Frankfeldt, 1997).

Consent Contracts

Many adoption agencies offer the option of *consent contracts* to natural parents. These contracts assure the agency that the parents will agree to be contacted if their children should search for them in the future. Such contracts, although they are not foolproof, eliminate some of the uncertainty of past years.

Some agencies also ask adoptive parents if they would be agreeable should their adopted child choose to search out his or her roots. It is felt that these procedures will help future adoptees in their searches.

Trends

Children Available for Adoption

The trend toward fewer infants available for adoption continues. However, there are numerous special needs children still in need of adoptive homes. The need for *homes for special needs children* places additional responsibilities on the adoption agency. Along with the homestudy, to determine if couples meet the required means to adopt, agencies also find that it is essential that couples be prepared for the magnitude of their new venture.

Parents adopting multiracial children, older children, or sibling groups must also be prepared for a change in their lifestyles. Whereas a baby means that one may not have the same freedom, children with special needs further complicate life by requiring additional doctors' or therapists' visits, an increased number of school meetings, and new stressors between adoptive parents.

Another source of children to meet the demand for adoptable infants will be through *independent adoptions*. Despite the inherent risks in nonagency-sponsored adoptions, ads continue to appear in newspapers ("couple seeks infant to adopt"), while attorneys and physicians continue to receive calls from those looking to adopt or place infants for adoption. The continuation of such practices will leave adoption open to the unscrupulous, who hope to make a profit from someone else's need. By the same token, the popularity of independently arranged adoptions may alert agencies to the need to reevaluate their own standards and practices.

As young children become less available in the United States, those hoping to adopt will more frequently seek *foreign-born children*. The Holt International Children's Fund reports that, despite the decrease in children available from Korea and other Asian countries, increasing numbers of children can be adopted from Central and South America, Mexico, and Canada. There is concern, however, about the lack of standardization of adoption practices in various countries.

The number of different types of children available for adoption has caused agencies to lean more toward *specialization in their adoption practices*. According to one adoption worker:

> It used to be that we placed mostly infants. We became experts at it. But today there are few infants and many other types of children—from the

*disabled and mentally retarded to sibling groups and children who have ex-
perienced severe trauma. It became too complicated for us—a small adoption
agency—to serve all types of children. So now we specialize. We place only
single healthy children under ten. It makes it much easier to address the
needs of all the parties involved. The staff also receives specific training to
help us do our job more effectively.*

For the most part, public child welfare agencies continue to see children
with a variety of backgrounds and needs. However, many have developed
units that are dedicated to handling particular types of children. As private
agencies become more specialized, larger agencies may also refer to them.
Some agencies specialize in helping older adoptees with their searches rather
than the actual placement of children.

Permanency Planning

Another trend that may make more children available for adoption is the
move toward *permanency planning,* which is

> *the systematic process of carrying out, within a limited period, a set of goal-
> directed activities designed to help children and youths live in families that
> offer continuity of relationships with nurturing parents or caretakers, and the
> opportunity to offer life-time relationships. (Maluccio et al., 1986, 5)*

The Adoption Assistance and Child Welfare Act of 1980 and the Adoption
and Safe Families Act of 1997 now mandate agencies to follow permanency
planning guidelines, attempting first to reunite families, or consider kinship
alternatives, and then to make other plans for children. The latter legislation,
however, pushes agencies to consider the health and safety of the child above
all. Only through compliance with these guidelines will they receive funds for
services.

Resources Available

Adoption resource exchanges provide one more method of finding homes for children, especially those who are hard to place. The first such exchange was developed in Ohio, but the concept has become not only a statewide, but a regional
and national idea as well. The Adoption Resource Exchange of North America
was credited with aiding in 1,760 adoptions during its first nine years of operation. In 1978, NAIES (National Adoption Information Exchange System) was
funded by the Adoption Reform Act; it is a fully computerized system to identify
children who need homes and the parents who wait for them.

Children in need of homes (usually hard-to-place children) are initially
registered with the statewide adoption resource exchange. This exchange is, in
turn, connected with the national service. In this way, a child on the East

Coast who has particular needs may find new parents as far away as the opposite coast. Thus, both children and adoptive parents are provided with many more opportunities for adoption placement.

Another resource that has gained increased popularity is *adoption subsidy.* This is based on data (Shyne and Schroeder, 1978) that estimated that over 100,000 children were legally freed for adoption, but their care would require more financial outlay than interested adoptive families could provide. These special financial burdens were often based on preexisting medical problems. The states, beginning with New York in 1968, enacted legislation providing adoption subsidies. By 1976, 42 states had enacted subsidy programs, but provisions and eligibility criteria varied widely. The Adoption Assistance and Child Welfare Act of 1980 (PL 96-272) provided more uniformity in subsidies as well as making special needs children eligible for Medicaid and, in some instances, Supplemental Security Income. In 1999, the Administration for Children and Families (AFCARS, 2001) estimated that 88% of the children adopted through public agencies received adoption subsidies (10).

Despite the fact that subsidies allow many children who might not otherwise have this opportunity to be adopted, there are several drawbacks for adoptive parents. First, some states base eligibility criteria not on children's needs but on the adoptive parents' income. And some states limit the duration of subsidy to three years, with the possibility of a two-year extension (Stein, 1981).

Subsidies are based on written agreements made with the adoptive parents at the time of placement. The subsidy cannot be more than state-set foster care payments. Although subsidized adoption has made it possible for many more children to be adopted and for those who were previously unable financially to become adoptive parents, the future of subsidized adoption is constantly debated due to a lack of funds (Adamec and Pierce, 2000).

Lifelong Services

Today there is increased recognition that adoption is a lifelong experience. Parent organizations support both adoptive parents and their adopted children in a variety of ways. These groups provide education, social supports, recruitment, and advocacy for other adoptive families. Many groups publish newsletters and hold support meetings, sometimes independently and sometimes working closely with agencies. One widely known national group, OURS (Organization for United Response), publishes a newsletter that contains all types of parenting experiences. These organizations are often provided with resources by such groups as the North American Council on Adoptable Children (NACAC), which publishes a newsletter (*Adoptable*) outlining activities, resources, and adoption news across the nation, and by the Council on Adoptive Parents (COAC). An adoptive mother states:

> *Our adoptive parent group was a great deal of help to us. Several members spoke with us during our home study and provided all sorts of help when we*

first got our child. They had a "help line" we could call if we had a question. It felt better to call someone who'd adopted than the agency. Later the group was a great deal of support when we needed some advocacy. Now I help out new adoptive parents and it feels great. Every time I talk to a new struggling parent, I am helped to work out my own issues.

In addition to input from parent groups, agencies are becoming increasingly aware of additional *lifelong support services*. Many agencies provide adoption-specific counseling. As one adoptive mother who is also a mental health clinician put it:

We professionals are just beginning to realize that what we thought were family problems are specifically adoption issues. We need to continue to develop our skills in counseling adolescent and adult adoptees. Adoption is not always a happily-ever-after story. It's work—like every other worthwhile relationship. But we have to learn to help adoptive families through the trials of adjustment throughout their lives!

When children are unable to adjust they may be removed from the adoptive home in later life. Only recently have theorists and clinicians begun to recognize adoption as a factor of importance in children's problems (Robinson, 1998; Simon and Altstein, 2001). The already turbulent teen years, when individuals strive to find their identity, can prove overwhelming for the adopted child. Biological parents and heredity can become such preoccupations that the adolescent's quest for understanding, combined with the insecurity felt by many adoptive parents, creates a dangerous imbalance in the family. The results usually seen in the adolescent—impulsive, provocative, aggressive, or antisocial behavior—can lead to placement outside the home (Grotevant and McRoy, 1998). Residential treatment centers across the country attest to the upsurge in the number of adolescents coming to them from adoptive families. Professionals treating these individuals are becoming increasingly aware that the experience of adoption cannot be ignored if one is to take a holistic approach to the adolescents' problem (Rosenberg, 2000).

As we consider the issues discussed in this chapter, it becomes obvious that the process of adoption is complex. There are so many variables that affect the successful outcome of this created family. Those in the field of adoption strive to improve services to all involved in the process.

Summary

Adoption has its roots in antiquity. Over the years the rationale for adoption shifted its primary focus from providing heirs for the titled to acknowledging every child's right to a home. While originally based on English law, adoption laws in the United States began to take shape in the mid-nineteenth century.

Different cultural groups influenced the evolution of these laws. Today, adoption practice is shaped largely by PL 96-272, the Federal Adoption Assistance and Child Welfare Act of 1980, and the Adoption and Safe Families Act of 1997, which emphasize permanency planning for every child.

Adoption can be divided into two categories: related and unrelated. Related adoptions encompass such arrangements as adoption by a relative or stepparent and, more recently, adoption by the biological father of a surrogate mother's child. Unrelated adoption can be agency sponsored or independent of agency involvement. Agencies are increasingly involved in the placement of special needs children which encompasses children with disabilities, cross-cultural adoptions, the adoption of children older than age 5, or of sibling groups. Subsidized adoption provides adoptive couples with a stipend to help them with the support of their special needs child. Some agencies allow single-parent adoptions, placing children in the homes of unmarried adoptive parents. In international adoptions children are brought from other countries to the homes of parents in the United States.

There are increasingly fewer white, healthy infants available for adoption. Perhaps the increase in birth control and abortion is one set of factors. In addition, teen parents are more likely to keep their children than in years past. The focus has therefore shifted to the placement of special needs children and to couples searching out and arranging their own independent adoptions. Both of these types of adoptions involve risks and require special thought on the part of adoptive couples.

The adoption process is complex. Birth parents must be recognized as having their own motivations for and feelings about placing their children for adoption. While some lose their children through abuse and neglect, others make a conscious, often painful, choice, recognizing that adoption provides a better alternative for their children. Race and culture may also influence the biological mother's decision and her ability to act on her choice. Parents who relinquish their children may feel out of control, inadequate, stigmatized, bitter and angry, or powerless. Agencies strive to help them with these feelings and enable them to make the choice with which they can feel relatively comfortable.

The children available for adoption may be healthy infants, older children, sibling groups, children with disabilities or medical problems, children from minority groups, or foreign-born children. Depending on who they are, they will present different issues for their adoptive families.

Adoptive applicants are recruited by agencies in different ways. Increasingly agencies have used churches and other civic organizations to improve their recruitment efforts. Applicants are motivated to adopt for varied reasons, some because they want to enlarge their families, others because they believe that there is a need for homes for specific types of children.

Potential adoptive couples are screened through a home study that evaluates their motivation and eligibility criteria, as well as educating them about the children available and the issues inherent in adoption. Children are then placed with appropriate families. Sometimes the children's ties with the past are maintained—called open adoption—while in other instances these ties are severed. Legalization means that the original records are sealed and the child legally becomes the child of the adoptive parents. Despite this finality, families are encouraged to keep the issue of adoption open and talked about at home.

Increasingly agencies are recognizing that legalization is not the end of the story. Families need postadoption support, and may return for counseling around adoption issues. Occasionally adoption placements will fail, necessitating further agency intervention and counseling.

Over the last few years there has been an increase in the number of adoptees who have searched for their biological parents. This upsurge in the interest in biological roots has stimulated further controversy over whether adoption records should continue to be sealed. Today, agencies often offer biological parents consent contracts, documents that state the parents' willingness to meet their offspring if that individual, as an adult, chooses to search.

Several trends can be seen in the field of adoption. These fall into three categories: the children available for adoption, resources currently available, and adoption as a lifelong issue. The children available are increasingly special needs children. Some adoptive applicants seek foreign adoptions instead. For this reason an increased number of couples are exploring independent adoption as an alternative. Various resources aid couples and children in their search for family life. Adoption resource exchanges unite children from one geographical area with parents from another. Adoption subsidies provide funds for adoptive parents who could not otherwise afford the expenses incurred by a particular child.

Finally, adoption must be seen as a lifelong issue. More and more services are recognizing this fact. Adoption is not an easy answer to a desire to augment one's family or to provide permanency for a child. But with resources, time, and support for all those involved, adoption can be a rewarding option.

EXPLORATION QUESTIONS

1. What was the original purpose of adoption in early history? How has that view changed?
2. What is meant by *permanency planning?* What legal statute influenced our current perception of adoption?
3. On what values is adoption practice based?
4. What are the types of adoption? Explain each briefly.
5. What is meant by independent adoption? What types of placements are there in this area? Why is this type of adoption seen as problematic?
6. Cite five issues prevalent in adoption literature today. Explain each briefly.
7. Why might a birth parent give up a child for adoption? What might she feel in making this decision?
8. Who are the children who are available for adoption?
9. Why might someone want to adopt a child? Outline a profile of those who apply to adopt.
10. Explain the adoption process.

11. What is meant by adoption disruption? Why might it happen?
12. Cite the trends in adoption today. Explain each briefly.

REFERENCES

Adamec, C. A., & Pierce, W. L. (2000). *The Encyclopedia of Adoption*. Facts on File, Inc.

Administration for Children and Families (AF-CARS). (2001). "AFCARS Report" at http://www.acf.dhhs.gov/programs.

Barry, M. (1990). "Preparing and Supporting Special Needs Adoptive Families: A Review of the Literature," *Child and Adolescent Social Work*, 7, 403–418.

Barth, R. P., & Berry, M. (1988). *Adoption and Disruption: Rates, Risks and Responses*. New York: Aldine De Gruyter.

Berger, M., & Hodges, J. (1982). "Some thoughts on the Question of When to Tell the Child That He Is Adopted," *Journal of Child Psychotherapy*, 8, 67–88.

Berry, M., & Barth, R. P. (1990). "A Study of Disrupted Adoptive Placements of Adolescents," *Child Welfare*, 69(3), 209–225.

Boersdorfer, R. K., Kaser, J. S., & Tremitier, W. C. (1986). *Guide to Local TEAM Programs*. York, PA: Tressler-Lutheran Associates.

Brace, C. L. (1872). *The Dangerous Classes in New York and Twenty Years' Work among Them*. New York: Wynkoop & Hallenbeck.

Brodzinsky, D. M., & Schechter, M. D. (Eds.). (1990). *The Psychology of Adoption*. New York: Oxford University Press.

Brodzinsky, D., Smith, D. W., & Brodzinsky, A. (1999). *Children's Adjustment to Adoption*. Thousand Oaks, CA: Sage.

Byrd, A. D. (1988). "The Case for Confidential Adoption," *Public Welfare*, 46(4), 20–23.

Carp, E. W. (1998). *Family Matters: Secrecy and Disclosure in the History of Adoption*. Cambridge, MA: Harvard University Press.

Carp, E. W., & Frankfeldt, G. (1997). *Family Matter: Secrecy and Disclosure in the History of Adoption*. Cambridge, MA: Harvard University Press.

Child Welfare League of America. (1978). *Standards of Adoption Service*. New York: Child Welfare League of America.

Child Welfare League of America (CWLA). (1998). *State Agency Survey*. Washington, DC: CWLA.

Cohen, N. (Ed.). (2000). *Child Welfare: A Multicultural Perspective*. Boston: Allyn and Bacon.

Cole, E. S. (1987). "Adoption." In A. Minahan (Ed.), *Encyclopedia of Social Work* (Vol. 1, 18th ed.). Silver Springs, MD: National Association of Social Workers.

Cole, J. (1995). *How I Was Adopted: Samantha's Story*. New York: Wm. Morrow.

Cole, E. S., & Donley, K. S. (1990). "History, Values & Placement Policy Issues in Adoption." In D. M. Brodzinsky & M. D. Schechter (Eds.), *The Psychology of Adoption*. New York: Oxford University Press.

Coleman, L. (1988). "The Search." In L. Coleman et al., (Eds.), *Working with Older Adoptees*. Portland, ME: University of Southern Maine.

Coleman, L., Tilbor, K., Hornby, H., & Boggis, C. (1988). *Working with Older Adoptees: A Sourcebook of Innovative Models*. Portland, ME: University of Southern Maine.

Crosson-Tower, C. (2003). *From the Eye of the Storm: The Experiences of a Child Welfare Worker*. Boston: Allyn and Bacon.

Cushman, L., Kalmuss, D., & Nameron, P. B. (1993). "Placing an Infant for Adoption: The Experiences of Young Birth Mothers," *Social Work*, 38(3), 264–272.

Dallas, C. M., & Chen, S. C. (2002). "Experiences of African-American Adolescent Fathers," *Western Journal of Nursing Research* 20(2), 210–223.

Dave Thomas Foundation for Adoption and Evan B. Donaldson Institute. (2002). *National Adoption Attitudes Survey* at http://www.davethomasfoundationforadoption.org.

Day, D. (1979). *The Adoption of Black Children*. Lexington, MA: Lexington Books.

Downs, S. W., Costin, L. B., Moore, E., & McFadden, E. J. (2000). *Child Welfare and*

Family Services: Policies and Practice. New York: Longman.

Feigelman, W., & Silverman, A. (1983). *Chosen Children: New Patterns of Adoptive Relationships.* New York: Praeger.

Festinger, T. B. (1986). *Necessary Risk—A Study of Adoptions and Disrupted Adoption Placements.* New York: Child Welfare League of America.

Festinger, T. (1990). "Adoption Disruption: Rates and Correlates." In D. M. Brodzinsky & M. D. Schechter, (Eds.), *The Psychology of Adoption.* New York: Oxford University Press.

Fish, A., & Speirs, C. (1990). "Biological Parents Choose Adoptive Parents: The Use of Profiles in Adoptions," *Child Welfare, 69,* 129–139.

Frey, L. (1988) "Making an Impact: Post-Adoption Crisis Counseling." In L. Coleman et al. (Eds.), *Working with Older Adoptees.* Portland, ME: University of Southern Maine.

Gibb, P. (2000). *Adopting Massachusetts.* Worcester, MA: Center for Adoption Research. University of Massachusetts.

Gitlin, H. (1987). *Adoptions: An Attorney's Guide to Helping Adoptive Parents.* Wilmette, IL: Callaghan.

Goodrich, W., Fullerton, C. S., Yates, B. T., & Berman, L. B. (1990). "The Residential Treatment of Severely Disturbed Adolescent Adoptees." In D. M. Brodzinsky & M. D. Schechter (Eds.), *The Psychology of Adoption.* New York: Oxford University Press.

Grotevant, H., & McRoy, R. G. (1998). *Openness in Adoption: Exploring Family Connections.* Thousand Oaks, CA: Sage.

Gruber, A. R. (1973). *Foster Home Care in Massachusetts.* Boston: Governor's Commission on Adoption & Foster Care.

Hartman, A., & Laird, J. (1990). "Family Treatment after Adoption: Common Themes" (221–239). In D. M. Brodzinsky & M. D. Schechter (Eds.), *The Psychology of Adoption.* New York: Oxford University Press.

Hegar, R. L., & Scannapieco, M. (1999). *Kinship Foster Care.* New York: Oxford University Press.

Helwig, A. A., & Ruthven, D. H. (1990). "Psychological Ramifications of Adoption and Implications for Counseling," *Journal of Mental Health Counseling, 12,* 24–37.

Hollingsworth, L. D. (1998). "Promoting Same-Race Adoption for Children of Color," *Social Work, 43*(2), 104–116. Holt International at http://www.holtintl.org.

Howe, R. W. (1983). "Adoption Practices, Issues and Laws. 1958–1983," *Family Law Quarterly, 17,* 173–197.

Kadushin, A., & Martin, J. A. (1988). *Child Welfare Services.* New York: Macmillan.

Koehler, P. (1997). *The Day We Met You.* New York: Aladdin Books.

Krementz, J. (1982). *How It Feels to Be Adopted.* New York: Alfred A. Knopf.

Levy, T., & Orlans, M. (1998). *Attachment, Trauma and Healing.* Washington, DC: Child Welfare League of America.

Livingston, C. (1978). *Why Was I Adopted?* Seacaucus, NJ: Lyle Stuart.

London, J. (1997). *A Koala for Katie: An Adoption Story.* Morton Grove, IL: Albert Whitman.

Maluccio, A. N., Fein, E., & Olmstead, K. A. (1986). *Permanency Planning for Children: Concepts and Methods.* London and New York: Routledge, Chapman, & Hall.

Marindin, H. (1987). *The Handbook for Single Adoptive Parents.* Chevy Chase, MD: Committee for Single Adoptive Parents.

Maza, P. L. (1990). "Trends in National Data on the Adoptions of Children with Handicaps," *Journal of Children in Contemporary Society, 21*(3–4), 119–138.

Mica, M. D., & Vosler, N. R. (1990). "Foster-Adoptive Programs in Public Social Service Agencies: Toward Flexible Family Resources," *Child Welfare, 69*(1), 433–446.

National Committee for Adoption. (1989). *Adoption Factbook: U.S. Data Issues Regulations and Resources.* Washington, DC: National Committee for Adoption.

Patton, S. (2000). *Birthmarks: Transracial Adoption in Contemporary America.* New York: New York University Press.

Pavao, J. M. (1998). *The Family of Adoption.* Boston: Beacon Press.

Pecora, P., Barth, R. P., Whittaker, J. K., Maluccio, A. N., & Plotnick, R. D. (2000). *The*

Child Welfare Challenge: Policy, Practice and Research. New York: Aldine De Gruyter.

Plumer, E. H. (1992). *When You Place a Child.* Springfield, IL: Charles C. Thomas.

Register, C. (1991). *Are Those Kids Yours? American Families with Children Adopted from Other Countries.* New York: Free Press.

Robinson, G. (1998). *Older Child Adoptions.* New York: Crossroad Publishing Group.

Rosenberg, E. B. (2000). *The Adoption Life Cycle.* New York: Free Press.

Rynearson, E. K. (1981). "Relinquishment and Its Maternal Complications," *American Journal of Psychiatry,* 139, 338–340.

Samuels, S. C. (1990). *Ideal Adoption: A Comprehensive Guide to Forming an Adoptive Family.* New York: Plenum Press.

Schechter, M. D., & Bertocci, D. (1990). "The Meaning of the Search." In D. M. Brodzinsky & M. D. Schechter (Eds.), *The Psychology of Adoption.* New York: Oxford University Press.

Shanley, M. L. (2002). *Making Babies, Making Families.* Boston: Beacon Press.

Shireman, J. F., & Johnson, P. R. (1976). "Single Persons as Adoptive Parents," *Social Service Review,* 50(1), 103–116.

Shireman, J. F., & Johnson, P. R. (1986). "A Longitudinal Study of Black Adoptions: Single Parents, Transracial & Traditional," *Social Work,* 31, 172–176.

Shyne, A., & Schroeder, A. (1978). *National Study of Social Services to Children and Their Families.* Washington, DC: DHEW.

Siegel, D. H. (1993). "Open Adoption of Infants: Adoptive Parents' Perceptions of Advantages and Disadvantages," *Social Work,* 38(1), 15–23.

Silverman, A. R., & Feigelman, W. (1990). "Adjustment in Interracial Adoptees: An Overview" (187–200). In D. M. Brodzinsky &

M. D. Schechter (Eds.), *The Psychology of Adoption.* New York: Oxford University Press.

Silverstein, D. N., & Kaplan, S. (1988). "Lifelong Issues in Adoption." In L. Coleman et al. (Eds.), *Working with Older Adoptees.* Portland, ME: University of Southern Maine.

Simon, R. J., & Altstein, H. (2000). *Adoption Across Borders.* Lanham, MD: Rowman & Littlefield.

Simon, R. J., & Roorda, R. M. (2000). *In Their Own Voices: Transracial Adoptees Tell Their Stories.* New York: Columbia University Press.

Skinner, K. (1989). "Counseling Issues in the Fostering & Adoption of Children at Risk of HIV Infection," *Counseling Psychology Quarterly,* 10, 89–92.

Sloan, I. J. (1988). *The Law of Adoption and Surrogate Parenting.* New York: Oceana Publications.

Smith, J., & Miroff, F. (1987). *You're Our Child: The Adoption Experience.* New York: Madison.

Sobol, M., & Cardiff, J. (1983). "A Socio-Psychological Investigation of Adult Adoptee's Search for Birth Parents," *Family Relations,* 32, 477–483.

Stein, L. M., & Hoopes, J. L. (1985). *Identity Formation in the Adopted Adolescents—The Delaware Family Study.* New York: Child Welfare League of America.

Stein, T. J. (1981). *Social Work Practice in Child Welfare.* Englewood Cliffs, NJ: Prentice Hall.

Steinberg, G., & Hallinan, B. (2000). *Inside Transracial Adoption.* Indianapolis, IN: Perspective Press.

Wieder, H. (1977). "On Being Told of Adoption," *Psychoanalytic Quarterly,* 46, 1–22.

Wingard, D. (1987). "Trends and Characteristics of California Adoptions, 1946–1982," *Child Welfare,* 66, 303–314.

13 Children in Residential Settings

Historical Perspective

Residential settings for children have evolved as society's view of children and their needs has changed. Early institutional care was based on the concept of providing homeless children with a place to stay. In France, in the fifteenth century, St. Vincent dePaul established homes for abandoned children (Kadushin and Martin, 1988). The first institution in the United States was founded by the Ursuline nuns of New Orleans to harbor children who were orphaned by the Natchez Indian Massacre (Pecora et al., 2000).

For many years, poor children resided with their parents in *almshouses*. But critics of these institutions felt that they were unhealthy for young souls and bodies and encouraged separate sections of almshouses, if not separate institutions, dedicated to the needs of children. In 1875, the state of New York mandated that children be removed from almshouses and placed in institutions specifically set up for children or in families. The movement toward the establishment of *orphanages* for children flourished, and by the early 1900s, there were close to 125,000 children in the United States living in orphanages (Kadushin and Martin, 1988). Most of the institutions built were designated for white children, with policies excluding African American children (Everett et al., 1992; Billingsley and Giovannoni, 1972). These orphanages, or asylums, built mostly by charitable, benevolent, or religious organizations, served to house and feed children as well as instilling in them a sense of order, good moral character, and obedience. The hope was to save "children from both physical and moral degradation" (Keith-Lucas and Sanford, 1977, 6).

As child care institutions increased and flourished into the mid-1900s, there came the rumblings of criticism of the effects of institutional care on the development of young children. In 1951, Bowlby, in *Maternal Care and Mental Health,* written as a United Nations Report, discussed considerable research demonstrating that institutional care had a negative effect on children. Goffman, in 1961, wrote his well-known *Asylums,* in which he argued that children brought up in institutions learned behaviors that actually inhibited their ability to adjust once they left the institutional setting (Kadushin and Martin, 1988).

While orphan asylums were built and debated about, another type of institution for children had its inception. The first *setting for juvenile delinquents,* the House of Refuge, was built in New York in the 1800s to be followed by similar institutions in Boston in 1826 and in Philadelphia in 1928. In Massachusetts, the Lyman School, a state-funded reform or training school for delinquent boys, opened its doors in 1847 and operated until the early 1970s on the model of the German agricultural reformatory (Pecora et al., 2000). The 1800s also saw the development of *institutions for the mentally retarded, deaf, blind, and physically handicapped* (Kadushin and Martin, 1988).

Another type of institution for children, the *residential treatment center,* began between the 1930s to 1950s. These settings were based on an increased interest in mental health and the recognition that for some children the family could not meet their needs. Emotionally disturbed children became a new interest of practitioners, and techniques to treat them as groups in congregate settings became popular.

Pecora and colleagues (2000) suggest that the history of residential care can be divided into four phases: (1) provision of separate institutions for children as opposed to mixing them with adults; (2) the move to cottage or family-style units as opposed to barrack-style living; (3) the psychological phase, which emphasized the introduction of treatment concepts as opposed to maintenance of children in institutions; and (4) the environmental or ecological phase, which emphasized evaluation of outcomes in residential care.

The history of one large institution, the Devereux Foundation, exemplifies how institutions for children developed in the United States. In the early 1900s, while the media of Philadelphia were expounding on the quality of local schools, there was little available to address the needs of children who had "fallen behind their classmates in school." One educator cognizant of this deficit was Helena Trafford Devereux, a young teacher who began to focus on these children with special needs. Initially, she was assigned to teach mentally retarded children within the public school system. In 1912, she began a program in her own home, designing an around-the-clock program for three children in a "homelike setting." In 1918, she moved the children to a home in Devon, Pennsylvania, and a year later was ready to expand her program into an adjoining house. Parents of special children began to seek out Miss Devereux and the school/residence expanded, until in 1924 it became the Devereux Schools. As Devereux's reputation grew, the program continued to expand. Additional components offered help to young men in their late teens to train them for trades, and a camp component offered "therapeutic programming and recreation for children and adolescents who were brain-damaged, mentally handicapped, and/or emotionally disturbed."

By 1938, the Commonwealth of Pennsylvania had granted a charter to the Devereux Foundation with the purpose of

studying, treating and carrying on research and educational work in connection with functional and nervous disorders; and educating and developing, and advancing boys and girls of any age along psychological and psychiatric lines, in addition to serving their intellectual, emotional, and vocational needs. (4)

During the 1940s, the Foundation opened centers in other areas of the United States as well as several new centers in Pennsylvania. From treating the mentally retarded and emotionally disturbed child, the Devereux Foundation expanded its programs to serve the newly diagnosed condition of autism. The 1950s saw additional expansion, and in 1958, the American Psychiatric Association made Helena Devereux an Honorary Fellow, the first woman without a medical degree to be so honored. By the 1970s, Devereux's standards in residential treatment had become the "benchmark by which other programs were measured" (7).

Today, the Devereux Foundation offers programs for mentally retarded children, emotionally disturbed and autistic children and adolescents, and individuals with head trauma. Programs serve 14 states and provide such services as residential treatment, group homes, supported apartment living, therapeutic foster care, day treatment, respite services, and partial and acute hospital facilities. In addition, the foundation carries out research and provides training for those interested in therapeutic work with a variety of populations. Although not all institutional programs for children have the components of the Devereux Foundation, many provide such services on a smaller scale.

The complexion of child care institutions has changed a good deal since the nineteenth and early twentieth centuries. The orphanage, at one time the most popular child care institution, has all but disappeared as a result of the recognition of the importance of a family setting to children's healthy development. The beginnings of this extinction came when cottage settings or family-style units began to replace the sterile barrack-style buildings of early orphanages. The deinstitutional movement of the mid-1900s continued the trend toward replicating family and community whenever possible. It is interesting that today's political leaders have spoken of the reestablishment of orphanages despite the lessons of the past.

Although some institutions for the handicapped do still exist, the move is toward having those who are able to live in the community as opposed to an institution. The emphasis on the least restrictive environment and the preservation of the family has significantly changed the nature of residential settings today.

Assumptions about Residential Care

CASE EXAMPLE

Nancy

Nancy was 12 years old when her mother was institutionalized. Before that, she had been in and out of foster care from the age of 4. "My mom had been sick for a long time," she recounts. "We never knew who she'd be and when. Sometimes she was like another kid and it was fun to be with her. We didn't get meals and stuff, but we got used to that. But sometimes she'd sleep all day or scream at us and curl up in a ball under the table. That was scary. It seems like every few months we'd end up in a foster home. I got sick of it."

When her mother was finally institutionalized, Nancy ran away and was gone for several days. When she returned she was once again placed in a foster home. "That was just it!" she explained. "I was sick of everyone telling me what to do, of new rules and new faces! The foster mother's kid really got to me. I couldn't stand the little brat! I got really mad one day and pulled a knife on him. I think I would've killed him, but the foster father grabbed me and the foster mother called the social worker. The next thing I know, I'm in this place with other kids who'd blown out of foster homes too."

A residential setting is seen as *the last alternative for children.* Children who are placed in such settings have either had difficulty in foster homes or demonstrate behavior that would be difficult to handle in a family setting. Some children have difficulty with attachment and forming relationships, therefore they may do better in a group than in the intimacy of a family (Levy and Orlans, 1998). Children who are extremely self-abusive or suicidal, children who cannot conform to family rules, children who are dangerous to others or are exceptionally destructive to property may be candidates for residential care. In addition to behaviors, some children have physical limitations that are difficult for families to handle. Jared, for instance, was born severely mentally retarded, deaf, and blind. Because of his disabilities, he was minimally responsive to his environment. At first, his parents kept him at home, but as he grew they found that they were no longer able to do so. "It was with a great deal of guilt that we placed him in the center," explained his mother tearfully. "But it got to be too much. We have four other children and we couldn't have any kind of a family life. I began to resent Jared and that wasn't fair to him either."

The trend is to place children in the *least restrictive setting*. Some settings are locked and the staff ratio is high. Others are more like a community setting and residents have a good deal of freedom. The needs of each child are considered when he or she is placed in residential care and the hope is that children will be placed in a situation where there is just enough structure to meet their needs.

What makes residential settings more beneficial than family environments for some children? First, having a staff of several people provides children with *opportunities for diluted emotional interaction with others*. Instead of one mother and one father, children in residential settings have choices as to the parenting figure to whom they are exposed. Attachment-disorderd children can feel comfortable with less intense relationships while they work on trying to learn to trust. They can also feel safe by knowing that there is structure with *consistent rules* that a family setting cannot always offer. For the staff, relating to the children and understanding their needs is their primary function while they are on duty. Thus, not faced with tasks of maintaining a family that foster parents have to contend with, child care *staff can be more focused on their charges' needs* (Whitaker et al., 1998; Kadushin and Martin, 1988).

Residential programs are *structured specifically to meet the needs of their residents*. The treatment environment can be orchestrated so that it addresses the therapeutic challenges of each child. The day of each child can be planned to be of maximum therapeutic benefit. If a child is having difficulty with his or her program, it can be adjusted. If there are problems with roommates or cottage mates, the unit can be rearranged. These changes might not be possible in a family setting. Educational programs can be geared to the abilities of the specific child and can be monitored closely if changes are necessary (Marohn, 1993).

Residential settings *can also accommodate a wider range of destructive behaviors*. Although most foster parents learn to child-proof their houses, the fact remains that they have more investment in the preservation of their furniture, house, and possessions than do staff in an institutional setting. Residences also tend to be furnished with almost indestructible furniture and a dearth of fragile items.

Granted, the attributes of residential treatment settings described previously represent the conditions in the best case scenario. In reality, staff is not always consistent and there is usually a high turnover rate. Training for child care staff is often not given as much time and emphasis as would be ideal. Funding may mean that school supplies are in short supply, and vandalism still does happen. (Additional problems will be discussed later in this chapter.) But, on the whole, for some children, the comparatively impersonal structure of a group residence provides a better opportunity for therapeutic intervention.

Types of Residential Settings

Currently residential group settings serve several different populations:

1. *Children who are in need of diagnostic services;*
2. *Children who are in need of intense therapeutic services due to being abused, neglected, or abandoned;*
3. *Children who are emotionally disturbed and require residential treatment;*
4. *Children who are adjudicated delinquent and require rehabilitative services;*
5. *Children who are severely mentally retarded or multiply handicapped. (Kadushin and Martin, 1988)*

It is important that residential setting not be seen as one entity and grouped together. In fact there are numerous types of facilities, each meeting the needs of a different type of population. In addition, not every type of residential service is provided by one specific agency. Many settings mix clients with various types of problems. For example, a large setting might have a cottage or program dedicated to diagnostic services, where children stay for a short period of time while a treatment strategy is being devised for them. That same center may have another section designed to treat children over a longer period of time, while working with their families and attempting to integrate them back into the community. Some centers have components that deal with children who are severely disabled and/or mentally retarded and others that deal with higher functioning children. There are also residential treatment settings that treat both the dependent child, who may be in the care of the social services agency, along with the child who has been adjudicated delinquent by the court. These centers also may see children on a short-term basis (often called an *emergency placement*) or on a longer ongoing basis. The combinations and possibilities are endless. There are also a few settings that specialize in certain types of problems. For example, increasingly, there are programs dedicated to the treatment of adolescent sexual offenders.

As we consider the types of services provided in residential settings, bear in mind that a center may either specialize or combine a variety of different services in one organization.

Diagnostic Services

When a child is in emotional distress, it is not always clear, what has caused his or her behavior, suicide attempt, depression, or other manifestation of disturbance, or what type of treatment will be most helpful to him or her. In order to best serve the child, this information must be discovered. Diagnostic centers, or diagnostic components of programs, observe children closely while having them participate in various types of testing and assessment interviews. Children stay in diagnostic centers from a day or two to several months, depending on their needs and the availability of services for them once they leave the diagnostic center. Some agencies use diagnostic programs not only as initial screening tools but also as evaluative services.

Intense Therapeutic Services for Dependent Children

Children who have been exposed to extreme trauma in their families may need treatment or respite before they are able to respond to another family experience such as a foster home. These children are usually young and their final plan may involve adoption.

CASE EXAMPLE

Shannon

Shannon was the oldest of four children, all of whom had been severely neglected by their natural mother. The girl was extremely protective of her younger siblings and adamant that they not be placed separately. Because a foster home could not be found for the entire group, the four children were placed in a small church-sponsored residential center. Shannon was helped to feel safe and to overcome some of the residual behaviors of her mother's neglect. Eventually, an adoptive home was found for all four siblings.

Possibly the closest modern thing to the old orphanage, these centers specialize in young children who are not so deeply affected by their abuse that they cannot return to a family setting. Often that family will not be their own.

Residential Treatment Centers

Residential treatment is perhaps the most common type of setting for children and adolescents today. These agencies specialize in the *therapeutic milieu,* combining therapeutic services from a residential, educational, and psychological perspective. Children and youths might be placed in residential treatment settings for a variety of reasons. The most common of these are to protect the child; to protect the community; or because the child's behavior cannot be managed in the home, school, or community. Some children become so involved in self-defeating or destructive behaviors that it is necessary to treat them on a round-the-clock basis. Their disturbance may also require professionals skilled in addressing such behaviors. Residential treatment also allows for the constant supervision and technical interventions that are not possible in the home.

Children with psychiatric problems or those who are in danger of hurting themselves or others are especially appropriate for such out-of-home placement.

The following descriptions illustrate the types of children who are appropriate for residential treatment:

- Rosemary is a 15-year-old girl who uses marijuana and crack cocaine. She is sexually active and has many older partners. Her parents are at a loss as to what to do with her. Recently, the school called home saying that Rosemary complained of "hearing voices." School officials were not sure if she was using drugs or psychiatrically disturbed, but did not feel that she should continue attending school. The school suggested that she be placed in residential treatment.
- Donald is 13 years old and has been involved in criminal activity. He has been seen by the juvenile court for breaking and entering, assault, truancy, and possession of drugs. His mother is dead and his father is an alcoholic who wants to "wash his hands of the kid." His older brother is serving time in prison. Donald can no longer live at home and refuses to go to a foster home. In addition, foster parents fear his violent temper. Therefore, the juvenile court has mandated that he be placed in residential treatment.
- Janis is 14 years old. She was severely sexually abused by her father and two of her uncles. She became pregnant at age 13 and gave up her child for adoption. Janis is extremely impulsive and very concerned with boys. She is bulemic and is into cutting herself with knives. Although Janis's mother is concerned, she does not feel that she can handle her daughter. This mother's hope is that a program will "knock some sense into her." Due to this mother's inability to cope with her daughter's behavior, the social service agency working with her has recommended residential treatment.

These scenarios also describe situations in which children might reach residential treatment. Usually, placement is initiated by one or more of four sources: the school, the social service agency (often CPS), the juvenile court, or the probation officer or agency dealing with delinquent behaviors or the child's parents. These referral sources are also those who may be responsible for paying for this placement.

Rehabilitative or Secure Treatment for Delinquents

CASE EXAMPLE

Harvey

Harvey was a 15-year-old who had a long history of delinquent acts. He had been in and out of the court system since he was age 10. When he pulled a knife on another student at school, he was arrested and again referred to the court. Harvey became out of control in the courtroom and threatened to "get that lousy kid who sent me here!" (the child on whom he had pulled the knife). Feeling that Harvey was a safety risk, the judge sent him to a secure detention center until further plans could be made. From there, he was placed in a locked setting for delinquent boys.

The goal of secure treatment is to protect the community from delinquents while trying to change their behavior until it is possible to place them in a less secure setting, usually a residential treatment center. Most secure settings are locked and have a high staff-to-student ratio. Residents are closely monitored, have educational services at the facility, and receive intensive therapeutic services. The hope is that the restrictive setting, combined with the intensity of the intervention services, will help the individuals gain sufficient control so that they can benefit from a less restrictive treatment program.

What determines if a child is placed in a secure setting or in a residential treatment setting that is less secure? There are several factors involved. First, the child's behavior must be assessed to determine how injurious it is to self or others and if it can be managed without constant attention from staff. Second, the child's potential for the development of inner controls is important. Can he or she monitor himself or herself to some extent or is it necessary for the controls to be totally external? Third, does the child have a history of running away? Many nonsecure centers have no recourse but to let the child run away. A locked center might be more appropriate for a chronic runner. Finally, the choice of where the child is placed may not be based as much on therapeutic considerations (although it should be) as on the institution that is able to take a child at a given time (Whitaker et al., 1998; Marohn, 1993).

Centers for Children with Severe Special Needs

When children have severe special needs, it may not be possible for their parents to care for them. For example, one center for brain-injured children took those who could not do any of their own self-care. Usually these children had become older, larger, and were too heavy or their needs too complex for their parents to handle. Many of these parents had been well intentioned when the children were little, and had expected to keep them at home. But time had taken its toll, and as their lives began to center exclusively around these children, many parents felt they could no longer care for them. This is not to say that many parents do not feel terribly guilty about their decision to place their child in a residential setting. But many also realize that the residence may be better equipped to deal with their child's issues. In addition, having a special needs child in a family can be difficult for other siblings. Sometimes it is the needs of other children that the parents must also consider.

Centers for mentally retarded or physically disabled children are usually staffed by a variety of professionals, including medical personnel. The facility may look like a hospital when the population is more severely disabled or it may look like any other institution, or even a large private home. Services usually include medical care, as well as residential and educational services for higher functioning clients. Some centers also have a day program in which children can spend the day, giving their parents respite to work or perform tasks for the rest of the family.

Children in Residential Settings

Reasons for Referral

What might point to placement of a child in residential care as opposed to placement in a foster home? Some answers to this question were alluded to in an earlier section (Assumptions about Residential Care). Basically, children are placed in these centers because their needs are beyond the domain of the foster care system. Some are placed due to the needs of the community and some due to the child's own specific needs.

Meeting Community Needs.   Some children are placed in order to protect the community. These children may be homicidal, fire-setters, sexually abusive, or otherwise injurious to others.

CASE EXAMPLE

Quentin

Quentin was 10 years old when he killed his younger brother. After a brief observation period, it was felt that he must be placed in a center for severely disturbed children. He had three other younger siblings and had also threatened other children in the neighborhood. His parents admitted that even they were afraid of him.

Meeting the Child's Specific Needs.   A child also might be placed for his or her own protection. Some children are suicidal or abuse substances to a degree that is unmanageable in a home environment.

CASE EXAMPLE

Wendell

Wendell was a 14-year-old who had been taking drugs and drinking since he was age 9. At that time, he and several friends stole cough syrup containing codeine and drank it in large quantities to enjoy the effect. Later,

Wendell graduated to street drugs and alcohol. By age 12, he was usually either drunk or "stoned" on some substance. A drug addict herself, with five other children, his mother had little control over his behavior. At age 13, he was removed from her home due to severe neglect. Then followed placement in seven foster homes within a year, until finally Wendell was placed in a secure residential setting.

Sometimes a child's behavior is not necessarily dangerous to others or himself or herself but is so disturbed that neither parents nor foster parents are able to manage it.

CASE EXAMPLE

Marina

At age 9, Marina, was diagnosed as psychotic. Her severely abusive background gave her little ability to trust adults, including the therapists who had tried to help her. She hallucinated and seemed unable to maintain touch with reality. After a series of placements in psychiatric hospitals, it seemed better, both emotionally and financially, to place her in a center for severely disturbed children.

There are also children who can benefit from the type of treatment provided in a residential setting. For those who have demonstrated a self-perpetuating cycle of dysfunctional behaviors that could not be dealt with in less restrictive settings, a residential program may be the answer.

In some cases, a child needs treatment that requires skills that the parents do not possess and residential placement may be the solution.

CASE EXAMPLE

Vivienne

Vivienne was adopted by the Reiners when she was 5 years old. It soon became clear from her bizarre behavior that she was having difficulty bonding with her new parents or with anyone else. Several diagnostic screenings made it clear to the distraught Reiners that Vivienne had "attachment disorder," a condition usually associated with early trauma that renders an individual unable to bond with others. As a result, the individual has little feelings or empathy for others and may actually harm them. All concerned felt that Vivienne should be placed in a residential setting that was a pioneer in the treatment of attachment disorders.

For such children, a residential setting is used when all other attempts have failed. Some children perceive this and strive to make good in this new setting. Others feel that this is the "end of the road" and have difficulty with their residential experience. Effective casework with these children can often help them to recognize that there is hope.

Adjustment to Placement

Often, placement in residential care is abrupt and children are given little opportunity to adjust to it. Even if they are allowed to accept the fact of placement by preplacement visits to the new site and given time to acclimate to the idea, children have feelings about the transition.

The predominant feeling among children who have been separated from their parents is that they are bad. This may be especially true when the placement is in an institution. Then children feel that they may have been "too bad" to live in a family setting. They may even feel that placement is a form of punishment. It may require intensive casework to help children recognize that there are problems but that it is possible for them to change their behavior.

We can probably all remember a time when we had to go from a family environment to an impersonal setting and how that felt. Perhaps when you went to college was the first time that you were suddenly alone in a room with the bathroom down the hall and none of the little personal touches of a private home. Further, it may seem that there is no one there who cares exclusively about you. Children in residential settings may also have this isolated, impersonal feeling, but often at a much younger age. One way to help children who are placed to overcome this is to allow them to bring personal items from home, such as special toys or other objects. These are sometimes referred to as *transitional objects*.

The feelings of aloneness may cause some children to isolate themselves from their peers. It may take time and help with learning to recognize their own and others' needs before the child acclimates himself or herself to congregate living. However, such living can provide valuable lessons in the development of social skills.

Life in a Residential Setting

Every residential setting interprets its mission differently. In general a residential setting can be seen as an environment that strives to provide a safe, structured atmosphere for children, one that is dedicated to helping them to gain insight into and overcome their issues. At the same time, these centers work with families both to understand and to manage their children's problems when the children return home. The intent of a residential treatment facility is to move the child, through treatment, to a less restrictive setting, preferably his or her home or a foster home. The child's stay in the residence is meant to be temporary, usually no more than several months to a year or two. Residences for more chronically involved children may expect to keep them until their majority, although this is the exception rather than the rule.

Components of a Residential Setting

There are three components of a residential setting: residential, educational, and clinical. Although they are designed to work together in a total program for each child, called *the therapeutic milieu,* each component of group care provides a different service (see Figure 13.1). The *residential* component is made

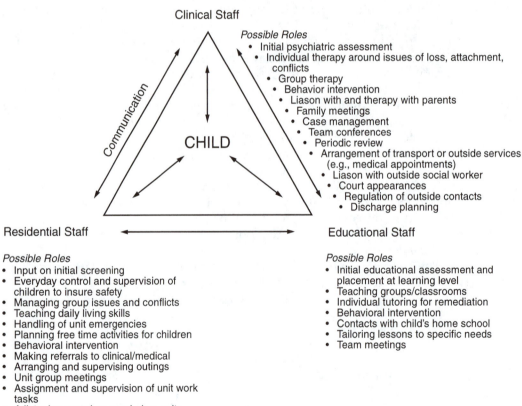

Clinical Staff

Possible Roles
- Initial psychiatric assessment
- Individual therapy around issues of loss, attachment, conflicts
- Group therapy
- Behavior intervention
- Liason with and therapy with parents
- Family meetings
- Case management
- Team conferences
- Periodic review
- Arrangement of transport or outside services (e.g., medical appointments)
- Liason with outside social worker
- Court appearances
- Regulation of outside contacts
- Discharge planning

CHILD

Communication

Residential Staff

Possible Roles
- Input on initial screening
- Everyday control and supervision of children to insure safety
- Managing group issues and conflicts
- Teaching daily living skills
- Handling of unit emergencies
- Planning free time activities for children
- Behavioral intervention
- Making referrals to clinical/medical
- Arranging and supervising outings
- Unit group meetings
- Assignment and supervision of unit work tasks
- A listening ear when needed on unit
- Team meetings

Educational Staff

Possible Roles
- Initial educational assessment and placement at learning level
- Teaching groups/classrooms
- Individual tutoring for remediation
- Behavioral intervention
- Contacts with child's home school
- Tailoring lessons to specific needs
- Team meetings

FIGURE 13.1 Milieu Therapy

up of those staff members who interact with children in their living space and who guide them through daily routines (meals, bedtime, etc.), ensuring that the environment is stable, safe, and as consistent as possible, seeing that peers interact appropriately and providing residents with positive caring adult role models and opportunities to interact with these adults. It is not always easy to maintain consistency or positive relationships with children who have behavior problems. The role of residential staff can be as challenging as it can be rewarding (Arieli, 1997; Frost and Stein, 1999).

Children may live in dorms with child care workers who monitor them while they are in this setting. Child care workers may continue to be with their charges at any time when they are not either with their therapists or in school. Or children may reside in smaller, more homelike settings, often referred to as *cottages* or *houses.* In these settings there may be houseparents who act almost like surrogate parents. The type of setting children reside in differs from agency to agency and is sometimes based on the children's ability to function independently. For example, one residence for disturbed girls operates on a level system. When a girl first comes to the agency, she is placed in a dorm with child care workers who monitor her progress. When the girl has integrated into the program and seems to be following the rules, she achieves a higher level and may be moved to a residential setting that is more like a cottage. Here, there are houseparents, but the girl has more freedom. When a girl is almost ready to leave the center, she moves to a house that operates like an apartment. Although there is a housemother, the girls are expected to care for themselves as they would in an apartment setting. This prepares them for living on their own.

The *educational* component is designed to provide specialized instruction to the children to enable them to realize their scholastic potential. Many children who come to residential settings are behind educationally—because their individual problem has hindered their ability to learn, they have missed too much school, or the school they attended found them difficult to teach due to behavior problems. For this reason, children are tested scholastically and their educational plan is geared toward their own level, often requiring remedial work. Teachers also maintain close contact with both residential and clinical staff to ensure that they are aware of any nonscholastic issues (e.g., residual issues from the past, disputes with peers, etc.) that are impeding the student's learning or ability to concentrate (Marohn, 1993).

The *clinical* component is dedicated to counseling services to help children understand themselves and their needs. Children are seen, both on an individual and a group basis, by staff trained in social work and psychology. Some programs offer a once- or twice-a-week individual therapy session as well as group sessions that deal with a variety of issues. Other centers offer more intensive therapeutic services. For example, one program for boys of latency age offers individual therapy with a caseworker for an hour three times a week. The boys are also involved with at least one group a day on weekdays. The groups address such issues as anger management and understanding their past abuse; there is a group for boys who show signs of sexually abusing others, a group that addresses substance abuse issues, and a group that helps them understand how to live and deal with each other in the residential setting. Almost all programs feature groups designed to enhance children's social skills, and an increasing number of programs have groups to help children deal with their past abuse in their homes.

Token Economy and Phase System

Most residential centers, especially those for disturbed or delinquent children, are set up along behavior modification lines. These programs use points or tokens as rewards when children are abiding by the rules or following their treatment plans. There are also levels, usually based on how much independence children are allowed. When children have earned a certain number of points, they may progress to the next level and be given more privileges.

For example, when a child comes to the Holyrood Center, he is on Level 1. This means that he resides in House #1 (Forrest Hall), where there is a high level of supervision and structure. While he is in this house, he cannot receive outside phone calls or leave the grounds, and is not allowed visitors. Most boys, by following the rules, progress to Level 2 fairly quickly. This enables them to move to House #2 (Sherwood Hall), where they can decorate their room with their personal items, make two outside phone calls a week, and have visits from parents and siblings. Although they may leave the grounds, they must be accompanied by a staff member. Boys who achieve Level 3 move to House #3 (Garland Hall), where they have a good deal of independence. They can make off-campus calls and receive visitors at any time when they have free time. The atmosphere at Garland House is collegial and informal and the boys learn to do a great many of the house tasks themselves. They can leave campus alone with permission. If children in this system do not continue to make progress, they can be dropped back down a level. It is not uncommon for children to move back and forth between levels as the events in their lives put a great deal of stress on them.

CASE EXAMPLE

Judy

Judy had been in the residential treatment center for nine months. She had done well and had progressed to the highest level. Judy had come to the center after her 80-year-old grandmother had found her behavior too difficult to manage and Judy had been unable to adjust to two foster homes. She enjoyed the residential setting and it was expected that, due to her excellent progress, she would be returned to the last foster home. Shortly before Judy was released, her mother, who had abandoned her as a toddler, returned and wanted to resume a relationship with her daughter. Judy, angry and confused by the attention of a woman who she had always assumed "did not want her," began to act up in the residence. She fought with her peers and finally pulled a knife on one of them. Feeling that she needed much more supervision to contain her behavior, the residence dropped her back to Level 1. It took numerous family meetings between Judy, her grandmother, and her mother before Judy was able to control her behavior to the extent that she could progress again to a higher level.

Children often feel safer with a token economy because they can measure the progress they are making. Some centers use tangible rewards like chips, but more use points, which are accounted for on a chart.

The Influence of Peer Culture

A major factor in the rehabilitative process for children in residential treatment is their contact with their peers. These are usually children whose relations with others have been extremely problematic. Now they are faced with a group of other children all of whom have had similar negative experiences. These children are often hyperactive, overly aggressive, antisocial, and impulsive, and have a variety of other ego deficits. Even though the peer interaction may be negative, the development of the ability to interact with these peers helps children to develop many skills (Arieli, 1997; Frost and Stein, 1999).

Understandably, peer interactions may have negative as well as positive influences. For example, children may learn antisocial and aggressive behaviors from one another or negative behaviors may be reinforced by peer acceptance. It becomes the task of staff to intervene in such circumstances so that peer interactions reinforce functional rather than dysfunctional behaviors.

Peer culture can also have a positive influence. In their peers, children find examples of others who have had similar backgrounds of abuse and family dysfunction. There is a safety in knowing that others have shared your experiences, despite the fact that children may not recognize or admit it. Further, peers give children an opportunity to try out a variety of relational styles in the relative safety of a structured environment. A former treatment center resident remembers fondly her housemates at the residential setting where she stayed for two years:

> They were my best friends! "I didn't have to be embarrassed with them because my Mom drank and my Dad sexually abused me. Those things happened to them, too. And living with a bunch of girls made it feel like family. I never really had a family so it was really good to have them. I still write to a couple of the other kids.

Whether the peer culture teaches children negative attitudes or behavior or provides support for them, it does play an extremely important role in their rehabilitation.

Handling Crises in Residential Settings

What is a crisis when you are dealing with a group of disturbed or delinquent children? The term *crisis* is often used to describe when a child or children lose control. Children who feel especially vulnerable may express it by losing control. Sometimes staff can predict what might cause a child to lose control and prevent it. A crisis often occurs when staff are unprepared for the acting-out behavior.

CASE EXAMPLE

Dillon

Dillon had not had a self-abusive episode for months. The staff had begun to relax and not keep up their constant vigilance. When Henry was admitted to the center, his intake profile had not mentioned any self-abusive behavior, but Henry got into a fight with Yanus and became very angry. He grabbed a bottle someone had left in the kitchen, slammed it against the refrigerator to break it, and began cutting himself. Dillon, observing the scene, began to gouge deep cuts in his arm with his fingernails. Yanus, who was petrified of the sight of blood, began to scream and run around the room.

Clearly, the two staff members who were in the kitchen area saw this as a crisis and called for help. But crises are not always as unpredictable or dramatic. Holidays, for example, often cause crises for children in residential settings. Christmas, Easter, Thanksgiving, and birthdays may not have been the happy times most of us remember. Instead, these days, surrounded by the excitement usually associated with them, may have served to point out for children who are eventually placed in a residential setting that life is not as idyllic as they perceive the lives of other children to be. This may create in them anger or sadness and these feelings are often acted out. Anniversary reactions (anniversary dates of deaths or traumas from the past) may also send children into crisis.

Everyday events may also contribute to crises. Katz (1988) cites several instances that can increase the risk of some children going into crisis.

1. *Lack of sufficient structure.* Structure is an important part of residential treatment. When there is less structure than usual or less supervision, children may feel vulnerable, unsafe, and then lose control.

2. *Competitive situations.* Children who have a history of failures are often oversensitive to being put in positions where they feel they can fail again.

Whether the event is a sports competition or doing school work and being compared to others, these fears may cause them to lose control.

3. *Contact with family.* Children in residential settings have usually had problematic relations with their family members. Seeing them again, whether it is during home visits or family sessions, can generate feelings of anger, rage, sadness, and longing. These vulnerable feelings must be denied by hurt children and the way they deny is often to act out. This out-of-control behavior can either precede or follow these contacts.

4. *Changes in relationships with staff.* Children who have finally allowed themselves to trust another, to whatever small degree, are often overly sensitive when staff leave, are not consistent, or in some way change. Sometimes staff will discover a change in the behavior of the children when they know that a staff member is getting married. "It's like she was no longer just ours," explained one adolescent girl when her social worker returned from her honeymoon. The girls had been particularly difficult in therapy and it soon became obvious that they were jealous of the new husband.

5. *Ability to deal with stress.* It is not always easy for children in residential treatment to deal with stressful situations. Instead of being able to handle them calmly, they may overreact and lose control. The stressful events can be minor or major and even happy events can cause children's behavior to escalate. "Not only holidays but the end of school is hard at this center," explained one child care worker. "The kids know there will be an award ceremony and they are excited to find out who got awards. And many of them will go home in the summer and these changes always create crises."

In handling crisis events, it may be necessary to physically restrain children who are so out-of-control that words cannot calm them. Although not all agencies use physical restraints, most do have some preferred method. Staff are usually trained when they are hired in whatever method the center uses. Most techniques stress a continuum of restraint, teaching the worker first to try to de-escalate the problematic behavior and, if all else fails, to physically restrain in a manner that will not endanger either the child or the staff member.

Staff in residential centers learn that they can often anticipate problematic behavior. If they can recognize the child's precursors to out-of-control behavior, they can sometimes prevent it. In time, they may also be able to teach the child how to recognize what leads to crisis and seek help or activate his or her inner controls before things get out of hand (Katz, 1988).

Sexually Acting Out in Residential Care

One of the most difficult problems for staff in residential care to handle is the issue of residents sexually acting out (see Braga and Schimmer, 1993; Northrup, 1994; Plach, 1993; Farmer and Pollock, 1998). Crenshaw (1988) postulates that sexually acting out should be seen in a broader Freudian psychosocial framework. In the course of their development, children experience sexuality in different ways. Psychosocial theory maintains that the first area of sexuality is the mouth, as oral gratification is the child's first contact with the world. If that contact is inconsistent or unsatisfactory, the child can develop an oral fixation. Because many children in residential treatment have experienced neglect, abuse, or a lack of attention at the hands of caregivers in their early years, food becomes an issue. Thus, the tendency to withhold food as a form of punishment (e.g., "You'll go to your room with no dinner" or "You'll miss your snack") can actually be extremely countertherapeutic for the orally deprived child.

A child's oral deprivation may also account for the problems many centers have in enlisting his or her cooperation in taking medication by mouth. Staff may assume that a child does not want to take the drug that will help him or her with depression, hyperactivity, or seizures. Yet it is not necessarily the effect of the drug that the child is avoiding; he or she may be experiencing conflict about the dispensing of it. Medication is often dispensed by a female nurse who appears to be the mother figure from whom the child did not receive early nurturing. Thus, the anger and rage about this early deprivation is often unconsciously centered on this medical person (Crenshaw, 1988).

During later development, the bowels and elimination become the focus of psychosexual development. Thus, for children traumatized in this period of their development (between 1 to 3 years), the smearing of feces or urination or inappropriate elimination is not uncommon. In addition, control becomes paramount and children can go to seemingly extraordinary means to control child care staff (Crenshaw, 1988).

CASE EXAMPLE

Juanita

Juanita, a 14-year-old who had been severely abused as a toddler, was a staff favorite. She was small for her age and had leg braces that impeded some of her activities. She sought the help and attention of staff and usually got it. She did not get on as well with peers and took a particular dislike to Dawn, a new girl on the unit. After an especially heated fight between the two girls, staff sent both to their rooms. When she was allowed to come out, Juanita was at first sullen and then extremely clingy and manipulative with staff. That night at bedtime, Dawn came crying hysterically to the staff member in charge saying that "there was crap in her room!" Indeed, there was a pile of feces placed neatly on her pillow. Staff questioned everyone but could not uncover the culprit. Two days later, there was another deposit of feces. Several days after that, Juanita started another fight with Dawn. This night, Dawn's whole bed was smeared with feces and staff began to recognize a pattern. Each time, Juanita had been particularly endearing to staff after she had apparently placed the feces in Dawn's room.

In the course of psychosocial development, the years of 3 to 6 are characterized by a preoccupation with the genital area. Masturbation can be practiced often and it is not uncommon for children to masturbate openly in front of others. This may also translate into a desire for genital contact with others, usually exhibitionism, touching, or competitive activities (e.g., "My penis is bigger than yours"). Sex talk is common. For children who are fixated in this period of development, genital preoccupation is quite common. One of the most difficult tasks for residential staff is to determine what types of behavior involving exposure, mutual viewing, and touching are curiosity and exploration and what behaviors are exploitive (Crenshaw, 1988). Most residential treatment settings prohibit all interactive sexual contact. Some permit solo masturbation for teens when they are alone in their bedrooms. Other centers frown on this.

It is expected, for several reasons, that there will be some sexual acting out in residential settings. First, most of the children in these settings have had inappropriate models for sexuality or insufficient or inappropriate sexual education. Children who observe parents having sex with each other or with someone else are usually traumatized by the experience. Children who are sexually abused are not allowed to develop sexual attitudes and behavior normally. And children who are shielded from even healthy information about sex may develop their own distorted ideas and need to try them out. Second, children who learn about sexuality by being victimized or watching others in adult sexual pursuits become confused. This confusion may result in a need to "try out" this behavior on others (Johnson and Aoki, 1993), or they may have a psychological need to replicate the relationship they had with their parents or caregivers by setting up that same type of relationship (including the sexuality) with their current care providers (Charles et al., 1993). Also, children who have not been taught appropriate sexuality may confuse it with attention or caring or use sexuality to act out rage, control, or dehumanization. And finally, because staff do not want to "jump to conclusions," they may not intervene with debatable sexually acting out (e.g., brushing past a staff member somewhat seductively, touching other areas of the body like the hair or the back) until the behaviors are quite obviously sexual. This is often because either the staff member was abused himself or herself and cannot recognize the behavior or because the staff member has been sheltered from abusive situations and is inexperienced at the job.

The types of sexual behaviors that staff in residential settings usually identify are masturbation, especially in the presence of others, profane sexual talk, participating in sexual interactions with other residents, exhibitionism, and exploitive sexual contact with others (Powers, 1993). It is vitally important that staff be given adequate training to deal with these various behaviors. In addition, Powers suggests that the staff may actually contribute to sexual acting out by not having resolved their own sexual conflicts, breaking boundaries by talking about their own sexual prowess or pursuits to residents, being seductive with the children in their care or with other staff members in front of the children, wearing seductive clothing, and inappropriately touching children, which, although not sexual, could be misinterpreted as being so by the children (33–34).

Increasingly, the treatment of youthful sexual offenders is undertaken in group homes. Although there is some question if grouping youthful offenders together is the best method of treatment, the reality is that they usually cannot be handled at home or in foster homes. Thus, the move has been to create centers, or at least units, that specialize in their rehabilitation (Burnett and Rathburn, 1994; Ross and deViller, 1993; Breer, 1996; Cunningham and MacFarlane, 1997). Certainly, placing children who have sexually abused other children with others who have done the same involves some serious considerations.

Screening, Training, and Supervision of Staff. It is vital that the staff working with abuse issues and youthful sexual offenders be thoroughly screened for their past involvement with sexual abuse issues and attitudes toward sexuality. Punitive attitudes or unresolved sexual conflicts in staff leave young offenders vulnerable to being revictimized, as they have themselves been early victims of abuse. In addition, staff must be well trained not only in sexual abuse issues but in behavior management. And, due to the fact that sexual abuse may well bring up personal issues for staff members, careful supervision is a must (West, 1998; Ross and deViller, 1993; Arieli, 1997).

Managing the Living Space. Sexual offenders should be housed separately from those without a history of sexual aggression. In addition, most programs for youthful offenders strive to provide single rooms whenever possible. When single rooms are not an option, careful supervision of residents is necessary (Ross and deViller, 1993).

Adequate Treatment Plans. Sexual offenders require intensive treatment, including both group and individual counseling (Burnett and Rathburn, 1994; Ross and deViller, 1993; Breer, 1996). Burnett and Rathburn (1994) suggest that this therapy should include groups led by both a male and female therapist. The treatment should address such issues as denial, the offender as a victim, victim personalization (seeing the victim as a person and trying to understand how he or she might feel), social skill training, human sexuality, and relapse prevention (60–62).

Staff Protection. There are some youthful offenders who may pose a threat to staff members. Thus, in addition to screening for such offenders, the center must be careful to ensure that staff members are never placed in a vulnerable position. For example, a staff member should not be alone with a child or enter a bedroom or shower area without being "covered" by another staff member. The agency must be careful to protect staff boundaries, such as home addresses and phone numbers. And when incidents do occur, they must be dealt with immediately and staff members supported in this (West, 1998; Lemmond and Verhaagen, 2001).

Sexual Abuse of Children in Residential Care

Although the residential care system is set up to protect children and have a therapeutic effect on their lives, it is always possible for someone who is in the role of the helper to further victimize the child (see Braga, 1993; Plach, 1993; Johnson, 1997; Stanley and Manthorpe, 1999). Sexual abuse in institutions has been documented by numerous studies (Johnson, 1997; Stanley and Manthorpe, 1999) and continues to be a concern necessitating careful screening of employees.

What causes someone who cares for children to sexually abuse them? First, those who have the inclination to sexually abuse will be attracted to settings that give them close proximity to children and the opportunity to have access to them. Second, the frustrations of the job, along with the closeness to children, may bring out tendencies in some to abuse that they did not realize they had. Third, child care workers, especially, are among the poorest paid in the mental health field. Agencies do not always have an easy time finding staff due to the low pay and long hours, and so may not do sufficient screening.

CASE EXAMPLE

Horace

Horace Milner was sexually abused as a child by his father, a priest, and two uncles. He had forgotten much of the abuse (and was not to think of it until he ended up in therapy years later for sexually abusing two children). When Horace was in his early twenties, he knew he wanted to help kids. He had finished a stint in the army and was looking for a job he could do while he went back to school. A local home for disturbed boys had been having a difficult time finding staff for the night shift. When Horace applied, they asked if he could start immediately. Horace enjoyed the contact with the boys. The dependence some of them developed on him made him feel needed.

For Horace, extremely needy himself, the neediness of these boys fed into a part of his pathology of which he was as yet unaware. Several weeks after he began working at the center, several boys reported that he was sexually abusing another boy. The reports turned out to be true.

It is clear that centers must recognize that abuse can happen and make provisions for the safety of both children and staff. Many institutions now have processes whereby both child and staff are heard and fair attention is given to the allegations and reports of each.

Working with Families of Children in Residential Care

Work with the families of the children in institutional care can be one of the most frustrating—and is often the least emphasized—parts of the therapeutic process (see Powell, 2000). Yet, if we recognize that the child may well return to this family someday, the importance of such work cannot be underestimated. The focus of family work is usually threefold: to help the family maintain a functional relationship with the child in placement; to aid the family in preparing for the return of the child (if this is the plan); and to help the family sort out and cope with the dysfunction that caused the placement of the child in residential care. All of these factors are usually intertwined.

Motivation of Parents

The attitudes of parents of placed children range from the very concerned and involved parents to the disengaged parents, who would prefer to forget that they have a child in placement. Before we criticize the latter parents, however, we must remember that by the time a child gets to residential care, many other solutions have probably been tried. The parents may have invested heavily in those attempts at solving their problems but to no avail. Now the parents are most likely at the end of their patience and resources. To have someone else responsible for this child may seem like a relief.

Van Hagen (1988) divides parents into several categories: absent, ambivalent, impoverished, addicted, and abusive. The *absent parent* is not available because of mental illness or incarceration. The lack of parental visits may be a problem for the child, who feels abandoned and resentful. The child may also harbor fantasies about the absent parent and therapeutic work with that child may focus on the resolution of these fantasies. A powerful example of such fantasies was told in Hayden's *The Tiger's Child* (1995). Sheila, the tiger's child of Hayden's story, was abandoned when she was 4 years old by her mother, who left her at the side of the road. After several foster homes, Sheila was placed in a group home. Intermittently in touch with Hayden, a former special education teacher and mentor, Sheila has shared fantasies of finding and being reunited with her mother. While in the group home, she sends an ad to a California paper to attempt to locate her mother. A letter arrives from a woman claiming to be her mother, a woman whom Hayden quickly recognizes as being disturbed. Trying gently to alert Sheila to the danger of getting her hopes up does not work and Sheila runs away to find her mother. Defeated and disillusioned, but wiser, Sheila eventually returns to contact Hayden. The woman was indeed disturbed and was not her mother. But the fantasies had been a powerful motivator for the child.

A second type of parent identified by Van Hagen (1988) is the *ambivalent parent*. The child may have spent a good amount of time outside of the home and reunification efforts may have been tried before. The ambivalent parent feels exhausted by these efforts and is not sure whether she or he wants the child at home. Sometimes the placed child is scapegoated and all the family ills are attributed to him or her. The family has deluded itself into thinking that, if this child is gone, the family will be fine.

CASE EXAMPLE

Coraleen

When Coraleen was placed in residential care, it was almost as if her family breathed a collective sigh of relief. The family had been dysfunctional for years. The father, now dead, had sexually abused his two daughters and physically abused his son and wife. But the family had guarded the secret of its pathology. The oldest girl had been the "good child" and had excelled in school, and the boy had remained quiet, drawing little attention to himself. Then Coraleen gave up the family secret in her attempts to deal with her own eating disorder. The family was furious with her for "tarnishing the name of the father." After years of rejection by them, Coraleen began to act out and, after a brush with the juvenile justice system, was placed in residential care. Visits to her were constantly postponed or cancelled by the mother, who found one conflict after another. Not having Coraleen at home gave the family the opportunity to pretend that the secret had never come out. Although the mother loved her daughter and wanted to see that she was well cared for, the burden of having her home was too great.

The problem for such families is that placement is rarely permanent and they will need to come to terms with the fact that the child may come home.

The *impoverished parent* (Van Hagen, 1988) is overwhelmed by a whole set of external problems that require the family to put a great deal of effort into merely surviving.

CASE EXAMPLE

The Harbingers

The Harbingers were beset by a myriad of problems. Although a steady worker, Mr. Harbinger found it difficult to make enough to support his six children, who ranged in age from 20 to 9. The oldest child, Ned, had suffered a spinal injury and was now quadriplegic and living at home. Seventeen-year-old Fran had just announced that she was pregnant and that the father was HIV-positive. Fifteen-year-old Justine had recently been placed in residential care after years of running away and using drugs. Fourteen-year-old Suzie appeared to be copying her sister's drug abuse. Twelve-year-old Gary and nine-year-old Farley appeared to have no problems as yet, but the Harbingers were sure they would in time. In addition to their other problems, Mrs. Harbinger's father, who had sexually abused her as a child and who she suspected of abusing at least one of the older girls, was living with them. He had recently been diagnosed with Alzheimers and could no longer live alone.

For this overwhelmed family, the placement of Justine seemed like a respite from one small part of their problems. Although they worked diligently with the social worker at the residential treatment setting, it was clear that they had little investment in having her home.

The *addicted parent* is often too caught up in her or his addiction to be much of a resource for the child. Only after he or she is willing to deal with this problem can work with the family be effective. And the *abusive parent* may be a threat to the child if he or she is returned home. Such a parent will need additional services in order to be an appropriate resource for the child (Van Hagen, 1988).

Some parents are most interested in having their children home and work well with agencies.

CASE EXAMPLE

The DeRosas

The DeRosas adopted Angela when she was 3 years old. As a young adolescent, Angela became quite difficult. She would not go to school, and she was promiscuous and generally difficult to handle. The school recommended that she be placed in residential treatment. Unsure of what else to do, the DeRosas agreed. After a year of intensive family work, Angela returned home.

For Angela and her parents, family therapy proved quite effective. The more successful the work with the family, the more smoothly the child's transition from the institution to the home will be.

Types of Family Treatment

Each agency has a different commitment to family treatment and therefore different techniques and procedures. Some see families once a week or even once a month, depending on the needs of the family and their availability to come to the center. Families may be seen individually or with their institutionalized child. All members may be present or just one parent. Sometimes, one parent is comfortable working with a therapist while the other is not. There are also some agencies that feature group treatment for parents or parenting skills classes.

It is not only therapy sessions but also visits that are part of family work. Families are usually encouraged to visit so that the child will not feel abandoned. Visits may be made at the center or the child may be allowed to have supervised visits off-site or at home. When children progress in their program, they may be allowed home visits for a day, a weekend, or over a holiday or vacation.

Visits can be extremely conflictual for both parents and children. Children may harbor a variety of resentments toward their parents that have not been resolved. They may feel that they were abandoned and feel angry. If parents cancel at the last minute, children feel betrayed, or they may not want to see their parents at all. It is not uncommon for the day preceding or following visits to be difficult emotionally for children.

Parents, too, might feel some ambivalence. After all, this is the child whose problem seemed to cause them a great deal of trouble in the recent past. This is the child who has caused society to question them as parents and who has made them feel inadequate. They may feel anger toward this child or they may not trust the child and may be fearful about how the child will behave. For parents, visits may be as much of an adjustment as they are for their children. Often, much social worker time is dedicated to helping both parents and children with visiting issues.

What if a child does not have a family that is willing to visit or available for the child's return? These children are either kept in long-term residential placement or, more likely, placed in a foster home when they are ready to return home. Some agencies provide children who do not have visits from parents with a *visiting resource*. This visiting resource might be an adult friend or family member, a concerned member of the community who volunteers to do so, or a potential foster parent who may someday receive them in placement. When children will not be returning to their own homes, but rather leaving placement to be on their own, they are prepared by the agency for independent living (see Chapter 11 for discussion of independent living).

Problems in Working with Families

Parents whose children have been placed in any type of setting may *feel ambivalence*. The fact that their child is not home with them may make them *feel as though they have failed*. They believe that people in the community will criticize them and many parents do not tell their neighbors that their child is in placement. They may *feel hurt* if their child is doing better in residential care than he or she was at home. For all these reasons parents might act in a variety of ways. They may *approach the agency with hostility*. Some parents, either consciously or unconsciously, *sabotage their child's treatment*.

CASE EXAMPLE

Sabotage

Kelly was extremely obese when she came to the center. One of her problems was that she was so ostracized by her peers that she became angry and would try to hurt them. At the center, she was put on a rigid diet, a plan with which she cooperated well. After a month of placement and 10 lost pounds, she went on her first home visit. When she returned, she came back with a large selection of sweets bought for her by her mother, who was fully aware of the treatment plan. When the mother was confronted about this, she apologized, saying that she had "forgotten." But after every subsequent visit, the same thing happened. Kelly, formerly motivated, but now confused about her loyalties, became difficult and would not comply with her treatment plan. It took several months of intensive casework before the social worker was able to enlist the mother's full cooperation. Having been pregnant herself at age 15, the mother was finally able to recognize that she feared the same would happen to Kelly if she became "too attractive and desirable." The mother was helped to see that there were others ways to break the pattern.

Family work can also create difficulties for staff, whether they are working directly with the family or dealing primarily with the child. For clinical staff who work with the family, the missed appointments, the parents who arrive drunk or high, the hostility, and the sabotage can take its toll. The staff members must remember how difficult it may be for these parents to cope with the fact that they have lost control over their children's lives. For all staff who see a child who has been maltreated, rejected, or hurt in some other manner, they may have difficulty understanding the parents' motivation. Staff may feel a need to protect the child from further abuse from these parents. The reality is that the parents are an integral part of the child and it is not possible to separate the two entirely.

The Role of Staff in a Residential Setting

The roles performed by staff members in a residential setting differ according to the department they are involved with and the agency itself. As previously discussed, most agencies are composed of three departments organized by function: residential, educational, and clinical.

Residential Staff

The residential component oversees the children's everyday life, from their waking hours to bedtime and through the night. Child care workers or residential counselors are the backbone of the residential component and work in shifts similar to those of nurses. It is these staff members who help the children get up and get ready for the day. They are often responsible for preparing or serving breakfast. Some residences serve all meals in a common dining room; in others, the children eat some or all of their meals at their living units. If not responsible for the preparation of food, workers must monitor the children's behavior while they eat in the dining hall.

While the children go to school, whether on grounds or off, the residential staff either help with transitions, help the educational staff, or return to their units to do housekeeping in anticipation of the children's return. After-school and evening hours may be punctuated by a series of activities or groups, often led by child care workers. If the children have therapeutic activities, such as counseling appointments or therapy groups, child care staff are usually responsible for getting the children there. Although this may not sound like much of a task, the reality is that many children have difficulties with transitional periods.

Bedtime, too, can be problematic, especially for sexually abused children who do not remember their beds as being safe places. Child care workers report talking to children before they go to bed and comforting them after they wake with distressing nightmares. Night terrors can be a common occurrence for children whose early lives have been filled with trauma.

Despite the fact that child care workers spend most of their time with children and can be one of the most influential aspects of their therapeutic program, they are often the youngest, most inexperienced, and most poorly trained of all agency staff. This can be problematic for all involved. As Kagan (1988) comments:

> *Children from troubled families repeat behavioral patterns experienced in their homes and previous placements. Children in group care, in effect, reenact family dilemmas with staff. Accordingly, the child who has experienced abuse, abandonment, and neglect will often provoke the same interactions with staff members. (160)*

Child care workers are usually supervised by a staff member who oversees their work. In turn, these supervisors may answer to a program director or the agency director, depending on the size and organization of the agency.

Instead of child care workers, some agencies use housemothers or houseparents, with a single woman (or man) or a married couple acting as surrogate parents. They are relieved for time off by other staff, but remain the primary resource for child care responsibilities. Although these individuals may have more life experience, they too are usually undertrained.

The training required for each staff position differs according to the population served, the organization and needs of the agency, and, in some cases, supply and demand (West, 1998). Most agencies will hire child care workers with little experience or education if their need is great enough and the applicant seems qualified. Many college students have worked as evening or overnight child care staff while they pursue their degree. Increasingly, agencies are asking for workers who have had more education or experience with children. Retired people or parents can bring parenting skills to a residential setting, but without training they may not be prepared for the fact that the children placed in residential care may present many more challenges to patience than their own children did.

Educational Staff

Children in residential settings are usually educated on the grounds of the agency, although there are exceptions—that is, some children attend local schools. Those who teach them on-site are usually teachers trained in special education techniques. It is true, however, that many states do not have as stringent regulations requiring the hiring of licensed teachers for residences as they do for public schools. Teachers may also use aides, as it is important that the teacher-to-child ratio be small enough to promote optimum learning.

Children are usually tested when they enter a residence to determine their educational level and their remedial needs, if they have any. Then teachers work with children to help them achieve their academic potential. Classes may be organized according to ability rather than age or grade-level equivalent to public school.

Teaching in a residential setting is not dedicated just to academics. A significant part of a teacher's role may be removing the barriers to learning that have prevented the child from achieving on the outside. Children who come to residences often feel that they have failed and may exhibit behavioral problems in reaction to this perception. They may also have difficulty with their peers and therefore cause trouble in the organized classroom.

Gordon Howly, for example, had taught in a public high school for 10 years. He relates his experience teaching in a residential setting:

I just needed a new challenge when I took a job in a residential center for disabled and disturbed kids. I had completed most of a Master's in Special Education and thought I would really like to work with kids like this. I taught History and English and the kids rotated classes. I had about five adolescents in a class with an aide. The aide was there mostly because some of the kids needed help with manual tasks. Each child had different educational needs and I found myself working with most of them individually. For example, one child had cerebral palsy and couldn't talk. He used a board with letters to communicate. He would spell things by pointing to the letters. But he got frustrated very easily and when he was not understood, he would hurl the board across the room. I learned to duck very quickly. But all in all, I loved the job. The drive that some of those kids had was an inspiration!

In addition to teachers, most educational departments have administrators and other educational staff who oversee the child's academic progress.

Clinical Staff

Social workers, as well as counselors, psychologists, and psychiatrists, make up an agency's clinical component. These individuals may be on staff or they may operate on a consultant or part-time basis. For example, one residential treatment center had three social workers who did therapy both individually and in groups with the children on a weekly basis. These social workers also saw the families, arranged home visits, and kept in touch with the residential and educational staff to monitor the progress of each child. In addition, a psychologist was hired on a part-time basis to do psychological testing and make treatment recommendations. She came to the agency twice a week. A psychiatrist from a nearby mental health clinic reviewed the medications of the children on a once-a-week basis and prescribed other medications as needed. He would also see children for a screening interview if the staff had questions about treatment.

The number of clinical staff depends largely on the mission of the agency and the population served. As clinical staff may be the most highly trained, and therefore command higher salaries, fiscal constraints may mean that there are fewer clinicians than would be optimal.

Clinicians see children on a regular basis to help them sort out and understand the issues that brought them into care. These issues may be their own behaviors, family dysfunction, or abuse/neglect issues. In addition to individual meetings with children, clinicians may hold groups to help children with such issues as anger management, divorced families, abuse/neglect, substance abuse, social skills, and a variety of other concerns. In centers for juvenile offenders, groups help them confront their problems, understand their victims, understand their own cycles, and take steps to interrupt their abusive patterns (Braga and Schimmer, 1993; Burnett and Rathburn, 1994; Farmer and Pollack, 1998; Lemmond and Verhaagen, 2001). Group work in these settings is an integral part of treatment.

Todd, with a Master's in Social Work, is a therapist in a residential setting for sexually abusive boys. Formerly, he worked for a protective services agency studying families in which abuse had occurred: "I was always fascinated by the motivation of the offender, especially when he or she was young. I find doing groups with these kids very enlightening. It is amazing that being a victim is so traumatic for some of these kids that victimizing someone else is the only way they see to escape that victim role."

Since the treatment of children in residential settings requires communication among the components, it is often the role of the clinician or case manager to facilitate this communication. He or she, with knowledge of abnormal psychology, might also consult with staff in other components to help them understand children's behaviors and problems.

Other Staff Functions

There are important functions, and therefore integral staff members, who may not fit neatly into the previously mentioned categories.

The *nurse* is extremely important in residential settings. Although sometimes one person fills this role, with contracted services from the outside as needed, other agencies have whole medical units. For example, a residence for physically disabled residents might require a larger medical component than a center in which physical health is not the primary issue.

The program to rehabilitate children must be carefully planned, and many agencies hire a *program director* and often other program staff to perform this function. These individuals may be part of the previously mentioned components or may make up a component by themselves. The administrative staff of an agency cannot be underestimated. It is these individuals who not only oversee the running of the agency, but may also need to raise funds for its continued existence. The *director,* especially, may set the tone of how an agency operates.

Some agencies also have a training component responsible for in-service training for all staff, and many larger centers have instituted quality control specialists or units to ensure that the quality of service remains consistent and high.

No residential agency could function without some form of intake. The *admissions specialist* or unit is assigned the task of reviewing applicant files, interviewing children and their parents before acceptance, and determining if the agency can meet the needs of this potential client.

Other support personnel, such as chaplains, transportation specialists, and visiting coordinators, may figure in a particular agency's plan. Other agencies operate with a minimum of staff who perform a variety of different roles.

The Frustrations of Staff

One of the most widely discussed frustrations for staff in residential settings is the work itself. Children who are placed have had lives filled with abuse and injustices and they know nothing else but to mirror the way they have been treated in their treatment of others. In addition, it is difficult to constantly be a secondhand witness to the inhumanity that has been perpetrated on so many children. Their pain is not easy to watch and burnout is not uncommon (Corcoran, 1988).

Corcoran (1988) describes *burnout* as a phenomenon peculiar to professions that have one-to-one contact with people who have problems. A practitioner becomes burned out when he or she experiences "the depletion of emotional energies needed to perform one's job" (252). Dealing with problems daily can leave one short-tempered and emotionally exhausted. Although this can be true with any type of helping profession, residential treatment, because of the close proximity with clients on a continual basis, can make one especially vulnerable to burnout.

The *turnover of staff* in line positions (child care worker) can be especially high. Some centers estimate that they will be able to keep a child care worker for between 6 to 18 months. It is not surprising, for this reason, that many centers do not invest a great deal of time in training such transient staff members.

Yet, some would argue that better trained workers would not burn out as quickly (Whitaker et al., 1998; Bertolino and Thompson, 1999).

The high turnover rate can be a frustration for staff members as well as administration. When the work is taxing, it is important to trust and depend on one's fellow workers. When there are constantly new faces to relate to, workers feel isolated and perhaps more vulnerable.

Another issue for both staff and residents is the *inconsistency among child care practices*. Each staff member has a different idea of how children should be dealt with. As shifts change, so do the approaches of the staff. Thus, the very thing needed most by the child—consistency—is lacking (Kadushin and Martin, 1988). Consistency requires good communication as well as adequate training. When there is poor communication, staff become frustrated and children feel unsafe.

Although there are frustrations in residential settings, many staff say that the rewards outweigh them. "Just to see a child who is so out of control at intake become a more stable, happier child is worth all the insults and grief you get while that's happening," reports one child care worker. Staff often report that being prepared for the frustrations at the onset through an effective orientation program goes a long way toward helping them deal with their jobs.

Termination

Where do children go when they leave a residential setting? Children leave a residence usually for one of several settings: home, a foster home, a less restrictive residence, a more restrictive residence, hospitalization, or independent living.

Return Home

Children who return to their own homes may do so because the center feels that the child is now able to control his or her behavior sufficiently and/or the parents are able to handle the child's problems. This step is not undertaken without a great deal of thought. Usually, the parents have participated in family therapy and the child has progressed well in the residence. The agency social worker has met with the school, and school staff feel able to provide educational services. Other therapeutic resources, such as therapists or support groups or remedial help, have been arranged. This planning has probably taken weeks or even months. The parties are motivated and feel that the child's return will be a success. This is a "best case scenario" and unfortunately does not always happen. Even when it does, the plan may or may not be successful.

There are other reasons why children return home. Residential treatment is funded by the social service agency or the child's school department and, though very rarely, the parents. If any of these parties feel that they are unable to continue funding the placement or any other out-of-home placement, the child may return home. In these situations, it is unusual for a sufficient amount of progress to have been made and the child is often the one who suffers.

Children occasionally return home because the parent does not feel that the child is being well served by the agency. This may be a reality or the parent may find that the problems are not as easy as she or he first thought.

CASE EXAMPLE

Mrs. Kaiser

Mary Kaiser urged the school to place her daughter, Stephanie, because neither the teachers nor the mother could handle her oppositional behavior. After several psychiatric evaluations, the school agreed to fund a placement in a residential center for disturbed girls. Soon after placement, Stephanie became a model resident, obeying all the rules and complying with her treatment plan. In family sessions with Mrs. Kaiser, the agency social worker tried to explore the reasons why this mother and daughter had such a troubled relationship that the daughter became uncontrollable when at home. Mrs. Kaiser was incensed that the center was "blaming her" and immediately removed her daughter from placement.

Family work becomes an extremely important aspect of treatment if it is expected that the child will return home. Without such intervention, the problems that brought the child to placement often go unsolved. As one director of a residence explained about family work: "I have seen some very concerned, motivated families try their best to raise a child and find that the child ends up in placement. It might not even be what the family is doing that is the problem, but how the child interprets it. So often it is communication, or the lack of it, that is at the core of family problems."

Placement in a Foster Home or a Less Restrictive Environment

Some children progress in the residence but are not yet ready to return home. For example, a child might be placed in a secure setting because he or she might be a danger to himself or herself or others. As treatment progresses, it becomes clear that he or she can benefit from a less restrictive setting in which internalized controls are necessary. From this new setting, the child might return either to home or to a foster home. Or, if he or she is not ready for the amount of freedom given, the child might again return to a more restrictive setting.

A child may no longer need the structure of a residential setting but cannot yet cope with the issues at home. Or some children may not have a home to return to, for whatever reason. In these instances, children may be placed in a foster home until they can return home or until they are able to live on their own. The foster parents often work with the residential center during the transition period to acclimate the child to the new foster home. The child may visit the home prior to placement to facilitate the move.

Placement in a More Restrictive Setting

As previously mentioned, some children need more structure than was anticipated when they were originally placed in a residential setting. There are several factors that might alert staff to this fact. A child may run away from the center. Less restrictive centers may have little recourse if a child decides to run away. Says one residential worker:

> *We are trained that if we see a child who is threatening to run, we will try to talk him out of it. If you see a kid who you know is on his way off grounds, you can call him back, but you cannot go after him. Different centers have different policies. Some actually chase the kid, but we don't. But most kids don't threaten when they are going to run. They just leave, and then it is our policy to call the police.*

Children who run away may need a locked facility or an environment in which there is a higher staff-to-child ratio.

Sometimes children become so out of control that they are abusive to other residents, to themselves, or to staff. These children may require a more highly structured environment to ensure their safety. When children begin to act out their sexual abuse history by abusing other children, they may be moved to settings that provide better treatment for these issues.

The more structured settings to which children are transferred may be more secure residential facilities or even psychiatric hospital units.

Hospitalization

Children who are in residential settings may require hospitalization in psychiatric facilities. It may be that some aspect of the treatment process throws the child so off balance that he or she cannot cope.

CASE EXAMPLE

Lana

Lana had been ritualistically sexually abused by her father. She had forgotten much of the abuse, but the residual effects came out in her oppositional behavior. When she was placed in the residential center, she had been in three foster homes previously. None of these families felt capable of dealing with her. Probably due to the less intensive relationships, Lana settled easily into the residential setting. She was assigned a therapist and the two began to work on helping her understand her past. Then the memories began to return. At first they came through in terrifying dreams. Eventually Lana began remembering in therapy sessions. But these memories were too frightening, too overwhelming. Lana became so terrified that she curled up in a ball and could not be reached. After numerous unsuccessful attempts, the decision was made to hospitalize the child.

Children who are hospitalized usually stay there for only a short period of time while they are stabilized. After this, they may be returned to the same residential setting or to another.

Independent Living

It may be that a child remains in a residential setting until he or she is old enough to become independent. Increasingly, centers, much like foster care agencies, are developing programs for this possibility. Centers may have job readiness programs or teach specific independent living skills. They may also transfer teens who are almost ready for emancipation to small group homes that are often off the main campus of the residential center. These homes operate much like an apartment and give the teen a chance to try out such tasks as buying food and keeping house. Such programs are found to be fairly successful.

A former resident recalls her experiences:

What was it like to be a kid in a residential treatment center? I guess I have a lot of responses to that!! Some parts were great but some weren't.

When I was 8 years old, my brothers [ages 6 and 4] and I were taken away from our mother. She was always boozed up and used to bring men into the apartment. We were neglected and one of her boyfriends actually sexually abused me. One night my mom and this guy got into a fight and someone called the police. I guess when they saw our place (it was a real pigpen) the cops figured we shouldn't be there, so they took us to a foster home. We stayed in foster homes for a couple of years until my mom got her act together. Then she got us back. But that didn't last long. The guys started coming again and this time she did drugs as well as booze. But before the child welfare people could take us again, she shipped us off to an aunt. That was really bad news and I ran away. When they found me, I was put in a foster home by myself. But I was real angry and hated it and the other two after that. I wouldn't go to school, and finally some kids and I stole a car but they caught us. They bailed me out and the foster parents took me back but I was real angry by then. I said I was going to kill myself and when the foster mother tried to stop me I turned the knife on her.

There was a mess of legal and court stuff, but then they sent me off to this place for girls way out in the country. No one was going to tell me what to do, and at first I guess I gave them a real hard time. I was about 15 but I was a big kid and I think some of them were afraid of me. At first I was on this unit with about six other kids. They watched us every minute. It was awful. We had to eat in the unit and sleep there. We went to school on the grounds, too. The classes were small and we got a lot of attention, but at that point I was so angry at the world that I didn't care. There was this one teacher I liked though. She was young and could make stuff real interesting. She used to bring me books to read from her house—like her own books, I mean. That made me feel good, like someone trusted me.

I saw a social worker once a week and we tried to figure out what had gotten me there. She was also supposed to see my mother, but Mom only came when she felt like it, which wasn't too often. She was pregnant again and sick a lot and then she had the baby and that was her excuse. The social worker also helped me learn how angry I was at Mom. We talked about that a lot.

The director of the place was great too. He was an older guy who had had daughters, but they were grown. They came down sometimes to see the kids at the center. One of them had a little kid she used to bring, too. I played with him a lot and figured out that I liked little kids. And I made a bunch of friends there too. The kids were from all over the state. They were in there for lots of different stuff like running away and drugs and just being obnoxious to people. I still write to one of the girls.

After I'd been there a couple of years and they couldn't get my Mom to straighten out, they transferred me to a group home. I was 17 and it looked like I could never go home. The group home was a house with six girls, each in her own room. We were supposed to think of it like an apartment. We got jobs after school and had to pay rent. It wasn't much. It just was supposed to teach us to budget and stuff. They also made us take classes on budgeting and other things we had to do on our own, like cooking and that stuff.

A week before I was eighteen, I found out that I was pregnant. I was going to leave the home when I was 18 and I think I was a little scared. The guy who got me pregnant was 26 and I figured we'd get married. Right! When he found out I was pregnant he took off and I never saw him again. So the center helped me get welfare and an apartment until I got a job at this fast food place.

That was five years ago. My daughter and I are doing pretty well. It's tough being a parent, but I'm going to be a better one than my mother! Looking back, the center was probably better than any of the foster homes I was in. But who knows? I don't think I gave any of them a chance.

Problems in Residential Settings

As in any service, there are problems associated with residential treatment. These can be both internal and external.

Staff Issues

A variety of issues associated with staff in residential treatment can be problematic. Many of these have been discussed earlier but it is useful to summarize them here.

The *high staff turnover* can undermine the consistency that is the objective of many residential settings. As mentioned earlier, *burnout* occurs frequently due to the complexity and intensity of the job. Even when there is not a high turnover rate, *staff members have different styles* that can confuse and frustrate the residents. These differences also make it easier for children to play one staff member against another unless the agency is dedicated to good communication.

There can also be an *overlap in staff roles*. For example, a child care worker confronted with a child at bedtime who wants to talk about his or her abuse may not feel it is appropriate to tell the child to wait to speak to the social worker the next day. Yet, child care staff are often not trained in counseling and to counsel under these circumstances might not be therapeutic. Once again, communication between the two staff components is essential.

Abuse in Residential Settings

The amount of contact between children and staff members gives ample opportunity for both physical and sexual abuse to occur. Increasingly, centers are concerned with proper screening of new staff members. Many states require potential workers to be processed through a criminal records check, but these files usually identify a sexual offender only if he or she has been prosecuted. Current antidiscrimination practices and laws also prohibit asking some of the questions that might identify someone as a person who would abuse children. Agencies are finding that it is within their authority to use case scenarios and ask applicants to respond to these. The scenarios would have to be written with a knowledge of behaviors and attitudes that correlate with abusive behavior, however, and some critics argue that there is no way to anticipate an abuser no matter what techniques of evaluation are available. And so the dilemma of how to protect children in residential settings continues to be debated.

Once staff have been hired, many agencies today safeguard their populations by insisting that no staff member be alone with a child. This may work in some situations. Better training might be given to staff to help them to avoid the temptation of using physical punishment to cope with problematic behavior. Severe penalties for abusive practices might serve as another deterrent.

Community Support

Another issue often faced by residential centers is the lack of support within the community. For example, the St. Joseph's Center used to bring the residential care kids to community events in a big blue van. Recounts one resident of a small town in which there was a 40-bed facility for disturbed boys, "When the van would drive up, everyone would whisper 'Here come the St. Joe's kids.' It was as if everyone expected them to get into trouble. I felt sorry for the kids."

The mentality of "not in my community" can surround the presence of a residential treatment center in a given area (Rose, 1998). How well the center is accepted within the community can be the most challenging public relations issue for any center. Some agencies find that giving back to the community helps its public image. For example, one residence was in close proximity to a nursing home. The agency began a program in which the more high functioning of the residents would volunteer time at the nursing home to read to the elders, sort mail, do light chores, or just provide a listening ear. The program was so successful that the community awarded the agency a public service award. Unfortunately, all residential centers are not as well received. This stigma can have a great impact on children who already have lives filled with rejection.

Trends

Population Served

At one time, the child served by many residential settings tended to be the child who was unmanageable in a home; however, the problems being seen in centers today are much more severe. Many children have been involved with the court system for years before placement. This may mean that their attitudes make treatment challenging. Substance abuse is now a common problem necessitating residential treatment. The seriousness of these problems calls for better staff training and more creative methods of handling the residents. Clinical staff as well as residential and educational staff will require more sophisticated training to deal with these children in the most effective and therapeutic manner.

In addition to the severity of problems, an increasingly high percentage of children in residential settings come from a variety of minority groups. Thus, centers are called on to provide bilingual and bicultural staff to help the children in their care. Additional staff training will also be needed to understand the variety of cultural attitudes and customs that residents bring with them into care.

Restriction in Funding

Residential treatment is usually funded by several sources: the public child welfare agency, the school system, the mental health system, or the parents and/or their insurance. As funds become more restricted, the funding of this service is more in question. Child welfare agency budgets have been drastically cut from state to state, meaning that these agencies seek the least expensive means to treat their clients. School budgets have been decreased, leaving schools to look for the most cost-effective ways of dealing with students.

Managed care has also played a role in the provision of residential services. As insurance companies become more selective and advocate the least restrictive and least expensive settings, parents find that they are unable to afford residential treatment for their children no matter how desperate their need may be.

These constraints will put a great deal of pressure on residential centers and necessitate that they do more active recruiting, cut their costs and services, and seek creative ways to continue to function.

More Effective Evaluation

As residential settings face their critics, they will be called on to demonstrate the efficacy of their services. Yet, how effectively children have been treated cannot always be measured by the children's future directions. The question of "what if" is always at issue. For example, what if Jennifer (in "A Former Resident Remembers.") had not been influenced by the residential setting in which she was placed? Would she have become a substance abuser, following in her mother's footsteps? Or did the fact that she became pregnant before leaving the center mean that treatment and therefore the attempt to help her live a productive life were unsuccessful?

Mordock (1988) contends that "evaluative efforts in residential treatment centers should now focus less on outcome and more on monitoring treatment environments" (243). Children from dysfunctional backgrounds may not have an easy time, but rather than looking at their life as a whole, it will be important to monitor the coping mechanisms they have developed as a result of residential treatment. It is the challenge of the future to devise evaluation techniques that are accurate in assessing the efficacy of this type of service.

Family Involvement

As the emphasis continues to shift away from institutional settings and toward community treatment, it will be necessary to develop creative ways to involve parents in the discharge planning for children in residential settings. Some feel that involving an overwhelmed parent who has given up on being able to handle a child in the planning of that child's return home is futile. And yet, the child will need to return to the community more quickly than in years past. Thus, residential treatment must be seen as merely a step toward that goal. Parental involvement will be a critical part of the therapeutic picture.

The twenty-first century offers numerous challenges inherent in the provision of child welfare services. With the increased emphasis on our nation's failure to support the family, residential treatment centers will have their work cut out for them in justifying their existence.

Summary

Residential settings for children have roots that go back as far as the fifteenth century. Initially, orphan asylums met the needs of dependent children, while centers for delinquents attempted to rehabilitate and secure juveniles. There were also settings for disabled children and those who were mentally retarded. Over the years, they evolved to meet many different needs.

In considering residential care for children today, two assumptions are made: a residential setting is the last alternative and the least restrictive setting is best. Residential settings give children an opportunity for diluted emotional interaction with others and programs are structured to try to meet the individual needs of children, many of whom exhibit destructive behaviors.

Residential settings range from those designed to be diagnostic, those designed to provide treatment for both the emotionally disturbed and the disabled, and those designed to rehabilitate juvenile offenders. Children are referred to such settings as a way of removing them from the community or because their individual problems necessitate specialized treatment.

Residential settings are usually made up of three components: residential, educational, and clinical. Most centers use a token economy that reinforces children for acceptable behavior. An important part of group treatment is the influence that the residents have on each other. Many centers work with the families of the children in their care. Families range from those who are invested in their children to those who either do not become involved with their children's care or who attempt to sabotage the treatment efforts made by professionals.

Children leave residential centers for a variety of reasons. Some return home, some are placed in a less or more restrictive environment, and some are placed temporarily in psychiatric facilities. In some situations, children leave residential care to live on their own.

Over the last few years, the types of children placed in residential centers have been more of a challenge. In addition, funding has decreased, placing more pressure on centers to provided comprehensive programs. The future of group care must be marked by more creative ways of operating if residential centers are to meet the needs of the children of the future.

EXPLORATION QUESTIONS

1. How did residential centers begin? Outline the history of the movement.
2. Cite six assumptions about residential care.
3. What are the types of residential settings? What is the function of each?
4. What are the three components of residential treatment? What role does each play in the therapeutic milieu?
5. What instances can induce crisis situations in residential settings?
6. What are some issues regarding sexual acting out in residential settings? How can they be handled?
7. What are some considerations when working with the parents of children in residential care?
8. What roles do staff members take in residential settings? What are some of their frustrations?
9. Why might a child leave residential care?
10. What are the problems inherent in residential care?
11. What trends characterize residential care in the future?

REFERENCES

Arieli, M. (1997). *The Occupational Experience of Residential Child and Youth Care Workers: Caring and Its Discontents*. New York: Haworth Press.

Bertolino, B., & Thompson, K. (1999). *The Residential Youth Care Worker in Action*. New York: Haworth.

Billingsley, A., & Giovannoni, J. (1972). *Children of the Storm: Black Children and American Child Welfare*. New York: Harcourt Brace Jonvanovich.

Bloom, R., Denton, I. R, & Caflish, C. (1991). "Institutional Sexual Abuse: A Crisis in Trust" (48–49). In *Contributions to Residential Treatment*, AACRC.

Bowlby, J. (1951). *Maternal Care and Mental Health*. Geneva: World Health Organization.

Braga, W. (1993). "Experience with Alleged Sexual Abuse in Residential Programs: Problems in the Management of Allegations" (99–116). In W. Braga & R. Schimmer (Eds.), *Sexual Abuse and Residential Treatment*. New York: Haworth Press.

Braga, W., & Schimmer, R. (Eds.). (1993). *Sexual Abuse and Residential Treatment*. New York: Haworth Press.

Breer, W. (1996). *The Adolescent Molester*. Springfield, IL: Charles C. Thomas.

Burnett, R., & Rathbun, C. (1994). "Discovery and Treatment of Adolescent Sexual Offenders in a Residential Treatment Center" (57–64). In G. Northrup (Ed.), *The Management of Sexuality in Residential Treatment*. New York: Haworth Press.

Charles, G., Coleman, H., & Matheson, J. (1993). "Staff Reactions to Young People Who Have Been Sexually Abused" (9–21). In G. Northrup (Ed.), *The Management of Sexuality in Residential Treatment*. New York: Haworth Press.

Corcoran, K. J. (1988). "Understanding and Coping with Burnout" (251–262). In C. E. Schaefer & A. J. Swanson (Eds.), *Children in Residential Care: Critical Issues in Treatment*. New York: Van Nostrand Reinhold.

Crenshaw, D. A. (1988). "Responding to Sexual Acting-Out" (50–76). In C. E. Schaefer & A. J. Swanson (Eds.), *Children in Residential Care: Critical Issues in Treatment*. New York: Van Nostrand Reinhold.

Cunningham, C., & MacFarlane, K. (1997). *When Children Abuse*. Brandon, VT: Safer Society Press.

Devereux Foundation. (1987). "The Devereux Legacy in the Seventy-Fifth Annual Report." Devon, PA: The Devereux Foundation.

Everett, J. E., Chipungu, S. S. & Leashore, B. R. (Eds.). (1992). *Child Welfare: An Africentric Perspective*. New Brunswick, NJ: Rutgers University Press.

Farmer, E., & Pollock, S. (1998). *Sexually Abused and Abusing Children in Substitute Care*. Chichester, UK. J. Wiley.

Frost, N., & Stein, M. (1999) *Understanding Residential Care*. Burlington, VT: Ashgate.

Gambrill, E, & Stein, T. J. (Eds.). (1994). *Controversial Issues in Child Welfare*. Boston: Allyn and Bacon.

Goffman, E. (1961). *Asylums*. Garden City, NY: Anchor.

Hayden, T. (1995). *The Tiger's Child*. New York: Avon.

Johnson, T. C. (1997). *Sexual, Physical and Emotional Abuse in Out-of-Home Care*. New York: Haworth.

Johnson, T. C., & Aoki, W. T. (1993). "Sexual Behaviors of Latency Age Children in Residential Treatment" (1–22). In W. Braga & R. Schimmer (Eds.), *Sexual Abuse and Residential Treatment*. New York: Haworth Press.

Kadushin, A., & Martin, J. A. (1988). *Child Welfare Services*. New York: Macmillan.

Kagan, R. M. (1988). "Professional Development for a Therapeutic Environment" (160–174). In C. E. Schaefer & A. J. Swanson (Eds.), *Children in Residential Care: Clinical Issues in Treatment*. New York: Van Nostrand Reinhold.

Katz, M. (1988). "Crisis Intervention in Residential Care" (30–49). In C. E. Schaefer & A. J. Swanson (Eds.). *Children in Residential Care: Clinical Issues in Treatment*. New York: Van Nostrand Reinhold.

Keith-Lucas, A., & Sanford, C. (1977). *Group Child Care as a Family Service.* Chapel Hill, NC: University of North Carolina Press.

Lemmond, T., and Verhaagen, D. A. (2001). *Sexually Aggressive Youth: A Guide to Comprehensive Residential Treatment.* Westport, CT: Greenhouse.

Levy, T., & Orlans, M. (1998). *Attachment, Trauma and Healing.* Washington, DC: Child Welfare League of America.

Marohn, R. C. (1993). "Residential Services" (453–466). In P. H. Tolan & B. J. Cohler (Eds.), *Handbook of Clinical Research and Practice with Adolescents.* New York: John Wiley and Sons.

Mordock, J. B. (1988). "Evaluating Treatment Effectiveness" (219–250). In C. E. Schaefer & A. J. Swanson (Eds.), *Children in Residential Care: Clinical Issues in Treatment.* New York: Van Nostrand Reinhold.

Northrup, G. (Ed.). (1994). *The Management of Sexuality in Residential Treatment.* New York: Haworth Press.

Pecora, P., Barth, R. P., Whittaker, J. K., Maluccio, A. N., with Barth, R. P., & Plotnick, R. D. (2000). *The Child Welfare Challenge: Policy, Practice and Research.* New York: Aldine De Gruyter.

Plach, T. A. (1993). *Residential Treatment and the Sexually Abused Child.* Springfield, IL: Charles C. Thomas.

Powell, J. Y. (2000). *Family-Centered Services in Residential Treatment.* New York: Haworth.

Powers, D. (1993). "Some Medical Implications of Sexuality in Residential Centers" (23–36). In G. Northrup (Ed.), *The Management of Sexuality in Residential Treatment.* New York: Haworth Press.

Rose, M. (1998). "The Management of Boundaries and an Organization's Therapeutic Task," *Therapeutic Communities: International Journal for Therapeutic and Supportive Organizations,* 19(2), 107–121.

Ross, J. E., & deViller, M. P. (1993). "Safety Considerations in Developing an Adolescent Sex Offender Program in Residential Treatment" (37–47). In W. Braga & R. Schimmer (Eds.), *Sexual Abuse and Residential Treatment.* New York: Haworth Press.

Stanley, N., & Manthorpe, J. (Eds.). (1999). *Institutional Abuse: Perspectives Across the Life Course.* New York: Routledge.

Van Hagan, J. (1988). "Family Work in Residential Treatment" (134–144). In C. E. Schaefer & A. J. Swanson (Eds.), *Children in Residential Care: Clinical Issues in Treatment.* New York: Van Nostrand Reinhold.

West, J. G. (1998). "Designing an Orientation Program for the Direct Care Staff of a Children's Residential Treatment Center," *Residential Treatment of Children and Youth,* 16(1), 21–32.

Whitaker, D., Archer, L., & Hicks, L. (1998). *Working in Children's Homes: Challenges and Complexities.* New York: John Wiley.

14 Our Children's Future

What Is in Our Children's Future?

Our children's future depends largely on the formation of policies and programs that ensure that their rights are protected and their needs are met. The status of today's children suggests that this is not being done adequately. The number of children in poverty has increased. Our protective services agencies are seeing more and more maltreated children and teens. Our juvenile courts are overworked, and the protection of children's health is regulated largely by those who can and will pay the bills. These facts do not present a favorable picture for the future of children.

Solutions to the problems that face children are far from easy. One impediment to finding adequate solutions is the fact that Americans are often split on a number of questions that impact our youngest citizens. For example, the controversy over welfare reform, the educational reform law, the reinstitution of orphanages, and the child abuse reporting backlash represent only a few of the difficulties we have on agreeing about the issues.

The resolution of the dilemma of how best to serve our children may fall largely on the shoulders of the next generation of citizens, policymakers, and child welfare advocates and workers. For this reason, a text on child welfare would be remiss if it did not give consideration to the issues at hand. The issues discussed here will be children's status, poverty, children at risk, health issues, and educational concerns. This list is in no way exhaustive but does cover some of the areas in which there is currently debate.

Children's Status

"If I was taller, bigger, and my voice had changed," my 10-year-old son told me recently, "people would listen to what I had to say. But as soon as they see a small person and recognize me as a child, my views are discounted and everyone assumes that I know nothing. I do know how I feel and what I need. In this world of consumer rights, I think adults have forgotten one group of important consumers—kids!" The old expression "out of the mouths of babes" comes to mind as we read the words of an articulate 10-year-old. How many times has a child dreaded unsupervised visits with a sexually abusive parent only to have the court, unable to prove beyond the child's word that the abuse has occurred, order that the visit must take place? And how many children have told their parents by their behaviors that they are not comfortable in a particular setting, but not being "heard" they are sent anyway?

Admittedly, today's world is not always a friendly place for adults either, but so often the needs of the adult come first. For example, in many families, both parents must work in order to support their family's needs. But, even given this reality, the daycare services provided for children across the United States are at best uneven and at worse grossly inadequate (Scarr, 1998). Currently there are no national standards for centers providing daycare, and many states have few, if any, guidelines about teacher qualifications or group size. Not only are children as a group not "heard" in terms of their needs, but in some areas there are marked gender and cultural differences in the services available. For example, several studies found that boys were more likely than girls to commit suicide or drop out of school and yet there are no more services offered for one gender than the other (Garfinkel et al., 1996).

Why are children discounted? The most obvious answer is that, in a democratic society, they cannot vote. If one cannot vote, one's rights and needs may be overlooked. It falls to those working with and advocating for children then to bring forward their causes. This also necessitates that those advocating for children be listening to them. This is not always easy for adults who have learned that money is what drives the mechanisms to provide service, and marketing is what creates the money. Thus, even if children are "heard," what they need may not be provided.

The first and most involved advocates for children can be their parents. When parents can make themselves heard, children can benefit. Thus, support groups for parents that empower parents to help their children go a long way toward making sure that children's needs are met. One neighborhood of concerned parents proved this point. A nearby intersection had become busy, but it was the only route to school for neighborhood children. The children had expressed their fear of crossing the street, even when monitored by parents, but the city took no action. Finally, the concerned parents took a stand. Through an intense community awareness effort, they convinced the city of the need for a stoplight. It was a proud group of parents that watched the light being put up so that their children could cross in safety.

Although a stoplight may seem minor in the total lives of children, it may have taken on a different emphasis if a child had been hurt or killed by oncoming traffic. For this group of low-income parents, who had never felt in control of their own lives, advocating in this manner was not only beneficial for their children but a lesson in empowerment for them. Parents must be helped to recognize that they have the power to speak for their children.

When parents are not able to speak for children, others may need to. Advocacy for children necessitates recognizing and weighing all the issues. One agency that has been especially effective in advocating for children is the Children's Defense Fund. Knitzer (as cited in Downs et al., 1996), of the Children's Defense Fund, identifies several underlying assumptions about advocating for children:

1. *Advocacy assumes that people have, or ought to have, certain basic rights;*
2. *Advocacy assumes that rights are enforceable by statutes, administration, or judicial procedure;*
3. *Advocacy efforts are focused on institutional failures that produce or aggravate individual problems;*
4. *Advocacy is inherently political;*
5. *Advocacy is most effective when it is focused on specific issues;*
6. *Advocacy is different from the provision of direct services. (Downs et al., 1996, 445–446)*

Changing the status of children will require serious attitudinal changes on the part of society. This may never happen. In the meantime, it is up to child advocates to exert sufficient influence to protect children's rights.

Children in Poverty

Poverty among children and their families is a major problem in the United States (see Chapter 3). Not only does poverty cause health and educational problems, but some argue that it can create conditions in which maltreatment of children by parents is likely as well (see Ambert, 1997; Milner, 1994; Pelton, 1994). What would be involved in ending poverty?

Baker (1995) suggests the adoption of Canada's child allowances and tax concessions for families. The child allowance would give each family with children a certain amount of money for the care of each child. Administrative costs are actually lower because of the elimination of eligibility testing. Feminists argue that this gives mothers more freedom, and those who choose to stay home to raise their children could do so. The disadvantage with such a program is the higher cost of providing money for all children rather than just those whose parents cannot adequately provide for them.

Instead of child allowances, some countries are increasing tax concessions (i.e., exemptions, deductions, or credits) for those who have children. These are less visible to the public, and eligibility can be determined without the stigma of welfare eligibility determination procedures. The United States is one of the only industrialized countries that provides tax concessions instead of a child allowance. Baker (1995) comments that "American children fare considerably worse in terms of poverty rates than do their counterparts in Western Europe" (150). Noel and Whyte in Chapter 3 suggest other strategies to reduce poverty in the United States. All of these programs will impact children in some manner.

Paradoxically, while programs are being instituted that attempt to reduce poverty, other legislation may have a more deleterious influence on poverty-stricken parents and their children. Welfare reform and specifically welfare-to-work programs directed at teenage parents have not improved the economic well-being of the teens in whom proponents of the legislation had hoped to instill motivation and discourage childbearing. In fact, the program has done neither (Aber et al., 1995). The solutions to child poverty are extremely complex. New and creative solutions are the only possibilities that might interrupt the cycle (see Chapter 3 for additional solutions).

Children at Risk

When we speak of *children at risk,* we think first of children who are at risk for abuse and neglect. Over the last few years, there has been much debate over what is best for maltreated children. Costin and colleagues (1996) contend that current "child abuse policy contains dangerous contradictions that contribute to the breakdown of the system" (6). Further, these authors feel that the current method of protecting children is less than effective and requires revisions. The media, attracted to high-spectacle events, does not help to raise the consciousness of Americans about the realities of child abuse effectively (Freeman-Longo and Blanchard, 1998). Instead, reporters focus on the well-known perpetrator and the bizarre or sadistic case. This distorts the picture of maltreatment and almost negates the seriousness of the plight of the low-income child.

Costin and colleagues (1996) also criticize what they refer to as the "child abuse industry" or the network of agencies and services designed to intervene in abusive situations. Caught up in bureaucracy, political disputes, legislative rhetoric, and debates over false versus repressed memories, the mechanisms do not always serve the children. The legal system, too, can do more damage than good with court delays and grandstand courtroom tactics.

Drake (1996) points out that even the semantics can be in question. The term *substantiated* is given to a case that the Child Protective Services feels warrants further investigation because, according to the evidence available, maltreatment appears to have taken place. *Unsubstantiation* is often misinterpreted to mean that there was no abuse or neglect. In fact, the term *unsubstantiated* can indicate that there was insufficient evidence or insufficient harm to the child, without necessarily meaning that there was no such abuse. In such situations, the child may be just as much in danger but is not protected by an agency. Drake suggests that further research is needed in the areas of screening accuracy and overreporting. Giovannoni (1989) feels that *unsubstantiated* should be clearly defined and divided into two categories: *unsubstantiated,* no further action taken, and *unsubstantiated,* services provided or arranged (317). Whatever the area considered, the protection of children from maltreatment must be better addressed and researched in the future.

Waldfogel (2001) contends that the current child welfare system emphasizes the "front end" of intervention too much—placing more emphasis on reporting and investigation than on treatment. She suggests a "narrowed" approach that customizes services to families and brings in other community agencies to collaborate more fully.

Maltreated children are not the only ones covered by the phrase *at risk.* The term has been broadened to include children whose dysfunctional family or whose poverty puts them at risk for a variety of social service needs. Since the late 1980s, the literature has been filled with the term as well as proposed ways to deal with the problem of children at risk. Throughout this text, we have considered different ways that children are put at risk and possible solutions to protect them. But Swadener and Lubeck (1995) contend that the phrase has become a "buzzword" that emphasizes the negative and in no way accentuates the positive or builds on the family's strengths. These authors suggest that this "deficit model" often results in blaming the victim. When we blame someone for their own victimization, we then feel justified in not helping them. Swadener and Lubeck (1995) suggest the term *at promise* rather than *at risk.* "At promise" would consider all the possibilities for all children whatever their socioeconomic class, race, gender, or age.

> *Perhaps the time has finally come to move beyond the dominant culture assumptions and deficit-model thinking that have so separated students and educators alike, particularly as they create barriers to building the sort of culturally inclusive alliances which authentic change will require. Such alliances for children can begin to transcend the internalized oppression which is a major by-product of the deficiency model embodied in the construct "children and families at risk." (41)*

These authors suggest that plans for children's well-being would be done in partnerships with parents, who would be empowered to meet their children's needs and seek out resources for the needs that they are unable to meet. As the authors put it: "By viewing parents and children as 'at promise' we enhance the possibilities of constructing authentic relations where we actively *listen* and learn from one another" (42).

Although an attitudinal change is not a complete solution to protecting children from harm, it may well enhance our ability to find solutions. Instead of looking to "fix" broken families, would not such a reframing cause us to be more creative and proactive about services for children?

Children and Health

There is no area in need of adopting a proactive state of mind more than health care. One problem for poor children seeking medical care is finding a doctor who will accept Medicaid. A high percentage of doctors refuse to accept Medicaid due to the long delays in reimbursement (Chase-Lansdale and Brooks-Gunn, 1995; Brown, 1994; Sherman, 1994). One pediatrician from a particularly deprived low-income area commented:

> *It got so I literally could not pay my bills. With 90 percent of my patients covered by Medicaid and the very long delays before I was reimbursed, I could be seeing patients for weeks with no income at all. I am certainly not in medicine for the money. If I was, I would not be practicing where I do, but I also need to feed my family.*

Poor families who are not eligible for Medicaid may have trouble paying medical fees. Even middle-income families who have no or minimal insurance coverage may find themselves bankrupted by one medical crisis. Even regular checkups may not be done when a family has difficulty meeting the costs.

Landrigan and Carlson (1995) emphasize that it is not only routine health and organic illness that threatens children. Increasingly, environmental hazards take their toll on human beings, and children are actually more vulnerable for several reasons:

1. *Children have greater exposure to toxins than adults. As they grow, children actually take in more food and water and breathe more air than their adult counterparts.*
2. *Children's metabolic pathways, especially in the first months after birth, are immature compared to those of adults. This means that their ability to detoxify harmful substances is less than adults.*
3. *Children are undergoing rapid growth and development, and their delicate developmental processes are easily disrupted.*
4. *Because children have more future years than adults, they have more time to develop any chronic diseases that may be triggered by early environmental exposures. (36)*

Attention to environmental policy-making may also be crucial to the protection of the future health of children.

Provisions under the Family Support Act of 1988 do offer some opportunity to study health issues for children thought to be at particular risk. Lear (1996) outlines a plan for a school health care center that would link "existing efforts in primary care, public health, school health, and health education with emerging systems of managed health care to ensure that the health care requirements of the neediest children are met" (176). But more could be done for all children. It will be the challenge of the next generation of child welfare professionals to advocate for primary health care for every child.

Children and Education

Another area of much controversy has been our educational system. Innovations in the inclusion of special needs children as well as the total Educational Reform Act have sought to make the educational experience a rewarding one for every child. But we are far from that goal.

Some learning in school goes beyond reading, writing, and math. Children come to their learning environment with a set of cultural values as well as familial values. Increasingly, it has become important for educators to be sensitized to the diversity brought to the educational experience by each child. In addition, Mosteller (1995) found, in a study of Tennessee schools, that children taught in smaller classes, especially in the lower grades, performed better than children in larger class groups, even when a classroom aide was present. In addition, school violence must be curbed so that schools are a *safe* place to learn.

Children also come to school with a variety of barriers to learning. The residual effects of abuse and neglect, the conflict over domestic violence in the home, the scars of poverty, health issues, and the threat of community violence all affect a child's ability to learn. It is not until we fully address these other social issues that we can truly remove the barriers to learning for all children. In the meantime, educators must develop a sensitivity that goes beyond the ability to communicate information. As one educator put it:

> When it was suggested that the teachers at our school go to a child prevention program, a number of my colleagues protested. "We don't even have time to teach the basics!" retorted one veteran teacher, "and now we have to train to detect child abuse!" My response was that she should wake up! Teaching today is not just about the "three R's"! When a child comes in hungry or hurting from the beating he got, he's not going to care about the spelling words for the day. Until you deal with his safety or hunger issues, there is no way that child will learn to his full potential!

Fortunately, more teachers are recognizing their need to become aware of the whole child and to gear education toward *that* child. Increasingly, educators value and use the services provided within the school system (see Chapter

5) and within the community. Preparation for the future necessitates that educational as well as health and child welfare professionals work together for the whole child within his or her total environment.

Preparing Those Who Help Children

The role of the child welfare worker, no matter what the discipline or the agency, is an important one. For this reason, it is vital that child welfare professionals be well trained, not only in their particular job but also to understand every issue concerning children. The child welfare worker should have training in the following areas at the very least:

- Child development
- Interviewing skills (especially as they apply to children)
- Child welfare services
- Child abuse and neglect
- Systems theory (so that there is recognition that the child is part of the family system, the neighborhood, the community, etc.)
- Other theories, such as crisis intervention, attachment theory, functional theory (emphasizes strengths)
- Formulation of social policy and grant writing
- State, urban, and federal government
- Cultural diversity
- Computer skills

Many of these areas should be covered in college courses. Agencies do not always train their workers in skills or knowledge beyond the definition of their particular jobs. Thus, when a worker is faced with interviewing a young child for the first time, he or she may be hampered by a lack of knowledge of either child development and/or interviewing. Or, when an agency needs a new program to better serve clients, the worker would be well advised to have knowledge in grant writing and/or the political working of the community to be in the best position to apply for or negotiate for such a program. And, most agencies are now computerized and require that workers do their own documentation on a personal computer. Thus, a familiarity with computer skills can be invaluable.

Training, once one is hired by an agency, may be thorough but is more likely to be brief and often incomplete. For example, consider this inexperienced social worker's thoughts:

When I started as a worker in a foster care agency, I had just graduated from college as an English major. I could do great dictation, but I didn't have a clue if a child was acting normal for his or her age or not. I started work on Monday, got a brief training in forms and policies on Monday and Tuesday, and was sent to my first foster home visit on Wednesday. I had no idea what to say or how to talk to young children. Later my supervisor told me that we were short-staffed that day or they would have let me shadow a worker for a day. Even a day would not have done it!

Training is vital to child welfare staff, especially in the field of child abuse and neglect. The training environment should be well organized with attention to such things as selection of the trainers, seating arrangement, timing, and group interaction. "Good training also promotes a good team," explains one agency director. "My agency training consists of team building right at the on-set. Experienced workers join new workers in training groups and we do problem-solving exercises. This helps the new workers see how the work is done without just talking at them. I have had workers come to me years after they have been with us, telling me what a valuable experience that training was."

Child welfare workers also have ongoing supervision and the quality of this supervision is extremely important. "I tell my workers that quality supervison is their right! If they aren't getting it, I'd like to know why," asserted the same agency director. It is in supervision that one learns how to prioritize difficult cases adeptly, receives support to make decisions, learns more about the agency, and has an opportunity to process one's own feelings about particular cases. "One case was giving me a lot of trouble," said one new child welfare worker. "I couldn't figure out why. It was only after supervision that I realized that this mother was pushing old 'buttons' in me that reminded me of things I hated when I was growing up."

In addition to weekly training, many agencies provide ongoing in-service training or give workers the opportunity to take workshops, training sessions outside the agency, or courses at a local college. This is a valuable chance to keep up one's knowledge in the field. The preparation of child welfare workers cannot be taken too lightly. It is these individuals who may be responsible for major decisions in the lives of children.

Child Welfare in the Twenty-First Century

The challenge of social workers of the twenty-first century is to fully tailor the services we provide to children to their needs. Many experts express concern that the efforts to preserve families have not been working. Granted, the divorce rate may have stabilized and the rate of unwed pregnancies lessened slightly, but there are many stresses still causing family breakdown. Some critics (see Hegar and Scannapieco, 1999; Alstein & McCoy, 2000) argue that intensive family preservation services have been ineffective and that these services should be refined and evaluated in the future. Hegar and Scannapieco (1999) suggest an expansion of and additional legislative support for kinship care as one way of redefining family preservation. New models to address child protection issues are much needed. Changes must take place, not only within child protection agencies but also within the larger community—businesses, churches, schools, and neighborhoods. Freeman-Longo and Blanchard (1998) contend that new approaches to prevention are vital. Siegel and Senna (2000) stress the importance of continued reform of the juvenile justice system. Some feel that welfare reform will aid needy families and stimulate additional services, whereas others insist that the more stringent requirements for receiving financial support will only add to the burden of impoverished families and children.

There are some positive projections for the future. Demographic trends indicate that there will be fewer unwanted children (see Chapter 7), which may influence the number of children being abused or neglected. Improved medical care and biotechnology may result in fewer medical problems and developmental disabilities for children. In addition, the medical and social service community, with updated research, will be better able to deal with children who have these problems. And as women rise higher in institutions and various influential professions, more attention will be paid to the needs of children (Finkelhor, 1991).

Whatever the demographics tell us, experience has made us aware that the only hope we have of meeting the needs of all citizens, but especially children, is through a *unified* team approach. We cannot afford the luxury of turf-ism—in which each profession stakes out a territory that it fiercely guards. Only through sharing our knowledge and ideas with others who are concerned for children can we solve the problems that we all face in the provision of services for them.

You have read this text probably because you are considering child welfare as a career goal or teaching those for whom this is an option. Providing services for children is an exciting and challenging endeavor. It falls to you and others like you to make a difference for our children. Holocaust survivor and noted writer Elie Wiesel (1995) spoke of the future being assured by building a moral society.

> *In a moral society, people listen to each other and care about the other person. No person may be sacrificed for any goal.... A primary difference between an immoral society and a moral society is that in an immoral society, people don't listen. [They] know everything, know the question, know the answer to the question. Clichés are used. But in a moral society, there is a sense of wonder at the presence of someone else. I am free because other people are free. No cliches are used. (3)*

It is up to all of us to build a moral society in which even children can be heard. As those who advocate for children, we must help children be heard. This may involve promoting pro-child/pro-family federal legislation or searching for creative agency responses or supporting clients to empower themselves, or a variety of other responses. It will mean not seeing our clients as doomed to fail, but rather filled with promise. Only when we begin to recognize the importance of children as our future, and value the strengths their families can provide for them, will today's children receive adequate services. Being a voice for the children is the *only* way we can help them be heard. It will be a challenge, but one well worth meeting.

Summary

The future of child welfare is dependent largely on the policies and programs that are designed to protect and serve children. Responsibility for the formulation and implementation of policies that work falls on the shoulders of those about to enter the field as well as veteran advocates and policymakers. Therefore, it is important for new child welfare workers to know the issues and begin to search proactively for solutions.

Several issues immediately present themselves in a discussion of the future of child welfare. First, how can we improve the status of children? Children are often discounted because they are unable to vote. Therefore, it will be important to develop effective advocacy on behalf of children. Second, how can we elevate children and their families above the poverty level? Increased financial allocations is one possibility. Unlike the United States, which depends on tax concessions, some countries give parents a child allowance to help them care for their children. Next, how can we protect children at risk? *At risk* can be seen as being at risk for maltreatment or at risk for a variety of other reasons. Some believe that the phrase *at risk* emphasizes the negative rather than allowing for the strengths that families and children have. We need also to think about how we can improve both health care and education for children.

It is also imperative that those who work with children be adequately trained, both at the college level and within the agency. Beyond training, effective supervision is also vital. It will fall to the child welfare worker of tomorrow, if not to each citizen, to protect children and speak for them so that their needs will be met and the services they need will be provided.

EXPLORATION QUESTIONS

1. What are some areas of controversy among those considering services to children?
2. What accounts for the status that children have in society? How could it be improved?
3. What is meant by *advocacy?* What are some basic assumptions about advocacy?
4. What are some possible solutions for poverty among children and their families?
5. What is meant by *children at risk?* Why might they be at risk?
6. What is the criticism of the term *at risk?* What is an alternative?
7. Why are environmental factors such a concern with respect to children's health?
8. What needs to be considered when discussing education in the future?
9. What type of preparation should child welfare workers have?
10. What are some projections for this new century?

REFERENCES

Aber, J. L., Brooks-Gunn, J., & Maynard, R. A. (1995). "Effects of Welfare Reform on Teenage Parents and Their Children" (53–71). In R. E. Behrman (Ed.), *The Future of Children*, 5(2). Los Altos, CA: Center for the Future of Children, David and Lucille Packard Foundation.

Ambert, A. (1997). *The Web of Poverty*. New York: Haworth.

Altstein, H., & McCoy, R. (2000). *Does Family Preservation Serve a Child's Best Interests?* Washington, DC: Georgetown University Press.

Baker, M. (1995). *Canadian Family Policies: Cross-National Comparisons*. Toronto: University of Toronto Press.

Behrman, R. E. (Ed.). (1995). *The Future of Children*, 5(2). Los Altos, CA: Center for the Future of Children, David and Lucille Packard Foundation.

Brown, R. (Ed.). (1994). *Children in Crisis*. New York: H. W. Wilson Co.

Chase-Lansdale, P. L., & Brooks-Gunn, J. (Eds.). (1995). *Escape from Poverty: What Makes a Difference to Children?* Cambridge: Cambridge University Press.

Clinton, B. (1996). "Proclamation 6626—National Children's Day, 1993." In *Weekly Compilation of Presidential Documents*, Nov. 22, 1993, 29(46), 2393–94, as cited in I. Garfinkel, J. L. Hochschild, & S. S. McLanahan (Eds.), *Social Policies for Children*. Washington, DC: The Brookings Institution.

Costin, L. B., Kerger, H. J., & Stoesz, D. (1996). *The Politics of Child Abuse in America*. New York: Oxford University Press.

Downs, S. W., Costin, L. B., & McFadden, E. J. (1996). *Child Welfare and Family Services: Policies and Practice*. New York: Longman.

Drake, B. (1996). "Unraveling 'Unsubstantiated,'" *Child Maltreatment*, 1(3), 261–271.

English, D. J., & Pecora, P. J. (1994). "Risk Assessment as a Practice Method in Child Protective Services," *Child Welfare*, 73(5), 451–473.

Finkelhor, D. (1991). "The Lazy Revolutionary's Guide to the Prospects for Reforming Child Welfare," *Child Abuse and Neglect*, 15 (suppl. 1), 17–23.

Freeman-Longo, R. E., & Blanchard, G. T. (1998). *Sexual Abuse in America: Epidemic of the 21st Century*. Brandon, VT: Safer Society Press.

Gambrill, E., & Stein, T. J. (Eds.). (1994). *Controversial Issues in Child Welfare*. Boston: Allyn and Bacon.

Garfinkel, I., Hochschild, J. L., & McLanahan, S. S. (Eds.). (1996). *Social Policies for Children*. Washington, DC: The Brookings Institution.

Giovannoni, J. (1989). "Substantiated and Unsubstantiated Reports of Child Maltreatment," *Children and Youth Services Review*, 11, 299–318.

Graves, C. (1994). "Jackson Urges Youths to Look to the Future," *Star Tribune*, Feb. 13, 7b.

Hegar, R. L., & Scannapieco, M. (1999). *Kinship Foster Care*. New York: Oxford University Press.

Knitzer, J. E. (1996). "Child Advocacy: A Perspective," *American Journal of Orthopsychiatry*, 46(2), 200–216, as cited in S. W. Downs, L. B. Costin, & E. J. McFadden, *Child Welfare and Family Services: Policies and Practice*. White Plains, NY: Longman.

Landrigan, P. J., & Carlson, J. E. (1995). "Environmental Policy and Children's Health" (34–52). In R. E. Behrman (Ed.), *The Future of Children*, 5(2). Los Altos, CA: Center for the Future of Children, David and Lucille Packard Foundation.

Lear, J. G. (1996). "Health Care Goes to School: An Untidy Strategy to Improve the Well-Being of School Age Children" (173–201). In I. Garfinkel, J. L. Hochschild, & S. S. McLanahan, (Eds.), *Social Policies for Children*. Washington, DC: The Brookings Institution.

MacPherson, A. (1993). "Parent-Professional Partnership: A Review and Discussion of Issues," *Early Child Development and Care*, 86, 61–77.

Milner, J. S. (1994). "Is Poverty a Key Contributor to Child Abuse? No" (23–26). In E. Gambrill & T. J. Stein, (Eds.), *Controversial Issues in Child Welfare*. Boston: Allyn and Bacon.

Mosteller, F. (1995). "The Tennessee Study of Class Size in the Early School Grades" (113–127). In R. E. Behrman (Ed.), *The Future of Children,* 5(2). Los Altos, CA: Center for the Future of Children, David and Lucille Packard Foundation.

Pecora, P. J. (1994). "Are Intensive Family Preservation Services Effective? Yes" (290–301). In E. Gambrill & T. J. Stein (Eds.), *Controversial Issues in Child Welfare.* Boston: Allyn and Bacon.

Pelton, L. H. (1994). "Is Poverty a Key Contributor to Child Abuse? Yes" (16–22). In E. Gambrill & T. J. Stein (Eds.), *Controversial Issues in Child Welfare.* Boston: Allyn and Bacon.

Roberts, D. (1991). "Child Protection in the 21st Century," *Child Abuse and Neglect,* 15(1), 25–30.

Scarr, S. (1998). "American Child Care Today," *American Psychologist,* 53(2), 95–108.

Schwartz, I. M. (1991). "Out-of-Home Placement of Children: Selected Issues and Prospects for the Future," *Behavioral Sciences and the Law,* 9(2), 189–199.

Sherman, A. (1994). *Wasting America's Future.* Boston: Beacon Press.

Siegel, L. J., & Senna, J. J. (2000). *Juvenile Delinquency: Theory, Practice, and Law.* Belmont, CA: Wadsworth.

Smith, G. (1993). *Systematic Approaches to Training in Child Protection.* London: Karnac Books.

Smith, S. (1995). "Two-Generation Programs: A New Intervention Strategy and Directions for Future Research" (299–314). In P. L. Chase-Lansdale & J. Brooks-Gunn, (Eds.), *Escape from Poverty: What Makes a Difference to Children?* Cambridge: Cambridge University Press.

Swadener, B. B., & Lubeck, S. (Eds.). (1995). *Children and Families "at Promise."* Albany, NY: State University of New York Press.

Waldfogel, J. (2001). *The Future of Child Protection.* Cambridge, MA: Harvard University Press.

Wiesel, E. (1995). "Building a Moral Society." Lecture at the Provost's Forum, Kent State University, Kent, Ohio, April 1989, as cited in B. B. Swadener & S. Lubeck (Eds.), *Children and Families "at Promise."* Albany, NY: State University of New York Press.

NAME INDEX

SUBJECT INDEX

443